AN EXPLANATION OF THE THIRTY-NINE ARTICLES

AN EXPLANATION OF THE THIRTY-NINE ARTICLES

Alexander Penrose Forbes

BISHOP OF BRECHIN

with an Epistle Dedicatpry

First Published in Two Volumes in 1867
Re-Issued as One Volume
2023

with a new Foreword
by
C.P. Collister

Foreword

by C.P. Collister

The Catholic revival in the Church of England responded to changing cultural circumstances by calling men to return to the fullness of the Christian faith. Pusey, an Old Testament scholar at The University of Oxford and disciple of the Anglican divines and Church Fathers, marshaled reams of evidence from the Anglican tradition and early Church to reawaken contemporaries to the Apostolic authority of the Catholic Church, including the Church of England, the inspiration of Scripture, and Christ's saving grace given in the regeneration of baptism and the real presence of communion. As a writer, pastor, and professor, he inspired many to give their lives to the cause of the Oxford Movement, dedicating themselves to the service of Christ and his Church. Alexander Penrose Forbes (1817-1875), the first Tractarian bishop in the United Kingdom, was one such student. In the introduction to *An Explanation of the 39 Articles*, he thanks Pusey in the most reverential terms:

> You have devoted your time and your talents, and the varied gifts which God has bestowed upon you, to adorn the Church of England ; by bringing forward in her service your varied stores of patristic learning ; by the evolution of a more accurate theology ; by the publication of heart-stirring and thoughtful sermons; by placing within the reach of her members adapted editions of the devout works of spiritual authors in other communions; by supplying to the student of Holy Scripture the beginning of a deep, affective, and exhaustive commentary on the Word of

God ; by the development of the dogmatic element in the Church's teaching as the strongest bulwark against rationalism and infidelity ; by defending the authenticity and inspiration of that Prophet whose work has been the battle-ground of modern criticism[…][1]

As Pusey's protégé, Forbes shared his spiritual father's desire to contribute to the "evolution of a more accurate theology" and "development of the dogmatic element in the Church's teaching."[2] To this end, he wrote *A Short Explanation of the Nicene Creed* for students of theology in the Church of England.

"[A]mid the great revival of the last twenty years,"Forbes recounts , "as deeper views of God's truth have by His mercy been accorded to our aching hearts, a desire of a more systematic theology has almost of necessity been engendered."[3] The Catholic revival persuaded many that "an exact theology is at once the most reverent and the most satisfactory" and "the only sure guarantee for orthodoxy of faith."[4] Forbes believes that "the faith of our own Church, on the subjects that were left as open questions, has shriveled and withered away," and it is this conviction that underlies his work as a theologian.[5]

---

1   A.P. Forbes, *An Explanation of the 39 Articles*, Oxford: J.H. Parker, 1871, 13.

2   Forbes, *Articles*, 13.

3   A.P. Forbes, *A Short Explanation of the Nicene Creed*, Oxford: J.H. Parker, 1852, Preface

4   Forbes, *Creed*, Preface

5   Forbes, *Creed*, Preface

Through his commentaries on the Creed and the Articles, Forbes expounds a systematic theology for Evangelical Catholics. This dogmatic theology holds to the Evangelical conviction that the inspired Word of God contains all things necessary for salvation, and the Catholic conviction that God is guiding the whole Church into all truth. "Our Lord has promised, " I am with you always, even to the end of the world;" "but He has not promised to be always present in the same degree or the same way,."[6] And we can only come to understand the relationship between doctrinal development and the rule of faith when we see how God relates to his people in different ways in different times and places. By distinguishing between the ways that the Holy Spirit has guided the Church throughout her history, he clarifies the relationship between Scripture and the great tradition in his explanation of how God uniquely acted through the Apostles: "they spake as "moved by the Holy Ghost," so that what they spake were the words of God, and have been, ever since, a fountain of truth to the Church of Christ, such as no words, since spoken through men, are or can be. This does not mean that Christ abandoned his Church, or the Holy Spirit ceased to lead her into all truth. Instead, Forbes observes that "He has been with the Church, in different degrees, since, according to her faithfulness."[7]

Forbes turns to the Vincentian canon to determine what beliefs are essential to the Catholic Christian faith. Considering the faith and practice of the original Christians,  as this faith and worship spread among Christians around the world and across the ages, demands careful study of the Bible and Church history. In his commentary on the Articles, he

---

6 Forbes, *Creed*, 289

7 Forbes, *Creed*, 289

contrasts Newman's theory of development with the posture of Roman Catholics and Protestants writing at the outset of the reformation:

> The theory of development had not yet been used as the master-key to explain all existing phenomena. It had been propounded in Lerins in the fifth century, and in a very modified manner taught by St. Thomas Aquinas: but neither had Catholics used it to account for the dissidences between primitive practice and the actual state of things; nor did the Protestants use it to justify their novelties. Both parties appealed to antiquity.[8]

Contrasting the Roman Catholic theory of development and Anglican principles, Newman argues that St Vincent's claim that what has always been believed is impracticable as part of the rule of faith because so much remained unclear and undecided among the first Christians. Forbes shows that historically both Romans and Protestants claimed to hold a faith in harmony with that of the early Church, and both claimed to appealed to a Catholic Biblical faith: "The Roman Church to Scripture and coordinate tradition, as expounded by the living Church, especially by the successor of St. Peter; the Anglican to Scripture, witnessed to and expounded by the tradition of the Church."[9] Forbes sees parallels between the historic approaches of Romans and Anglicans absent in Newman's method.

The Articles of Religion, according to Forbes, address early modern debates in a manner that assumes the faith of the Bible, as represented and explained in the Church's tradition.

---

8   Forbes, *Articles*, 45

9   Forbes, *Articles*, 45.

His purpose in commenting on the Articles is to display how they can be turned from "the transitory controversies of the sixteenth century to those immutable truths which have been taught in the Church, and by the Church, in all ages[.]"[10] As Newman sought to explain apparent inconsistencies encountered when Christians faced different kinds of cultural conflicts and contexts, Forbes seeks to show that its possible to develop doctrine in such a way as to address new challenges while holding fast to unchanging truths. Both theologians sought to guide faithful Christians as they strive to stay on the straight and narrow despite the controversies obscuring the way.

Forbes casts light on what might be called the Evangelical Catholic rule of faith in his explanations of the Articles focusing on the doctrines of Scripture and the Church. First, he looks at the sufficiency of Scripture described in Article VI: "Holy Scripture containeth all things necessary to salvation: so that whatsoever is not read therein, nor may be proved thereby, is not to be required of any man, that it should be believed as an article of the Faith, or be thought requisite or necessary to salvation." The Article delineates the parameters of the Church's teaching office in a limited manner: "It defines the sense in which it means that Holy Scripture contains all things necessary to salvation, by the most important qualifications. It leaves the amplest room for the deductions which tradition or even individual doctors may gather from it,"[11] The scope of this article maintains the Church's traditional role as "guardian and the expounder" of the Scriptures.[12]

---

10   Forbes, *Articles*, 12

11   Forbes, *Articles*, 98

12   Forbes, *Articles*, 98

God once and for all reveals himself in the person of Christ and the Scriptures, Forbes maintains, and Christianity should not be confused with progressive sciences. Doctrinal development occurs in response to heresies in order to more clearly annunciate or definitely define the truths handed down in the Apostolic deposit. It also occurs when saints meditate on the mysteries of the faith, and by the grace of God, the Holy Spirit guides them into a more vivid description of those mysteries.[13]

Second, Article XX further clarifies the relationship between Church and Scripture, the Church has "authority in Controversies of Faith: And yet it is not lawful for the Church to ordain any thing that is contrary to God's Word written, neither may it so expound one place of Scripture, that it be repugnant to another." Forbes sees the Church "expounding" Scripture in such a way as to authoritatively decide "controversies in matters of faith." These matters of faith, particularly of what beliefs are necessary for salvation, arise out of the matter of Scripture. In the Church's teaching office, she explains which beliefs are essential parts of the Catholic faith and how Christians should interpret the passages that speak to such doctrines when adjudicating between contradictory and mutually exclusive interpretations. Forbes looks to Christ's promise that the Father has sent him into the world, so he analogously sends the disciples. He commissions them to do the sort of thing that he did and assures them that he will always be with them (Jn 20:21). According to Christ's commission, Forbes concludes, "[W]hen He ascended, He left His mystical Body

---

13   A.P. Forbes, *A Primary Charge Given to the Clergy of His Diocese* -Eucharistic Sacrifice and
Real Presence], London: Joseph Masters, 1858, 7

a society which in its turn should be the living expositor of the truth and represent Him."[14] Jesus Christ provides true interpretations of the Old Testament and answers passing controversies with immutable truths. He commissions the Apostles, as overseers and representative members of the Church, to do the same.

The Church, therefore, represents Christ across time and space: "The Church is the Body of the Lord; it is in its universality His visible form, His permanent ever renovated Humanity, His eternal revelation. He dwells in the community. All His promises and gifts are bequeathed to it, but to no individual, as such, since the days of the Apostles."[15] Forbes final point in this description of the Church raises a question. If the teaching office of the Church, the reliable voice of Christ, does not rest in, say, the bishop of Rome or the bishop of Canterbury, where can the faithful look to reliably find Christian truth?

"Christian Tradition" includes, Forbes contends, 'the concurrent testimony of antiquity, universality, and consent." St Vincent saw that "A doctrine which the Church has received and taught in every age, in every country, and concurrently by all, must be, as agreeable with the Divine Scripture, infallibly true." And Forbes recovers this canon to contest Newman's theory of development.[16] In doing so, he offers a rejoinder to Newman's argument against the Vincentian canon on the basis of the absence of certain terms integral to the doctrine of God among the first Christians: "inasmuch as the Church is indwelt by God the Holy Ghost, it is no mere concocter

---

14   Forbes, *Articles*, 270.

15   Forbes, *Articles*, 280.

16   Forbes, *Articles*, 281.

of formularies after a mechanical and lifeless fashion; it has been guided to express wisely and rightly the form of faith, and therefore has availed itself of new terms, such as " the consubstantial," rejecting it in. the wrong sense, accepting it in the right. [17] The Church develops terms and explanations to refute heresy and clarify orthodoxy, and she does so with infallibility in certain cases.

The Church stamps the decisions of Ecumenical Councils as infallible interpretations of Scripture and developments of Christian doctrine. Forbes discovers the origins of faith in the correspondence of unity and truth in the teaching of St Paul (Eph 4), more scientifically define in St Cyprian's *The Unity of the Church*, and a key to understanding the organ of the Church's teaching office in the Body of Christ: "So long as the Church was undivided, the organ was in perfection and did its work. The decisions of the ecumenical Church are the voice of the Holy Ghost; nothing can exaggerate the veneration or submission with which they ought to be received."[18] Disunity appears as an illness that impairs the healthy action of this organ. After the great schism of East and West, the Church's teaching office is more or less "limited to the authorization, inculcation, and application of truths already infallibly defined, or to the declaration of truth which had not yet that test of infallibility, the reception by the whole Church of Christ."[19]

---

17   Forbes, *Articles*, 281.

18   See Forbes, *Articles*, 286 and also Cyprian, *The Lapsed: Unity of the* Church, trans. Maurice Bevenot, Westminster, MD: Newman Press, 1957 for what Forbes considers the first scientific treatise on the subject.

19   Forbes, *Articles*, 286.

The Articles on the authority of Scripture and the Church explain where Christians should look as they search for the truth. They can find Christ revealed in the inspired scriptures, and guiding the faithful in the correct interpretation of this revelation through the tradition of the whole Church, especially in the creeds and decisions of Ecumenical Councils.

Forbes contrasts the Catholic decisions of the Church marked as infallible by the conclusions of ecumenical councils received by the whole Body of Christ with peculiar Roman innovations:

> [I]t is another thing, that a new growth of doctrine should spring up beside the Catholic Faith, that anthropomorphic tendencies should be gathered into the Church under a licensed image-worship, that the sympathetic nature of woman should be canonized in "the delegated omnipotency" of Mary, and that the dread of the next world and the shrinking of the natural instinct from the idea of eternal punishment for temporal sin should have shaped itself into such a theory of indulgences and purgatory as, practically speaking, in the case of those who die in the Church tends to obscure the notion of hell.[20]

Forbes proposes a test for Anglicans to apply when determining whether or not doctrinal developments measure up to the Evangelical Catholic rule of faith. This test should inform all legitimate decisions of the Church of England: "No decision is morally binding which is founded on one of these sources to the prejudice of the rest. Direct depravation of an article or contradiction of the Prayer Book, or of Holy Scripture, or of the concurrent voice of catholic antiquity[.]"[21]

---

20   Forbes, *Real Presence*, 8

21   Forbes, Real Presence, 9

Newman rightly challenges Roman Catholics and Anglican Orthodox to give an account for the faith within them in the face of apparent inconsistencies in the Church's tradition. A.P. Forbes, in explanations of the Creed and Articles, shows that such an account can, and should, uphold the Apostolic deposit, development of doctrine according to the rule of faith, and genuine Catholicity, what has been believed everywhere, always, and by all the faithful.

However Rome, Constantinople, or Canterbury err under the pressures of transitory controversies, the rule of faith ensures that Christians have a way to return to the form of Catholic Orthodoxy, the shape and boundaries of the Body of Christ. In an era when progressive dogmatism and multi-cultural relativism conquer more hearts, minds, and institutions by the day, we can take comfort in the truth that Jesus Christ is the way, the truth, and the life (Jn 14:6), and he remains with the faithful, even until the end of the age (Mt 28:20). Political leaders fail us, bishops fail us, but Christ, present at the right hand of the Father, present in Holy Communion, and present in his One, Holy, Catholic, and Apostolic Church never fails. And the gates of hell will not prevail against the advances of his church (Mt 16:17).

AN EXPLANATION OF THE THIRTY-NINE ARTICLES

Alexander Penrose Forbes

EPISTLE DEDICATORY

TO THE

REV. E. B. PUSEY, D.D.

My dearest Friend,

THERE seems a moral fitness, in the permission which you have so kindly accorded to me, that a work, undertaken at your suggestion, and assisted by your learning and counsel in each step of its progress to maturity, should be, with every assurance of the most devoted affection, dedicated to you. This enables me to express, in however inadequate terms, the veneration in which I hold you; and to acknowledge the deep debt of gratitude which I owe you, for the many benefits which you have bestowed upon me, during a friendship which has lasted for more than twenty years, and which has been one of my greatest earthly blessings. To have been trained in your school of thought has been the best discipline for the discharge of the onerous duties of the Episcopate: to have been admitted to your intimacy has been the greatest social and spiritual privilege I could have desired. It is the prerogative of noble and affectionate characters, that they who know them best love them most; and you have the mighty gift of a tender sympathy for those devoted friends from whom

a 2

you draw forth the sentiments of the most loyal and sincere attachment. Among those friends, there is none that you have distinguished with a more affectionate regard than myself. I can only say that I am deeply grateful. Moreover, to no one else can a book, which seeks to place the Anglican position on a philosophic and ecclesiastical basis, be more appropriately dedicated. You have devoted your time and your talents, and the varied gifts which God has bestowed upon you, to adorn the Church of England; by bringing forward in her service your varied stores of patristic learning; by the evolution of a more accurate theology; by the publication of heart-stirring and thoughtful sermons; by placing within the reach of her members adapted editions of the devout works of spiritual authors in other communions; by supplying to the student of Holy Scripture the beginning of a deep, affective, and exhaustive commentary on the Word of God; by the development of the dogmatic element in the Church's teaching as the strongest bulwark against rationalism and infidelity; by defending the authenticity and inspiration of that work which has been the battle-ground of modern criticism; by giving comfort to many perplexed, weary, doubting, and sin-laden hearts, both in the more special ministrations of your holy office and in less formal intercourse with those who have needed consolation; by the guiding of individual souls into the higher life; and by the foundation of religious communities, in which devout persons may serve God in the double way of contemplation and work. By all this and more you have earned the gratitude of all true members of the Church of England. Trained and disciplined within her sheltering care, you have acted upon the advice of the oracle in the thoughtful heathen story, and have adorned that Sparta in which the Providence of God has placed you.

The Thirty-nine Articles have suffered from having been always treated controversially. It is natural that they should be so treated, considering the circumstances under which they were put forth. They were to secure uniformity; in other words, " for the avoiding of diversities of opinions, and for the establishing of consent touching true religion," but uniformity on the basis of a protest against certain errors. The consequence is, that their first aspect is polemical, and this has led to their having been treated polemically. In the expositions of their contents which have been put forth, an undue proportion has been given to the negative side of theology, and this is to be regretted. The soul cannot live on negations. "I do not believe," is poor food for intellect or heart. No doubt error must be protested against, and there is a proper place for the negative as for the positive side in theology, just as we see the anathematisms at the end of the first draft of the Nicene Creed, and just as Councils often accompanied their positive enactments with the condemnation of errors, (the bare negative of such condemnation being all that comes rigorously to be believed as *de fide*); but still an undue proportion may be given to this, and it is right not to lose sight of the fact that the true way to confute falsehood is to build up and illustrate the opposite truth.

My aim, therefore, in the ensuing pages, is not so much to dwell on the condemnations of errors, as to elucidate and evolve the positive doctrines, the excesses and perversions of which doctrines are the subjects of the censure of the Articles. Almost all the errors touched on in the Articles are perversions or exaggerations of Gospel truths, and it is to illustrate these Gospel truths without these exaggerations that this attempt is made. For example, the Romish doctrine of pardons, alluded to in Article XXII., was a perversion of the belief and practice of the penitential discipline of the Church. It shall be my duty to shew what that penitential discipline was, and so of the rest. In short, this exposition shall be constructive, not destructive.

Viewed from this point, it will be seen what a vast amount of Christian truth the Articles of Religion cover; how they may be turned from the transitory controversies of the sixteenth century to those immutable truths which have been taught in the Church, and by the Church, in all ages; how they may be made the means of supplying that great want from which our divines at present suffer, the want of an accurate theology; for it cannot be denied that much of the vague, incorrect, and imperfect statement of the truth in the present day, is the result not of unbelief, or misbelief, or any conscious perversity of will in the matter of divine faith, but simply of want of clear-headedness and precision.

Ten years ago [a] I made the following remarks upon the position of the Articles of Religion, in their relation to the convictions of members of the Anglican Communion :—

"The outward expression of this [reaction] was exhibited in the Thirty-nine Articles, but it is to be observed that their loose and unsystematic structure precludes the idea of their ever having been intended to

[a] Primary Charge, delivered in 1857.

be the *sole* rule of faith. They are rather statements about truths, than the truths themselves. They assume an implicit substructure of the old catholicity, and therefore they do not define terms which, without a knowledge of the scholastic theology of the day, must have been unintelligible, and which actually, from the lack of such knowledge, have given rise to the most absurd mistakes, as may be seen by much which has been said about grace of condignity and congruity. The great doubts that have been entertained with regard to the true meaning of the Articles, are in themselves sufficient to prove that they could never have been intended to be the sole rule of faith in the Church. The possibility of Arian subscription was much discussed at the beginning of this century and at the end of the last. The great German theologian, Möhler, assumes that they are Calvinistic, though he bears testimony to the moderation of their expressions. Archbishop Laurence labours, in the Bampton Lectures of 1804, to shew that they are purely Lutheran. Sancta Clara asserts that, by the exercise of allowable casuistry, they are compatible with Tridentine doctrine; whereas Paley maintains that the legislature of the 13th Elizabeth being the imposer, its animus was 'to exclude abettors of Popery, Anabaptists, and Puritans,' and by saying that 'whoever finds himself comprehended within these descriptions ought not to subscribe,' seems almost to imply by the limitation that any one else may do so [b]."

" With such a diversity of opinion as this, it is absurd to hold that a set of propositions, drawn up with a certain object, to meet a peculiar state of circumstances, and swayed by very different influences, (for we find

[b] Vol. iii. p. 144.

the Queen, two parties of the clergy, and the Parliament, severally leaving their impress upon these documents,) is the only rule of faith in the Church. Unless we are prepared to allow that the legislature of the day is the ultimate reference in matters of faith, we must assign to the Articles but a subordinate place in their claim upon our submission. They cannot be looked upon as a Creed: they are Articles of Religion, that is, of obligation, binding under certain circumstances of holding office in the Church; not Articles of Faith in any strict sense, that is, of submission to God and His Church [c]."

On serious re-consideration I have no wish to modify or to alter the substance of what I then said on this subject; but since these words were written, it is to be observed, that an influential school in the Church of England has made an attempt, and to a degree succeeded, in modifying in some instances the stringency of subscription. With some this is almost confessedly an attempt to introduce the thin end of the wedge to abolish subscription altogether. I confess that, in the present circumstances of our Church, I am not prepared to advocate so sweeping a measure, though I am fully alive to the fact that the Articles are not only trying to the consciences of many individuals, who feel a natural difficulty in acquiescing in so many propositions imposed by a human authority, but that they have also a lowering effect upon men's apprehension of divine truth, from the way in which some of them are worded. I can sign them myself "in the literal and grammatical sense," that is, taking sentence by sentence as a lawyer would do, and where "the plain

[c] "Charge," pp. 3, 4, ed. 2.

and full meaning" alluded to in the Declaration is
doubtful, I supplement any deficiency by the interpretation of the other subscriptions which I have
made, and the documents I am bound to: so that, not
having the necessity to call in to my aid more than
the most moderate help of such laws of explanation as
all men practically need in the interpretation of every
oath, obligation, pledge, or subscription, I feel that I
am in the position of being able to come to a pretty
impartial opinion on the subject of relaxation, and
that opinion is, in the present circumstances of the
English Church, that subscription to the Articles
should be maintained; for some test, having a *quasi*
dogmatic character, seems necessary to our position;
and the difficulties of any substitution seem, at this
moment, insuperable.

I admit the hardship of demanding men's assent
to a document which, being uninspired, can claim no
heaven-directed guarantee for its truth. I acknowledge the halting in the argument which would impose
as a condition of ministering in the everlasting Church
of Christ, subscription to a formula which has received
modifications and alterations. I mislike the tone of some
individual Articles, and the inaccurate wording and
ambiguity of others; but I should have more sympathy
with those who are now clamouring for a change, if I
did not think that in attacking the Articles, they were
attacking the general dogmatic character of Christian
confessions.

But while I bear all this in mind, I think that in
remembering their history, we get a practical solution
of some of our difficulties; and for the illogical English mind, this is enough. Confessedly a compromise in

the forms of their expressions, the Articles do not affect to declare absolute truth. There is no one Christian confession that they absolutely make for. They cannot satisfy the pure Calvinist, (however often they are ignorantly claimed for them, even by so great a writer as Möhler,) for not one of the five points of Calvinism is expressly stated in them, and some, such as Perseverance and the Indefectibility of Grace (Art. XVI.), are actually contradicted. They cannot be said to symbolize with the Confession of Augsburg, inasmuch as they give no countenance to the crucial doctrine of Luther, justification by mere imputation, or by that faith which believes itself justified. The High Church party have never concealed their depreciation of them in comparison with the *lex supplicandi lex credendi* of the Book of Common Prayer, while they are silent on, if not contradictory to, many of the Shibboleths of modern Evangelicalism. The name or idea of sensible conversion does not occur from beginning to end, neither is there mention of the renouncing of our own merits as the formal cause of our justification, or of assurance, as the end to be sought for in the spiritual life. The Articles give no countenance to the idea, that if a man dies happy, (as the saying is,) he is safe.

It is very difficult now to throw oneself into the mind of the framers of the Articles at their last revision. We know that there were many contrariant opinions to conciliate. The political and religious state of England, in 1562 and 1571, was made up of many factors, and all these told profoundly on the composition of the Articles.

The problem was to construct a Confession for the National Church of England. England had cast off the jurisdiction of the Bishop of Rome, and had thrown herself on the right that every individual and nation has, of reforming his ways, if he have erred, as France had, in a less degree, actually done one hundred years before, when, at the Council of Bourges, the Pragmatic Sanction gathered up the results of that of Constance. What was to be the common basis of belief on which the National Church was henceforth to stand? The factors, as I said, were many and various. There was the old pre-Reformation dislike of foreign, and especially of Italian interference—there was the stench of the fires of Smithfield still fresh in the nostrils of the people—there was the fear of the predominant influence of Spain—there was the germ of the democratic spirit which afterwards expressed itself in English Puritanism—there was the marked religious influence of the Marian Exiles, and of their friends the foreign Reformers. Luther and Melanchthon told strongly in one direction; Calvin had his representatives in both the Universities; and the nation had already been committed to a certain tone of thought in the earlier Articles, some Acts of Parliament, and the two Prayer-books of Edward VI. On the other hand, one half of England was still, practically speaking, in a state of traditionary Catholicism: a school of theologians, represented by Cheyney, Bishop of Gloucester [d], to whom we may add, Alley, of Exeter, and Gheast, of Rochester, with others, such as Baron and Barrett at Cambridge, had sustained itself in a more or less constant appeal to Antiquity and Church authority from the time of Ridley, the germ in fact of the afterwards distinguished school of Andrewes and the Caroline di-

[d] Vide Collier's Hist., vi. 488.

vines: the Court, as represented by Cecil and Bacon, really inclined to the *via media;* and Elizabeth's own proclivities, never indulged indeed at the expense of her interest, were probably in the direction of the old religion [e].

But the foundation of the school may be traced further back than Cheyney. It is the outcome of that school of thought which all through the Middle Ages existed, representing the national as against the papal tone of thought among the clergy. The history of the passing of the Act of Supremacy shews that there were no Protestant elements at work in that act. Under the influence of the strong will of Henry VIII., it was the act of men who most of them ended their lives in communion with the see of Rome. These men, represented chiefly by Gardiner, Bishop of Winchester, were driven into the fiercest reaction by the acts of Edward VI. What the political foresight of More, and the spiritual instinct of Fisher had revealed to them, they found out too late, that to separate from the rest of the Latin Church, even on justifiable grounds, involved consequences of the most momentous character. Though they might have continued in the Church of England as left by Henry VIII., there was no room for them in that of his successor; and accordingly we see the course they adopted during the brief restoration of the old religion in Queen Mary's time. The blinded cruelties of that unhappy reign are written in letters of fire and blood in the annals of England. Among other miseries, it prevented any reconciliation of parties among those actually implicated in them, when Queen Elizabeth succeeded.

[e] Vide Hallam's Const. Hist., vol. i. p. 234; Strype's Parker, p. 227.

But still, in the case of the rank and file of the Church, the old spirit remained [f]. Suppressed and crushed, it formed the vivifying influence when the Catholic opinions began to re-assert themselves. The Lower House of Convocation, we know, at the beginning of her reign, spoke out in the ancient voice; and though much was done to destroy that spirit, yet there is no doubt that it continued to exist, gradually, during Elizabeth's reign, overcome by the growing Puritanism, but destined to rise from its ashes in the time of her successor, when, after giving birth to the belief of such men as Andrewes, Montague, and Donne, it developed into the great school of the Caroline divines.

Meanwhile the Council of Trent had just concluded its sittings, and the last sessions having been strongly affected by the influence of Laynez and the Jesuits, had ceased to exhibit that wise moderation and dread of giving unnecessary scandal which had distinguished those canons which had been drawn up at the earlier period of its history, before Charles V. was dead, and all hope of curing the schism had died away. There was, therefore, no great inclination on the part of the English to modify any strong expressions that might have been used on the points controverted between the Churches, though we do find some instances of a milder phraseology; nay, as the breach seemed now incurable, the same process that affected the Fathers at Trent would naturally affect the English in an opposite direction, and while the Romanist occupied his time and thought in securing (as he believed) the Church doctrine against the insidious and plausible sophistries of the Reformers, the Church of England was naturally tempted to retain strong

[f] Strype's Annals, vol. i. p. 166.

language with regard to those popular superstitions and corruptions of the old faith, the abuses and scandals, in short, which formed her only justification for infringing existing theories of the unity of the Body of Christ. On this point all who were concerned in making the Articles would be agreed, for the English Roman Catholic prelates necessarily took no part in their construction; and though Elizabeth never intended to shut the door so as to prevent a possible reconciliation with the see of Rome [s], yet just at this time the irritation was increasing, and the temporary friendship of Philip II. turning into the deadliest hate.

The times were not favourable for symbolizing the results of religious thought. The reign of Elizabeth, of all the periods of English history, has suffered most from historical investigation. For a long time the assumed advocacy of certain popular and successful ideas invested Elizabeth with a factitious glory, and the contrast of her reign with that of her successors added to her fame. But truth in the long run vindicates herself. "Non semper pendet inter latrones crucifixa veritas." The revelations of the State Paper Office, and still more the confidential papers of the Spanish ambassador laid up at Simancas, have made a sad alteration in the estimate of that epoch. They exhibit a condition of things very sad: hand to mouth legislation, political pyrrhonism, unbounded profligacy characterize the upper classes of England. The Queen, loving Dudley much, but power more, is found to be jealous and self-willed as her father, avaricious and selfish as Henry VII. The nobility, uncertain as to the future succession, from the Queen's reluctance

____

[s] Vide Froude's History, vol. ix. p. 325.

to marry, are involved in constant intrigue, and desirous of opening the way for reunion with Rome[h], while the Church settlement is too recent to inspire any well-founded confidence. With some noble exceptions—Matthew Parker was of blameless life and great learning, and in later days[i] Carleton, though a Puritan, was an excellent man—the Elizabethan bishops were far from being perfect types of the episcopal character[k]. The remains of Church property, left by the sacrilege of Edward the Sixth's time, were jobbed in a disgraceful way[l]. A persecuting spirit prevailed, although the severities greatly increased as Elizabeth grew older[m]. The parish churches were shamefully neglected; even the cathedral closes lay in squalor and decay[n]. There is almost a relief in the thought of the rise of a certain earnest Puritanism, which, though containing within itself the seeds of heresy and political danger, at least redeemed England from religious stagnation. Dull and narrow was the thought, still it was religious thought, and its earnestness in due time touched the heart of England.

I say advisedly in due time, for during the most of Elizabeth's reign its influence was confined to London and the wealthy country towns. The great mass of England was implicitly Catholic[o], even in the case of those who had submitted to the new-made changes. Most of the peers of old creation were either avowed

---

[h] Froude, vol. ix. p. 414.   [i] Hallam's Const. Hist., vol. i. pp. 154, 163.

[k] Hallam's Const. Hist., vol. i. p. 274.   [l] Fuller, vol. ii. p. 498.

[m] Hallam's Const. Hist., vol. i. p. 204.

[n] Calendar of State Papers, 1587—1589, vol. lxxiii. 68; Sept. 12, 1570, vol. lxxi. 58, p. 385; March 12, 1562, p. 196, vol. xvii. 32, p. 177.

[o] Ibid., 1547—1589, vol. lxxiii. 36, p. 390.

Roman Catholics or had sympathies in that direction [p]. The country squires, the tenants of land, and the labourers, were less influenced by the change in London than we can imagine [q]. Putting out of the question the feeling of the people, as illustrated by the different rebellions, the great mass went on very much as they had done before. The struggle between the old and new theology was long, and the event sometimes seemed doubtful. "There were two extreme parties prepared to act with cruelty, or to suffer with resolution. Between them lay, during a considerable time, a middle party, which blended very illogically, but by no means unnaturally, lessons learned in the nursery with the sermons of the modern evangelists, and while clinging with fondness to old observances, yet detected abuses with which these observances were closely connected [r]." They had never liked the foreign influences, therefore they did not miss the prayers for the Pope and "hys trewe cardinallys:" they had seen their churches emptied of images, and a number of symbolical rites, which to them had ceased to be symbols, given up; they had gained somewhat in having the services and homilies, such as they were, in the vernacular, and therefore in a language which they could understand; the clergy were living in half-respected marriage rather than in tolerated concubinage, though the legality of such marriages was still doubtful, Parker having to obtain letters of legitimation for his own offspring [s]. The poor looked back with fond regrets to the days when the ever-ready dole was given at each convent door, and

---

[p] Froude, vol. x. p. 110.   [q] Ibid., vol. ix. p. 506.   [r] Macaulay, Hist., vol. i. p. 49.   [s] Hallam's Const. Hist., vol. i. p. 236.

they retained most of the practices of devotion to which
they were used in childhood. They still made reverence to the altar, though the blessed Sacrament was
no longer habitually there; they still invoked the four
Evangelists in a form that has come down to the nineteenth century among the poor.

Even in the classes of the more intelligent—except
of course where the Puritan element was generated—
the same traditional religion long maintained itself.
This is very evident from Shakspeare's plays. The
religion of that great man has long been the subject of
discussion. Some have maintained that he was a Roman
Catholic; a great scholar has written a book to prove
that he was an Anglican of the modern type; while
an eminent review would have it that his great mind
soared above all distinctive forms of religious belief.
I believe that none of these views are entirely true.
I believe that Shakspeare—making some allowance, of
course, for the costume of the characters he portrayed—
exhibited what was the current religion among the mass
of the people in Elizabeth's time, a faith in which the
great features of the old religion remained, modified
and stripped of excesses and superstitions, but still in
tone and temper Catholic in the main.

If, however, it be said that the evidence from Shakspeare is inconclusive, we have a much more distinct
proof of our position in the diary of Henry Machyn,
Citizen and Merchant Taylor in London, which he kept
between the years A.D. 1550 and A.D. 1563. This individual conducted the funerals of many of the great
personages of that epoch, and the journal begins with
a mere chronicle of these. Gradually, however, he
takes to recording the public events as they occur, and

although we find no profound or farsighted speculations
on those stormy times, yet we have an accurate account
of the extraordinary occurrences, the deprivations, consecrations, imprisonment, trials, and executions which
distinguished them. "On religious matters his information is valuable, so far as it represents the sentiments
and behaviour of the common people at this vacillating
period of our ecclesiastical history. It is evident from
numerous passages that his own sympathies were inclined to the old form of worship. . . . It is instructive,
however, to observe, that in common with the population at large, he afterwards took great interest in the
public sermons which were so zealously multiplied by
the new preachers [t]."

[t] Preface, pp. ix., x.

Machyn's diary records the complete public restoration of the rites of
the Roman Catholic religion during Queen Mary's time. Every procession, festival, funeral, and even sermon is carefully recorded. Nothing
could be more complete than the re-establishment of the old religion in
all its pomp. At last comes the notice of the Queen's death: "The
xvii of November, betwyn v and vi in the morning, ded quen Mare, the
vj yere of here grace's rayne, the wych Jhesu have mercy on her solle!
Amen." Then he goes on to detail the events in Queen Elizabeth's
reign, and here we get evidence how few and how gradual were the
changes. On the 22nd of November, 1558, there is "morow-masse" at
the funeral of Robert Jonsun: so at that of Lady Chamley, on the 7th
of December, "and she had iiij baners of santtes (saints)." Cardinal Pole's
body is carried in procession to Canterbury "with iiij baners of saints in
oil." On the 28th of December, at Bishop Christopherson's funeral,
"v bisshopes dyd offer (at) the masse, and iij songe masse that day." On
the 23rd was "durge and morow-masse" to Charles V. On the xv
January there is mass at Q. Elizabeth's coronation. The Lent of 1558-9
is strictly kept. On the vii of April, 1559, he records 'the first use of the
English Burial service;' yet on the xii of April, at the funeral of Sir
Richard Monsfeld, there are "24 prests clarks, prayers all latin and
durge." At the burial of Lady Barnes "there was a xx clarkes singing
afor her to the Church, with blake and arms: and after Master Horne

But a better witness than that of Shakspeare and of Machyn to the current belief of England is to be found

mad a sermon, and after the Clarks song *Te Deum Laudamus* in English, and after bered with a songe, and a-for songe the Englys precessyon." On the xi June, 1559, "the postulle masse mad an end that day, and mass a Powlles was non that day, and the new Dene took possessyon. . . . and the same night they had no evensong at Powlles." It records of the deprivations and substitutions of the bishops, and the departure of the religious in June and July, 1559. Machyn styles the bishops of the new succession exactly as their predecessors are styled. "The xiii day of August dyd pryche at Powlles Crose the bysshop of Harford Skore." On the xxiv of August, 1559, two "gret bonfires of roods and Mares, and John and oder images, these they were burnyd with great wonder." On the vii September "Dirge is sung for the French King." On the iv of November "was a prest mared with a prest's widow ;" and "one West, a new doctr, raylyd of the rod-loft." He records the election and consecration of the new bishops. On the 25th January, "were mayd at Powlles by the new Bp. of London lx prestes, ministers, and decons, and more." On the 30th January, "dyd prech Master Juell, the new Bp. of Salesby, and there he said playnley that there was no pergatore." In March the bishops are mentioned as preaching "in Rochett and Chymere ;" and Dr. Byll, preacher in the Queen's chapel, where "the Cross and two candylls borning, and the tabulle were standing auterwyse." On Palm Sunday, 1562, Parker preached "a nobull sermon." In the Rogation week, 1560, "they whent a processyon in dyvers places." On the other hand, Jan. 17, 1560, Master Flammocke was "carred to church without synging or clarks, and at the church a Psalm-song after Genevay, and a sermon and bered contennente." In the beginning of Lent, Master Adams, "dwellyng in Lyttel Est chepe, is fined for killing iii oxen." On the xvi April all the altars in Henry VII. chapel are taken down, and the stones carried "where Queen Mare was bered." On the 23rd of April, St. George's Day, "the quen's court chaplains in copes, to the number of xxx, sang the Litany in procession." On the 18th of May, they do so again, in grey amices. Machyn notes that the destruction of St. Paul's takes place on the eve of Corpus Christi. He mentions Elizabeth's banishment of the prebendaries' wives from out the colleges, and the restoration of daily service at St. Paul's, "was begon the serves at Powlles to synge, and there was a great communion there begun." On Nov. 1, there is a torchlight service there. At the burial of John Brun's wife, "20 clarks carry their sorplices on their arms."

in the Homilies themselves. These works, written in the interest of the "new learning," and not without some of the Shibboleths of the Reformation—authorized by Cranmer and Jewel—are yet full of testimonies to the continued prevalence of many of the ancient doctrines [u]. The inspiration of the Apocrypha, the authority of Councils and of the primitive Church, as well as of the ancient Church doctors and Catholic Saints and Fathers, the Presence of Christ in the Eucharist, the recognition of Order and Matrimony as Sacraments, the reign of the Saints in heaven with God, the purifying and cleansing effect of alms-deeds, the power of the keys, are all assumed as principles. How could it have been otherwise? The Marian clergy were not exterminated; they conformed, partly in hope of better times, partly from fear of the Government, partly moved by a sincere desire for reformation; but still the traditions of a whole lifetime cannot be destroyed in a moment, and any great shock to their feelings would have led them to act as the eighty rectors, fifty prebendaries, fifteen masters of colleges, twelve archdeacons, twelve deans, and six abbots and abbesses, actually did, that is, abandon their preferments [x]. We are left to the dilemma that either the great mass of the lower clergy were a set of unprincipled self-seekers, or that the changes, interpreted by custom and previous usage, were so small, that no real violence was done to their consciences.

To approach, therefore, the subject of the interpretation of the Articles, it is necessary to place ourselves in the position of those who first accepted them. They must be read with the gloss of antecedent faith

[u] Vide *Apologia pro Vita mea*, p. 164.
[x] Fuller's Church History, vol. ii. p. 451.

and preconceived notion. Just as in our own time men have read them with the preconceived notion of the Low Church School, and so have imported into them meanings which their letter will not bear: so at the time of their enforcement they must have been read with the deep consciousness of the old traditional Christianity, which had obtained in England since the days of St. Augustine of Canterbury, which had animated the faith of Lanfranc and of St. Anselm, had warmed the affection of St. Thomas Cantilupe and of St. Stephen Harding, but which, chilled and overshadowed by the corruption of the fourteenth and fifteenth centuries, now cried out for a fresh outpouring of the Holy Spirit of God.

In no other way can we account for the rise of the Caroline school. This line of thought never ceased to be represented in the Universities, and protected by some of the bishops. When the Puritan element began in the next reign to disturb the State, here was found the material for reaction. There is nothing in Bishop Andrewes' works to shew that his views were those of a counter-Reformation, as we find later in the time of Laud. Educated in such a religion as I have attempted to describe, he applied his learning to develope his position, and the reverence in which he was held in the next generation, as well as during his lifetime, shews that his views had the strength and consistency of a hereditary position.

So much for the elements that went to make up the mind of the English Church in the days of Elizabeth. It would be unfair not to say somewhat as to the form of its expression. That form was suggested by the numerous Confessions which were put forth by the

Protestants. Such Confessions are the fruits of the Reformation, the necessary results of a system which, in attacking what was then considered the ancient belief, needed to consolidate its existence on the basis of human conscience. When as a Church it could no longer impose its distinctive teachings as the voice of the Holy Ghost, when it gave to its determinations only a collateral authority, that it was in accordance with the Word of God, it was necessary to call in the element of individual good faith to maintain the position. A man no longer submitted his reason to the teaching of the body to which he belonged, he now belonged to the body because he believed in its teaching. This was the only reasonable attitude which the right of private judgment permitted, and therefore all the Protestant bodies of necessity put forth their Confessions.

England, while retaining her organic and sacramental connexion with the old Church, through the episcopal consecrations and perpetuation of the orders of the Church Catholic, was from her position obliged in a degree to follow in this course, and, as was natural, not only adopted the same form as the Continental Reformers, but actually borrowed much from them. An interesting parallelism might be drawn between the Articles, and many of the Lutheran and Calvinistic formulas, especially the Confession of Augsburg; and the result would be, that while the likeness is in many respects confessed, the Protestant Shibboleths are in the main left out, and a form of words of exceeding moderation, and to which succeeding ages have rightly or wrongly assigned an ambidextrous character, is left to us, purposely made to include the greatest number of adherents, a process which has resulted in the acknowledged fact of the co-existence of a Catholic and Protestant element within the pale of the Anglican Church, which has continued to this very day.

On the other hand, it will be observed, that many of the sentences are almost in the very words of approved Church doctors and schoolmen. Not to mention the reference to St. Jerome in the Sixth, and to the Pseudo-Augustine in the Twenty-ninth Articles, we shall find that many of the Articles enunciate truth in authoritative language. The Seventeenth Article is a concise summary of St. Augustine's teaching, the end of that on free-will is in his own words, and the corroboration of the opinion of grave divines may be adduced for some of the most startling of the propositions. Before the Council of Trent, the line was not drawn so sharply as afterwards. Individual doctors allowed themselves considerable latitude in matters not authoritatively ruled by the Church; and it is no reproach to the English Church that she availed herself of a latitude of belief claimed by or conceded to Peter Lombard or Cajetan. Denying the authority of the Council of Trent that shut up this liberty, she felt herself free to use it. The Councils of the thirteenth century, which England by Provincial Councils had already accepted, had not defined anything which clashes with the English Articles. A writer, much approved by the English bishops, says: "In the first Lateran Council, there was no decree on faith;" in the second, "nothing except what was laudable was done in matter of faith;" in the third, "there was no decree on faith, except that the heretics, called Cathari, &c., were for very good reasons excommunicated." "No *decisions on* faith seem to have been made in the first Synod of Lyons." "The only decree on faith made by Gregory in the second synod of Lyons was a definition that the Holy Ghost proceeds from the Father and the Son as from one principle." "The Synod of Vienne made decrees, which seem to have been generally laudable [y]." At Constance, the reception in one kind was not laid down as a law. It was only decreed that the custom of receiving was not to be rejected by man's private judgment *without the authority of the Church*. No part of the Council of Basle is now accepted by any one. The Council of Florence, according to the last eminent editor of the Councils, laid down nothing new on the authority of the Pope, but only declared whence it may be ascertained what the power of the Pope is [z]. The Cardinal of Lorraine, Launoi, (in the name of the Gallican Church,) and others following them, denied that it was Œcumenical. But, in fact, with the exception of doctrines on Transubstantiation and Purgatory, (of which more hereafter,) there was no controverted doctrine then ruled as *de fide* which the Anglican Articles had to do with.

Another point to be observed is, that the Articles are not systematic. They do not evolve one theory of God's dealings with mankind. Lutheranism is a system rolling round its cardinal doctrine of *fiducia*, that justifying faith is the faith that believes itself to be justified. It is a whole in which other doctrines exist only in the bearing upon this. So Calvinism is a system in which all turns on election and reprobation, all other doctrines being subordinated to and influenced by this; but the English position in the

---

[y] Palmer on the Church, p. iv. c. ii. t. ii. p. 216, sqq.

[z] Mansi, *Animad. in Alex. Natal.*, Diss. x. Art. vii. § 4. cit. Ffoulkes.

Articles is the reformation of certain abuses. The old Creed is everywhere assumed, as well as the abuse in reference to it, and then a statement is made in correction or modification:—"Vitium vel abusus corrigi debet et non status destrui, vel suis debitis juribus defraudari: sicut boni medici est ab infirmo morbum tollere et non infirmum corpus destruere [a]."

For the right understanding of the Articles, it is of paramount importance to remember the organic identity of the Church of England before and after the Reformation. The Church of England is older than the State of England. It was a unity when England was a Heptarchy. There was a chief bishop of Canterbury before there was a king of England. The spiritualty and temporalty of the nation was a complete whole, organized and regulated, while the political necessities of the country, the talent and ambition of individual rulers, were gradually forming the State. The *nexus* of the Church was found, in the hierarchy, in the succession of Church officers. They were the *personæ* of the Church of England. The personality was further maintained both by ecclesiastical laws and by civil laws recognising the Church. So far as the organic character of the Church is concerned, the Reformation was nothing but the alteration of some of the ecclesiastical and civil laws affecting it. As there was a *persona* of the Church of England in each living before the Reformation, so there was a *persona* of the same Church of England in each living after the Reformation, and the alteration in doctrine and discipline within certain limits did not affect this. I say advisedly within certain limits, for changes might be caused which would destroy the

[a] Peter D'Ailly, *de Ref. Eccl. c. de ref. cap.*

identity of the two bodies, utterly divide the pre-Reformation from the post-Reformation Churches, as actually for a time took place in Scotland. When the old religion was abolished in 1560 in Scotland, its hierarchy came to an end. The bishops of the old succession consecrated no successors. The Reformers, claiming to be the true Church of Christ, started their General Assembly, which excommunicated those who differed from it. Only the most earthly accidents of Church property, such as teinds, manses, &c. were assumed as identical [b].

In England it was very different. The organic identity was carefully preserved, as may be seen from the efforts made by Elizabeth towards securing the continuation of the old succession. Parker threw himself back upon the forms and processes used in Cranmer's Pontificale, which were the old canonical forms (excluding, of course, what referred to the Pope) used in the election of Bishops before the institution of papal provisions in the thirteenth and fourteenth centuries. These forms had been always in use for the election of Abbots, and in the reign of Henry V., during the vacancy of the Popedom in 1416, had been used in the case of Bishops. They were still and always canonical, but superseded in each vacancy by a distinct act of the Pope. What had been lawful, or eventually allowed then, must be lawful or eventually allowable now. The essence of the old forms was retained; what was given up was held to be superfluous. Organically, then, the Church before and after the Reformation was one.

[b] Yet when the hierarchy was restored by the English consecrations, the old diocesan arrangements were strictly adhered to.

But the other element had to be considered also. It is of the essence of the Church that it teach the Catholic faith. As the Church had been Catholic before the Reformation, (though in the eyes of the Reformers corrupted,) so it was Catholic after the Reformation, (in the eyes of the Reformers purified). This is founded in truth. Had such a change taken place at the Reformation as would have altered the integrity of the faith, e.g. had the Church taught Arianism, it would have ceased to be the same Church as before, it would have become a new Church. Organic identity depends upon dogmatic identity. If the Church of England in any true sense is the Church before the Reformation, there must be a certain dogmatic identity. Roman Catholics deny this—maintain that the changes made were in essentials, and so destructive of all identity. The only logical basis of Anglicanism is the maintenance of the identity, the Protestant notion of a new primitive Church, teaching the Shibboleths of modern religionism, for the moment extemporized, being historically and philosophically false: hence, in proportion as the foundation of a theoretical Anglicanism is deeply laid, so in that measure must the organic identity be maximized, and by consequence the theological differences of the same Church in its two phases be minimized. "Turpis fit pars quæ suo non congruit universo."

Such minimization would be the natural effect of the working, or existence, of the Marian clergy who conformed in Elizabeth's time. We know that they effectually prevented the other party going into extremes. The Queen had also the convocation of York, still addicted to the old learning, to consider. It would be her wish that as little violence as possible should be done to their consciences, though the Bishops acted in a high-handed way in dealing with some of the mediæval practices.

After all, even theologically, there was much to be said for the position. Mediæval corruptions were assumed, perhaps exaggerated, if we may judge by some passages in the Homilies, but then mediæval corruptions had been assumed by all the Reformers within the Church from the time of the Council of Basle. The great work of Erasmus had been simply destructive of these. Colet followed in his steps; and even the great and holy More, in his earlier days, had been deeply convinced of the necessity of some reformation, and only rushed into reaction when he saw what way the Reformation was likely to go.

Given, then, the existence of mediæval corruptions, there was a fair issue between the two learnings. The theory of development had not yet been used as the master-key to explain all existing phenomena. It had been propounded in Lerins in the fifth century, and in a very modified manner taught by St. Thomas Aquinas: but neither had Catholics used it to account for the dissidences between primitive practice and the actual state of things; nor did the Protestants use it to justify their novelties. Both parties appealed to antiquity. The Roman Church to Scripture and co-ordinate tradition, as expounded by the living Church, especially by the successor of St. Peter; the Anglican to Scripture, witnessed to and expounded by the tradition of the Church.

Staking, therefore, the question on this issue, the Reforming Bishops had a good deal to say for themselves. It is doubtful whether all the statements in

Jewel's Apology are theologically defensible, still there are some blots which he distinctly hits, and at any rate he indicates a line of thought which may successfully be carried to its conclusion.

The founder of the existing Church of England, at the Reformation as now, is Pope St. Gregory the Great, a writer of great sagacity, earnestness, and orthodoxy, from whose writings we may easily cull what were the doctrines which St. Augustine of Canterbury preached to the men of Kent, and what is of more importance, what he imposed upon them as conditions of communion—as things to be held as *de fide*. If we find him asserting his prerogative of successor of St. Peter, Patriarch of the West, Primate of the suburbicarian Churches, we find him in his dispute with John Nesteutes, of Constantinople, laying down such canons of ecclesiastical hierarchy as contradict both mediæval Papalism and modern Ultramontanism. If we find him strongly asserting the efficacy of the Eucharistic Sacrifice, we find no countenance for transubstantiation; his very public Liturgy recognising the existence of the *munus temporale* in the Sacrament as well as the *cœleste remedium*. If we find him ordaining litanies and invocations to the saints, we discover very little mention of the prerogatives of the mother of God, and the strongest assertions of Christ being the only sinless One. If we find him (assuming the authenticity of the Dialogues) living in a very atmosphere of miracle, we find the strictest prohibitions of anything like picture-worship. If he stoutly asserts a power of ruling and administration in his own see, we find that he bases the faith upon Scripture, and upon the four Councils recognised by the Church of England. There is in all his works not a word in favour of indulgences, or of communion under one kind, or of the *thesaurus meritorum;* while positively in his dealings with the Emperor Phocas he accepts somewhat of the Anglican position with regard to the civil power, and in his answers to St. Augustine, admits the position in reference to the separate rites and customs of "the Churches of Italy, France, Spain, and Germany," described in the Canons of 1604.

It may be said, of course, that while the details of the teaching of St. Gregory support the Anglican system, the spirit is Roman; that the hands are the hands of Esau, the voice the voice of Jacob; in other words, that while the formal outline of St. Gregory's faith coincides with that of the Anglican Church, the teaching is practically Roman, only not in a developed state. To this the satisfactory answer is, that we must distinguish between St. Gregory's private opinions and his official and public belief. St. Gregory, as an individual doctor, is one person; St. Gregory, as the official representative of the Church, is another.

To sum up, then, and to conclude, I venture in the following work to assume,—that the position of the Anglican Church requires that the Articles shall be interpreted in the Catholic Sense; that this sense exposes us to fewer difficulties than any other canon of explanation; and, that historically there is support for this theory.

Lastly, convinced that a divided Christendom will not be able to stand the assaults of infidelity, as a house divided against itself cannot stand, I therefore, in all that I have written, have had in view the future reunion of the Church. Recognising the pro-

vidential position of the Anglican Church, as stretch-
ing forth one hand to the Protestant bodies, and the
other to the Latin and Greek Churches, I have tried
to do justice to that position, by acknowledging on
the one hand the great necessity for a reform in morals
and discipline at the time of the separation, and on the
other by minimizing the points of dissidence between
ourselves and those venerable institutions. It is no
longer a question of opinions on either side. The basis
of reunion must be on that which is ruled as *de fide*,
and of this nothing is to be assumed as such, but the
contrary of what is published under anathema. This
reduces the difficulty, and leaves a wide margin for
negociation and explanation. May God in His good
time incline men's hearts to this, and let the heavens
rejoice, and the earth be glad, for that the wall of partition is broken down.

Believe me,
Ever affectionately yours,
THE AUTHOR.

DUNDEE,
May 8, 1867.

SYNCHRONISTICAL TABLE.

1562.

England.	Scotland.	France.	Portugal.	Spain.	Italy.	Naples.	States of the Church.	Nether-lands.	Holy Roman Empire.	Sweden.	Poland.	Turkey.
Elizabeth reigning from 1568-1603. Thirty-nine Articles ratified. Establishment of Poor Law. 1566, Queen resists enforcing the Articles by Act of Parliament.	Mary, 1567. Revolt of Huntley. Battle of Corrichie.	Charles IX., 1560-1574. The Huguenots protected. Synod of Poissy, 1561. Slaughter of Huguenots at Vassi. Beginning of religious civil wars.	Sebastian, 1557-1578. Cardinal Henry Regent. The kingdom begins to decline.	Philip II., 1556-1598. Persecution Arbitrary taxation. Preparation for building the Escurial.	Cosmo dei Medici, 1569. In tranquillity for sixty-six years, under Spanish ascendency.	Philip II. governs by Viceroys.	Pius IV. (Medici), 1559-1566, re-assembles the Council of Trent.	Philip II. Cardinal Grandvelle Minister.	Ferdinand I., 1558-1564. Relinquishes the custom of the Emperor being crowned by the Pope. Truce with the Turks, 1568. Conference of Altenburg.	Eric XIV., 1560-1568. War with Russia and Poland.	Sigismund Augustus, 1562. Diet of Wilna. Next year admits the Protestants to the dignities of the kingdom.	Soliman the Magnificent. Military power of the Turks at its greatest height. Truce of eight years with the German Empire.

1571.

England.	Scotland.	France.	Portugal.	Spain.	Italy.	Naples.	States of the Church.	Nether-lands.	Holy Roman Empire.	Sweden.	Poland.	Turkey.
Conspiracy of Norfolk. Money and troops sent to help the Huguenots.	Morton succeeded Murray as Regent.	1567, Massacre of St. Bartholomew.	Universal peace.	The battle of Lepanto.	Cyprus reduced by the Turks.	The Pope unsuccessfully claims jurisdiction over Sicily.	Pius V. (Ghislieri) excommunicates Queen Elizabeth. Gregory XIII., (Buoncompagni,) succeeds, 1572.	Alva's reign of terror. 8,000 artizans emigrate to England in 1569.	Maximilian II., 1564-1576. Universal religious toleration in Austria.	1570, Peace of Stettin. Mutual concessions between Denmark and Sweden.	1573, Extinction of the Jagellans.	Selim II., 1566-1574. 1570, First encounter between the Turks and Russians on the Volga.

DATES OF THE DIFFERENT EVENTS

BEARING ON THE

CONSTITUTION AND INTERPRETATION OF THE THIRTY-NINE ARTICLES.

Those specially relating to the English Church are printed in italics.

———

A.D.

1500. Birth of Charles V.

1521. Diet of Worms.

1529. Conference at Marburg between Lutherans and Zwinglians (Oct. 3).

—— Schwaback Articles, in number XVII. (Oct. 15).

1530. Torgau Articles.

—— Augsburg Confession presented to Charles V. (June 25).

—— Confutation thereof by Eck, Wimpere, Faber, and Cochlæus (Aug. 3).

—— Final breach with Lutherans brought about by Campeggius (Aug. 16).

1531. *Gardiner made Bishop of Winchester.*

1532-3. *Statute of 24 Henry VIII., harbinger of Reformation.*

1533. *Cranmer made Archbishop of Canterbury.*

1534. *Deliberations in the two Provincial Synods of Canterbury and York on the jurisdiction of the Bishop of Rome, and its rejection.*

—— League of Schmalkald (Dec. 24): *Fox and Heath present.*

1536. Calvin's Institutes published.

A.D.

1536. Conferences at Wittenburg (Jan. 15).

—— *"Articles devyzed by the Kinges Highnes Majestie to stablyshe Christen quietnes and unitie among us," and consequent Rebellion in Lincolnshire.*

1537. *Institution of a Christian Man.*

1538. *Lutheran Embassy to England (May 12), and consequent XIII Articles.*

—— *Royal Commission contra Anabaptistas (Oct. 1).*

—— Select Committee de Emendendâ Ecclesiâ, appointed by Paul III.

1539. *Statute of the Six Articles.*

1540. Foundation of the Company of Jesus.

1541. Colloquy of Ratisbon under Contarini.

1543. *Necessary Doctrine for any Christian Man.*

—— *Repressive Act, 34 and 35 Henry VIII., for the advancement of true religion.*

1547. First Session of Council of Trent.

—— *Death of Henry VIII.*

—— *First Book of Homilies.*

1548. *Cranmer puts forth a Lutheran Catechism.*

1549. First draft of some Articles (Feb. 27).

—— *First Service-book of King Edward VI., (Whitsunday).*

—— Consensus Tigurinus reconciles Calvin and the Germans on the Eucharist.

1550. *Royal Commission against Anabaptists (Jan. 18).*

—— *Contest between Hooper and Ridley about vestments.*

1551. *English Prayer-book first used in Ireland.*

—— New Session of Council of Trent.

1552. The Confession of Wurtemberg.

—— *Hooper's Articles, in number fifty (July 6).*

—— Commission against the Family of Love (Sept.)

1553. Publication of XLII Articles (May 20) *with a Catechism.*

A.D.

1553. *Subscription publicly enjoined* (June 15).
——— *Death of Edward VI.* (July 6).
1555. *Gardiner's XV Articles* (April 1).
1558. *Southern Convocation emit five definitions.*
——— *Queen Elizabeth proclaimed* (Nov. 17).
1559. *The Eleven Articles of Religion.*
——— *Royal Commission visits all the Dioceses.*
1560. The Pope's jurisdiction renounced in Scotland.
1562. Fresh Session of Council of Trent (Jan. 18).
——— THE SYNOD PASSES THE XXXIX ARTICLES.
1564. Bull confirming the Council of Trent (Jan. 6).
1566. *The Eleven Articles enjoined in Ireland* (Jan. 6).
1566-7. *Elizabeth resists enforcing the Articles by Act of Parliament* (Jan. 2).
1567. *The first Conventicle organized.*
1568. Conference of Altenberg between Flacconists and Electorals.
1571. *The XXXIX Articles enjoined on all the English Clergy.*
——— *Elizabeth yields to Parliament.*
1572. *Puritan "Admonition to the Parliament."*
1595-6. *The Lambeth Articles.*
1604. Rise of Arminiansim in the Low Countries. Quin-quarticular Controversy.
——— *Fruitless effort to engraft the Lambeth Articles on the XXXIX.*
——— *Hampton Court Conference.*
1605. *The Northern Convocation of York formally accept the XXXIX Articles.*
1610. The Dutch Remonstrance of Episcopius.
1615. *Irish Articles.*
1618. The Synod of Dort.
1625. *Charles I. comes to the Throne.*
1626. *Proclamation about Calvinism.*

A.D.

1628. *His Majesty's Declaration prefixed to the XXXIX Articles.*

1635. *XXXIX Articles accepted by the Church of Ireland.*

1689. *Certain of the Articles signed by Nonconformists (1 Gul. et Mar., c. 18, § 18).*

1771. *Blackburn's Movement.*

1772. *Feathers Tavern Petition* (Feb. 6).

1801. American Church, with modifications, adopts the Articles.

1804. Synod of Scotch Church at Laurencekirk adopts the Articles.

1818. *Wix of St. Bartholomew's interpretation.*

1841. *Tract XC. published.*

1863. *Alteration of terms of Subscription.*

1864. *Dr. Pusey's Eirenicon.*

HIS MAJESTY'S DECLARATION.

"BEING by God's ordinance, according to Our just title, Defender of the Faith, and Supreme Governor of the Church, within these our Dominions, We hold it most agreeable to this Our Kingly Office, and Our own religious Zeal, to conserve and maintain the Church committed to Our Charge, in unity of true Religion, and in the Bond of Peace; and not to suffer unnecessary Disputations, Altercations, or Questions to be raised, which may nourish Faction both in the Church and Commonwealth. We have, therefore, upon mature Deliberation, and with the Advice of so many of our Bishops as might conveniently be called together, thought fit to make this Declaration following.

"That the Articles of the Church of England—which have been allowed and authorized heretofore, and which our Clergy generally have subscribed unto—do contain the true Doctrine of the Church of England, agreeable to God's Word: which We do therefore ratify and confirm, requiring all Our loving Subjects to continue in the uniform Profession thereof, and prohibiting the least difference from the said Articles; which to that end We command to be new printed, and this Our Declaration to be published therewith.

"That We are Supreme Governor of the Church of England: and that if any Difference arise about the external Policy, concerning the Injunctions, Canons, and other Constitutions whatsoever thereto belonging, the Clergy in their Convocation is to order and settle them, having first obtained leave under Our Broad Seal so to do; and We approving their said Ordinances and Constitutions; providing that none be made contrary to the Laws and Customs of the Land.

"That out of Our Princely care that the Churchmen may do the work which is proper unto them, the Bishops and Clergy, from time to time in Convocation, upon their humble Desire, shall have Licence under Our Broad Seal, to deliberate of, and to do all such things, as being made plain by them, and assented unto by Us, shall concern the settled Continuance of the Doctrine and Discipline of the Church of England, now established; from which We will not endure any varying or departing in the least Degree.

"That for the present, though some differences have been ill raised, yet We take comfort in this, that all Clergymen within Our Realm have always most willingly subscribed to the Articles established; which is an argument to Us, that they all agree in the true, usual, literal meaning of the said Articles; and that even in those curious points, in which the present differences lie, men of all sorts take the Articles of the Church of England to be for them; which is an argument again, that none of them intend any desertion of the Articles established.

"That, therefore, in these both curious and unhappy differences, which have for so many hundred years, in different times and places, exercised the Church of Christ, We will, that all further curious search be laid aside, and these disputes shut up in God's promises, as they be generally set forth to us in the Holy Scriptures, and the general meaning of the Articles of the Church of England according to them. And that no man hereafter shall either print or preach, to draw the Article aside any way, but shall submit to it in the plain and full meaning thereof; and shall not put his own sense or comment to be the meaning of the Article, but shall take it in the literal and grammatical sense.

" That if any public Reader in either of our Universities, or any Head or Master of a College, or any other person respectively in either of them, shall affix any new sense to any Article, or shall publicly read, determine, or hold any public Disputation, or suffer any such to be held either way, in either the Universities or Colleges respectively; or if any Divine in the Universities shall preach or print anything either way, other than is already established in Convocation with Our Royal assent; he or they, the offenders, shall be liable to Our displeasure, and the Church's censure in Our Commission Ecclesiastical, as well as any other: and We will see there shall be due execution upon them."

The ill-advised step of King James I. of sending deputies to the Synod of Dort, (a course very inconsistent in the friend of Montague and Andrewes, but caused partly by dislike of Vorstius, partly by political friendship for the Prince of Orange,) issued in the fiercest theological disturbance in England. Though the English delegates did what they could to mediate, their efforts were unavailing, and no sooner did they return home than the controversy began to rage. An active school, in all the energy of youth, maintained the tenets of Arminius, which drove the opposite party into the wildest Calvinism. In vain did the King charge Archbishop Abbot to issue directions concerning preachers. They were deliberately ignored. On the accession of Charles I., in concert with the Bishops, he issued the memorable proclamation of 1626, against "the sharp and indiscreet handling of some of either party." This did good in the Universities, but in the country the evil continued, wherefore it was deemed fit to issue a reprint of the Thirty-Nine Articles, with the Declaration which has ever since attached to them. It was resisted by the Calvinistic clergy, who saw in it a special condemnation of their teaching, and in the House of Commons, a debate on the Royal Declaration avowed the sense of the Articles, " which, by the public act of the Church of England, and by the general and current expositions of the writers of our Church, have been delivered to us. And we reject the sense of Jesuits and Arminians, and all others, wherein they differ from us [a]."

The Caroline Bishops knew very well what they were doing, so did the Puritans. No wonder that these latter sought to stigmatize the sense as Jesuitical[b] and Arminian. The instinct of Puritanism was naturally aroused, the Declaration was the enunciation of the Catholic sense of the Articles; Tract XC. and the Eirenicon are legitimate outcomes of the King's Declaration.

[a] Hardwick's "History of Articles of Religion," ed. 1859, p. 206. See, also, Sir John Elliot's Speech, at p. 204, and Rushworth, i. 652.

[b] This could not allude to Santa Clara's Book, which was not published till 1634.

THIRTY-NINE ARTICLES OF RELIGION.

ARTICLE I.

I. DE FIDE IN SACRO-SANCTAM TRINITATEM[a].

UNUS est vivus et verus Deus, æternus, incorporeus, impartibilis, impassibilis, immensæ potentiæ, sapientiæ, ac bonitatis, creator et conservator omnium, tum visibilium, tum invisibilium. Et in unitate hujus divinæ naturæ, tres sunt personæ, ejusdem essentiæ, potentiæ, ac æternitatis, Pater, Filius, et Spiritus Sanctus.

Of Faith in the Holy Trinity.

"There is but one living and true God, everlasting, without body, parts, or passions; of infinite power, wisdom, and goodness, the Maker and Preserver of all things both visible and invisible. And in unity of this Godhead there be three persons, of one substance, power, and eternity; the Father, the Son, and the Holy Ghost."

---

1. SINCE God is incomprehensible and ineffable, we cannot define Him by any expression which perfectly

---

[a] The author having at some length gone into the subjects of Articles I., II., III., IV., V., XI., XVII., XIX., XX., XXVII., in his "Short Explanation of the Nicene Creed," would wish it to be understood that what is now put forth is in some sense, but not entirely, supplementary to what he has written in that volume. In some cases it has been necessary to go over the same ground, but generally the matter is treated from a different point of view.

describes His nature. Yet, since man can in an imperfect way know Him, such descriptions as, The most Perfect Being, the Supreme and Independent Being, the Infinite Being, the Being than whom nothing greater can be imagined, the Being by Himself, or from Himself, are given of Him. Thus in Exod. iii. 14, "I am that I am. Thus shalt thou say unto the children of Israel, I am hath sent me unto you."

To be of Himself, to exist by the power of His own Being, therefore, is a constituent idea of God, seeing that to be of Himself belongs only to God, and is the first conception we form of Him.

That God is, is proved by many places in Holy Scripture, and by natural reason itself. The existence of God cannot be proved by *à priori* arguments [b], because in that way of proof the effect is proved by its cause, but God has no cause of His existence. But, *à posteriori*, God's existence may be proved by the existence of His creatures. "The invisible things from the creation of the world are known by those things which are made; even His eternal power and Godhead [c]:" or, to follow out the thought more clearly,—it is certain to every man that he exists; but he does not exist of himself, but of some other being, therefore of God; or by some other being, who again exists of some other, and so by advance we come to a first being, who is from Himself. There can be no infinity

---

[b] We do not here use *à priori* in the Kantian, but in the Scholastic sense. Kant held that God's existence is proved *à priori* from the practical reason.   [c] Rom. i. 20.

in such a process; for it implies all posterior or middle causes, and a posterior cause cannot be granted unless a prior and then a first be granted also.

Another argument may be adduced from the movement of creatures. Whatever moves is moved by another; therefore, it is moved by an unmoving motor, who is God; or by a moving motor, which again is moved by another; and so, as the process cannot be infinite, we come to the first Motor, who moves and is not moved.

Next, the existence of God is proved by the consent of all nations, the fulfilment of prophecies, miracles, the hankering after the infinite good, the remorse of conscience in case of sin, the wondrous formation and preservation of all things, which distinctly imply the existence of a supremely intelligent being.

2. Holy Scripture asserts the unity of God: "See, I am alone, there is none other God beside Me [d]." This also is proved by reason. If there were more Gods than one, either one would be subject to another or not; if subject, then the one so subject would not be God, the most perfect Being; if he was not subject, then neither would be God, neither would be perfect, the perfection belonging to the one being by so much taken away from the other.

Having proved His Being, we now come to His attributes. An attribute is that which is determined by, and flows from essence; or, in other words, a divine attribute is a perfection which, in our way of conceiving

[d] Deut. xxxii. 39.

it, follows as a property the divine essence. Attributes are divided into absolute and relative. Absolute attributes are they which have no relation to any one else, as simplicity, eternity. Relative attributes are divided again into attributes *ad intra*, such as paternity, filiation, spiration; and attributes *ad extra*, such as creation, preservation, and the like. Attributes, again, are either positive or negative. Positive attributes are they which impute to God, wisdom, goodness, &c.; negative, are they which deny Him imperfection, as to be uncreate, incorporeal, infinite, incomprehensible, immutable, immense, invincible, ineffable. All the attributes of God are in reality one with the divine essence, and one with each other, except the relative attributes *ad intra*, between which there is the opposition of relation, as between paternity and filiation. Thus the justice of God is His mercy, His will is His intellect; and yet, as we may not say that God punishes men in His mercy, so we must admit a sort of distinction in regard to the fact that our minds, on account of their imperfection and limitation, cannot in one conception grasp the whole perfection of the divine essence, and so we form diverse, imperfect conceptions of God from the analogies of creation, which we correct by faith and reflection,—conceptions which are not erroneous, but imperfect.

3. The first attribute predicated in the Article of the one living and true God, is His eternity. That eternity is defined as the entire, simultaneous, and perfect possession of an interminable life. In that it is

defined as entire and simultaneous, the idea of division and succession is excluded: for in eternity there is one instant, ever-present and existent. In that it is perfect, it excludes the thought of the imperfection and transitoriness of an instant of time, though that instant be without divisibility. By the thought of possession, we understand stability and unfailingness. Such eternity as this belongs only to God. "I live for ever[e]." "Thou art the same, and Thy years shall not fail[f]." It differs from time in that eternity hath no beginning, no change, either substantial or accidental.

When Holy Scripture attributes a past and future to God, it does not mean that the works of God in creation are so described in the way of the action of God, but in the way of results and terms which begin to be and cease. So when in Scripture such a passage occurs as "Before the morning watch I begat Thee[g]," it does not signify that the generation of the Son has just passed, for that never has, and never will have an end, being always present, but there is a certain accommodation to our imperfect way of understanding things who have to measure all things by time.

4. Next, God is without body, parts, or passions. The uncompounded nature of God is of faith. It is proved, first, by the thought that there is no physical composition of matter or form, for God is a Spirit, therefore immaterial and indivisible. Neither is there

---

[e] Deut. xxxiii. 40.　　　[f] Ps. cii. 27.　　　[g] Ps. cx. 3, Vulg.

in God metaphysical composition of action and power, for God is the purest act, and therefore in God there cannot be power, to which anything is added by which it may be made perfect; neither is there composition of essence and existence; for otherwise essence would be in the power to exist, which may not be said, since essence includes in itself necessary existence, nay is constituted by itself in its own being; neither is there composition of nature and personality, for in God personality is not distinguished from nature.

Neither in Him is there logical composition, because genus is something perfectible and limitable by difference, also genus implies some one thing existing in many, whereas whatsoever is in God, is so His, that it cannot in the same sense be held to be shared with any other being.

5. The power of God is the productive principle of all things. In God there can only be admitted one active power, which is the very essence of God in action, or in the divine act itself. In our way of speaking, the power of God is distinguished from His knowledge, providence, or will; in that by His knowledge He is apprehended as intelligent, by His providence as directing, by His will as governing, by His power as executing. In God the power and the act are not distinguishable. His power is infinite, as illustrated by creation, for the distance between being and not being is infinite.

God is called Omnipotent, for He can do all things that do not involve imperfection; therefore God cannot sin, because to be able to sin is to be able to be imperfect in action.

His wisdom and knowledge are perfect: "The Lord is the Lord of knowledge [h];" and this again is not accident or habit, but pure act and the essence of God Himself.

All philosophers of the highest order have demonstrated in the same manner the existence of God. All have recognised the existence of a moral obstacle which conceals the light from the spirit, and must be removed. All have recognised an inner and divine sense, the allurement and charm of the desirable and the intelligible, which, when the obstacle is removed, becomes the resort of the reason. All have found the point of rest, the ποῦ στῶ of that first start of the reason in the spectacle of things created, either world or soul. All have understood that this point of departure is in no sense a principle whence the reason can deduce the existence of God; but simply a point of departure whence the reason raises itself to the principle of all things which contains no point of departure. All have recognised that the process is not syllogistical, and that it is one of the two essential processes of the reason; that which seeks the major, not that which draws the consequences; all have described this process as an operation of the reason, which regarding finite being, either world or soul, sees, by the mournful contrast, in this finite the necessary existence of the Infinite, and knows the Infinite

[h] 1 Sam. ii. 3.

by negation, in denying the limits of every finite being and every limited perfection.

It is clear that this being granted, the process gives a demonstration of the existence of God and a knowledge of His attributes. For God can be demonstrated only so far as He is demonstrated as endowed with His essential attributes, without which there would be the demonstration of the existence of something else, not God. The demonstration of the existence of God gives His attributes at the same time, and furthermore reason can enlighten and develope the idea of God in two ways, as well as know His attributes. It can either obtain them at starting, from the consideration of creation, on the principle that the perfections of God are those of His creatures, only without limit; or, granting but one of the attributes of God, it can deduce the rest by way of identity. The Schoolmen held that what they termed the metaphysical essence of God was the attribute which implied all the rest, but we saw just now that there is no real distinction between God and His attributes, therefore reason may take any one, and argue to the absolute identity of all that is in God, a principle which belongs to Him alone, and not to Him with His creatures.

Granted one attribute of God, one can take it as a principle, and by way of syllogistic consequence and algebraic identity, deduce the others. Thus to start from the attribute of God implied in the words " I am that I am." From the idea of ' Being,' as from the proposition ' Being is,' we can deduce the metaphysical attributes of God. We suppose that it is purely, simply, and absolutely true that Being is, and it is equally clear that when we thus speak of Being we mean the absolute Being, not relative beings.

i. This granted, if the Being is simply and absolutely, it is not a finite Being, because a finite being is only to a certain point and not further. It has its limits and conditions: it is not simply and absolutely. Therefore, if the Being be not finite, it is infinite.

ii. Again, if the Being be infinite, it must be infinite in all senses, because if it ceased to be infinite in one sense, in that sense it would be finite, and therefore not infinite. In the sense it was limited, in that sense it would cease to be the Being.

iii. If Being is, it is all that is possible, otherwise it would not be absolute. It is all that is possible, and that infinitely so, for if it were not so, there would be, in that manner of being and in that sense, a limit in which it would not be so. If it is, it is infinitely all-possible.

iv. The same reasoning applies to immensity and eternity. If it was not eternal, there would have been a time when it was not: if it was not immense, there would be a place where it was not. It therefore would not *be* purely, simply, absolutely.

v. Furthermore, if Being is, it must be necessary. If it is, it cannot not be. There never has been a choice between Being and not being, for Being is eternal. An absolute being must always have been. To conceive a doubt as to the non-existence of the Being is not to have the idea of it : it is not to know the value of the word. Hence it follows that all that is not the Being, might not have been. All that has not been from eternity might not have been, and is contingent.

vi. If the Being is, it is by itself, otherwise it would be a relative, not an absolute Being. To be necessary, and to be by itself, is the same idea under two different forms.

vii. It is rigorously true, though truly inconceivable, as are many algebraic deductions in their application to geometry, that the Being, because It is eternal and immense, is really present in all points of time and space. We can conceive to a certain point His immensity in space, but we cannot conceive His omnipresence in all time. And yet this is the case. For God there is no past or future : He sees and contains all things in an eternal present. The past, present, and future co-exist in the infinite, as in a single point unextended and simple, the two extreme points in the centre of an infinitesimal element.

viii. If God is absolutely, He is simple and uncompounded. Were He not simple, He would be composite. If He was composite, He would have parts. These parts might be physical or spiritual. If He had physical parts, He could not be wholly in one point. He could not be so absolutely. If He had spiritual parts, they would be separate attributes, of which the one would not be the other, nor would they be in Him entire, but limited by each other. If, then, God is not composite, He is absolutely simple, and therefore His attributes are identical with each other and with His essence. God is His own essence. In God, Being and Essence are one. His will is His Essence. God is His Life. God is His own Beatitude.

ɪx. God, then, being absolutely simple is one—nay, unity itself. All created things have their unity in Him, an approximative unity, an image of unity, but the Infinite is alone One, He is the only concrete unity.

x. Nay, He is so simple and one in Himself, that in a sense there is but one absolute Being. There cannot be two absolute beings, for there cannot be two infinites. Infinity + infinity has no sense in algebra, or means exactly infinity also. Infinity + infinity = infinity.

xi. He who is, is unchangeable. To change is to be what one was not, or to cease to be what one was. To cease to be implies some loss, therefore Being is not absolute. If God is, He is unchangeable. There is no increase in Him. He is not like us, partly in act, partly in power. He is all act, *actus purissimus*. If so, He is all His possible unfolded. He is all actually present. He is living.

xii. Lastly, if we only grant that there are outside of the Absolute Being finite and relative beings, it is true that they could not become such of themselves alone, nor commence if nothing was yet, nor be but by the Being that was already. Therefore the Being had the power to produce all that is produced: and as the beings which are were not, it follows that He made them out of nothing, or created them: which implies infinite power. No finite power could create things out of nothing. Therefore God is almighty.

6. So far we have deduced from the idea of Being what are termed the metaphysical attributes of God; but there are beside these, moral attributes and intellectual attributes, and here we come to the question between atheists and ourselves. Atheism will allow a physical, geometrical, mechanical God, who is to the Infinite all that one meets with in nature and its laws; but between such a God and an Infinite Intelligence there is a gulph fixed. Intelligence is another face, another dimension of Being.

But this is not the only gulph which reason encounters. Given an absolute Being, eternal, immense, immutable; given intelligence, given infinite power, there still lack liberty, will, goodness. Is this infinitely powerful and intelligent Being free? wills He? loves He? If we look into ourselves, we find these powers, and we justly carry them on to God, and attribute them to Him in an infinite degree; or, if we reason from what we know of Him, we say He is infinite; whence it follows that all perfections everywhere found in created things must be superabundantly and originally found in Him. If all perfections of every sort pre-exist in Him, needs must be that He is intelligent, free, with the power of will and love. Thus the intellectual attributes are revealed to the understanding by the understanding, and the moral attributes by the heart and by the conscience; and our conception of these first is only limited by the imperfections of these last.

For to continue the development of the idea of Being, we come to find it identical with power, intelligence, will, liberty, love. Take away one of these and you destroy Being. You take the heart out of that which is. You say in so many words, There is no Being above us. We are better ourselves than such a ruined God. He is no longer the Absolute. Therefore—

God is free, good, and He loves: and this with reference to the world implies Providence, the paternal government of the world.

7. He must have a distorted vision who in the visible creation sees not the hand of God. Such, alas! there have been, and will be to the end, but they have not been the highest intelligences. One must lose one's reason, and abdicate one's senses, not to acknowledge that the eye was given to see with, the members to move with: not to comprehend that a profound knowledge and goodness, sustained by infinite power, has made our bodies and the world, and left its mark and signature, not only on the whole, but on each detail. Who can study the infinite strength, delicacy, and beauty of the structure of any of these parts of our own constitution and not say, This is the work of God? or take the world and think how out of nebula it has gradually, through countless ages, been prepared for the habitation of man, ages passing and yet a constant advance to perfection, without confessing, not merely the cold abstraction of an overruling Providence, but the work of a tender Father, who made me, loves me, guards me,

who reads my secret thoughts, rules the beatings of my heart, trains me for heaven, even in the smallest details of my life? Thus it is with all men. Such is the providential work of God in the history of humanity. He awaits the harvest. Even death, in His hands, is the light that transfigures all here below, and gives it an eternal sense, for it is the prelude of eternal life in the presence and enjoyment of God.

8. Having said thus much on the triple distinction of God's attributes into metaphysical, intellectual, and moral, one must remark that they seem to correspond with the Divine Persons in the adorable Trinity, if it be true, as we believe, that the Holy Trinity is distinguished, according to a procession of the Word from Him who uttered it, and of Love from both. Pantheists may have perverted this into a support of their system, but still there is a true philosophical side to the doctrine, and it has applications which bear upon the science of humanity and of the world. As Christian philosophy developes itself, men will come to know that power, intelligence, and love, being three radical distinctions, are to the absolute Being what the three dimensions, breadth, height, and length, are to the body, and that they constitute an unity, as the product of the three unities of dimension constitute the unity of solidity: that they no more destroy simplicity, than the simplicity of the infinitesimal element of solidity is destroyed, because one ought there to distinguish the elements of the three dimensions: and that, finally, if it be true that in living organisms, the highest per-

fection consists in the maximum of individuality, or in unity, joined to the maximum of distinction of organs, in the absolute life, perfection consists in absolute unity united to absolute distinction. But absolute unity is simplicity, and absolute distinction is the distinction of person from person, so that one understands what theologians mean when they say that the distinction of the Persons, in God, is the condition, not the negation, of simplicity. In God, transcendental unity and transcendental plurality are identical. Our God is not solitary, though He be One, is the teaching of S. Hilary of Poitiers. And in thus seeking by study and contemplation to sound the unfathomable depths of the mystery, let us above all dwell on the adoration and worship which it calls forth. Here is the source of all knowledge, all virtue, even life and immortality. Here is the heart of Christianity, the last prayer of our Lord, " that they may be one as we are." Here is the perfection of each soul, the organization of the world to come, and of the ideal society of heaven, which will be, according to that prayer, a plurality of persons in one [1].

The Holy Trinity is the Substance of three divine Persons in one and the same nature. The Holy Trinity is God the Father, God the Son, God the Holy Ghost, three Persons, one God. In dwelling upon It, we have to consider :—

1. The question of Procession, which is nothing else than the production or emanation of one Person from

---

[1] Cf. Gratry, *de la Connaissance de Dieu*, tom. ii. p. 135.

another, as the river flows from the source. It is either *ad extra*, or *ad intra*. Procession *ad extra* is transient, as when that which is produced is placed outside its principle; thus, the child proceeds from its father. In this sense, all creatures proceed from God. The other procession is immanent, where the term produced abides within its principle, as an act of understanding remains in the faculty of the understanding. Of this kind is the Procession in God, which may be theologically defined as the emanation of one Person from another, as from a productive principle, not a productive cause, which would imply that it had a being distinct from that whence it proceeds, that it depended on it, and that it was posterior to it; thus, "Thou art My Son; this day have I begotten Thee[k];" "I came forth from God[l]." The divine essence, whereby God is of Himself (*a se*), is numerically the same in the three Persons, and therefore each Person by reason of its being, though not by reason of its Person, is *a se* and God.

In God there are only two processions *ad intra*, the one by the understanding, whereby the Son proceedeth from the Father, the other by the will, whereby the Holy Ghost proceedeth from the Father and the Son, according to the two immanent actions in God, which are to know and to will.

There is a double principle of action, the *principium quod*, which is the operating Person, and the *princi-*

[k] Ps. ii. 7.　　　　　　　　[l] St. John viii. 42.

pium quo, whereby the Person worketh. This, again, is divided into the *principium quo remotum*, whereby He worketh mediately, and the *principium quo proximum*, by which He worketh immediately. Thus when a man understandeth, the *principium quod* is man; the *principium quo remotum* is his intellectual nature, and the *principium quo proximum* is the intellect itself; in God the *principium quod* of the processions are the producing Persons; that is, the Person of the Father in respect of the Son, and the Persons of the Father and Son in respect of the Holy Ghost. The *principium quo remotum* is the divine Nature understanding and willing. The *principium quo proximum* are the intellect and will, as the relations of paternity and active spiration indicate them as necessary conditions.

The Son does not produce another Son, because intellect in the Son is no longer fertile, because it is expended in the production of the Son by the production of an infinite term, for one action can produce but one adequate term. Therefore the Holy Ghost cannot generate; and so the Holy Ghost, though having the same will with the Father and the Son, does not produce another Spirit, for *to will* in Him has not the character of spiration or fertility, seeing that in the Father and the Son, it has produced its adequate and complete term, i.e. the Holy Ghost Himself.

While we call the Procession of the Son from the Father, Generation, we do not give that name to the Procession of the Holy Ghost, because production by will differs from production by intellect inasmuch as it is not formally assimilative, which is the essence of the other.

Theologians in treating of the three Divine Persons of the ever-blessed Trinity, are accustomed to speak of the Father as the first, the Son as the second, and the Holy Ghost as the third Person of the Holy Trinity, and this not because one Person "is afore or after other," either in time or duration, but because there is in the nature of the Godhead a certain order of source or origin; an order, as St. Augustine says, "not by which one may be before the other, but by which one is from the other[m]." Hence it is not allowable to speak of any of the divine Persons having a principle or beginning as to *time*, though we may speak of the second and third as having a principle of production, i.e. they do not exist from nothing, but have from all eternity had their being communicated to them. Hence, too, we may not call the Father "before" the Son in *nature*, but "before" Him in source or origin. All three Persons are equally wise, powerful, and eternal, for the whole perfection of the divine nature is in each.

Some persons stumble at the words of our Lord, "My Father is greater than I[n];" but St. Thomas[o], with many other theologians, maintains that the previous words of the text, "I go unto the Father," make it sufficiently clear that our Lord was speaking simply of His sacred humanity. Neither do our Lord's words,

[m] St. Aug., cont. Max., c. 4. [n] St. John xiv. 28.
[o] St. Thomas, Part I. 9, xlii. qu. &c.

"The Son can do nothing of Himself[p]," oppose this doctrine, for they merely signify that the Son having, by His generation, the same power and essence with the Father, can do nothing to the exclusion of the Father; every power which the Father has, the Son has likewise with Him, though sometimes with a different relation; e.g. the power by which the Father generates, is in the Son, the Father having it as *giving*, the Son as *receiving*.

The mutual inexistence of the divine Persons, one in the other, of which our Blessed Lord speaks[q], is called by theologians, Circuminsession.

In speaking of "mission" with reference to the Persons of the Blessed Trinity, theologians are to be understood to mean; the "procession" of one Person from another, having relation to some temporal effect. Two things are required in "mission" thus understood; 1. That the Person sent proceed from Him who sends; 2. That the Person sent stands in a new relation to the object to which (*terminus ad quem*) He is sent. Hence we gather;—

That the Father can be sent of none, for He proceeds from none.

That the Son is sent of the Father only[r].

That the Holy Ghost is sent by the Father and by the Son[s].

That the Holy Ghost, as neither of the Persons proceeds from Him, so neither of them are sent by Him.

[p] St. John v. 19.   [q] Ibid. xiv. 11; xvii. 21.
[r] St. John vi. 57.   [s] Compare St. John xiv. 26, with xv. 26.

Although we cannot speak of the Father as *sent*, yet it is lawful to speak both of Him and of the whole Trinity as "given" to men, to dwell in them by grace [t]. When we speak of "mission" putting one of the Divine Persons in a new relation, we must remember that the *change* is in the relation of the creature to whom the Person is sent, and not in the Person; "mission," be it also remembered, is the term specially used to denote not the *eternal* generation or spiration, but the "sending forth" of one of the Persons to work certain effects *in time*.

Mission is—1. *Invisible*, when the effect to work which the Person is sent is invisible and not seen outwardly; thus, as by grace our souls are conformed to the image of the Son, the Son may be said to be invisibly "sent" to us. St. Augustine [u] says, "the Son is then invisibly sent to any one, when He is known and apprehended by him;" so also the Holy Ghost is invisibly sent, when by hallowing grace He comes to dwell in the hearts of the just [v].

2. *Visible*, when it is accompanied by some effect sensibly appearing, and representing the Person sent; thus the Son was visibly sent in the Incarnation [x]; we frequently read of the Holy Ghost being visibly sent, as a Dove [y]; as a bright Cloud [z]; as a Breath [a]; as Tongues like as of fire [b]; nor should the missions to the

---

[t] Vide St. John xiv. 23.   [u] lib. 4. de Trin., c. 20.   [v] Gal. iv. 6.   [x] St. John iii. 17; St. Luke iv. 18; Rom. viii. 3.   [y] St. Matt. iii. 16.   [z] St. Matt. xvii. 5.   [a] St. John xx. 22.   [b] Acts ii. 3.

first Christians be forgotten as recorded in Acts viii. 18; x. 44; xix. 6, and in other places.

It is not strictly correct to speak of men "sending," or "giving" the Holy Ghost by administering the Sacraments; it is safer to say that they give the Holy Ghost *ministerially,* i.e. that *God* uses their ministry to give the Holy Ghost[c].

Such is the great God as He is revealed to us in our most holy faith, ineffable, incomprehensible, known to us for certain only so far as He is revealed to us, above time and beyond space, His own law, His own sufficiency, His own centre, His own end. "Canst thou by searching find out God?" Yet so soon as He is made known to us in His beauty, goodness, and power, our souls, made originally to contemplate and enjoy Him, rise to the conception of His eternal attributes, and in the image of Him thus formed in the still waters of the human heart we cannot fail to own Him, as the true Lord of heaven and earth, as the blessed and only Potentate, the eternal Father, Whom to know is to live, Whom to serve is to reign.

[c] Vide St. Thomas, pt. I. qu. xliii. Compare with this the words of the Ordinal at the consecration of Archbishop Parker: "Take the Holy Ghost."

ARTICLE II.

De Verbo, sive Filio Dei, qui verus
homo factus est.

Filius, qui est verbum Patris, ab æterno a Patre genitus, verus et æternus Deus, ac Patri consubstantialis, in utero beatæ Virginis, ex illius substantiâ, naturam humanam assumpsit : ita ut duæ naturæ, divina et humana, integre atque perfecte in unitate personæ fuerint inseparabiliter conjunctæ, ex quibus est unus Christus, verus Deus et verus homo, qui vere passus est, crucifixus, mortuus, et sepultus, ut Patrem nobis reconciliaret, essetque hostia, non tantum pro culpâ originis, verum etiam pro omnibus actualibus hominum peccatis.

Of the Word, or Son of God, which was made very Man.

"The Son, which is the Word of the Father, begotten from everlasting of the Father, the very and eternal God, of one substance with the Father, took man's nature in the womb of the blessed Virgin, of her substance : so that two whole and perfect natures, that is to say, the Godhead and Manhood, were joined together in one Person, never to be divided, whereof is one Christ, very God and very Man, who truly suffered, was crucified, dead, and buried, to reconcile His Father to us ; and to be a sacrifice, not only for original guilt, but also for all actual sins of men."

---

1. Although some of the ancients, such as Lactantius and Tertullian, from want of precision called God the

Word or the Person of the Son, the Holy Spirit, and though some of the early heretics distinguished God the Word from the Son of God by nature, yet the Church hath ever held that the Son and the Word are two terms describing that divine Person Who, eternally begotten by the Father by way of thought, is the ultimate term of the intellect of God.

There are many names in Holy Scripture which apply to the Son, some of which refer to His divine substance, others to the nature He assumed, and some to the Person, which embraces both. Thus St. Ambrose says, "There are some names which evidently shew forth the properties of deity; others which express the similitude of the Father and the Son; others the unity of the divine Majesty. Those which express properties are generation, God, Son, Word. Those which express similitude, are splendour, character, mirror, image. Those which signify the eternal unity are wisdom, power, breath, life,—twelve names corresponding to the twelve gems which glittered on the breastplate of the High-Priest[a]." The name Word was happily chosen as expressing the two characters of the eternal Son, being at once ἐν Θεῷ and ἐκ Θεοῦ.

2. "Begotten from everlasting of the Father." If there be one part of religion which demands from us a simple faith on authority rather than a comprehension from reason, it is this truth, which is so recondite and abstract, that all we know from the Holy Scripture is, that there is a Father who begets, and a Son who is

[a] De Fide, lib. ii. § 3, vol. ii. p. 471.

begotten. God is not the object of investigation, but He is the object of knowledge. Perfect knowledge is so to know Him as to say that none can declare Him, yet all must know Him. He is to be believed, He is to be known, He is to be adored. St. Athanasius says, " It is unmeet to ask how the Word exists from God; or how He is the brightness of God; or how God begets; or what is the mode of that generation. He were mad, who so dared to declare in speech that which is unexplorable, a property of the divine nature, known only to God and to His Son [b]." And St. Basil, " Dost thou believe that He is begotten, ask not how. If it be right to ask how the unbegotten is the unbegotten, then you may ask how the begotten is begotten. But if the first is not subject of question, so neither is the second [c]." All that we dare to say is, that it is—1. Incomprehensible, being beyond our ken; 2. Perfect, because no sterility can be predicated of God; 3. Substantial, as proceeding from a cause or principle; 4. Producing similarity, in that that which is begotten is like the begotten; 5. That there be communication of the substance of the Begotten. On this very profound subject we can do no better than quote the lines in which Prudentius [d] sums up all that is known or revealed on the subject :—

" Hoc solum scimus, quod traditur esse Deum quem
　　Non genitus Genitor generaverit, unus et unum,
　　Integer integrum, non cœptum, sed tamen ortum,

[b] Orat. Cont. Arian, ii. § 36.　　　　　[c] Bas., Hom. 29.
[d] Apotheosis, 268.

Et comperpetuum retrò Patris, et Patre natum.
Sed nec decisus Pater est, ut pars Patris esset
Filius : extendens nec se substantia tractim
Produxit, minuitve aliquid de numine pleno;
Dum mutata novum procudit portio Natum.
Non convertibilis, nec demutabilis unquam
Est Deus, aut gignendo aliquid sibi detrahit : atqui
Totus et ex toto Deus est, de lumine lumen.
Quando autem lumen sine lumine ? quando refulgens
Lux fulgore caret ? quando est ut proditus ignis
Ignem deminuat ? Quando Pater et Deus et lux
Non lucis Deus et Pater est ? qui, si Pater olim
Non fuit, et serum genuit post tempore Natum
Fit novus, inque novum jus proficit.   Absit ut unquam
Plenus proficiat, qui non eget incremento.
Et Deus et genitor, lumenque et gloria semper
Ille fuit : nec post sibi contulit, ut Pater esset.
Sic fit ut æternum credamus cum Patre Christum
Illo auctore satum, cui nullus præfuit auctor."

3. "The very and eternal God." This is an assertion
that in theological language the Son is αὐτόθεος.   In
St. Athanasius[e] we find αὐτοσοφία, αὐτολόγος, αὐτο-
δύναμις, αὐτοφῶς, and such like, just as the Holy Ghost,
in Gregory Nazianzen, is termed αὐτοκίνητον and αὐτο-
δύναμον; and yet in another sense Athanasius denies
that He is αὐτοσοφία or αὐτολόγος.   These contradictions are easily reconciled if we consider the force
of αὐτο in composition. If it mean that He proceedeth
from no principle, but is an unbegotten substance, then
He is not αὐτοσοφία, for that were Sabellianism, which

<hr>

[e] Contra Gentes, § 46.

is to admit neither difference nor origin of Persons; but if the *αὐτο* be taken to mean that He hath not the divinity or the wisdom by participation or relatively, in this sense the expression is correct. He is wisdom itself, inasmuch as He possesseth all these things not by participation, nor by external gift, as those who are partakers of it, and become wise and powerful and reasonable by Him; but He is the very Wisdom, the very Reason or Word, the very power of the Father, the very truth, the very light, the very righteousness, the very virtue: "As the Father hath life in Himself, so hath He given to the Son to have life in Himself'."

4. The term 'consubstantial' was objected to by the Arians as unscriptural, and was accused both of materialism and Sabellianism. The word *οὐσία*, in the language of Aristotle, stood for an individual substance numerically one, which is producible of nothing but itself. Improperly it stood for a species or genus. Based on this, Christianity took it in a sense of its own, such as we have no example of in things created, viz., that of a Being numerically one existing in three Persons; so that the word is producible, or in one sense *universal*, without ceasing to be individual. Heretics objected to the term in the philosophical sense, and then, as applied to Father and Son, it either implied parts of a *material* subject, or involved no real distinction of persons. Hence the Homoousion. It was denied by Arians before the Nicene Synod, and was rejected at the Council of Antioch, when it was taken in a wrong

<hr>

' St. John v. 26; cf. 1 St. John v. 11.

sense by Paul of Samosata. "They who deposed Samo-satene took 'one in substance' in a bodily sense, because Paul had attempted sophistry, and said, 'unless Christ has of man become God it follows that He is one in substance with the Father: and if so, of necessity there are three substances, one the previous substance, and the other two from it,' and therefore guarding against this, they said with good reason that Christ was not one in sub-stance. For the Son is not related to the Father as he imagined. But the bishops who anathematized the Arian heresy, understanding Paul's craft, and reflecting that the word 'one in substance' has not this meaning when used of things immaterial, and especially of God, and acknowledging that the Word is not a creature, but an offspring from the substance, and that the Father's substance was the origin, and root, and fountain of the Son, and that He was of very truth the Father's like-ness, and not of another nature, as we are, and separate from the Father, but that as being from Him, He exists as Son indivisible, as radiance is with respect to light,— and knowing too the illustrations used in Dionysius' case, (the fountain) and the defence of 'one in substance,' and before that the Saviour's saying, symbolical of oneness, 'I and My Father are one, and he that hath seen Me hath seen the Father,'—on these grounds, reasonably asserted on their part, that the Son was one in substance [g]." Yet though the word thus admirably describes the truth, though it was all-important that the word should be used in the Council, yet the Church

[g] Athan., *Conc. Arim. et Sel.*, Oxf. Tr. p. 144.

was very tender in enforcing it. The next generation
of bishops were more sparing in using it: even St.
Athanasius himself did not insist upon it unreason-
ably :—" It should be observed how careful the Fathers
of the day were not to mix up the question of doctrine
which rested on Catholic tradition with that of the
adoption of a term which rested on a Catholic injunction. Not that the term was not in duty to be received,
but it was to be received on account of its Catholic
sense, and where the Catholic sense was held, the word
might even by a sort of dispensation be waived[h]."

5. The astonishing truth that the Word had assumed human nature was stoutly denied by many of
the early heretics. Hence we find how necessary it
was for the Evangelists to lay such store by the
human actions of our Lord. The Docetæ denied that
our Lord was man, and maintained that He was but
a phantasm. In appearance only was He born and
crucified. So also held the disciples of Simon Magus,
adding that Simon the Cyrenian had suffered in His
stead. Valentinus divided Christ from Jesus, holding
that the first was born of Unigena, the latter of all
the Æons at once. He called Him Christ and Saviour, said that He passed through Mary, but had
received nothing of her. The Ophites said that Christ
was the serpent that had deceived Eve, and worshipped
it. They hated Jesus the Son of the Virgin Mary,
into whom they said that Christ descended: so taught
some of the Manichees, and that to delude men's senses,

[h] Athan., ib., p. 157, n.

He appeared and simulated a death and resurrection. The Priscillianists denied that Christ had a pure existence, and asserted that He had not the true nature of man. Neither Arius nor Apollinaris admitted that our Lord was true man. Eutyches did not believe that our Lord was true and perfect man after His Ascension, and his followers believed that the human nature was absorbed into the divine, some before, some after the Resurrection; others, again, held a composite nature.

Against these manifold errors, the Church of God,—resting on the sure word of Holy Scripture, which asserts that "the Word was made flesh[i];" that Christ "was made according to the flesh of the seed of David[j];" that "Every spirit that confesseth that Christ is come in the flesh, is of God[k];" and that, "Forasmuch then as the children are partakers of flesh and blood, He also took part in the same[l];"— has ever maintained that our Lord Christ was a true and perfect man, composed of a reasonable soul and human body. That human body was assumed as the instrument whereby the actions through which the world is saved have been wrought. The Word is said to have donned human nature, never more to doff it, to shew that without any change in itself, there is made the accession of another nature to itself, and in being so assumed, human nature has been deified, and has become life-giving, because it belongs to the Word.

[i] St. John i. 14. [j] Rom. i. 3. [k] 1 St. John iv. 3.
[l] Heb. ii. 14.

Nor is this deification merely relative; nor on the other hand is the humanity turned into divinity, but it is as subsisting in the Word.

Yet we must not hold with the Lutherans that the humanity of our Lord is ubiquitous, for the humanity of our Lord is in heaven, in a certain local circumscribed place.

6. "In the womb of the Blessed Virgin, of her substance." As the unenlightened and carnal nature of man shrank from recognising in the meek and lowly Jesus of Nazareth the Word made flesh, and so twisted and contorted itself on every side if so be that it might rid itself of this astounding conception, so it was a sore trial to it to believe that any daughter of man, however holy, should be brought into that awful proximity with the nature of God, which the true doctrine of the Incarnation implies. Yet no earthly son was ever so completely the son of his mother, as God the Son is the Son of His. For in earthly generations there are two human parents who jointly give life and being to their offspring: whereas in Christ, the entire pure manhood came from the substance of His mother only.

The exaggerated and daily intensifying language of Roman divines on the subject of the present office of the Blessed Virgin,—(language peculiarly significant when we are assured on very high authority that we may be sure, that "whatsoever is prevalent in the Church under the eye of its public authority, practised by the people, and not censured by its pastors, is at least conformable to faith, and innocent as to morals [m],")—such as that all graces come through her as the neck which unites Christ the Head with the Church the Body, or that she is our 'Co-redemptrix,' the 'Authoress of our everlasting salvation,' have prevented Anglicans doing justice to the position of the Holy Virgin in the order of grace. They have shrunk from looking the doctrine concerning her fairly in the face. They have not allowed their minds to dwell on the incomparable singularity, on the incommunicable prerogative of Divine Maternity. While they freely dwell on the gifts of God in other saints, in the patriarchs under the old law for instance, they shrink from resting on the sweet and holy images which surround the name of Mary. This is in every way wrong. A theology that is afraid of possible consequences is sure to err. We must state the absolute truth, and leave consequences to God. To eliminate from our moral theology the idea of the Blessed Virgin, is to strip it of some of its most delicate bloom. What does not civilization, what does not woman owe to the sublime and tender conception of Mary, which has done more to tame the rude social life of Europe in the middle ages than any other one idea! And what more constraining motive to purity of soul, next of course to the thought of Him Who is the great Exemplar of all virtues, can there exist than the idea of such perfect spotless womanhood as a grateful Christendom recognises in our Lady! But there is a still more serious thought. After making every allowance for the re-action against

[m] Pastoral, on Reunion of Christendom, by Manning, p. 65.

the distressing language of certain popular Roman devotions, there is a danger lest the shrinking from a due appreciation of the dignity of the Mother, may not generate an imperfect belief in the divine personality of the Son, and no error is so deadly as that which seeks to touch the person of Jesus. For just consider how much is bound up in the thought expressed in our Article, that " the Word took man's nature in the womb of the Blessed Virgin, of her substance." It implies all those tremendous consequences that are involved in the term Θεοτόκος, " Mother of God," a term asserted to be of apostolical tradition, certainly employed at a very early period in the Church, and endorsed by the sanction of a General Council. That term, (the underlying truth of which was denied by the Ebionites, by Leporius and the Pelagians, and by the followers of Nestorius, and shared also by Eutyches from a different point of view, by Felix and Elipandus, the Adoptionists, and, lastly, by some ill-instructed Protestants,) implies that Mary, not by the power of nature, but by the overshadowing of the Holy Ghost, brought forth in the flesh Christ, the true God, the Son of God by nature, so that she is just as truly and as properly Θεοτόκος, as Christ is truly and properly Θεός.

No wonder that the pious sentiment of Christendom in the contemplation of this stupendous dignity should have burst forth in finding paraphrases for this wondrous term, that it should awake to the conception of an ideal of female holiness, such as no mere human reason could attain unto. No wonder that poetry has strained her utmost to find words to describe the celestial glories of her whom all generations call blessed, or that the art of the limner and sculptor should have been taxed to the full to embody in external expression those marvellous combinations of lowliness and glory, of gentleness and power, of grace and strength, which attend on the idea of the creature-mother of the Creator-Son.

> "Thou maide and mother, daughter of thy Son,
> Thou well of mercy, sinful soules cure,
> In whom that God of bounty chees to won;
> Thou humble and high over every creature,
> Thou nobledst so far forth our nature,
> That no disdaine the Maker had of kinde,
> His Son in blood and flesh to clothe and winde.
>
> Within the cloister blisful of thy sides,
> Toke mannes shape the eternal love and pees
> That of the trine compas Lord and gide is,
> Whom erthe, and see, and heven, out of relees
> Ay herien; and thou virgine wemmiles,
> Bare of thy body (and dwellest maides pure,)
> The creatore of evry creature[n]."—*Chaucer*.

[n] "It hath been said of me, O Latimer, nay, as for him, I will never believe him while I live, nor never trust him, for he likened our Blessed Lady to a saffron-bag! when indeed I never used that similitude. But in case I had used this similitude, it had not been to be reproved, but might have been without reproach. For I might have said thus: as the saffron-bag that hath been full of saffron, or hath had saffron in it, doth ever after savour and smell of the sweet saffron that it contained, so our Blessed Lady which conceived and bare Christ in her

7. The mystery of the Incarnation is the vastest and most profound of all the ways of God. It reaches to the heavens above; it descends to the depths beneath. It solves a multitude of problems, which but for it were insoluble; it gives a master key to all history, and enters into the individual life of every human soul brought within reach of it. Yet how past finding out are God's judgments! God made man, the Eternal Word made flesh, the Creator and Governor of the universe born of a lowly woman, in a little town, in a little country of our little planet; the Infinite reduced within the proportions of the finite, the Uncircumscript held in space. "How can these things be?" If the mystery explains all things, it is at the price of being inexplicable itself: it is no rest to the human mind that this last problem, like Moses' rod, should swallow all the rest that vex and perplex the spirit of man.

The mind of the great poet-philosopher of Italy, in speaking of the mystery of the Trinity says, that he is mad who wishes to know how three Persons can be in one substance, and then he adds, "O human race, stay contented at the *quia*—the fact. If we knew that, there were no need that Mary should have given birth to a Son." In the same spirit, Theodotus speaking of the mystery of which we are treating, says, "If thou

womb, did ever after resemble the manners and virtues of that precious babe that she bare. And what had our Blessed Lady been the worse for this? or what dishonour was this to our Blessed Lady?"—*Latimer's* "*Sermon of the Plough.*"

wouldest know, learn the *quia*, the fact that He was made; the alone worker of miracles, God, knoweth the *how, quomodo* [o]."

This runs through all God's dealings with us. We may know His purpose; we cannot know His method of operation. These are the two sides of the cloud which led the children of Israel through the desert. It is a property, even in mathematics, that things which explain other things are themselves inexplicable; nay, they explain in the measure that they cannot be explained; therefore that which explains all things, God, must, of all things, be the most inexplicable. Things cannot be explained but after the things which are anterior to them, and consequently That which is anterior to all, cannot be explained after anything. Moreover the Infinite is the archetype of the finite, which therein receives the rationale of its existence, as its actual existence. Thus we can explain the world and creation only by God, the Creator, but we cannot explain Him; and we can explain the moral and social world, man and humanity, only by the solution afforded it by the Incarnation, but no one can explain that Incarnation. However, though nothing can explain the Infinite and His operation, all things bear witness to Him. God explains the world, and the world proves God: in biblical language, " The heavens declare the glory of God, and the firmament sheweth His handywork." Much more is this the case with reference to the Incarnation, where the Infinite is

[o] See a grand passage on the *quomodo*, in St. Cyril, in Joan., 359, 360.

not only in operation, but in person; both object and subject; both cause and effect: "Abyssus inscrutabilis, Sacramentum Divinæ Incarnationis [p]."

But a person may say, I admit to the full the idea of mystery in religion, and the mystery of the Incarnation charms me by its beauty, and the rich morality of its economy, but it seems to me to involve contradiction; How can the Infinite be at the same time finite? how can the Omnipresent God quit one place for another? how can the uncircumscript God become measured by space? how can the Eternal God be born, the Impassible God die? how can Greatness and Majesty become man? Let us take these difficulties in their order.

I. How can the Infinite be at the same time finite; Creator and Creature, God and Man in Jesus Christ? In Jesus Christ are two natures, the infinite and the finite, but one single Person, the person of God the Son. If these two natures made one nature, there would be a contradiction, as one could not conceive the finite and the infinite as one thing; but the two natures remain two natures, as distinct after as before the union. There is no contradiction here. Neither is there any from the thought that one person cannot be composed of two natures so as to complete it, for the Personality of Jesus Christ is what it is, that of God the Son, without the help of the human nature. Containing all perfection it can receive no increase; it is

---

[p] St. Bernard, *In Annunc. B. M. De Septiformi Spiritu in Christo. Serm. II. § 6.*

joined to human nature not to perfect itself, but to perfect that human nature. It holds the place of all; gives all, receives nothing. The divinity does not enter into composition with the manhood in Jesus Christ. This is emphatically union; an imperfect analogy may be derived from ourselves. Had such a thing never been formed, had there never been but pure spirits and animal bodies, it would have been difficult to have conceived a being which united the qualities of both, which could be at once flesh and spirit, which could live in the highest metaphysical abstraction, and yet be under the influence of the lowest and basest earthly sensations. Yet this is what man is, and so the Son of God is the object of a still more transcendent union: "What is man? a rational soul joined to a body; what is Christ? the Word of God joined to man." Here is mystery, profound mystery, but no contradiction.

II. But it may be said, How can one conceive that God, who is universal, should have quitted a place to come to another: have been "sent," come upon earth, come down and re-ascended? But the Son of God has never quitted any place. This is but a way of speaking in accommodation to our frailty. The Son of Man was in heaven when He sat with Nicodemus[q]. The Incarnation is not a migration, it is an exhibition of the Godhead. As the Eternal Son proceeds eternally from the Father without leaving His bosom, so His appearance in the midst of us is a visible extension

[q] St. John iii. 2, and 13.

of that invisible extension which hath made the Son
the Sent of the Father, as the ray is sent forth from
the sun.

III. Or it may be asked, How can God, who is
uncircumscript and invisible, localize Himself in His
entirety in Jesus Christ, in the ineffable union of
the holy Incarnation? To this we answer, that in
Christ dwelleth all the fulness of the Godhead bodily,
and yet that Divinity filleth all things, and by its
immensity passes beyond the whole universe of creatures. It is all entire in one, without separation from
any other. Just as in the case of a person speaking,
he utters a word which goes in its entirety to one
auditor, and also in its entirety to all the auditory.
One possesses it in its generality and it overflows among
the multitude, who all possess it complete : so it is not
surprising that God, all complete in heaven and in the
universe, should at the same time be all complete in
the Humanity of the Word.

IV. Next, one may ask how can one say God is
born, or God died? How can the Son, born from all
eternity of the Father, be born a second time of
Mary? How can the Impassible One die? All this
is of faith, not a jot or tittle of its sharpness can be
taken from it, but it is incomprehensible : Yes, but
not irrational.

When one speaks of any one, He is born, he is dead,
it is the individual, the person, of whom one speaks, as
indicated by the personal pronoun *he*. The body and
soul have reference to a personal subject, who is the

Ego. But in Jesus Christ there is but one Person, one *Ego*, and that *Ego* is the Word, God of God. It is, then, God who is born, and who has died in Jesus Christ.

But in the Word, the Son of God, there is the divine nature and the Person. The Person and the Nature are distinct. The divine nature is common to the Divine Persons in the Holy Trinity, and the Person is the means of being of that nature which differs in the Father, or the Son, or the Holy Ghost. When we say person, we do not mean Nature. The Person is God, the nature is Deity.

When speaking of the Word we say God is born, we do not say the Deity is born, for then it would be the Divine Nature which was subject to birth and death, and both the Father and the Holy Ghost would be predicated of in the same way, which were heresy. But, it may be asked, what has this to do in helping the difficulty, since if the Person be God, it is the Deity personified? It is the Divinity which is born and dies. This is not the case, for by the birth from Mary, that which is already God takes human nature, appropriates a humanity, and this appropriation of humanity one calls birth, so that it is equally true, that He who is born is God, and yet He is not born as God. The divine existence hath not to do with that birth and death, being entirely distinct from the human nature, only joined to it by personal communication.

Such is the mystery of the Incarnation; mystery, indeed, if ever there were mystery, but such as ought and must be, when God is its subject.

V. There remains the fifth difficulty. How could God, without derogating from the dignity of His nature, come to assume ours in the womb of one of His creatures? How can we conceive that He for whom the heavens are not great enough, should become man, should be made flesh? While the heart accepts the thought of this divine charity in abasement, the reason revolts against it, even as the greatest manifestation of love, and sees in it contradiction, and a sort of rational impossibility.

" Do not be ever quoting the members of a virgin as a dishonour to the Divinity. For by their nature they have nothing unworthy. Had they been unworthy, or a dishonour to God, He would not have made them with His divine hands; for God maketh nothing but good, and there is no disgrace in God indwelling in His own handiwork.

"But you add that to you it seemeth inappropriate, that He who inhabiteth the heavens should take up His abode in man. Yet here thou judgest rather by passion and by prejudice, than by right reason. Tell me, except heaven, what is greater than man. Stop not to consider the splendour of the material world,— let not the grace of colour and form which thou seest in nature seduce thee,—be not dazzled by the magnificence of the rays of the sun; confuse not thyself at the thought that God is clothed in flesh and skin, as Job beareth witness. But consider the excellence of the reasonable soul, the moral constitution of man, and thou canst not fail to admire this divine being.

He hath received as gifts hands, the ministers of his thought, whereby he can do wonders. Alone, of all the animals, he has been constituted free, alone he hath been created in the power of will. The sun obeys its laws, and circulates in its orbit; it is without freedom or will; but man doth what he willeth. The sun is a slave, thou art free. Is it, then, surprising that God should come to dwell in man, whom He hath so graciously made in His own image, declaring thereby from the beginning His delight to be with him?

"It is true He took dust to form thy body, while He made thy soul the image of His divinity. Wherefore willed He to form of so base a stuff that which He vouchsafed so to adorn? Why took He not the glory of the sun when He willed to make man, and not the very dust of the earth? He did it to keep man humble, that the baseness of his origin should be a counterpoise to the might of his destination; that he might recognise that it was from no merit of his own, but from the munificence of his Maker, that thus he came to be.

"So noble a creature is man, however fallen into ignominy by sin. Judge him not as fallen, but in his original righteousness, and thou wilt see no dishonour in the good God, for the good of such a creature, condescending to communicate with it, as He hath done [r]."

Thus are resolved all the difficulties of apparent con-

---

[r] Serm. Theod. Anc. ap. Concil. Eph., tom. iii. 1016, 1017, ed. Labbe et Cossart.

tradiction in the mystery of the Incarnation, those only which one may venture to try to solve, and this by rigorous comparisons and reasons, rather than by explanations, shewing us that there are mysteries in the natural order, and analogies that can clear our thoughts.

But this is all. The mystery is not less a mystery. The depth is still as unfathomed, in which all vain conceptions come to be cast into the Omnipotence of the Infinite, of which the incomprehensibility itself becomes the evidence. One may say, in this sense, that, freed from all false notions concerning it, and vindicated from the impossibilities of reason, which men fancy they see in it, the mystery of the Incarnation proves itself, by its depth, by its height, by its infinity [s].

One end of the Incarnation is in this Article stated to be the reversal of the penalty of the Fall, and the annulling of the handwriting that was against man. The expression, " to reconcile the Father to us," which is not a Scriptural one, must be taken *metonymicé*, just as we find human emotions, e.g. repentance and change of purpose, frequently in the Old Testament attributed to God. The Scriptural expression is always the other way. The change is on the part of man. "Who hath reconciled *us* to Himself by Jesus Christ [t];" "We pray you in Christ's stead be

[s] Cf. the thoughtful Appendix on the Incarnation in M. Nicolas' work on the Blessed Virgin Mary.

[t] 2 Cor. v. 18.

ye reconciled to God [u];" "By Him to reconcile all things unto Himself [v];" "God was in Christ reconciling the world unto Himself [w]." Yet we may not blame the expression because God who is great without quantity, good without quality, allows us to employ words with regard to Him which though not absolutely true, represent the truth concerning Him, and His dealings with us, in the most real way that we are capable of receiving it. And this is one aspect of the fruits of the Incarnation, that in some mysterious way, for the merits of Jesus Christ, God is pleased to look upon us in mercy.

The extreme intellectual difficulties which attend on a belief in the vicarious satisfaction of Christ, whereby the just has died for the unjust, have been aggravated by the coarse and disproportionate manner in which that doctrine has been taught. The analogy of the faith has been violated by the suppression of other balancing truths. The truth itself has not been carried out into its logical consequences, and notions of *à priori* fitness have been imported into it in a way totally unnecessary. Thus a sort of discordance of will between the First and Second Persons in the adorable Trinity has been assumed; the Father fierce and longing to punish, the Son all mercy and indulgence, whereas they may not be separated in will, even in thought; and while the Father never ceases to be our Father, yearning over the wayward creation of His own hands,

[u] 2 Cor. v. 20.   [v] Col. i. 21.   [w] 2 Cor. v. 19.

the Son is still the revelation of the righteousness of God, and we believe that He shall come to be our judge.

Yet both Holy Scripture and the ancient doctors unanimously attribute to the life, and especially to the death, of our Lord, the character of an expiatory sacrifice. As one with the Holy Eucharist, our Lord says, "This is My Blood of the New Testament, which is shed for many for the remission of sins [x]." Predicting the same holy mystery, He elsewhere says, "The Bread that I will give is My Flesh, which I will give for the life of the world [y]." So St. Paul: "Christ our Passover is sacrificed for us [z];" "Christ hath given Himself for us an offering and a sacrifice to God for a sweet-smelling savour [a]." The main part of the argument of the Epistle to the Hebrews turns on the idea, and the notion of λύτρον and ἱλασμός runs through all the Gospel expositions of this mysterious but most blessed work.

> "Non potea l'uomo ne' termini suoi
> Mai soddisfar, per non potere ir giuso
> Con umiltate, obediendo poi,
>
> Quanto disubbidendo intese ir suso;
> E questa è la ragion perchè l'uom fue
> Da poter soddisfar per se dischiuso.
>
> Dunque a Dio convenia con le vie sue
> Riparar l'uomo a sua intera vita,
> Dico con l'una o ver con ambedue.

[x] St. Matt. xxvi. 28. [y] St. John vi. 51. [z] 1 Cor. v. 7. [a] Eph. v. 2.

Ma perchè l'opra tanto è più gradita
Dell' operante quanto più appresenta
Della bontà del cuor' onde è uscita,

La divina bontà che 'l mondo imprenta
Di proceder per tutte le sue vie
A rilevarvi suso fu contenta:

Nè tra l'ultima notte e 'l primo die
Si alto e si magnifico processo
O per l'una o per l'altro fue o fie;

Che più largo fu Dìo a dar se stesso
In far l'uom sufficiente a rilevarsi
Che s'egli avesse sol da se dimesso,

E tutti gli altri modi erano scarsi
Alla giustizia, si'l Figliuol di Dio
Non fosse umiliato ad incarnarsi [b]."

Dante, Par. vii. 97.

[b] "Man in himself had ever lacked the means
Of satisfaction, for he could not stoop
Obeying, in humility so low,
As high, he, disobeying thought to soar:
And for this reason he had vainly tried,
Out of his own sufficiency, to pay
The rigid satisfaction.   Then behoved
That God should by His own ways lead him back
Unto the life from whence he fell, restored:
By both his ways, I mean, or one alone.
But here the deed is ever prized the more,
The more the Doer's good intent appears;
Goodness celestial, whose broad signature
Is on the universe, of all its ways
To raise ye up, was fain to leave out none,
Nor aught so vast, or so magnificent,

The idea of Sacrifice is a necessary result of the relation between the Creator and His creature. The creature owes everything to his Maker, and therefore the self-devotion of his whole being is that Maker's due. This is the primary idea of Sacrifice. It is the incommunicable privilege of God alone, and therefore is the highest form of worship. Yet this sacrifice is imperfect, if only because the creature hath nothing purely his own wherewith to propitiate his God. But beyond this there is a new idea introduced when we come to deal with sin. The relations of the Creator with the creature are not only those of the disproportion that must always exist between the Infinite and the finite; they are now complicated by the absence of these qualities which, stated positively, are explained by the term "sin." A debt has been incurred which must be paid to the Honour of God; a stain has been imprinted which must be cleansed; an offence has been given that must be removed; a guilt incurred which must be atoned. Therefore into man's creaturely relations with his Maker there comes in the element of reparation.

> Either for Him who gave or who received,
> Between the last night and the primal day,
> Was or can be. For God more bounty shewed,
> Giving Himself to make man capable
> Of his return to life, than had the terms
> Been mere and unconditional release.
> And for His justice, every method else
> Were all too scant, had not the Son of God
> Humbled Himself to put on mortal flesh."
>
> *Cary's Dante.*

Man's sacrifice is, therefore, now doubly imperfect, and therefore a full and perfect sacrifice, oblation, and satisfaction can only be found in one who is more than mere man. The life and death of one not only innocent, but the fountain and source of innocency, is required to the realization of this idea. Such a condition is only to be found in the God-man, and therefore, from the beginning, He was the Lamb slain, in purpose, from the foundation of the world, and all the patriarchal and Jewish rites received what grace they had from Him whom they foreshewed. And still more is this the case now that the Word has actually taken flesh, now that the human nature has been assumed into the unity of the Person of the divine Word, and consequently the actions of our Lord are the actions of His divine Person. The elements, therefore, of eternity and omnipotence now accrue to the acts of Christ; His very human acts, because done by a divine Person, savour of the attributes of Divinity, and thus there is no limit to the efficacy of His eternal Sacrifice, which, being thus superabundant and fulfilling all the ends of such sacrifice[c], is in itself:—1. the highest possible worship, praise, and adoration to God the Holy Trinity; 2. the only, the fullest, and most complete Propitiation for sin; 3. the most grateful and acceptable *Eucharistia* or thank-offering which humanity in its head and members can render to its God; and 4, lastly,

[c] "Et in quel che, forato da la lancia
Et poscia et prima tanto soddisfece
Che d'ogni culpa vince ta bilancia."—*Pas.* xiii. 40.

the most efficacious impetration of all blessings, mercies, and graces which humanity can require.

Thus it will be seen that our Lord's Sacrifice reaches to every sin. It was discussed in the Middle Ages, whether the Passion was chiefly for the destruction of original or of actual sin, and the conclusion was, that

"Although Christ came into this world to destroy all sins, yet He came more especially to take away original than actual sin; for that sin by which the whole human race is infected, is greater than that which is peculiar to individual man." And this conclusion was mainly based upon the consideration that

"It is certain that Christ came into this world not only to destroy that sin which originally passed upon Adam's posterity, but also to destroy all sins which in a manner are superadded to it ; not that all are destroyed, (which arises from defect in men who are not in Christ, according to the words of St. John iii. 19, 'Light is come into the world, and men loved darkness rather than light,') but because He shewed that He was able to destroy all sins. Wherefore it is said in Rom. v. 15, 'Not as the offence, so also is the free gift : for the judgment was by one to condemnation, but the free gift is of many offences unto justification.' But the greater any sin is, the more especially did Christ come into the world for the destruction of that sin. Now a thing may be said to be 'greater' in two ways ; in one way, *intensively*, as where we say greater, that is, more intense, whiteness. And in this way actual is greater than original sin, because it has more of the nature of voluntary agency. In another way a thing is said to be greater *extensively ;* as where we say greater whiteness, meaning a larger superficies. And in this way original sin, by which the whole race of man is infected, is greater than any actual sin which is peculiar to individuals."

Another question in the Middle Ages was, whether the Incarnation would have taken place irrespective of sin and of the fall, but the Article does not enter upon this tempting field of speculation. It views the matter from the practical light of accomplished facts. It assumes the sad truths of sin having entered into the world and death by sin, and here announces the all-powerful Remedy.

ARTICLE III.

DE DESCENSU CHRISTI AD INFEROS.

QUEMADMODUM Christus pro nobis mortuus est, et sepultus, ita est etiam credendus ad Inferos descendisse.

Of the going down of Christ into Hell.

" As Christ died for us, and was buried, so also it is to be believed that He went down into hell."

The minds of men at the time of the Reformation turned much upon this mysterious subject. " There have been in my diocese," says Bishop Alley, of Exeter, " great invectives between the preachers, one against another, and also partakers with them; some holding that the going down of Christ His soul to hell was nothing else but the virtue and strength of Christ His own death, to be made manifest and known to them that were dead before. Others say that *descendit in infera* is nothing else but that Christ did suffer upon the cross the infernal pains of hell. . . . Finally, others preach that the Article is not contained in other symbols, neither in the symbol of Cyprian or rather Rufinus. The contrary side bring for them the universal consent of all the Fathers of both Churches, both of the Greeks and of the Latins [a].

Moreover from a very early period, in an uncritical

---

[a] Alley, cit. Hardwick, Articles, 137. Perkins expounded the descent into hell of our Lord's mental sufferings in the place of the damned. (Hardwick, 171.)

age, the influence of the false gospel of Nicodemus had been profoundly felt in the Church. In that there was a most graphic description of the descent of our Lord into the lower parts of the earth, given with circumstances particular enough to excite the imagination and to impress the soul :—

"Cap. xxi. And while Satan and Hades thus communed together, there came a great voice, like thunder, saying, 'Lift up your gates, ye princes! and be ye lift up, ye everlasting doors, and the King of Glory shall come in!' And Hades, hearing it, said to Satan, 'Go forth now, if thou art able, and make stand against him.' And Satan went forth. Then Hades saith to his demons, 'Make fast the gates of brass and the bolts of iron, and secure me the locks, and watch, all of you, standing on tiptoe, for if this man enter, woe betides us.'

"And hearing these things, the forefathers began to upbraid him, saying, 'All-devouring and insatiate! open, that the King of Glory may come in!' And David, the prophet, saith, 'Knowest thou not, blind one! that, while still in life, I prophesied these self-same words, "Lift up your gates, ye princes?"' And Isaiah said, 'I too foresaw this, and wrote by the Spirit, "The dead shall stand up, and those who are in the tombs shall be awakened." And, "Where is thy sting, O death? Where, O grave! thy victory?"'

"Then came again the voice, saying, 'Lift up your gates, ye princes! and be ye lift up, ye everlasting doors, and the King of Glory shall come in!'

"And Hades, hearing the voice the second time, answered, as one forsooth unwilling, 'Who is this King of Glory?' And the angels of the Lord answered, 'The Lord strong and mighty, the Lord mighty in battle.'

"And straightway, with that word, the brazen gates were broken, and the bolts of iron torn asunder, and the bound in death were loosed from their chains, and we with them. And the King of Glory entered, in form even as a man, and all the dark places of Hades were lighted up.

"Cap. xxii. And straightway Hades cried out, 'We are conquered. Woe unto us! But who art thou, that hast such power and privilege? And what art thou that comest hither without sin, small in seeming but excellent in power, the humble and the great, slave at once and master, soldier and king, wielding power over the dead and the living; nailed to the cross, and yet the destroyer of our power? Truly thou art the Jesus, of whom the Archsatrap Satan spake to us, that by thy cross and death thou shouldest purchase the universe!' Then the King of Glory, holding Satan by the head, delivered him to the angels, and said, 'Bind his hands and feet, and neck and mouth, with irons.' And, giving him over to Hades, he said, 'Receive, and keep him surely until My Second Advent.' . . .

"Cap. xxiv. Then the King of Glory stretched out His right hand, and took the forefather, Adam, and raised him up, and turning to the rest also, he said, 'Come with Me, all of you, as many as have died by

the wood which this man eat of; for lo! I upraise ye all
by the wood of the cross!' After these things He
brought them all forth. And the forefather, Adam,
filled with exceeding joy, said, ' I render Thee thanks,
O Lord, that Thou hast brought me up from the depths
of Hades.' Thus, too, said all the prophets and saints :
' We thank Thee, O Christ, Saviour of the world, that
Thou hast redeemed our life from corruption.' And
while they were saying these things, the Saviour
blessed Adam in the forehead with the sign of the
cross, and did the like to the patriarchs and the prophets, and the martyrs and forefathers, and taking
them with Him, He rose up out of Hades. And as He
journeyed, the holy fathers, accompanying Him, sang,
' Praised be He Who hath come in the name of the
Lord. Hallelujah [b].' "

When scenes like this passed, for the very fact, as we
find it all assumed as such even so late as the time of
the great preacher, Luiz of Grenada, it is not to be
wondered that it should occupy men's thoughts. " The
harrowing of hell," as it was technically called in English, became a favourite subject of the religious art of
the fourteenth and fifteenth centuries, as may be seen
in the works of Taddeo Gaddi and Simone Memmi, in
the chapter-house of Santa Maria Novella at Florence.
But this was not all. Calvin pushed his theory of the
satisfaction of Christ to such a pass, that he maintained
that our Lord not only descended into hell, but actually
suffered the tortures of the damned.

[b] Lord Lindsay's " Christian Art," vol. i. p. lvii.

Although this truth is not expressed either in the Nicene or Constantinopolitan Creeds, we find it in many of the most ancient, such as the Roman and Apostles' Creeds, and before all in the Creed of Aquileia, as Rufinus testifies:—"Rufinus mentions that it was not found in the contemporary creed of the Church of Rome. It occurs in the Athanasian (A.D. 430), but we do not meet it again till we find it in the Creed of Venantius Fortunatus (A.D. 570.) Thenceforward it is of very frequent occurrence. It is found in an Arian Creed, which appeared in three forms in the years 359 and 360, and is known as the third Sirmian Creed. It was adopted at Nicé in Thrace [not Nicæa], and next year in a council held at Constantinople. King supposes that the Article relating to our Lord's descent into hell was introduced into it by the Arians, the more effectually to blind the eyes of the orthodox, that by proposing a doctrine which by implication overthrew a doctrine which many of their sect held, viz. that Christ was without a human soul, the Λόγος supplying the place of soul, they might get the whole creed to pass without suspicion. These are the only creeds in which the clause is found previously to Rufinus's time. But the fact of our Lord's descent seems to have been ordinarily delivered, in connection with the other great facts of the Gospel history, in the elementary instruction communicated to the new converts. In the summary of faith which Eusebius says he translated from the Syriac, and which he states to have been rehearsed by Thaddæus to Agbarus of Edessa, we have the following: ‘He was crucified and went down into hell, and broke down the partition which had never been broken.’ Whatever opinion may be formed as to the authenticity of the narrative, at any rate the summary of faith in which these words occur is a witness to the elementary teaching of very early times[c].” It is founded on two remarkable passages in Scripture, the 16th Psalm, as expounded by St. Peter in Acts ii., “Thou shalt not leave my soul in hell, neither shalt Thou suffer Thy holy one to see corruption;” and secondly, 1 Pet. iii. 18, 19, where our Lord is said to have come in the spirit, and to have preached to the souls in prison; to which may be added the 81st Psalm, as a prophecy of this mystery, Christ alone being He who is free among the dead.

The chief questions which have been raised on this matter are, Did our Lord descend into hell? For what end in the order of redemption did He so descend? Whom did He rescue therefrom? Besides, there is the great question whether, on the dissolution of the vital union in Christ, the hypostatic union still was maintained?

Now that our Lord descended, was taught from the very beginning of Christianity by the holy Fathers. Justin Martyr[d] applies to this truth that text of Jeremiah which is not found in our version, but is quoted also by S. Irenæus: “The Lord God remembered His dead from Israel that slept in the earth of the sepulchre,

---

[c] Heurtley’s *Harmonia Symbolica*, pp. 135, sqq. Oxf. 1858.
[d] *Dial. Tryph.* § 72, p. 164, Oxf. Tr.

and He came down to them to preach His salvation."
Justin accused the Jews of suppressing this passage.
Irenæus says, "He went down to see with His eyes *id
quod erat inoperatum conditiones* [e];" also to announce
His coming, and extending the remission of punisment
to those that believed in Him [f]; and that for three days
He passed the time where the dead were, and descended
to them to bring them out and save them [g].

Clement Alexandrinus asserts "that our Lord descended for no other reason than to preach the Gospel [h]," and his disciple Origen says, " the soul of Christ
disembodied conversed with disembodied spirits [i];" "that
for the salvation of the world He went down and
brought back Adam [k]." Eusebius, commenting on the
16th Psalm : " He was present for the sake of the souls
who were detained in hell; who for many ages had
expected His coming. He descended to break the
brazen gates, and burst the iron bonds, that He might
set those free who had been hitherto bound beneath [l]."
St. Athanasius uses the doctrine as an argument against
Apollinaris, who denied that our Lord had assumed a
human soul. St. Cyril of Jerusalem elucidates the doctrine in the practical teaching of his Catechism, and
St. Epiphanius in his refutation of the heresies of the
Herodians and Arians. To this truth also, in magnificent diction, St. Chrysostom, in the beginning of his
homilies on St. Matthew, alludes, where he says: "Thou

---

[e] *Iren.* iv. 39.   [f] Ibid. iv. 48.   [g] Ibid. v. 31.   [h] Strom.
vi. 6, p. 762, ed. Potter.   [i] Cont. Cel. ii. § 43, p. 419.   [k] Hom.
xv. Gen.   [l] Eus. *Dem. Ev.* x. B., p. 501, ed. Col. 1688.

shalt likewise see the tyrant here bound, and the multitude of the captives following, and the citadel from which that unholy demon overran all things in time past. Thou wilt see the hiding-places and the dens of the robber, for even there also was our King present [m]." The Latin fathers are equally unanimous in their testimony, and no one goes into the question more thoroughly than St. Augustine, who, in his 99th Epistle, treats of the interpretation of the obscure passage of St. Peter. St. Jerome [n] also developes the doctrine. He makes St. John Baptist, in sending his disciples to our Lord, reason,—" I know that Thou art He who hath come to take away the sins of the world, but because I am going to descend into hell, I also ask, whether Thou also art to descend thither; or is it impious to think this of the Son of God, and so wilt Thou send another? I desire to know whether, as I have announced Thee on earth, I am also to announce Thee beneath." So, in his "Commentary on the Epistle to the Ephesians [o]," he says, "The Son of God therefore descended into the lower parts of the earth, and ascended up also; not only that He might fulfil the law and the prophets, but also obtain other occult dispensations, known only to the Father and Himself. For we cannot know how the Blood of Christ profited the angels, and those that were in hell, and yet we cannot be ignorant that It did profit them. He descended therefore into hell, and ascended into heaven, that He might fill those who were in those regions, according as they could receive."

[m] Hom. ii. 18, Oxf. Tr.   [n] Ep. cli. *ad Algasiam.*   [o] iv. 10.

Fulgentius [p]: "It remained therefore for the full effect of our redemption, that thither sinless man assumed by God might descend, whither sinful man separated from God deservedly had fallen; that is, into hell, where the soul of the wicked was used to be tormented; and to the tomb, where the flesh of the wicked was used to be corrupted; yet in such wise that neither the flesh of Christ was corrupted in the tomb, nor the soul of Christ tortured by the pains of hell; because that Soul free from sin was not liable to punishment, and corruption dared not touch the sinless flesh."

He meets the question of the dissolution of the vital union [q]: "In the sepulchre the same God made man lay; and the same God made man rose from hell on the third day; but in the sepulchre the same God lay only according to the flesh, and descended into hell solely according to the soul."

His disciple Ferrandus [r] developes this thought: "Whole (*totus*) Christ is everywhere, in that He is the Word; but the whole which He is (*totum*) is not everywhere: for the rational soul and flesh are not everywhere; with which He is one. He was in hell according to His rational soul, but not the whole of Him, for His flesh was not there, which went to constitute the whole. Whole Christ was in the grave according to the flesh; but not the whole of Him,

[p] *Ad Trasimundum,* lib. iii. 30, *init. Bibl. Patr.* ix. 65.   [q] *Lib. de Fid. ad Petr.,* cap. iii., *B. Patr.* ix. 74 B.   [r] *Ad Severum Scholast. B. Patr.* ix. 512 E.

because the rational soul, which goes to constitute the whole, was not there. But the Word of God was both with the soul in hell, and with the body in the grave, because naturally it is everywhere diffused, and was never wanting either to His soul or His flesh."

Some of the Fathers, from the expression "nethermost hell," in the Psalms, imagine that there are two mansions, one in which the souls of the saints were detained, and one in which the wicked are tormented. Whether our Lord went to both is a question on which the consent is not perfect. St. Gregory, in his Morals, would have that our Lord went to the first only; St. Augustine[s] and, as we have seen already, his disciple Fulgentius, to the second.

As regards the question what souls our Lord freed, the author of the treatise *De Paschate*, attributed to St. Ambrose, asserts that all sinners were freed by Christ; and to this St. Gregory Nazianzen, in his Paschal Sermon (xlii.), alludes, where he says: "If He descended into hell, descend with Him. Learn the mysteries of Christ that are enacted even there; what is the secret of that double descent, what was its reason? Did He save all without exception by His advent, or those only who believed in Him?" The large-hearted Alexandrian school, with its intense love of heathen learning, and with its theory of the providential development of the Greek philosophy, rather inclined to the opinion that our Lord freed all; but the common belief of the

[s] *De Gen. ad lit.* xii.

Church has been that our Lord, descending into hell, imparted salvation to those only who, while they lived, by faith and righteousness had rendered themselves worthy of that favour. This would seem to be the interpretation of the extremely obscure passage in the Epistle of St. Peter, viz. that our Lord in the Spirit, descending into hell, mercifully bestowed His grace upon the dead, and called to the knowledge and veneration of Himself, not all, but those who from the beginning of the world had died in the grace and friendship of God, not only under the law, but from the most ancient times, even before the Flood. Therefore he specially dwells on their case, that he might exhibit. the fact that the beneficent power of the Redeemer told backward, and that he might have a fitting opportunity of making mention of baptism, which the Flood prefigured [t].

[t] *Vide* Petavius, *de Incarnatione ad locum.*

ARTICLE IV.

DE RESURRECTIONE CHRISTI.

CHRISTUS vere a mortuis resurrexit, suumque corpus cum carne, ossibus, omnibusque ad integritatem humanæ naturæ pertinentibus, recepit : cum quibus in cœlum ascendit, ibique residet quoad extremo die ad judicandos homines reversurus sit.

Of the Resurrection of Christ.

" Christ did truly rise again from death, and took again His body, with flesh, bones, and all things appertaining to the perfection of man's nature; wherewith He ascended into heaven, and there sitteth, until He return to judge all men at the last day."

"The same stone which the builders rejected is become the Head of the Corner." The same argument which the Apostles used when, inspired by the Holy Ghost on the day of Pentecost, they went forth to conquer the world to the obedience of faith, is the turning-point in the great contest between Faith and Infidelity, which is being waged in the midst of the civilization of the nineteenth century. Grant the Resurrection, and the whole Catholic Creed follows; reject the Resurrection, and there remains no basis for Christianity, however long a pietistic sentiment may seek to feed the dead embers of a defunct and extinguished faith.

Observe the course of persuasion used by the first propagators of the faith. They distinctly assert that Jesus of Nazareth, who had been seen and known by many to whom they spake, whose public Crucifixion was recorded in the Criminal Procedure of the State, actually had risen from the dead, in accordance with such a distinct promise that He was to do so, as that on the fulfilment of such promise He had all along staked His pretensions as a Divine Teacher. The apostolic college is filled up specially with a view to a " witness with us of His resurrection[a]." St. Peter's sermon on the day of Pentecost turns on this fact: "This Jesus hath God raised up, whereof we all are witnesses[b]." So at the Beautiful Gate of the Temple, "The Prince of Life whom God hath raised from the dead, whereof we are witnesses[c];" so before the Sanhedrin, "Whom God raised from the dead, even by Him doth this man stand before you whole[d];" so in the preaching after that, "With great power gave the Apostles witness of the Resurrection of the Lord Jesus[e];" so in the presence of Gamaliel, "Him hath God exalted with His right hand to be a Prince and a Saviour, for to give repentance unto Israel and forgiveness of sins[f];" so St. Stephen saw the Son of Man in heaven, whereon the people "cried with a loud voice and stopped their ears[g];" so at the baptism of Cornelius, to the Gentiles the astounding fact is declared, " Him God raised up the third day, and shewed Him openly[h];" so in St.

---

[a] Acts i. 22.   [b] Ibid. ii. 32.   [c] Ibid. iii. 15.   [d] Ibid. iv. 10.
[e] Ibid. iv. 33.   [f] Ibid. v. 31.   [g] Ibid. vii. 57.   [h] Ibid. x. 40.

Paul's first sermon at Antioch[i], and at Thessalonica[k], and specially at Athens, the Resurrection is the subject of his teaching[l]. When charged before the Sanhedrin, he claims the sympathy of the Pharisees, and at the same time states the very centre of his teaching, when he says, "Of the hope and of the resurrection of the dead, I am called in question[m]." And the practical and unsupernatural Festus states the matter from his point of view, when he speaks of the complaints against Paul, being " of one Jesus which was dead, whom Paul affirmed to be alive[n];" as indeed the blessed Apostle himself makes plain in his solemn address to Agrippa[o]. In short, the whole of the Acts testify to the truth that the early disciples made this the very kernel of their teaching.

As might be expected, the early Christian apologists urge this argument. St. Justin[p] says : "After His crucifixion, then, even they that were acquainted with Him all denied and forsook Him ; but afterwards, when He rose from the dead, and was seen by them, and taught them to read the prophecies in which all these things were foretold to happen, and when they had seen Him go up into heaven, and had believed and received power from thence, which was sent them from Him, they went forth to the whole race of men and taught these things, and received the name of Apostles." And Tertullian shews how the belief in our

[i] Acts xiii. 30.   [k] Ibid. xvii. 3.   [l] Ibid. xvii. 19.
[m] Ibid. xxiii. 6.   [n] Ibid. xxv. 19.   [o] Ibid. xxvi. 23.
[p] Apol., 50.

Lord's resurrection is bound up with the hope of our own: "Believing the resurrection of Christ, we believe also in our own, for whom He died and rose again. When, therefore, we are sure of the resurrection of the dead, the sorrow of death is voided, as well as the impatience of pain [q];" and, conversely, "weaken the faith in the Resurrection of our Lord, and that of ourselves is injured also [r]." St. Chrysostom [s] shews how all the different mysteries hang upon each other: "For if He (Christ) truly took not upon Him our flesh, He neither was crucified, dead, nor buried, neither did He rise again. If He did not rise again, the whole reason of the Dispensation is overthrown. Thou seest into what inconsequence they fall who will not follow the canon of the Holy Scripture, but who twist everything in their individual reasonings."

Now in the modern controversies, this truth, as has been said, is the Crucial one. We must begin by assuming God, therefore an omnipotent God, therefore a God who ruleth and governeth all things in heaven and earth. This granted, there can be no limit to His power, and however contrary to our experience, there is no antecedent improbability that He may not act by what we term 'miraculous intervention.' We have a right, therefore, on the ground that all natural phenomena are the result of the operation of a perfect will, to assume the propriety of a general fixity, but also the power of an occasional disturbance of the order

[q] *De Patientia*, p. 165, ed. Rigalt. Paris, 1641.   [r] Ibid., p. 484.
[s] In Gen. Hom. 58, n. 3.

of being. Brute matter can have no law within itself, else it would cease to be brute matter. Matter, therefore, is either the Pantheistic God, or it has no inherent laws of its own constitution outside the will of its maker. But that brute matter is the Pantheistic God is a supposition surrounded by great difficulties. We therefore may safely choose the only other alternative.

Assuming, then, the possibility of miracle, we have in the Resurrection of our Lord to face the fact of the greatest objective miracle which has ever been preached to the world. If mankind have been deceived in giving credence to this, Christianity must fall; for both its apologetic and its ethical position is bound up in the truth of the fact. On the other hand, accept the Resurrection of our Lord, and all other mysteries follow in its train. When the soul has bowed itself before the truth of the Resurrection, it is only inconsistency which keeps men back from accepting all the mysteries of the faith. It is only a little more or a little less. In principle the point has been yielded.

This being the case, the historical truth of what is asserted of our Lord's rising again must be submitted to the severest historical criticism. There is no true kindness in blinking any fact with regard to it. It is too serious a matter not to be probed to the quick. And here such works as the Trial of the Witnesses come in good stead. The acutest minds have devoted themselves to pick holes in the Gospel narrative of this sacred event, and the result is that, given the authenticity of the documents, there is not only no contradiction such as can destroy their historic worth, but actually there is no escape for an unprejudiced mind in accepting the truth on the historic testimony.

The chief modern attempt at evasion is that of Dr. Strauss, whose theory of a mythic accretion around a really historic personage is a very subtle device of the evil one. The main points on which he rests are— i. an exaggeration of the difficulty of systematizing the records of the different appearances of our Lord during the forty great days, and thereby the infusion of a doubt as to the trustworthiness of the testimony; or, ii. the philosophical difficulty as to the nature of the Resurrection of Body.

i. Following the authority of Mr. Greswell[t], we seem to find that the following chronology harmonizes the different accounts of our Lord's Resurrection, and of such of His apparitions as it has pleased the Holy Ghost to reveal to us in the Gospels and Epistles.

1. On Sunday morning the sixteenth of Nisan, corresponding with the sixth of April, the two Maries and Salome, who had bought spices, went very early to the tomb. An earthquake takes place. An angel of the Lord comes down and rolls back the stone, and sits upon it; as the women approach, they ask who is to roll back the stone, and on arriving they find that this has actually taken place. An angel announces the Resurrection, and invites them to enter the tomb; there they see a young man sitting on the right in a shining garment, who encourages them, and again

---

[t] *Harmonia Evangelica*, p. 393.

Arians on the one side, and Marcellus of Ancyra on the other, sought to veil their heresies by dwelling on the true doctrines which they also acknowledged [c].

After the Constantinopolitan Creed had been sanctioned by a General Council, we find no further change in the unchanging East; but in the West the expression *Deum de Deo*, which had been in the Nicene formula, was probably restored by a Spanish Council, either that of Braga, A.D. 411, or of Galicia, A.D. 447. It is certain that the expression occurs in the formulæ of the three Councils of Toledo, A.D. 589.

Here also occurs the other more important addition of the Filioque which has been fraught with such momentous consequences to the Church of God. This Toledan Creed moreover agrees with the present English Form, in which 'holy' is missed out before the Catholic and Apostolic, as well as the preposition 'in' in the same clause.

It is a remarkable thought how, in the history of Christianity, God has used works of anonymous or doubtful authorship to produce the most profound effects upon the intellect of the Church. Putting out of sight, on the grounds of reverence, any discussion as to the Epistle to the Hebrews, we find various works telling markedly on the religious consciousness of the times, on the authorship of which no certainty has been arrived at. The Apostolic Constitutions, though probably the embodiment of a very early phase of Church discipline, are no longer attributed to is-apo-

[c] See Tertullian, Oxf. Ed. note P. p. 496.

stolic times. The treatise on the Heavenly Hierarchy, ascribed to Dionysius the Areopagite, is certainly not his work, but has been a storehouse for pious meditation for many centuries. No one can positively say who wrote the *Te Deum*, and in later times, the authorship of the " Imitation of Christ" is still controverted. Thus it is that God uses servants unknown to man for His purposes, and thus the words of some unknown individual, unrewarded by human commendation on earth, receive the blessing from the Most High, and the praise not of man, but of God.

This is the case with what is termed the Creed of St. Athanasius. It certainly is no Eastern Creed at all, for although now printed in some of the *Euchologia* of the Greek Church, it is nowhere found in Greek before the twelfth century, and is evidently the result of purely Latin influence. Neither in the West was it promulgated by any council, or by any authority of the see of Rome. Its origin is probably from Gaul. St. Hilary of Arles was long reputed to be its author. Modern criticism bestows the honour upon Victricius of Rouen. This, at least, is certain, that it was commented upon in company with the Lord's Prayer and Apostles' Creed by Venantius Fortunatus about A.D. 570, and that in France it generally was called the Faith of St. Athanasius the Bishop, the exposition of the Catholic Faith of Athanasius, the Sermon of St. Athanasius of Faith, the Symbol of Athanasius, the Little Book of Athanasius of Faith, the Sermon of the Catholic Faith. About the year 1050, we have

Gualdo of Corby calling it the Catholic Faith ascribed to Athanasius (*quem composuisse fertur B. Athanasius*). Honorius of Arles calls it the Faith *Quicunque vult*. The Schoolmen generally attribute it to Athanasius, but in the twelfth century there appears a more critical spirit in the title. A German MS. of Leipzig, A.D. 1180, calls it *Fides Anastasii Papæ;* so in 1120, a Harleian MS. A MS. of the Friar Minors in France has *Canticum Bonefacii, ce Chant fust St. Anaistaise qui Apostoilles de Rome*, and in a Bodleian MS. of 1400 we have *Anastasii Expositio Symboli Apostolorum. Laud. Misc.*, 490.

All that we can gather is, that it was written in Gaul before the Council of Chalcedon, that it specially referred to the Apollinarian heresy which appeared about A.D. 360, and that its author was deeply imbued with St. Augustine's teaching, especially as expressed in his treatise *De Trinitate*.

The essence of a revelation is that it must be definite. We cannot conceive God announcing anything to His creatures which is not precise. There may be question whether a fact is really revealed or not, but there can be no question as to the obligation of accepting the entire conception, if it really be so. Moreover this applies not only to this or that doctrine or faith. It applies to the whole body of truth that claims to be communicated by God. There is no scope for selection of this or that doctrine, which speaks especially to this or that soul. The one question is, What is the sum of revelation?

Now, not only has the Christian religion ever maintained that God in sundry measure, πολυμερῶς [d], and divers manners, πολυτρόπως, spake in times past to the human race, communicating so much divine knowledge as He thought good for them, or as they were able to bear,—as to Adam, Noah, and Moses; but it has asserted that one of the offices of the God-man, one of the objects of the Incarnation, was to communicate a fresh and fuller measure of certain truths by the Holy Spirit, which was sent as a consequence of His ascension. Of the gifts for men which He obtained, none was so important as that of the Paraclete, for His indwelling in the Church organic, and in the soul and body of the individual believer, was not only as a principle of love and holiness, but as a principle of divine faith. "No one can say that Jesus is the Lord but by the Holy Ghost."

But how did the Spirit work? Of course the work was supernatural, and even its manifestations were such as we now see no more; but its more obvious external manifestations were :—1. the direction of the Apostles, as a corporation, to declare certain Divine truths, the belief in which constituted the right of belonging to the new community, and the participation of the spiritual privileges deposited therein, and 2. the illumination of the minds, the memories, and all the inward powers of certain of their number to record more fully the supernatural events of the Life of the Founder and His teaching.

From these two sources spring the two authorities

---

[d] Vide Alford on the Epistle to the Hebrews, *init.*

of the Creeds and the Scriptures. We have already touched upon the second, it remains to say somewhat of the first.

Before a page of the New Testament was written, Christianity was an organized polity. Like every other polity, it had its laws, its privileges, its penalties, its conditions of membership. Of these last, the necessity of receiving Baptism was the initiatory. But this implied certain requirements. A thorough repentance of all past sin, and a renunciation of the three great enemies of Christ and His people were not sufficient. Beyond this there was the *de fide* acceptance of certain historic facts, certain theological truths (very simple indeed and rudimentary, but still definite and precise) concerning God. His unity and existence as against Polytheism, His creative energy against Pantheism, the personal existence of His Word against Emanationism, the Incarnation of the Word as the distinctive truth of the new religion; the historic facts of the Birth, Life, Suffering, Death, Rising, Ascension, and Assession of the Word in His Human Nature; the existence of the Holy Spirit, was what their Founder had laid down as the terms of knowledge required in those who were to be baptized in the Name of the Father, and of the Son, and of the Holy Ghost. Moreover we find that close to this primary faith required in the baptized, there were certain " principles of the doctrine of Christ," " the foundation of repentance from dead works, and of faith toward God, of the doctrine of baptisms, and of laying on of hands, and of resurrection of the dead, and of eternal judgment[e]," which went to make up the sum of necessary convictions on their part. It will be seen at once that these in substance suggest the Sacraments of the Church, and correspond with the Articles of the Creed, when actually formalized. Such was "the form of sound words," to which allusion is made in the Pastoral Epistles of St. Paul, and the παρακαταθήκη or deposit.

From that day to this, these articles have been the sum and substance of Christianity. Nothing less than that is sufficient. Nothing more than that is of absolute necessity to salvation. When a child is baptized, the Church demands no more of him, or of his sponsors, than an assent to the Apostles' Creed—and when the Christian soul is going out of the world to meet its Judge, it is in the terms of the same Creed that the dying man is interrogated[f].

In the present day there is a great jealousy of the principle of dogma. It is imagined that a true Christian morality, a holy Christian sentiment can exist without it; that Creeds, professing to give us very definite statements on supernatural subjects, are by the very imperfection of language and thought, only trammels to the soul, which is thereby kept from aspiring to the indefinite. Yet this is unreasonable, for there can be no Christian morals without Christian definite faith. Dogma is to morals as cause to effect, will to motion. Christian morality is dogma in action, or practical faith. Indeed, to make men receive and prac-

---

[e] Heb. vi. 1, 2. [f] Office of Visitation of the Sick.

tise a morality severe and painful to human nature, one must give great and positive reasons for so doing: when the morality is superhuman, the motives must be so also. Virtues imply beliefs. Nay more, the very fact of Christian morality and its realization in the world implies a set of dogmas at its back, perfect like unto itself. "By their fruits ye shall know them," said our Lord, and the common sense of mankind has accepted the dictum. As we gather an argument for the existence of God from the contemplation of the divine beauty of things created, so we obtain a proof of the supernatural truths of religion from the lives of those who believe and practise it.

Hence proceeded the deficiency of motive, that is, of definite belief or dogma, which weakened the moral conceptions of the heathen. Their notions of God, the soul, and a retribution, were so feeble that they could not resist the onslaught of the passions; but our Lord, manifesting Himself as the Logos, as the Archetypal Reason, whence human reason has ever derived its truths, came to strip the spiritual edifice of the encumbering ruins that choked man's understanding; to restore in all their primitive purity and strength those enfeebled truths; to communicate fresh notions destined to aid man's weakness, and finally to place all these things beyond attack, on the impregnable fortress of His own authority, so that the incessant assaults of nineteen centuries have failed to touch the sacred treasure.

With Him every new precept has been a fresh reve-

lation of truth. He has rested the one upon the other.
He has made men touch the invisible by faith. Faith
has bound dogma to practice, as the bond between the
two—partaking in the first by its object, in the latter
by its principle—the link between the creature and
the Creator. In Christianity there is a precise adjust-
ment between the work of the intellect and the work
of the heart. It is not a speculative system. We know
that we may act: we act because we know. Where
our conception surpasses our power of practice, we have
evidence of a fall in an originally grand nature ; but
in the original intention of God, in the restoration of
humanity in Christ, there is a holy proportion between
the province of the understanding and the province of
the heart : just as the intellect and will in God, the
Son and the Spirit, are hypostatically separate, but
essentially one [g].

And such has been the course of the world—such
the history of the progress of Christianity. From certain convictions, so strong that many have died for
them, has proceeded the whole of the supernatural life,
which has distinguished the true faith from all others.
Because men have held, not as speculations, but with
the grim tenacity of a struggle for life, certain truths,
the Christian world is what it is.

And this is no slavery, but rather emancipation.
The human soul must think on the relations in the
adorable Trinity. This teaches one to think safely,

[g] Vide Nicolas, *Études Philosophiques sur le Christianisme*, vol. ii.
p. 367.

and safety ever gives the sense of freedom and expansion. The greatest of human minds has found sufficient scope for the most abstract speculation on the dogmas of revealed faith, and in such speculation has been aided by the possession of an infallible starting-point in the Creeds. Without Creeds speculation is apt to run into mysticism: with Creeds it is the exercise of the Spirit-illumined faculty, the grandest use of that divine reason which God has implanted in the master-work of His Hands.

And the same Creed which has this mighty office with the profound thinker, has a no less holy one with regard to every Christian. As a fund of pious meditation, we have here the mysteries of the faith presented to us in the briefest form, the great verities brought before us day by day so as to enter into the very substance of the soul. Hence the benefit of making the Creed a part of man's daily devotion. The repetition of our belief is an act of faith, and we are justified by faith. St. Augustine says : " Say it daily; when you rise, when you betake yourself to sleep, say your Creed; say it to the Lord. Do not say, I said it yesterday, I said it to-day, I daily say it, I have it perfect. Call to mind thy faith, examine thyself. Let thy Creed be thy mirror. In it see if thou believest all that thou confessest thou believest, and rejoice in thy faith [h]."

Speaking of the Council of Nicæa, an eloquent author remarks : " That Asia Minor, where the Christian

[h] Serm. lviii. tom. v.

Church had just held her grand assizes, had been for many centuries the birthplace of all superstitions and of all systems. Philosophy and fable had alike their favoured abode there. The southern coast of that same land was strewn with the ruins of Troy, the brilliant country of the gods of Homer. There was not one of all the flourishing cities along the margin of the Ionian sea, not one of the islands of her archipelago, which could not at the same time boast of a god, and the birth of a sage. Samos had the temple of Neptune and the cradle of Pythagoras. The Apollo of Claros and the Diana of Ephesus were adored on the same shores where Thales and Anaximander had taught, and where Heraclitus first saw the light. But this long labour of the same people to conceive the thought or the image of God, had only produced, till that day, dreams, idols, and monsters. And in less than six weeks, three hundred men unknown to one another, arriving from opposite ends of the world, speaking in different tongues, had been able to give a nervous and concise formula of the Divine nature, destined to traverse all oceans and all ages! And at this day, after fifteen centuries have passed away, from one extremity of the civilized world to the other, in the lonely hamlets of the Alps, in unknown isles of ocean discovered by modern science, when the solemnity of the Sunday lifts towards heaven brows bent earthward by labour, is heard a concert of rustic voices repeating in one and the same tone the hymn of the Divine Unity: 'I believe in one God the Father Almighty, Maker of all things visible and invisible; and in one Lord Jesus Christ, the only-begotten Son of God, begotten of His Father before all worlds, God of God, Light of Light, Very God of very God, Begotten not made, Being of one substance with the Father, by Whom all things were made, Who for us men and for our salvation came down from heaven, And was incarnate, and was made man; He suffered and rose again on the third day; and ascended into heaven, and shall come again to judge ... And I believe in the Holy Ghost[i].'"

[i] De Broglie, *L'église et l'empire Romain au 4' ieme siècle*, t. ii. p. 68.

ARTICLE IX.

De Peccato Originali.

Peccatum originis non est (ut fabulantur Pelagiani) in imitatione Adami situm, sed est vitium, et depravatio naturæ, cujuslibet hominis ex Adamo naturaliter propagati: qua fit, ut ab originali justitia quam longissime distet, ad malum sua natura propendeat, et caro semper adversus spiritum concupiscat, unde in unoquoque nascentium, iram Dei atque damnationem meretur. Manet etiam in renatis hæc naturæ depravatio. Qua fit, ut affectus carnis, Græce φρόνημα σαρκὸς (quod alii sapientiam, alii sensum, alii affectum, alii studium carnis interpretantur) legi Dei non subjiciatur. Et quanquam renatis et credentibus, nulla propter Christum est condemnatio, peccati tamen in sese rationem habere concupiscentiam, fatetur Apostolus.

" Of Original or Birth-Sin.

"Original sin standeth not in the following of Adam, (as the Pelagians do vainly talk,) but it is the fault and the corruption of the nature of every man that naturally is engendered of the offspring of Adam, whereby man is very far gone from original righteousness, and is of his own nature inclined to evil, so that the flesh lusteth always contrary to the Spirit; and, therefore, in every person born into this world, it deserveth God's wrath and damnation. And this infection of nature doth remain, yea, in them that are regenerated; whereby the lust of the flesh, called in Greek, φρόνημα σαρκὸς, which some do expound the wisdom, some sensuality, some the affection, some the desire of the flesh, is not subject to the law of God. And although there is no condemnation for them that believe and are baptized, yet the Apostle doth confess, that concupiscence and lust hath of itself the nature of sin."

In approaching the subject of the Ninth Article of religion, we have to bear in mind, that at the Reformation, the Church had to deal 1. with those who denied original sin, and 2. with those who mistook its nature and unduly magnified its consequences. The Family of Love affirmed that the elect and regenerate sin not. The Adamites maintained that they were in as good a state as Adam before the Fall, therefore without original sin. The older sect of the Begards (condemned in the Council of Vienne under Clement V. A.D. 1311) maintained that man in the present life can attain unto so great a measure of perfection, that he is rendered absolutely impeccable, and cannot grow more in grace. The Socinians very soon developed the doctrine of the denial of original sin. On the contrary side, as will be seen, men ran into the opposite extreme.

The learned Möhler, in treating of the doctrine of original sin, states that the Confession of the Anglican Church on every point endeavours to avoid a tone of exaggeration[a]. Exaggeration on this subject was the cardinal error of the Reformers of the sixteenth century.

In order to estimate what is the meaning of original sin, it becomes necessary in the first place to consider what was the primitive state of man, in what condition, endowed with what faculties, did he come forth from his Maker's hands? Now we can only attain to this knowledge by directing our view to the renewal of the fallen creature in Jesus Christ, because as regeneration consists in the re-establishment of our primæval condition, the insight into what Christ has given us back affords us the desired knowledge of what was originally imparted to us. Moreover, the Holy Scriptures tell us "that God made man upright." Man in Paradise was blessed with pre-eminent gifts of body and soul. He was a spiritual being endowed with freedom, capable of knowing and loving God, and of viewing all things in Him. He was formed in God's image and likeness. His lower faculties acted under the guidance of his reason, as his reason was in obedience to God, and thus he lived in blessed harmony with himself and his Creator. He had also the great gift of immortality, even in his earthly part, and an exemption from disease and the ills that lead to death, and all this by a special divine gift, for it is one thing not to be able to die, and another thing to be able not to die, as St. Augustine

[a] Symbolism, vol. i. p. 110, ed. 1843.

bears witness. This condition of things is the state of "original righteousness," a state, which by no means merely implies that man was unpolluted by any alloy adverse to God, but what is more, that he stood in the most interior and closest communion with his Maker, and such a state and condition cannot be attained or upheld by the natural powers; in short, no created being can be holy but by the Holy Spirit, and no finite essence can live in loving communion with God but through Him. Therefore the relation of Adam to God, as it raised him above human nature, and made him partaker of that of God, was caused by a supernatural gift of divine grace superadded to the endowments of nature. Had these gifts been natural, they would have survived sin, as those of the demons: and it is necessary to distinguish between the state of pure nature, and the superadded gifts which in one sense are accidental qualities. Though, as a matter of fact, both existed together in the unfallen man, it is necessary for theological precision to bear the distinction very clearly in mind.

Some theologians hold that on Adam the supernatural superadded gifts were bestowed simultaneously with his natural endowments, i.e. in the first moment of his creation; others, distinguishing between holiness and justice, prefer the opinion that Adam was created in a sound, pure, and unpolluted nature; and that he was favoured with the supernatural gift of communion with God after he had by his efforts rendered himself worthy of its reception. Both theories sharply distinguish alike between the provinces of nature and grace.

Luther's cardinal error was, that he mistook the distinction between the natural and the superadded gifts, maintaining that Adam's acceptableness with God was natural, and an integral constitutive part of his nature. He failed to distinguish between the nature itself of the mind and will, created by God alone without us; and the virtue and uprightness, which are perfected by our co-operation with the grace of God. Divines called the former " the image," the latter " the likeness of God." The importance of this distinction is obvious. Moreover, Luther and many of his followers denied the freedom of the will in fallen man. Though Melanchthon at one time held with his master, he afterwards perceived the abyss into which such a doctrine must plunge the Church, and abandoned it. Yet the servitude of the human will, as it was termed, profoundly influenced the Lutheran system. Calvin's paradisaic man was also devoid of supernatural gifts, but he allowed him free-will. How this is compatible with an actual predestination of all things, even of the Fall itself, is unintelligible.

What has gone before is necessary to the elucidation of the Doctrine of Original Sin. Our Article tells first of all what it is not. " It consisteth not in the following or imitation of Adam." The rise of the Pelagian heresy in the fifth century is the beginning of a new epoch in the history of doctrine.

Till this period, the mind of man had occupied itself with Christology, with the conditions of the existence of the Son of God; for the earlier heresies, if we except Gnosticism and Manicheism, had chiefly concerned themselves with His Divine Person and Natures. Theology began now to deal with the subjective. Anthropology, the science of man, became its subject. It remained for St. Augustine to re-exhibit those wonderful doctrines of the grace of God so precisely stated before by St. Cyprian, which, expressed with the most subtle analysis by St. Paul, had not been drawn out with precision by the Fathers, either in the epoch of the apologies to the heathen, or in the age of persecution, or in that of the controversies on the mode of existence of the Word made Flesh. Perhaps the Christian was occupied in defending the faith against the heathen public opinion that surrounded him, in strengthening himself and his friends to die for Christ, and in humbly meditating on that Lord, who was all in all to him, rather than concerning himself about his own nature in the eyes of Almighty God, or Christians held the faith implicitly; else they would not have been started by the errors of Pelagius, when he appeared, as something new. St. Augustine shews that it was stated in terms by eminent fathers and bishops in all parts of the world who preceded him [b]. But the truth was fenced more precisely to meet the errors of Pelagius. Said to be of Welch or Scottish extraction, it seems strange that the scion of

[b] c. Julian, l. ii.

a race, ever most susceptible of supernatural ideas, should have been the first promulgator of a system, whose error was a too great reliance on the rectitude and power of the human will. Aided by Celestius and by Julian, he maintained with exceeding acuteness the thesis that man by his natural powers is able to merit eternal life, and that consequently the Fall was hurtful only from causing the possibility of the imitation of Adam's sin, and that to all intents and purposes there was no such thing as original sin. These errors were met by St. Augustine, who maintained the power, the freeness, and the efficacy of divine grace; in which he was followed by St. Fulgentius, and his teaching became so authoritative, that it was formalized and sanctioned by the Council of Orange, in language which has been ever since accepted by the Catholic Church of Christ. It is to the effect that Adam, by sin, lost his original righteousness and holiness, drew down upon himself the anger of the Almighty, incurred the penalty of death, and in body and soul became deteriorated; that this sinful condition is transmitted to all his posterity, through natural generation, entailing the consequences that man is of himself incapable of doing acts well-pleasing to God, or of being in any way justified before Him, save only by the merit of Jesus Christ, the one Mediator between God and man.

To state the matter scientifically: " as between things opposite there is an opposite relation, so from original righteousness, original sin its opposite, may be ex-

plained. But the order of original righteousness consisted in this, that the will of man was obedient to God;
and it is the province of the will to direct and rule all
the other parts of the soul in conformity to this. Hence,
when the will fell away from God, disorder in all the
other faculties ensued. Hence, the deprivation of original righteousness is the formal cause of original sin,
and the disorder in all the faculties of the soul, the
material cause; and that disorder manifests itself in the
perverted affection for transitory good, which we call
concupiscence."

" Now this disorder or displacement is called the
wound of nature, and it is chiefly felt in the four
powers of the soul, which become the conduits of
virtue, viz. reason wherein is prudence, will wherein
is justice, the faculty of exertion wherein is courage,
the faculty of desire wherein is temperance. Reason
wounded suffers from ignorance, justice or righteousness wounded suffers from wickedness, the faculty of
exertion wounded results in frailty, and that of desire
in concupiscence."

The inheritance of a nature marred both by punishment and guilt is manifest in the want of the intuition
of God, which presupposes guilt; for no one can be deprived of that eternal good for which he was created,
unless there be in him something which renders him
unworthy to stand in the divine Presence; in the
ignominy which hangs upon the reason, for that reason
is now ashamed of certain motions of the flesh; and in
the preponderance of concupiscence, because man must

be guilty unless the spirit be in subjection to God, and the flesh and the animal faculties in subjection to the spirit. Here faith, philosophy, and daily experience concur. It is undeniable that the soul of each one from his birth is perverted, and this perverted state is guilt, as the right state of the soul is righteousness. Hence the Apostle, speaking in the person of fallen humanity, says: "I see another law in my members striving against the law of the Spirit, and holding me captive under the law of sin." Then he exclaims: "O wretched man that I am, who shall deliver me from the body of this death?" Then he replies: "Thanks be to God—or better, the grace of God—through Jesus Christ our Lord."

Let it never be forgotten that all this is a great mystery. How the soul created by God, and created in all soundness, purity, and integrity, should at the moment of its union with the body not only be deprived of all its supernatural gifts, but be deeply wounded in its natural faculties, is a very great difficulty; yet this, which involves the doctrine of Creatianism, that souls are created by God, must be accepted rather than the opinion called Traducianism, that souls are transmitted through generation by the parent to the children.

The error which Luther maintained with regard to the state of man in Paradise told profoundly on his view of original sin. If Adam's acceptableness with God was natural, by the Fall he lost certain natural powers. According to this school fallen man no longer possessed even the mere faculty to understand God and

His holy will, and in conformity to that knowledge to direct his own will. The image of God, according to Luther's definition, the natural capacity in man to love God, to fear Him, and to confide in Him, was utterly effaced; the image of the devil was substituted. The freedom of will is only an external freedom, non-existent in spiritual things; man is now a mere earthly power. Luther maintained that original sin was a substance; Melanchthon, that it was an innate power. At last it was held that original sin was the very substance of fallen man.

While we cannot fail to respect that sense of human misery and sin, as well as of the need of redemption, which prompted these notions, we must guard against an error, which by making man the mere mechanical instrument of God's actions, by obliterating a spiritual faculty, transforms moral into physical evil. How can man sin when he has not the faintest idea of God, when he has no faculty to will, when he is devoid of freedom?

It will be seen that all true morality must rest on a certain limitation of the idea of the magnitude of the effect of original sin. If all the higher spiritual faculties be utterly destroyed, how can man really grieve over his shortcomings, if God has deprived him of all power of overcoming and avoiding these shortcomings? Deeply penetrated as the Church is with the enormity and misery of that hereditary evil which affects our race, she would be false to the experience of life, as well as to precise theology, if she were to allow sentiment to take the place of reason in this respect, and by exaggeration to undermine the foundation of Christian ethics by the destruction of moral responsibility. Man is only responsible in the measure that he is free, and the utter destruction of the spiritual faculties in fallen man necessarily acquits him of the misguiding of such faculties.

The Calvinists did not run into such extremes as these. They took warning from the mistakes of the earlier Reformers. They recovered themselves to a degree, but still the language of some of the confessions is very exaggerated and false. For example, the Westminster Confession:—" By this sinne (our first parents) fell from their original righteousness and communion with God, and so became dead in sin, and wholly defiled in all the faculties and parts of soul and body. From this original corruption, whereby we are utterly indisposed, disabled, and made opposite to all good, and wholly inclined to all evil, do proceed all actual transgression[c]."

Very different is the tone of our own Article: " It is the fault and corruption of the nature of every man, that naturally is engendered of the offspring of Adam, whereby man is very far gone from original righteousness[d], and is of his own nature inclined to evil, so that

[c] The Confession of Faith, p. 22, ed. 1658.

[d] " Very far gone from original righteousness."—The assembly of divines of 1643, in the criticisms which were required of them by Parliament, preferred the phrase, " *Wholly* deprived of original righteousness," which would have brought the Article into harmony with the statements of the earlier Lutherans, and the general tenor of the Calvinistic Confessions. Cf. Hardwick, p. 376.

the flesh lusteth always contrary to the spirit." Now some of the Schoolmen taught that a destructive and infectious quality was introduced into the human body, and that this quality, propagated by generation, contaminated the soul at the moment of its union with the body. Such a theory, which involves the absurdity of the existence of a positive bad quality, of an essential evil substance, is not taught in the Article; on the contrary, the words " fault and corruption" are both privative words, implying the lesion of something good in itself by the abstraction of a certain condition; and this helps us to understand what follows, " that this infection of the nature remains even in the regenerate," which, as held by Luther, and in his sense, constituted one of his quarrels with the Church. Luther by this meant, that all that he implied by original sin,—the utter inability to think, to believe, to will, the entire deadness to good, the obliteration of the image of God and the substitution of the image of the devil,—remained even in the regenerate or baptised; whereas the Anglican Article, by its expression " whereby the lust of the flesh is not subject to the law of God," limits it to the continuance of concupiscence, a fact which to his sorrow every one must admit.

Now concupiscence or evil desire, being the disorder of the natural powers, was by the Reformers stated to be actual sin, the true image of the devil, which through the loss of the image of God is propagated by generation in man: whereas our Article, following the Apostle, says " that it is of the nature of sin [e]," inasmuch as, at least, it provokes to sin. We cannot be wrong in using St. Paul's words, though we recognise the distinctive teaching of our great father in the faith, St. Gregory, who, in answer to the questions of St. Austin, of England, lays down distinctly the different stages in sin. Following the teaching of St. James, he shews how there is first the suggestion, then the delight, and then the consent to sin; and till the consent is given the sin is not complete. The expression that there is no condemnation for them that believe and are baptised, while it cuts at the root of the unsacramental teachings of the present day, is nearly equivalent to the statement that God hates nothing in the regenerate; condemnation and the hatred of God being to all intents and purposes the same.

It will be seen that the estimate of the nature and effects of original sin forms the turning-point between the ancient faith of the Church and the systems of the sixteenth century. If all the germs of good be extirpated in fallen man, there can be no co-operation on his part with the work of divine grace. There can be no response to the operations of God upon the soul, therefore man becomes passive in the

---

[e] "This corruption of nature during this life doth remain in those that are regenerated; and although it be through Christ pardoned and justified, yet both itself and all the motives thereof are truly and properly sin."—Westminster Conf., p. 24.

The Assembly of Divines suggest, "It is truly and properly sin."—Hardwick, 376.

work of regeneration, his justification becomes of necessity the mere imputation of the righteousness of
another, there can be no correspondence with God's
work by man in the life of the Christian. On the
other hand, grant that in fallen man, though "læsus
in naturalibus, destitutus in gratuitis," there still exists
the capacity for the love of God, there remains full
scope for a supernatural transfiguration. Divine grace
stoops to this lowliness, imparts to the free-will and
sin-polluted faculties a heavenly consecration, really
cleanses, strengthens, and matures the soul, leads him
on from strength to strength, making him daily better,
holier, and more Christ-like, till the hour of his trial
is accomplished [f].

[f] Vide Möhler, Symbolism, 31—134.

ARTICLE X.

De Libero Arbitrio.

Ea est hominis post lapsum Adæ conditio, ut sese natura-
libus suis viribus, et bonis operibus, ad fidem et invo-
cationem Dei convertere ac præparare non possit. Quare
absque gratia Dei (quæ per Christum est) nos præve-
niente, ut velimus, et cooperante, dum volumus, ad pie-
tatis opera facienda, quæ Deo grata sunt et accepta,
nihil valemus.

" Of Free-Will.

" The condition of man after the fall of *Adam* is
such, that he cannot turn and prepare himself, by his
own natural strength and good works, to faith and
calling upon God: wherefore we have no power to do
good works, pleasant and acceptable to God, without
the grace of God by Christ preventing us, that we
may have a good will, and working with us, when we
have that good will."

This is one of the instances in which the title of the
Article does not correspond accurately with its contents. In the Article there is no direct assertion of the
free-will of man, nor definition of its meaning, though
it is implied in its very limitation. The Article ought
really to be termed, " Of the necessity of Divine grace."
The whole of man's responsibility rests on the freedom
of his will. Some philosophers have maintained that

the only argument for the existence of God is to be found in that responsibility. It is therefore one of the gravest of doctrines. If there is no freedom, there can be no virtue nor vice, no merit nor fault, no moral government of the universe. The opposite of freedom is necessity. Once grant necessity, and the idea of God is nearly eliminated from our system. And so with regard to ourselves, under the domination of an imperious necessity we become mere machines. "No inanimate creatures, neither any irrational animals, but all rational and intellectual beings, whether angels or men, have free-will. Free-will is not a habit, whether natural or acquired, but an appetitive power, the principal and proper act of which is election. Will and free-will, *θέλησις καὶ βούλησις*, *voluntas et lib. arb.*, are not two powers, but different acts of the same power. Will has immediate reference to the final cause, free-will to secondary or intermediate causes. Free-will never chooses evil, but always good, or apparent good [a]."

"Deadly sin, which is an act of free-will, as the choice of that which is absolutely bad, arises from ignorance or error. Venial sin, as the choice of that which is in itself good, but without due order of measure and rule, arises from absence of consideration. Doubting is not of the essence of election, but is an accident of its exercise in an erring nature. The will is always convertible in this life, but the converting power may be withdrawn. In the future life, the will of the

[a] Cf. St. Aug., *De Grat. et Lib. Arbit.*, c. xvii. al. xxxiii.

blessed will be confirmed in good; the will of the reprobate obstinately established in evil. Christ's human will was as the will of the blessed saints. In respect of His own goodness, which God wills of necessity, He has not free-will, but in respect of contingent events God is said to have free-will [b]."

And yet the subject is most mysterious. The reconciliation of the knowledge and ordination of God with the freedom of the human will is one of those mysteries which has occupied the subtlest intellects, and when those intellects have worked to the uttermost, the question is left where it was at the beginning. It is therefore enough for us to maintain the two truths, and leave their reconciliation to a higher state of intelligence. Yet, while philosophical thought sustains these two apparently contrariant truths both floating in the mind, there will always be tendencies one way or the other. Some minds will lean rather to the side of freedom, and the excess of that will be Pelagianism; other minds will lean to that which takes an exaggerated view of the province granted by God to grace, and that excess will lead to Lutheranism and Jansenism. The Church of God has to hold the balance between the two. On the one hand, she seeks to develope to the highest degree the sense of individual responsibility, seeking to convince every soul of the unspeakable importance of the passing of each hour, making our eternity to depend on the good or evil use of time: on the other hand, she systematizes

[b] St. Thos., 1^{mi} 2^{dæ}, qy. 58.

the beautiful doctrine of grace ; maintains that all that is great and of good report in man is the result of a condescendence on the part of God to the creation of His hands; that the beginning, middle, and end of man's salvation is influenced by God ; and that there is a perpetual everflowing effluence from the Person of our Lord and from His Spirit, sanctifying, illumining the soul of man, and aiding him in the search for truth, and in the operation of good. Thus it will be seen that in every good action, there are two factors— a divine and a human. As is right, God's holy work goes first, suggesting, exciting, quickening ; then follows man, freely yielding himself to the divine impulse. God offers freely and man accepts, and the double work becomes a unity. For His own good purposes, God respects human freedom. He does not force things. Man may resist grace, for the moral order of the world is founded in liberty.

Luther, however, from his view of original sin, was driven to deny the freedom of the will. In spiritual and divine things, according to him, man is as the pillar of salt into which Lot's wife was turned ; yea, he is like a stick or stone, which is lifeless, and has no use of eyes or mouth, or any organ of the senses [c]. Calvinists, while by their juster view of original sin they were able to admit the co-operation of man in the work of salvation, denied however that grace could be resisted [d]. According to them it was not in the power of man to receive or reject the action of God. When

[c] Luther in Genes., c. xix.   [d] Calv. Inst., lib. ii. c. 3, n. 6.

divine grace knocks, the door must be opened. It works invincibly, and those who enter not into life have never had grace, a theory which lands us at the door of the doctrine of predestination. The controversy with these, as well as with the Jansenists, turns on this phase in the question.

The only-begotten Son of God assumed our nature, among other reasons, that He might rescue mankind from that infection and penalty, which by the fault of our first parents it had contracted, and to recall it to communion with God, and raise it to eternal felicity. For God proposed " in the dispensation of the fulness of times, that He might gather together in one all things in Christ, both which are in heaven, and which are on earth; even in Him [e]." This gathering together, chiefly consists in the justification of the sinner, and in the aids and assistances whereby man is able to attain to this, and to persevere in it so attained, and to bring forth the fruits thereof, till he attain to everlasting life.

This at once brings us to the consideration of grace, of which the efficient cause is God, the meritorious cause our Lord Jesus Christ, and the final cause everlasting.

By grace, taken in its widest sense, we mean every gift or benefit either external or internal which is bestowed out of the mere liberality of God upon the rational creature. In this sense creation, preservation, and their accompanying blessings, — much more, law,

[e] Eph. i. 10.

teaching, good example, and such like,—may be called by the name of grace. Again, the word may be applied to supernatural gifts, and to those miraculous powers which are bestowed rather for the benefit of others than for our own sakes (*gratia gratis data*). But the true and rigorous sense of grace (*gratia gratum faciens*) is that inward help, freely bestowed, which God for the merits of Christ grants to fallen man, both to help his infirmity in the way of abstaining from that which is evil and doing that which is good; so also to raise him to the supernatural state, in making him fit to perform supernatural actions, so that he may attain unto justification; and having so attained may persevere until he come to everlasting life.

This again is divided into habitual and actual. Habitual grace is a supernatural quality permanently inhering in man, making him well pleasing to God by formally and intrinsically sanctifying him. Actual grace is a certain motion within us excited by God, by which, first, the intellect is led to recognise good and evil, and then the will is led to follow the one and avoid the other in order to the blessed life of heaven.

Habitual sanctifying grace is twofold: first and second :—

First grace is that by which the sinner is first justified, and from being an enemy is made the friend of God. It is called 'first,' because it presupposes no other habitual grace, being itself expulsive of sin, and is conferred by baptism and penance.

Second grace is the increase of the first, it preserves the first grace, being given to him who has thus received it. It is conferred by Confirmation, the Holy Eucharist, Orders, the Anointing of the Sick, and Matrimony. Moreover, by prayer, by meditation, by the reading of God's Word, by deeds of mercy, and by every good action done in a state of grace do we acquire it.

Actual sanctifying grace is threefold :—

i. Prevenient, antecedent, or exciting grace;

ii. Assisting, co-operating, or concomitant grace;

iii. Subsequent, or completing grace.

1. Prevenient grace is a supernatural motion of the soul, to will what is good, and to nill what is evil.

2. Assisting grace is that by which God, when we will and so will that we do, co-operates with us to will and do that which He had previously stirred us up to.

3. Subsequent grace is that which follows, strengthens, and confirms the consent of the free-will.

Again, grace is divided into sufficient and efficacious grace :—

Sufficient grace, taken specifically, is that which, although it affords sufficient power to produce an effect for which it is ultimately given, does not produce it in defect of the consent of man.

Efficacious grace is that which always and infallibly infers the ultimate result, and the co-operation of the free-will.

Holy Scripture makes mention of both these graces :

of sufficient—" My grace is sufficient for thee [f]." " I can do all things through Christ that strengtheneth me [g]." Ezekiel mentions efficacious grace, " I will put My spirit upon you, that ye may walk in My commandments [h] ;" and St. Paul, " It is God that worketh in us, both to will and to do of His good pleasure [i]."

It is a true proposition, that to fallen man grace merely sufficient is granted, which, in defect of the consent of his free-will, is frustrated of the effect ultimately intended by God.

Pelagians denied this, rejecting all grace; Calvin and Luther willed that all grace was efficacious, so efficacious that the will acted under compulsion. Baius and Jansen agreed with them. Yet the Scripture goes to prove the contrary, as e. g. Isaiah v.: " O ye inhabitants of Jerusalem, and men of Judah, judge between Me and My vineyard; what more could I have done to My vineyard that I have not done in it? I waited for grapes, and behold it brought forth wild grapes." " O Jerusalem, which killest the prophets, how often would I have gathered thy sons [k]," &c. " I stretched forth My hands all the day long to a rebellious and gainsaying people [l]." " Ye do always resist the Holy Ghost [m]." " We beseech you that ye receive not the grace of God in vain [n]."

Sufficient grace is bestowed on all men : " That was the true light, which, coming into the world,

[f] 2 Cor. xii. 9.   [g] Phil. iv. 13.   [h] Ezek. xxxvi. 27.
[i] Phil. ii. 13.   [k] St. Matt. xxiii. 37.   [l] Rom. x. 21; Isa. lxv. 2.
[m] Acts vii. 51.   [n] 2 Cor. vi. 1.

lighteth all men [o]." " God willeth that all men should be saved, and should come to the knowledge of the truth [p]." " There is nothing hid from the heat thereof [q]."

As corollaries of this we may deduce the following propositions :—

1. Man, aided by the grace of God, which is wanting to no man, can keep the commandments of God, as did Zacharias and Elisabeth, walking in all the ordinances of the Lord blameless.

2. He who does what in him lies by the power of grace, grace shall not be denied to him, as in the case of the conversion of Cornelius.

3. No one by his natural powers can obtain actual grace, or the beginning of spiritual life. " No man can come unto Me except the Father who sent Me draw him [r]." " Without Me ye can do nothing [s]."

4. An equal grace may be sufficient in one case, and efficacious in another, as in our Lord's denunciation of Chorazin and Bethsaida in contrast with 'Tyre and Sidon.

5. Nay, sometimes less grace converts men, while under the influence of higher grace others remain hardened, as the men of Nineveh were converted by the grace given through Jonas, and the Jews resisted the grace offered by our Lord Himself. So the fallen angels and Judas may be presumed to have received greater grace than many who are saved. Hence we

---

[o] St. John i. 9.   [p] 1 Tim. ii. 4.   [q] Ps. xix. 6.

[r] St. John vi. 44.   [s] St. John xv. 5.

gather that grace in the second stage is rendered efficacious by the co-operation of the human will elevated by assisting grace. Thus St. Paul exhorts us not to receive the grace of God in vain: words which clearly warn us to give efficacy to grace by our co-operation, yet that co-operation is not a bare naked co-operation, but a co-operation elevated by grace.

6. Grace causes no constraint to the will, for it can be resisted. If man is not free, he cannot deserve nor fail in deserving, nor be rewarded nor be punished. Scotus, with a sort of grim pleasantry, and in the spirit of his age, proposes, that they who deny free-will should be exposed to tortures, until they learn that it is possible that they cannot be tortured.

The question of grace was not only discussed in the fourth and fifth centuries against the Pelagians and semi-Pelagians, and in the sixteenth against the Socinians, but since the Reformation the question has again and again come up; among Protestants in the case of the Arminians and Socinians, among Roman Catholics in the case of the Jansenists and Molinists [t].

[t] The error of Jansenism will best be understood by transcribing the five condemned propositions of the Augustinus. Whether the propositions were in the book or not, is not the question now with us. It will be seen that the Church's instinct was wise in stigmatizing them:—

I. Some precepts of God are, according to the present powers bestowed on man, impossible to those who are just, willing, and striving; also the grace is wanting to them whereby they may become possible.

II. In the state of fallen nature, inward grace is never resisted.

III. For merit or demerit, in the state of fallen nature, there is not required in man liberty from necessity, but liberty from compulsion only (co-actione).

IV. The semi-Pelagians admitted the necessity of prevenient inward

Although much has been done in the elucidation of the various truths which hinge upon it, it may be said that the matter is by no means exhausted, and the relations of man to the Sacraments, the discrimination of the orders of nature and grace, the relation between theology and medicine in some questions of morals, and many similar questions, still require development and exposition.

When we speak of the state of grace, by the word 'state' we technically mean that condition under which human nature is conceived of, in reference to its ultimate end according to the laws of Providence. It is divided into the *status termini*, the condition of those who possess and enjoy the end of man; and the *status viæ*, the condition of those who are militant here upon earth.

The *status viæ* is threefold—1. the state of innocence, 2. the state of fallen nature, and 3. the state of nature restored by Christ.

1. The state of nature is that in which Adam was placed by God, free from sorrow, misery, and death, with that integrity of nature by which the senses and affections were perfectly subject to the empire of reason, and with original righteousness, and ●ctifying grace.

grace for every act, one by one, even for the beginning of faith; and in this they were heretics, that they denied that grace to be such as the human will can resist or obey.

V. It is semi-Pelagian to say that Christ in effect (*omnino*) died and shed His blood for all men.

2. The state of fallen nature is that miserable condition of the posterity of Adam, who are not yet freed by baptism from the original " culpa" which it receives from him.

3. The state of repaired nature is that in which men are set free and redeemed by the grace of Christ.

These are all the conditions in which man *in viâ* can be or has been; but to elucidate the subject more, theologians have discussed what are termed possible states, e.g. :—

1. Whether a state of pure nature is possible, in which man can be without vice, and without grace, subject however to the infirmities and miseries to which we are subject.

2. Whether a state of perfect (*integra*) nature is possible, in which man might be destitute of supernatural aid, and not raised to supreme blessedness, yet gifted with such aids of nature as to be free from our miseries, and by the natural virtues to obtain a blessedness corresponding with them.

3. Lastly, whether a state of fallen nature, not to be repaired, is possible, in which man would have been after the sin of Adam if God in His infinite mercy had not freed him.

Now to state clearly the errors on these subjects :—

The Pelagians, in the beginning of the fifth century, denying original sin, and asserting that Adam was constituted by God as men are now born, without any aid of nature, and without the auxiliary of supernatural grace.

This heresy was revived in the sixteenth century by the Socinians, who, denying original guilt, taught that Adam was created mortal and liable to all our present miseries.

A close approach to this is the Arminian doctrine which, as expounded by Limborch, acknowledges in Adam no supernatural gift, no *indebita prærogativa*, although they allow that he was gifted with a certain knowledge necessary to him in his then estate, and with a rectitude which precluded inordinate concupiscence, and even concupiscence itself, inasmuch as, there being no law, there might be without guilt the most free exercise of the will.

Although contrary to the Pelagians and Socinians, they teach that Adam might have been free from death in virtue of the fruit of the tree of life; they nevertheless maintain that man, by virtue of even his present natural powers, might tend towards, arrive at, and possess God as his last end and highest good; and, moreover, that Adam's sin, save as a bad example, has in no way done damage to the race of man.

Calvin, Luther, Baius, and the Jansenists agree with the Pelagians and Socinians as to man's original lack of supernatural gifts and graces, and the original sufficiency of his natural powers; but they go farther, and declare him to be now despoiled of some of the properties and perfections of that nature.

Quesnel held that the grace of Adam was subsequent to his creation, was due to the integrity of his nature, and produced only human merit. According to him

Adam's integrity, sanctity, and all other his prerogatives were conditions inseparable from, and properties due to nature not yet depraved by guilt.

The orthodox faith teaches that Adam, as constituted in the estate of innocence, was endowed with supernatural grace, was established in righteousness and holiness, was free from misery and death, was subject to neither concupiscence nor passion. And had his every affection entirely under the control of his reason.

As to the miserable estate of fallen human nature, in which the race of man now finds itself by reason of Adam's sin,—deprived of the *indebita dona* of nature, subject to our present miseries, to concupiscence, to the powers of the devil and to the wrath of God, and infected with Adam's guilt, propagated by generation,—the orthodox faith teaches that all men descending from Adam, even the children of the faithful, are born infected with original sin, deprived of their right to eternal felicity, children of wrath and vengeance, and liable to everlasting damnation.

Baius, Jansenius, and Quesnel, taught that in man, after Adam's sin, *libertas indifferentiæ* was wanting; that for merit or demerit it was sufficient to be free from compulsion, not to be free from antecedent and inevitable necessity. Hence, *inter alia*, they say that men are guilty of deadly sin even in things which they cannot avoid, and that the involuntary motions of concupiscence are real sins; that God commands impossibilities; and that even to just men some of His precepts are impossible [n].

Such is the doctrine of the grace of God, as it has been formulised by the Church in opposition to contrariant errors. It is the work of the Divine Word in His Incarnate Nature, the universal Truth, the Eternal Beauty, the Light that shineth into the soul of man. He, the Light of celestial spirits, speaks by an inward voice in the ears of all men; and as without the sun the universe would be in night and death, so without the Word the kingdom of the powers of the next world would be without life and heat. Grace is that mighty aid to holy action, added to what we are and to what we know by the inspiration of the most burning and enlightened charity [x]. For the love of God is shed abroad in our hearts, that the soul now made whole may work, not from the fear of punishment, but from the love of righteousness. Of grace it is said: "The mountains shall drop sweet wine, and all the hills shall melt;" for the mountains and hills of Judah, with their terraced, vine-clad sides, are but a faint shadow of the joys and real delight and glad fruitfulness of this supereminent gift of God. Of grace it is said: "Thou shalt prevent him with the blessings of goodness," for the blessings of goodness are the grace of God whereby He works in us, that we delight in and love that which He teaches us; so that if God

[n] Ferraris, *Bibliotheca de Gratia*, Venice, 1770.
[x] St. Augustine, vol. x. p. 246 D.

hath not anticipated us in this respect, not only is the spiritual life not perfect in us, but actually not begun. For if " without Him we can do nothing," certainly we can neither begin His work nor bring it to an end. For of the beginning it is said, " His mercy shall go before me ;" and of the end it is said, " His mercy shall follow me all the days of my life [y]."

[y] St. Augustine, vol. x. p. 445 B.

ARTICLE XI.

De Hominis Justificatione.

Tantum propter meritum Domini ac Servatoris nostri Jesu Christi, per fidem, non propter opera et merita nostra, justi coram Deo reputamur. Quare sola fide nos justificari doctrina est saluberrima, ac consolationis plenissima, ut in homilia de justificatione hominis fusius explicatur.

" Of the Justification of Man.

" WE are accounted righteous before God only for the merit of our Lord and Saviour Jesus Christ, by faith, and not for our own works, or deservings. Wherefore, that we are justified by faith only, is a most wholesome doctrine, and very full of comfort, as more largely is expressed in the Homily of Justification."

How man may be accounted righteous in the eyes of the all-holy and righteous God is the most important question that can concern him. For the truth of God requires that in some sense what He accounts righteous must be righteous. The doctrine, therefore, hinges on the relation of the creature to its Creator, on the spiritual condition of man in reference to his eternal destinies. It is no mere theological discussion, nor argument of the Schools; it is the mighty question, how is fallen man brought into relation with God in Christ, and when thus brought, what are the conditions of that relation?

But not only is the question most important in view of its intrinsic merit, it has for us the additional element that historically justification was one of the rallying cries of the Reformation. At one particular phase of that event all other questions became subsidiary to it. The Schoolmen had perhaps carried system to its fullest legitimate result, and what followed? The age of the great mediæval saints [a], of the earlier School-divines, and of the great intellectual Popes, was now past. The renaissance had set in. The triumph over the Hussites at the two great Councils of Basle and Constance had put to silence all public opposition to the Church. The fifteenth century is eminently barren in saints; men were occupied with the fresh surging of political thought, and the sensual glories of heathendom; the classic authors for the scholar, and the pagan sculptures for the artist, really possessed men's souls. The real leaders of European thought were no longer the pupils of Aquinas or Buonaventura, but Politian, and Marsilius Ficinus, and the Medici. The higher intellects sneered at those ceremonies and beliefs, which they as princes and prelates were paid to maintain. Among the baser sort, "the love of the many had

---

[a] It is remarkable that the greater number of the saints of this period illustrate the first half only of the fifteenth century. St. Antoninus of Florence died in 1459; St. Bernardinus of Siena in 1444; St. Laurence Giustiniani in 1431; St. Vincent Ferrer in 1414, and St. John Capistran in 1456.

waxed cold," but they were in general sedulous in the
external profession of religion. Dimmed as their spiritual perceptions were, the belief in the great objective
truths of religion remained unimpaired. They continued to place great faith in the external ordinances
of religion, while divorcing them from their end as
means of grace. And so they went on through life in
an infructuous round of barren observances, till they
came to the close of a life of alternative sacrament
and sin.

And if the deep instincts of the regenerate soul, never
entirely faithless to the grace of baptism, did from time
to time acknowledge the hollowness of this condition of
things, they were softened by an application of the
coarsest form of the power of the keys, by the indulgences of Tetzel and his companions.

It was in opposition to this corrupt state of things
that a potent voice through Europe was heard proclaiming "justification by faith," justification in the
true sense of the Apostle Paul. It thrilled through
Christendom, it penetrated even the precincts of the
Vatican; and Pole and Contarini[b], and the Theatines,
felt its power. It was a mighty reaction, and like
most reactions it went too far, nay, ran into heresy.
The power got into the hands of the more violent.
The truths that God worked objectively in the soul
through the Sacraments, as *media* between Himself and

[b] "'You have brought to light the jewel which the Church kept half-
concealed,' was Cardinal Pole's comment on a treatise on Justification
by Contarini."—Ranke, vol. i. p. 138, ed. 1840.

man,—and that man, responding to grace, whether given in or out of the Sacraments, must needs have a personal, immediate, and individual relation to God, which had peacefully co-existed in the minds of Christians for sixteen hundred years, were precipitated into the sharpest opposition. Again, St. Paul was arrayed against St. James, no doubt to the intense astonishment of those blessed Beings in their glorious home in heaven; and in reaction against the coarseness of Tetzel was marshalled the coarseness of Luther.

But the treatment of the doctrine by Luther soon led into great error. First of all, from his conception of the effects of original sin, he was obliged to eliminate all co-operation on the part of man in the work of salvation. If man be utterly ruined by the Fall, the operation of God finds as little response in him as in the irrational brute. Secondly, he was obliged to maintain that justification was only a judicial act of God, whereby the believing sinner is delivered from the punishment of sin, but not from sin itself. All righteousness is external to us[c]. It remains in Christ, and passes not into the inward life of the believer. Thirdly, concupiscence was regarded as subsisting original sin, no distinction being made between feeling it and consenting to it. Fourthly, he had to hold that all sins in themselves, whatever be their nature, accuse men equally before the tribunal of Christ; faith being the only decisive distinction between sinners in the eyes of God. Lastly, on the ground that the faithful, on

[c] *Solid. Declar.* iii. *de Fid. Justif.* § 11. p. 665, § 48. p. 664.

account of the obedience of Christ, are looked upon as just, although by virtue of corrupt nature they be truly sinners, and remain such unto death[d]; it follows that no internal and essential difference as to moral being is recognised between the converted and the unconverted; the Scriptural antithesis of the old and new man, the old and new creation, lose their point and significance; the notion of penitence, whereby the transition is brought about, is mistaken; and the impressive teachings of Holy Writ, about a real deliverance from sin, wrought through Christ, and a real mortification or killing of sin in believers[e], becomes the occasion of self-delusion. Furthermore, the doctrine became dangerous, in that it was made to usurp the place of the Sacraments, that it swallowed up all the other factors in the life of the soul, and was substituted as the ground of man's assurance, in place of these Sacraments, which not only are pledges to assure us of grace, but which themselves keep alive and nourish faith and grace within the soul. It was emphatically one-sided and imperfect, in that it ignored all those blessed truths that are conveyed to us by St. John, when he teaches us that we are branches of the True Vine, each branch partaking of the life and sap of that from whence it springs, the merit and grace and virtue of Christ flowing forth from Him into all His members.

As there is no source of error so copious as a misunderstanding of terms, when we proceed to treat of the very important question of justification it becomes

---

[d] Ibid. § 15. p. 657.   [e] Rom. vi.; viii. 1—4.

our first duty to define the term. In its literal sense it means a making just or righteous, just as rectification is a making right, or sanctification a making saintly or holy. And this subdivides itself into three acceptations. 1. As, in human affairs, the word must be restricted to a forensic sense, because man cannot alter or affect the heart, the term 'to justify' is sometimes taken for to pronounce just, as when in the courts of law one who has been tried is absolved from the accusation and pronounced innocent of the crime by the judge. Thus in the Gospels: " He, willing to justify himself[f];" or, " He that justifieth the wicked, and he that condemneth the just, even they both are abomination to the Lord[g]." 2. To justify, in the strict sense of the term, and with reference to the work of God, is to make just. Thus St. Paul, contrasting the crimes of the Corinthians before their conversion with their after condition, says : " But ye are washed, but ye are sanctified, but ye are justified in the name of the Lord Jesus Christ, and by the Spirit of our God," words which distinctly refer to the final justification, if we have respect to the use of the Aorist in the original. 3. To justify, is sometimes in Holy Scripture taken for to advance in justice or righteousness. Thus, " He that is righteous, let him be righteous still; and he that is holy, let him be holy still[h]."

The word ' justification' is also taken actively and passively. It is taken actively, when it is described

---

f St. Luke x. 29.   g Prov. xvii. 15.

h 1 Cor. vi. 11; and Rev. xxii. 11, δικαιωθήτω.

as the proper work of God; passively, when it is described as a certain change in the right hand of the Most High, by which man from being unjust becomes just.

Now the second is the genuine theological sense of the word 'justification.' It is a real and not an imaginary process, which takes place in the soul by the operation of God. That process is both external and internal; man is declared and accounted righteous because he is made righteous. Hence St. Paul describes the justified state as a change from the state of sinfulness into the state of habitual grace and of Sonship, as, "Who hath delivered us from the power of darkness, and hath translated us into the kingdom of His dear Son[1]." It is the destruction of the alliance between the human will and the old Adam, the removal of original sin, and every other sin committed previously to itself. It is the contraction of a real and living fellowship with Christ the Righteous and Holy One; such fellowship-implying the remission of sin and the infusion of sanctification. It is the making over and imparting of the righteousness of Christ, so as to become inherent in the believer, who thus, no doubt imperfectly, becomes really just and well-pleasing to God. It restores him to the original righteousness in which he was constituted, by means of communion with the second Adam Jesus Christ. By it faith, hope, and charity, with an infinite power of increase, are infused into the soul, and the love of God shed abroad in our hearts

---

[1] Col. i. 13.

by the operation of the Holy Spirit. These blessings, in technical language, may be summed up under four heads:—1. Reconciliation with God, Who instead of slaves now treats us as friends. 2. The remission of sin, so far as the eternal punishment is concerned. 3. The rénovation of the inner man, whereby we who were stained and foul by sin, weakened and diseased, stripped of spiritual goods and half dead, become beautiful in God's eyes, members of Christ, so closely united to Him, that what is done by and in us is by Him in us done: "I live, yet not I, but Christ liveth in me; I merit, yet not I, but Christ meriteth in me; I satisfy, yet not I, but Christ satisfieth in me." 4. Our right and title to eternal life.

From what has been stated, it will be seen that justification may be divided into—1. First, 2. Second.

First justification is that whereby the unjust becomes just. Actively, it is a certain admirable and supernatural act whereby God makes the unjust just. Passively it is a certain supernatural change by which a man from being unjust becomes just. By this a man, from being hateful and unpleasing to God, becomes dear to Him; instead of an enemy to Him, His friend; instead of impious, pious; instead of wicked, holy; instead of the slave of sin, the servant of righteousness; instead of guilty of eternal death, the heir of the kingdom of heaven.

The second justification, actively, is the operation of God whereby He makes the righteous, righteous still, more pleasing, more holy; passively, it is the supernatural change whereby man becomes still more righteous, still more holy; as it is written, " And grace for grace."

Having defined the term ' justification,' we now advance to the first proposition of the Article,—that its meritorious cause is the Lord Jesus Christ. We are accounted righteous before God only for the merits (*propter meritum*) of our Lord Jesus Christ by (*per*) faith, and not for (*propter*) our own works or deservings; and this is founded on the theological truth that He with His own most precious Blood has most fully satisfied for us to our Father in heaven, and, having rendered a perfect obedience to Him in His most holy life, willed that these should subserve to our justification. By His excellent virtues, by His endurance, toils, and labours, by His blessed good-will to us, He not only has satisfied superabundantly for our sins, but He has reconciled us to God, and merited our justification.

Nay, He not only merited our justification,—whereby we are restored to the grace of God, our sins are remitted, our spirits renewed, and our adoption and heirship bestowed upon us,—but He merited 1. that the Sacraments should have a power of justifying, and that the good works which are necessary to the justification of adults should be sufficient for the purpose; and 2. that adults should have grace sufficient for such work, for unless these things happened to us for the merits of Christ, and had their sufficiency from Him, we could not say that we were accounted righteous for the merits of Christ, but only by the law and grace of Christ,

who of His great mercy freely appointed these remedies for us who could in nowise obtain them of ourselves; whereas it cannot be doubted that Christ has
actually satisfied for us, *ad condignum*, and merited
justification for us, *de condigno* and according to the
severity of justice, giving, as He has done, more than
we owed by our sins; for His life was better than our
sins were bad; seeing that His life was the life of God
and of Man, infinitely well-pleasing to God. And His
death was more dear in the sight of God than our
offences were hateful[j].

The next point to be considered is the office of faith
in justification. Following the teaching of St. Paul,

---

[j] The sum of our hope and justification is this: "For He hath made
Him to be sin for us, who knew no sin: that we might be made the
righteousness of God in Him," (2 Cor. v. 21). Nor can there be any other
victim well-pleasing to God, or sacrifice for others, save the Word made
flesh; of whom the Apostle says, "God was in Christ, reconciling the
world to Himself, not imputing their trespasses unto them;" (ver. 19).
For He imputeth not, who not only pardoneth freely, but truly giveth
righteousness and holiness.

That the righteousness of Christ is imputed to us, and that that imputation is necessary for justification is quite true, but we must not
say that men are justified solely by the imputation of the righteousness
of Christ to the exclusion of grace, whereby He makes us just by the
Holy Spirit, the love of God being shed abroad in our hearts. Moreover, the merits of Christ are by faith not only imputed to us, but are
applied and communicated to us; by which process not only our sins are
remitted, but a righteousness transmitted from Christ is poured into our
souls. This is the justification of the new man. St. Augustine says,
"We read that they are justified in Christ who believe in Him, by
a hidden communication and inspiration of spiritual grace."—Lib. i.
de pec. mer. et rem., c. x. n. 11. Bossuet, *Proj. de Réunion entre les Ca-
tholiques et les Protestants d'Allemagne. Œuvres*, tom. xxvi. 19.

that we are justified freely, the Article asserts that we are accounted righteous for the merits of our Lord by faith.

Observe distinctly that the Article is here speaking of the first justification, viz. that whereby from being unjust man is made just, and that the faith here spoken of is not the *fiducia* of Luther, the confidence that one's own sins are remitted, neither is it a bare speculative assent to the supernatural truths of religion, such as exists in the demons; but it is that beginning and root of the spiritual life, whereby we savingly believe that God is, that He is the rewarder of them that diligently seek Him, and that He hath sent His only Son for the redemption of all men; without which it is impossible to please Him; the hand whereby God's grace is apprehended; the intellectual power of soul which lays hold on revealed truth; the root whence springs the holy life, nay, which is the holy life itself in germ and possibility. It is a divine gift of God in the soul, a supernatural infused virtue.

It must be laid down as a principle that this first justification is the free gift of God. We are justified freely by faith, as the Apostle bears witness. St. Augustine says, " Wherefore grace, because it is given gratis : wherefore is it given gratis ? because thy merits have not gone before, but the benefits of God have anticipated thee." Elsewhere he says [k], " The grace of Christ, without which neither infants nor adults can be saved, is not given as the reward of merit, but is

[k] cap. 4. *De Natura et Gratia.*

given gratis, wherefore it is called grace, ‘being justified freely by His grace[1].’ ” This he says, explaining the words of St. Paul—“Who shall deliver me from the body of this death? the grace of God, through Jesus Christ our Lord.”

This faith is not mere speculative, but practical. Love is its vivifying principle. It does not, however, merit, it impetrates justification.

The justifying faith of Lutheranism, however, is not this. According to this system man has faith when he believes that he has been received by God into grace; and that for Christ’s sake, who by His death hath offered atonement for our sins, he receives forgiveness of the same. Therefore no sin can damn a man, but unbelief alone; and the word faith changes its meaning into confidence[m].

The Article now proceeds:—

“ And not for our own works and deservings.” The emphatic word here is *for* (*propter*). The antithesis is between the merit of Christ and our merit. We are said to be justified by the one and not by the other. That is to say, our works are not the meritorious causes

[1] Rom. iii. 24.

[m] “ Gratis justificantur propter Christum per fidem, cum credunt se in gratiam recipi et peccata remitti propter Christum qui pro peccatis nostris satisfecit.”—Confess. Aug., Art. iv.

The form which this doctrine takes in modern English Evangelicalism seems to be of this nature:—“ We do not misrepresent their doctrinal system by stating it as follows: St. Paul tells us, that a man is justified by faith; that is, by having faith, and by the faith which he has. But when has a man this faith? Is it sufficient that he has love to Christ, and puts his trust in His merits for salvation? ‘Not necessarily,’ it is replied,

of our justification. There is no antithesis between by
(*per*) faith, and for (*propter*) our works; so that the
question between faith and works ought not strictly to
be imported into an explanation of the letter of the
Article, though the close connection of the two subjects
tempts one to consider their relation. It is clear that,
the first justification being the act whereby we are in-
grafted into Christ, before the justice or righteousness
becomes habitual, faith must precede merit, which is
the fruit of God the Holy Ghost working in those who
are already in Christ.

It is next stated that the opinion that "we are justified by faith only is a most wholesome doctrine, and
very full of comfort, as more largely is expressed in
the Homily of Justification." If faith is taken in an
objective sense, that is to say, as an establishment instituted by God in Jesus Christ, in opposition to Ju-
daism, or any human and arbitrary system of religion,
and the modes of thinking, feeling, and acting, which
such religions prescribe; then it is absolutely, and with-

'because he may be putting some trust in himself too.' What, then, is
necessary to constitute him the possessor of this saving faith? 'He
must throw himself upon Christ's merits *entirely*,' is the answer. But
what is the test whereby to judge whether he does trust in Christ thus
entirely, or wherein does the entirety of his trust consist, and what is
its essence? 'It consists *in his renouncing his own merits*. When
a man does this, then and not till then he believes in Christ; then and
not till then he throws himself upon his Saviour's merits; then and not
till then he has saving faith.'

"First of all, the conviction is a negative one; and, secondly, the
conviction is no profound spiritual truth, but something about the man
himself."—Christian Remembrancer, vol. lxiv. p. 353.

out restriction, true, that faith alone justifies. Thereby alone man is able to acquire God's favour: "There is none other Name given unto man whereby he may be saved, but only the Name of the Lord Jesus." It is *only* through the mercy of God that this Name is given, without any merit on the part of mankind in general, or of individual man in particular [n].

"Very many of the Fathers affirm that we are justified by faith alone [o]. By the word 'alone,' the Fathers never intended simply to exclude all works of faith and grace from the causes of justification and eternal salvation: but in the first place the laws of nature and of Moses; secondly, all works done in our own strength, without faith in Christ, and His preventing grace; thirdly, a false faith or heresy, to which and not to works they oppose faith; fourthly, the absolute necessity of external works, even those which are done through grace, as love, penitence, the reception of the Sacraments, and the like, whenever the power or the opportunity to do such works is absent: for then faith alone, without external works, is sufficient, yet not

[n] Möhler, *Symbolik*, vol. i, p. 211.

[o] Origen in cap. 3 ad Rom. § 9; St. Hilary of Poitiers, Canon 8 in Matt. § 6, movet Scribas; St. Basil, Hom. de Humilitate, § 3, t. 2, p. 158. The author of the Commentaries on St. Paul in cap. 3, Rom. v. 24, t. ii. p. 46 D; St. Greg. Nazianzen, *Orat.* n. 32, § 25. t. i. p. 596 C; St. Chrysostom in 3 Gal. § 5, t. x. p. 699; St. Hieronymus in cap. 4. ad Rom. v. 3, v. 5, v. 11. Theodoret. Therapeut. 7, t. 4, p. 892; St. Augustinus Cont. 2. Ep. Pelag., lib. i. c. 21, § 39, t. x. p. 429. St. Cyril of Alexandria, lib. x. in Joh. cap. 18; Pope St. Leo, Ep. 70. Serm. iv. Epiph. St. Peter Chrys. Serm. xxxiv. *Bib. Patr.*, t. vii. p. 872; St. Prosper of Aquitaine, t. i. p. 334.

without some good affections of penitence and charity, which are internal works; fifthly and lastly, all vain assurance and boasting of our works of whatever sort, not only those preceding faith, but those done, either externally or internally, from the grace of faith[p]."

Again, the expression is, though not used in Scripture, true and undeniable, if we understand by faith, not a faith segregated from love and hope, and other virtues, no mere union of the phantasy or feelings with Christ, no barren recognition of Christian truth or conviction about our own spiritual state; but a new, living spirit, a new divine sentiment regulating the whole man, forming an inseparable unity with charity, "the very bond of peace and of all virtue, without which whosoever liveth is counted dead before God." While an element of hope and trust accompanies this informed faith, its essence does not consist in an assurance of divine grace in Jesus Christ, nor in a confidence in the merits of the Redeemer, by the power of which sins are forgiven. Neither must we hold up this confidence as being able entirely of itself, and abstractedly, to win for its possessors the favour of God. This doctrine has no solid foundation in Holy Scripture; and it is a striking circumstance that, while this Article bears evident traces of having been founded upon a similar one in the Confession of Augsburg, the peculiar symbol of Lutheranism, that a man is justified, if he believes that he is justified (an expression which occurs at least

---

[p] Forbesii Consid., vol. i. p. 58, Oxf. ed.

seven times in that document) has been rejected from the Anglican Formulary.

The Article, in its close, sums up this teaching by saying that it is a most wholesome doctrine, and full of comfort, that we are justified by faith only; and refers to the Homily of Justification. There is no Homily of Justification in either Book, but perhaps the Homily on the salvation of all men may be meant, as expressing this same teaching more largely. On this there is no point of controversy. Any question which would possibly arise, must relate not to our being justified by faith only, but to the character of the faith whereby we are justified. And on this all must be agreed. Faith, which had not love, would be the faith of devils, and this, of course, would justify none: faith, which had not the purpose of living to God, and according to His law, would be self-deceit [q].

"We nowhere expressly read in Scripture 'That the righteousness of Christ is imputed to us for righteousness.' We read, indeed, in Scripture that 'faith is imputed unto us for righteousness, that because of Christ's righteousness God does not impute to us our sins,' and

[q] Yet Bossuet puts the question, "Does faith alone justify?" He answers, "In regard to the mercy of God and the merits of Christ, there is no doubt but that they truly justify us. But when the Lutherans, with this most excellent author (Molanus), agree that faith justifies, not a bare faith, or alone, in the sense of being solitary and destitute of the purpose of doing well, they would entirely satisfy Catholics."—*Projet de Réunion*, t. xxv. p. 377.

Molanus had stated, "the word 'alone' (*sola*) is not to be taken for 'solitary,' i.e. for a dead faith, or a faith destitute of good works, or, at least, of the purpose of doing well."—Ib., p. 286.

that 'righteousness is imputed to us;' but the Scripture nowhere expressly says that God 'imputes to us for righteousness the righteousness of Christ.' ... That the righteousness, i. e. the obedience of Christ, is imputed to us, as to effect and fruit, i. e. remission of sins, inherent righteousness, and acceptance to everlasting life; that it is communicated, attributed, and given to us, is, in fact, said in Scripture wherever it is expressly asserted that by the obedience and death of Christ righteousness and salvation have been obtained for us, or that we have been redeemed from sin and reconciled to God: or when it is taught that Christ is of God made unto us righteousness: or that for us He is made sin, that in Him we might be made the righteousness of God: or that by His righteousness and obedience we are made just before God. Yet it would not be safe to say that the righteousness of Christ is the formal cause of our justification. It is more rightly held that Christ's righteousness or obedience, imputed or applied to us, is the meritorious and impulsive cause of our justification:' that is, it is the external and objective cause, as opposed to an internal and subjective one[r]. If imputation mean the collation of the gifts of Christ, the expression is a sound one; but if it mean that Christ's righteousness is taken instead of our righteousness— that His obedience takes the place of ours—it is subversive of Christian morality."

It was said at the beginning of this Article, that a school of Catholic theologians, headed by Contarini

[r] Forbesii Consid. Mod., vol. i. p. 113.

and Pole, resting mainly on the necessity of a stronger subjectivity in religion, and relying on such authority as that of St. Bernard, had taught a theology in which many elements of Protestant thought existed. A little later, also, we have Catharinus, Cassander, and the eminent Groper, attempting an Eirenikon; but logically such Eirenikon could not stand. Justification in the Catholic sense, as a real though imperfect deliverance from sin or stain, was incompatible with a covering of a sin-stained soul with the merits of Christ, so that the soul still remains sinful in itself, though for Christ's sake the punishment is remitted. It was impossible to reconcile two such contrary theories, as one which makes the work of Christ in the soul a real process of right-making and holy-making, with a system which consisted merely in a feeling, a reflective act of the soul that it is certainly in a state of grace. Accordingly, a distinct separation took place[a].

[a] On the continent, also, justification by imputation was the turning-point of the Reformation; yet hardly a single scientific Protestant theologian now maintains it. (See a remarkable enumeration of Protestant theologians, in number exceeding forty-two, who have abandoned the doctrine of justification, as it is set forth in the *Formula Concordiæ* and the Heidelberg Catechism, in fact the prevalent doctrine till 1760.—Dollinger's " Church and Churches," ed. Maccabe, p. 295.) And in England, though during the latter days of Elizabeth and the first of James, it was the dominant teaching in the Schools, it was so thoroughly demolished by Bull, Hammond, and Thorndike, within the Church, and by Baxter among the Nonconformists, its contradictions and destructive consequences have been shewn to be so glaring, that it has ceased to maintain itself theologically; though a class of amiable writers—Toplady, Venn, Newton, and Hervey—are still quoted with admiration by their followers, who have specially adapted themselves to the well-to-do comfortable Englishman, who desires an intelligible, consolatory, and tranquillizing

Thus we have endeavoured to expound the holy and blessed doctrine of Justification by Faith, as it has been held in the Church of God from the beginning. From first to last the gift of God, like all His gifts, it blesses mankind by the elevation of every faculty of the soul. Consecrating the free-will to the glorious service of religion, it developes the notion of responsibility, and so puts Christian ethics on a solid basis, at the same time recognising its absolute need of divine grace in every stage of its process; it renders high praise to God, from whom descendeth every perfect gift. Herein also is the Son glorified, as the sole meritorious cause; and the Holy Ghost honoured, through whose potent operation alone we are able to will and to do of God's good pleasure.

system. This he finds in the doctrine of justification by imputation. A man is there taught that by an act of mere imputation of the righteousness of Another, one may pass into a state of perfect security and certainty of salvation; that by being clothed with the merits and righteousness of the Saviour he may be regarded by God as righteous, although inwardly he is not so; that he can never forfeit this state of grace, for that he is one of the elect. All this depends on his having a completely favourable opinion of his own state. This is assurance. Men announce the immediate and certain forgiveness of all sins, and assurance of safety, as the price of momentary excitement and concentration of feeling. This is called 'Preaching the Gospel in its fulness and freedom.' "—Vide Dollinger, "Church and Churches," pp. 114, 175.

In short, to sum the matter up scientifically, "it is not faith but the imputation of the sufferings of Christ, which makes man appear justified before God, or that the process of justification is therewith fulfilled, that God attributes to man the sufferings and the fulfilment of the law by Christ, as if man himself had yielded the same obedience; and that man, through faith, knows and becomes assured of this imputation."—p. 299, note.

ARTICLE XII.

De Bonis Operibus.

*Bona opera, quæ sunt fructus fidei, et justificatos sequun-
tur, quanquam peccata nostra expiare, et divini judicii
severitatem ferre non possunt; Deo tamen grata sunt,
et accepta in Christo, atque ex vera et viva fide necessario
profluunt, ut plane ex illis æque fides viva cognosci possit,
atque arbor ex fructu judicari.*

"*Of Good Works.*

"ALBEIT that good works, which are the fruits of
faith and follow after justification, cannot put away
our sins, and endure the severity of God's judgment,
yet are they pleasing and acceptable to God in Christ,
and do spring out necessarily of a true and lively
faith; insomuch that by them a lively faith may be
as evidently known as a tree discerned by the fruit."

This Article is a protest against the opinion of Luther,
that every so-called good work of man, is, when considered in itself, an act of sin, though by reason of faith
it is remitted to him[a]; that of Melanchthon, that all
our works, all our endeavours, are nothing but sin[b];
and finally, that of Calvin[c], who states the same, only
in milder language. On the other hand, it asserts that

---

[a] Op., tom. ii. fol. 325 b.   [b] *Loc. Theol.*, p. 108.
[c] Calv. Inst., *in edit.*, lib. ii. c. 8, § 59; lib. iii. c. 4, § 28.

they cannot take the place of Christ in putting away or expiating our sins, neither can they endure the severity of God's judgment.

1. First, then, good works are the fruits of faith. This follows from what was said before, that faith is the beginning, and root, and foundation of all our justification. Faith being the beginning of the spiritual life, good works must of course spring out of it. When the child is baptized it seeketh from the Church faith, and then and there receives the graces necessary to act rightly. Faith is the root of good works, in that the root and the rest of the tree being of the same substance, these two are in fact one, different expressions of the same habit of soul: the living faith is the good work still silently shut up in the soul, and the good Christian work is nothing other than the faith brought to light. Hence in Holy Scripture salvation is attributed sometimes to work, sometimes to faith. Lastly, it is the foundation, for faith comes first in the order of intellectual conception, and the moral work rests on the intellectual; for before a man can come to God—and so much the more, before a man can follow out the consequences of that coming to God—he must be convinced of His existence, and of the other truths with regard to Himself which He has graciously revealed.

2. Next, it is said that good works follow after justification. This proposition is self-evident, if we consider what has been said on this subject under the preceding Article. The state of light and grace, which is the justified state, will be one of actions done in union with

Jesus Christ, into whose fellowship we are already entered. Nay, the good works will become the measures, as well as the promoters of the necessary justification, according as it is written, " He that is holy, let him be holy still."

The Latin version here indicates that the Article follows the mind of St. Augustine. The expression " follow after justification" is rendered "justificatos sequuntur," and evidently refers to the celebrated passage in the *De Fide et Operibus* of that Father, " Good works follow a justified person, but do not go before in one about to be justified" (*sequi justificatum non autem præcedere justificandum* [d]); a passage which has been much misunderstood, for the Saint is here speaking of works of righteousness, which, "after the faith has been received and professed," are henceforth to be performed; or of those works which are performed by habitual righteousness, i.e. which are implied in the act of justification, and so are inherent and habitual: not of those good works which, through the assisting or preparing grace of the Holy Ghost, dispose to justification.

3. Yet they cannot put away our sins, i.e. expiate (*expiare*) them. Christ alone is the Lamb of God that taketh away the sins of the world, and we cannot set so much good work against so much past sin. We cannot keep a debtor and creditor account with God, and pay for the sins we love by certain acts, even the best. This is almost a truism; for the justified man, inhering, as he does, in the True Vine, even when he falls into great

[d] cap. 14, § 21, t. vi. p. 177.

and terrible sins, will allow no such thoughts to enter his soul. His sense of the offence to God is too great to think that he may thus destroy his guilt; but this passage must by no means be taken to exclude the necessity of penitential acts whereby, when forgiven, we would seek to discipline ourselves after sin, whereby we would seek to shew to Almighty God that we would, if we could, by a holy revenge, undo the hated past.

Good works cannot put away sin. " One must distinguish first in what state the works are done, whether in a state of mortal sin, or in a state of grace; and so one must distinguish in 'putting away,' whether it refer to *culpa* or *pœna*."

" We say, then, 1st. That none of our works can put away sin *quoad culpam*, because if they are done in mortal sin they do not satisfy God for the offence against Him; and if they are done in the state of grace, that state of grace implies the abolition of the *offensa* and the *culpa*, by the divine aid, from the satisfaction of Christ, who satisfied for the offences whereby we offend God, by offering up His own Life on the altar of the Cross.

" Secondly, we say, that no works of ours done in mortal sin are satisfactory to God for the *pœna* due to our sins, even those already absolved in the Sacrament of Penance; because when a sin is remitted by God, so far as the offence is concerned, the sinner, from an enemy, becomes the friend of God, and therefore is no longer to be punished as an enemy, i.e. eternally: yet if the measure of grace bestowed to any so meriting, as that with the remission of the *culpa* there is not full remission of the *pœna*, the sinner remains bound as a friend to pay the rest of the *pœna*; and if he falls into sin again, and becomes again the enemy of God, before he have paid the penalty of that relapse, his works are works in a hostile state, he cannot pay as a friend, and therefore cannot satisfy for that *pœna*.

" Thirdly, we say, the work of our persevering in the friendship of God, has no impediment in the way of satisfying for that residuum of *pœna*. In this the Lutherans err doubly, 1. in teaching that when sin is remitted *quoad offensam* it is remitted also *quoad pœnam*, in the teeth of the example of David. 2. They take away from the works of the living members of Christ any power that may satisfy for *pœna* not yet remitted. For this were to contradict the power of Christ the Head in us: for I satisfy, yet not I, but Christ satisfieth in me. It were also to contradict the practice of the Church which is used to impose salutary satisfactions, by the ministry of priests, on those who, being truly penitents, have confessed their sins [e]."

4. An extreme school of the Reformers held that even the most excellent acts of the just are defiled with sin, and are of themselves worthy of eternal death, although done by the grace of Christ. Every work of ours is an abomination. The expression of the filthy rags in Isaiah lxiv. 6, (in which the Jewish Church, polluted by idolatry and apostasy, complains mournfully of the severity of the punishments laid on her, and, confessing her sins, alludes to the things

[e] Cajetan, *Opuscula*, tom. iii. p. 169. Antwerp, 1612.

she had done during her public alienation from God,) was applied by them to the actions of the holiest of Christians.

This dogmatic use of the text is, of course, wholly independent of a pious employment of it, made, at all times, by holy souls, who in sight of the Infinite holiness of God and their own coming short of their own ideal of what is due from the creature to the Creator, have not found words strong enough to express their own sense of unworthiness.

This opinion of the Reformers as above stated, is opposed to Scripture, to tradition, to right reason. In the Word of God, the works of the just are called "good[f];" "works of light[g];" "sacrifices acceptable and well-pleasing to God[h];" "clean robes[i];" "fine linen[k];" and they who here have lived holily, are said to have done "works of righteousness, and kept their garments undefiled[l];" also, to those who walk aright is promised a great reward, "both in this world, and in that which is to come[m];" and St. James says, "In many things we all offend[n]," therefore not in all things.

So even those Fathers, who are most opposed to Pelagius, though they denied that a just man would entirely avoid all sin for his whole life, or even for a long portion of his life, yet granted that the just could do so, at least for a short time.

Lastly, in view of right reason. Can anything be

[f] St. Matt. v. 16.   [g] Eph. v. 8, 9.   [h] Phil. iv. 18; comp. Heb. xiii. 16.   [i] Rev. vii. 13.   [k] Rev. xix. 8.   [l] Rev. ii. 4, iii. 4.   [m] 1 Tim. iv. 8; comp. St. Matt. v. 12.   [n] St. James iii. 2.

so despiteful to the grace of Christ, which has freed us not only from liability to punishment for our innate corruption, but from the dominion of it? Certainly those who maintain this opinion, although they seem to themselves to extol God's mercy and grace, do, in fact, though unwittingly, exalt the strength of the old Adam, and of indwelling sin more.

We of the Church of England content ourselves with the affirmation that none of our works can endure the *severity* of the judgment of God. It is enough that they can endure God's judgment, as tempered with grace and mercy on account of Christ; but we are not so ungrateful or unjust to that grace, as to assert that nothing whatever can here be performed by us through its strength, which is in view of human frailty not in some way defiled by sin [o].

If God should strictly judge our works, they might be said to be vices, and our just works to be unjust; because many things which are now just, good, and meritorious, would be truly vices, and bad, and unjust, if they were brought to the standard of that sanctity and purity wherewith we ought to serve God, and which God might rigorously exact from us, as well on account of His own goodness, as on account of the excellent benefits He has conferred upon us. For not only is it true that the life of every one of the just is defiled by many venial sins, but also the very works of the perfect fall very far short of that goodness wherewith we ought to worship, praise, and honour

[o] Forbesii Consid., vol. i. p. 407.

O

God; for they are joined during this life to much imperfection, nor are they so pure, holy, or fervent, as the greatness of the divine goodness towards us requires. And whereas God, on account of His exceeding kindness and graciousness towards us, does not at present impute to us these defects and imperfections even as a venial fault, yet He might reckon them as a fault if He willed to treat us strictly, and apart from His graciousness and benignity [p].

While it was right to re-assert the existence of the divine work in the justification of man, and that in one sense eternal life is emphatically the free gift of God, it cannot be doubted that some of the Reformers ran into extremes on the want of value of man's part in the mighty co-operation with the grace of God in making his calling and election sure. Luther by his theory of faith, Calvin by his exaggerated teaching of predestination, went far to destroy man's faith in what he had to do. Moreover, the matter did not rest with the authors of these teachings: their followers very much surpassed them, and a deep Antinomian spirit became very prevalent. It was to meet this that the Article was framed. No such Article is found in the code of 1553. It is the result of Archbishop Parker's first endeavour to restore a patristic line of thought. He guards indeed the other side, where he says that they cannot expiate sin, or take the place of our Lord's Blood, and where he asserts that they cannot endure the severity of God's judgment; but he goes on to

[p] Vega, *de Justificatione,* ii. 38, cit. Forbes.

assert that they are 1. *grata et accepta,* and 2. that they spring from faith. Both these are distinctly Christian propositions.

1. The good deeds of those who sent offerings to Jerusalem are called a sacrifice, a sweet savour, well-pleasing to God: and various other passages in the Bible enforce this upon us. Indeed, no such severe blow has ever been struck at Christian morality as the one-sided conception of the Reformation on this head. It has tended, first of all, to stunting the spiritual life in preventing great ventures in faith. It has destroyed self-sacrifice. It has crippled those usages of self-dedications where men from the love of God have given themselves up to spend and to be spent in His service. It has taken away the motives for self-discipline and watchfulness, tending to substitute sentiment for principle. It has tended to a certain softening of the soul, and to an idolatry of comfort and respectability. In short, it is a mistake to seek to be wiser than Jesus Christ. If He makes the joys of the next world to be the reward of good deeds on earth, who are we that we should seek to place Christian action on a supposed higher platform? No man can purchase heaven by his good actions, but actions done in the power of Christ, by His grace, with the aid of His Spirit, are the things which determine our position and measure of glory in the life to come,—God thus crowning His own gifts in us, so that to Him and to Him alone belongs the glory.

Although the first grace ever comes from God, and

precedes all on man's part, yet faith is the first in order of time in all supernatural acts; nay, more, it is the source from whence they flow: and, as the Article says, they tell back on their source, the holy act being but the embodied conviction, and the strong impression of the soul welling forth and expressing itself in the outward act.

A true faith here is mentioned in contradistinction to a false faith; the faith of heretics, as such, has no justifying power. Hence the severity with which the Church has always regarded intellectual errors. All religious truth finds its ultimate term in Christ, who is the Eternal Truth. He it is who warrants all revelation. It is on His authority, as the Revealer of God's will and purpose, that we accept any proposition laid before us. And if the Church be His Body, and the Bible His Word, then those dogmas which we accept on their joint authority come to us on His authority.

And, next, it is a "lively," a living faith, which is spoken of. This is the same as the formed faith of the Schoolmen. The form of a thing is that which causes it to be what it is; the life of a thing is that which gives it the power of motion and energy, of fulfilling the end for which it was created. By a formed faith the Schoolmen understood a faith that had love as its soul, its vivifying, plastic principle, its life, in short, and on this account it was termed *fides charitate formata, animata, fides viva, fides vivida,* a lively faith. This is that higher faith which brings man into a real vital communion with Christ, fills him with an infinite devotion to God, with the strongest confidence in Him, with the deepest humility and love towards Him, liberates him from sin, and causes all creatures to be viewed and loved in God [q].

It would be improper to pass over the word 'merit,' which so often occurs in theology, as men have justly dreaded a theory of the meritoriousness of good works out of Christ. They have rightly said that the best of man's good deeds, in themselves, are filthy rags. They have dwelt upon the evidence of that imperfection which clings to the actions of man, and taints all efforts done in his own strength.

But, on the other hand, we must not forget that God in many parts of Holy Scripture makes the eternal life the reward of a holy life here on earth, and that great promises, both in this life and in the world to come, are held out to obedience. Sometimes merit is taken strictly and in the rigorous sense of the word, and means a free action, to which, out of justice, is due a certain reward or premium. At other times it is taken in a wider sense, as a free action entitled to a certain reward, either in terms of debt, or compact, or condition, or bargain, or even for grace: and generally it is taken for any work which impetrates any reward, and is the cause of its bestowal [r]. Now, theo-

---

[q] Möhler, vol. i. p. 171.

The sentiment of this Article is in accordance with the formula agreed upon between Protestants and Catholics at Ratisbon, in 1541:—" It is a settled and sound doctrine, that sinful man is justified by living and active faith: for by it we are rendered agreeable and well-pleasing unto God for Christ's sake."

[r] Vega, *de Justif.*, lib. viii. p. 192, ed. 1672.

logically speaking, it is a voluntary work, either internal or external, to which in right a reward is due, according to the Apostle[s]: "To him that worketh is the reward not reckoned of grace, but of debt." So that four parties concur to the establishment of merit: 1. The person who merits; 2. the voluntary work, which is the merit; 3. the reward due; 4. the Rewarder.

However, the question becomes complicated when we deal with the relation which exists between us and God, for it seems difficult to conceive how in justice our work should be rewarded by God, since no absolute and simple right can exist between us: " In Thy sight shall no man living be justified." It can only be a relative right at best, a *jus secundum quid*, like the relations of master and slave, only infinitely less than that. Yet this feeble right is of divine ordination, and thus God owes, not to man but to Himself, to reward good actions with eternal life. Moreover, both under the old and new Law we find evidence of covenants made between God and man, and just as in a covenant between master and slave, an actual right is generated, so it is between God and man; yet even then, God is not a debtor to us, but to Himself, to His own will, which induced Him to enter into covenant with us[t].

The word ' merit' is hardly to be found in Holy Scripture, though there are expressions nearly equivalent to it, as where we read "worthy," or " to be accounted worthy[u]." Yet it is of frequent occurrence in the

[s] Rom. iv. 4.   [t] Cajetan, tom. iii. p. 168.
[u] St. Luke xxi. 36; 2 Thess. i. 5; Apoc. iii. 4.

Latin Fathers of the best and purest ages, e.g. St. Cyprian, having nearly the same sense as to obtain, or to become apt and fitted for obtaining; so as nothing is detracted from God's grace, from which all merits arise.

The word is used in this sense in the Latin classics: "Sequi gloria, non appeti, debet, nec si casu aliquo non sequatur, idcirco quod gloriam non meruit, minus pulchrum est [x]."

But the true philosophy of the matter rests on the truth, that the merit of eternal life is not our work, but the work of Christ our Head in us and by us. Men by grace are made the living members of Christ. The sufferings of the body are the sufferings of the Head: "Why persecutest thou Me?" Christ spoke in Paul, and Paul lived, yet not he, but Christ lived in him [y]. Hence we may say, "I merit, yet not I, but Christ meriteth in me." "I fast, yet not I, but Christ fasteth in me."

So that while baptized infants are saved purely by the merit of Christ's life and death, in the case of adults eternal life is due in two ways: 1. by right of the merit of Christ, which He earned in His own person; 2. by right of the merit of Christ, which Christ the Head earns in the adult and by the adult, it being suitable to the divine liberality that in both ways He should communicate to adults the merit of eternal life, as it is written, "Them He did predestinate to be conformed to the image of His Son [z]." And men are so conformed

---

[x] Pliny, Ep., lib. viii. cp. 13, ap. Facciolat.   [y] Gal. ii. 20.

[z] Rom. viii. 29.

to the image of Christ by having the merit of eternal
life in both ways: for He had glory also in two ways,
1. by virtue of the hypostatic union, and this was without merit; and 2. by virtue of His obedience unto
death [a], wherefore in a meritorious sense "God also
hath highly exalted Him, and given Him a name that
is above every name [b]."

And this in no wise contradicts what the Apostle
says, that "eternal life is the gracious gift ($\chi\acute{a}\rho\iota\sigma\mu a$)
of God in Christ Jesus," i.e. to those who are in Christ.
For first, the foundation of all is that we are *in* Christ,
not our mere natural selves only; eternal life is bestowed upon us because we are in Christ; then, the
grace of God, whereby we do good works, is the free
gift of God; whence, as St. Augustine says, "When
God crowneth our merits, what else crowneth He but
His own gifts?" Then, as Theodoret says, "There is
no proportion between temporal evils and those eternal
goods." St. Augustine strikingly sums up, "That to
which eternal life is owed, is true righteousness. But,
if it is true righteousness, it is not of thee; for it
cometh down from above, from the Father of Light.
That thou mightest have it, if indeed thou hast it,
thou hast in truth received it. For what hast thou
which thou hast not received? Wherefore, O man, if
thou art to receive eternal life, it is, indeed, the wages
of righteousness; but to *thee* it is grace, for to thee
righteousness itself too is grace. For it would be
given to thee as a debt, if thou hadst the righteous-

---

[a] Phil. ii. 8, 9.   [b] Cajetan, iii. Tract. x. p. 169.

ness, to which it is owed, from thyself. But now from His fulness we have received not only the grace, whereby we now live righteously, in our labour, to the very end, but also grace for His grace, that we should live hereafter in rest without end [c]."

[c] Epist. 194, *ad Test.*, n. 21.

ARTICLE XIII.

De Operibus ante Justificationem.

Opera quæ fiunt ante gratiam Christi, et Spiritus ejus afflatum, cum ex fide Jesu Christi non prodeant, minime Deo grata sunt, neque gratiam (ut multi vocant) de congruo merentur. Immo cum non sunt facta, ut Deus illa fieri voluit et præcepit, peccati rationem habere non dubitamus.

" Of Works before Justification.

"Works done before the grace of Christ and the inspiration of His Spirit, are not pleasant to God, forasmuch as they spring not of faith in Jesus Christ, neither do they make men meet to receive grace, or (as the School-authors say) deserve grace of congruity: yea rather, for that they are not done as God hath willed and commanded them to be done, we doubt not but they have the nature of sin."

That which tended to produce confusion concerning the relation between faith and good works, was the explanation of several passages of St. Paul; e. g. Rom. iii. 28, where it is said, that not through works of the law, but through faith, a man is justified. St. Paul here contends against the Jews of his own epoch, who obstinately defended the eternal duration of the law of Moses, and asserted that not needing a Redeemer from sin, they became righteous and acceptable before God by that law alone. In opposition to this, he lays down the maxim that it is not by the works of the law, i.e. not by a life regulated merely by the Mosaic precepts, that man is able to obtain the favour of Heaven; but only through faith in Christ, which has been imparted to us by God, for wisdom, for sanctification, for righteousness, and for redemption. On the one hand, an unbelief in the Redeemer, and confidence in the fulfilment of the law performed solely through the natural powers; on the other hand, a faith in the Redeemer and the righteousness to be conferred by God. This is the opposition described by the Apostle. He accurately distinguishes between the works of the law and good works; the former are wrought without faith in Christ, and without His grace; the latter, with the grace and in the spirit of Christ.

The Thirteenth Article is another instance where the title does not correspond with its contents. It would be correct if it were worded "Of some works before Justification." There are some works done before justification which are not pleasant to God. There are others of which it would be the most extreme want of charity to predicate such a thing. Again, of works done before justification, some are done before the grace of Christ and the inspiration of His Spirit; other works done before justification, are done by that grace and with that inspiration. Cornelius was not justified till the Holy Ghost fell on him and he was baptized, but no one can deny that, according to the express words of the Angel, his prayers and alms went up as a memorial before God, and impetrated his justification.

It is very important to bear in mind, that the effect of the death of our Lord Jesus Christ extends to all those for whom He died, in the way of sufficient grace being freely imparted to all men. Beyond His covenant, outside His Church, to Pagan and to Jew, to those who have heard of His Name, and to those who have never heard of Him, grace is given before faith. God wills that we should pray for all men, on the ground that He willeth that all men should be saved, and come to the knowledge of His truth[a]. Again, treating of the divine Word, St. John says: "That was the true light, which lighteth every man that cometh into the world;" of which words St. Chrysostom asks: "If It lighteth every man coming into the world, how do men remain without light?" He answers, "It is true so far as It is concerned, but if any, wilfully shutting the eyes of their minds, refuse to recognise the rays of this light, it is not from the nature of the light that they remain in darkness but from their own wickedness, who wilfully deprive themselves of this light. For grace is poured forth upon all men[b]." Thus also St. Ambrose: "That mystic Sun of Righteousness hath risen on all, hath come to all, hath suffered for all, and hath risen again for all[c]."

[a] 1 Tim. ii. 4.   [b] Homily on St. John, vol. viii. p. 48.   [c] Cf. *In Psalm* cxviii. p. 1077, § viii. 57 ; p. 1220, § xix. 39. Ed. Paris, 1686.

This grace is termed medicinal grace, aided by which the heathen are able to fulfil the natural law, and to overcome the difficulties which stand in the way of its observance; works done by the aid of such assistance come within the order of moral rectitude. If the heathen correspond with these graces, greater helps are given them, until God of His free mercy calls them to the supernatural end of life by the beginning of faith, either by missionaries sent for the purpose, or by the whispering of their good angel, or inwardly by Himself, or in such other way as seems good to Him.

Premising this, a sound theology will map out the acts of the unjustified man into several distinct divisions :—

1. Acts in which neither the grace of Christ nor the inspiration of the Spirit have aught to do, such as the good works of heathen men done from the tradition and custom of their race, from the fear of the public opinion of those by whom they are surrounded.

2. The *splendida vitia* of the heathen, those acts of continence and generosity, performed from simple self-respect, and which may be referred for a motive to pride.

3. Those acts which may be said to be by the grace of Christ, who is the light of every man that cometh into the world; as where a heathen follows his conscience, does actions from a sense of duty, and gives free scope to the feelings of benevolence which survive in all men since the fall.

4. Actions such as those of Cornelius, where a person brought up and trained in an inferior system, lives up to his light, and by so doing draws down blessings upon himself.

It is with regard to the first class that we must understand the wording of the Article in its absolute literal sense.

With regard to the second, one must hesitate to say that such acts in a manner are not pleasant to God. Nay, St. Augustine would rather maintain that the just God would be bound to reward them with temporal advantages, just as He gave to the Romans the domination of the earth as a return for their early frugality, adding, however, the significant words, " perceperunt mercedem suam[d]." Still, so far as regards the supernatural kingdom of Christ, these works are valueless, and therefore they also, in a less proper sense, come under the condemnation of the Article.

Touching the third, we are not called on to pass any judgment. How God will deal with the heathen who have never heard His name, is not for us to say. It opens up an immense question, on which there has been no decision by the Church. While charity hopeth all things, no lax view should affect our sense of the duty of missionary exertion, or diminish our value for those assertions which attach the attainment of everlasting life to such conditions as faith, baptism, and holiness.

The last class of actions of the unjustified man do not come under the condemnation of the Article; for the

---

[d] *De Civ. Dei*, lib. v. cap. 15.

proposition that grace does not act outside the Church has been justly condemned, and it is false to assert that the grace of Christ and the inspiration of the Holy Ghost do not concur with the free-will of man before he is justified.

In fact, before justification, a mighty process goes on. The grace of Christ, and the inspiration of the Holy Ghost, are not lacking. First of all, grace touches the sinner, for no sinner can of himself turn to God. The first movement towards justification is the free and gratuitous work of God. Christ speaks to the heart, as the abiding Teacher. He announces the Gospel by His Word and by His Church; God the Holy Ghost rouses the soul by preventive grace. If the free-will responds to this influence, a faith in God's Word is the first result of this. He becomes convinced of the supernatural order of things. He is touched with it, and especially with the thought of the love of God in Christ. He compares himself as he is with what he ought to be. He measures himself by the new standard, with which the Passion of Christ supplies him. He returns to himself and conceives the holy fear of God. Then turning to the thought of Jesus Christ dying for him, he begins to hope that God, for the Redeemer's merits, will pardon him; he begins to love God and to hate sin; he believed, he now repents. All this precedes justification.

2. The next question is, Do these works deserve grace *de congruo?* "Works of grace and special aid, which concur with faith, and dispose to regeneration and the

forgiveness of sins, are not excluded from justification :
but though they are said to concur with faith, they do
not in any sense merit the first justification, for merit
de congruo is now almost excluded from Catholic
Schools[e]." This notion tallies with what the Holy
Scripture says of our being justified freely, and by
grace : also with what is taught therefrom by St. Augustine : but while we admit this, we must not assert
that these disposing acts have no influence whatever in
the process. Unless we distort the word of God[f], we
must concede that they are in some way efficient causes
of justification ; not in the way of merit, but solely from
the benignity and gratuitous promise of God[g].

Sufficient weight, in the consideration of this Article,
has not been given to the fact that the only works excluded from merit *de congruo* by its terms are those
done before the grace of Christ and the inspiration of
the Spirit : consequently it does not prejudge the
question whether other works, those which are the
fruit of faith, do or do not dispose us in some way to
justification, and *de congruo* (though not *de condigno*)
merit the grace of justification, according to the teaching of St. Augustine[h]. At the same time it must be
observed, that no Church has ever asserted the doctrine
of grace *de congruo*, and that the Dominican Order has
always held that it had a Pelagianizing tendency[i].

---

[e] Stapleton, *de Justif.*, lib. viii. c. 16, cit. Forbes.　　　[f] Ezek.
xviii. 21; St. Luke xiii. 3; Acts ii. 38, iii. 19; 1 St. John i. 7—9.
[g] Forbesii Consid., vol. i. p. 28.　　　[h] Ep. 105.　　　[i] See Sarpi,
i. 344, quoted by Hardwick, p. 101.

ARTICLE XIV.

De Operibus Supererogationis.

Opera quæ supererogationis appellant, non possunt sine arrogantia et impietate prædicari. Nam illis declarant homines, non tantum se Deo reddere, quæ tenentur, sed plus in ejus gratiam facere, quam deberent, cum aperte Christus dicat; Cum feceritis omnia quæcunque præcepta sunt vobis, dicite, servi inutiles sumus.

" Of Works of Supererogation.

" VOLUNTARY works besides, over and above, God's commandments, which they call works of supererogation, cannot be taught without arrogancy and impiety. For by them men do declare, that they do not only render unto God as much as they are bound to do, but that they do more for His sake, than of bounden duty is required: whereas Christ saith plainly, When ye have done all that are commanded to you, say, We are unprofitable servants."

There are two ways of putting every subject. A fact may be so stated as to appear false; a doctrine so enunciated as to be deemed an error: or again, certain results of a course of action may be stated to flow from it, as in the common fallacious argument against use from abuse. Lastly, imperfect reasons may be adduced for a perfectly reasonable course of action.

Now all these things must be borne in mind when

we discuss the question of what are termed works of supererogation. In the Bible there are plainly laid down certain counsels of perfection. Over and above what is demanded and expected of every baptized man, there are narrower paths in the narrow way, which all are not required to follow, not so demanded or expected. Certain souls have an exceptional religious destiny laid out before them. Some are called to one work, some to another. All souls are not called to Christian heroism, but some are so; and it is an imperfect view of Christianity which does not give due space for such vocations. It is obvious, e.g. at first sight, that every one is not called upon to be a missionary, or to forsake houses, or brethren, or father, or mother, or wife, or children, or land, for His Name's sake. And yet all of us know of some who have given up some of these things for Jesus' sake.

While the great mass of Christians are bound to keep their Baptismal and Confirmation vows, others of their own free-will add to them those of Matrimony and Orders. Each of these conditions has the necessary graces for their fulfilment attached to them, and these constitute the general obligations of the Christian life. But beyond this, under the Gospel, a higher state of things is borne witness to both by our Lord and His Apostles. Certain injunctions are laid on men; not on all, but on such as can bear it. Certain things are promised, in addition to the ordinary blessings of God, on those who make certain renunciations. Again, St. Paul recommends a certain line of conduct as wise in the present necessity. All this higher law is gathered under the heads of Counsels of Perfection, of which the main branches are Poverty, Chastity, and Obedience.

The teacher of ecclesiastical dogma must pursue his way towards the heights of the revelation of God, having to deal with the science whereby men, through the God-enlightened faculty of knowledge, are brought back to Him. He must necessarily touch upon subjects which his own religious experience may never have realized, and therefore his humbler task is with regard to the higher teachings of Christianity, merely to reproduce what saints have taught on these recondite themes.

It is in this spirit and with bated breath that one would venture to speak first of perfection, and secondly of its counsels.

Perfection consisteth not in gifts bestowed by God for the benefit of others, not even in those great spiritual gifts, healings, tongues, and the like, which were bestowed upon the early Christians. It is not to be found in austerities or abnegations, nor in sensible consolations; rather is it the way whereby we travel to our Eternal Fatherland—the course we steer towards the "haven where we would be." It is not hindered by those duties which are undertaken in the spirit of obedience and love, nay, rather is aided thereby. It consisteth in the keeping of the commandments of God; for perfection is the perfect health of the soul, the chiefest of the gifts of God, and it is summed up in the words of our Saviour, " Thou shalt love the Lord thy God with all thy soul."

Thus it will be seen that ' Counsels of Perfection' are not perfection itself, nay, they are rather means to that end. Counsels are ways of attaining to everlasting salvation; not necessary for all, but very helpful to those whom God calls to them. The word ' counsels' stands in opposition to the ' precepts' of God; the fulfilment of which is of necessity to salvation; and no counsel can take the place of exact obedience to precept, or be excused for its non-observance. " Except ye repent, ye shall all likewise perish [a];" " Every tree that bringeth not forth good fruit shall be hewn down, and cast into the fire [b]." On the other hand, counsel is that which is referred to by our Lord: " If thou wilt be perfect, go and sell all that thou hast and give to the poor."

There are many Evangelical counsels which need not be referred to here, but there are three, all boasting about which is especially condemned by the Article. The first is that of Poverty, or the giving up of worldly goods, whereby, disencumbered and free from care, we may follow Christ. It is of this that the Apostles spake when they said, " Behold, we have left all, and followed Thee; what shall we have therefore [c]?"

The second is Chastity, of body and soul, whereby is fulfilled that counsel of St. Paul: " He that is un-married careth for the things of the Lord, how he may

---

[a] St. Luke xiii. 3, 5.　　　[b] Ibid. iii. 9.　　　[c] St. Matt. xix. 27.

please the Lord. The unmarried woman careth for the things of the Lord, how she may be holy both in body and in spirit." Its special safeguard is humility. But we need also all things that tame the flesh, such as fasting and watching, and similar austerities. This helps to cleanse us from all defilement, both of the flesh and spirit, and to perfect holiness in the fear of God.

The third is Obedience, whereby we mortify our own wills and submit to others, in imitation of Him who "came not to do His own will, but the will of His Father which is in heaven."

Not in these counsels is the substance of perfection, for perfection is the end of the spiritual life; it is that which, according to its own nature, unites our wills to God, who is our last End.

But they are the mighty means whereby that perfection is most easily attained unto. Happy are all they who keep God's commandments, who, for the merits of Christ, shall attain unto everlasting life, in the end being made perfect; but happier are they who, while still in life, seek to anticipate perfection by exceptional sacrifices for God. They shall enter into glory, and beyond that, with the saints and mighty men who have conquered themselves and all things earthly, shall enter into the incomprehensible joy of their Lord.

Now fully admitting that the Counsels of Perfection have their place in Christianity, we may not call them "besides, over and above God's commandments" because in the exceptional cases where men are called to them, to these they become God's commandments. Woe be to that soul, which is called to a Counsel of Perfection, has received the grace for a Counsel of Perfection, and fails to fulfil its high destiny! This, true as it is, could not be taught without arrogancy and impiety, if by it people meant to express, that "by them men do declare, that they do not only render unto God as much as they are bound to do"—that is arrogancy; or that "they do more for His sake than of bounden duty is required," a sentiment here stigmatized as impiety. It is arrogancy to maintain that there is a certain fixed measure of obedience, which God requires of us, seeing that nothing short of the Perfection of God, and the Standard of Christ, is our great exemplar. It is impious to say that any one, for the sake of Christ, does more than is required; for the whole heart, and soul, and time, and habits are His, and at His service. His claim upon us is illimitable: our best obedience most imperfect, and therefore at best we are unprofitable servants. Unprofitable servants! what but unprofitable servants can we repute ourselves, when we measure our very best performances with that which God requires of us: when we call to mind that nothing short of the perfection of God is the standard whereby we shall be measured, and that in Him lie hidden not only all possible perfections that are or ever have been in any of His creatures, but that beyond that there is the inscrutable perfection which is His own attribute: when we remember that the Blessed Humanity of our Lord is that great exemplar upon which the Christian is to form himself; and that the virtues of the

Son of God made man, are the mirrors whereat he is to dress himself? Unprofitable servants! what but unprofitable, in view of the truth that God needs not one of us, that He is in Himself complete in all things, and that the addition or subtraction of an universe adds nothing to, takes nothing from His perfection? And yet He never calls us to impossibilities, never withholds the grace to do what He desires; every individual soul is dear to Him, in the mystery of redemption, His money, His sheep; and therefore in the order of grace, we are dear and precious in His sight: "And they shall be Mine, saith the Lord of Hosts, in that day when I make up My jewels [d]."

[d] Mal. iii. 17.

ARTICLE XV.

DE CHRISTO, QUI SOLUS EST SINE PECCATO.

CHRISTUS in nostræ naturæ veritate per omnia similis factus est nobis, excepto peccato, a quo prorsus erat immunis, tum in carne, tum in spiritu. Venit ut agnus, absque macula, qui mundi peccata per immolationem sui semel factam, tolleret, et peccatum (ut inquit Johannes) in eo non erat : sed nos reliqui etiam baptizati, et in Christo regenerati, in multis tamen offendimus omnes. Et si dixerimus, quod peccatum non habemus, nos ipsos seducimus, et veritas in nobis non est.

" Of Christ alone without Sin.

" CHRIST, in the truth of our nature, was made like unto us in all things, sin only except, from which He was clearly void, both in His flesh and in His Spirit. He came to be the Lamb without spot, who, by sacrifice of Himself once made, should take away the sins of the world, and sin (as St. John saith) was not in Him. But all we the rest, although baptized, and born again in Christ, yet offend in many things ; and if we say we have no sin, we deceive ourselves, and the truth is not in us."

After laying down positively the blessed truth of a Homoüsia between our Lord and us,—in that He has actually assumed our nature, with all its attributes, its sinless infirmities, its faculties, and powers, into His divine person, so that as He has become a sharer in human nature, we have become partakers of the divine, —the Article goes on to state the one abatement that must necessarily be made to the statement in its breadth which is involved in the exclusion of any thought of sin in connection with Him.

It is first stated negatively that Christ is without sin; we have therefore in the first place to consider the doctrine of the sanctity of our Lord in His incarnate nature. By sanctity, we mean that quality which is contrary to what is profane or polluted,— which is opposed to sin,—which is a state of the soul free from the contagion of deadly crime,—which is pure, incorrupt, and adorned with the splendour of divine grace. Now our Lord by Gabriel was emphatically called the holy thing that was to be born of Mary; and this took place in three ways: 1. by the gift of sinlessness, the absence of the power of falling; 2. by the perpetuity of that gift; and 3. by the plenitude of grace. If the first Adam was made upright, how much more the second Adam, who, as to body, was formed and confected out of the most pure and perfect flesh and blood of the Virgin Mary, and whose soul was formed on the likeness of the archetypal Word of God, which was taken by Him and proposed as the example of holiness to all the saints; for " whom God did foreknow, them He did predestinate to be conformed to the image of His Son, that He might be the firstborn among many brethren [a]." Hence it is in His human nature, assumed into the unity of His Divine Person, that our Lord is the head of the Church, and the author of holiness, which are necessary conditions of the due discharge of His offices of Mediator, Saviour, and High-Priest [b]; and, duly to estimate the plenitude of this grace, we must bear in mind that this special gift was not accidental or communicated, but inherent in Himself. In Him was the fountain of grace, infinite and uncircumscript. And if we ask the awful question, What was the formal cause of this holiness? we have to answer that the actual divinity of the Word by itself sanctifies the human nature assumed into consortship with the same Person; that the human nature by union with the Word is deified and holy by an archetypal holiness: that the unction of the humanity of Christ has been effected by the Word sanctifying the flesh, by the Father working through the Word, and by the Holy Ghost causing the union of the Word and the Flesh. Hence the laws of the impeccancy of Christ [c].

The testimony of the ancients to the truth that sin is not to be predicated of our Lord is very ample. Some assert that Christ alone is without any sin, without specifying original sin: others that, Christ alone excepted, all men are defiled with that original sin.

1. St. Augustine, in the controversy on original sin with Julian, asks him whether he would venture to say,

---

[a] Rom. viii. 29.   [b] Heb. ii. 17, iii. 2.
[c] Petavius, *de Incarnatione*, xi. 10, 1.

to St. Ambrose too, that because he excepted Christ alone from the bonds of a guilty generation, in that He was born of a virgin, whereas all others descended from Adam were born in the bond of sin, he made the devil the creator of all born after the ordinary law of nature. " Charge him," he says, " as a condemner of marriage, who said that the Virgin's Son was alone born without sin [d]."

" Christ was the first and only man upon earth that did not commit sin, neither was guile found in His mouth [e]."

2. " No one of the saints, of whatever virtues he may be full, yet being gathered from that blackness of the world, can be equalled to Him of whom it is written, ' The holy Thing which shall be born of thee shall be called the Son of God.' For we, although we are made saints, yet are not born saints, because we are constrained by the very condition of our corruptible nature to say with the Prophet, ' Behold, I was shapen in iniquity ; and in sin did my mother conceive me.' But He alone was truly born holy, who, that He might overcome the condition itself of corruptible nature, was not conceived in the ordinary way of nature [f]."

The doctrine of the sinlessness of our Lord is very important, when regarded in its relation to other truths of the Gospel.

I. The conception of a perfectly sinless character was never attained to by the unassisted reason of man.

[d] Cont. Jul. ii. 2. tom. v. p. 18. c. ii.

[e] Cyril Alex., *de Recta Fide ad Theodos.*,

[f] S. Greg. in Job, l. xviii. c. 52. tom. i. p. 598.

II. Impeccancy has never been claimed by any teacher save by our Lord, but He rests His divine mission on it: " Which of you convinceth Me of sin ?" If He is not sinless, on His own shewing, He has no claim on us.

III. It infuses an element of meritoriousness and sacrificial power into the fact of our Lord's life and death. He was made a curse for us. He bore our sins in His own Body on the tree, whereas in the case of all us, the rest, " the wages of sin is death."

IV. The teaching office of our Lord is closely connected with His sinlessness. In proportion as sin prevails, it clouds the higher part of the intellect, and the moral taint will tell upon the belief. Not only does our Lord rest His teaching office, that is, His right to be listened to, on the fact that they could not convince Him of sin, but He claims to be the Truth itself.

V. It makes the perfection of the Christian to be ever advancing; for if no standard short of the pattern of a sinless Christ be that to which mankind is invited to look as the *Species eximia pulchritudinis*, it follows that there is no room for boasting, however highly any one may seem to have attained. Between the perfection even of the Blessed Virgin herself and the perfection of her Son,—who alone is, by His own nature, impeccable, because His Manhood is One Person with God the Word, and so holy with an uncreated holiness,—there is a great gulph fixed.

VI. The sinlessness of Christ has a most important bearing on ourselves. If our justification be the imparting to us of an actual righteousness, and that actual righteousness be the righteousness of a sinless Person, it will be seen what a standard is placed before us. Lastly :—

VII. It infuses into the soul a high sense of the destinies of that creation which now, and for a season, is made subject to vanity. Not only in body, but in soul and in spirit, are we destined to be changed into His likeness. The second Man, which is the Lord from heaven, who operates upon us here sacramentally, as the Food of our souls, is the sinless Christ, and it is into His image that we shall be changed from glory to glory.

The Article here rises from simple dogmatic statement into something like religious fervour. It goes on from the assertion of the sinlessness of our Lord to deduce the conveniency of His being the eternal Victim for sin. Priest and Victim in one, in order to fulfil the necessary conditions of our propitiation, the requirement of sinless life enters into both natures. His priesthood must be pure, " For such an High-Priest became us, who is holy, harmless, undefiled, separate from sinners, and made higher than the heavens ; who needed not daily, as those high-priests, to offer up sacrifice first for His own sins, and then for the people [g]." A sinless Sacrifice is the antitype of a lamb without spot. It was a lamb, or a kid of the goats without blemish, that was to be taken for the sacrificial feast ; and so Christ our Passover must needs be sinless. For

[g] Heb. vii. 26, 27.

we are redeemed from our corrupt conversation by the precious Blood of Christ, as of a Lamb without spot, "who did no sin, neither was guile found in His mouth [h]."

The impeccable nature of our Lord supplies the special aptitude for His sacrificial function. The perfectness of the victim under the old law presignified this condition in its antitype, and foreshadowed in no dark similitude that the victim that was to take away the sins of the world must have no sins of its own to atone for. Herein was the difference between priest and victim under the old law. There the priest was emphatically sinful, he had to offer both for his own sins and for the sins of the people; but the victim must be perfect, the first-born, free from all defect, otherwise it was not worthy to be offered to God. Under the new dispensation both Priest and Victim are one, wherefore if the Victim be pure, the Priest is pure also; in short, fulfilling the conditions laid down in the Epistle to the Hebrews, " holy, harmless, undefiled, separate from sinners."

And this sacrificial aspect of Christ's mediation cannot sufficiently be borne in mind; for, from the obscuration of Eucharistic truth which has prevailed since the Reformation, our Lord's intercession has been looked upon much more as an act of prayer than of sacrifice. Hereby the whole typology of the Books of Moses—as representing the ceremonies of the great day of atonement, whereby the atonement by slaying being made

[h] 1 Pet. ii. 22.

outside the veil, the blood was carried, still as atonement, by the high-priest into the holy of holies once a-year—is entirely lost[1]; a poverty of conception with regard to the present work of Christ—the continued presentation of those Sacred wounds, of that glorious Body which once hung upon the tree, and now, without words, pleads by its very presence within the Holy of Holies— at the Father's right hand is engendered; and the deep cry of the Church, involving its belief in the everlasting propitiation of the Son of God, loses its significance. "Agnus Dei qui tollis peccata mundi, miserere nobis."

The Article goes on to assert in broad terms the actual sinfulness of mankind. In spite of our high privileges in the Gospel; of our being taken out of the state of nature and put in the state of grace; of our being by baptism buried and risen with Christ; of our being born again of water and of the Holy Ghost; it is certain that we shall not escape all sins. Though God gives us grace to fulfil His law, though He enables us to meet each temptation as it arises, though He bestows on us sufficient helps to serve Him; as a matter of fact, we do not do so. To take an analogy in the things of this life: just as with sufficient knowledge of arithmetic to sum up a set of figures rightly, we know that if we do so a great many times we shall certainly make a mistake; just as out of a certain number of letters, there are a certain number and average that will be misdirected, so in our own individual case, we may be sure that we shall fall into some sin. The Article does not speak of exceptional

---

[1] See Theological Defence for the Bishop of Brechin.

cases. It says, "all we the rest." It does not commit itself to what may be the case with regard to saints whom God may by a special prerogative save from sin; as was the case, under the old law, with Zacharias and Elisabeth, who (albeit they might not have been free from infirmities) walked in *all* the ordinances of the Lord blameless, or as must be the case with regard to His own Holy Mother, of whom, though we may imagine imperfections as possible, yet, with whom, for the honour of her Son, we can associate no idea of sin[k]. To imagine that even for one moment the Blessed Virgin, by a wilful sin, was hateful to her Son, or that by a deliberate evil wish she took the part of Satan against her Son, and conspired to dethrone Him (both which notions are bound up in the idea of sin), is a thought revolting to the pious instinct.

Closely connected with this is the important question, whether, by that measure of grace which God metes out in this life, the saints can fulfil the law of God. The matter was discussed in St. Augustine's time, and he expresses himself with great hesitation on the subject. When discussing with Pelagius where Abraham's bosom was, he was unwilling to contend about the power of living without sin by the grace of Christ, although he thought that no one could be shewn who had done it[l]. Proceeding from the power to the act, he expressly affirms that he does not wish strenuously to dispute whether there are not some who arrive here at such a perfection of righteousness as to

---

[k] *Vide* Forbesii Considerationes, ed. Oxf. 1850, t. i. pp. 339—377.

[l] Lib. ii. *de Peccat. Merit.*, c. 6—8, t. x. p. 43 c.

be without sin, although it seemed to him the true
view that there are none [m]; and in the celebrated letter
sent by four African bishops (of whom the Saint was
one) to Pope Innocent, it is confessed that there are
Catholics to whom it seems not contrary to truth that
there are some persons who through grace are able to
fulfil in this life the law of God without sin; that, *if
they err,* they err more tolerably than Pelagius; but
that for them it is enough that no one of the faithful is
found in the Church of God, in however high a state of
advance and excellency of righteousness, who can dare
to say that the petition in the Lord's Prayer, " Forgive
us, &c.," is not necessary for him, and that he has " no
sin," although he now lives blamelessly [n]?

That the Blessed Virgin is not included necessarily
in this condemnation, may be inferred from the language of the rest of the formularies. The Collect for
Christmas dwells on our Lord's birth from " a pure
virgin." The Preface, " that He was made very man
of her substance, and that without spot of sin." The
Homily on Repentance, in a short dogmatic statement,
speaks of " Jesus Christ, who being true and natural
God, equal and of one substance with the Father, did
at the time appointed take upon Him our frail nature,
in the Blessed Virgin's womb, and that of her undefiled substance, so that He might be a mediator between God and us, and pacify His wrath." In that
on Wilful Rebellion [o] it speaks of " the obedience of

---

[m] *De Nat. et Gratia,* 59, 69, t. x. p. 157 d.

[n] Ep. 95, num. 177, 16, 18.   [o] Part II.

this most Noble and most Virtuous Lady, which doth well teach us who in comparison to her are most base and vile." Of course, between the perfection of God and the perfection of the noblest of His creatures, there is the gulph of infinity fixed. Between essential Sanctity, the Sanctity that is the same as Being, and the most exalted sanctity that is a gift, there can be no possible comparison. There can be no comparison between that which is the attribute of the Creator and the gift to the creature.

Indeed, as regards the Blessed Virgin, one's first thought with regard to her is a jealousy for the honour of the Lord God of Hosts. Anything that approaches Him must be zealously fended off. We cannot endure that the idea of any created thing, however great and holy, shall be compared unto Him. He is supreme, and His honour we must not give unto another. Therefore the soul shrinks with an infinite loathing from any of those expressions which seem to trench upon His incommunicable glory.

But on the other hand, viewed rightly and in the analogy of faith, the great honour bestowed on Mary, the recognition of her place in the order of grace, tends very directly to a proper estimate of the glory of God. As in Alpine scenes one can never estimate the vast distances and enormous magnitudes of the glorious objects by which we are surrounded, from the fact that we have no measure or power of comparison till we see some tree or human form, the comparative insignificance of which forms that measure, so it is with the infinitude of God. We ascend towards it through the contemplation of the saints. Take the Virgin as the highest of them all, estimate her pure as Eve at the moment of her creation, add to that the miraculous idea of divine maternity, exhaust all thought and all positive language in the conception and expression of her august prerogatives, and yet, when you have reached the height, God is still infinitely greater. Thus she becomes a height of created nature, whence to rise to the Divine Humanity of her Son, and thence to the infinitude of God, and the higher ideal we have of her, the more complete is our all-imperfect estimate of Him.

Christ is the glorious sun of righteousness, shining in His strength, glorious and radiant, from whose heat nothing is hidden; and He shines all the more gloriously and radiantly, by reason of and in comparison with those derived fires, the saints who shine in the firmament as the stars of heaven, and specially with her whom an imaginative and poetic Christianity, playing upon a fancied interpretation of her lovely name, has designated as the Star of the Sea.

But the question of her immaculate conception is beside the honour due to her. Unless we assume the theory of development as the only intellectual basis for our faith, it cannot be denied that this doctrine has little support in antiquity. While the ancient liturgies freely testify to her being undefiled, while Holy Scripture denies the possibility of bringing what is clean out of that which is unclean, and St. Augustine from the honour due to our Lord, refuses to connect the notion of sin with her mother, the notion of a suspension of the law of the fall in this individual case is a middle-age conception. The festival was opposed by St. Bernard as a novelty, and as involving the doctrine of the Immaculate Conception, but in so doing he submitted himself beforehand to any contrary judgment from Rome. The festival spread, however, with the deepening devotion to the Blessed Virgin, and its supporters resented opposition to it as a slight upon her. In this country, it was upheld, alas! by what are now known to have been forgeries,—the relation of a vision in which the Blessed Virgin is herself stated to have enjoined its observance, and a letter of St. Anselm enforcing it on the credit of that revelation. The Schoolmen on St. Augustine's principles and tradition continued to oppose it, until Duns Scotus, mainly on abstract grounds, turned the tide, and gained the University of Paris in its favour. The Feast of her Conception began with the Greeks, and was brought by them to Sicily and to Italy. Its object was, to celebrate the first moment of her existence, who was to be the Mother of the Redeemer of the world. Accordingly the day was fixed on Dec. 8, just nine months before that upon which her nativity was celebrated. It was a natural expression of piety. The Council of Basle charged Turrecremata, the master of the Sacred Palace under Eugenius IV., to make a report on a subject so fiercely contested among theologians. Afterwards, Turrecremata retiring with the more moderate party of the Council, the Council put forth a decree in every sense in accordance with the opinion of the University of Paris; and, although at this time, being in opposition to Pope Eugenius, it was held to be a schismatical Council, its decree was, by many, (e.g. Gabriel Biel,) accounted to be the voice of the Church. The Council of Trent contented itself with asserting that it had no intention of including the Blessed Virgin Mary in its decree on original sin, and renewed the bulls published on the subject by Sixtus IV. Efforts were from time to time made both by the Franciscan Order, and by the kings of Spain, Philip III. under Paul V., and Philip IV. under Gregory XV., to have the doctrine declared to be dogma; but it was reserved for Pius IX. on Dec. 8, 1854, by the Bull *Ineffabilis*, to do what he could in this respect. Whether the interests of Christianity have gained by the increase of honour which hereby accrues to the Holy Virgin, and by the additional prominence given to the idea of the Suprasensual in the mystery of redemption, or have lost by the divorce in sentiment between the past and present Church, by the dissidence between the Old Traditional Faith and the Developed Sentiment of the Living Church, is a question which suggests the gravest consideration, and excites the deepest anxiety.

ARTICLE XVI.

De Peccato post Baptismum.

Non omne peccatum mortale post Baptismum voluntarie perpetratum, est peccatum in Spiritum Sanctum, et irremissibile. Proinde lapsis a Baptismo in peccata, locus pœnitentiæ non est negandus. Post acceptum Spiritum Sanctum possumus a gratia data recedere, atque peccare, denuoque per gratiam Dei resurgere, ac resipiscere; ideoque illi damnandi sunt, qui se quamdiu hic vivant, amplius non posse peccare affirmant, aut vere resipiscentibus veniæ locum denegant.

"Of Sin after Baptism.

"Not every deadly sin willingly committed after baptism is sin against the Holy Ghost, and unpardonable. Wherefore the grant of repentance is not to be denied to such as fall into sin after baptism. After we have received the Holy Ghost, we may depart from grace given, and fall into sin, and by the grace of God we may arise again, and amend our lives. And therefore they are to be condemned which say, they can no more sin as long as they live here, or deny the place of forgiveness to such as truly repent."

One heavy impenetrable cloud hangs over the Gospel of our Lord and Saviour Jesus Christ. One appalling thought there is beyond all others terrible, which, revealed to us in mercy, yet blanches the cheek and terrifies the soul. It is that in the order of God's providence there is one sin, for which the Eternal Son, the Redeemer of all men, has declared there is no remission: "Wherefore I say unto you, All manner of sin and blasphemy shall be forgiven unto men; but the blasphemy against the Holy Ghost shall not be forgiven unto men. And whosoever speaketh a word against the Son of Man, it shall be forgiven him; but whosoever speaketh against the Holy Ghost, it shall not be forgiven him, neither in this world, nor in the world to come[a]." What that sin is, has never yet been declared by authority. Some have thought that it was the imputation of a diabolic origin to the miracles of our Lord, though one cannot see how that can be the sin, for the Spirit was not yet given. Others have held that it is final impenitency, but it is left in a terrible suspense that men may fear the judgment of God.

There is another very awful text in the Epistle to the Hebrews, when the author uses the expression that it "is impossible," i.e. impossible for man, though possible for God, (as we see from the use $\dot{a}\nu a\kappa a\iota\nu i\zeta\epsilon\iota\nu$, rather $\dot{a}\nu a\kappa a\iota\nu\epsilon\sigma\theta a\grave{\iota}$,) "to renew to repentance those who were once enlightened (been baptized), and have tasted of the heavenly gift (of the Holy Eucharist), and were made partakers of the Holy Ghost (in confirmation), and have tasted the good Word of God (the Holy Scripture), and the powers of the world to come," " seeing that they

[a] St. Matt. xii. 31.

crucify to themselves the Son of God afresh, and put Him to an open shame." This passage, which is commonly interpreted of the exceeding great difficulty of a return after an open apostacy from God, has its special importance in these days, when men think so lightly of loss of faith; when they tamper with doubts and bad books, and imagine themselves none the worse for intellectual sins. It is no carnal sin that is here alluded to, it is not avarice, nor ambition, nor envy. It is the loss of faith, which being not only a divinely infused gift, but a moral habit, follows the laws of all moral habits, and shall be judged accordingly.

On these two texts, Novatian of Rome, urged on by Novatus of Carthage, established his false system. He maintained that "after baptism, there is no room for penitence; that the Church cannot pardon mortal sin further; that she herself perishes by the very receiving of sinners[b]." He denied the commission of the priesthood to pardon and absolve, the right use of ecclesiastical discipline, and the power of the keys. Nay, he went so far as to say that those who had fallen into apostacy, had no more hope of salvation, and could not be restored, even after penance[c]. The occasion of the separation of the Novatians from the Church was that they would not communicate with those who had fallen in the Decian persecution. In all other respects they held the true doctrine, though they mocked at the martyrs, and re-baptized those

[b] S. Pac. Ep. iii.
[c] Tillemont, *Mémoires pour Servir*, &c., vol. iii. p. 472.

who joined their sect. It is probable that the author of the *Philosophumena* was of this school, and the Church historian Socrates shews great sympathy for it. Their orders were recognised in the sense that their bishops on being reconciled were received as bishops. They died out in the seventh century. The last mention of them as existent is about the year A.D. 672.

But at the Reformation the same texts suggested another phase of error. One extreme form of Calvinism was that the saints can never fall away. The doctrine of final perseverance, coupled with the doctrine of a capricious election, necessarily resulted in this; and although many good people merely found in a speculative view of this kind a sense of comforting assurance, it cannot be doubted that, in the case of some of the fierce sectaries in Germany, Holland, and England, during the Commonwealth, the most fearful excesses were committed under the cloak of this dangerous error. We all know that it was the anodyne which soothed the perturbed deathbed of Oliver Cromwell.

Now, for the sake of correctness, the first step is to define what sin is; secondly, to describe its effect; thirdly, to illustrate its relation to Baptism; and lastly, to dwell upon sin committed after Baptism.

1. Sin is variously defined as "an act, deviating from what is ordered for the end of man, contrary to the rule of nature, or of reason, or of eternal law [d]:" or negatively, it is "every defect in action which implies

[d] S. Thos. 1ᵐᵃ. qu. 63, 1.

violation of order;" " it is the death of the soul by the withdrawal of grace ; it is to fall away from good, and therefore every defect in duty is of the nature of sin ; it is to neglect the next world for this ; it is anything said, done, or desired against the eternal law ; it is the breaking of the law of God ; the will to retain or to follow what justice forbids.

It is contrary to the nature of the human mind in its integrity, but according to the nature of the human mind in its fall. It is twofold, that of omission and that of commission ; which last is subdivided into sin of thought, of word, and of deed.

2. Next, as to the effect of sin. The soul of man, turning away from its eternal, uncreated, and incommutable good, converting itself and cleaving to temporal, created, and commutable goods, loses a twofold lustre, which it formerly possessed. One, the refulgence of the natural light of reason ; the other, the refulgence of the supernatural light of the Divine wisdom and grace. This loss of lustre is the *macula animæ*, the stain of the soul ; and it remains in the soul till by a retrogressive motion of the will the man returns to the light of reason and the Divine law, which he does by grace. In the case of mortal sin, by a fresh infusion of habitual grace ; and in the case of venial sin, which, however, does not really stain the soul, by any act of that habitual grace which it has not destroyed.

The act of aversion from the Creator, an inordinate conversion to the creature, constitutes the *culpa peccati*, the guilt of sin: mortal, if aversion ; venial, if conversion.

The punishment of sin, *pœna peccati*, is proportioned to both. The punishment of a mortal sin, that sin as an aversion from the Infinite and Eternal, being itself also infinite, must be infinite and eternal. The punishment of a venial sin, that sin being but an inordinate conversion to the temporal and finite, and so itself temporal and finite, requires to be but temporal and finite. The act of guilt may have passed away, the lustre of the soul may have been renewed, and so its stain removed, and yet the liability to punishment may remain to restore the balance and satisfy the demands of justice.

Venial and original sin are visited, the one with the pain of sense, *pœna sensus,* the other with the pain of loss, *pœna damni;* mortal sin with both.

Punishment must be—1. contrary to the will; 2. afflictive; 3. inflicted by reason of guilt. And it may be 1. satisfactory; 2. remedial; or, 3. simply penal [e].

It has ever been held that the Sacrament of Baptism is the specially ordained rite whereby the grace of God, working in the power of the Passion of our Lord, destroys and takes away all sins, past and present. It removes in all, equally the entire guilt of sin, and all necessity of future penitence. The baptized person is wholly a new creature in Christ Jesus. It also acts as a check upon future sin in the way of prevention [f]. Baptism is principally ordained as a remedy against original sin [g]. It at once takes away its penal-

---

[e] S. Thomas, 1ma. 2^{dæ}. qu. 86.   [f] 3 p. q. 67, 3 c. q. 68, 2, 2. m. 3, 3.

[g] 3 q. 66, 9, c.f.

ties and its infection so far as the individual is concerned, but not so far as the nature is concerned, save only in the end[h]. It cleanses the flesh from all pollution, contracted so far as regards the individual, but not so far as regards the nature. By it the stains of sin, *culpa*, are washed out, the fire of its incentive mitigated by grace; but this fire is not wholly quenched in the present life. Baptism absolves us from all penalty, so far as that penalty is inflicted by God, but it does not take away penalty so far as inflicted by man.

3. The fall from the supernatural state, the return to sin after this complete cleansing, the re-engagement in the service of the powers of darkness, the deliberate choice of the will in opposition to the will of God, the ingratitude to the best and kindest of Fathers, who has translated us out of darkness into the kingdom of His dear Son, is surely very grievous. Of necessity the sins of Christians, being sins against grace and light, are infinitely more heinous than those of the heathen. Grace done despite to, conscience violated, the deliberate choice of evil rather than God's law, are bound up in the idea of post-baptismal sin.

So strongly was this felt in the fourth and fifth centuries, that men were apt to put off their baptism until the hour of death. There are various canons to prevent this vicious practice. All this illustrates how deeply the thought of the danger of violating the baptismal obligations had penetrated into the consciousness of the Christian community.

<hr>

[h] 1, 2. q. Art. 5, 31, 32.

But here there was danger of running into excess. Several of the early heresies erred in the direction of over-strictness; especially the Novatians, against whom this Article is primarily directed. To doubt the grace and mercy of God is most unpleasing to Him. The very Gospel, by its terms, is a Gospel of reconciliation and forgiveness. God is ever more ready to hear than we to pray, and is wont to give more than either we desire or deserve. The freest, the fullest forgiveness is held forth to us for the sake of the Death and Passion of our Lord and only Saviour Jesus Christ, and there is no sin that we can now commit which, if sincerely repented, can resist the effect of His atoning Blood. Therefore, while the Church would seek to deepen within us the sense of the malignity of the deliberate sins of Christians, she assures us that "not every deadly sin committed after Baptism is unpardonable, or sin against the Holy Ghost."

Besides this statement of doctrine, we may observe certain corollaries from the structure and doctrine of the Article. 1. The expression 'deadly sin' implies the distinction between deadly and venial sin, with all the consequences of that distinction. 2. The very denial that sin after baptism is the sin against the Holy Ghost, refutes the notions of those who would reduce the Sacrament of Baptism to a mere admission into the visible Church. Were it such, no person could ever have supposed post-baptismal sin to be so terrible. The heinousness of its dishonour, is the measure of the greatness of its efficacy. That must be a very high state of grace indeed, which could involve such a result from its violation. 3. Observe the metonymy. After speaking of the fall after baptism in the negative form,—the grant of repentance is not to be denied to those who fall after baptism,—the same proposition is enumerated positively, and in so doing, baptism is said to be "receiving the Holy Ghost." In the Article, "receiving the Holy Ghost" is equivalent to "being baptized." It is true that some of the Reformers took an exaggerated view on this point, since, according to them, the power of regeneration worked no extirpation of sin, the original and carnal sin, as such, remaining in them; it follows that sin does not dissolve the state of grace received in baptism, or break the fellowship with Christ. Baptism thus not only imparted the assurance that all our sins committed before baptism were remitted, but gave the pledge of the remission of sins hereafter to be committed.

Now the true doctrine of repentance is taught not only in these Articles, but in the Commination Service: " Let us return unto the Lord our God with all *contrition* and meekness of heart: bewailing and lamenting our sinful life, acknowledging and *confessing* our offences, and seeking to bring forth worthy fruits of *penance*[1]."

Observe the italicized words. They divide the process into three, the contrition of the heart, the confession of the mouth, and the worthy fruits of penance

[1] Commination Service.

as the satisfaction of the life; and this is in accordance
not only with the teaching of the Church, but with the
deepest necessities of human nature.

1. Repentance cannot spring from the mere fear of
hell torments. This is not the only path that leads
men back to God. We must take a high view of what
we are to Christ, and what Christ is to us, and from
this thought must spring the emotion which brings
us back to Him. Faith and confidence must precede
repentance, and from these, hatred to sin and a faint
love of God is unfolded. Attrition, as the sorrow for
the consequences of sin, is only an incitement to repentance; it requires something more, namely, contrition,—a profound detestation of sin springing from
an awakened love of God, with the determination never
wilfully to sin again.

2. But repentance rests not there. What is interior
must be outwardly expressed; as our inward love to
Christ is outwardly manifested in acts of charity to His
poor, so our deep inward energetic contrition will seek
an external manifestation in confession. A reconciliation between two friends cannot take place without
mutual avowals, and this avowal must be definite. So
when we confess our sins, it must not be a vague declaration of our sinfulness, but a specific, definite detail
of our transgressions—to Christ, or His anointed servant.
Yet on the other hand, it must be recollected that
perfect contrition takes the place of all outward ordinances.

3. But this is not all; if, in confession, internal

repentance is manifested, the Church acts back on the offender by the claim of satisfaction. It may refer either to the past or to the future. 1. If a man has offended human justice, he must make restitution either to the sufferers, or if that is impossible, in the way indicated by his spiritual adviser. 2. As regards the future, satisfaction becomes medicinal, in short, a strengthening remedy to restore the power of the soul debilitated by sin. Yet this is not all, penitential exercises must be looked on also as real punishment. By sin man contracts a debt which he is quite unfit to pay. Christ has paid it, and to all who enter into real living communion with Him the debt is remitted; but it is not God's will to remit the temporal consequences of the penitent's previous acts, and justice requires the imposition of those penalties, especially in believers who, having been made members of His Body by baptism, have received grace both to perceive what they ought to do, and strength and power to perform it. All this is the work of Christ. By this His merits are in no ways infringed upon. All our satisfactions must be done in Him. We who of ourselves, as of ourselves, can do nothing, in Him who strengtheneth us, can do all things. Therefore all our glory is in the cross of our Lord Jesus Christ, in Whom we live and move, and have our being.

Although the errors against which the Article was directed have passed away, yet something similar has lately reproduced itself in Plymouthism. While one cannot fail to respect every effort at the restoration of

Pentecostal simplicity, and respect those who in view of the salvation of their souls withdraw themselves from the world into a stricter community, it must be recollected that many of the heresies of the early Church sprang from an attempt to be stricter than the Church of God. Montanism, Novatianism, and Donatism, are special instances of this, and therefore the same laws which guided the Church in her treatment of these errors apply now. No doubt the best confutation of such errors lies in orthodox Christians leading daily stricter lives, for the cause of the uprise of these errors is the laxity of the Church; God scourging His own Elect by those exaggerations of suppressed truth and neglected practices, which constitute the peculiarity of such sectaries as we describe.

The rise of Plymouthism may be traced 1. to the worldly lives of those who profess the doctrines of the Church, and 2. to the neglect of preaching the Counsels of Perfection. Did a more simple and charitable habit of life prevail, we should not have those attempts at Communism and equality, which must be bad for master, and worse for servant; neither should we have such a condition of mind as is implied by such propositions as the following :—

1. All that are sanctified are so perfect, that there is no room for confession of sin.

2. Because we are saved by faith and by grace, a pure and holy life is not necessary that we should attain to glory.

3. Because our Lord has delivered us by His Resur-

rection, therefore we ought not to pray for deliverance from His wrath. Because the believer has passed from death unto life, we ought no longer to pray for deliverance in the hour of death and at the day of judgment.

4. Because peace is the essential privilege of the believer, it is superfluous to pray for peace; because we are saved, it is wrong to ask God to make speed to save us; because God hath made such meet to be partakers of the inheritance of the saints in light, we may not pray in the language of the *Te Deum* "make them to be numbered with Thy saints."

5. For that God hath granted unto the Gentiles repentance unto life, we ought not to pray for repentance.

6. All prayer for the Holy Spirit is superfluous, because already given.

All these propositions spring from the confusion of thought which mixes up the Objective with the Subjective in the work of man's salvation. God on His part, by the manifestation of His dear Son, has supplied a satisfaction, superabundant enough to take away the sins of ten thousand worlds. Nothing is wanting to that entire and complete redemption. Hereby the hopes of glory are held forth to every child of Adam. Jesus is our only Hope, our only Refuge, our Treasure, our End, our All. But now comes another thought. We are free agents, free to choose evil and good, under certain limitation. Life is a trial, in which they only shall be crowned who strive. All will not be saved, though our Lord died for all. All may be saved, because our Lord died for all. It depends upon the way in which we respond to the grace of God, whether we be saved or not. God gives sufficient grace to all, but grace does not obliterate free-will, rather it strengthens and elevates it.

To answer then the six propositions, one must say,—

1. That our Lord has indeed perfected those that are sanctified, but sanctification is a progressive act, day by day, through God's grace, increasing till we come to the perfect man, to the measure of the stature of the fulness of Christ; and the more we are sanctified, the more humble we necessarily become; and the more humble we become, the more we see ourselves as the All Pure One sees us, the more in the spirit of lowliness shall we be able to rejoice in saying in deed and in truth that there is no health in us, and be thrown more and more on the resources of prayer.

2. The descriptions of the awards of the last day shew us that heaven is a reward, the reward of a holy life. We cannot merit heaven without the grace of God, but God crowns His own work within us with the gift of Eternal Life.

3. The act of our Lord's Resurrection has delivered us from the wrath to come, has caused our justification, and has opened the kingdom of heaven to all believers; but we must still pray for deliverance, for what God has predestinated to give to each of us, He hath willed shall be obtained through the instrumentality of prayer and the Sacraments. Pity that poor soul, who, when

the death-sweat is on his brow, and the world failing him, can find no comfort in a prayer for deliverance to Him who alone is mighty to save.

4 and 5. This goes on the assumption that the believer cannot forfeit peace. When one sees the faults of the best around us, faults that in the sight of God are grievous sins, one is amazed that any frame of mind can exist, in which daily repentance is not exercised, daily restoration of the measure of grace lost by frailties, not implored.

6. This is the most marvellous of all the logical results of the system. If there be diversities of gifts, but the same spirit,—if there be no possible condition of the spiritual man from the first groan of attrition to the most extatic realization of the Presence of God, which is not caused, and may not be increased, by God the Holy Ghost,—to pray for His *charismata*, and to His Person, is the duty of every Christian at all times. It is the error of the sect that the state of grace cannot be increased, being perfect. Alas! what is the best perfection of man when measured and weighed by the standard of Him who charges the angels with folly!

ARTICLE XVII.

De Præstinatione et Electione.

Prædestinatio ad vitam, est æternum Dei propositum, quo ante jacta mundi fundamenta, suo consilio, nobis quidem occulto, constanter decrevit, eos quos in Christo elegit ex hominum genere, a maledicto et exitio liberare, atque (ut vasa in honorem efficta) per Christum ad æternam salutem adducere. Unde qui tam præclaro Dei beneficio sunt donati, illi spiritu ejus opportuno tempore operante, secundum propositum ejus vocantur, vocationi per gratiam parent, justificantur gratis, adoptantur in filios Dei, unigeniti ejus filii Jesu Christi imagini efficiuntur conformes, in bonis operibus sancte ambulant, et demum ex Dei misericordia pertingunt ad sempiternam felicitatem.

Quemadmodum prædestinationis et electionis nostræ in Christo pia consideratio, dulcis, suavis, et ineffabilis consolationis plena est, vere piis, et his qui sentiunt in se vim Spiritus Christi, facta carnis, et membra, quæ adhuc sunt super terram, mortificantem, animumque ad cœlestia et superna rapientem; tum quia fidem nostram de æterna salute consequenda per Christum plurimum stabilit atque confirmat, tum quia amorem nostrum in Deum, vehementer accendit: Ita hominibus curiosis, carnalibus, et Spiritu Christi destitutis, ob oculos perpetuo versari prædestinationis Dei sententiam, perniciosissimum est præcipitium unde illos diabolus protrudit, vel in desperationem, vel in æque perniciosam impurissimæ vitæ securitatem. Deinde promissiones divinas sic amplecti oportet, ut nobis in sacris literis generaliter propositæ sunt, et Dei voluntas in nostris actionibus ea sequenda est, quam in verbo Dei habemus diserte revelatam.

" Of Predestination and Election.

" Predestination to life is the everlasting purpose of God, whereby (before the foundations of the world were laid) He hath constantly decreed by His counsel, secret to us, to deliver from curse and damnation those whom He hath chosen in Christ out of mankind, and to bring them by Christ to everlasting salvation, as vessels made to honour. Wherefore they which be endued with so excellent a benefit of God, be called, according to God's purpose, by His Spirit working in due season : they through grace obey the calling : they be justified freely : they be made sons of God by adoption : they be made like the image of His only-begotten Son, Jesus Christ : they walk religiously in good works, and at length, by God's mercy, they attain to everlasting felicity.

" As the godly consideration of predestination, and our election in Christ, is full of sweet, pleasant, and unspeakable comfort to godly persons, and such as feel in themselves the working of the Spirit of Christ, mortifying the works of the flesh, and their earthly members, and drawing up their mind to high and heavenly things, as well because it doth greatly establish and confirm their faith of eternal salvation, to be enjoyed through Christ, as because it doth fervently kindle their love towards God : so, for curious and carnal persons, lacking the Spirit of Christ, to have continually before their eyes the sentence of God's predestination, is a most dangerous downfall, whereby the devil doth thrust them either into desperation, or into wretchlessness of most unclean living, no less perilous than desperation.

"Furthermore, we must receive God's promises in such wise as they be generally set forth to us in Holy Scripture. And in our doings, that will of God is to be followed, which we have expressly declared unto us in the Word of God."

The educated thought of the nineteenth century, with some notable exceptions, is content to recognise the existence of the truths of the perfect knowledge and power of God on the one hand, and of the freedom of the human will on the other, and to sit down contentedly under the utter impossibility of reconciling them.

> " La contingenza, che fuor del quaderno
>   Della vostra materia non si stende,
>   Tutta e depinta nel cospetto eterno.
>   Necessità però quindi non prende
>   Se non come dal viso, in che si specchia
>   Nave, che per torrente giù discende*."

The question is now taken out of the region of pure intellect, and relegated into that of morals; in other words,. the truths are looked upon now only in a practical point of view. How do their co-existence and

* Par. xvii. 40.

mutual modification tell upon the life? Does a disproportionate estimate of the first of these factors deny or cripple the notion of human exertion? Does the undue influence of the second, destroy that abiding rest in the Creator, which is one of the first principles of nature and of revealed religion?

But it was not so at the time of the Reformation. Both the good side and the bad side of that event tended to throw the thoughts of men disproportionately on the Divine side of the work in man's salvation. If the great gain of the Reformation was that men were won from an undue trust in the external practices of religion, from the belief that doing certain acts, in themselves would secure man's salvation; it was natural that in reaction men should throw themselves exclusively on the thought of God's work in them, to the exclusion of all co-operation of man. On the other hand, if the loss at the Reformation, especially on the Continent, was the faith in the Church as an institution, as the one ordinary channel of God's grace, as the appointed harbour of souls, it followed that a new law of mercy must be found, a new theory of salvation, and that was sought in a theory of absolute predestination.

A reasoning on the nature and attributes of God, certain texts of St. Paul, and the great authority of St. Augustine in the Western Church, combined to familiarize men's minds with the thought of a certain predestination in the Divine mind, whereby those are set free who are set free. It was God's will that all men should be saved; yet all, as a matter of fact, are not saved. How was such a state of things as this to be accounted for?

The question was answered diversely. One school held that there could be no limitation to the power of God, that whatever He willed He must will efficaciously, and therefore, seeing that all men are not saved, it could not be His purpose that all men should be saved. The other school held that God willed that all men should be saved, but leaving man's will in some sense free to choose good or evil, his final salvation was the reward of those good deeds which God predestined him to do.

" The Church," says Möhler [b], speaking of the enticing field opened to human speculation on the subject of predestination, " has deemed it her duty to set certain limitations to this spirit. For God can be exhibited in such wise over-against man as to make him entirely disappear; or man again may be conceived in such a position relating to God, as to subvert the notion of the Almighty as the dispenser of grace. According to the first view, God appears also to act with a cruel caprice, which cannot be conceived by man : according to the second, so to be ruled by the caprice of man, that He ceases to be He who is, and through whom all goodness flows. Accordingly the Catholic Church alike rejects an overruling of God on the part of man, to impart sanctifying and saving grace; and an overruling of man, on the part of God, to compel the former to become this or that. On the contrary, she

[b] Symbolism, vol. i. p. 137.

teaches, in the former case, that Divine grace is unmerited ; in the latter, that it is offered to all men, their condemnation depending on the free rejection of redeeming aid."

Calvin expresses himself thus :—" We assert that by an eternal and unchangeable decree God hath determined whom He shall one day permit to have a share in eternal felicity, and whom He shall doom to destruction. In respect of the elect, the decree is founded in His unmerited mercy, without any regard to human worthiness: but those whom He delivers up to damnation, are by a just and irreprehensible judgment excluded from all access to eternal life." " It is scarcely credible to what truly blasphemous shifts Calvin resorts in order to impart to his doctrine an air of solidity, and to secure it against objections. As faith is by him considered a gift of the Divine mercy, and yet, as he is unable to deny, that many are represented in the Gospel to be believers, in whom Christ found no earnestness and no perseverance, and whom consequently He did not recognise to be the elect, Calvin asserts that God intentionally produced within them an apparent faith; that He insinuated Himself into the souls of the reprobate, in order to render them less excusable [c]. Instead of acknowledging in the above facts the readiness of the Almighty to confer His grace on all who only wish it, he explains them by the supposition of intentional deceit, which he lays to the charge of the Almighty. Equally strange is the reason assigned

[c] Instit., lib. iii. c. 2. n. 11.

for the doctrine of predestination. That God wishes to manifest His mercy towards the elect, His justice towards the condemned; as if the two Divine qualities were separated from each other, and mutually ignored each other. God will be at once just and merciful to all without exception; not just merely to these, and merciful only to those, as prejudiced judges in this world are wont to be. We must also bear in mind that even the notion of justice, considered in itself, cannot be upheld where no fault exists; and no fault can be charged to the reprobate, if without possessing the use of freedom they are condemned from all eternity. Equally baseless would be the notion of mercy, as it has necessarily for its object sinners who, by free determination of their own will, and accordingly not by extraneous compulsion, have transgressed the Divine moral law, in order thereupon to receive pardon; for in this case the whole process would be a mere absurd farce [d]."

Now the moderation and cautiousness of the Article is a remarkable contrast to this language [e]. As a matter of history we know that the Article never contented the Puritans. The very fact of the attempt to ingraft the Lambeth Articles in the present code, during the

[d] Möhler, Symb., vol. i. p. 140.

[e] The very history of the process of the construction of the present Article is significant. In the earlier Articles of Edward VI. we find the formula, " licet praedestinationis decreta sint nobis ignota;" and in the curious documents preserved in C.C.C., Cambridge, and published by Dr. Lamb, we find these words, as they occur in the latter part of the draft copy of the Article, actually erased by the minium pencil of Matthew Parker.

time of the dominance of the Calvinistic party at the beginning of the seventeenth century, is a proof of this.   In fact, the Article is Augustinian, and not Calvinistic.

In treating of this tremendous mystery, the Article keeps itself closely to the word of Scripture.   It first states the fact of a predestination in the divine mind, very much in the language of St. Paul: " According as He hath chosen us in Him before the foundation of the world, that we may be holy and without blame before Him in love: having predestinated us unto the adoption by Jesus Christ Himself, according to the good pleasure of His will, to the praise and glory of His grace, wherein He hath made us accepted in the beloved ʳ."   It then goes on, still in Biblical language, to describe the processes which attend on this predestination: 1. vocation, 2. obedience to vocation through grace, 3. free justification, 4. sonship by adoption, 5. conformity to the image of our Lord, 6. a religious life, and 7. finally eternal felicity.   " For whom He did foreknow, He did also predestinate to be conformed to the image of His Son, that He might be the First-born among many brethren.   Moreover, whom He did predestinate, them He also called: and whom He called, them He also justified: and whom He justified, them He also glorified ˢ."   Having done its duty to Biblical truth by stating almost in its own words the doctrine and its way of working, the Article goes on through the rest of its clauses to guard men against its abuse.

ʳ Eph. i. 4.   ˢ Rom. viii. 29.

While all God's truth, and this among others, tends to comfort, there is the double danger of desperation and recklessness, to be guarded against in the case of bad men. As a matter of fact, we know that, at the time of the Reformation, when men's minds ran in an undue degree upon these abstract subjects, these two opposite results actually did occur; and the immoral condition of the peasantry in Scotland, where notions of predestination are much exaggerated, may be adduced in confirmation of the necessity of the caution expressed in the Article. The Article concludes with two canons of interpretation of Holy Writ, also with a view to correcting the abuses of this mystery; 1. that God's promises are to be received *generaliter*, that is, as applying to all; and 2. the will of God that is expressly declared in Holy Scripture is to be followed: and that will is "that all men should be saved, and come unto the knowledge of the truth [h];" "that the Gospel should be preached to every creature [i];" "that God sent His Son, that the world through Him might be saved [k];" and "that all who are weary and heavy laden, should come to the Lord Christ for rest [l]."

> "O Predestinazion, quanto remota
>   E la radice tua de quegli aspetti:
>   Che la prima cagion non veggion tota!
>   E voi, mortali, tenetevi stretti
>   A guidicar: chè noi, che Dio vedemo,
>   Non conosciam ancor tutti gli Eletti:

[h] 1 Tim. ii. 4.   [i] St. Mark xvi. 15.

[k] St. John iii. 17.   [l] St. Matt. xi. 28.

> Et enne dolce così fatto scemo,
> Perchè 'l ben nostro in questo ben s'affina
> Chè quel, che vuole Dio e noi volemo."

In order to avoid inconsistency, no interpretation of this Article can be the right one which is at variance with the statements in Article XXXI., "that the offering of Christ is that perfect redemption, propitiation, and satisfaction for *all* sins of the *whole world*, both original and actual;" and in Article V., "that eternal life is offered to *mankind* in Christ;" and in Article XI., "that Christ is the Lamb who, by the sacrifice of Himself, should take away the sins of the *world*." We are therefore compelled to reconcile what is here said of predestination with the truth taught elsewhere of the universality of the effect of the death of Christ. Hence the Calvinistic notion, which confines the benefit of our Lord's death to certain individuals, is not the right interpretation of the Article. God's predestination is bestowed on every baptized Christian. "It is the good will of our heavenly Father declared towards" each such baptized. The fact of God bringing men to baptism is synonymous with His choosing them in Christ out of mankind — with His calling them according to His purpose by His special working in due season. In baptism they become "His own children by adoption," in the very words of the Article[m]. Thus God's predestination is in one sense His pledge

[m] The Church prays for the child about to be baptized, that it may ever "*remain* in the number of" His "faithful and elect children." —(Public Baptism of Infants.)

of the gift of sufficient grace, and so the consideration of such a predestination is full of most pleasant and unspeakable comfort to those who are conscientiously using that grace. It says, in exact opposition to Calvinism, that God will not act in a tyrannical, arbitrary way, but according to His mingled justice and mercy; that we may comfort ourselves in the thought of His predestination for us, His preparation of good things in store for us, with full assurance and trust, only never leaving out of sight, that, as a result of our free-will, we may make vain all that He has put in our power.

And so with regard to the salvation of others, we are not called on to judge any. "God's ways are not as our ways," and "many shall come from the East and from the West, and shall sit down with Abraham, and Isaac, and Jacob; and the children of the kingdom shall be shut out."

Of the practical effect of Calvinism, it remains for me to speak; its power as a dominant idea cannot be gainsayed. If the value of a religion be the measure of assurance which it can bestow, we have here that assurance held out to us in its most positive form. According to the Westminster Confession, man, by the hearing of preaching, receives the soul-saving faith, that he from all eternity is one of the elect; and that God will impart to him, as if himself had rendered it, the obedience of Christ. This unfading assurance of salvation is never lost, though transitory doubts and obscurities may for a time arise. He believes that he is under the power of irresistible grace, the consistent result of which is, that, whereinsoever he fails, it is God's fault, not his. If he sin, he is still one of the elect, and irrevocably in a state of grace, just as happened to David. By such sins the certainty of· salvation may be shaken and obscured, but the life of faith and seed of God is never entirely lost to the believer. Man being the passive instrument of God's will, the measure of which is the free agency of man, whereby he admits it, a very deep sense of the awful sinfulness of sin, and its terrible consequences, in itself, comes necessarily to be weakened.

Again, it tends to destroy all belief in Sacramental Grace. Without pushing the doctrine to its fatalistic consequences, which would destroy belief in all grace whatsoever save itself, this teaching, though held inconsistently together with other truths, tends to hurt the belief in the Sacraments; for with it there is no place for Sacraments in the divine order of the Church. A Calvinist cannot look upon Baptism as of any vital importance, if man's salvation depends on an irrespective election; for he will not grant that grace reaches any but the elect, and as all are not elect, there are many who are baptized who never receive grace. Grace may be given, but, according to this view, grace is not necessarily linked to the Sacrament, even when (as in the case of infants) there can be no hindrance to the reception of that grace on the part of the receiver. If there is an inner circle of election within the great body of the baptized, baptism can be of no real value, and its continued use is illogical, continued merely out of deference to the letter of Scripture, and to an instinct of piety, which corrects the logic of the mind.

So with regard to the Blessed Eucharist. A belief in a real Presence of Christ cannot co-exist with a theory of irrespective predestination, and of its consequence, irresistible grace. For if the Body and Blood of Christ, and the grace of Christ therewith, were given through the Sacraments, then since grace, according to them, is irresistible, it would necessarily overpower all who received the Sacrament; which is patently contrary to what Holy Scripture says of those who "eat and drink damnation to themselves," and to what we cannot fail to see with our own eyes in the case of careless and indevout receivers. The presence of Christ must then, according to them, not be in the Sacrament, but in the believing recipient; and that, in a way not peculiar to the Sacrament, nor in any way higher than that, in which any devout Christian may at any time, mentally and spiritually feed on Christ. As it is only to the elect that the Divine gift is imparted, and the rest are passed over by God, so grace must by no means be connected with the visible sign.

ARTICLE XVIII.

DE SPERANDA ÆTERNA SALUTE TANTUM IN NOMINE CHRISTI.

*SUNT et illi anathematizandi, qui dicere audent unum-
quemque in lege aut secta quam profitetur esse servan-
dum, modo juxta illam, et lumen naturæ accurate vix-
erit, cum sacræ literæ tantum Jesu Christi nomen præ-
dicent, in quo salvos fieri homines oporteat.*

" Of obtaining eternal Salvation only by the Name of Christ.

" THEY also are to be had accursed, that presume to
say, that every man shall be saved by the law or sect
which he professeth, so that he be diligent to frame his
life according to that law, and the light of nature.
For Holy Scripture doth set out unto us only the
name of Jesus Christ, whereby men must be saved."

The provisional attitude of the Church of England
is exhibited in the remarkable fact that she has generally avoided enforcing her teachings under the penalty
of anathema. Unlike the general and provincial Councils,—which, not content with defining the truth, have
guarded that truth by anathema, in which anathema
lies the essence of what is to be guarded against, and

per contra, what is to be believed,—the Church of England has in the main been contented with stating her convictions, insisting on subscription to them as a condition of ministering at her altars, but has not gone so far as to brand the non-reception of her teaching with spiritual denunciations. If the conjecture is right that in 1562 the door of reconciliation was purposely left ajar, the wisdom and charity of such a course as this is evident. To have to retract anything is difficult for man or Church; to explain is what the most sensitive conscience can condescend to. Besides, in avoiding anathematisms, a fertile source of irritation is obviously avoided. We are not disposed to be conciliatory to those who have expressed themselves in the sense that our errors peril our immortal welfare.

But there is one remarkable exception to this moderation, and it is that which is the subject of the present Article. The Church of England anathematizes one error, one spiritual sin, the sin of latitudinarianism; and this, because the latitudinarian spirit finds its logical basis in the abnegation of all objective truth whatsoever. Latitudinarianism is not a tender judgment of the motives of others. It is not a disposition to find excuses, as from the imperfect demonstration of the truth to individuals, inveterate prejudice, peculiarities of intellectual training, or the like, with which it regards the erring. It is the principle that nothing is so certain in religion that it need be insisted on; that one view is as good as another view; that it does not much matter what people believe, if their morals be good; in short, that there are no truths for which a man ought to be prepared to die, no revealed will of God, to deflect from which, is ruin to the spiritual nature.   In the presence of latitudinarianism, Church authority obviously disappears, Creeds are necessarily mistakes, Holy Scripture becomes an instrument on which one may play any tune, certainty as to religion vanishes.

Latitudinarianism is the logical consequence of the denial of a Divine authority, lodged in the Church, although many by a happy inconsistency, who have denied that authority, have stopped short of this consequence.   There have ever been bigotry and persecution on the part of those whose position made bigotry absurd, and persecution a sin.   When once the divine authority of the Church is given up, there is no reasonable alternative but the human authority of the individual.   It may be sought to uphold conclusively another divine authority, that of the Holy Scriptures, a process which actually took place, but experience has shewn that this also resolves itself into the judgment of the individual; the Holy Word of God, as a fact, having been differently understood, so that " private judgment" appeals, in fact, to the individual's, enlightened or unenlightened, interpretation of that word.

Closely connected with this, one must consider the cognate question of the practice of the Christian Church to enforce certain truths under pain of anathema.   The popular English form of this question exhibits itself in the defence or reprobation of the damnatory clauses in the Athanasian Creed. It is said, "Why impose a complex formula on the most recondite subjects upon the conscience under so tremendous a censure?" In answer it must be said first of all, that here is no question of those who never heard the name of Christ, nor of those who have not had the truth persuasively and intellectually placed before them, but of those who, having the dogmas of religion plainly and explicitly taught to them, do perversely set up their judgments against the teaching of God's holy truth, and deliberately reject those truths, on the mental acceptance of which our blessed Lord and His Apostles made salvation, in one sense, to depend. And that such is the case, must be admitted by all who confess the authenticity of the last chapter of St. Mark's Gospel: "He that believeth and is baptized shall be saved; he that believeth not shall be damned." In principle the Athanasian Creed says no more nor no less than this.

The Article then asserts that, in order to attain to everlasting life, it is not sufficient for a man to follow the dictates of his natural conscience. Not only is it asserted that man cannot be saved by the sect or law he professeth, i. e. that there is no objective grace in such law or sect: but it makes the further assertion that the strictest obedience to such a law, though it may obtain temporal rewards, will not affect eternal life: for this reason, that there are certain supernatural gifts which are linked to the manifestation of the Son of God in the flesh. In rigorous justice man has no right as against

God; therefore he has no right to everlasting life[a]. Everlasting life is a free gift to man on the part of God, and He has willed that that gift shall stand connected in the way of cause and effect with the economy of grace. One of the ends of the Incarnation was to open the way to heaven; our access to God is through Christ; and conversely there is no access to God save through Him. The power of His Passion may extend to many who never heard His Name. We have no right to limit the extent of His works, but it must be laid down as a fundamental truth, that whatever grace here or glory hereafter is held forth to sinful man, is held forth in virtue of the merits of the God-man Jesus Christ.

The Article here rises into fervour as it dwells upon the gracious Name of our Saviour, that Name which is as unguent poured out, which whosoever seeketh shall be saved. "He Himself said, 'Except a grain of wheat fall to the ground and die, it abideth alone: but if it die it bringeth forth much fruit.' Let the grain die, and let the corn of the Gentiles spring up. 'It behoved Christ to die and to rise from the dead, and that repentance and remission of sins should be preached in His Name,' not only in Judea but among all people, so that from that one Man, which is Christ, thousands and thousands of believers should be called Christians, and should say, 'Thy Name is as unguent poured out.' O Blessed Name! O unguent everywhere poured out! And whither? From Heaven to Judea, and thence it

[a] Vide *supra*, p. 198.

flows through all the earth, and the Church everywhere says, 'Thy name is as unguent poured out,' not only in Heaven and Earth but even in Hell, for 'at the name of Jesus every knee shall bow, of things in Heaven and things in earth, and things under the earth, and every tongue confess, and say, 'Thy Name is as unguent poured out.' Behold Christ! behold Jesus! Both poured out upon angels, both poured out upon men, and upon those men who, like the brutes, were defiled in their own vileness, God 'saving both man and beast,' 'for His mercy endureth for ever.' How dear! how cheap! cheap, but health-giving! were it not cheap, it would not be poured out for me; if it were not health-giving, it would benefit me nothing. I am a sharer in the Name, yea, of the inheritance. I am a Christian, I am the brother of Christ. If I am what I am called, I am the heir of God and the joint-heir with Christ. And what wonder if the Name of the Bridegroom is poured out, when He Himself is poured out, 'For He humbled Himself, taking upon Himself the form of a servant,' and at last He says, 'I am poured out like water.' The fulness of the Godhead dwelling bodily upon earth is poured out, that all we who bear about with us 'the body of this death' should receive of His fulness, and, filled with the odour of life, should say, 'Thy name is as unguent poured out [b].' "

[b] St. Bernard in Cant., Serm. xv. 4.

ARTICLE XIX.

De Ecclesia.

*Ecclesia Christi visibilis est cœtus fidelium, in quo verbun
Dei purum prædicatur, et sacramenta quoad ea quæ
necessario exigantur, juxta Christi institutum recte ad-
ministrantur. Sicut erravit Ecclesia Hierosolymitana,
Alexandrina, et Antiochena ; ita et erravit Ecclesia Romana, non solum quoad agenda, et cæremoniarum ritus,
verum in his etiam quæ credenda sunt.*

" Of the Church.

" THE visible Church of Christ is a congregation of
faithful men, in the which the pure word of God is
preached, and the sacraments be duly ministered according to Christ's ordinance, in all those things that
of necessity are requisite to the same.

" As the Church of *Jerusalem, Alexandria,* and *Antioch* have erred, so also the Church of *Rome* hath erred,
not only in their living and manner of ceremonies, but
also in matters of faith."

From the beginning, under the name of the Church,
many have understood, in its more restricted sense, the
reunion of those who, believing and professing the faith
of Jesus Christ, are members of the society established
by Him and in Him on earth, in view of salvation. In
its larger sense, it is the society of God's creatures who

have a share on earth in the effects of redemption, or who in heaven have remained faithful to God.

This idea of the Church is expressed in Holy Scripture by figures setting forth its nature and destiny ; as " the kingdom of God," " the city of God," " the house of God ;" but the most sacred and mysterious conception is that of St. Paul, " the Body of Christ [a]."

The first notion with regard to the Church is its visibility. This is in accordance with the teaching of the early Church. It is a light [b], the city set upon a hill [c]. It is the visible means whereby we attain to Christ who is invisible [d], whereby we keep His life in ourselves, whose pattern we have no longer before our eyes [e].

" The ultimate reason of the visibility of the Church is to be found in the Incarnation of the Divine Word. Had that Word descended into the hearts of men, without taking the form of a servant, and accordingly without appearing in a corporeal shape, then only an internal invisible Church would have been established. But since the Word became *flesh*, it expressed itself in an outward perceptible and human manner. It spoke as man to man, and suffered and worked after the fashion of men, in order to win them to the kingdom of God, so that the means selected for the attain-

---

[a] Klee, *Histoire des Dogmes Chrétiens*, i. 76. [b] S. Iren. v. 20. n. 1. *S. Cypr. de Unit.* [c] S. Chrys. *in Jes. Hom.* ii. n. 3 ; S. Aug. *Unit.*, c. xvi. n. 40; *Cont. Litt. Petiliani*, ii. 104. n. 239. [d] S. Aug. Serm. 238. 3. [e] Aug. *de Fide Rer. quæ non videntur*, c. iv. n. 7. Klee, *Hist. des Dogmes Chrétiens*, vol. i. p. 94.

ment of this object fully corresponded to the general method of instruction and education determined by the nature and the wants of men. This decided the nature of those means whereby the Son of God, even after He had withdrawn Himself from the eyes of the world, willed still to work in the world and for the world. The Godhead in Christ having put forth its operations under the ordinary way of humanity, the form also in which His work was to be continued, was thereby traced out. The preaching of His doctrine needed then a visible human medium, and must be entrusted to visible envoys, teaching and instructing after the wonted method; men must speak to men, in order to convey to them the Word of God. And as in the world nothing can attain to greatness but in society, so Christ established a community; and His divine Word, His living will, and the love emanating from Him, exerted an internal uniting power upon His followers, so that an impulse implanted by Him in the hearts of believers corresponded to His outward institution. And thus a living, well-connected, visible association of the faithful sprang up, whereof it might be said, There they are, there is His Church, His institution, wherein He continueth to live, His Spirit continueth to work, and the Word uttered by Him eternally resounds. Thus the visible Church, from the point of view here taken, is the Son of God Himself, everlastingly manifesting Himself among men in human form, eternally renewing His youth, the permanent Incarnation of the same, as in Holy Writ the faithful, too, are called the Body of Christ. Hence it is evident that the Church, though composed of men, is yet not purely human; nay, as in Christ the Divinity and the Humanity are clearly to be distinguished, although both are bound in unity; so is He in undivided entireness perpetuated in the Church. The Church, His permanent manifestation, is at once divine and human; she is the union of both. He it is who, concealed under earthly and human forms, works in the Church; and therefore she has a divine and a human side, yet in both undivided; so that the divine cannot be separated from the human, nor the human from the divine. Hence these two sides change their predicates. If the divine, the living Christ and His Spirit, constitute undoubtedly that which is infallible and eternally inerrable in the Church, so also the human is inerrable and infallible in the same way, because the divine without the human has no existence for us; yet the human is not inerrable in itself, but only as the organ and manifestation of the divine [f].

This leads us on to the next term in the definition: "In the Church the pure Word of God is preached, and the Sacraments duly administered."

If Christ the eternal Truth hath built the Church; truth, transformed by the Spirit into love, is become living among men. The Divine truth, embodied in Jesus Christ, must thereby be bodied forth in an outward and living phenomenon, and become a deciding authority if it is to seize deeply on the whole man,

[f] Möhler, *Symbolik*, vol. ii. p. 7.

and put an end to pagan scepticism,—that sinful uncertainty of the mind, which stands on as low a grade
as ignorance [g].   It is, then, the duty of the Church to
preach the pure Word of God; to communicate, on the
authority of God, those truths with regard to the nature
of God and the destinies of creation which He has revealed; to impress upon the intellects of men the true
doctrine of Christ,—by oral instruction, by the development of a school of theology, by symbolical and suggestive rites, by catechetical instruction, by preserving
and interpreting Holy Writ.   Its emphatic office, so
far as regards the intellects of men, is to impress upon
the minds of men an abiding conviction of certain
truths; which truths not merely *lead* to a holy life
here and to salvation hereafter, but of which the
mental acceptance is itself a part of the integral
Christian life, one phase of that supernatural life
which, begun in this life, receives its fulness in the
eternal world.   Thus one department of the Church is
to be the *Ecclesia docens*.   To the hierarchy, as distinguished from the great body of Christians, is committed the duty of handing down and communicating
these truths,—not merely as spiritual nourishment to
those within the fold but also to those without,—to
heathens and strangers, that they may be brought to
share in the supernatural blessings which attach themselves to this blessed γνῶσις.

But this is not all.   When we come to consider the
question of the Sacraments, we shall see that these are

[g] Möhler, vol. ii. p. 12, 15.

the channels whereby the virtue that proceeds from Christ our Head flows into His Body in general, that is, the Church Catholic, and into us the members in particular. From all antiquity the custody of the Sacraments has always been attributed to the Church; in fact, they are among other things *tesseræ* of membership with her. And, given this custody, it is the duty of the Church to administer them. Next to the teaching office of the Church comes the ministerial: next to the appeal to the intellect and heart comes the appeal to the purely spiritual part of the nature, and this is made by the Sacraments. A Sacrament does not appeal to the intellect. It does not move the soul by any intellectual consideration. It only *per accidens* touches the heart. It works solely by virtue of the institution of Christ. It derives its power from Him, nay, in a primary sense He Himself operates in all the Sacraments as the High-Priest of the new law, using the earthly minister as the organ only.

But the Sacraments are so far influenced by the elements of the world that they have their proper matter and form; that is, there are certain conditions that must be observed, very simple ones indeed, but still definite, which go to give validity to each ordinance. Therefore the Article makes it a note of the Church that in it the Sacraments are duly administered according to Christ's ordinance; that all the necessary conditions to a valid Sacrament are observed. Thus there is no true baptism without the water and certain words; the water alone, or the words alone, are not sufficient:

moreover, only certain definite words may be used with profit and effect. So, to a valid consecration of the Holy Eucharist, in addition to a definite matter, that is, bread and wine, and a definite form of words, there must be the action of a priest, episcopally ordained, else the Body of Christ is not consecrated (*conficitur*).

" As the Church of Jerusalem, Alexandria, and Antioch have erred, so also the Church of Rome hath erred, not only in *their* living and manner of ceremonies, but also in matters of faith."

The emphatic word here is *their*. It refers to the human side of the Church, or rather to the individuals in the Church who do not live up to the graces bestowed on them. " The Church as the institution of Christ hath never erred, hath never become wicked, and never loses its energy; which it ever preserves, although the proof may not always be so obvious to the eyes. To exhibit the kingdom of God upon earth, and also to train mankind for the same, she has to deal with men who were all born sinners, and were taken from a more or less corrupt mass. Thus she can never work outside of the sphere of evil; nay, her destination requires her to enter into the midst of evil, and to put her renovating power continually to the test [h]."

Individuals will never " in their living" come up to the perfect ideal, and the moral taint will tell upon the belief. It will affect the acceptance by the intellect of those truths which belong to it, not to grasp, but

[h] Möhler, vol. ii. p. 29.

to yield a reverent submission to. Hence corruption of life will always be correlative to corruption of doctrine, and in proportion as men fail to practise the moral and practical parts of the Christian religion, in that measure will they fail to apprehend those delicate intuitions which are the fruits of a true faith. A man who lives as though there were no retribution, though he may in words acknowledge what the Creed says on the subject, can, in only a most imperfect sense, be said to believe it; and still more will that be the case with regard to the finer truths. Practical love to God will alone enable a man really to believe in the Holy Ghost, the love of the Father and of the Son; and practical righteousness and Christian wisdom alone enable a man to realize the righteousness and wisdom of God.

The Article is then directed against the practical and doctrinal corruptions of " members" of the Church of Rome, and these errors are declared to be similar to the errors in the Churches of Jerusalem, Alexandria, and Antioch. Now by these terms we are not to understand the Jacobite communities which devastate these provinces with the miserable heresy of Eutyches. These, having been cut off from the Church by the Council of Chalcedon, which the Church of England acknowledges, cannot by her be termed in any sense the Churches of those countries. The errors in the Church of Rome, therefore, are compared with any errors of the orthodox and believing remnants that have remained in the East testifying to the faith of Jesus. Now, not only has the Church of England never taken any formal step against the orthodox Eastern Church, but it has always acknowledged the East as a true branch of the Church of Christ, not without many corruptions, the effects of ignorance, and practical deformities, but still honourable and venerable in the highest degree; and therefore the censure here passed upon the members of the Church of Rome must be compatible with this view of the subject. In short, such censure only is intended as was implied in the general cry for reformation which prevailed all through Europe at the time of the publication of the Articles, and which the Council of Trent, partially indeed and imperfectly, but still in a measure actually, tended to correct.

Since no doctrine formerly received by the Orthodox Eastern Patriarchates can be pointed out, which the Church of England can be held to have had in view when it declared that those Patriarchates had erred, then neither, by the force of the terms, is any doctrine formerly received of the Latin Church intended, when it says that the Church of Rome had erred. The two clauses are strictly antithetical, and the same degree of error must be meant in both. It may be that the writers of the Article had in their minds tacitly to protest against the infallibility of the Church of Rome by itself: it may be, that they meant to convey that corruptions had crept into the Roman Church too, which required reformation. But neither statement lies in the words of the Article. All which the Article states is an historical fact as to the past. It says of the Church of Rome that it has erred in time past; "*hath* erred;" as it says of the other Patriarchates that they "*have* erred." The Article binds to nothing more than this fact. Whatever lies beyond it must not be imported into the Article, since it says nothing thereon.

The "living" of the members of the Church of Rome was, unhappily, notoriously bad. If Florence was the Athens, and Venice the Corinth of mediæval Italy, the imperial city and metropolis of the Church did not escape the contaminating influences of the times. Italy was at the head of the civilization and refinement of Europe, and alas, of its wickedness. Macchiavelli had destroyed its political morality. The secession to Avignon, and the great schism, shook the confidence of Europe in the Papal See. The Borgias and Pope Julius were strange vindicators of the spiritual kingdom of Christ. The heathen movement, from Nicholas V.'s time, when the Vatican Library was founded in 1447, and Laurentius Valla began that bright galaxy of scholars which culminated in the time of Leo X., shocked the moral sense of the Church. Complications, caused by the union of the temporal and ecclesiastical powers, such as certain sanitary arrangements in which the moral health of the community was sacrificed to the physical, became scandals. The spirit of paganism pervaded the *Curia Romana*.

Yet, that error should creep into the different Churches, had long been recognised as possible. As early as the days of St. Pacian of Barcelona, who died in extreme old age before A.D. 392, and who represented the mind of St. Cyprian, we read such words as these: "Therefore she (the Church Catholic) is also a fruitful and rich vine, with many branches, and the varied tresses of many a tendril. Look! Are there everywhere large clusters, is every grape full swelled? Have none of these suffered from the winter cold? Have none endured the rough hail? Have none to accuse the burning heat of summer? One bud is studded thicker with shoots; another is stronger; another clearer: one bursts forth into fruit; another only into exuberance of leaves. Yet is she a vine, in every part beautiful [1]." Moreover, sufficient stress has not been laid upon the note of sanctity, and its operation on the organic Church; perhaps because, inasmuch as God only knows those who are His, men prefer to deal with that which is tangible and visible. They therefore appeal, perhaps too exclusively, to the note of unity. And yet surely the same laws affect both. If man's free-will can affect the sanctity of the Church, so it may affect the unity; and the same laws and circumstances that affect the one, may affect the other. The distinction between the objective and subjective in sanctity and unity must be maintained: the one, that wrought by God only; the other, that which is produced by the co-operation of man. Men ever come short of God's gracious purpose with regard to them, and this applies to the Church as well as individuals.

The whole of the latter part of the Article is pro-

[1] Ep. iii. 30, Oxf. Tr. 300.

bably best illustrated by a thoughtful study of the Epistles to the Seven Churches in the Apocalypse. Those words of the Divine Head of the Church—with the exception of those addressed to St. Paul, standing alone in their pre-eminent majesty and significance as the only words spoken by the Son of Man *during the Christian dispensation*—seem to lift the veil of His dealing with the Church, and to shew that the trials, and failings of the local portions of the One Church Ca-. tholic may be widely different in kind, and their consequences diverse in degree.

To those whose strong polemical instincts lead them to be perpetually inclined to " unchurch"—be it the Church of Rome, or be it our own,—it might prove a not unsoothing study to meditate at times upon the patience of our Divine Lord, not only in His Passion, but in His ascended glory, remembering that in the local portions of the Church Catholic, even in the " earliest and purest ages," we find :—" failure of first love ;" " toleration of the doctrine of Balaam ;" " immoral living introduced by a false prophetess ;" " a church which had need to strengthen the things that remain that are ready to die ;" and " lukewarm and self-complacent Laodicea." And yet each and all were then integral portions of the Church Catholic, and the merciful word was still, " I will !"

ARTICLE XX.

DE ECCLESIÆ AUTHORITATE.

[*HABET Ecclesia ritus sive cæremonias statuendi jus, et in fidei controversiis authoritatem; quamvis*] *Ecclesiæ non licet quicquam instituere, quod verbo Dei* [*scripto*] *adversetur, nec unum scripturæ locum sic exponere potest, ut alteri contradicat. Quare licet Ecclesia sit divinorum librorum testis, et conservatrix, attamen ut adversus eos nihil decernere, ita præter illos, nihil credendum de necessitate salutis debet obtrudere.*

" Of the Authority of the Church.

"THE Church hath power to decree rites or ceremonies, and authority in controversies of faith[a]: and yet it is not lawful for the Church to ordain any thing that is contrary to God's Word written, neither may it so expound one place of Scripture that it be repugnant to another. Wherefore, although the Church be a witness and a keeper of Holy Writ, yet, as it ought not to decree any thing against the same, so besides the same ought it not to enforce any thing to be believed for necessity of salvation."

The end of revelation requires a Church, one and visible. The divine truth embodied in Jesus Christ,

---

[a] For the history of the first clause in Article XX., which gave rise to so much discussion in the time of Archbishop Laud, see Collyer's Church History, vol. vi. p. 364—377, and Hardwick's History of the Articles, p. 143.

the eternal Truth, and thereby exhibited in an outward and living phenomenon, is of course a deciding authority; but when He ascended, He left His mystical Body—a society which in its turn should be the living expositor of the truth, and represent Him. " As My Father sent Me, so send I you. I am with you always, even unto the end of the world."

We never can attain to an external authority, like Christ, by purely spiritual means. The attempt would involve a contradiction, which must be disposed of in one of two ways. Either we must renounce the idea that in Christ God manifested Himself in history, to the end that the conduct of men might be permanently determined by Him; or we must learn that fact through a living, definite, vouching fact. Authority must have authority for its medium. Christ established a credible institution, in order to render the true faith in Him perpetually possible. Immediately founded by Him, its existence is the *de facto* proof of what He really was. How doth man attain to the true knowledge of Christ? The Scripture is God's unerring word, but *we* are not exempt from error; we only become so, when we have unerringly received the Word, which in itself is inerrable. In this reception of the Word, human activity, which is fallible, has necessarily a part. But in order that in this transit of the Divine contents of Scripture into the human mind there be no illusion, it is taught that the Holy Spirit supplies, in His union with the human spirit in the Church, a peculiarly Christian tact, and deep sure-guiding feeling.

By confiding attachment to the perpetuated Apostolate, by education in the Church, by "hearing," as St. Paul would say, a deep, interior sense is formed, which alone is fitted for the reception and acceptance of the written Word, because it entirely coincides with the sense in which the Scriptures were composed.

Where misunderstandings as to the meaning of the Divine Word arise, the Church must interpret Holy Scripture. The Church is the Body of the Lord; it is in its universality His visible form, His permanent ever-renovated Humanity, His eternal revelation. He dwells in the community. All His promises and gifts are bequeathed to it, but to no individual, as such, since the days of the Apostles. This general sense is the ἐκκλησιαστικὸν φρόνημα of Eusebius, the *ecclesiastica intelligentia* and *catholicus sensus* of Vincentius Lirinensis. To this sense the interpretation of Holy Writ is entrusted. The declaration which it pronounces on any controverted sense is the judgment of the Church, and therefore the Church is *Judex controversiarum,* an "authority in controversies of faith[b]."

This being so, the first question that suggests itself is the law whereby she is to be the judge of controversies. We have in a previous Article laid down the relations between the Church and Holy Scripture. We have now to add the other great authority which the Church takes as her guide, in expounding

---

[b] Möhler: but the author identifies the *ecclesiasticus sensus* with tradition, which seems incorrect, as tradition is a *definite thing,* the *sensus* the power of judging of that thing.

that Holy Scripture, and which constitutes the second great factor in her decisions. This is Christian Tradition, the concurrent testimony of antiquity, universality, and consent. A doctrine which the Church has received and taught in every age, in every country, and concurrently by all, must be, as agreeable with the Divine Scripture, infallibly true. These two powers, Holy Scripture and ecclesiastical tradition, have historically been the sources from whence men ascertained the truth [c].

But, secondly, inasmuch as the Church is indwelt by God the Holy Ghost, it is no mere concocter of formularies after a mechanical and lifeless fashion; it has been guided to express wisely and rightly the form of faith, and therefore has availed itself of new terms, such as " the consubstantial" rejecting it in the wrong sense, accepting it in the right. And so in later times, in regard to the sacred doctrines of the Natures and Person of our Lord, it exercised the Divine gift in dictating the precise terms whereby man might in

[c] See Dr. Pusey's Sermon on the " Rule of Faith," p. 34. The Fathers at Nicea wrote concerning the Easter, ' *it seemed good* as follows,' for it did seem good that there should be a general compliance; but about the faith they wrote not ' it seemed good,' but ' thus believes the Catholic Church;' and thereupon they confessed how the faith lay, in order to shew that their own sentiments were not novel, but apostolical; and what they wrote down was no discovery of theirs, but is the same as was taught by the Apostles: " so at Chalcedon, in their decree the Bishops are careful to shew that they set forth no other faith than that of the Fathers, that they are not even devising anew aught lacking to the faith, but considering what is useful for the things newly invented by these heretics."

reverence and truth speak of those holy mysteries. But it is not derogatory either to the Church, or to the Office of God the Holy Ghost in her, to maintain that, in some periods, this gift has been less vividly present than at others.

As man is the microcosm of the universe, so the individual, faithful man, is that of the universal Church. As in the individual the faith whereby he believeth unto salvation is, as we have seen, a faith informed and animated by love; and as his faith stands in relation to, and is profoundly affected by his moral nature, (so that love and good works are an integral part of vivid faith, and, correspondingly, faith is quickened by a holy life, and expires under the indulgence of certain sins,) so something of this kind, limited of course by Christ's promise of indefectibility and the Holy Spirit's guidance, must take place in the Church. There must be a similar process. The divine perception of truth will be quickened in the body of the faithful, in periods of revival and refreshment. The eye of the Church will wax dull when the moral state of society, and especially of its teachers, is at the lowest. Is it impious to believe that the Christianizing of the Empire, by increasing the material interests, by silencing the delator's tongue, by bringing into the net plenty of bad fishes, weakened the spirituality of the Church? Is it not in the nature of things, that when the old society, before the fresh blood of the barbarians gave it new youth, was actually dying out, the divine ray should become dimmed by the fetid exhalations from a putrifying civilization? Would the great schism ever have been permitted, had men not lost their sense of the necessity of Christian unity and of the transcendental truths in the Divine nature, on which that Christian unity depends? Surely as under the old law we find a shortening of God's merciful hand caused by the sins of His people, so, even in the dispensation of the Spirit, in the Catholic Church of Christ, we may believe that the depraved use of man's free-will may have worked to the distinct detriment of her teaching office, if faith and works be different aspects of the same habit.

Hence it may have been, in the providence of God, that no heresy arose in those awful times, when "Christ seemed to be fast asleep in the bark, and the ship was covered with waves, and He Himself seemed to allow of the evils which He did not avenge[d]." And we cannot think that it was without His providence that almost all the heresies which could emerge in the great, central doctrines of the Holy Trinity and the Incarnation, (and we might say also as to the grace of God,) did emerge in those first centuries of strong faith and fresh tradition, so that the highest truths of faith were ruled in the undivided Church.

It is even remarkable how very little was defined between the fourth General Council and the Council of Florence. The lawfulness of the religious use of images, established in the second Council of Nice, has scarcely the character of a dogma. The Council of

[d] Baron. H. E. A.D. 912.

Frankfort, in condemning Felix and Adoptianism, had no new definition to make. In the fourth Lateran Council, transubstantiation is rather practically taught in view of the Real Presence, than defined in itself[e]. Perhaps the one great exception is, that in regard to the Procession of God the Holy Ghost, the heresy imputed by Photius of old, that the Latin doctrine involved two Ἄρχαι in the Deity, is rejected in the second Council of Lyons; and the decision of the Council of Florence, that the language used by the Greek and Latin Fathers meant the same, was anticipated. Even in the Council of Trent it is remarkable how very little is defined upon some of the subjects which perhaps mainly occasioned the Reformation,—e.g. indulgences, purgatory, the cultus of the saints.

In fact, the short-comings of sinful humanity have crippled the operation of this divinely-ordered system. So long as the Church was undivided, the organ was in perfection and did its work. The decisions of the Œcumenical Church are the voice of the Holy Ghost; nothing can exaggerate the veneration or submission with which they ought to be received. But when, for the sins of Christendom, God permitted the great schism between the East and the West, the teaching office of the Church was, for the most part, limited to the authorization, inculcation, and application of truths already infallibly defined, or to the declaration of truth which had not yet that test of infallibility, the reception by the whole Church of Christ. We cannot

[e] See further on, Article XXVIII.

dispose of this fact as we can of the casting forth of Nestorianism or Eutychianism, or even of the Novatian schism in earlier times. On the one hand, no heresy can be charged against the orthodox Easterns; and on the other, the position of the East was founded in no negation of unity or catholicity. Novatianism had a theory of its own—a false one. The Greek Church became separated by circumstances over which it had no control. From the time of the establishment of the Empire at Byzantium, the elements of the future scission began to work—the human passions of the Popes and Patriarchs gave force to a dissidence which probably had its roots in the totally different temperaments and minds of their respective subjects; and in the final quarrel about Bulgaria, which occasioned the actual split, it is very difficult to award the meed of praise or blame to either party. If the Easterns, on the plea of the decrees of the Councils, arrogated for the Patriarchs a power to which they had no right, the Westerns were equally bold in asserting the prerogatives of St. Peter. The establishment of the Latin Emperors, and the aggression of a Latin Church at Constantinople, were not to be justified. In short, it is impossible to say that either side was quite right, or that either side had not much to say for itself; and therefore we cannot aver that either party is cut off from the true Vine, or that either section has ceased to be a part of the Catholic Church of Christ.

And this assertion has not only been held by individual doctors of the Western Church, but actually has been admitted by its most authoritative organs. On no other theory could the Councils of Lyons, Sienna, Ferrara, or Florence ever have been held. If modern theories be true, the Church can only deal with the individual members of separated communities. In the eyes of the Church such communities, according to these theories, have no corporate existence at all. It was not so in those great Councils, nay, it was not so in any of the prior attempts at reconciliation, some of which from time to time were actually successful. One must deny history, if one would assert that the Latins never treated the separated Greeks as a Church. Except by the Ultramontane School, the Orthodox Eastern Church has ever been regarded as a Church, with orders, sacraments, miracles, and jurisdiction, which has never fallen into heresy—in short, a real Church, the schism notwithstanding.

We find that, long after the time of Cerularius, a certain degree of communion still existed between the East and the West. Leo Allatius has produced several proofs that the act of Cerularius did not prevent the unity of the Churches: and the author of the *Perpétuité de la Foi*, says, " that even in the twelfth century, the schism was not yet so formed as that all the Greeks were generally rejected by all the Latins, and all the Latins by the Greeks, and there appeared among many of them marks of ecclesiastical communion ."

Again, it must be observed, that in the present day the authority of the Church is made to rest mainly

---

[f] Palmer's " Treatise on the Church," vol. i. p. 189.

on unity. It is said that the Church cannot speak authoritatively except it be one. And yet it is infallibility, not authority, of which the reception by the whole Church is the test, which reception is hindered when intercommunion is suspended. There may be many degrees of authority, adequate to guide us to the faith, short of absolute infallibility. When a heresy had been rejected of old in a local Church, there was guidance enough for its members, before the universal adoption of its decrees stamped its judgment with infallibility. But apart from this, many years elapsed before it was brought out that unity was the guarantee for authority. Even after the luminous exposition of the unity of the Church by St. Paul, we find centuries elapse before it is brought out scientifically by St. Cyprian. Before that, bishops excommunicated each other, and, resting on the goodness of their respective causes, died in separation, without a doubt as to their eternal safety. Such was the case in the matter of Pope Victor and the Eastern Bishops. Even St. Cyprian, who, as a doctor, has done more than any other for the scientific development of the idea of Church unity, actually felt it his duty not to give up the re-baptizing of heretics, which he and a large African Council had ordained, in conformity to an African tradition, although Pope Stephen renounced his communion for it, and the great St. Firmilian confirmed him in this, saying that Pope Stephen had rejected, not St. Cyprian, but himself[g]. Except when controversy embittered men's hearts, the mere

[g] In St. Cypr. Epp., Ep. 75, n. 25, Oxf. Tr.

fact of separation was not looked upon as crucial, as we may judge by the way in which the Meletians at Antioch were regarded. So also Lucifer of Cagliari, though the founder of a sect, is always spoken of with the greatest reverence; and St. Leo, after the death of his great opponent Hilary of Arles, speaks of him as "of blessed memory." The Donatists were heretics as well as schismatics. So that, although St. Augustine dwells very prominently on the fact of the schism, it was not pure schism, (such as that between the East and West,) of which he says, that men without the Church may have everything but salvation.

Nay, the converse of the proposition may be asserted, that the testimony of different Churches, agreeing in handing down the deposit, was regarded as of more importance in way of corroboration of truth, than a concurrent testimony of two Churches closely united. It was more like the witness we now claim for certain truths from the immemorial practice of the ancient heretical communities. It was the bringing together of witness which was specially called for, as a basis for authoritative declaration. It will be seen that the hinge of the two notions turns on the prominence given to the theory of doctrinal development.

That the plenary and absolute authority of the organ for deciding controversies should be thus temporarily limited is no doubt a startling fact. The philosophizing Christian may rejoice in the thought that the Church is thereby saved from the danger of over-definition. The Catholic Christian will mourn. The mournful fact itself is clear from what has gone before. Inerrancy is not the gift of any individual Church, but of the Church Œcumenical; and if the Eastern Church be, as we have shewn, a real Church, then, while the East is separate from the West, the power of inerrancy cannot be set in motion or promoted; all that has been decreed in either branch of the Church since the schism is liable to revision, and the promise of guidance given to the Apostles remains restrained as to its present use, in consequence of the perversity of the human will.

And yet the Church still remains a witness to the truth, even if for the time she has ceased to declare infallibly fresh truth. She testifies as to the old, if she cannot sanction the imposition of new dogma. While the schism lasts, we must be content with this, and in the meantime, it is our duty to labour and pray for unity, that God, in the way He thinks fit, may build up the breaches in the walls of Zion, may unite the scattered limbs of His mystical Body, may mend the rents in His holy coat, may restore Pentecostal unity, and then the long silent voice will again be heard, and the Urim and the Thummim be restored, and the heavens shall rejoice, and the earth exult, that the wall of separation is pulled down, that peace and concord have returned, and that Christ the corner-stone, Who out of two hath made one, hath united in the bonds of love both walls, and held them together in the covenant of eternal unity [h].

[h] *Bulla Eugenii IV., Hard. Act. Conc. Flor.,* tom. ix. p. 985.

ARTICLE XXI.

De Authoritate Conciliorum Generalium.

Generalia Concilia, sine jussu, et voluntate principum congregari non possunt; et ubi convenerint, quia ex hominibus constant, qui non omnes spiritu, et verbo Dei, reguntur, et errare possunt, et interdum errarunt etiam in his quæ ad normam pietatis (al. ad Deum) pertinent; ideoque quæ ab illis constituuntur, ut ad salutem necessaria, neque robur habent, neque authoritatem, nisi ostendi possint e sacris literis esse desumpta.

" Of the Authority of General Councils.

" General Councils may not be gathered together without the commandment and will of princes; and when they be gathered together (forasmuch as they be an assembly of men, whereof all be not governed with the Spirit and Word of God) they may err, and sometimes have erred, even in things pertaining unto God. Wherefore things ordained by them as necessary to salvation, have neither strength nor authority, unless it may be declared that they be taken out of Holy Scripture."

It having been shewn in the preceding Article that the *Ecclesia docens* hath power to decree rites and ceremonies, and hath authority in controversies of faith, we come to consider one great channel or organ of that power—the Œcumenical Council[a]. Given that the Church has this power, by whom or how is it to be exercised? By whom but by the Apostolic ministry who are appointed "for the perfecting of the saints, for the work of the ministry, for the edifying of the body of Christ;" by those to whom was committed the power of the keys, who had among other duties connected with admission to communion to test the orthodoxy of applicants; by those whose important office it was to hand on the form of sound words which they had received, to their successors. Each bishop held individually what belonged to all *in solidum*. A paramount authority, therefore, belonged to each Bishop in his diocese, by containing in his single person the authority of the whole body. This is the basis of the Cyprianic theory.

But a state of things like this was not sufficient, in view of the constant efforts of Satan to sow tares amid the good wheat. The restless activity of the human mind, and the hatred which the sinful intellect bears to the true doctrine of the Incarnation, early necessitated a stronger organization. Error often was too powerful for a single bishop to cope with in his own diocese. Error extended beyond the diocese. Nay, error infected the Bishop himself. Moreover, questions arose which could not be settled by the

[a] "Synodi vel Concilii nomine majores nostri semper intellexerunt sacerdotes, præsertim episcopos, in locum anum congregatos, ut causas eas scilicet definirent, quæ ad ecclesiæ fidem seu mores pertinerent."—*Melch. Can. de loc. Theo.*, p. 146, ed. Patav. 1734.

appeal to the sure practice of the Apostles and their followers. The very lapse of time weakened the individual appeal to antiquity. Something else was necessary, and accordingly—acting on the precedent of the Acts of the Apostles, when the Apostles and Elders came together to settle the terms of admission of the Gentile converts into the infant Church—we find that before the days of Tertullian, "Throughout Greece were held Councils out of all Churches, by means of which matters of importance were treated in common, and the representation of the whole Christian name celebrated with great veneration [b]." Furthermore, it was held in accordance with our Lord's promise, "that where two or three were gathered together in His Name, He was in the midst of them;" and men dwelt upon other promises of special guidance, that He, the Word, and the Holy Ghost, were specially present on such occasions to control and direct the proceedings, to save them from error, and to bless the deliberations.

The earliest record which we have of a Council, after that mentioned in the Acts of the holy Apostles, is a Sicilian Council held in the year A.D. 125, on the subject of an error respecting the impossibility of a fall after baptism [c]. Soon after the synodicon mentions a synod at Rome, in the time of Pope Victor, against Theodotus of Byzantium, who not only had sacrificed in persecution, but had denied the divinity of our Lord [d]. At Pergamos, in A.D. 152, a synod of

---

[b] *De Jejun.*, c. 13. [c] Labbe, i. 558. [d] Ib. 568.

seven bishops anathematized a form of Gnosticism called the Colorbasian heresy; in the East, in A.D. 160, Cerdon was thus condemned; at Rome, in A.D. 170 and 198, the Quarto-decimans; at Hierapolis, in A.D. 173, Montanus and Maximilla; and in Palestine, in Pontus, at Lyons, in A.D. 198, the Quarto-decimans again. The Roman synod against Sabellius and Nortus was probably held about A.D. 258[e].

During these early times, from the constant liability of persecution, and the fact of the empire being still heathen, the action of the Church was by small local Councils in different parts, as questions happened to arise, and these, as they got accepted by the other Churches, became the voice of the whole Church.

In short, during this period we find that every question that arose was settled by local Councils, increasing in importance and weight, till the State-establishment, under Constantine, allowed a representation in a large sense of the whole Church of God in the great Œcumenical Synod of Nicæa. The language with regard to its authority is very strong, and it is remarkable that in spite of the efforts of the Arians and the Arianizing emperors to establish counter synods, and in spite of the crucial word the omoüsion not having been universally enforced, that Council had a grasp upon the conscience of the Church which none of its rivals succeeded in effecting.

So great was its effect, that henceforward the autho-

---

[e] Baring, *Nov. Coll. in* Conc. i. 848, Col.

rity of the episcopate became merged in the representative institution of Councils. In the midst of much human feeling, violence, and fraud, God used this form of legislation to preserve the truth once declared to the saints. While the intellect of the East surged up and down, a very sea of speculation on the most recondite mysteries of the faith, it was always felt that the decision of a General Council closed the matter for ever; they who could not agree continued in their error, but outside the Catholic Church. Thus the Nestorians were cut off after the decision at Ephesus; and the Cophts, refusing the decree of Chalcedon, to this day remain separate from the orthodox Eastern Church.

However, from the date of the Council of Nicæa, another power had been asserting itself in the Church, the power of the successor of St. Peter. Often resisted successfully, often urged upon inconsistent and false grounds, that power was gradually more and more felt, especially when the Eastern Empire became weak, and the Western Church, by the conversion of the barbarians, had placed itself at the head of the new civilization. The question eventually was a question between the authority of the General Council and the authority of the Apostolic See. Following up the teaching of the false decretals, the Lateran Councils did all they could to support the Papal authority; but in the next century, the dreadful corruption and schism induced the princes of Europe to insist on the summoning of the synods of Constance and Basle. There the doctrine was asserted, and acted on, that the Pope is inferior to the Council. The rival Councils of Ferrara and Florence were in the interests of the Papacy. The Council of Trent left the question unsolved.

1. The first proposition in the Article does not touch the marrow of the question. It is a mere matter of policy. Under the Empire it was of course an impossibility that large bodies of bishops, with their attendants, should be allowed to assemble in any city without the cognizance of the civil power. Religious questions then, were what political questions are now. There was the same, or greater excitement prevailing with regard to the question of the Divinity of our Lord or the double Procession, as there is now regarding the most hotly discussed question of secular government; and just as the first duty of the State is to maintain tranquillity at any price, so it was the duty of the Emperors to maintain peace in their dominions by the exercise of a control over the assembling of Councils.

Moreover, recognising as they did the authority of the Council—though in after times we see, as in the case of Zeno and the Henoticon, that they did seek, unsuccessfully indeed, to impose formulas by the authority of the civil power—they used the Councils as great State engines for the welfare of their people. It was by their own will and suggestion that the General Councils were actually called. This power, in the West in abeyance for many centuries, was evoked again in the instance of Constance and Basle, though the forms of a certain deference to the ecclesiastical authority were maintained on the score of a long prescription.

It is the same at the present moment. However much a General Council might be desired on the part of the Church authorities, no Council worthy of that name could really be called without the concurrence of the civil powers of Christendom. Even those assemblages of prelates of the Latin Communion which from time to time have been summoned, have been controlled by the civil authorities of the different countries; much more a Council, such as that of Florence, where free access was given to all to state their claims, would need to have the moral support and sanction of the authorities of the different nationalities. No doubt the union between Church and State is loosening all over Christendom, and the time might come when such a condition of things should be possible; but at this moment, in the present condition of the Church and of civil society, it may be safely admitted that a Council ought not to be assembled " without the commandment and will of princes f."

The proposition in the Article has distinct historical support. From the time that the Emperors were converted by Christianity, the affairs of the Church were mightily affected by them, and the most important Councils took place at their will g.

f Vide Dr. Pusey's " Royal Supremacy."
g Socrates, *Hist.*, lib. v., *proœm.* v. *Jus. G. E.* 317.

Constantine the Great summoned that of Nicæa[h]; Theodosius that of Constantinople[i]; Theodosius the Younger, that of Ephesus[k]; Martian and Valentinian, that of Chalcedon[l]; Justinian, the fifth, at Constantinople[m]; Justinian II., that in Trullo[n]; Constantine and Irene the second Nicene[o]; and Basil, the eighth, which was held at Constantinople[p].

Yet the Emperors, even as representing the laity, were checked in their interference in Councils. Hosius, Bishop of Cordova, writes to the Emperor: "Mix not thyself in ecclesiastical affairs, and lay not on us commands concerning them, but rather learn from us. God has given the *imperium* to thee, to us the *ecclesiastical* power[q]." St. Ambrose asks Valentinian the Younger[r], "When, O most clement Emperor, did laics judge a bishop in matters of faith?" Theodosius the Younger, when he sent Count Candidian to the Council of Ephesus, lays this principle down in his commission.

2. The second point to be considered is the relation between the decisions of a General Council and Holy Scripture. That relation was symbolized by a copy of the holy Gospels being put on a throne in the midst of the assembly as the type of the blessed

---

[h] Euseb., *Vit. Const.*, lib. iii. c. 6.   [i] Socr., *Hist.*, lib. v. c. 8.   [k] Evagrius, c. 3.   [l] Leontius, *de Sectis*, p. 462.   [m] Nicephorus, *Hist.*, lib. xvii. c. 27.   [n] Balsamon, *De Eâ Synodo quæ dicitur* 6ᵗᵃ *Beveregii, Synod.*, tom. i. p. 151.   [o] *Conc. Nicen.*, init.   [p] *Concil. Const.*, Harduin, vol. v. p. 1025.   [q] *Ep. ad Const. ap. S. Athan.*, tom. i. p. 371.   [r] *Ep.* 21.

Spirit. It was always assumed that the duty of a Council was to declare what had been the faith from the beginning, not to propound new objects of belief. A Council might make that matter of explicit faith, which before, being matter of implicit faith only, might in ignorance be contradicted without sin, but it could only give authority to it as a portion of the original deposit and revelation. It must witness to a continuous tradition, and give authority to its enunciation, but it could teach nothing as of divine faith which it did not trace up to the Holy Scriptures. The Council of Carthage (A.D. 348) declares that it makes its decrees "mindful of the divine precepts, and of the magisterial authority of the divine Scriptures[s]."

3. The next point asserted is that General Councils may err, and sometimes have erred, in things pertaining to God. This proposition is strictly true, for it may be proved by the evidence of ecclesiastical history. Not to speak of such Councils as the Arian Councils of Sirmium, that of Ariminum reached the proportions of a general synod; more than 400 Bishops were assembled there; a number beyond that at Nice; much more beyond those of Constantinople. And yet the Synod of Ariminum erred in things pertaining to God. But there is a much stronger instance in the Latrocinium of Ephesus. It was duly summoned with all the appropriate forms; there was present an immense representation of the Church of God, yet it

---

[s] Labbe, Conc., tom. ii. p. 747; cit. Owen's "Dogmatic Theology," p. 14.

went wrong. The inerrancy of a Council can never be guaranteed at the moment. The test of the value of a Council is its after-reception by the Church. Synods of very limited numbers, in very obscure places, have by after reception assumed the weight of an Œcumenical Council, as, for example, that of Orange on the question of grace; on the other hand, one act of the holiest of all Councils, that of Jerusalem in the Acts of the Apostles, in the matter of things strangled, has in the West become obsolete. Again, some canons of a Council are accepted, and some reprobated. Discipline also may change, so that in the matter of authority there is not only an after verdict on the part of the living Church, but there is also a constant correction, or rather corrective process, on its part going on, in matters of discipline, which certainly pertain to God; of course, in the case of dogma, the decision of an approbated Œcumenical Council forecloses the matter for ever.

To the understanding of the Article, another most important distinction must be borne in mind. It speaks of General Councils, not of Œcumenical Councils. Now, though in the strict sense of the term, General, Universal, Œcumenical, are the same, yet the term Œcumenical has been consecrated by usage to mean 'a General Council, lawful, approved, and received by all the Church.' A Council may be general without being lawful. To be General, all the bishops of the world should be summoned to it, and no one excluded but heretics and excommunicated persons.

To be lawful and truly Œcumenical, it is necessary that all that occurs should be done regularly, and that the Church should receive it. Hence there have been Councils, general in their convocation, but not so in their acts or event; such as the Council of Milan, held in the case of St. Athanasius in A.D. 354, and others [t].

While the Church, then, is in her present rended condition, local Churches must be content to make local decrees, and these may hereafter either by reception by the whole Church become part of the Church's living teaching, or receive a certain modification.

As to the number of Councils, the Churches are not agreed as to their number. The Anglican Church in some of her documents refers to St. Gregory's four, in others to six. The Greek Church holds seven, though Barlaam, in A.D. 1339, treating with Benedict XII., mentions only six [u]. The Latin Church is not at one with itself on the subject. Some doctors count twenty-one; that is, two of Nicæa, four of Constantinople, one of Ephesus, one of Chalcedon, five of Lateran, two of Lyons, one of Vienna, one of Pisa, one of Constance, one of Basle, one of Florence, and one of Trent. Others count only eighteen, cutting off Pisa, Basle and Constance, and later sessions. This is the common opinion of the Italians. The French do not consider either the fifth Lateran or that of Florence Œcumenical [x].

[t] Richard, *Analyse de Conciles*, tom. i. p. 4. Paris, 1772.

[u] Palmer, ii. p. 203.   [x] Richard, *Analyse de Conciles*, t. i. p. 108.

The Council of Florence was styled by its editor the eighth Œcumenical, and is so termed in the Papal licence [y]. Gaspar Contarini styles the ninth Œcumenical [z].

[y] *Launoius Epistolæ*, part viii. ep. xi. p. 563, ed. 1571, cit. Palmer.

[z] *Opera Contareni.*

Printed by James Parker and Co., Cornmarket, Oxford.

ON THE
THIRTY-NINE ARTICLES OF RELIGION.

ARTICLE XXII.

DE PURGATORIO.

DOCTRINA Romanensium [a] *de purgatorio, de indulgentiis, de veneratione, et adoratione, tum imaginum, tum reliquiarum, necnon de invocatione sanctorum, res est futilis, inaniter conficta, et nullis Scripturarum testimoniis innititur : immo verbo Dei contradicit.*

" *Of Purgatory.*

" THE Romish doctrine concerning purgatory, pardons, worshipping and adoration, as well of images as of reliques, and also invocation of saints, is a fond thing vainly invented, and grounded upon no warranty of Scripture, but rather repugnant to the Word of God."

Whatever dissidence may be imagined to exist between the preceding Articles and the doctrines as promulgated by the Council of Trent, there is none with regard to the subjects mentioned in the present one; for while the points formerly touched on were ruled

---

[a] " The words *Romanenses* and *Romanistæ* were already used as far back as 1520 by Luther and Ulrich von Hutten to designate the *extreme* Mediæval party." Hardwick, p. 389. Just as in modern French literature, the expression *parti romaniste* is used for the more pronounced section of the Ultramontanes. Observe that the harsh word *perniciosa* of the early Articles is entirely dropped in the later version.

x

by the Church of England subsequently to the earlier
decrees of the Council, the questions of Purgatory and
Pardons were not discussed for many months after
the publication of the Article. The Article, therefore,
cannot be strained into a condemnation and contradiction of that which did not exist at the time; and
we must come to the conviction that it was not the
formulized doctrine, but a current and corrupt practice in the Latin or Western Church, which is here
declared to be " fond" and " vainly invented."

This distinction is a very important one. People are
apt to ignore the real reformation which took place
within the Latin Church, the wise and scientific treatment to which many points were subjected, and the
abuses and scandals which were discountenanced. No
doubt the reform might with effect have been carried
further. Points vitally affecting our own position, e.g. all
questions of jurisdiction, might have been defined; the
disciplinary enactments for dioceses might have been
extended to the Papal Court; still a real reform did
take place, and it is unscientific or uncandid to ignore
it. The reform, such as it was, only came too late. We
cannot say what in the Providence of God would have
been the results, if the Popes had yielded sooner to the
clamours of Europe for a free and Œcumenical Council; but they feared similar results to those of Constance and Basle, and so the time passed, till all hopes
of reconciliation had disappeared. Still the Council
did a mighty work [b], and such men as St. Carlo Bor-

[b] Cantù, *Histoire des Italiens*, t. viii. p. 394, also p. 441.

romeo, Archbishop of Milan, St. Thomas of Villa-
nueva, Archbishop of Valencia, Rusticucci, Salviati,
Sartorio, Gaspar Contarini, Fra Bernardino Ochino
da Siena, Bonomo, Bishop of Vercelli, Paul of Arezzo,
Bishop of Piacenza, Ypolito Galantino, the silk-
worker of Florence, S. Filippo Neri, and a host of
others, who carried on the work, exhibit in their
own persons the results that were effected.

The points against which this Article is directed may
be discerned in any of the satires which immediately
preceded the Reformation, such as the *Epistolæ Obscu-
rorum Virorum*, the history of Dill Eulenspiegel, or the
Colloquies of Erasmus. These exhibit the picture of a
great decay of practical religion, corruption and avarice
reigning among the clergy, nothing done to stem the
flood of immorality, and, beside this, a round of ceremonies and puerile superstitions. Nothing is so remarkable as the way in which holy names and holy
mysteries are placed by Chaucer in the mouths of those
who are perpetrating the foulest deeds. It would seem
as if morality and religion had got so divorced that
there seemed no incongruity in their association. Erasmus' account of his visit with Colet to Canterbury, and,
again, his description of the shrine of Our Lady of Walsingham well repay perusal, and are specially important
in considering the Article, as they exhibit the prevalent
habit of thought of the time, the every-day devotional
life of the people, as seen by the eyes of one of the most
intelligent of men.

Indeed, the one refreshing aspect of the English

Reformation is that which exhibits to us the way in which the scandals that brought it on were dealt with, how the objects of superstition were cast to the winds, and the gainful frauds exposed and scorned. Even in the reign of Henry VIII. the semi-heathen image of Darvel Gatheren, which had in Wales promoted a horrid cultus, such as is said to have existed till the seventeenth century among the cognate race of the Bretons, was destroyed[c]. The miraculous rood of Boxley, which was said to move its eyes and lips, and to sweat blood, was broken up among the jeers of the people[d]; and through the length and breadth of the land, the instruments of fanaticism were cast into the fire or the water. Even the bones of the saints, the temples of the Holy Ghost, the shrines of the grace of God, were mixed up in the common ruin. Because discredited by a base coinage, the true mintage was destroyed. Because mixed up with manifold impostures, the real authentic relics were dishonoured, and one common grave received the lying and fraudulent objects which had been used to keep alive the failing piety of the preceding ages of declension, and the blessed remains of those holy men who had been the vessels of the favour of God, and His lights in their several generations.

Excess always leads to re-action. Superstition is closer to irreligion than men think for, and the

---

[c] Vide Froude's History, vol. iii. p. 294.

[d] Vide Fuller's Church History, bk. vi. 8—10, p. 244, ed. 1837; also Froude, iii. 288.

misery is, that you can hardly prune away the one without promoting the other. Tear the ivy off the mouldering church wall, and you will bring away part of the wall with it. So it was at the Reformation. It was impossible to reform and not to deform; and, as a fact, much that had been once good, and in time abused, was for the time lost. Solemn rites that had lost their significance, or been veiled in an unknown tongue, were cast aside as useless; edifying ceremonies, such as the washing of poor men's feet, nay, the unction for the sick, which had the support of the Inspired Word itself, were ignored; doctrines, such as the Communion of Saints, the witness of God to innocence in the case of ordeal, the horrible watchful skill and constant infestation of evil spirits, dropped out of sight, and a one-sided view of God's truth was advocated and enforced. This was specially the case with regard to the subject of the Article. "The Romish doctrine," in the earlier type of the Article termed " the scholastic doctrine," was hereby condemned. It only was condemned, but somehow people seemed to forget that besides the Romish doctrine on these subjects, there was a Catholic doctrine also; that the errors lay rather in the exaggeration and want of proportion of the statements, than in the substance, and that as formerly there had been danger from excess, there now was danger in defect, in the way of suppressing important truths of the Gospel.

For on every one of the points mentioned there is an underlying Christian truth, and it is necessary to the right understanding of the Article to know what this is. We cannot tell what the Article means till we know what it condemns; and we cannot know what it condemns till we know the doctrine, the perversion of which drew forth the condemnation.

But before proceeding to this, historic truth and candour demand that we should say that the protest in the Article is still needed. One does not here speak of those ancient mountain-shrines in the Tyrol or in Switzerland, where the simple, loving herdsman toils his weary way over brake and fell, encountering danger and real hardship, till he falls down before the Marien-bild, or other object of veneration, to which his steps have been directed. God forbid that we should sit in judgment on the simple faith which prompts the prayer, which, perhaps misdirected, God rewards and hears, as if offered immediately to Himself; but the protest is still needed, because it cannot be denied that superstition is still tolerated, if not actually encouraged by the authorities of the Church abroad. At Rome itself, in the church of the Ara Cœli, the people are blessed by the elevation of the Bambino, a doll of the infant Saviour, a sort of parody of the solemn rite of benediction with the most Holy Sacrament. At Calcata, a place near Civita Castellana, the exhibition of a certain relic[e] violates the first instincts of decency and

---

[e] Vide *Narrazione critica storica della reliquia pregiosissima del Sanctissimo prepuzio di N. S. G. C. che si venera nella Chiesa Parrochiale di Calcata, diocesi di Civita Castellana, e Fendo dell' Eminentissima Casa Sinibaldi. Ristampata ed accresciuta per ordine di S. E.*

reverence ; and Loretto still draws her gains from the credulity of the faithful. Nay, even in France, where the battle of the faith is being fought by an able body of clergy, whose tone in some respects presents a very marked contrast to that of the moderate and learned school of divines who adorned the Church of France before the first Revolution, it is to be feared that, as in the notorious instance of the shrine of La Salette, too many are using the weapon of superstition to combat the growing irreligion.

I. The doctrine of Purgatory, against which the Article excepts, is that which is made patent to the eye of every traveller as he passes from Germany into Italy. The wayside shrines which so edify him still continue, but the subjects are changed. In place of the affecting representation of the sufferings of the Eternal Son, and the touching impersonations of the Lord crowned with thorns, with the purple robe and the reed in His hand, which speak to the soul of the wayfarer, terrible representations of the holy souls in flames appal him. They are the predominant, although not the exclusive subject. Sometimes the Madonna is placed in relation to those souls, but oftener still they are by themselves, appealing for a few pence to the awakened sympathies of the passers by. They say, " Have mercy upon me, have mercy upon me, oh my friends; for the hand of the Lord hath touched me." The popular

il Sign. Marchese Cesare Sinibaldi Gambalunga, Barone e Signore della detta terra. Roma, 1862, presso Vincenzo Poggioli. Con approvazione.

doctrine thus symbolized prevailed in England at the time of the Reformation. Probably, as is believed to be the case in New Spain, it had come to take the place of a living faith in the eternal pains of hell in the case of most men. It was also mixed up largely with interested motives on the part of the clergy. There was a perfect traffic in masses for the souls, and men fancied that by leaving money to the Church at the hour of death, and at the expense of their heirs, they might purchase mitigation or exemption from pains, which in degree, though not in duration, were said to equal the pains of hell. The English were very strongly affected by these teachings, for several of the most striking and romantic legends, e.g. the dream of St. Fursæus and the vision of Drithelm, as recorded in Bede's History[f], which had contributed much to fix in the minds of the faithful a conviction of this doctrine, were of British origin, and accordingly the number of endowed chantries which were founded, that priests might, in the sweet language of the time, "sing for souls," was immense. Of these, the college of All Souls', Oxford, which was established with the idea of study subordinated to that of prayer for those who perished in the French wars in Henry the Fifth's time, saved by the scholastic endowment attached to it, has survived the shock of the Reformation. In the foundation, too, of Lincoln College, Oxford, the same duty of prayers for the departed was made co-extensive with that of theological study. The popular doctrine

---

[f] Vide *Bedæ Historia*, book iii. c. xix., book v. c. xii.

of the day is laid down in Sir Thomas More's "Supplication of Souls," a work in which he answered the "Supplication of Beggars," a political brochure, which pleaded for the suppression of the chantries, on the ground that so much was taken from the poor. The chantries were in due time suppressed, but it may be doubted whether the poor profited much by the transaction.

"If ye pity the poor, there is none so poor as we, that have not a bratte to put upon our backs. If ye pity the blind, there is none so blind as we, which are here in the dark, saving for sights unpleasant and lothsome, till some comfort come. If yo pity the lame, there is none so lame as we, that can neither creep one foot out of the fire, nor have one hand at liberty to defend our face from the flame. Finally, if ye pity any man in pain, never knew ye pain comparable to ours; whose fire as far passeth in heat all the fires that ever burned on earth, as the hottest of all that passed a feigned fire painted on a wall. If ever ye lay sick, or thought the night long and longed for day, while every hour seemed longer than five, bethink you then what a long night we sely souls endure, that lie slepeless, restless, burning and broiling in the dark fire one long night of many days, of many weeks, of many years together. You walter, peradventure, and tolter in sickness from side to side, and find little rest in any part of the bed; we lie bound to the brands, and cannot lift up our heads. You have your physicians with you, that sometimes cure and heal you; no physic will help

our pain, nor no plaisters coole our heat. Your keepers do you great ease, and put you in good comfort; our
keepers are such as God keep you from—cruel, doomed
spirites, odious, envious, and hateful, despiteous enemies
and dispiteful tormentors, and their company more
terrible and grievous to us than is the pain itself; and
the intolerable torment that they do us, wherewith from
top to toe they cease not continually to tear us[s]."

It was strongly felt at the Reformation - period
that the doctrine of Purgatory had been so taught
as to invalidate the power of the Passion of Christ.
With the usual confusion of the objective and subjective of those times, on the one hand it was coarsely
taught that so much suffering would do its work,
independent of the merit of Christ, in the way of
cleansing so much sin; on the other hand, according to
the new learning, it was supposed that our Lord's death
took away the temporal as well as the eternal punishment for sin, a mistake, as every day's experience
teaches us; for the application of Christ's Blood by the
deepest repentance will not restore the lost health to
the profligate, nor the squandered wealth to the spend-
thrift. Moreover, a divorce in thought had practically
taken place between the Sacrifice of Christ and the
applicative and commemorating Sacrifice, so that the
souls were thought to be succoured by masses, to the
exclusion of the thought of that adorable Passion
which was pleaded in and by those masses.

[s] More's "Supplication of Souls," Works, p. 337, Cawood, London,
ed. 1557.

Now the true doctrine, of which the opinion condemned in this Article is an exaggeration and excess, is founded on the tenderest and deepest sympathies of our common human nature. Mankind will not endure the thought that at the moment of death all concern for those loved ones who are riven from us by death comes to an end. We firmly resist the heathen notion, which the inverted torch and the broken column symbolize, that henceforward they are nothing to us, or we to them; nay, we go so far as to say, that though the tree must lie as it falls, and though death puts an end to each man's probation, so far as he is concerned, yet that Infinite love pursues the soul beyond the grave, and there has dealings with it, in which we who survive have still our co-operation. To pray for the departed is a deep instinct of natural piety, but it is much more than that, it is one of the best-attested doctrines of the primitive Church. The Jews at the time of our Saviour, as they do to-day, prayed for the dead, and there is not a word proceeding from the lips of our Lord which can be tortured into a condemnation of it. There is little doubt that St. Paul prayed for Onesiphorus when dead: for the Greek phrase for "his household" implies his absence; and he prays for no grace for this life, but only, "The Lord grant unto him, that he may find mercy of the Lord in that day [h]." The early Liturgies of the Church, which, traced back to the Apostolic times, bear witness to the public teaching of the most remote antiquity, are unanimous in this

[h] 2 Tim. i. 18.

respect. That of Jerusalem prays:—" Remember, O Lord God, the spirits and all flesh, those of right faith whom we have mentioned and whom we have not mentioned, from Abel the Just to this day. Do Thou Thyself give them rest [or refresh them] in the region of the living, in Thy kingdom, in the delights of Paradise, in the bosoms of our holy Fathers Abraham, Isaac, and Jacob, whence sorrow, grief, and lamentation are banished away, where the light of God's countenance visits and shines continually[1]." That of Alexandria prays:—" Rest [or refresh] the souls of our fathers and brethren who have fallen asleep before us in the faith of Christ, remembering the forefathers, fathers, patriarchs, prophets, apostles, martyrs, confessors, bishops, saints, just, every soul perfected in the faith of Christ; and those whom on this present day we commemorate, and our holy Father Mark, the Apostle and Evangelist, who shewed us the way of faith," [then after reading the diptychs of the departed,] "and of all these rest [or refresh] the souls in the tabernacles of Thy saints in Thy kingdom, granting them the good things of Thy promises which eye hath not seen, &c. Refresh their souls, and vouchsafe to them the kingdom of heaven[J]." That of Constantinople separates off " the oblation for the forefathers, fathers, patriarchs," &c., with the clause " at whose intercessions may God visit us;" and proceeds, "And remember all who are fallen asleep before us in the hope of the resurrection unto eternal life; and rest [or refresh] them where the

---

[1] Assem., *Cod. Lit.*, v. 46.   [J] Ass., vii. 24—26.

light of Thy countenance visits." The Liturgy of St. Chrysostom, now "in use through the four Patriarchates and Russia, except on the few days on which St. Basil's Liturgy is said," has no special form for those mentioned in the diptychs of the departed. That of St. Basil provides a prayer "For the rest and forgiveness of the soul of Thy servant *N.* In a lightsome place, where grief and lamentation are fled away, rest [or refresh] him."

In the Roman Liturgy, the prayers are more varied. In the Canon of the Mass is a prayer "upon the diptychs" (occurring in a different place, in the Sacramentary of St. Gregory):—"Remember also, O Lord, Thy servants and handmaidens (*N.* and *N.*) who have gone before us with the seal of faith, and sleep in the sleep of peace. To them, O Lord, and to all who are at rest in Christ, we intreat Thee to grant a place of refreshment, of light and peace [k]." Other prayers, after the pattern of St. Paul's for Onesiphorus, were for a merciful judgment[l]; that God would "save the souls of the departed from hell," "from the judgment of vengeance," "from the mouth of the lion," from "the hands of the enemy;" that they endure not "everlasting punishments," "the fire of Gehenna and the flame of hell [m]." Or, again, that they may "have part in the

---

[k] Opp., iii. p. 4. Ben. Comp. p. 289, n. 70.

[l] Gelas. Sacram. *Orat.*, n. 91, *post Sepulturam*, p. 751, Murat. :—"That before the throne of the glory of Thy Christ, severed with those on the right, we may have nothing in common with those on the left." (S. Greg., t. v. p. 233.)

[m] "From the gates of hell deliver their souls, O Lord." (Breviary.)

first resurrection[n]," or " have a blessed resurrec-

"Absolve, O Lord, the souls of all the faithful departed from all bond of sin, and, Thy grace succouring them, let them attain [*mereantur*] to escape the judgment of vengeance, and enjoy the bliss of eternal light." (*Missæ pro Def. Tractus.*) "O Lord Jesus Christ, King of Glory, deliver the souls of all the faithful departed from the punishment of hell, and from the lake profound; deliver them from the mouth of the lion, lest hell (*tartarus*) swallow them up, lest they fall into darkness; but let St. Michael, the Captain, present them to that holy light, which Thou hast promised to Abraham and his seed." (*Offert.*) "Deliver it [the soul of one buried] not into the hands of the enemy, nor forget him for ever; but command him to be received by the holy angels, and to be brought to the house of Paradise; that, since he hoped and believed in Thee, he may not endure the punishment of hell [*inferni*] or everlasting punishments," [it used to be *pænas eternas* in old Missals, as *Missale Rom.*, Paris, 1521, Ussher,] " but may possess everlasting joys;" [ib., "on the day of death or of burial"], "that it may escape the place of punishment and the fire of Gehenna, and the flame of hell, in the land of the living." (Gelasian Sacram., n. 91; *post obit. Hom.*, p. 748, Mur.) "May he pass the gates of hell and the ways of darkness," (p. 749). "Deliver him, O Lord, from the princes of darkness and the places of punishment" (p. 750), "that he may be free from the burning of eternal fire" (p. 751). "That thou wouldest deliver him from the torments of hell." (Greg. Sacram., *post lavat. Corp.*, ib., p. 215 and 216). "Let him be severed from the fierce burning of the boiling Gehenna." (*Post sepult. Corpus*, p. 217.) "Grant him to escape the flames of eternal punishment, and gain the rewards of eternal life." (*Miss. Ambros. in Pam. Lit.*, i. 450.) So also in the Jacobite Liturgy of St. James :—" Freeing them from the infinite damnation to come, and making them worthy of the joy which is in the bosom of Abraham, Isaac, and Jacob." (Renaud., ii. 38.) "Spare the sinners in the day of judgment," (ibid., 39). "Forgive those sins especially for which in eternity condemnation is prepared," &c., (ibid., 196). "Let them be hidden under the wings of Thy grace, and not be condemned," (ibid., 222). "Give rest in the habitation of Thy kingdom to all who have fallen asleep in hope of Thee, and free them and us from the unquenchable fire and the worm that dieth not," (ibid., 339; add ibid., 350, 364, 378, 405, 520).

[n] Gelasian Sacram., n. 91, *post obit. Hom. in* pp. 749, bis. 750, bis. Murat.; add Gallic. Sacram. *Miss. pro defunct.*, ibid., p. 950; S. Greg.

tion °," " or that they may obtain eternal felicity in
the congregation of the saints;" "may be enrolled in

Opp., t. v. p. 228, Paris; *Missale Goth.*, p. 394, ed. Thomas. Mur. " That,
severed from the horror of hell [*horrore tartareo*], placed in Abraham's
bosom, the Almighty would vouchsafe to resuscitate them in the first
resurrection, which He shall effect." Tertullian, in reasoning against
second marriages, asks how she is to pray for the two husbands, the
old and the new; and states the boon demanded for the dead one,
" refreshment and a share in the first resurrection." (*De Monog.*, x.)

° " May he rise again among those who rise, and among those who
receive their bodies in the day of resurrection may he receive his body,
and with the blessed who come at the right hand of God the Father
may he come, and among those who possess eternal life may he possess
it." (*Sacr. Gelas.*, l. c., p. 749.) " Let us deprecate the mercy of Almighty
God for the spirit of our dear *N.*, whose burial is celebrated to-day, that
He would receive him in eternal rest, and restore him by a blessed
resurrection." (Ibid.) " Let his soul receive no injury, but when that great
day of resurrection and reward cometh, vouchsafe, Lord, to raise him
with Thy saints and Thine elect; forgive him transgressions and sins
'to the last farthing,' and let him obtain a life of immortality and an
eternal kingdom with Thee." (Ibid., 750.) " Eternal God, Who hast
given us in Christ, Thy Only-begotten, our Lord, the hope of a blessed
resurrection; grant that the souls of Thy servants, for whom we offer
to Thy Majesty this sacrifice of our redemption, may be found meet,
through Thy mercy, to attain with Thy saints to the rest of a blessed
resurrection." (*Praef. Ant. in Pamel. Lit.*, ii. 609.) " That Thou wouldest
command the soul of Thy servant *N.* to be carried by the hands of Thy
holy angels to the bosom of the Patriarch Abraham Thy friend, to be
raised up in the last day of the great judgment." (*Sacram. Greg.*, n. 104,
p. 214, Murat.) " And may be found meet to be raised among the saints
and elect in the glory of the resurrection." (Ibid., and in another
prayer, at the grave before interment, p. 215.) " Let us pray that the pity
of the Lord would vouchsafe to place him in the bosom of Abraham,
Isaac, and Jacob; that when the day of judgment shall come, He may
cause him to be raised, and be placed among His saints and elect,"
after interment." (Ibid.) The Jacobite Liturgy prays for the person's
resurrection (Ren. ii. 167), " Raise them, O Lord, in that last Day, and
be Thy face calm towards them: and forgive for Thy mercy's sake
their sins and failings."

the number of the saints who pleased God." There are prayers also for the recently baptised [p], and for eternal remission to those who desired penance, but were cut off by death [q]. There were also the well-known prayers for St. Leo I. and St. Gregory I. specifically [r].

Perhaps it may not be an improbable conjecture, that the Church at first prayed for all the departed in one tenour [s], without discriminating, leaving it to God

[p] Sacram. Gelas., n. 96, p. 755, ed. Mur.

[q] Ibid., n. 98, p. 756.

[r] " Grant to us, Lord, that this oblation, by immolating which Thou didst grant that the offences of the whole world should be pardoned, may profit the soul of Thy servant Leo, through," &c., (*Sacram. Gregor.*, p. 101, ed. Murat.); and, substituting the name Gregory, (ibid., p. 25).

[s] The ancient Office in the Apostolic Constitutions, prays :—" We offer to Thee also for all who, from the beginning, have pleased Thee, saints, patriarchs, prophets, just, apostles, martyrs, confessors, bishops, presbyters, deacons, sub-deacons, readers, singers, virgins, widows, laics, and all of whom Thou knowest the names." (*Const. Apost.* viii. 12, t. i. p. 403. Cotel.) The Liturgy of Theodorus, in use among the Nestorians, goes on in one tenour :—" O our Lord and God, receive from us by Thy grace this sacrifice of thanksgiving, the reasonable fruit of our lips, that there be before Thee a good memory of the ancient just, holy prophets, blessed apostles, martyrs and confessors, bishops, doctors, priests, deacons, and all the sons of the Holy Catholic Church, who in true faith passed out of this world; that through Thy grace, O Lord, Thou wouldest forgive them all the sins and offences which in this world, in their mortal body and soul subject to change, they sinned or offended against Thee; for there is no one who sinneth not." (Renaud., *Litt. Orient.*, ii. 620, 621.) The Armenian Liturgy prays collectively :—" Through this oblation grant health, peace, plenty, &c., through it give rest to all who have heretofore fallen asleep in Christ; to the patriarchs [Adam, Noah, Abraham, &c.], to the fathers, [of tribes, families, of the Armenian people, *antistites* in its secular sense, C. M.,] to the prophets, to the apostles, to the martyrs, to the bishops, to the elders [i.e. presbyters],

to hear her in whatever way He knew for each; and so, that the prayers for deliverance from hell,

to the deacons, and to the whole clergy of Thy Holy Church, and to all the laity, both men and women, who have ended (their life) in the faith," (said privately, then aloud,) "with whom we beseech Thee to visit us also." Then "of the Holy Virgin Mary, Mother of God, and of John Baptist, and of Stephen the first martyr, and of all the saints let there be remembrance in this holy oblation, we beseech Thee." Then, after full intercessions for the living, special mention of certain departed :—"Remember, O Lord, also the spirit of Thy servant *N. N.*, and have mercy on him according to Thy great mercy, and on (the day of Thy) visitation give him rest in the light of Thy countenance," (but if he be living, "save him from all snares of the soul and body"). "Remember, O Lord, also those who have recommended themselves to a mention of them in their prayers, both them that are in life, and them that rest in death; direct the intention [or "will"] of their requests unto Thee, and of our own to that which is right and that tends to salvation," &c. (Armenian Liturgy [Gregorian], translated by the Rev. C. Malan.) In the Jacobite Liturgy of the twelve apostles, the one prayer comprises all classes :—" Remember, O Lord, those also who pleased Thee from the beginning, especially the holy glorious Mother of God, Mary, John Baptist, &c. Remember also, Lord, all the faithful departed who have died of old and come to Thee. Receive these oblations which are offered for them to Thee this day, and make them rest in the blessed bosom of Abraham. With hope of Thy mercy, all the departed have received rest, and expect compassions of Thee, our adorable God. Grant that they may be found meet to hear that life-giving word, which shall call them and bring them, that they be invited to Thy kingdom." (Renaudot, ii. 173.) Alcuin has the like prayer in the offices which he framed, chiefly (it is related, *Monit. Præv. Alcuini*, Opp., t. ii. pt. i. p. 3, ed. Frob.) from the Sacramentaries of St. Gelasius and St. Gregory :—"We humbly pray Thee, O Lord, Holy Father, Almighty Everlasting God, for the spirits of Thy servants and hand-maidens, whom, *from the beginning of this world*, Thou hast commanded to be brought to Thyself, that Thou wouldest vouchsafe to give them a lightsome place, a place of refreshment and quiet; that it be allowed them to pass the gates of hell and the ways of darkness, and they may remain in the mansion of the saints and in the holy light which Thou

related to souls on whom the particular judgment
was not yet passed[t]; those for the saints were "for
increase of their glory," as was expressed in words
in a Gothic Missal, before the close of the eighth century[u]; on which also Innocent III., at the beginning
of the thirteenth, says, that "very many thought not

promisedst of old to Abraham and his seed. Let their souls receive no
injury, but when that great day of resurrection and retribution shall
come, Thou vouchsafe to raise them, O Lord, together with Thy saints
and Thine elect, and efface their transgressions and sins 'to the uttermost farthing,' that they may obtain immortal life and an eternal kingdom with Thee." (Ibid., p. 82.) That of Dioscorus in like way prays
God :—" Remember all who, from Adam until now, have had a conversation well-pleasing to Thee, who have departed unto Thee; especially
those who have excellently ministered and served before Thee, *faithful*
priests and deacons, who have purified their own souls and those of
the people," &c. (Ibid., p. 293.)

[t] They occur chiefly on the day of the death or burial (see above, notes
k, l, m). Since some are dying at every moment, the more general prayers
may perhaps relate to them, although not specified. Dieringer says of
these prayers :—" To regard these formularies as prayers for those engaged in the death-struggle is, even on this ground, inadmissible; that
this liturgy, in its central prayers, presupposes death as having already
occurred; but the expressions are too strong to be applied to Purgatory..
But if one brings before one's mind the whole contents of the liturgies in
question, that the Church in these prayers sets the departed before her,
as they undergo the last agony, are placed before their Judge, pine in
Purgatory, await the Resurrection and the Judgment of the world;
all this, in time severed, is to the praying Church, directly present, since
she may be certain that her intercessions and sacrifices, though as yet
future, are taken account of by God at the time when their benefits can
still avail to those who are the objects of them." (*Lehrb. d. Kath.
Dogm.*, § 142, p. 721, ed. 5.)

[u] "For the glory of the martyrs and the rest of the departed."
(*Missale Gothicum in Thomasius*, ".Codices Sacram. 900 annis vetus-
tiores," p. 393, Rom. 1680.)

unworthy [x]." The more common explanation was that they were thanksgivings [y], which suits the forms in which they were commemorated, yet does not fit in naturally with those in which they were prayed for. St. Epiphanius explains that these prayers were intended to mark the difference between the highest saints and God [z]. St. Cyril of Jerusalem, in explaining the Liturgy, apparently arranges the departed mentioned in it into three classes; 1. those who are commemorated and not prayed for—" patriarchs, prophets, apostles, martyrs, that at their prayers and intercessions God would receive our petition;" 2. the holy dead prayed for—"then also in behalf of ($\dot{v}\pi\grave{\epsilon}\rho$)

---

[x] "What is contained in a great many [*plerisque*], viz. 'let such an oblation profit [*prosit vel proficiat*], this or that saint to glory and honour,' ought to be understood, that it should profit to this end, that he should be more and more glorified on earth, or be honoured; although a great many [*plerique*] do not think it unworthy that the glory of the saint be augmented up to the judgment, and that therefore, meanwhile, the Church may wish for an increase of their glorifying." (*Innocent III. Archiep. Lugdun. in Decretal. Greg. IX.* l. iii. tit. 41, vel de celebr. Miss. c. 6. *Quum Marthæ*, p. 614, ed. Ritter.)

[y] *S. Aug. Enchirid.*, c. 109, in his Short Treatises, p. 151, Oxf. Tr., quoted by Innocent III., l. c.

[z] "The prayer for them [the departed] helpeth, although it cuts not off everything of accusation. We make mention of the just and for sinners. For the sinners, we entreat for the mercy of God. For the just, and fathers, and patriarchs, prophets, and apostles, and evangelists, and martyrs, and confessors, and bishops, and anchorites, and the whole Order, that we may separate the Lord Jesus Christ from the order of men through the honours to Him, and may render Him reverence; mindful that the Lord is not on a level with any among men, though any man be ten thousand fold or yet more in righteousness." (*Hær.* 75, n. 7, Opp. i. 911.)

the holy fathers and bishops;" and 3. of all universally who have fallen asleep among us, believing that it will be a very great advantage to the souls, in behalf of ($\dot{v}\pi\grave{\epsilon}\rho$) whom the supplication is put up while the "holy and most awful sacrifice lieth there."

St. Cyril thus meets the difficulty, which was in the mouths of "many," "What is a soul benefited, which departed out of this world with sins or without sins, if it be remembered at the prayer?" He answers the question as to "sinners" by an illustration :—"Now, surely if a king had banished certain who had offended him, and their relations, having woven a crown, should offer it to him on behalf of those under his vengeance, would he not grant relaxation of the punishments? In the same way we also, offering up to Him supplications on behalf of those who are fallen asleep before us, even though they be sinners, entwine no crown, but offer Christ sacrificed for our sins, propitiating both on their behalf and our own, God, the lover of mankind [a]."

When we turn to individual writers in the early Church, we find various statements with regard to the conditions of the souls of the departed : and those not only in different writers, but in the very same; and yet some of these writers are ordinarily so consistent, that their sayings have to be reconciled. Then, too, as to other minds, a concurrent language has great weight as representing some common tone of thought or belief in their period. Now, on the one side, we have broad

[a] Cat. xxiii. Mystag. v. n. 9, 10.

statements, which assume that there are but two abodes in the intermediate state, the one for the saved, the other for the lost; and that the abode of the saved is one of rest and refreshment[b]. They anticipate for

[b] "I affirm that souls never perish, for this would be a godsend to the wicked. What, then, befalls them? The souls of the good are consigned to a better place, and those of the unjust and evil to a worse, there to await the Day of Judgment." (St. Justin M., *Dial. c. Tryph.*, §. 5, p. 78, Oxf. Tr.)

"We will answer [Marcion], this very Scripture too [of Dives and Lazarus], which separates Abraham's bosom for the poor man from the *inferi*, refuting him. For the *inferi* are one place, I deem; Abraham's bosom, another. For he says that a great gulf intervenes between those regions, and forbids a passage on either side. Nor would the rich man have lifted up his eyes, and that from afar, unless unto an upper region. Whence it is clear to any wise man—that there is a certain bounded space called Abraham's bosom, for the reception of the souls of his sons—which shall yield meanwhile refreshment to the souls of the just, until the consummation of all things shall complete the fulness of reward at the resurrection of all; a temporary reception of the souls of the faithful, where an image of the future shall be delineated, and there be an anticipation of either judgment [of eternal death and salvation]." (Tert., *adv. Marc.* iv. 34.)

"Are all souls, then, in the *inferi?* sayest thou. Will you, nill you, thou hast there already both punishments and refreshments; the poor and the rich. For why shouldest thou not think that the soul is both punished and cherished in the *inferi*, under the expectation of either judgment, in a sort of anticipation of it?" (*De anima*, n. 58.)

"Passing which gate [of Hades], those who are brought down by the angels set over souls, go not by one way; but the just, light-led to the right, and hymned by the angels presiding in their place, are led to a lightsome spot, where dwell the just from the beginning, not constrained by necessity, but ever enjoying the gaze of the things which they behold, and gladdened with the expectation of the things ever new, and thinking them better than these; to whom their abode brings no troubles; no burning heat, no frost are there; but the sight of the righteous fathers which they see ever smiles upon them,

the departed the same comfort and peace which people commonly do now ; they console under sorrow for losses

while, after this spot, they await the rest and new eternal life in heaven. It is called Abraham's bosom.—But the unjust are dragged by avenging angels to the left" ("to the confines of hell"). (S. Hippol., *adv. Græc. et Plat.* n. 1, Gall. ii. 451, 452.)

" As those, who departing from this world according to the common death, are disposed of according to their acts and merits as they shall have been judged worthy ; some into the place called *Infernus*, some into Abraham's bosom, and in different places or mansions." (Origen, *de Princ.* iv. 23 (as revised by Rufinus), Opp. i. 185.)

" For neither are the places which lie below the earth themselves void of ordered and arranged powers. For there is a place where the souls of the godly and ungodly are led, feeling the foretastes of the judgment to come." (Novatian, *de Trin.*, c. i.)

" The vengeance of hell overtakes us at once, and, immediately we depart from the body, if we have so lived, 'we perish from the right way.' The rich and poor man in the Gospel shew us this ; the one placed by angels in the abode of the blessed and in Abraham's bosom, the other at once received into the place of punishment. So quickly did punishment come upon the dead, that even his brothers were still alive. There is no deferring or delaying there. For, as the day of judgment is the eternal award either of bliss or punishment, so the time of death orders the interval for every man by its own laws, committing every one to Abraham or to punishment till the judgment." (St. Hilary, in Psalm ii. § 48.)

" I think that I have to prove first of all, that our souls are not dissolved when they put off the body ; but, according to the quality of their deeds, some are banished to penal places, some are cherished in peaceful abodes." (St. Zeno, lib. i. tr. 16, n. 2, *de Resurr.*)

" Why mourn you so pertinaciously those who migrate out of this life to better things ?" (Ib., n. 6.)

" The brazen altar represents the earth, under which is the *Infernus*, a region removed from punishment and fires, and the rest of the saints ; in which the just are seen and heard by the ungodly, but they cannot pass thither." (Victorinus, *in Apoc.* vi. 9 ; *Gall.* ii. 57.) (Those spoken of by St. John are martyrs, but Victorinus has only the two classes, *sancti* and *impii*, of whom the saints are at rest.)

" Between death and the *inferi* there is this difference ; death it is,

with the same topics, not only that those departed rest from their labours, and have no more strife with sin, but that they are in peace[c]; they speak absolutely of

whereby the soul is departed from the body; *Infernus*, a place in which souls are laid up either in refreshment or in pains, according to the quality of their deserts." (S. Jerome, *in Os.* xiii. 14, t. vi. p. 152, Vall.)

"After the departure from the body, forthwith there takes place the distinction of the just and unjust. For they are led by the angels to the places meet for them; the souls of the just to Paradise, where is the converse and sight of angels and archangels, and of the Saviour Christ in vision, as is written, 'being absent from the body and present with the Lord.' But the souls of the unjust to the place of Hades," &c. (*Qu. et resp. ad Orthod.*, p. 75; in St. Justin M., App. p. 470.)

"We learn from the Scriptures that the souls of sinners are in Hades, below all earth and sea, as the Psalm (lxxxvii. [lxxxviii.] 7) says, and as is written in Job (x. 22). But the souls of the just, after the coming of Christ (as we learn from the robber on the cross) are in Paradise. For Christ our God did not open Paradise for the soul of the holy robber alone, but for all the souls of the holy thereafter." (*Quæstt. ad Antioch.*, q. 19, in St. Athanasius, Opp. ii. 272.)

The author of the *Carmen de judicio Domini* in Tertullian, pp. 808, 809, knew but of the two abodes. So Prudentius, Cathem. x. 151 —162, *de exeq. def.*

[c] "We injure Christ, when, as each is called away by Him, we bear it impatiently, as though they were to be pitied. 'I have a desire,' saith the Apostle, 'to be taken and to be with Christ.' But how much better doth he shew the desire of the Christians to be! Wherefore, if we impatiently mourn for others who have obtained this desire, we are unwilling to obtain it ourselves." (*Tertullian de Pat.*, n. 9, p. 340, O. T.) "It is for *him* to fear death, who willeth not to go to Christ: it is for *him* to will not to go to Christ, who believeth not that he beginneth to reign with Christ. For it is written, 'the just liveth by faith.' If thou art just and livest by faith, if thou truly believest in God, why, since thou art to be with Christ and art secure of the Lord's promise, dost thou not embrace thy being called by Christ, and congratulate thee that thou art rid of Satan? Simeon, rejoicing in the nearness now of death, said, 'Lord, now lettest Thou Thy servant depart in peace;' proving and

attesting that then have the servants of God peace, then free, then quiet rest, when, withdrawn from these storms of the world, we gain the haven of our everlasting rest and security." (*S. Cyprian de Mortal.*, n. 2.) "The righteous are called to a place of refreshment, the wicked are hurried to punishment" [by the pestilence]; "the multitude of those who are already believers is called to peace." (Ibid., n. 10.) " We should not regret nor deplore them, nor go into mourning for those who have already put on white raiment." (Ibid., 15.) "Embrace we the day which assigns each to his own domicile ; which restores us, rescued hence and freed from the chains of the world, to paradise and the kingdom of heaven." (Ibid., n. 20.)   "The good man shall go, rejoicing, to his everlasting house, but the wicked shall fill all with lamentations." *Greg. Neocæs. Metaphr. in Eccl.*, xii. 6. p. 95, Paris, 1622.) St. Macarius of Egypt even contemplates the perfecting of the imperfect in a moment by God. "Qu. But if a man, engaged in war, and having two sides in his soul, of sin and of grace, is removed from this world, whither goeth he, being held back on the two sides ? Ans. Where his mind hath its aim, where he loveth, there he goeth.   Only if affliction and war assail thee, thou oughtest to contradict and hate ; for, that the war cometh is not thine, but to hate is thine.   And then the Lord, looking at thy mind, that thou strivest and lovest Him with all thy soul, severeth death from thy soul in one hour (for this is not difficult for Him), and He receiveth thee to His bosom and to the light.   For He snatcheth thee, in an hour's turn, from the mouth of darkness, and forthwith translateth thee to His kingdom.   For to God all things are easy to do in an hour's turn, so thou have love for Him." (Hom. 26, pp. 151, 152, Par., 1622.) "On the two-fold condition of those who depart out of this life." " When the soul of man goeth forth from the body, a great mystery is accomplished there.   For if he be under the guilt of sin, bands of devils come, and angels of the left, and powers of darkness receive that soul, and hold it on their side.—See from the good side that this is so.   For to the holy servants of God there are from now, angels awaiting, and holy spirits encircling and guarding them, and when they go forth from the body, the choirs of angels receive their souls to their side, to the pure world, and thus they bring them to the Lord." (Id. Hom. 22, p. 133.) St. Hilary :—"This guardianship, (to be scorched neither by sun or moon, and to be preserved from all evil,) doth not belong to this time and this world, but is the expectation of the goods to come, when, departing out of the body, all the faithful shall be reserved, through the guardianship of the Lord, for that entrance of the heavenly kingdom, placed meanwhile in Abraham's bosom (whither the interposed gulf hinders the ungodly from approaching) until the time come of entering the kingdom of heaven. The Lord then 'shall guard their going out,' when, going out from the body, they rest, severed from the ungodly by the interposed gulf. The Lord shall 'guard their coming in,' bringing them into that eternal and blessed kingdom." (In Ps. cxx. fin., p. 383, Ben.) "The joy of each just one, as of Lazarus resting in Abraham's bosom, is shewn. For the joy of the just is when he seeth the vengeance (Ps. lvii. 11); because, when sinners are to be punished, he rejoices that he is carried by angels into eternal rest." (Ibid., in Ps. lvii. n. 6, p. 125, Ben.) "Let innocent religion have this confidence, that, if it be put to death unjustly, the soul, going forth from the habitation of the body, rests in the guardianship of God." (Ibid., in Ps. liii. n. 10.) The ancient author of the *de Virginitate* in St. Athanasius :— "If thou walkest in the world, thou walkest in death and out of God, according to the Divine Scripture; but if thou walk in righteousness, thou walkest in life, and death shall not hurt thee. With the just it is not death but translation. For they are translated from this world to the everlasting rest, and as one goeth out of prison, so do the saints go forth from this toilsome life to the good things prepared for them." (n. 8, in St. Ath., Opp. ii. 120, 121.) St. Ambrose :—" Death is in every way a good; because it puts away those principles in us which war against each other, and because it is *a sort of harbour for those* who, after tossing on the wide sea of this life, *seek for an anchorage of secure peace.*" (*De Bono Mortis*, 4.) "Unwise persons fear death as the greatest of ills; but the wise desire it, *as if a rest after toil and the end of ills.*" (Ibid., 8.) "Relying on these considerations, let us betake ourselves courageously to our Redeemer Jesus, courageously to the Council of Patriarchs, to our father Abraham, when our day shall arrive; courageously to that holy assembly and congregation of the just. We shall go to our fathers, to our preceptors in the faith; so that, though our works fail us, our faith may succour us, our birthright plead for us. We shall go where holy Abraham opens his arms to receive the poor, as he received Lazarus; where they rest who in this life endured heavy and sharp inflictions. . . . We shall go to those who sit down in the kingdom of God with Abraham, Isaac, and Jacob, because when asked to supper they did not excuse themselves. We shall go thither, where there is a paradise of delight, where Adam, who fell among thieves, has forgotten to lament his wounds, where, too, the thief himself rejoices in the fellowship of the kingdom of heaven; *where are no*

clouds, where no thunder, no lightning, no storm of wind, no darkness, no evening, no summer, no winter, will vary the seasons. There will be no cold, hail, rain, nor the presence of the sun, moon, or stars; but the brightness of light will alone shine forth." (Ibid., 12.) St. Chrysostom :—
" Think, to whom he is gone, and receive comfort; where Paul is, where Peter, where the whole choir of saints." (*In Illud de Dormientibus nolo*, Hom. 5, n. 3, t. i. p. 766.) "Nor then [when Joseph made the mourning Gen. l. 9—11] were the gates of hell broken, or the bands of death loosed, nor was death called a sleep. Wherefore, when they feared death, they did this; but now, for the grace of God, since death has become sleep, and the end rest, and there is much assurance of the resurrection, we exult and are glad, as removed from life to life. Why say I, 'from life to life?' From the worse to the better, from the temporal to the eternal, from the earthly to the heavenly." (Hom. 67, in Gen. n. 4, t. iv. p. 641.) " It is death no more, but a sleep and a journey, and a translation from worse to better. Wherefore also Paul crieth aloud, 'to depart and be with Christ is much better.' But this is now, since Christ is come, since the gates of brass have been broken, since the Sun of righteousness hath shone forth over the whole world. For then death had still a fearful aspect, and shook the mind of those righteous men." (Ibid., Hom. 45, n. 2, p. 459.) " Death is rest, freedom from labour, reward of toils, reward and crown of struggles. Wherefore, at first, there were wailings and laments for the dead; but now, hymns and psalmodies. For they wept Jacob forty days, and the Jews wept and mourned Moses forty other days. For then death was death; now, not so; but hymns and prayers and Psalms; all things shewing that the event hath pleasure. For Psalms are a symbol of cheerfulness : ' If any is of good cheer, let him sing Psalms.' Since, then, we are full of cheerfulness, we sing over the dead Psalms which bid us be of good courage as to the end. ' Turn again,' he saith, ' unto thy rest, O my soul, for the Lord hath dealt well with thee.' Thou seest that death is a benefit and rest. For he who entereth into that rest, hath rested from his works, as God from His." (*Hom. de S. Bernice*, &c., n. 3, t. ii. pp. 638, 639.) St. Jerome, to a mother on the death of a daughter :—
" Let the dead be lamented, but he whom Gehenna receiveth, whom hell devoureth, for whose pain the eternal fire blazes up. Let *us*, whose departure a company of angels attendeth, whom Christ cometh forth to meet, be rather grieved, if we dwell longer in this tabernacle of death, because, as long as we linger here, we are pilgrims from the Lord." (Ep. 39 *ad Paulam de ob. Blæs.*, n. 3, pp. 177, 178, Vall.) St. Augus-

those being at peace for whom they pray for rest[d]; they so speak not of individuals only, but of the great body of believers. (See above, p. 323, sqq.)

tine :—" Although it is not lawful to doubt that the souls of the just and pious departed live in rest." (*De Civ. D.*, iii. 19.) "Of which [our city of God] how that part had its birth, which is gathered out of mortal men to be associated to the immortal angels, and now is in its mortal pilgrimage on earth, or, in those who have died, rests in secret receptacles and abodes of souls, the same God creating them." (Id., ibid., xii. 9.) St. Cyril of Alexandria :—" The force of His words (' Father, into Thy hands I commend My Spirit') laid a beginning and foundation of good hope for ourselves too. For it ought, I deem, to be held fixed, and very justly, that the souls of the saints, departing from the earthly bodies, are deposited, as it were, in the goodness and loving-kindness of God, as into the hands of a most tenderly loving Father, and not, as some of the unbelievers think, linger in the tombs waiting for the libations there ; neither are they, like the sin-loving souls, conveyed to the place of boundless torment, i.e. Hades ; but rather they hasten to the hands of the Father of all, and of Christ our Saviour Who made for us this new way. For He gave up His soul into the hands of His Own Father, that we, too, having in this and through this received a beginning, may have bright hopes, firmly settled and believing, that we, when we have endured the death of the flesh, shall be in the hands of God, and in a far exceeding better state than we were in the flesh. Wherefore also the wise Paul writes to us, that it is ' better to depart and be with Christ.' " (On St. Joh., xix. 36, l. xii. Opp. iv. 1069, Aub.)

[d] Archbishop Ussher instances that St. Ambrose says of Valentinian :—" Believe we, that the stain of sin being wiped away, he mounts up cleansed, whom his faith washed and his prayers consecrated. Believe we, that he has ' mounted up from the wilderness,' i.e. this dry and uncultivated spot, to those flowery delights, where, united with his brothers, he enjoys the pleasure of eternal life." " Yet," he adds, " blessed both, if my orisons shall aught avail, no day shall pass you by in silence, no speech of mine shall pass you over unhonoured ; no night shall run by, some portion of my prayers unbestowed, I will frequent you in all my oblations." (*De Obit. Valent.*, n. 77, 78, Opp. ii. 1194.) Of Theodosius, St. Ambrose says :—" Freed from doubtful conflict, Theodosius, of august memory, now enjoys perpetual light, abiding tranquillity ; and, for the

This is the light, bright side. There are to be adjusted with this two sets of statements, both founded on Holy Scripture. 1. The one which unquestionably relates to the Day of Judgment, (whether the general judgment of all, or the particular judgment of the single soul, when it parts out of the body,) St. Paul's

things which he did in this body, he rejoices in the fruits of the Divine reward. Therefore, because he loved the Lord his God, he hath attained the fellowship of the saints." (*De Obit. Theod.*, n. 32, Opp. ii. 1206.) Then he prays, " Give perfect rest to Thy servant Theodosius ; that rest which Thou hast prepared for Thy saints. Let his soul turn thither, whence it came down, where it cannot feel the sting of death, where it may know that this death is the end, not of nature but of fault. For in that he died, he died to sin, that now there may be no more room for sin ; but he shall rise again, that life may be restored more perfect by a renewed gift. I loved him, and, therefore, I follow him to the land of the living ; nor will I forsake him until by my tears and prayers I bring the man, whither his merits call him, to the holy mount of God, where is perpetual life, where is no corruption, no contagion, no groan, no dolour, no society of the dead, the true land of the living, where this mortality puts on immortality, and this corruption puts on incorruption." (Ibid., n. 36, 37.) And then again :—"Theodosius there abideth in light, and glorieth in the assemblies of the saints." (Ibid., n. 39.) Of his own brother Satyrus, after setting forth his excellences, he says :—"He hath, then, entered the kingdom of heaven, because he believed the Word of God," (ibid., n. 61, Opp. ii. 28) ; and concludes the oration, " To Thee now, Almighty God, I commend the guiltless soul, to Thee I offer my sacrifice; receive, propitious and serene, the brother's gift, the sacrifice of the priest." (Ibid., n. 80.) And to Faustinus he contrasts his sister's death with the perpetual decay of earthly things ; she, " a holy and admirable woman, who is for a time snatched from us, but is passing a better life *there ;*" " so then," he adds, " I think that she is not so much to be mourned, as to be followed by orisons ; nor is she, I deem, to be saddened by many tears, but rather her soul is to be commended to the Lord." (Ep. 39, Opp. ii. 944.) St. Ephrem, in his Canons for the Departed, prays for those whose prayers he had asked, e.g. Can. 16, Opp. Syr. iii. 259, 261.

description of that fire which shall try every man's work, when they whose work shall be burned shall escape, yet so as by fire. 2. The other, our blessed Lord's words of that prison, into which they who shall be "cast, shall not come forth till" they have "paid the uttermost farthing," which, while some interpreted of hell, others conceived to be a temporary prison; the debt being paid, not by anything which we can do, but by suffering.

1. Of the first class, St. Clement of Alexandria says, "*We* say that fire purifies not flesh but sinful souls, speaking not of that all-devouring and common fire, but of that discriminating fire, which penetrates the soul which passes through the fire[e]." Origen pursues this with much fuller reference to St. Paul's words : "If, after the remission of sins and the dispensation of the washing of regeneration, we sin, (as we most of us do who are not perfected like the Apostles,) and after or with this sinning do some things as we ought, what awaits us? If, after the foundation Christ Jesus, thou hast gold, much or little, silver, precious stone, but also wood, hay, stubble, what wouldest thou should happen to thee after thy departure? Enter into the holies, with thy wood, hay, and stubble, to defile the kingdom of God? Or again, abide in the fire for the hay, wood, stubble, and receive nothing for the gold, silver, precious stone? Neither were this equitable. What, then, followeth, to receive first for the wood? Plainly, that the fire consumeth the wood, hay, stubble.

[e] Strom. vii. 6, p. 851.

For God, Who is a consuming fire, consumed not His own image and likeness, but the wood, hay, stubble, superbuilded[f]."   Origen is followed in this by St. Ambrose, who believed that the Day of Judgment would be prolonged so that all but great saints would have suffering in it.

" 'Thou hast proved us by fire,' says David, therefore we shall be proved by fire; therefore the sons of Levi will be purged by fire; *by fire, Ezekiel; by fire, Daniel.*   But these, though proved by fire, yet shall say, ' We *passed* through fire and water,' (Ps. lxvi. 12). Others shall remain in the fire; and the fire shall be as dew to them (Song of Three Children, 27), as to the Hebrew children who were exposed to the fire of the burning furnace.   But the avenging flame shall consume the ministers of impiety.   Woe is me, should my work be burned, and I suffer this worsting of my labour! Although the Lord will save His servants, we shall be saved by faith, but so saved as by fire.   Although we shall not be burned up, yet we shall be burned.   But how some remain in the fire, others escape through it, learn from another Scripture.   The Egyptians were drowned in the Red Sea, the Israelites passed over; Moses passed through, Pharaoh sank, for his heavy sins drowned him.   In like manner the irreligious will sink in the lake of burning fire[g]."

[f] *In Jerem.* Hom. xvi. n. 5, 6, t. iii., pp. 231, 232 (abridged); *in Num.* Hom. xxv. t. ii. p. 368; also, *in Lev.* Hom. xiv. n. 3, p. 259.

[g] In Ps. xxxvi. n. 26, i. 790, *Ben.*   Again;—"*All must be proved*

St. Hilary also, probably, here as elsewhere [h], followed Origen ; the more so, since he, with Origen [i], combines with St. Paul's words our Lord's saying, " He shall baptize you with the Holy Ghost and with fire;" " for," he adds, " to those baptized in the Holy Ghost it remains to be consummated by the fire of judgment [k]." " Since we are to give an account for every

through fire, as many as desire to return to paradise ; for it is not said for nothing, that, when Adam and Eve were expelled from Paradise, God placed at the outlet of Paradise a fiery sword which turned every way. *All must pass through the flames, whether he be John the Evangelist*, whom the Lord so loved as to say to Peter of him, 'If I wish him to tarry,—what is that to thee ? Follow thou Me ?' Some have doubted of his death ; of his passage through the fire we cannot doubt, for he is in Paradise, not separated from Christ. Or, *whether he be Peter*, he who received the keys of the Kingdom of Heaven, who walked upon the sea, must still say, ' We passed through fire and water, and Thou broughtest us out into a place of refreshment.' But the fiery sword will soon be turned by St. John, for iniquity is not found in him whom Righteousness loved. Whatever human defect was in him, Divine Love melted it away, for ' her wings are as the wings of fire ?' (Cant. viii. 6.) He who possesses here the fire of love, will have no cause to fear there the fiery sword. But he shall be tried as silver, I, as lead ; *I shall burn till the lead melts away.* If no silver be found in me, ah me ! I shall be plunged down into the lowest pit, or consume entire as the stubble. Should ought of gold or silver be found in me, not for my works, but through the mercy and grace of Christ, by the ministry of the priesthood, I shall peradventure say, 'They that hope in Thee shall not be ashamed.' The fiery sword, then, shall consume iniquity, which is placed on the leaden scale. One, then, only could not feel that fire, Christ the Righteousness of God, because He did no sin ; for the fire found nought in Him which it might consume." (In Ps. cxviii. Serm. xx. n. 12—14, i. 1225, B.)

[h] See *Bened. Praef.*, n. 29.

[i] *Hom. 24, in Luc.*, Opp. iii., 961, 962, De la Rue.

[k] *In Matt.* ii. § 4, p. 616 ; add *In Ps.* cxviii. Lit. iii. n. 5.

idle word, shall we desire the Day of Judgment, in which we must undergo that unspent fire, and those heavy penalties for expiating the soul from its sins? The sword will pass through the soul of blessed Mary, that the thoughts of many hearts may be revealed. If that Virgin, who could contain God, shall come into the severity of the judgment, who shall dare desire to be judged of God [1]?"

St. Gregory Nazianzen says, of those who rejected the penitent: "Let these, if they will, go my way and Christ's; if not, their own. Perchance then they will be baptized with the fire, the last baptism, the more painful and longer, which devours what is coarse, like hay, and consumes the lightness of all vice [m]." He says, in a doubtful case of acting: "The end of these things I will remit to the last fire, which convicts and purifies all things with judgment, if by some craft we escape notice here [n]."

St. Ephrem, since he did not know Greek [o], is plainly independent. He says, "Both the just and the unjust shall pass through the fire which is to try them, and

---

[1] *In Ps.* cxviii. Lit. iii. n. 12.

[m] *Orat.* xxxix. in *SS. Lum.*, n. 19, p. 690, Ben. He uses the word τυχόν in the same way of himself:—"Perchance, I shall hereafter be moulded by another moulding, *cleansed by the friendly fire.*" *De seipso,* v. 496, p. 48, Toll. In Orat. iii. n. vii. p. 71, he exhorts to "build on the foundation of faith, not wood, nor hay, nor stubble,—matter unresisting and easily consumed, when what is ours is judged by the fire or purified—but gold, silver, precious stones, which abide and are stable."

[n] *De seipso,* 10—13.

[o] See Dr. Pusey, "Doctrine of the Real Presence," pp. 411, 412.

shall be proved by it; the righteous pass and the flame is quiet; but it burneth the wicked and snatcheth him away [p]:" and "What shall I do, who must pass over the burning flame? How shall I be able to soar high above it [q]?" St. Ephrem connects this fire with the fire of hell, which he prays may shrink back "through the precious Body and Blood of Christ, which" "the saved had received; and that the Cross of the Son of the living God may be a bridge over the sea of fire [r]."

St. Jerome, in answer to Jovinian, (who maintained the paradox, that, as there were only two classes, those on the right hand and those on the left, all the saved would have the same reward,) alleged, among other places, those words of St. Paul: "If he whose work was burned and perished, shall lose indeed the reward of his labour, but himself be saved, yet not without the probation of fire; then, he whose work abides, which he built on the foundation, will be saved without the probation of fire, and so there will be some difference between the salvation of each [s]."

St. Augustine expresses himself as strongly as any other fathers as to the benefit of prayers for the de-

[p] *Canon* xlii., Opp. Syr., t. vi. p. 298; Burgess's Hymns of St. Ephr., p. 32.

[q] *Can.* ix., ib. 236; Burg., p. 18.

[r] See *Canon* lxxxi. init., p. 355; *Paræn.* iii. p. 386, P. xiii. p. 432; P. xxiii. pp. 458, 459; P. lxiv. p. 535; in Dr. Pusey's "Real Presence," pp. 124, 418—422.

[s] *Adv. Jov.*, lib. ii. n. 22; t. ii. p. 360, Vall. His words on Am. vii. 4, seem to me to belong to this life.

parted, and enumerates it among the errors of the Arian Aerius, that he said that oblation "ought not to be made for those asleep[t]." In regard to the purifying fire at the judgment, he used the same language as the others, briefly but undoubtingly in earlier works, and has the well-known passage on its awfulness: "'Rebuke me not, O Lord, in Thine indignation.' Let me not be among those to whom Thou wilt say, 'Go into fire everlasting, which is prepared for the devil and his angels.' 'Nor rebuke me in Thy wrath,' but purge me in this life and make me such that I shall no longer need the amending fire. (This he says) on account of those 'who shall be saved, yet so as by fire.' Why, but because here they build on the .foundation wood, hay, stubble? If they would build gold, silver, precious stones, they would have no fear as to either fire, not only that eternal fire which shall to eternity torment the ungodly, but that also which shall amend those who shall be saved by fire. For it is said, 'Yet himself shall be saved, but so as by fire.' And because it is said, himself shall be saved, that fire is despised. Yet, although they shall be saved by fire, more grievous will be that fire, than whatever men can suffer in this life[u]." In his latest works he

---

[t] *De Hares.*, n. 53, t. viii. p. 55.

[u] *In Ps.* xxxvii. n. 3, t. iv. p. 295. He adds, that in this life good or bad, the martyr and the malefactor, suffer alike the same things. More briefly, *de Gen. c. Man.* ii. 30, Opp. i. 677. "He who cultivates not this field, but allows it to be choked with thorns, has in this life the curse upon his 'earth' in all his works, and after this life will have either a fire of purgation or eternal punishment. Thus no one

somehow throws a doubt on the interpretation, explaining the "fire" primarily of tribulation in this life[x]. Even in that last book, *De Civitate Dei*[y], he writes thus doubtfully: "After the death of this body, until the arrival of that last day of condemnation and reward after the resurrection of the bodies, should it be said that in this interval the spirits of the dead suffer

escapes that sentence (Gen. iii. 17).'' "All are rebuked in the Day of Judgment, who have not the Foundation, which is Christ. But *they* are amended, i.e. purged, who, on this foundation, build up wood, hay, stubble. For they 'will suffer loss, yet shall be saved so as by fire.' What, then, prayeth he who willeth not in the anger of the Lord to be either rebuked or amended ? What but that he be healed ? For where health is, neither is death to be feared, nor the physician's hand, burning or cutting." *In Ps.* vi. n. 3, Opp. iv. 26. "If he shall have built on the foundation, wood, hay, stubble ; that is, if he has built on the foundation of his faith worldly love ; yet, if Christ be in the foundation, so as to have the first place in his heart, and nothing whatever be preferred to Him, such are endured, are suffered. The furnace shall come and shall burn the wood, hay, and stubble ; and 'he shall be saved, yet so as by fire.' This will the furnace (from Gen. xv. 17) do ; it will separate off some to the left ; others it will in a manner strain off unto the right ;—the birds it did not divide." *In Ps.* ciii. n. 5, ib. 1154. He gives the same explanation of Abraham's vision, *de Civ. Dei*, xvi. 24. 4, "By that fire is signified the Day of Judgment, severing the carnal who are to be saved by fire or condemned in fire ;" and xx. 26 : "From these things it seems to appear more evidently, that in their judgment there will be some purifying punishments of some ;" and xxi. 16 : "Let him opine that there will be no purifying punishments, save before that last and tremendous judgment."

[x] Sufferings in this life are put prominent and in the first place, as an adequate meaning of 1 Cor. iii. 11 sqq., with an expression of uncertainty as to any further fulfilment of the words "after this life," *de fide et oper.*, c. 16, pp. 62—65, Oxf. Tr. (about A.D. 413, Ben. Preface), in the *Enchiridion* (not earlier than 421, Ben. Pref.), c. 68, 69, elaborately in the *de 8 Dulcitii quæst.* [A.D. 422 or 425, Ben. Pref.] q. i. n. 6.   [y] xxi. 26, 4.

such a fire, which *they* do not feel who had not habits and likings in the life of this body, which require their wood, hay, and stubble, to be burned up; but *they* feel who have carried with them the like worldly tabernacles, whether there only, or here and there, or not there because here, though they experience the fire of transitory tribulation, rescuing venial offences from damnation by consuming them, I do not oppose, for *perchance* it is true."

St. Paulinus, of Nola :—" 'Our God is a consuming fire.' The Lord grant unto me here, that in me, too, for me, He be a consuming fire. May my heart burn for me with this fire to life eternal, lest my soul burn with it to perpetual punishment. For in this fire shall the day of the Lord be revealed, and 'the fire shall try every man's work, of what sort it is.'—If we dwell in the city of God by those works, whereby we become meet to be citizens with the saints, our work shall not be burned; and that sagacious fire will, when we pass through its ordeal, surround us with no severe heat of punishment; but, as if we were commended to its care, it will play around us with a kind caress, so that we may say, 'We have passed through fire and water, and Thou hast brought us to a place of refreshment '.' "

The other passage,—of a prison, where one who is cast shall pay the very last mite,—if not interpreted of

---

* *Epist.* xxviii. *ad Sever.*, n. 1—3, i. 176, Paris, 1085. So also the author of the *Ep. ad Marc.*, n. 7; ib. App. ii. 6. Lactantius (though no authority) expresses much the same.

hell, as some fathers do, would imply the existence of a place, where those souls should be detained, who although saved, were not yet (on account of their previous misdeeds or neglect of God) admitted to behold Him.

The very ancient Acts of St. Perpetua and St. Felicitas have been thought to have been written by Tertullian [a], and, if so, when a Montanist. In them St. Perpetua relates her being called suddenly to pray for her brother Dinocrates, to have seen him with tokens of distress in darkness, and pining for something withheld. After her prolonged prayers night and day she saw him in light, cleansed, refreshed [b]. In answer to the Pelagians, who quoted this vision, in proof that those who died without baptism might gain its benefits through the prayers of others, St. Augustine answers, (1) that it is not Canonical Scripture [c], from which, in questions of this sort, testimonies ought to be produced; (2) that "perhaps after baptism he had been in time of persecution alienated from Christ through idolatry," "for which he was in punishment, whence he was freed by his sister's prayers [d]." . St.

---

[a] Maintained in a letter to Valesius their editor. Ruinart leaves this doubtful, denies their being Montanist, which Valesius thought, and which to me seems most natural. Tertullian, *de Anima*, c. 55, refers to one of the visions, so they are very old anyhow.

[b] *Acta*, n. 7, 8.   [c] *De Anima*, i. 10, iii. 9, Opp. x. 343, 380.

[d] *ll. cc.* In i. 10, St. Augustine uses the stronger language : "for which he went into the damnation of death, nor went forth, but as granted to the prayers of his sister about to die for Christ." St. Augustine's conjecture of the nature of the sin falls in with the expression in the Acts, "I grieved, remembering his fall."

Augustine entirely believed the Acts, and speaks of "the exhortations of the martyrs in Divine revelations [e]."

St. Cyprian [f], in maintaining that the clemency of the Church in restoring extreme cases of sin, as of adulterers or of those who in persecution had denied the Lord, would not unnerve devotedness or continence, seems to combine both passages. He contrasts "being tortured with long anguish for sins, and long cleansed and purged by fire," with "having purged all sins by suffering" (martyrdom); the "being cast into prison, not to go hence until one has paid the last farthing," with "receiving at once the reward of faith and courage." He adds a contrast yet more awful, "to wait in suspense until the Day of Judgment for the Lord's sentence," and being "crowned at once" by Him.

St. Ambrose, explaining this passage, says, "that the offence is either redeemed by the price of charity, or the punishment relaxed by the estimation of the injury; and that the sin of each is washed away, when the guilty is so long tried by punishment as to pay the penalty of the fault committed [g]."

Eusebius, of Gaul, also connects this text with the fires of judgment: "Thou who hast done things worthy of temporal punishment, to whom is addressed the

---

[e] *Serm.* 280, beg., t. v. 1134.

[f] *Epist.* 55, *ad Antonian.*, n. 16, p. 128, Oxf. Tr.

[g] *In S. Luc.*, lib. vii. n. 156, 157, t. i. 1448. I omit Origen on this place, t. iii. Hom. xxv. p. 975; because, speaking of "infinite ages," in the payment of the 10,000 talents, he, probably, is substituting temporal for eternal punishment.

Word of God, 'that they go not out thence until they pay the uttermost farthing,' through the fiery stream, which the prophetic spirit mentions. In proportion to the matter of the sin, will be the lingering in the passage; in proportion to the growth of the fault, will be the discipline of the discerning flame; in proportion to the things which iniquity in its folly has wrought, will be the severity of the wise punishment [h]."

St. Jerome also explains the text briefly: "What He says means this: 'Thou shalt not go forth from prison, until thou hast paid for even the least sins [i].'"

St. Chrysologus says, on the words of Abraham, "Nor can any one pass hence to you:" "The hearing of this voice terrifies me, brethren, terrifies exceedingly; shewing that, after death, those who have been consigned to penal custody in hell cannot be transferred to the rest of the saints, unless, having been already redeemed by the grace of Christ, they be freed from this hopelessness by the intercession of holy Church. So that what the sentence [of the Judge] denies them, the Church may obtain, grace bestow [k]." He seems to contemplate some extreme cases, in which, but for the foreseen intercession of the Church, sinners would have been left to hell, but were delivered from it through those foreseen intercessions.

St. Paulinus asks prayers for his brother who had died "as a debtor" to God in spiritual negligence. "We mourn his death more truly, because we perceive

---

[h] *De Epiph.*, Hom. iii. Bibl. P. vi. 625.
[i] *ad loc.* vii. 28, Vall.   [k] *Serm.* 123, Bibl. P. vii. 943.

from those things which were done or ordered by him
to his end, he did what corresponded more to our sins
than to our prayers, so that he chose to pass to the
Lord, a debtor rather than free." St. Paulinus then
begged St. Amandus to pray with others earnestly to
God, "that through your prayers He may refresh his
soul with drops of His mercy. For as 'a fire kindled
by Him will burn down to hell below,' so doubtless
the dew also of His forgiveness will penetrate to hell,
so that when scorched in the kindled darkness he be
refreshed with the dewy light of His pity[l]." To
Delphinus, who had converted him, he speaks of his
"spiritual negligence," whereby he provided for his
sons in this world, rather than remedies for the world
to come, "preferring what ought to be secondary,
making secondary what was to be preferred." For
him he asks, in allusion to the history of Dives and
Lazarus, that he would pray lest "we should bring
to shame your piety, which gloried in us your sons,
a portion of the inheritance being wasted, but rather
that it be granted to your prayers, that a drop of
refreshment distilling even from the little finger of
your holiness may sprinkle his soul[m]."

These two aspects of the intermediate state require

---

[l] *Ep.* xxxvi. *ad Amand.*, n. 2, pp. 224, 225.

[m] *Ep.* xxxv. p. 223. St. Nilus speaks of praying for everlasting mercy
for the departed: "He that believes that the just buried will rise again
from the dead, will be strengthened by hope, will give thanks unto God,
will change lamentations into cheerfulness, will pray that the departed
may obtain everlasting mercy, will turn to the correction of their own
stumbling." (*Ep.* i. 101, p. 105.)

reconciliation; the more so, since each is founded upon Holy Scripture. On the one side it says, " Blessed are the dead who die in the Lord! Amen, saith the Spirit, for they rest from their labours." For, although it is primarily said "from their labours," i.e. from the toils of this continual strife with infirmities, passions, temptations, sin, it could hardly have been said that " they rest" at all, if, as More said in the names of the departed souls, " when ye rest, *which we do never.*" On the other side, there are those awful descriptions of the judgment, especially that of St. Paul, in which he speaks of a destruction of the building which some who still built upon Christ had raised during their lives, the loss which these endure, the saving of the man himself so as by fire. Then there are our Lord's awful words, as to that gradation of punishment on breaches of charity (which are the more terrible, if that gradation be understood of eternal punishment only); as to the prison, where " the uttermost farthing" is to be paid; as to the account to be taken of every idle word. Truly, this throws a very awful light upon the Judgment. If every idle word is to be taken account of, what a very individual, searching thing, judgment must be; and this before Him, and by Him, Who loved us and Whom we offended! Awakened conscience and love can imagine no such suffering as this, short of hell. What if the soul be, for a time, or even a prolonged time, uncertain of the issue! Each such moment would be like a lifetime. St. Macarius of Alexandria says, as by Divine revelation, that forty days elapsed before the judgment, and that then, according to its works, the Judge commanded the place of the soul's custody; and this the Angels are related to have assigned to him as the reason why "the Church prayed for the souls of the departed on the fortieth day[n]." St. Cyprian speaks of waiting in suspense to the Day of Judgment[o]. St. Ambrose says, that "the soul is freed from the body, and yet after this life still hangs in suspense through the uncertainty of the future judgment[p]." St. Gregory of Nyssa, uniting in one the particular and the general judgments, describes how, in the sight of the glories of heaven and the punishment of hell, the whole human race, from the first creation to the consummation of all things, shall stand in suspense between fear and hope of the future, trembling oftentimes at the events of the things looked-for either way, and they who have lived with a good conscience, mistrusting what shall be, when they see others dragged down to fearful darkness by an evil conscience as by an executioner[q]. The description of the destruction of the wood, hay, stubble, in the fire of the Judgment Day, was thought, not unnaturally, by Origen and others, to imply a more or less prolonged suffering in that Day, according to the greater or less gravity of the things to be destroyed in those who are saved.

Christian instinct agrees with this. It cannot ima-

<hr>

[n] *De excessu just. et peccat.*, n. 4, Gall. vii. 239.
[o] *Ep.* lv. *ad Anton.*, n. 16.   [p] *De Cain*, ii. 2.
[q] *De beatitud.*, i. 809.

gine that all this history of sin in those who are saved, can be without some great meaning for eternity. And yet in this life none, probably, but the greatest saints, have any conception what sin is. Then it must be revealed to them in judgment.

Again, the human instincts of persons of no depth of Christianity,—in view of the great mass of imperfect, ill-taught, erring humanity, the sheep that have gone astray having no shepherd, living and dying as the great mass of men in our large towns live and die—has turned aside from the idea of hell, and sought comfort in the deadly error of its denial. Yet the false doctrine does not lie in the assertion of a temporal penal abode, but in the denial of an eternal one. The deep instincts of humanity, combined of pity and of justice, demand a belief in some punishment, but deprecate eternal punishment, in the case of many who go out of this world; and here such teaching as has been cited from the early Church comes in to our aid. Nay, not such as those poor outcasts only whom men have most in their eyes and their minds, because their sins are more tangible and coarse, but—and even yet more than these—rich and educated men and women, who have more light than they, yet who, to outward appearance, live mere natural lives, immersed in worldliness, yet not altogether, it is hoped, separated from God, are, as they are, seemingly ripe neither for heaven or hell. God alone knows whether they have deserved hell; yet their whole tastes, thoughts, feelings, tone of mind, would seem to fit them more for a Grecian Elysium than for the Christian's heaven and for the sight of God, of Whom they have scarce thought, save to hope that He would not cast them into hell. Will God think it best for them at once to admit them into His presence, which they have never desired? Or would they be fit to enjoy it, if He did? But if not, and if, when the soul is parted from all earthly distractions, it comes to see that God is its only Good, and is yet withheld from His beatific sight, that it may learn to long for Him, this is at once what the schools have called the *pœna damni;* and this awakened, unsatisfied longing, with the sense that, through its own fault, it remains in this darkness as to God, may be intenser pain than any, or than all the pain which could be accumulated in one in this life. We know what pain separation from an object of deep human love occasions. What may it not be, of God? This falls in singularly with St. Cyril of Jerusalem's remarkable expression, " His banished," as though banishment were a chief suffering.

The very theory of the morality of the Gospel, the notion that justification and sanctification are real, though in the individual often imperfect processes, the belief that salvation depends on obedience[r], conduct us to this thought that the work of Christ in us whereby we are saved, being individually imperfect, in view of our insufficient co-operation with it, shall continue to work in us, so that at the day of judg-

r Matt. v. 1, xxv. 34; Rom. viii. 17.

ment we may be found pure in Him; that having had grace to keep the law of God and having failed to do so, yet having died in His faith and fear, God will carry on the process of our being made fit for heaven, not by the gift of fresh grace, but by the same purifying process of adversity whereby He fines our souls in this life. We know that we have in us passive bad habits, unheavenly tastes, which the soul contracts through sin, and which remain after the guilt of sin is remitted, and that these must be removed before our entrance into heaven, into which nothing that is impure or imperfect may enter. St. Macarius thought that these were removed by God in an instant[s]. The same has been held by very thoughtful minds, who yet had a deep perception of the holiness of God's love[t]. Others may think it more probable that God removes the stain gradually, as it was gradually contracted, and that man's cleansing after death will bear some relation to his cleansing in this life, as St. Augustine often suggests. Only as regards the eternal condition, as the tree has fallen so will it lie; and the eternal distinction between the lost and saved is not confused by the process.

But not only is this thought a source of comfort, in view of such as we have mentioned, it is also fraught with unspeakable consolation in the case of all those who try to do their duty, and who put their whole trust in their Lord's Passion, and yet are conscious of many short-comings, of want of depth and reality

[s] Hom. xxvi. n. 18, in Gall. vii. 29.   [t] Suarez, Disp. xlvii. 1—6.

in their contrition. To such, the idea that after death, although they will have no choice of their own, they will be so conformed to the just will of God, that they may joyfully endure that which is to prepare them for the eternal vision and fruition of Him Whom in their poor way they love above all things, is not only not appalling, however terrible, but actually conducive to holy peace. That true humility which ever seeketh the lowest room, will extend beyond the grave; and to bear the indignation of the Lord because one has sinned against Him, is a disposition of soul well-pleasing to Him.

To sum up what has gone before: while our Church has justly stigmatized popular practices which had become gainful superstitions, she has not condemned either the devotions of the primitive Church, or the deep truths on which those devotions are grounded. Recognising the fact that prayer for the dead, as taught in the Jewish schools, was nowhere reprehended by our Lord; that it was most probably practised by St. Paul, and certainly embodied in all the early liturgies; knowing that the soul does not sleep in the interval before the resurrection; and that, although the Christian's trial ends at the moment of death, there is no ground to think that the soul is simply perfected at once, as it shall be at the coming of the Lord Jesus; deeply convinced that the general tone of the teaching of antiquity goes beyond a mere prayer for consummation of bliss both in body and soul, and probably extends to actual forgiveness for

some sins (perhaps at the foreseen prayers of the
Church), and the mitigation of some penalties; she
has formed her Burial Service on a theory, of which
this doctrine is the only interpretation: that words of
hope may be used with regard to all whom she does
not know to have died not in the state of grace, that
is, all save the unbaptized, the suicide, and the excommunicate[n]—and that therefore by implication, with regard to all save them, however basely they may have
lived, if (which God alone knows) they but died in
a state of grace, the door of salvation is not closed,—
that prayer and Eucharist for them are still available,
—and that with trembling hearts we may in the case
of those we love, who have been riven from us by
death, cast ourselves on the ineffable mercy of Jesus.
And so, with regard to the imperfect Christian, who
has gone to his account, we may rejoice in the thought
that God's love is preparing the soul for perfect fruition, and that, through the fire of suffering and the
water of affliction, He is bringing him into a wealthy
place[x].

Our English minds have so shrunk from the popular

[n] The Burial Service is framed for those who die in Christ; the unbaptized are excluded, because they have not been made members of
Christ, and therefore prayers cannot be said over them, which express
that they had been; the suicide and excommunicate, as having ceased
to be so.

[x] For the legality of prayer for the dead, see case of Woolfrey *v.*
Breeks, Stephen's "Clergy Law," i. 191. The acquittal of Mr. Wilson
was on the ground of his own defence, that all that he meant was, that
in the case of the erring and imperfect, the infinite love of God might
pursue them beyond the grave.

doctrine of Purgatory, because, in the representations of it, physical suffering, and *that* the suffering of fire, (equal perhaps to that of hell, except in its duration,) has been the one thought brought before us. How could the souls be at rest there? But the very same Fathers, who speak of suffering after death, speak also of the souls being in real rest and peace, as our Service for the Burial of the Dead says, that "the souls of the faithful, after they are delivered from the burden of the flesh, are in joy and felicity." They believed, then, that their sufferings, however great, did not interfere with that joy. And so Bellarmine, too, says: "Joy and rest are given immediately upon death, to all who depart in charity. For presently all become certain of their eternal salvation, which brings great joy." "Yet," he adds, "that joy is not given in the same way but diversely, according to the diversity of merits. For to some it is given without admixture of dolour, to others, not without admixture of temporal sufferings, as the same St. Augustine very often teaches [y]." The same has been said yet more boldly, because in the language of devotion.

The treatise of St. Catherine of Genoa brought out the happy side of the state of souls, detained, for a time, through their own fault when in the flesh, from the sight of God. "I do not believe," she says [z], "it would be possible to find any joy comparable to that of a soul in purgatory, except the joy of the blessed

---

[y] *De Purg.*, i. 9, t. i. col. 1894.

[z] Treatise on Purgatory, edited by Abp. Manning, c. 2, p. 3.

in paradise—a joy which goes on increasing day by day as God more and more flows in upon the soul, which He does abundantly, in proportion as every hindrance to His entrance is consumed away." "The souls in purgatory, having their wills perfectly conformed to the will of God, and hence partaking of His goodness, remain satisfied with their condition, which is one of entire freedom from the guilt of sin. Cleansed thus from all sin, and united in will to God, they see God clearly according to the light He imparts to them; they are conscious, too, what a good it is to enjoy God, that for this very end souls are created. Again, there is in them a conformity of will so uniting them to God, so drawing them to Him through that natural instinct whereby God is, as it were, bound up with the soul, that no description, no figure, no example, can give a clear idea of it, as it is actually felt and apprehended by inward consciousness[a]." "When the soul, by interior illumination, perceives that God is drawing it with such loving ardour to Himself, straightway there springs up within it a corresponding fire of love for its most sweet Lord and God, which causes it wholly to melt away: it sees in the Divine light how considerately, and with what unfailing providence God is ever leading it to its full perfection, and that He does it all through pure love; it feels itself stopped by sin and unable to follow the heavenly attraction. I mean that look which God casts on it to bring it into union with Himself, and

[a] Treatise on Purgatory, edited by Abp. Manning, c. 5.

A a

this sense of the grievousness of being kept from beholding the Divine light, coupled with that instinctive
longing which would fain be without hindrance to
follow the enticing look; these things, I say, make
up the pains of purgatory. Not that they think anything of their pains, however great they be; they
think far more of the opposition they are making to
the will of God, which they see clearly is burning
intensely with pure love to them. God meanwhile
goes on drawing the soul to Himself mightily, and,
as it were, with undivided energy : this the soul knows
well; and could it find another purgatory greater than
this, by which it could sooner remove so great an
obstacle, it would immediately plunge therein, im-
pelled by that conforming love which is between God
and the soul[b]." " It is true that the overflowing love
of God bestows upon the souls in purgatory a happiness beyond expression great; but then this happiness
does not in the least diminish the pain, rather the pain
is constituted by this love finding itself impeded; the
more perfect the love, of which God makes the soul
capable, the greater the pain. In this manner, the
souls in purgatory at the same time experience the
greatest happiness and the most excessive pain; and
one does not prevent the other[c]."

Had this been even *an* aspect of Purgatory, presented to the minds of the framers of our Articles,
as a possible authoritative exposition of the doctrine,
who would say that "the Romish doctrine of Purga-

[b] Treatise on Purgatory, c. 9.   [c] Ibid., c. 14.

tory" would ever have been censured in it? Anyhow, *this* doctrine was not included in that censure, since it was not taught. But what heart, which has known but a little of the love of Jesus, and has hated its own sin, would not respond to the thought:—

"It is the face of the Incarnate God
  Shall smite thee with that keen and subtle pain;
And yet the memory which it leaves will be
A sovereign febrifuge to heal the wound;
And yet withal it will the wound provoke,
And aggravate and widen it the more.—
When, then, (if such thy lot,) thou seest thy Judge,
The sight of Him will kindle in thy heart,
All tender, gracious, reverential thoughts.
Thou wilt be sick with love, and yearn for Him,
And feel as though thou could'st but pity Him,
That one so sweet should e'er have placed Himself
At disadvantage such, as to be used
So vilely by a being so vile as thee.
There is a piercing in His pensive eyes,
Will pierce thee to the quick, and trouble thee.
And thou will hate and loathe thyself; for, though
Now sinless, thou wilt feel that thou hast sinned,
As never didst thou feel; and wilt desire
To slink away, and hide thee from His sight;
And yet wilt have a longing, aye to dwell
Within the beauty of His countenance.
And these two pains, so counter and so keen,—
The longing for Him, when thou seest Him not;
The shame of self at thought of seeing Him,—
Will be thy veriest, sharpest purgatory[d]."

[d] The Dream of Gerontius, pp. 43, 44.

II. It is a well-known historical fact that it was the shameless traffic in indulgences which burst the barrier which had long pent up the dissatisfaction which prevailed on account of the scandals and corruptions in the Church. The reforming Councils had no power to stem the increasing corruption; and the expensive tastes of the Roman Curia demanding more and more money, a doctrine, which had its roots in primitive antiquity, was preached in a way to destroy all Christian morality. To the Dominican and Franciscan Orders, now fallen from their first purity, much of the blame is due, though it is fair to state that they were not the only guilty persons. A hundred years before the promulgation of the Articles, this practice had pointed the satire of the poet; and those acquainted with the literature of the period are familiar with Chaucer's and Sir David Lindsay's pictures of the " Pardonere."

To call this a " fond thing, vainly invented, and repugnant to the Word of God," is a mild censure. Gardiner himself describes them as " the devil's craft[e]." At the close of the thirteenth century the fervent Franciscan preacher, Berthold, called the " Penny Preachers" "favourite servants of the devil," and said that " they crowned the devil daily with many thousand souls[f]." In theory, the practice was an application of the power to bind and to loose on earth, which was given by our Lord to St. Peter and to the rest of the

[e] Against Joye, cit. Hardwick, p. 390.   [f] *Deutsche Pred.*, p. 384, ed. Kl.

Apostles [g]; as exercised by St. Paul at Corinth [h], when he forgave in the person of Christ. Such power was inseparable from all canonical penance upon deadly sin, the "godly discipline," the loss of which the English Church yearly laments, when "such persons as stood convicted of notorious sin were put to open penance and punished in this world, that their souls might be saved in the Day of the Lord [i]." For it is essential to law, that the same offence should be subjected to the same penalty. But equity alike and mercy required that this severity should be mitigated in view of the subsequent conduct, penitence, and circumstances of the offender. And this the rather, because the question related, not only to the remission of canonical penance, appointed to certain sins, but (and that chiefly) to the restoration to the communion of the Body and Blood of Christ. Hence it was provided in most cases that communion should be given, in dangerous illness, to those excommunicate, yet under penitential discipline; and on the approach of a new persecution in St. Cyprian's time, the lapsed were restored universally, that they "might be fortified with the protection of the Body and Blood of Christ [k]." And, more generally, (as was reasonable,) the period of penitence was abridged, on evidence of more than usual sorrow for the sins [l]; as, contrariwise, it was prolonged to the

[g] St. Matt. xvi. 10 *sqq.*, xviii. 18.   [h] 2 Cor. ii. 4—10.

[i] Comm. Service.   [k] St. Cypr., *Ep.* lvii. *ad Corn.*

[l] "*Conc. Neocæs.*, can. 3.   *Conc. Anc.*, c. 2, 7, 16.   *Nic.* i. c. 12. *Arelat.* ii., c. 10. Canons of St. Basil, *Ep. ad Amphil.*, c. 4, 7, 53, 74, 84. St. Greg. Nyss., *Ep. Can. ad Letoium*, can. 8—11, 13, 18, 20." St. Leo, Ep. 79, c. 5.

impenitent [m]. " When fervour and discipline were weakened, the Church, both in East and West, substituted lighter penances, sooner than the penitent should refuse all acts of penitence, and so risk the loss of his soul [n]." Penitents were also restored to communion, either altogether, or at an earlier period, at the solicitation of those who were about to die, or had suffered for Jesus Christ; in other words, at the instance of martyrs and confessors. Sometimes that restoration was delayed until the martyrdom was accomplished. The martyrs at Vienne obtained restoration for all the lapsed at once, yet at the hands of the Bishop [o]. St. Dionysius notices the carefulness of the Alexandrian martyrs in recommending those whose " conversion and penitence they discerned [p]." In Tertullian's time, not the lapsed, but those excommunicated for adultery, &c., sought restoration from the martyrs in prison [q]. In St. Cyprian's time the indiscriminate largess of restoration to the lapsed by certain confessors, threatened an utter overthrow of discipline, but was moderated and guided by the loving wisdom of St. Cyprian [r]. St. Gregory of Nyssa regulated by canon [s], that " to those who were zealous in penitence all

[m] *Conc. Carth.* iv., can. 75.

[n] In the East by Joannes Jejunator and Joannes Monachus, in their Penitentials (*ap. Amort, Hist. Ind.,* P. i. p. 32); as also in Bede, Theodore, Burchard, the Roman.

[o] Ep. Eccl. Lugd., &c., in Eus. H. E., v. 1.

[p] St. Dion. *Epist.,* in Eus. H. E., vi. 41, 42.

[q] Tert. *de pudic.,* c. i. and xxii.

[r] See his Epistles xv.—xxiii., xxv.—xxvii., xxx., xxxii.—xxxv., lv.; and those of the Roman Clergy, Ep. xxx., xxxvi.

[s] *Ad Letoium,* can. 8, P. ii. p. 119.

the stages of the public penitence might be abridged by him who was over this matter." Pope Innocent laid down that the ordinary term of remission, the Thursday before Easter, might be anticipated for those in whom " the Priests saw fitting satisfaction[t]." By the Council of Ancyra, bishops might deal ($\phi\iota\lambda\alpha\nu$-$\theta\rho\omega\pi\epsilon\acute{\nu}\epsilon\sigma\theta\alpha\iota$) indulgently with those who had taken part in idol-sacrifices[u].

The Crusades awoke through Europe a deep sense of religion among all classes; and when religion affects all classes, it has been well said that needs must it be, that it should become coarse. As an inducement to make men take up the cross, the privileges which the Church was said to hold within her treasuries were freely unlocked to the faithful. It was said that as our Lord and the saints have merited more than was necessary, there was a disposable stock of merits, which the Church could bestow on all who were fitly prepared to receive the benefit, and remission of sin was freely pronounced to all who joined the army that was marching against the Saracens; and these indulgences were declared to be available not only for the living but for the dead. When the Crusades ceased, actual service being no longer possible, the permission to buy oneself off the Crusade was allowed to the indulgences, and they became marketable. To this day in Spain you may obtain a dispensation for fasting, except on three days in the year, by the

---

[t] *Ep.* xxv. *ad Decentium.*　　　　　　　　　　[u] Can. 5.

purchase of the Bull of the Crusade for five-pence, if a lay person.

Indulgences were, from the middle of the eleventh century, granted on the occasion of the dedication of churches and canonization of saints. On the occasion of the re-consecration of the Portiuncula, in the time of St. Francis of Assissi, A.D. 1221, the first *plenary* indulgence seems to have been granted by Pope Honorius III [x].

In the beginning of the fourteenth century, a new phase of the doctrine manifested itself in the system of jubilees. In 1300, Boniface VIII. issued a Bull of Jubilee, inviting the faithful to frequent the Basilicas of St. Peter and St. Paul, promising to all who approached them reverently, being truly penitent and contrite, or who shall be penitent, or shall confess in the present or in any future year of the century, not only plenary, but larger, yea, the fullest pardon of all their sins, "non solum plenam, sed largiorem, imo plenissimam omnium suorum concedimus veniam peccatorum [y]." The system was found so profitable, that the period of the jubilee was reduced to fifty, thirty-three, and twenty-five years.

It was from such a state of discipline as this, that, after the dark ages, the corruptions we have stated were developed. When the Articles were promulgated, they were in all their abomination. It is but fair to say, that the Council of Trent, while it main-

---

[x] On its genuineness, see Amort, p. 149.
[y] *In Amort, Hist. Ind.*, P. i. p. 80.

tained the practice, as being the exercise of a power given to the Church by God, and used in the most ancient times also, set itself to check the abuses which it acknowledged[z]. How far this last has succeeded, one has no power of judging; but moderate theologians have since that time generally expressed themselves with great candour on the subject, holding indulgences in the primitive sense to be only the relaxation of those canonical penalties, which, in proportion to the gravity of his offence, the sinner ought to endure; and that in the case of those for the dead, they are but the prayers of the Universal Church, which the Pope and all bishops offer in the name of the Church to God, and which God hears, or hears not, as seemeth good to Him.

Mabillon says that "there are three degrees of indulgences: 1. In the time of the Apostles, the relaxation from excommunication, as in the case of the incestuous Corinthian; 2. In the time of the martyrs, when at the instance of their prayers the public penance was relaxed; and 3. at the time of the failure of the public penance which in the ninth century began to be not a little diminished. From that time certain indulgences, some more ample than others, were granted, for the remission of the penalty imposed upon or due to sin. The use of public penance was still in force in those times; but it could be bought off either by Masses and other suffrages, or by alms,

---

[z] Session xxv. *De Indulgentiis.*

or by pilgrimages, or by pious works[a]. The Council of Cloveshoe (A.D. 747) thought the buying off of penance by alms, a new invention, a dangerous custom ('nova adinventio, periculosa consuetudo'). By degrees, however, this method of redemption prevailed."

"In A.D. 878, indulgences were for the first time granted to the dead. Pope John VIII. granted in that year an indulgence to those who fell or were to fall in battle with the Pagans; and the Bishops of Bavaria besought the same favour for the soul of the Emperor Arnulph, which they desired should be absolved by his authority[b]." The notion of a war against the infidels being a directly religious act, involved as a sequence that death in such a war was a sort of martyrdom; accordingly plenary forgiveness of sins was freely promised. The Bull of the Crusade against the Saracens (A.D. 1118) ran in these terms: "And since ye have determined to expose both yourselves and the things belonging to you to the most extreme perils, if any of you, having accepted the penance for your sins, shall die in the expedition, we, by the merits of the saints

---

[a] *Præf. ad Sæc.* 5, *Benedictin*, n. 107.

[b] Ibid. Amort, however, doubts whether these were strictly indulgences. He observes that, 1. "John VIII. says, 'we absolve them, *quantum fas est;*' 2. the absolution was from their *sins;* 3. the Pope adds, 'and we commend them by prayers to the Lord.' 4. The Bavarian Bishops asked for that *same* indulgence for Arnulph. 5. Card. Ostiensis, A.D. 1260, thought that such indulgences were only absolutions from censures, to the effect that the faithful might be free to pray for them in the church," (Hist. Indulg., p. ii. S. v. § 1). See the letter to the French bishops as given from Baronius, A. 878, xxxiv. ib.

and by the prayers of the whole Catholic Church, absolve him from the chains of his sins [c]." That of
A.D. 1122 says: "that to those who go to Jerusalem
to defend the Christians, and to aid in breaking down
the tyranny of the infidels, we concede the remission
of all their sins [d]."

However much the Council of Trent may have cleared
away the difficulties with regard to pardons, by defining
them to be only a remission of the canonical discipline
of the Church, it cannot be denied that at the promulgation of the Article there was a substantial abuse
which well deserved its reprobation. What that abuse
was will best be seen from Erasmus' tract, *De Utilitate
Colloquiorum*, where he defends the line he took with regard to them: "Nor do I, then, condemn papal indulgences and bulls; but I censure that greatest of triflers
who, thinking nothing of amendment of life, presumes
to place his whole trust on human pardon." So in
the colloquy "Rash Vows," speaking of one who died
on pilgrimage:—

"*Con.* Was he, then, so pious?

"*Am.* Nay, the greatest trifler imaginable.

"*Con.* Whence, then, do you draw the conclusion
(that he is now in heaven)?

"*Am.* Because he had his satchel stuffed full of the
most ample indulgences."

[c] In Baronius, A. 1118, xviii. That against Roger, Count of Sicily,
in like way, "remitted all sins" under the same terms. Baron., A.
1127, v.

[d] Given by Calixtus II. in the Council of Lateran, A.D. 1122,
can. 11.

Thus in the Vision of Piers Ploughman :—

> " Then preched a pardoner, as he a prest were,
> Brought forth a bulle, with many bishope's seles,
> And seide that himself might assolven them all
> Of falshod, of fastynge, of a-vowes y-broken."

These indulgences were not granted by the Pope only, but by all bishops[e].

" The 'Questionarius,' 'Pardoner,' or 'Preacher,' was already so scandalous, that the antipope, Clement VII., in granting indulgences for building the nave of the cathedral of Aberdeen, A.D. 1380, declares that they shall be of no force if hawked about by these spiritual pedlars: ' Presentes autem mitti per Questuarios districtius inhibemus, eas si secus actum fuerit carere viribus decernentes[f].'

"The Quæstor, Quèstuarius, or Questionarius, the Pardoner, or Rome-raker as he was called, had now fallen on evil days. Even in his better state, when he played something like the part of the travelling deputation of the popular religious society of our own time, the Synod of Exeter, A.D. 1287, could describe him as ' Communiter idiota, vitæ pariter inhonestæ, confingens se peritum et vitæ sanctitatem exterius prætendens ... ut sic simplicium alliciat animos ad majores eleemosynas largiendas, quas postea in ebrietatibus et luxuriis in omnium conspectu prodigaliter consumere non erubescit[g].' He was the constant butt of ridicule from the fourteenth century downwards. He figures

---

[e] Vide J. G. Nichols' "Pilgrimage of St. Mary of Walsingham," p. 98, London, 1849.   [f] Robertson's *Statuta Eccl. Scot.*, vol. ii. p. 266.   [g] Wilkins' *Concilia*, vol. ii. p. 154.

in the 'flighting' of Kennedy and Dunbar, in 'the Satire of the Three Estates,' and in 'Symmie and his brother;' but no portrait of him can be compared with that drawn by the master-hand of Chaucer. Lindsay paints him as disheartened and discredited:—

> 'But now alace! our gret abusion
> Is cleirly knawen till our confusion
>   Quhilk I may sair repent.
> Of all credence I am now guyte,
> For ith man holds me in despyte,
>   That reids the New Testament [h].'

"The Council of Trent silenced him in 1546, and suppressed him altogether in 1562 [i]."

III. "Worshipping and adoration, as well of images as of relics," is the next point excepted against. In the state of ignorance in which the common people were for some time before the Reformation, it is not surprising that this should be so. There is always a danger of religion among the unlettered becoming superstitious, and even in northern nations, there is a tendency to turn objects of faith into anthropomorphic forms. The employment of Christian art, necessary and advisable as it was, to keep alive a belief among the poor, on St. Gregory's principle, that pictures are the books of the ignorant, had of course its dangerous tendency; and, as a matter of fact, a cultus of images had grown up which required

---

[h] Poet. Works, tom. ii. p. 9, 27. [i] Robertson's *Statuta Eccl. Scot.*, vol. ii. p. 288.

to be checked, and all its coarser manifestations to be condemned. That condemnation is still due where men of education, in the nineteenth century, have gone so far as to attribute a sort of quasi-sacramental value to images, as is said to be the case with some recent theologians. On the other hand, the absence of pictures can alone account for the gross ignorance of religion so prevalent among the peasantry of England.

The whole history of the employment of art in religion is intensely interesting. In the earliest times there is an entire absence of images, though not of pictures, from the worship of the Christians. Tertullian seems to deny that any images were used. Origen and the apologists follow in the same line[k], and so long as heathenism was an existing fact, there was great reserve in the Church in this respect. In the Catacombs, though there are figures of our Lord and His Mother, most of the decorations are symbolical, e.g. Orpheus drawing the beasts to him, to typify our Lord drawing all hearts to Him, and Moses striking the rock, and the multiplication of the loaves, to indicate the two principal sacraments. The early writers held that no image of God was to be made[l]; they maintained the bindingness of the literal sense of the Second Commandment[m]; some censured painting

---

[k] Orig. *c. Cels.*, viii. 17. Cæcilius in Minut. F., p. 91. Arnobius, lib. vi., Lact. *de mort. Persec.*, 12.

[l] St. Clem. Al., *Strom.*, vii. 5; Orig. *c. Cels.*, l. c.; Minut. F., p. 313; Lact. ii. 2; and, in regard to God the Father, Greg. II., *Ep. 2, ad Leon. Is.* in 7 Syn., p. 503 A; St. Aug., *de fide et Symb.*, c. 7.

[m] St. Clem. Al., *Strom.*, v. 5; Orig. *c. Cels.*, v. 6, vi. 14, vii. 64; Tert.

and sculpture altogether [a]; yet Tertullian himself mentions the symbol of the Good Shepherd on the chalice [o]; and the Encratites were blamed for a certain heathenish cultus to the images of Christ [p]. The statue at Cæsarea Philippi which Eusebius relates, " they *say*, is the image of Jesus," set up by the woman whom our Lord had healed of the issue of blood; and the pictures of St. Peter and St. Paul are said, at least by him, to have been made "after a Gentile custom of so honouring benefactors [q]." Then, however, the *vetri Christiani*, and other articles in the Christian museums, shew that gradually the use of art in aid of religion asserted itself. It did not do so, without conciliar resistance, as in the celebrated Canon of Elvira : " We will not have pictures placed in churches, lest that to which our worship is directed be seen on the walls." There is the history of St. Epiphanius destroying in Palestine the " picture as of Christ or some saint" (he remembered not which), and his request to John, Bishop of Jerusalem, to enjoin that " such veils which are against our religion, should not be

---

de Spect., 23 ; *de Idol.*, 3, 4; St. Cypr. *Test.*, iii. 59. St. Augustine held all the Decalogue to be binding on Christians except as to the Sabbath ; *c. Faust.*, xv. 4, 7, xix. 8; *con.* 2 *Epp. Pelag.*, iii. 4.

[a] Clem. Al., *Protr.*, n. 4, p. 18; Orig. *c. Cels.*, iv. 31 ; Tert., *de idol.*, 3, 4; *c. Hermog.*, init.

[o] *De Pudic.*, c, 6, 10. In note 28, on St. Paulinus, *Ep.* xi., it is said "under this form Christ occurs in the Roman Hagioglypta." St. Paulin., Opp., t. ii. p. 35. Constantine set them up in the market-places. —*Eus. de Vit. Const.*, iii. 49.

[p] St. Iren. i. 25, 6. [q] H. E., vii. 18.

hung up in the Church of Christ;" and St. Augustine
denies that Christians had images in Churches[r], and
speaks strongly against them[s].   On the other hand,
we have St. Paulinus of Nola's praise of Sulpicius
Severus[t], for having had St. Martin as "a perfect
imitation of Christ," painted "in the place where man
is formed anew" [the Baptistery] as "an object of imitation." Out of modesty, he blames him for representing
himself[u].   St. Paulinus himself had pictures of Job
with his sores, Tobit in his blindness, Esther and
Judith on two side doors of the Basilica of St. Felix,
and figures of Martyrs on the centre door.   In the
interior he mentions symbols only in mosaic; Christ
as a Lamb; a hand with a crown, symbolizing the presence of the Father; the Dove, probably on the Cross;
the Cross in a globe of light; or, standing on a rock
whence issued four streams, the Four Gospels[v].

A favourite type was Abraham's sacrifice of Isaac[w].
Then there were the representations of martyrdoms, as
of St. Cassian[x] and St. Hippolytus[y] in Prudentius;
St. Theodorus in St. Gregory of Nyssa[z]; St. Euphemia
(in a piece of exquisite beauty) in St. Asterius[a].   St.
Gregory of Nyssa, too, seems to speak as if the pic-

---

[r] *In Ps.* cxiii. n. 6.   [s] Ib., and *de cons. Evang.*, i. 10.

[t] *Ep.* xxxii. *ad Sev.*, n. 2, 3, pp. 199, 200.

[u] *Natal. S. Felic.*, x. 20—27, *Poem.*, pp. 159, 160.

[v] *Ep.* xxxii. *ad Sev.*, n. 10, p. 206, and notes, pp. 66—70.

[w] St. Greg. Nyss., *Orat. de Fil. et Sp. Div.*, iii. 476, painted in so
many places; Aug. c. *Faust.*, xxii. 73.   [x] *Perist.*, ix. 5 *sqq.*

[y] Ib., xi. 126 *sqq.*   [z] T. iii. p. 579.

[a] *Enarr. in Mart. D. Euphem. in Combefis*, i. 207—210.

tures of the martyrdoms, such as that basilica had, were to be found commonly in the basilicas of martyrs[b]. Evidently at first these paintings were historical, and St. Gregory, in his Epistle to Serenus, Bishop of Marseilles, commends him for having broken and cast out some images: "I praise thee that thou wert zealous, that nothing made with hands shall be worshipped[c]." Then he distinguished between their use for instruction, and their abuse for worship.

From the time of Constantine the cross continued more and more to be honoured; he himself set it up in many places[d]; it was worn as a protection by St. Macrina, the sister of St. Gregory of Nyssa[e]; it was defended as an object of honour by blessed Jerome of Jerusalem[f].　St. Nilus recommends for the decoration of a church one and one only cross, in the sanctuary to the East[g], and histories contained in the Old and New Testament on every side, done by the hand of the most skilful painter, in order that they who are unable to read the Divine Scriptures, may have a remembrancer of the worthy actions of those who have

[b] "Whoso cometh unto some spot like this, where is a memorial of the just, and a holy relic, his soul," &c. (Ibid.)

[c] Epp. ix. 105, xi. 13.

[d] *De laud. Const.*, c. ix. p. 740.

[e] *Ep. ad Johan. Hieros.*, translated into Latin by St. Jerome, Ep. lx. He uses stronger language in relation to the image made of the Blessed Virgin by the Collyridians, Hær. 79, p. 447. Another statement of the unlawfulness of images was quoted from him in *Conc. Const. in Act.* vi.; t. v. *Conc. Nic.*, ii.

[f] Galland., tom. vii. p. 530.

[g] Lib. iv. Ep. lxi. p. 491, 2.

B b

nobly served the true God, and be excited to emulate their "glorious excellencies." In the accusation against Ibas in the Council of Chalcedon, mention is made of "the crosses of silver and gold offered and dedicated [h]."

The history of the enlarged use of images is obscure. Of their use apart from churches, there is the memorable instance of St. Meletius, whose image, St. Chrysostom relates, was placed by the Antiochenes on rings, seals, cups, and chamber-walls [i]. Theodoret mentions a report that small images of St. Symeon Stylites were set up at the entrances of all the workshops, as a protection [k]. St. Chrysostom speaks of $\dot{a}\gamma\dot{a}\lambda\mu\alpha\tau\alpha$ which stood in the church [l], which some think to have been the Cross. In the Canons of the Quini-sext Council it is asserted that our Lord should be represented under the human figure, rather than under that of the Lamb [m]. Pope Hadrian says at the time of the sixth General Council (A.D. 680) that "sacred images and painted histories had *of old time* been reverenced [n]." The popular excitement at the insult, when Leo Isauricus had an image of our Lord cast down, evinces what an outrage they felt it to be to Himself. The Iconoclast troubles were Eutychian in their origin [o], carried on by godless Emperors, and settled by the second Council of Nice. The protest

---

[h] n. 8, Conc. iv. 650, Labbe.
[i] Hom. 10, *in Eph.*, n. 2, t. xi. p. 89.
[n] *Conc.*, t. vi. p. 136.

[l] *Hom. de S. Meletio,* t. ii. p. 519, Ben.
[k] *Hist. Relig.*, c. 26, t. iii. p. 1272.
[m] Can. 82.
[o] See Petav. *de Inc.*, xv. 11.

of the Council of Frankfort rested probably on the misinformation that the Council of Nice had enacted that they who did not pay to the images of the saints service " or adoration, in the same way as to the Deific Trinity, should be adjudged anathema [p]."

The dark ages set in, then commences the time of those miraculous and rudely-carved representations which still hold their places in some countries,—the Volto Santo at Luca, and the like. Many sacred images were brought from the East in the times of the Iconoclastic troubles, and formed centres of devotion in the West: God probably blessing the poor ignorant creatures who came to Him with what imperfect faith they had. Nor them only, for from that rude Byzantine art sprung the unspeakable devotional glories of the early Tuscan and Sienese schools; the pictures that speak to the soul as very symbols of divine truth; which pourtray, as no human hand before or since has done, the purity of the Virgin Mother; the ever young, ever fresh bliss of the saints in glory, the ineffable sufferings of God made man for us. God is to be praised for the gifts which He bestowed, obtained by prayer and sacramental communion, on Beato Angelico da Fiesole, and on those who have toiled in the same spirit, Sano di Pietro Duccio, and Gentil da Fabriano. Next to the development of a Christian philosophy, the greatest desideratum of the times is the development of a school of Christian art.

Of the *having* images or pictures, nothing is said in

[p] Conc. Francof., can. 2, quoted ib.

the Article, only of worshipping them. It was a common saying among many schoolmen, that "the same honour was due to the image as to the original, and so that the image of Christ was to be worshipped with *latria*, that of the Blessed Mary with *hyperdulia*, that of the saints with *dulia* [q]." But this language was easily misunderstood; and probably nothing more was intended than what was expressed in the very opposite way, viz. that "the image was nowise to be worshipped in itself, but only the original was to be worshipped before the image [r]," according to the lines engraven in a church at Venice, contemporary, it is thought, with the second Council of Nice :—

> "Nam Deus est, quod imago docet, sed non Deus ipsa ;
> Hanc videas, sed mente colas quod cernis in ipsa [s]."

And the Council of Nice, which they all acknowledged, had said that "images were to be worshipped, but not with *latria* [t];" and Basil of Ancyra, and Constantine, who recanted before the Council, said "that they received and worshipped images, but not with *latria* [u]." Whence Bellarmine, too, says, "As to the mode of speaking, especially in sermons to the people, it is not to be said, that any images are to be adored with *latria*, but contrariwise that they are not to be so adored." In support of this, he quotes two Councils

---

[q] Quoted by Bellarm., *Contr. de Imag. Sanct.*, ii. 20, t. i. col. 2146.
[r] Ibid.   [s] Ibid.   [t] Act. vii.
[u] Act. i. and iii., quoted by Bell. *l. c.*, c. 22.

of his own time, which said, "that the people ought to be admonished by preachers not to adore images [x]."

A vivid representation calls forth in us the feelings which are felt towards the original. It is so in feelings merely human. People kiss the picture or some relic of one whom they deeply love, as if it were the person. The picture of a friend speaks to us, and people speak to it, as if it were himself. If one kissed the feet of the Crucifix, it would be accompanied by a mental act to our crucified Redeemer, such as St. Mary Magdalene's when she kissed His feet in the feast; it would be an act of humble penitence and adoring love to Himself as our Redeemer. The act would be addressed to our Lord Himself, although elicited by the image.

The homilies illustrate what it was, in regard to the veneration or worship of images, which the framers of the Articles had before their eyes [y]. The Council of Trent reformed in the direction which our writers wished, but, by reforming, owned the existence of the evils complained of :—

"Into these holy and salutary observances should

[x] *Conc. Senon.*, c. 14; *Mogunt.*, c. 41, ib.

[y] See Tract XC., p. 32—37, ed. Pusey. "Thus there was a rood at Boxley, in Kent, made with devices to move the eyes and lips (but not to see and speak), which, in the year 1538, was publickly shewn at S. Paul's by the preacher, then Bishop of Rochester, and there broken to pieces; the people laughing at that which they adored but an hour before. Such imposture was also used at Hailes Abbey, in Gloucestershire, where the blood of a duck (for such it appeared at the dissolving of the house) was so cunningly conveyed that it spirted or sprung up, to the great amazement of common people, accounting it the blood of our Saviour." (Fuller, Ch. Hist., book vi. sect. iv. 8—10, vol. ii. p. 244, ed. 1837.)

any abuses creep, of these the Holy Council strongly [*vehementer*] desires the utter extinction; so that no images of a false doctrine, and supplying to the uninstructed opportunity of perilous error, should be set up. All superstition, too, in invocation of saints, veneration of relics, and sacred use of images be put away; all filthy lucre be cast out of doors; and all wantonness be avoided; so that images be not painted or adorned with an immodest beauty; or the celebration of saints and attendance on relics be abused to revelries and drunkenness; as though festival days were kept in honqur of saints by luxury and lasciviousness."

IV. The worshipping and adoration of relics, is the next subject of condemnation of the Article. The shameless frauds of the Friars at the time of the Reformation are well exposed in the writings of the time, and the undue veneration in which the relics of the saints were held is one of its most powerful chapters. Yet the principle that lay at the bottom of the sentiment was not in itself vicious, and had early established itself in the Church. They who see nothing incredible in the mantle of Elias dividing Jordan, in the bones of Elisha restoring a man to life, in the handkerchiefs and aprons that had touched St. Paul healing disease and casting out evil spirits, will see no antecedent improbability in some of the effects which well-authenticated Church history alleges to have been wrought by God, in connection with the remains of some of His most distinguished servants.

To attach a sanctity to the bodies of the saints, which
in life had been the temples of the Holy Ghost, which
had carried Christ formed within them, was one of the
earliest feelings of the Church[z]. To save the bodies
of the martyrs, after their Passions, became the privilege
of the early Christians. The more solid parts of St.
Ignatius, torn by wild beasts, were carried to Antioch,
wrapped in linen, and bequeathed to the Church[a]. The
Church of Smyrna collected the bones of St. Polycarp
from the fire, where they had been cast to prevent his
body being carried off[b]. St. Saturus plunged a ring
into his wound and gave it to Pudens as a memorial[c].
Clothes stained with the sweat of St. Cyprian were
eagerly coveted[d]. At the martyrdom of St. Vincentius,
the multitude received the blood in linen cloths with
sacred veneration, to be a benefit to their posterity[e].
The governor Maximus gave notice that he would
not allow the relics of St. Tarachus and others to be
carried away, but was defeated by the Christians'
prayers[f]. St. Ambrose, St. Augustine, and Paulinus of
Milan, agree in attesting the miracle of the restoration
of a well-known blind-born man to sight, when he

[z] See a magnificent passage in the peroration of St. Chrys. Comm. on
the Romans. Hom. 32, p. 757, ed. Mont.

[a] *Martyr. S. Ignat.*, n. vii.

[b] *Ep. Encycl. Eccl. Smyrn. de mart. S. Polyc.*, n. 17, 18.

[c] *Pass. SS. Perp. et Fel.*, n. 21, p. 96, Ruin.

[d] *Vit. et pass. St. Cypr.*, in Ruin., p. 214.

[e] *Pass. St. Vincent.*, ib., p. 395. Prudentius says the same, probably from the Acts, *Hymn.* v. *Pass. St. Vincent.*, 341—44.

[f] *Pass. St. Tarachi*, &c., Ruinart., p. 490, 491.

touched the hem of the garment which covered the newly-discovered relics of St. Gervasius and Protasius [g]. The miracle stopped the persecution against St. Ambrose. St. Cyril of Jerusalem mentions that the world was filled with wood of the Holy Cross which was dis-covered there in his time [h]. The depositing of the relics of martyrs, as an honour of basilicas, is mentioned by Eusebius [i], by Nilus [k], the eye-witness of the martyrdom of St. Theodotus, by St. Gregory of Nyssa on the Martyr Theodorus [l], and on the forty martyrs [m], and by St. Ambrose [n]. St. Basil promises to assist the zeal of Arcadius by sending him some martyrs' relics, if he can discover them [o]; he asks Soranus to send him some, "since the persecution in your parts even now makes martyrs unto the Lord [p]." St. Paulinus writes— "Our brother Victor has informed me, that you, as is worthy of your faith and grace, want, for the basilica which you have built, the blessing from the sacred relics of saints, whereby your Church should be adorned. The Lord is my witness, that if I had even

---

[g] St. Ambrose, *Ep.* xxii. *Sorori*, t. ii. 874, 848, embodying his discourse to the people; St. Augustine, *Conf.*, ix. 7, n. 16 (see note, Oxf. Tr.) *Serm.* 286, n. 4, 5, (where he says, "I was there; I was at Milan,") t. v. p. 1689; *de Civ. D.*, xxii. 7, t. vii. p. 1057, 1058; Paulinus, *Vit. S. Ambr.*, n. 14.

[h] *Cat.* x. 19.   [i] *Vit. Const.*, ii. 40.
[k] In Gall., iv. 119.   [l] T. iii. p. 579, 580.

[m] *Orat. in xl. Mart.*, t. ii. p. 213. He says, that "well-nigh the whole earth is blessed with the remains of the forty martyrs," p. 211.

[n] *Exh. Virg.*, n. 1. *Ep.* xxii. *Sorori*, t. ii. pp. 874—878.

[o] *Ep.* xlix. *Arcad.*, t. iii. p. 203.

[p] *Ep.* clv. *Sorano*, p. 354.

a scruple of sacred ashes more than I need for dedicating the basilica which will soon be completed in the Name of the Lord, I would have sent it to you [q]."

St. Jerome asks Vigilantius whether it is ill done of the Bishop of Rome, who, over the venerable bodies of the departed Peter and Paul, offers sacrifice to the Lord, and accounts their tombs Christ's altars; and not the Bishop of one city only, but the Bishops of the whole world who go into the basilicas of dead men, &c. He relates that the Emperor Constantius " translated to Constantinople the relics of Andrew, Luke, Timothy,— before whose relics demons howl; that Arcadius translated the bones of blessed Samuel from Judæa into Thrace; while from Palestine to Chalcedon the crowds were as one mighty hive, and lifted on high with one voice the praise of Christ [r]."   In the fourth century the system was distinctly recognised and regulated by Canon, as in the 5th Council of Carthage, A.D. 398, which legislated in regard to the wayside altars erected as memories of the martyrs [s]. The coarse attack of the inn-keeper Vigilantius was not of a nature to gain him followers, or to disturb the tide of pious feeling. Eminent fathers believed that there resided power in the bodies also of the just, which had so long been the temples of the Holy Ghost [t], that God witnessed to

---

[q] *Ep.* xxxi. *ad Sever.*, init.   [r] *Adv. Vigil.*, n. 4.

[s] Can. xiv. It directs that the bishops should overthrow those in which it should be proved that there was no body or relic of martyrs.

[t] St. Cyril Jerus., *Cat.* xviii. 16. "There reposes in that body a power greater than that of the soul itself,—the grace of the Holy

them who had witnessed to Him, and that He shewed, in this way also, that "right dear in the sight of the Lord is the death of His saints," that prayers were answered near the bodies of the martyrs, and that the touch of their relics dispelled disease. The evidence is irresistible [u]. Modern theorists will solve

Spirit, which, by the miracles which it performs, gives proof to all of the resurrection." (St. Chrys. *de St. Babyl.*, t. ii. p. 635.)

[u] St. Hilary says :—" Everywhere was the holy blood of the martyrs received, and daily are their venerable bones a testimony, while demons howl at them, while sicknesses are dispelled, while wonderful works are seen." (*Cont. Const. Imp.*, n. 8.) " The tombs of the apostles and martyrs, by the operations of miracles, speak of Him [Christ]." (*De Trin.*, l. xi. n. 3, p. 1084.) St. Gregory of Nazianzum:—"By them devils are cast out and maladies cured ; whose bodies, even alone, whether touched or honoured, can effect as much as their holy souls ; even whose drops of blood alone, and the minute symbols of their passion, can do as much as their bodies." (*Adv. Julian. Orat.* iii., t. i. p. 76.) " The driving away of evil spirits, the removal of diseases, the foreknowledge of future events—all which the very dust of Cyprian can effect, where there is faith, as they know who have made trial, and have transmitted the miracle even to us, and will deliver it to future ages." (*Orat.* xviii. *de S. Cypr.*, p. 285.) " What if I should speak of diseases and demons expelled in a manner surpassing belief, so as to amount to miracles ?" (*Carm. Iamb.* xviii.) St. Ambrose :—" It is a source of joy unto all to touch but the extremest portion of the linen that covers them ; and whoso touches is healed." (*Ep.* xxii. *Sorori*, t. ii. p. 87.) St. Augustine :—" What does God, by performing marvellous works near the bodies of the saints, but furnish a testimony that what dies perishes not to Him ? and it may hence be understood in what honour He holds the souls of the saints who are with Him when the soul-bereft flesh is adorned with so mighty an operation of the Divinity." (*Serm.* 275, *in Nat. S. Vincent.*, n. 3, t. v. col. 1631.) " Think what things God reserves for us in the land of the living, He who bestows things so great from the dust of the dead." (*Serm.* 317, n. i. *de S. Steph.*, ib., 1870.) St. Isidore of Pelusium :—" Ask those who are cured by those martyrs, and learn to how many they vouchsafe remedies." (*Ep.* i. 55. *Hieraci.*)

the knot by believing that the cures were wrought by the subjective excitation of spirit and the heated imagination of the ignorant votary. It is a humbler and surer line to take, to say that God, dealing with a rude and unlettered race, permitted that these relics should be the *media* of His own mercy in cure.

All through the dark ages relic-worship prevailed, but it was after the Crusades that it arrived at its intensity. The thought of the Holy Land filled all Europe with the tenderest sentiments of love and compassion, from the contemplation of the Life and Sufferings of the Saviour; and the soldiers of the Cross brought home objects which purported to be of the most sacred nature. Beautiful churches, in the purest taste of the first Pointed style were erected to receive them, and the skill of the goldsmith and enameller enlisted to do honour to the blessed objects in a style which still excites our admiration. At first, no doubt, the sight of these relics advanced

St. Victricius, A.D. 396 :—" Do they [the particles of the relics] afford healing to the miserable, in a different way in the East, at Constantinople, Antioch, Thessalonica, Neissa, Rome, in Italy ? Are the suffering bodies cleansed in different ways ? John Evangelist heals at Ephesus, and in many other places; and with us is his same medicine. At Bologna heals Proculus, Agricola, and here too we see their majesty ; Antoninus heals at Placentia ; Saturninus heals, Trajan heals in Macedonia. Nazarius healeth at Milan ; Mutius, Alexander, Datysus, Chyndeus, infuse the grace of health with abundant virtue. Healeth Rogata, Leonida, Anastasia, Anatoclia. I ask, is the remedy of the saints one with us, another with others ? But if all the saints everywhere defend with like tenderness those who reverence them [*cultores*], *cultus* is to be added, not majesty to be discussed." (*De laud. Sanct.*, n. xi. Gall. viii. 232; see also Theodoret, below, pp. 413, 414.)

piety. Who would not feel his heart burn within him at the sight of a real Thorn that once pierced that Sacred Brow? But where will not the idolatry of gain creep in ? Even St. Augustine had to complain of the sale of relics, probably fictitious. The enemy " hath dispersed on every side so many hypocrites, under the garb of monks, strolling about the provinces, nowhere sent, nowhere settled, nowhere standing, nowhere sitting. Some hawk about the limbs of martyrs, if indeed they be martyrs [x]." So now, too, the trade in relics led to the discovery of impostures, and there was a reaction. In vain the Friars preached them up; the feeling turned against them, and at the Reformation in England and Scotland, well nigh everything which had formerly excited the devotion of the people—all well-nigh, but the body of Edward the Confessor, saved no doubt on account of his royal dignity—was ruthlessly destroyed.

It is again to be remarked that the Article relates, not to the reverence of the relics, (we reverence the remains of any holy dead, much more of those who bore witness to Christ through sufferings which we can hardly imagine), but to " superstitions in their veneration" which the Council of Trent had to forbid. St. Jerome had to distinguish the honour to relics from the worship due to the Creator [y]. " We worship not, we adore not, I say not relics only, but not even

---

[x] *De Monach.*, c. 28 ; Short Treatises, p. 509, Oxf. Tr.
[y] *Ep.* cix. *ad Riparium*, n. 1.

sun and moon, nor angels, nor archangels, nor cherubim, nor seraphim, lest we serve the creature more than the Creator Who is blessed for evermore. But we honour the relics of martyrs, that we may adore Him Whose martyrs they are. We honour the servants, that the honour of the servants may redound to the Lord, Who says, 'He that receiveth you, receiveth Me.'"

V. Of all the points of difference between unreformed Churches and ourselves, there is none which has practically widened the difference so much as the invocation of saints. The divergence has operated on both sides. Roman Catholics and Orthodox Easterns regard the disuse of this practice as an evidence of great want of faith, and of the presence of an impious unsupernatural temper on the part of the reformed, while these in return have accused of superstition, and even idolatry, the having recourse to any created being in the way of prayer[s]. One cannot help honouring both sentiments, however contrariant their practical results. To live in an atmosphere of faith, to recognise in a very loving and practical way the Communion of Saints, to have faith and confidence even in the most subordinate powers of the unseen world, sheds a beautiful light over the Christian life of those who have been trained in such devotions; on the other hand, one respects that jealousy for the honour and incommunicable privileges of God which sees danger where

---

[s] Palmer's Essay "On Orthodox Communion."

others find food for faith, and which centres all its thought on the one Supreme invisible Object of the aspirations of the believing soul.

Viewing the matter from this dispassionate light, it shall be our duty, first to assert the truth of the literal meaning of the Article, that the doctrine of Romanists "on the Invocation of Saints" is "a fond thing, vainly invented, and grounded upon no warranty of Scripture, but rather repugnant to the Word of God;" and then, to shew what has been the real mind of the ancient Church upon this point of doctrine.

There will always be a tendency in human nature to rest in something short of the pure essence of God. His unapproachable holiness bears down upon the human spirit with a crushing weight. Anything that will satisfy the religious instinct, and at the same time prevent the soul from too great a proximity to Him Who is a consuming fire, will be eagerly hailed by those who recognise what God is and what they are, till the correctives supplied by the true faith, in the images of love and mercy revealed in the Gospel, make themselves living truths within the soul. It was in this spirit that the Jews in the wilderness desired Moses to stand between them and God.

Even in Mahomedanism, the centre of the philosophy of which is the unphilosophical belief in an unipersonal God, the worship of the Ooleys or Saints has developed itself. The votary of Islam, maintaining that "God hath not begotten, is not begotten," consistently refuses to worship the Only-Begotten. He cannot accept the blessed truths of a God united to human nature, and so human nature has avenged itself, and he is now given over to the cultus of men who ought not to be worshipped, and the devotion to Ali, Hooseyn, and Hooseyn, has avenged the neglect of the true God and our Saviour Jesus Christ.

Again, not merely are there deep principles in the human mind which lead to a resting in secondary worship, but the political condition of a people will strongly influence belief in this respect. It cannot be doubted that the state of the old heathenism, at the time of the State-establishment by Constantine, told sensibly in the direction of the development of saint-worship. In Italy, specially, the old Pagan ideas got baptized, and the religious devotion of the vulgar was transformed from the elder forms of heathenism to the purer cultus of the personages of the Holy Gospel and of the Church. That the world gained immensely by the change, the most bigoted religionist must admit. To withdraw the mind from the sensual images that belonged to the beautiful but corrupt Nature-worship of the heathen, to those of the self-denying heroism of the martyrs, must be acknowledged as an immense gain by all those who hold that the imagination exercises power over the whole man ; but still, beneficial as the process was, it cannot be doubted that it carried a danger within it, and that it laid the foundation of a state of things, in which a lower standard of religious morality came to be tolerated, and the idea of the one true God to be obscured. Not that either result of necessity took place. M. Comte maintains* that, at no time have Monotheistic ideas been so prevalent or strong, as in the full sunlight of the Virgin-worship of the eleventh and twelfth centuries; but still the religion of the vulgar will always exaggerate tendencies, and therefore such a warning as that contained in the Article is specially salutary.

At the time of the Reformation all this had specially to be insisted upon. The popularity of some devotions must have been very great, if the offerings at St. Thomas's shrine at Canterbury in one year amounted to £954 6s. 3d.; while that at our Lord's was nothing, and at Our Lady's £4 1s. 8d. The gross immorality which was everywhere prevalent found a satisfaction for those spiritual aspirations which never die, even in the bad, in the cultus of some easy saint.

But there is another aspect of the practice, which it would be uncandid and unphilosophical to pass over. There are certain high-strung souls, of whose undivided and entire love to God there can be no doubt, whose intense personal devotion to our Lord is the warmest, and who realize His Passion in a measure into which our cold hearts cannot enter, to whom this devotion is congenial. In them it exists in entire subordination to the feelings which the incommunicable right of God to our entire selves engenders and cultivates. We may not be able to understand them, but such they are. There must, therefore, be some aspect of this practice which appeals to a very high part of our

---

* *Comte Politique Positive*, pp. 428—433. Paris, 1823.

nature, and therefore well deserves our careful consideration. This can best be attained by tracing out
the development of the doctrine in the history of the
Church. We have, then, to ask two questions: 1. Did
the Early Church believe in the intercession of those
holy persons who have gone to their rest? and 2. Did
the Early Church think it right to address words of
petition to them? With regard to the first of these
questions, there is not a shadow of a doubt. But,
before entering into the details of evidence, it may be
as well to point out that it is not only in conformity
to all our Christian instincts of love, but that it is
a truth of Scripture. All creatures are, of course,
alike at an infinite distance from God. The highest
creature which God could create must be a creature
still; and, as a creature, finite; and everything finite
is alike distant from the Infinite. But God, "who has
ordained and constituted the services of angels and
men in wonderful order," has made their mutual
ministries a part of the harmony of love in His creation. Not only does Holy Scripture declare, that they
are "all ministering spirits, sent forth to minister for
them who shall be heirs of salvation [b]," but it speaks
of offices which they render, the higher to the lower,
and individually to ourselves [c]. "Twice, in Daniel's
visions, an angel enquireth of one most exalted angel,
(who yet himself is a creature, for he swears by the
living God [d],) and receives an answer [e]." In Zechariah

[b] Heb. i. 14.

[c] Dan. xii. 6, viii. 13.

[d] Ibid. xii. 7.

[e] Dr. Pusey, Daniel the Prophet, p. 521.

C C

we see that angels whom God had sent to "walk to and fro on the earth," give account to "the angel of the Lord [f]." A superior angel, in another vision, directs another angel to instruct Zechariah [g]. In regard to ourselves, it is our Lord Who told us of the angels of the little ones, "their angels," "always beholding the face of His Father in heaven [h]," as a ground of our reverent care not to offend them. It was the Apostolic body which, thinking it impossible that Peter himself, whom they knew to have been in prison, could be at the door, said, "it is his angel [i]." They were mistaken as to the fact, but they gave expression to their belief. Our Lord Himself allowed His angels to minister to Him, either together [k], or in an individual relation to Him. In His dread agony, He admitted of the strengthening of an angel to His Manhood [l]. The Old Testament revealed that they were interested in our race. They all "burst forth into jubilee [m]" at the prospect of our birth; God gave them charge of His own to "keep them in all their ways [n]," "ascending and descending [o]" from heaven to earth. We know how they ministered to the patriarchs and defended Elisha [p]; how one especially "stood up to protect the people of Israel [q]." The angel of the Lord prayed for Jerusalem [r];" and, although "the angel of the Lord" in the Old Testament is mostly a manifestation

[f] Zech. i. 10—12.　　　　　　　[g] ii. 7, 8 Heb.; 3, 4, Eng.
[h] St. Matt. xviii. 10.　　　　　　[i] Acts xii. 15.
[k] St. Matt. iv. 11.　　[l] St. Luke xxii. 43.　　[m] Job xxxviii. 7.
[n] Ps. xci. 11.　　[o] Gen. xxviii. 12, 13.　　[p] 2 Kings vi. 17.
[q] Dan. xii. 1.　　　　　　　　　[r] Zech. i. 12.

of God, yet since the angel prayed he must have had a created existence [s]. God's declaration, "Though Moses and Samuel stand before Me, My mind is not towards this people [t]," by the force of the words implies that they could intercede, though, doubtless, knowing the will of God, they did not. Isaiah's appeal to God implies the same, "For Thou art our Father, though [or, for] Abraham knoweth us not, and Israel will not acknowledge us [u]." For the belief that God would own them as their Father, though for their misdeeds the fathers of their race should give them up, implies that these ordinarily did remember them. The prophet contrasts the endurance of God's love with the possible failure of any manifestation of man's. But then this implies a real care on the part of man, although, like Abraham's intercession for Sodom and Gomorrah, it had to come to an end at last. This belief continued on, after the Canon of the Old Testament was closed. In Tobit the angel Raphael says, "When thou didst pray, I offered thy prayer to the Lord [x]," and says that he is one of the seven holy angels who present the prayers of the saints, and enter into the presence of the glory of the Holy One [y]. And Judas sees, in a vision,

[s] Job xxxiii. 23, is probably an anticipation of our Lord's coming in the flesh. See Pusey on Daniel, p. 519.

[t] Jer. xv. 1. The words are אם יעמד, not לו. Comp. Jer. v. 2; Is. i. 18, x. 22; Am. v. 22; Job ix. 20. Even when spoken of things impossible (Jer. xxii. 24; Ps. cxxxix. 8) אם presupposes them as possible, since it speaks of what would follow.

[u] Is. lxiii. 16.   [x] Tobit xii. 12.

[y] Ibid. 15. These (with 2 Macc.) are alleged in proof by Origen, *de Orat.*, n. 11, t. i. p. 213; *in Joann.*, t. 13, n. 57, Opp. iv. 273.

Onias, "the High Priest who prayed for all the people of the Jews," and Jeremiah, "environed with great beauty and majesty;" of whom Onias saith, "This is a lover of his brethren and of the people of Israel; this is he that prayeth much for the people and for all the holy city, Jeremiah the prophet of God[x]." Both are confirmed in the New Testament, where heaven is opened to us and we see "the angel[a]," who "stood before the altar, having a golden censer, and there was given to him much incense, that he should offer of the prayers of all saints upon the golden altar, which was before the throne; and the smoke of the incense, with the prayers of the saints, ascended up before God out of the angel's hands;" and not he only, but they who are represented by "the four beasts and the four-and-twenty elders," who fall down before the Lamb, and every one of them had harps, "and golden vials full of odours, which are the prayers of the saints[b]." And those, who so present the prayers of the saints, must themselves be of our race; for in their "new song" their thanksgiving is, "Thou hast redeemed us to God by Thy Blood out of every kindred and tongue and people and nation, and hast made us to our God kings and priests." Heaven and earth are joined in one in Christ our Head. "The heavenly Jerusalem," to which, Scripture says, "we are come," counts in it, we are told in the same place, "an innumerable company of angels, the general assembly and Church of the first-born,

[x] 2 Macc. xv. 12—14.   [a] Rev. viii. 3, 4.   [b] Ibid. v. 8.

which are written in heaven, and the spirits of just men made perfect[c]." In Jesus, our Head, are "united things in earth and things in heaven[d]." Angels and men are one family. The " Jerusalem which is above" is the mother of us all[e]. But then, not of us on earth only is that true, that "we, being many, are one body in Christ, and every one members one of another[f]," and that "the members should have the same care one for another; and whether one member suffer, all the members suffer with it; or one member be honoured, all the members rejoice in it; now ye are the body of Christ, and members in particular[g]." As our blessed Lord says that He is persecuted in His members, or receives our benefits in them, so they who are perfected must have a care for us, who are yet in our pilgrimage, and are beset by infirmities, and whose crown is as yet unwon; and we rejoice in the glory and honour of those who have attained. Since the angels rejoice over one sinner that repenteth, they must have a very individual love for those of our race, and know much of our individual histories; and so then must those of our race, who are admitted among them, and are "like unto the angels." Angels and saints are one body, Scripture saith. It is, at least, a pious belief, that, out of the redeemed, every rank of the angels shall be filled up, or, if none fell from it[h], shall be enlarged. Nay, as our Divine Lord

---

[c] Heb. xii. 22, 23.   [d] Col. i. 20.   [e] Gal. iv. 26.
[f] Rom. xii. 5.   [g] 1 Cor. xii. 25—27.

[h] The seraphim, with their burning love. Satan, the chief of those who fell, is thought to have been one of the Cherubim. (Ezek. xxviii. 14.)

for ever in-oned with His Divine Nature this our poor human nature, the lowest of His rational creation, so, in the nearest possible relation to His Godhead has He, from our same race, placed her, whom, by His grace, He prepared for that unspeakable nearness to Himself; whom, through those her early years, He formed to be the sacred shrine for His Deity; whom He taught to believe what was in human sight impossible, yet which, if brought to pass, involved the peril of utter shame; her, through whose obedience the curse of Eve's disobedience was annulled; from whose "Behold the handmaid of the Lord, be it unto me according to Thy word," her own redemption and the redemption of the world had its beginning. No titles, which the eloquence of human reverence and love have culled for her, reach the majestic simplicity of that, which, in barest truth, utters the mystery of the Incarnation declared in our Creeds, "conceived of the Virgin Mary," that "she bare God," Theotokos. And since no Divine mystery ends with this world, then, in that closest relation to Himself, higher than the Seraphim, or whatever is highest in the host of heaven, is she, His creature, as God, but, as God-Man, His Mother still. Well, then, may we think of angels and saints as one body under Him, our Head, since He, their Head, is God-Man, and nearest to Himself is His human Mother. Our Lord calls them, too, "like to the angels[1];" nay, He has admitted them to His own throne, as He says, "To him that overcometh will

---

[1] St. Mark xii. 25.

I grant to sit with Me in My throne; even as I also overcame, and am set down with My Father in His throne[k]; "he that overcometh and keepeth My works unto the end, to him will I give power over the nations: and he shall rule them with a rod of iron; as the vessels of a potter shall they be broken to shivers, even as I received of My Father[l]."

It may almost seem superfluous to adduce passages from the fathers to shew that they taught that angels and saints pray for us. Yet it may have its use. First, then, as to the angels. Clement of Alexandria says[m]:— "The Gnostic prays with angels, as being already the equal of angels; nor does he ever come to be out of the holy guardianship; even though he pray alone, he has the choir of the holy one standing with him." Tertullian speaks of the indecency of sitting at prayer, while the angel of prayer standeth by[n]. Origen unites the angels and the departed saints: "But not the High-Priest [our Lord] alone prays with those who pray sincerely, but also the angels who 'joy in heaven over one sinner who repenteth more than over ninety-and-nine just persons who need no repentance,' and the souls of the saints who have fallen asleep before (us)[o]." He says, "The angel of each one, even

---

[k] Rev. iii. 21.   [l] Ibid. ii. 26, 27.
[m] *Strom.*, vii. p. 879.   [n] *De Orat.*, 16, p. 310, Oxf. Tr.
[o] *De Orat.*, n. 11, t. i. p. 213. "It is likely that the angelic powers are present at the assemblies of the faithful, and the power of our Lord and Saviour, yea, too, of the holy spirits, and I think too, even of those who have fallen asleep before (us), and undoubtedly also of

of the little ones in the Church, both prays with us,
and acts with us in those things about which we pray,
wherein it is possible [p]."   "If the angel of the Lord
'encamp round about them that fear him, and shall
deliver them,' and Jacob speaks truly, not concerning
himself only, but all besides devoted to God, saying
to him that understands, 'The angel that delivered
me from all evils,' it is likely that when many are
assembled together sincerely unto the glory of Christ,
the angel of each one 'encamps round' each of those
who fear; with that man, that is, whom he has been
entrusted to guard and minister to; so as to be, when
the saints are assembled, a twofold Church, one of
men and another of angels."   "The power of Jesus,
and the spirits of Paul and such as he, and the angels
of the Lord that encamp round about each of the
saints, concur with and come together with those who
are assembled in sincerity [q]."   And in answer to Celsus,
who said, "we must render" to angels "first-fruits
and prayers, as long as we live, that we may gain
their friendliness," Origen says [r], "To Whom we give
the first-fruits, to Him we send up the prayers also,
having a great High-Priest, Who hath entered into the
heavens, Jesus, the Son of God, and we hold the confession while we live, having God favourable to us and
His Only-Begotten Son, Jesus, manifested among us.

those who are still living, even though the 'how' it is not easy to
declare." Ibid., n. 31, p. 269.

[p] *De Orat.*, p. 215.   [q] Ibid., n. 31, p. 269.
[r] *c. Cels.*, viii. 34, t. i. p. 766, 7.

But if we long for a multitude, too, whom we wish to be friendly to us, we learn that thousands of thousands stand by Him, and ten thousand times ten thousand minister to Him, who, looking at those who imitate their piety to God as kinsmen and friends, co-operate to their salvation who call upon God and pray sincerely, appearing to [them] and thinking that they themselves ought to obey them, and as by one compact, to be present for the benefit and salvation of those who pray to God, to Whom themselves also pray. For they are all ministering spirits sent forth," &c. : and, " The one God over all we must thoroughly propitiate, and have Him propitious Whose entire good will is gained by piety and all virtues; but if he (Celsus) will have it, that certain others are to be so propitiated by us after the God over all, let him observe that as the motion of its shadow followeth the body when moved, in like way upon the propitiation of the God Who is above all it followeth, that one has all His friends, angels, and souls, and spirits, propitious; and not only do they, too, become propitious to those who are worthy, but they also co-operate with those who wish to serve the God Who is above all, and gain His favour, and comprecate, and co-petition; so that we may dare to say, that with those who deliberately prefer the better part when they pray to God, many myriads of holy powers, *uncalled*, pray with them*."

Origen supports his own belief by that of one of the " older masters :"—" I so deem that all those fathers

* *c. Cels.*, n. 64, pp. 789, 790.

who fell asleep before us fight with us and help us by their prayers. For so also did I hear one of the older masters saying[t]." He exhorts Ambrose not to fear martyrdom on account of wife and children; for by thus "becoming the friend of God, thou wilt have greater power to help them." "Then thou wilt love them with more perfect knowledge, and wilt pray for them with greater wisdom[u]." He asks, "Who doubts that all the holy fathers help us by prayers[x]," &c. And there is the passage, well known for the beauty of the thought, that since knowledge is perfected in the life to come, so also other virtues, especially love. "But one of the principal virtues, according to the Divine word, is charity towards our neighbour, which we must needs think is felt by the departed saints towards those who are struggling in this life, more exceedingly than by those who are yet in human infirmity, and are struggling together with those who need aid[y]."

St. Dionysius, of Alexandria:—"They who are about to struggle in the sacred conflict of suffering for righteousness, have angels bringing them aid from heaven[z]." St. Gregory Thaumaturgus speaks incidentally of "the holy angel of God, who had as his lot, with great judgment to govern and tend me and be my guardian from boyhood, who nourisheth me from my youth; him, who in addition to the common governors of all men, is, whoever he may be, specially the attendant

---

[t] *In Jos., Hom.* 16, t. ii. p. 437. [u] *De Mart.,* n. 37, 38, t. i. p. 299. [x] *In Num., Hom.* 26, n. 6, t. ii. p. 373. [y] *De Orat.,* n. 11, t. i. p. 214. [z] *De Martyr.,* pp. 40, 41.

teacher of me who am a child, who, being in all besides, everywhere and in all things, my bringer up, stood in charge of me of old, and now, too, rears me up and instructs me and leads me by the hand [a]." Even Eusebius says :—" How shall we give thanks (for the Death of Christ for us)? Our tongues, our mouths, suffice not, though we had a thousand. We suffice not; let us seek helpers; let angels help us; let archangels, too, give thanks with us, that they, too, may rejoice [b]." Didymus, of Alexandria :—" It is the longing of perfect men, coming to the consummation of sanctity, to become equal to the angels. For angels give aid to men, not men to angels, ministering to them salvation, and announcing to them larger benefits of God [c]." St. James, of Nisibis :—" Let not the hatred thou hast against any re-enter thy mind whilst thou prayest. Be assured that thy prayers will be left before the altar, and that he who offers prayer will not receive and raise it from the earth. For he examines thy gift, whether it be polluted. If the prayer be holy, he raises it and offers it in the sight of God. But if he find thee saying in thy prayer, ' Forgive me, I too forgive,' he that raises prayer will answer thee who prayest, ' First forgive thou thy debtor, and then I will raise thy prayer to the Lord,

[a] *Orat. Paneg. in Orig.*, n. 4, Gall. iii. 418. St. Methodius says :—" We have received, in the God-inspired writings, that these children, though born of adultery, are delivered over to guardian angels." (*Conv.*, ii. 7, Gall. iii. 682.)

[b] *De fide adv. Sabell.*, l. i., Gall. iv. 473.

[c] *De Sp. S.*, n. 7, Gall. vi. 266.

Whose debtor thou art [d].' "　St. Basil :—" Of the holy spiritual powers who have their places in heaven, some are called eyes, from being intrusted to watch over us ; others, ears, from receiving our prayers [e]." St. Ambrose comments on the words in the Revelations :—" which incense, the prayers of saints, is carried by an angel unto that golden altar which is before the throne of God, and glows like a sweet ointment of pious prayer [f]."　St. Hilary :—" The angels of the little ones day by day see God, because the Son of Man came to 'save what was lost.'　Therefore both the Son of Man saves, and angels see God and are angels of ' the little ones.'　The authority is absolute that angels preside over the prayers of the faithful ; wherefore angels day by day offer up to God the prayers of those who are saved by Christ.　Therefore it is dangerous to despise him, whose desires and supplications are borne to the eternal and invisible God by the lofty service and ministry of angels [g]."

So also in regard to those who, of our race, were perfected ; those especially who had borne testimony to Jesus by their deaths.　In the very earliest times we find such testimony as this.　In the account of the martyrdom of St. Ignatius, many profess that they saw him praying over them [h].　Origen says, " It will not be

[d] Serm. iv. n. 7, Gall. v., xxx.

[e] *Hom. in Ps.* xxxiii., n. 11, t. i. p. 154.　On the Guardian Angel, see further St. Basil, ib., p. 148.

[f] *De Isaac et anima*, c. 5, n. 44, t. i. p. 369.

[g] *In St. Matt.*, c. 18, n. 5, p. 758.

[h] *Patres Apostolici*, p. 116, ed. Hefele.

wrong to say, that all the Saints departed, retaining love for those who still are alive, take care of their salvation and them, by their prayers and by their intervention with God[1]." St. Cyprian suggests to St. Cornelius that whichever should first be vouchsafed martyrdom, should not cease our prayers for our brethren and sisters, in presence of the mercy of the Father; and asks the Virgins whom he exhorts to "remember him when virginity shall begin to be honoured in them [i.e. in person] [j]."

Eusebius relates how the martyr Potamiæna promised to a kind soldier to beg him from her Lord, and obtained his conversion by her prayers[k]; and how Theodosia came to the confessors in bonds, "both out of kindness, and, as is likely, to ask them to remember her when they came to the Lord[l]." St. Athanasius speaks of the holy Psalmists, "who communicated the words as ministers praying with us[m];" St. Antony says "that the saints use much prayer and gladness in exultation before our Creator. The Maker, too, of all rejoices in our works, and on account of the testimony of the saints gives us immense *charismata*[n]." Nilus, an eye-witness, relates how (about A.D. 303) the Martyr St. Theodotus, just before he was beheaded, bade the weeping Christians, "weep not, but glorify our Lord Jesus, who had enabled him to finish his course. For

---

[1] *In Cant.* iii. t. iii. p. 75.

[j] *De hab. Virg.*, 362; *Ep.* lvii. *fin.* Ben.

[k] H. E., vi. 14.   [l] *De Martyr. Pal.*, c. 7.

[m] n. 31, t. i. p. 1001.   [n] *Epist.* v. n. 1, in Gall. iv. 666.

I shall be with confidence unceasingly interceding
with God in heaven for you [o]." Eusebius himself says:
—"that it is probable that holy powers and choirs of
sacred angels pray with and over those who send up to
God, by prayers, spiritual and pure sacrifices," as it "was
probable that a choir of holy angels and men dear to
God, the sacred ministers of God, prayed with David [p]."
St. Cyril, of Jerusalem, says:—" that we commemorate
those who have fallen asleep before us, patriarchs, prophets, apostles, martyrs, that God, by their prayers
and intercessions, may receive our petitions [q]."   St.
Hilary says:—"that apostles, patriarchs, prophets, or
rather angels, with a kind of guard, fence round the
Church. Good, indeed, is an angel's protection, but
that of the Lord is better [r]."   St. Gregory, of Nazianzum, says of his father:—"I am persuaded that he
now (guards the flock) more effectually by his intercession, than he did formerly by his teaching, by how
much he is nigher to God [s]."   And of St. Basil: "His
body is assigned to the tomb of his fathers, and he is
joined, the high-priest to the priests, that grand voice
which still ringeth in my ears to the preachers, the
martyr to the martyrs; and now, indeed, he is in
heaven, and there, as I think, is offering up sacrifices
for us and praying for the people; for though he has
left us, yet has he not utterly deserted us [t]."   And of

[o] *Mart. S. Theod.*, n. 32, in Gall. iv. 128.

[p] *In Ps.* xix. 1, *Montf. Coll. Nov.*, i. 75.

[q] *Cat. Myst.*, v. 9.   [r] In Ps. cxxiv. n. 6.

[s] *Or.* xxviii. p. 332.   [t] *Orat.* xliii. p. 831.

St. Athanasius :—"He now, I well know, looks down from above upon our affairs, and reaches out his hand to those who toil for what is excellent, and so much the more that he is free from the bonds [of the flesh][u]." And of his mother Nonna:—"And now from heaven she greatly prays over our affairs[x]." St. Ambrose hopes that he might the sooner rejoin St. Satyrus by his intercessions[y]. St. Augustine holds that the souls of the martyrs reign with Christ. They chiefly reign, when dead, who have combated for the truth, even unto death.

St. Chrysostom ends a Lenten exhortation, "If we thus rule our lives, and, together with abstinence from meats, manifest abstinence from evil too, we, too, shall enjoy greater confidence and be admitted to a larger loving-kindness of God, both in the present life and in that coming awful day, by the prayers and intercession of those who have pleased Him, by the grace and loving-kindness of our Lord Jesus Christ, with Whom[z]," &c.

St. Asterius, a contemporary of St. Chrysostom, says :—" The freedom of speech of the martyrs accomplishes the intercession for the world; and the enemy unawares fell into the opposite of what he meant. For as many as he slew, having confessed the faith, so many succourers of men did he provide[a]."

---

[u] *Orat.* xxxiv. p. 620.   [x] *Carm.* xciv. 5, Gall. vi. 379. 288

[y] *De Fide Resur. carn. fin.*, t. ii. 1170.

[z] *Hom 9, in Gen. fin.*, t. iv. 71.

[a] *In SS. Mart. Combef. N. Auct.*, p. 192.

St. Leo nowhere uses invocations, but speaks very frequently of the value of the intercession of St. Peter and St. Paul; once, also, of St. Laurence. He appeals to his own experience and that of those before him: "But as we, too, experienced, and our ancestors have proved, we believe and are confident, amid all the toils of this life, that, to obtain the mercy of God, we shall ever be helped by the prayers of special patrons; that in proportion as we are sunk down by our own sins, we may be raised by Apostolic merits [b]." "Let us use for our amendment the lenity of Him who spares us, that blessed Peter and all the saints, who were present with us in many tribulations, may vouchsafe to aid our entreaties for you with the merciful God [c]." Of St. Laurence he says, "by whose prayer and patronage we trust that we are aided without ceasing [d]."

It was, then, an intense, stupid, loveless paradox, of Vigilantius, that, "while we are alive, we ever pray mutually for one another, but that when we have departed this life no one's prayer is heard for another [e]." "If the Apostles and martyrs," St. Jerome answers, "while yet placed in the flesh, can yet pray for others, while they must still be anxious for themselves, how much more after their crowns, victories, triumphs! — Paul the Apostle says that 'two hundred threescore and sixteen souls' were granted

[b] *Serm.* 82, *in Nat. SS. Pet. et Paul.*, pp. 326, 327.

[c] *Serm.* 84, *in Oct. App. Pet. et Paul.*, p. 337. He speaks of the prayers of St. Peter, *Serm.* 12, 14, 76, 86, 88, 90, 92, 94.

[d] *Serm.* 85, c. iv. p. 340.   [e] In St. Jerome *c. Vigilant.*, n. 7.

him in the ship; and after that, being dissolved, he has begun to be with Christ, shall he then close his mouth, and be unable to utter a word for those, who throughout the world believed at his Gospel?" St. Jerome himself speaks of it as certain that some departed pray for him. He says to Heliodorus, that, when he should himself be crowned, "then wilt thou pray for me too, who spurred thee on to conquer [f];" and to Paula of Blæsilla, "she prays to the Lord for thee, and impetrates for me, (certain I am of her mind,) the pardon of my sins [g];" and to Theodora, on the death of her husband:—"He, already safe and triumphant, beholds thee from on high, and aids thee in thy efforts, and prepares thee a place near himself [h]." St. Augustine says :—"For the faithful departed, prayers are offered; for Martyrs, not: for they departed so perfect, that they are not our clients but our advocates. Nor this in themselves, but in Him, to Whom, their Head, they, perfect members, cohered. For He is truly the One Advocate, Who intercedeth for us, sitting at the right hand of the Father; but He is our One Advocate, as also our One Shepherd [i]." As, then, His character of "the Shepherd of the sheep" does not exclude others being shepherds in and under Him, so neither does His being the One Advocate preclude others being advocates, in His body, with and through Himself. Sulpicius Severus, comforting

[f] *Ep.* xiv. n. 3, *ad Heliod.*, p. 29, Vall. [g] *Ep.* xxxix. n. 6, p. 183.
[h] *Ep.* lxxv. n. 2, *ad Theod. Vid.*, p. 448.
[i] *Serm.* 285, *in Nat. Martt. Casti et Æmil.*, n. 5, t. v. p. 1147.

a friend on the death of St. Martin, says:—"I cannot
command myself not to weep. I have, indeed, sent
before me a patron, but I have lost the solace of this
present life, although, if grief admitted of reason,
I ought to rejoice. For he is inserted among the
Apostles and Prophets. He will not be wanting to us,
believe me, he will not be wanting; he will be with
us discoursing of him; he will stand by us praying;
and what he has vouchsafed to do to-day, he will often
let us see him, and protect us with his continual
blessing, as he did just now[j]." Prudentius says of
St. Cyprian:—"Here below he is a teacher; above,
a martyr: here, he instructs men; thence, a patron, he
gives loving gifts[k]." St. Maximus says "that the
heathen aimed a blow at the Church by the martyrdom of St. Sixtus; but "that great Xystus, who had on
earth been a shepherd of the sheep committed to him
by God, was at hand, a patron from heaven[l]." At the
Council of Chalcedon, mention being made of Flavian,
all the Constantinopolitan Bishops said:—"Eternal
the memory of Flavian; of the orthodox, eternal the
memory—Flavian after death lives; the martyr will
pray for us[m]," &c. The Bishops, collectively, in their
synodical Relation to St. Leo, own some aid from
St. Euphemia, in whose church they assembled, in

[j] *Epist.* ii. *de ob. et app. B. Mart.*, Gall. viii. 400, 401. The allusions are to a dream which Severus had, just before he heard of
St. Martin's decease, in which St. Martin blessed him.

[k] *Hymn.* 13, fin. Gall. viii. 467.   [l] *Hom.* 2, *in Nat. S. Laur.*

[m] *Conc. Chalc.*, Act. xi. iv. 698, Labbe.

the happy accomplishment of their labours:—" It was God Who worked, and the victorious Euphemia who crowned the Council by her bridal-chamber; who, receiving the definition of the faith from us as her own confession, did, through the most pious king and the Christ-loving queen, present it to her Spouse, having lulled the whole confusion of the adversaries, and strengthened the love and confession of truth, and by hand and tongue, having put the question to the votes of all for demonstration [n]." The Bishops in the Council of Tours, A.D. 461, express their hope that "the intercession of the holy and most blessed bishop, St. Martin, which is acceptable to God, will obtain, that the constitution of our humility may, by the mercy of the Lord helping, be preserved [o]."

But, further, it is equally true and equally scriptural that, in prayer to God, they pleaded to Him the acceptableness of those to whom they stood in this relation of love. Thus Moses prayed to God, after the people's sin as to the calf:—" Remember Abraham, Isaac, and Israel, Thy servants, to whom Thou swarest by Thine own self, and saidst unto them, I will multiply your seed [p]," &c. He does not say simply, " Remember Thy promise;" but " Remember those to whom Thou didst make it." And God speaks of Himself as "keeping mercy for thousands [q];" and Jeremiah pleads to Him that His character "that shewest loving-kind-

---

[n] *Conc. Chalc.*, part iii. cap. 2 ; Labbe, tom. iv. p. 835.

[o] *Conc. Turon.*, Labbe, tom. iv. p. 1052, prima paginationis serie.

[p] Exod. xxxii. 13.   [q] Ib. xxxiv. 7.

ness to thousands[r]," i.e. that whereas He "visited iniquity to the third and fourth generation" only, He kept or retained His mercy to manifold more, if they would at last admit of it. And Solomon seems to have pleaded to God, " Lord remember David, and all his trouble," i.e. his laborious zeal for the House of God, and entreats Him, not for his own deserts, but " for Thy servant David's sake turn not away the face of Thine anointed[s]." And it is recorded that "for David's sake did the Lord his God give Abijam a lamp in Jerusalem, to set up his son after him, and to establish Jerusalem; because David did right in the eyes of the Lord, and turned not aside from anything that He commanded him all the days of his life, save only in the matter of Uriah the Hittite[t]." And St. Paul says of all Israel, "as touching the election, they are beloved for the fathers' sakes. For the gifts and calling of God are without repentance[u]."

Among the friends of God in the Church of Christ, an eminent place was early given to the Martyrs, as having borne witness to Christ " the True Witness[x]," as having been likenesses to His sufferings, in whom especially these words were fulfilled, " If we suffer with Him we shall also reign with Him[y];" and His promise, that " he that overcometh, to him will I grant to sit down on My throne[z]." Hence the title that they were σύνθρονοι, 'enthroned with' Christ. Hence came

---

[r] Jer. xxxii. 18.
[s] Ps. cxxxii. 1, 10; comp. 2 Chr. vi. 41, 42.
[t] 1 Kings xv. 4, 5.
[u] Rom. xi. 28, 29.
[x] Rev. iii. 14.
[y] 2 Tim. ii. 12.
[z] Rev. iii. 21.

the language, so often used of them, that they had much "boldness of speech" with Christ, as having suffered for Him. "I know," says St. Gregory of Nyssa of the forty martyrs[a], "how mighty they are, and what boldness of speech they have with God." "They," says St. Chrysostom, "have much boldness of speech, not when living only, but also having died, yea, much more, having died. For they now bear the *stigmata*[b], the marks of Christ; and, displaying those *stigmata*, they are able to persuade the King all things[c];" and "as soldiers, exhibiting wounds which they have received from the enemy, speak boldly to the king, so these [Juventinus and Maximin, martyrs,] bearing in their hands their severed heads, and bringing them in the midst, can with reason effect all they wish with the King of heaven[d]." Thus, also, Eusebius says, on Psalm lxxviii. [lxxix.:]—"We are instructed to say these things in prayers, instead of sacrifice and whole burnt offerings putting forward the blood of the holy martyrs, and sending up such supplications as these. We, indeed, have not been held worthy to strive unto death, nor to empty out our blood for God; but since we are the sons of those who suffered these things, glorying in our fathers' virtue, we beseech to be compassionated for their sakes[e];" and, at the close of his commentary on Isaiah:—"Of which (heavenly con-

---

[a] *Orat. in xl. Mart.*, Opp. ii. 211.   [b] Gal. vi. 17.
[c] *Hom. de SS. Bernice et Prosdoce fin.*, Opp. ii. 645.
[d] *In Juvent. et Maxim. fin.*, Opp. ii. 583.
[e] *Montf. Nov. Coll.*, i. 486, 487.

templation) may we, too, be deemed worthy by the merits and intercessions of all the saints[f]." And St. Gregory of Nazianzum :—" May my affairs be conducted how God wills; may they, by his [St. Basil's] intercessions, be conducted better[g]." And St. Gregory of Nyssa :—" May we, too, [as well as the forty martyrs,] enter Paradise, having been strengthened through their intercession unto the good confession of our Lord Jesus Christ; to Whom[h]," &c. And St. Ambrose to his brother :—" That this favour [a speedy reunion] may be conferred on me by thy intercessions, that thou mayest summon me, who long to join thee, more speedily[i]." St. Chrysostom closes his homily on St. Pelagia :—" May it be by the prayers of this holy martyr, and by those of the rest who wrestled with her, that you may retain in accurate remembrance these things and the rest which have been said, and shewing them all forth by your deeds, may in all things abide well pleasing to God; to Whom[k]," &c. And on the saying " God remembered Abraham, and sent just Lot out of the overthrow[l] :" " What, then ? one may say, was the just man saved on the ground of the intercession of the patriarch and not of his own righteousness ? Nay, for the intercession of the patriarch too. For, when we contribute our part too, does the intercession of the righteous most benefit us; since

[f] *Montf. Nov. Coll.*, t. ii. p. 593.　　[g] *Orat.* 43 *in laud. S. Basil.*, n. 25, t. i. p. 791.　　[h] *Orat.* ii. *in* xl. *Mart. fin.*, t. iii. p. 514.
[i] *De Res. fin.*, Opp. ii. 1170.　　[k] *Hom.* i. *in S. Pelag. fin.*, ii. 590.
[l] *Hom.* 44, *in Gen.*, n. 2, Opp. iv. 448, 449.

if we ourselves are remiss, and place the hope of our deliverance on them alone, we shall gain nothing. Not because the righteous are weak, but because we betray ourselves by our own remissness." Then, having contrasted God's forbidding Jeremiah to pray for Israel when obstinate in sin, he says, " knowing this, beloved, let us flee to the intercession of the saints, and exhort them to beseech for us; but let us not rely on their supplications alone, but let us also order, as is meet, our part, and hold fast to amendment of life; that we may give room for their intercession for us." He closes his oration on St. Meletius:—" Let us all pray in common, rulers and ruled, women and men, old and young, slaves and free, taking the blessed Meletius as sharer of this prayer, (for he has greater freedom of speech now, and his love to us is more glowing,) that this love may be increased, and that it be vouchsafed to us all, as we are now near this urn, so there, too, we may be near his everlasting tabernacles, and obtain the goods laid up there[m];" and, " Taking the holy martyrs as partakers of our prayers, let us pray for length of her [the empress's] life, cheerful old age, sons and sons' sons, and, above all these, that this zeal may be heightened, piety increased [n]," &c.

There remains the question,—"Apart from the prayer

---

[m] *Hom. in S. Melet. fin.*, Opp. ii. 523.

[n] *Hom.* ii. *ex* xi. *fin.*, Opp. xii. 334; "preached before the Empress and the whole city and magistrates, in the Martyrium, three miles from the city, after she had translated thither the relics of the martyrs at midnight."

to God to grant favours at the intercession of such or
such a martyr or saint; apart also from those instances
of rhetorical apostrophe with such expressions as εἴ τις
αἴσθησις, taken evidently from the form of the heathen
rhetoricians;—did the early Church think it right
directly to ask the saints to use those intercessions, in
whose efficacy they believed?" It is true that no instance can be quoted before the Council of Nicæa,
except the case related by St. Gregory Nazianzen, out
of Acts undoubtedly apocryphal, how Justina, fleeing
the assault of Cyprian the magician, (whom those
Acts confounded with the great African father and
martyr before his conversion,) "abandoning all other
hope, fled to God for refuge, and took as her defender
against that accursed passion Him to Whom she was
betrothed;" and after many such prayers "besought
the Virgin Mary to aid a virgin in danger°." Yet
it cannot be doubted that in the latter part of the
fourth century the great fathers, who secured and
transmitted our faith, practised it and taught it. St.
Ephrem, in his funeral canons for a departed bishop
(for whom yet he prays), asks him, in the vacancy
of the see, "Visit thy Church, father, by thy prayers
which are heard, and pray for it, like Moses, that
there may be a priest like Joshua; for David had
long departed and was not in the day of Hezekiah;
his prayer defended and delivered Jerusalem from
Sennacherib."—"Let thy prayers defend thy flock,
and entreat deliverance for it, and may the congre-

<hr>

° *Orat.* xxiv. n. 10, 11.

gation, which praises thy memory, be blessed by thy prayers; that thy people may rejoice in the (heavenly) chamber, and may say, Praise to Him Who chose thee[p]." And for a monk, for the forgiveness of whose sins he afterwards prays:—"Pray to and supplicate God for the congregation of thy beloved, that He would reward their tears, which they have shed for thee. Supplicate Him Who heareth thee, that He would forgive them their sins; raise up thy hand over thy congregation, which beareth thy corpse with honour, and bless it as thou wert wont in the name of the holy God; for very loved and precious is the prayer of the hour of departure. Remember the holy Church, and recall it in the general assembly; for as a mother she buried thee, and as a sister she honoured. thy death[q]." These, however, are not invocations of saints, but mutual deprecations. In another, the congregation says:—"Pray and beseech for all of us, that we may be worthy to behold thee in the (heavenly) courts, and with thee may rejoice and be glad[r]." There is also a short prayer:—"Apostles twelve, intercede for me; prophets and martyrs, entreat for me[s]:" and, "Martyrs, who endured resolutely, afflictions cheerfully, and received crowns perfectly, as is meet, justly, supplicate with us[t] conjointly, to Christ lordlily, that He would shew mercies abundantly, upon us all unceasingly."

[p] *Can.* 1, Opp. Syr. iii. 227. [q] *Can.* 16, p. 259.
[r] *Can.* 15 *fin.*, p. 255. [s] *Paræn. ad pænit.*, 33, *fin.*, ib., p. 486.
[t] Not "for us," as Ass. l. c.

St. Damasus, in his poems, says to a martyr :—" Now dweller with the Lord, who guardest the altars of Christ, I pray thee to favour the prayers of Damasus, illustrious martyr ᵘ." St. Gregory of Nyssa asks the martyr, St. Theodore :—" Intercede with our common King for thy country, for the martyr's country is the place of his passion. We anticipate afflictions; we expect danger; not far off are the wicked Scythians, in pangs with war against us. As a soldier fight for us; as a martyr use boldness of speech for thy fellow-servants. Ask for peace, that these public assemblies may not cease. That we have been preserved un-harmed, to thee we ascribe the benefit; but we ask for safety in the future too. If there be need of greater importunity, assemble the choir of thy brother martyrs; and implore with all. Let the prayers of many righte-ous loose the sins of peoples and districts. Remind Peter; arouse Paul; John too, the theologian and be-loved disciple, that they have a care for the Churches which they established ˣ," &c. He closes his panegyric on St. Ephrem, " Do thou, standing by the Divine altar, and ministering with angels to the life-giving and All-holy Trinity, remember us all, asking for us remission of sins, and the fruition of an everlasting kingdom in Christ our Lord ; to Whom ʸ," &c. St. Gregory of Nazianzum says to St. Cyprian :—" Do thou look down on us propitiously from above, and direct our speech and life, and shepherd or co-shepherd this

---

ᵘ *Carm.* 22, Gall. vi. 549.   ˣ *Hom. de S. Theod. fin.*, Opp. iii. 585, 586.   ʸ *De Vit. S. Ephr. fin.*, iii. 616.

holy flock; and, directing the rest, as far as may be, for the best, and driving away the grievous wolves, the hunters of syllables and phrases, and bestowing on us a more perfect and bright illumination of the Holy Trinity, by Whom thou standest, Whom we worship [z]," &c. And to St. Basil:—"Do thou, divine and sacred one, look down upon us, and by thy intercessions either stay the thorn of the flesh, given us by God, our discipline, or persuade us to endure it bravely, and direct our whole life for us for the best; and if we be removed thence, receive us in thy tabernacles, that, living together and together beholding the holy and blessed Trinity [a]," &c. St. Ambrose says: — " Angels are to be besought for us, who were given to us as a guard; martyrs are to be besought, whose patronage we seem to claim for ourselves by the pledge of the body. They can ask for our sins, who washed whatever sins they had with their own blood. For they are God's martyrs, our presiders, the surveyors of our life and actions. Be we not ashamed to employ them as intercessors for our infirmity, who knew the infirmity of the body even when they overcame [b]."

St. Chrysostom says to the people:—"Thou, then, when thou perceivest that God is chastening thee, fly not to his enemies the Jews, lest thou kindle His wrath the more against thee, but to His friends the

---

[z] *Orat.* 24, *fin.*, p. 450.

[a] *Or.* 43, *fin.*, p. 832. He also asks his father and mother, " Save me now, too, by mighty supplications." *Carm.* 97.

[b] *De Viduis,* c. 9, t. ii. p. 200.

martyrs, the holy and well-pleasing unto Him, who have also much freedom of speech [towards Him] [c]."

St. Jerome says to St. Paula:—"Help with thy prayers the extreme old age of thy devotee. Thy faith and works associate thee with Christ; present, thou wilt obtain more easily what thou askest [d]." St. Chrysostom exhorts the people:—"Not on this festival only, but on other days too, let us be at their side, let us invoke them; let us beg them to be our patronesses [e]" [S. Bernice and Prosdoce]. "Since they have such power and friendship with God, let us, making ourselves their familiars by constant attention and coming to them continually, draw on us, through them, the loving-kindness of God."

St. Augustine, in his beautiful *De Curâ pro Mortuis* [f], says, that the benefit of burying their friends at the Memorials of the Saints, was that the living " recollecting where are the bodies of those whom they love, may commend them to the same saints or patrons." At the second synod of Rome, A.D. 495, they exclaimed, " Lord Peter preserve him," (the Pope) [g].

But a far stronger impulse than the advice given by these reverenced fathers or their practice, lay in the facts of those days. For apparently (and, in face of the evidence, we cannot contradict it) it was God who encouraged it by the answers to prayer so addressed. Gibbon has scoffed at the fact that one of

---

[c] *Adv. Jud. Or.* 8, n. 6.   [d] *Ep.* cviii. *ad Eustoch.*

[e] Opp. ii. 645, Ben.   [f] c. iv. t. vi. p. 519.

[g] Labbe, tom. iv. pp. 137, 8.

the miracles very commonly dwelt upon was the casting out of devils. But if it were ever so much, that these persons who spoke as demoniacs, persons possessed, were simple maniacs, still the maniacs were healed. Were it ever so much, that, in some cases, the body was healed through the mind, this would leave a large residue, in which any mind, open to evidence, must acknowledge " the finger of God." St. Augustine says :—" If, to omit others, I would write the miracles of healing alone, which were wrought through this martyr, the glorious Stephen, in the colony of Calama and in ours, many books must be written. And yet all cannot be gathered in one, but those only, of which accounts have been sent in, to be recited before the people. For this we had done, seeing that Divine miracles, like those of old, were multiplied in our times, and that this ought not to be lost to the knowledge of many[h]." " Many know how great miracles take place in that city (Ancona) through the most blessed martyr Stephen[i]." " At Uzalis, where my brother Euodius is Bishop, how many miracles take place, seek and ye will find[k]." One which he guarantees, was the temporary restoration of an infant, who had died unbaptized, that it might be baptized[l]. He is careful to say that all was

---

[h] *De Civ. Dei,* xxii. 8.

[i] *Serm.* 323, *post libell. de S. Steph.,* n. 2.

[k] Ibid., n. 3.

[l] *Serm.* 324 : "The mother said, 'Holy martyr, thou seest I have no solace.—Thou knowest why I mourn. Restore me my son, that I may have him in the presence of Him who crowned thee.' The child revived, was baptized, and, all the sacraments now completed, was taken.

done by Christ:—"Ye who know how to love Stephen, love him in Christ.—Do we read, or can we read any where in sound doctrine, that Jesus did or doth miracles through the name of Stephen. Stephen did them, but by the name of Christ [m]. This he doth now, too. Whatever ye see done through the memorial of Stephen, it is done in the name of Christ, that Christ may be extolled, Christ adored, Christ expected as Judge of quick and dead [n]."

St. Gregory of Nyssa says:—"I placed the bodies of my parents near the reliques of the [forty] soldiers, that, at the time of the resurrection, they may be raised with those who have noble freedom of speech. For I know how mighty they are, and I have seen the evident demonstration of their freedom of speech with God." He then relates how "a soldier, long and almost incurably lame, being within the martyrium and the resting-place of the saints [the forty martyrs], having prayed to God, implored the intercession of the saints." The soldier was restored in a vision, his companions heard the sound of the re-setting of the bone. "He awoke and was whole." "This miracle," St. Gregory says, "I saw, falling in with the man, relating it to all, and proclaiming the good deed of the martyrs [o]."

St. Basil is less definite in regard to the forty martyrs. He attests only the number of the applicants: —"Forty are they, that send up harmonious prayer.

"When, then," St. Augustine sums up, "God wrought such a miracle through His martyr, could He not there [at Uzalis] cure these?"

[m] Acts vi. 8.   [n] *Serm.* 316, n. 1.

[o] *Orat. in* xl. *Mart.*, Opp. ii. 211, 212.

Where two or three are gathered together in the name of the Lord, there is He in the midst of them; and where forty are, who doubts of God's presence? The afflicted flies unto the forty, the gladdened runs unto them; the former to find escape from his troubles; the latter, that his prosperity may be preserved. Thus a pious woman is found praying for her children, asking a return for her husband when absent, health for him when sick. Let your prayers be with martyrs [p]." In regard to the martyr St. Mamas, he speaks more definitely :—" Remember for me the martyr, all who have benefited by him through dreams; all who lighting on this holy place, had him as co-operator to prayer; all to whom, called by name, he has stood by in their deeds; all whom he has raised from sickness; all to whom he has given back sons, when now dead; all to whom he lengthened the appointed term of life. Bring them all together; form a panegyric from the common contribution [q]." St. Gregory Nazianzen tells the Emperor Julian, "By them [the martyrs] devils are driven out and diseases cured [r]." St. Chrysostom says of the Egyptian martyrs :—" Many, both of the natives and of those who have come from elsewhere, know how great the power of these saints, who also bear witness to what I say, having learned through the experience itself, their free access to God [s]."

St. Asterius, Bishop of Amasea, relates :—"Those op-

<hr>

[p] *Hom. in* xl. *Mart.*, n. i. t. ii. pp. 209, 210.   [q] *Hom. in Mam. Mart.*, n. i. t. ii. pp. 259, 260.   [r] *Orat.* 4, n. 69, p. 108.
[s] Opp. ii. 700.

pressed by calamities incidental to man hasten, as to an asylum, to those places, where those thrice-blessed rest, and employ them as legates and mediators of their prayers and requests, on account of their boundless confidence with God; thence the poor are solaced;—the sacred temples of the martyrs are tranquil harbours amidst all tumults and storms of life. Thus father or mother taking the sick child—having come to any of the martyrs, through him offer up a prayer to the Lord, saying to her mediator, ' Thou hast suffered for Christ, intercede for one who suffers and is ill. Having freedom of speech, use it for thy fellow-servant [t].' "

Even Vigilantius appears to have admitted the fact of the miracles; for he argued about them : — " He argues against signs and miracles, which take place in the basilicas of the martyrs, and says that they benefit unbelievers, not believers; as though the question now were, for whom they take place, and not, by what power they take place." " Tell me not, they are 'signs for unbelievers,' but answer how in 'most vile dust and I know not what ashes' there is such presence of signs and wonders [u]." Rufinus relates, that the bodies of the martyr Apollonius and his companions " were buried in one sepulchre, by which up to the present time many miracles and wonderful signs are wrought for all. Yea, and the vows and prayers are received by them, and are fulfilled with the fruits of the petition [x]."

<hr>

[t] *In S. Mart.* in Combef. *Nov. Auct.*, i. 186, 187.　　[u] *S. Jer. cont. Vigil.*, n. 11, Opp. ii. 397.　　[x] *De vitis Patrum*, c. 19, *fin.*

Prudentius says to St. Laurence:—"What power is entrusted, what gifts granted, the joys of the Romans prove, to whom, asked, thou assentest. What every supplicant asketh, he beareth off obtained prosperously; they ask, are enriched, tell, and no one returns sad [y]."

Yet more remarkable are the statements of Theodoret, both as being himself of a dry matter-of-fact mind, and in regard to the extent of the facts which he states. For, in refuting Heathenism, he is contrasting the martyrs with all which the heathen held great, gods or men:—"Time, which withereth all things, hath preserved their glory unwithered. For the noble souls of the victorious (martyrs) traverse heaven, forming part of the incorporeal chorus, but their bodies— it is not a single tomb that conceals each one of them, but cities and villages, having shared them between them, style them the Preservers both of soul and body, and healers, and honour them as tutelars and guardians : and, employing them as intercessors with the Lord of all, by these means obtain divine gifts. And when the body is severed, the grace remains unsevered. And that small and tiniest relic hath the same power with the martyr who hath never been distributed. For the grace abounding distributeth the gifts [z]." "These are truly leaders, and champions and succourers of men, averters of evils, conducting away the injuries brought by demons [a]." "Those who were distinguished for piety, and were slain for it, we call

[y] *Perist.*, ii. 561—568. [z] *Græc. aff. cur.*, viii. t. iv. p. 902, Sch.
[a] Ibid., p. 912.

averters of evil and physicians, friends of God and benevolent servants, using freedom of speech, and announcing to us the harvest of good[b]."

"But the shrines of the martyrs glorious in their victory, are grand, magnificent, and conspicuous in size, and manifoldly adorned, and sending forth flashes of beauty. And to these, not once or twice in the year, nor even five times do we go, but ofttimes we hold solemn assemblies, and often every day offer hymns to their Lord; and they who are in health beg for the preservation of their health; they that are wrestling with any sickness ask a riddance from their sufferings; the childless men ask for offspring, and the barren women for children. And they who have gained this gift, ask that their gifts may be preserved perfect; and those who are setting out upon any journey, implore them to become their fellow-travellers and guides on the way; and they who have gained their return, offer the acknowledgment of the favour; drawing nigh to them not as gods, but approaching them as devout men, and beseeching them to be intercessors on their behalf. But that they who faithfully ask obtain the things which they ask, their votive offerings clearly testify, manifesting the healing; for some offer models of eyes, others of feet, and others of hands; and some of them fashioned of gold, others of silver. For their Lord receives the small and cheap things, too, measuring the gift by the power of the offerer. But the things which are there testify the ceasing of the suffer-

[b] Ibid., p. 915.

ings, whereby they are placed as memorials by those who have become whole. And these things proclaim the power of those buried there; and their power shews that their God is the true God[c]."

We have already seen St. Augustine, before his people, carefully referring to Christ the miracles done at the intercession of the martyrs. He does the same, in answer to the allegations of the heathen; that " their gods, too, had done some marvels" [the fables of a legendary antiquity]. He says that neither did the facts bear comparison, nor the ends for which they were done. For that the end of those things had been to obtain worship for creatures; " but the martyrs do these things, or rather God doth them, they either praying or co-operating, to the advancement of that faith whereby we believe that they are not our gods, but have one God with us. Lastly, they [heathen] both built temples and set up altars, and made priests and offered sacrifices to such gods of theirs; we build not to our martyrs temples as to gods, but memorials as to dead men, whose spirits live to God; and we erect altars therein, not to sacrifice to martyrs, but to the One God of the martyrs and of ourselves; at which Sacrifice, as men of God, who, in confessing Him, overcame the world, they are named in their place and order, yet are not invoked by the priest who sacrifices. For he sacrifices to God, not to them, although he sacrifices in their memorials; for he is God's priest, not theirs. But the sacrifice itself is the Body of Christ, which is

[c] Ibid., pp. 921, 922.

not offered to them, because they, too, are it [viz. Christ's mystical Body].''   He draws out more scientifically the contrast between the cultus done to Almighty God and that shewn to the martyrs (which, he says, was the same *in kind* as that to holy men on earth).   In his celebrated treatise against Faustus the Manichean, who charged the Church with having made an exchange for idols in the cultus of the martyrs, he says : — '' The Christian people unite in celebrating with religious solemnity the memories of the martyrs, both to excite to an imitation of them, and to be associated with their merits and aided by their prayers ; yet so, that to none of the martyrs, but to the God Himself of the Martyrs, although in places dedicated to martyrs, do we raise altars.   For what prelate, standing at the altar in the places of their holy bodies, ever said, ' we offer to thee, Peter, or Paul, or Cyprian ?'   But what is offered is offered to God Who crowned the martyrs, in the memorials of those whom He crowned ; that through the admonition of the places themselves, a greater affection may arise, to make our love keener both towards those whom we are able to imitate, and towards Him by Whose help we are able.   We, therefore, worship the martyrs with that worship of love and of fellowship with which even in this life holy men of God are worshipped, whose hearts we feel are prepared for the like suffering for Gospel truth ; but the martyrs the more devotedly, the safer it is, their conflicts ended ; as also with the more confident praise do we exalt those who are already conquerors in a happier life, than those who are still warring here below. But with that worship, which, in Greek, is called ' latria,' in Latin it cannot be expressed by one word, as it is a kind of service due and appropriate to the Divinity alone, we neither worship nor teach to worship other than the One God. But whereas to this worship appertains the oblation of sacrifice (whence *their* worship, who give this to idols, is called *idolatry*), we do not anywise offer, or teach to be offered anything of this kind, either to any martyr, to any holy soul, or to any angel; and whosoever falls into this error he is reproved by the sound teaching, either that he may amend or be avoided [d]."

And St. Jerome : — " Madman, who ever adored martyrs ? Who thought man to be God [e] ?"

And St. Cyril, of Alexandria, in answer to Julian : — " The holy martyrs we neither say are gods, nor are we wont to worship them, viz., with Divine worship, but

[d] *c. Faust*, xx., 21. And again :— " Even at the memorials of the holy martyrs, do we not offer to God ? The holy martyrs have an honourable place. Observe. In the recital at the altar of Christ, they are recited in a better place; yet they are not adored as Christ; whence their act who offer this too to idols is called *idolatry*. When heard ye it said by any other my brother and colleague, or any Presbyter, ' I offer to thee, holy Theogenis, or I offer to thee, Peter, I offer to thee, Paul.' Never have ye heard. It is not, it may not be. If it be said to thee, ' Dost thou worship Peter ?' answer what Eulogius [the deacon] said [to the heathen judge] of Fructuosus [his bishop, whose martyrdom he shared], ' I do not worship Peter, but God I worship, whom Peter too worships. Then Peter loves thee.' "—*Serm.* 273, *in Nat. Fruct. Aug. Eulog.*, n. 7. t. v. 1108.

[e] *c. Vigil.*, n. 5, t. ii. 391, Vall.

relatively and honorifically. But rather we crown them with the highest honours, as having striven nobly for the truth [f]."

St. Asterius, of Amasea, in like manner, says to the heathen :—" *We* worship not martyrs, but we honour them, as sincere worshippers of God. We do not worship men, but we admire those who, in time of persecution, nobly worshipped God.   We deposit them in beautiful shrines, and the houses of their repose we raise magnificent in structure, that we may zealously honour men who died gloriously. But we shew them not an unrequited zeal, but enjoy their patronage toward God. For since our prayer suffices not to importune God in time of necessity and calamity ; for our supplication is not an obsecration but a reminiscence of our sins, therefore we flee to those our fellow-servants, the beloved of the Lord, that they in their own good deeds may heal our transgressions. What censure is it that, honouring martyrs, we too are zealous to please God ? What accusation is it to flee to patrons [g] ?"

Such, then, being the authorities, for the practice of asking the prayers and intercessions of the saints, even those same great fathers who jealously guarded for us, and by their toils and sufferings transmitted to us the belief in the All-Holy Trinity and our Blessed Lord's Divine Person :—such being the testimony upon which they tested it ; viz., the experience of those, who had sought through the saints what God alone could

---

[f] l. vi. t. vi. p. 203.   [g] *Encom. in SS. Martt. in Combefis. N. Auct.*, pp. 191, 192. Paris, 1648.

give and had found it, we could have nothing, in principle, to except against it, if only those errors be guarded against, to which our poor nature is so easily inclined, of betaking ourselves to the saints, as to beings less holy, less awful, whom the soul ever approaches with less effort and less fear than Him, Who, being our Mediator, will also be our Judge. The Council of Trent itself desired that "all superstition in the invocation of saints should be removed." A learned writer said, "Many Christians sin for the most part in a thing which is good, in that they venerate the saints no otherwise than God. Nor, in many, do I see what difference there is between their opinion of the saints, and what the Gentiles thought of their gods[h]."

This is precisely what our homily (which illustrates this Article) excepts against, when, having spoken of the conduct of Paul and Barnabas at Lystra, and the monition of the angel in the Revelations to St. John, it sums up, "which examples declare unto us that the angels and saints in heaven will not have us to do any honour unto them, *that is due and proper unto God[l].*"

On the other side, Bellarmine, in treating on this subject, lays down formally these propositions[k]: "(1.) We may not ask the saints, that they, as authors of the Divine benefits, would grant us glory or grace, and other means to beatitude. (2.) Saints are not our imme-

---

[h] *Lud. Vives on S. Aug. de Civ. D.*, viii. *ult.*, quoted by Bp. W. Forbes' *Consid. Mod.*, t. ii. p. 310.

[l] Homily on Prayer, p. 277.   [k] *De Sanct. Beat.* i. 17.

diate intercessors with God, but whatever they impetrate for us from God, they impetrate through Christ." The first statement he proves (1.) from Holy Scripture:—"The Lord will give grace and glory;" and St. James, "Every good gift and every perfect gift cometh down from the Father of lights:" (2.) From the usage of the Church; for in the prayers read at mass, or in the office on the festival of the saints, we never ask anything else but that, at their prayers, benefits may be granted to us by God. (3.) From reason; for what we need surpasses the powers of the creature, and therefore even of saints; therefore we ought to ask nothing of saints beyond their impetrating from God what is profitable for us. (4.) From Augustine and Theodoret, who expressly teach that "saints are not to be invoked as gods, but as able to gain for men what they wish." Bellarmine, however, subjoins:—"When we say that nothing should be asked of saints, save that they should pray for us, the question is not about the words, but about the sense of the words. For, as far as the words go, it is lawful to say, 'St. Peter, have mercy upon me, save me,' &c., so that we understand, 'save me and have mercy upon me, by praying for me,' &c.; for so speaks Gregory Nazianzen and many other of the ancients, and the universal Church, &c. And, as the Apostle says of himself, Rom. xi. 'that I might save some of them,' and 1 Cor. ix."

St. Thomas Aquinas says:—"To Him alone, from Whom we hope to obtain what we pray for, do we, by praying, pay the cultus of religion, because in this we testify that He is the Author ¡of our good things; but not to those to whom we resort as our advocates with God[1]."

In principle, then, there is no question, herein, between us and any other portion of the Catholic Church. Even where the incommunicable attributes of God have, in expression at least, been invaded, the real underlying belief has been explained to be, that nothing is obtained for man, no grace, no aid, no gift for body, soul, or spirit, except through or from the One Mediator between God and Man, our adorable Lord, Christ Jesus. Prayer to the saints in heaven is explained, again and again, to be the same *in kind* as the prayers to the saints on earth; as St. Augustine speaks of the cultus of the saints in heaven being the same in kind as the cultus of saints on earth. "Since the mediation of the saints is not invoked like that of Christ, since their mediation is held to be only one of intercession not of redemption, since the effectualness of their intercession rests on God's free mercy and the merits of Christ, then the honour of Christ and the aloneness of His redemption is not in the least intrenched upon. If the intercession of believers on earth may be invoked, without injury to the honour of Christ as Mediator, why not also the intercession of the saints in heaven[m]?" Had this been

[1] 2. 2. q. 83, art. 4, ad 1.

[m] Klee, *Kath. Dogmatik.*, iii. 407, 408, ed. 3. "It is good and useful to apply to the saints for intercession and help. They are, namely, friends and beloved of God, whose intercession is effectual, and they being, by reason of their love, inclined to help us, then it is also praiseworthy and beneficial to apply for their intercession, *as for that of*

all, the Article never could have been written. Not
our own Divines only, but foreign reformers, too, have
seen nothing herein to reject[n]. The Church of Rome
has not stated the practice to be necessary to salvation,
nor required it of any, so that he deny not that, as
above explained, it is in itself good and useful. The
more this aspect is dwelt upon, the more we shall be
disposed to accept the conclusion of a pious Divine:—
" Let God alone be religiously adored; let Him alone
be prayed to through Christ, Who, truly and properly
speaking, is the sole and only Mediator between God
and man. Let not that most ancient custom, common
in the universal Church, as well Greek as Latin, of
addressing angels and saints in the way we have
said, be condemned or rejected, as impious, or as vain
and foolish. Let foul abuses and superstitions which
have crept in be taken away, and so shall peace hereafter be easily formed and ratified between the parties.
Which, may the God of peace and all holy concord,
vouchsafe to grant for the sake of His Only-Begotten
Son[o]."

the righteous living upon earth. Therefore the Church has of old
approved and recommended the invoking them, and only rejected the
saint-worship which obscured the merits of the Redeemer."—*Dieringer
Lehrb. d. Kath. Dogm.,* p. 733, ed. 5.

[n] Bishop William Forbes quotes even Luther (A. 1518 and 1522).
Œcolampadius, Bucer, Camerarius, apparently the author of the *Enchirid. Theol., Consid. Mod.,* t. ii. pp. 266, 274.

[o] Forbes, *Consid. Mod.,* ii. 513.

ARTICLE XXIII.

De Vocatione Ministrorum.

(*al.* De Ministrando in Ecclesia.)

Non licet cuiquam sumere sibi munus publice prædicandi, aut administrandi Sacramenta in Ecclesia, nisi prius fuerit ad hæc obeunda legitime vocatus et missus. Atque illos legitime vocatos et missos existimare debemus, qui per homines, quibus potestas vocandi ministros, atque mittendi in vineam Domini, publice concessa est in Ecclesia, cooptati fuerint et adsciti in hoc opus.

" Of Ministering in the Congregation.

"It is not lawful for any man to take upon him the office of public preaching, or ministering the sacraments in the congregation, before he be lawfully called and sent to execute the same. And those we ought to judge lawfully called and sent, which be chosen and called to this work by men who have public authority given unto them in the congregation, to call and send ministers into the Lord's vineyard."

The Article here treats of what is technically called Mission[a]. That the clergy should have such mission is affirmed, not only by implication in such terms as describe them as stewards and ambassadors, but also

---

[a] Vide S. Pacian, Ep. i. 12, Oxf. Tr. 325, 326.

in so many terms by St. Paul[b], where, in a beautiful anti-climax, he describes the order whereby men arrive at righteousness and salvation. First comes the mission of the preachers; then the actual preaching of the Gospel; then the faith of the hearers; then their worship and calling upon God; lastly, salvation in this life from the disease of sin, hereafter from death and corruption in glory everlasting. " Whosoever shall call upon the name of the Lord shall be saved." " How shall they call on Him in whom they have not believed? and how shall they believe on Him of whom they have not heard? and how shall they hear without a preacher? and how shall they preach unless they be sent? (ἀποσταλῶσι) except they be Apostles?"

Now mission is divided into two kinds, that which comes immediately and proximately from God, and which needs the authentication of miracles and signs; and that which comes mediately from Him, through those to whom the power of mission is given by the institution of Christ. Just as in the old Jewish Church these two powers existed side by side in the respective institutions of the prophetic and priestly offices, so in the primitive Church we recognise the same. The Epistle to the Corinthians is full of allusions to the supernatural consequences which ensued on the gift of the Holy Ghost, while in the Pastoral Epistles—those to Timothy and Titus, we have evidence of the formation of the ordinary hierarchy. Of this hierarchy the ἀποσταλῶσι, the mission, is the key-note, referring us

<hr>

[b] Rom. x. 14.

back to Him, Who is the Apostle and High Priest of
our Profession, as receiving mission from the Father,
for the purpose of transmitting it fresh to the twelve,
in whom He lodged all power and authority. The title
of Apostle was not confined to the twelve. Barnabas
and Paul are first assumed into the holy band to the
violation of the mystic number of twelve completed by
Matthias. Epaphroditus[c] is termed by St. Paul "my
brother, and companion in labour, and fellow soldier,
but your apostle," (ἀπόστολον). In the Corinthians,
not only does he recognise the existence of Apostles—
first in their capacity of recipients of supernatural
gifts—"He gave some Apostles," but we find certain
of his brethren recognised as " Apostles of Churches,
a glory of Christ," (ἀπόστολοι ἐκκλησιῶν, δόξα Χριστοῦ,) where their office and dignity is happily recog-.
nised in one pregnant sentence. Again, in Rom.
xvi. 7, Andronicus and Junia are said to be " of note
among the Apostles."

Meanwhile the discontent of the Hellenistic Jews,
who thought that their widows were neglected in the
distribution of alms, had evoked the institution of the
diaconate, and wherever the Apostles established a
Church, they ordained men who in the Jewish communities were called " elders," in the Gentile Churches
" overseers." The first title was one associated with
notions of great dignity among the Jews, as there were
elders in the Sanhedrin, assessors to the chief priests
and scribes, and every synagogue had a chief or pre-

<hr>

[c] Phil. ii. 25.

sident.   The title 'overseer' or 'bishop,' occurs in the Alexandrian version in the sense of an ecclesiastical and civil officer.   Thus there are three orders in the Church, —apostles, overseers or elders, and deacons.

But only a part of the Apostolic office was to be transmitted, and such part as was transmitted had to be regulated.   It was impossible that the solidarity of their power should continue, and there were certain prophetical powers which in the purpose of God and in the nature of things must cease.   Accordingly before the close of the Canon of Scripture, we find a certain monarchical power establishing itself in each Church. St. James exercised what we should now call episcopal jurisdiction over the city of Jerusalem; and the seven Churches of Asia have each an officer termed an angel. Timothy and Titus, from acting as Apostolic delegates of St. Paul, become diocesan bishops, the first of Ephesus, the second of Gortyna in Crete.

In the early quarrels and insubordination, e.g. of Novatians, the line taken, was not to dispute the office of the episcopate, but to set up an anti-bishop.

This state of things is exactly represented in the Epistle of St. Clement to the Corinthians, which belongs to the end of the first century.   He recognises three orders: 1. the Apostles, who, in prospect of contention arising about the office of ruling, appointed rulers, and ordained for the future after their death other tried men who should hold their office of appointing such persons; 2. presbyters or overseers; and 3. deacons.   He also quotes the threefold ministry as a type and parallel of the hierarchy of the old law. By the time of St. Ignatius, we find the title of Apostle dropped, out of reverence to those who first bore it; the name of Overseer apportioned to the apostolic office, and thus separated from the presbyteral; in this way the three orders are still maintained in their integral distinction. Nor is this the mere local usage of the Churches of Asia Minor. We have distinct evidence, at the end of the second century, that this hierarchical constitution prevailed universally, without any known exception, throughout the whole of Christendom. "The episcopate was a whole in which each enjoys possession in solidarity." All over the earth, from India to Spain, the episcopate was a definite organization. It is impossible to account for this hierarchical uniformity without pre-supposing an original Divine institution. If we consider the difficulty of the transmission of intelligence, the rarity of the occasions of communication, the deep-rooted ethnical peculiarities of the varying tribes which were converted to Christianity, we can in no way account for it save on the supposition of the threefold ministry being a part of the original constitution of the Christian Church.

No new form could thus have established itself universally without exciting some opposition; of that opposition there is no trace in any of the earlier records. In the fifth century, indeed, we find the existence of opposition on the part of Aerius and Vigilantius, but this opposition actually tests the universality of the organization. It was left to the religious exigencies of the foreign Reformers to frame, first, a theory of the non-necessity of bishops ; and then, to erect the platform of their polity without reference to them. By some, indeed, the new constitution was justified only on the plea of absolute necessity. Calvin regretted this imagined necessity.

The gravity of the matter consists in this. That while we are not in any way to limit the mercy of God, and therefore can understand that in exceptional circumstances, exceptional conditions of things may be allowed ; yet, in the course of the guidance of the Church, it is a truth universally accepted by all who have any pretensions to be sound theologians, that the validity of certain rites depends upon Episcopal ordination, i.e. upon the Apostolical Succession, and as a result of the character of Holy Order, none but one so appointed can bind or loose in the Name of Christ, or consecrate His Body. As a matter of fact, in the bodies who have not apostolic mission, the belief in both these functions has disappeared, and that disappearance is not the least terrible result of the schisms of the sixteenth century. "If the light that is in thee be darkness, how great is that darkness!"

ARTICLE XXIV.

De Precibus Publicis Dicendis in Lingua Vulgari.

(*al.* De Loquendo in Ecclesia Lingua quam Populus
intelligit.)

*Lingua populo non intellecta, publicas in ecclesia preces
peragere aut Sacramenta administrare, verbo Dei et
primitivæ Ecclesiæ consuetudini plane repugnat.*

---

*"Of Speaking in the Congregation in such a Tongue as
the People understandeth.*

"It is a thing plainly repugnant to the Word of
God, and the custom of the primitive Church, to have
public prayer in the church, or to minister the Sacraments, in a tongue not understanded of the people."

It seems strange that, considering what divine service is, it should have been necessary to ordain that it
should be in the language of the worshipper. Bearing
in mind that one great part of oral prayer is the elevation of the soul to God, one would hardly imagine
that the greater part of the Christian Church should
deem it right to offer it in a tongue not understanded
of the people. There must be some reason for what is
rightly declared in the Article to be " plainly repugnant to the Word of God and the custom of the primitive Church."

F f

And that this custom is thus repugnant, is manifest from the text of St. Paul, " Yet in the church I had rather speak five words to the edifying of the hearers, than ten thousand words in an unknown tongue[a]." So also, " Else when thou shalt bless with the spirit, how shall he that occupieth the room of the unlearned say Amen at the giving of thanks, seeing he understandeth not what thou sayest[b]?" Again, positively, we are told, " I will pray with my spirit, and I will pray with my understanding also." God's service is a reasonable service, λογικὴν λατρείαν ὑμῶν, a service in which the λόγος is concerned.

Though we have no trace of it remaining, except the 'Kyrie Eleison' before the Lord's Prayer, and the ' Agios o Theos' in the office for Good Friday, there can be no doubt that in the earliest ages the Liturgy of the Greek-speaking Roman Church was Greek, and continued such till the transference of the Empire to Byzantium. It is probable that the Latin Liturgy of St. Peter existed also from the very earliest times, if not in Rome, at least in Africa. The Eastern Church, of course, employed the Greek language, which also served for Palestine, where, in consequence of more than two centuries of Hellenism, it was so universally employed, that many scholars believe that it was the very language of our Lord and His Apostles. We have no knowledge of the offices which were used by the Apostles who carried the Gospel into India, Parthia, and other regions, but there is no reason for

<hr>

[a] 1 Cor. xiv. 19.   [b] Ibid., 16.

supposing that the services were in any other language than the vernacular of each region.

Martene says[c], "Although the modern use of the Church is that the mass shall only be celebrated in Greek, Latin, and Hebrew, and the reasons for proscribing the mother tongue are sufficient, yet it was not so in the beginning." In support of this he quotes the story of St. Anthony the Abbot, told by St. Athanasius, who, knowing nothing but the Egyptian idiom, entered the church, and hearing the Gospel read in which it is enjoined to sell all, straightway went and did so. Still more to the purpose is the history of the life of St. Theodosius the Archimandrite, who built in his monastery four churches, one for the Greeks, one for the *Bessi*, a third for the Armenians, and a fourth for those beset with evil spirits; so that it happened that they all (except the beset) carried on the services in their own tongues, so far as the Gospel, and then joined together in the great Greek Church, and hereupon were made partakers of the Divine mysteries.

A similar fact is narrated by Cyrillus Scythopolitanus, in his life of St. Saba.

In the ninth century, when the Slaves were converted to Christianity by St. Methodius, John VIII. highly praised their performing the service in the Slavonic tongue[d]. He, however, adds, that for the honour of Divine worship, the Gospel is to be read first in Latin and then translated, and if the Count and his

---

[c] *De Antiq. Eccl. Nat.*, lib. i. cap. iii. art. ii. tom. i. p. 101.

[d] *Ep.* 247. to Sfentopulcher, Count of Moravia.

judges like to hear it read in Latin they may do so. Before this, Methodius had introduced the vernacular among the Pannonians, with the consent of Pope John; but Gregory VII. forbad it when writing to Vratisloff, Duke of Bohemia. All the Slaves still use the Slavonic, and not only the schismatical communities in the East [e], but those in communion with the Latins, as the Maronites, who use Arabic or Chaldaic, worship in their own language.

It is unnecessary to allude to those mixed rites, where Latin was used in the East, and Greek in the West, sometimes to typify intercommunion, sometimes to meet the case of alien populations, as was specially common in Magna Græcia. A still more interesting question suggests itself, whether in the West the use of the vernacular ever obtained to any great extent. Martene mentions that in the Church of Soissons (Suessonensis), on the feast of St. Stephen, the Epistle was sung in Latin and in French, as also at St. Gatien's, at Tours, and he gives the beginning of it. It is a specimen of what are termed "farsuras," and in a philological point of view is eminently curious. He mentions that in some parishes in the diocese of Rheims they sang, in his own time, a piece in French, describing the life of . St. Stephen, which was forbidden by the existing archbishop.

Theodoret makes mention of the translation of the Bible into many tongues [f]; and the version of Ulphilas into Mæsogothic, A.D. 360, is the first that prevailed in

---

[e] Vide *Bona Rer. Lit.*, lib. i. c. 9. n. 4.   [f] *Græc. Affect.*, l. 5.

the West. But we know nothing of a Gothic Liturgy.
It is true the Church hymns, e. g. the *Te Deum*, were
rendered into German, as well as the Epistles and Gospels, in the ninth century; and by the Council of Leptines, A.D. 743, certain parts of the Baptismal Service
were appointed to be in the German language[g]. Still
there was always a tendency to enforce the Latin language in the West. As the fresh tribes from the north
were evangelized by the Roman clergy, it was natural
that the Roman clergy should employ and recommend
the rites to which they had been accustomed. It became the measure of the solidity of the conversion that
the Latin tongue was accepted. It was also a great
means for the consolidation of the Church's power.
Even in the Celtic tribes of Ireland and Scotland the
mass, though not the rubrics and hymns, was always
in Latin; and whatever may have been the polity and
nationality of the race who first raised to heaven the
prayers of the Mozarabic Rite, that glorious formulary
speaks to God in the language of the Romans.

The Eastern Church did not take this exclusive line.
Wedded as that Church has ever been to tradition, it
freely allowed of the translation of the Euchologia and
Liturgies. The great Slave races, who received their
knowledge of Christ from the East, as we have seen,
were freely allowed their Slavonic services. The Armenians and Georgians, Cophts and Syrians, were all
allowed to worship God in a tongue which they understood. Time, of course, has told on this arrange-

[g] Labbe and Cossart, *Conc.*, tom. viii. p. 278.

ment. The language of daily use has altered, while the Church language has remained as it was, so that now over the greater part of the Christian world the ignorant among the worshippers imperfectly understand what is said in church.

In extenuation of this state of things, it is urged 1. that it would be impossible to be eternally altering the service to suit the alterations of the language of common life; 2. that more is gained by the reverence which an ancient form inspires than is lost by a partial ignorance of it; 3. that in fact, by means of translation and explanation, the great mass of the faithful do adhibit a rational attention to the sense of that in which they are occupied; and 4. that it is most important to embalm the expression of doctrine in a language, which, by being dead, has got a definite meaning sealed to each word.

To sum up, it is desirable that, due precaution being taken for the conservation of the true doctrine by certain unalterable formulæ, the language of prayer and praise should be that which every ordinary educated person of average intelligence should be able to follow with perfect facility; and that in the mutation of language, the service-books should from time to time be corrected, but only when the amount of discrepancy between the archaic and ordinary tongues has become so great, that an intelligent rational worship is rendered difficult or impossible.

ARTICLE XXV.

De Sacramentis.

Sacramenta a Christo instituta, non tantum sunt notæ professionis Christianorum, sed certa quædam potius testimonia et efficacia signa gratiæ atque bonæ in nos voluntatis Dei, per quæ invisibiliter ipse in no[bi]s operatur, nostramque fidem in se non solum excitat, verum etiam confirmat.

Duo a Christo Domino nostro in Evangelio instituta sunt Sacramenta: scilicet, Baptismus, et Cœna Domini.

Quinque illa vulgo nominata Sacramenta, scilicet, confirmatio, pœnitentia, ordo, matrimonium, et extrema unctio, pro Sacramentis Evangelicis habenda non sunt, ut quæ, partim a prava Apostolorum imitatione profluxerunt, partim vitæ status sunt in Scripturis quidem probati, sed sacramentorum eandem cum Baptismo et Cœna Domini rationem non habentes, ut quæ signum aliquod visibile, seu cæremoniam, a Deo institutam, non habeant.

Sacramenta non in hoc instituta sunt a Christo ut spectarentur, aut circumferrentur, sed ut rite illis uteremur; et in his duntaxat qui digne percipiunt, salutarem habent effectum. Qui vero indigne percipiunt, damnationem (ut inquit Paulus) sibi ipsis acquirunt.

Of the Sacraments.

" Sacraments ordained of Christ, be not only badges or tokens of Christian men's profession, but rather they be certain sure witnesses and effectual signs of grace and God's good-will towards us, by the which He doth work invisibly in us, and doth not only quicken, but also strengthen and confirm our faith in Him.

"There are two Sacraments ordained of Christ our Lord in the Gospel, that is to say, Baptism, and the Supper of the Lord.

"Those five commonly called Sacraments, that is to say, Confirmation, Penance, Orders, Matrimony, and extreme Unction, are not to be counted Sacraments of the Gospel, being such as have grown partly of the corrupt following of the Apostles, partly are states of life allowed in the Scriptures: but yet have not like nature of Sacraments with Baptism and the Lord's Supper, for that they have not any visible sign or ceremony ordained of God.

"The Sacraments were not ordained of Christ to be gazed upon, or to be carried about, but that we should duly use them. And in such only as worthily receive the same, they have a wholesome effect or operation: but they that receive them unworthily, purchase to themselves damnation, as St. Paul saith."

The Article begins by stating that Sacraments ordained of Christ are something more than badges or tokens of Christian men's profession. This was the miserable conception of Zwingli. He maintained Sacraments to be signs of covenant between man and man, external things in no wise affecting the conscience, neither spiritual in themselves nor working anything spiritual in us, the tokens of those who are spiritual. Luther and Melanchthon's theory was also inadequate. They reduced the Sacraments to tokens of a covenant between God and man, to pledges of the truth of the divine promises for the forgiveness of sins, to means of assurance that the debt of the sins of the faithful receiver is remitted, and of peace to comfort and console him. All this springs from the one-sided conceptions of the justification of man before God. The effects of the Sacraments were confined to the subjective acts of the individual at the moment of reception. In fact, the objective character of the means of grace was lost. Luther's variations were endless. His permanent belief was, that they were a sort of visible preaching to kindle faith. But the Confession of Augsburg is not even fairly orthodox on this point.

Calvin's teaching was in most respects similar to that of Luther, but he carefully points out all the parts of what is understood by a Sacrament, and recommends, with much urgency, its use, but then he divorces the inward grace from the outward sign. This is the necessary result of his theory of election. If it is only to the elect that God's grace is tendered, the rest being passed over by God, it follows that grace is by no means necessarily connected with the outward sign. Hence, in Baptism, those who are not elected are only outwardly washed, and in the Lord's Supper receive mere bread and wine. According to him, Sacraments are merely obsignatory.

Having thus cleared the way to a definition, the Article goes on to state that Sacraments ordained by

Christ are "certain sure witnesses and effectual signs of grace and God's good-will towards us, by the which He doth work invisibly in us, and doth not only quicken, but strengthen and confirm our faith in Him." Observe the singular strength of these words, in comparison with those of the Confession of Augsburg: "Sacraments are the signs and testimonies of God's good-will towards us, bestowed for exciting and confirming the faith of those who use them." Again, we call Sacraments rites, which have the commandment of God, and to which is added the promise of grace. Our Article makes five assertions with regard to them: they are—1. sure witnesses of grace, and God's good-will towards us; 2. effectual signs of grace, and God's good-will towards us; 3. by Sacraments God works invisibly in us; 4. by Sacraments He quickens our faith in Him; 5. by Sacraments He strengthens and confirms that Faith. There is no point of Catholic teaching on the subject which is not amply and explicitly contained in these words.

1. The first point impressed upon us is, the sense of Sacraments being witnesses of grace, or, in stricter theological language, signifying grace. They are types of that holiness and righteousness which they convey. There is a celebrated passage in St. Augustine, where he says that "Sacraments are called the things which they signify, from a certain similarity and likeness." Thus they are the pledges of the divine will in regard to man, and sureties of the truth of God's promises. As God, under the Mosaic

dispensation, employed outward signs, and wonders, and tokens, to strengthen the trust of the Jews in the divine assurance, as in the words of Deut. vi. 20, "And when thy son asketh thee in time to come, saying, What mean the testimonies, and the statutes, and the judgments, which the Lord our God hath commanded you?" so our blessed Lord, the new Moses, the Legislator of a better covenant, instituted these rites as pledges of the forgiveness of sin, of the bestowal of grace, of communion with God. A pledge to assure us of the inward and spiritual grace given to us, is a necessary part of the definition. But this is not all.

2. The Article says further, that a Sacrament is an effectual sign of God's grace. It not only typifies, it conveys. It is not a bare sign, but an effectual sign, a sign that carries its effect along with it. It is the means whereby we receive the same grace, of which it is the outward visible sign.

3. By Sacraments God works invisibly in us. All grace flows from the Humanity of Jesus Christ, and the Sacraments are main channels whereby that grace flows into the soul. Christ is the chief and principal worker in all Sacraments, as a function of His everlasting priesthood. They work in us by means of the institution of Christ. He has merited for us all things necessary to salvation, and these are freely bestowed upon us by God, if our free-wills only consent to receive them. This consent to receive grace, in other words expresses itself as repentance and faith. Re-

pentance and faith make us susceptible of the grace of the Sacrament, which thus abide in the Absolute and the Objective.

4. Sacraments quicken or give life to faith. In the old rituals, the service of Baptism begins with this question to the sponsor in the name of the candidate, What seekest thou of the Church? and the answer is, Faith.

5. Sacraments strengthen and confirm faith. As a means of grace, they strengthen the whole soul, increase its spiritual capacities both as to the intellectual and the moral part of man's being, and therefore intimately affect the faith, which, though dwelling in the intellectual part of the soul, is intimately influenced by the morals. The power of increase in faith is indicated by our Lord in the similitude of the mustard seed. Faith exists in the faintest recognition of a superior Being amid the fetich worship of the ignorant savage; it rises to the keenest recognition of Divine truth in the perfected saint, and to the endurance of martyrdom for these holy convictions. A power so infinitely varying in degree must be profoundly affected by the means which God gives us of advancing in righteousness and holiness, so that the Sacraments act directly according to their own nature, and for their appointed purpose, when they confirm and strengthen the faith.

The Article adds that "the Sacraments were not ordained of Christ to be gazed upon, or to be carried about, but that we should duly use them." In this sentence the stress is on the words, "were not ordained of Christ to be," &c. The Article does not say, that the things spoken of may not be done, but that they were not *the* objects for which Christ ordained them. Had they been, they could not have been laid aside without sin. Being of ecclesiastical, not of Divine institution, they were mutable, not immutable. What it affirms is strictly historically true. By carrying the Sacraments about, we are probably to understand the Procession of the *Corpus Domini*. No person in his senses would say that this was ordained of Christ, but, though not actually ordained of Christ, the practice is not necessarily sinful, nay, if ordered by the Church, in accordance with His will, permissible and edifying. If "gazing" be supposed to imply assisting at the Eucharistic celebration without communicating, it must be recollected that from the very beginning, the penitents called *consistentes* were required to be present without communicating; and as love waxed cold, the Church thought it better that men should be present at the great Eucharistic Service without communion, rather than turn their backs upon the holy mysteries. But it was distinctly an accommodation to weakness in the beginning, and the normal order of the Church is still, that all present should be in a fit state to participate in the holy mysteries, and actually do so [a].

As regards the circumgestation of the blessed Sa-

---

[a] Both the Articles and Council of Trent agree in considering that private masses are the result of the coldness of Christians. Both condemn it, but both have failed in enforcing universal participation.

crament. From the beginning of the third century we have evidence of its being reserved in the Church. It was sometimes carried home by the faithful for private communion, but generally it rested in a ciborium, in the form of a dove hanging over the altar. It was then ready for the exigencies of the sick and dying, and Church history is full of records of the tremendous profanations it endured from the hands of the heathen, or even heretic Christians. At length, on the occasion of the upspring of a pantheistic school in Europe, headed by David de Dinant, and Amaury de Chartres [b], the doctrine of the Sacrament received additional consideration, and it was deemed expedient to carry the Sacrament through the streets, as a protest patent to every one against the dangerous errors of pantheism; and since those days the devotional use of the Lord's Body, as divorced from its Sacramental participation, has greatly increased in the Western Church, while the Greek Church and the English Church have refrained from developing in this direction.

It is observable that the framers of our present Article omitted a clause contained in the Forty-two Articles, founded upon a misconception, common at that time, of the theological meaning of the term, *opus operatum*. After the words, " in such only as worthily receive the same, they have a wholesome effect and operation;" there followed, " and yet that, not of this work wrought [*ex opere operato*] as some men speak; which word, as it is strange and un-

<hr>

[b] Möhler, *Symbolik*, vol. i. p. 350.

known to Holy Scripture, so it engendereth no godly but a very superstitious sense." This supposed sense was, that the Sacraments conferred the benefits attached to them, to all who received them, without any good dispositions on their part, *sine aliquo bono motu utentis,* as people used to say. Such an opinion could not be too strongly condemned, but nothing could be more alien from the meaning of the term. It is a well-known distinction of the Schoolmen; "Some receive both the Sacrament and the substance of the Sacrament" [viz. those who receive it worthily]; "some, the Sacrament and not the substance" [viz. those who receive it unworthily]; "some, the substance and not the Sacrament[c]" [viz. those who desire to receive it aright, but, in the ordering of God's Providence, are prevented]. This distinction in itself excludes the imputation that, according to this doctrine, the Sacraments benefited those who received them unworthily by their mere reception. Such, in the language of St. Augustine, "placed a bar" to the reception of their grace. And so those alone universally received the benefits of a Sacrament, who could place no bar. "The Sacrament and the substance together all, in fact, receive who in Baptism are cleansed from original sin." The phrase, *ex opere operato,* was devised in contrast with the *ex opere operantis,* and to distinguish the Sacraments of the new law from those of the old; to exclude human merits, not worthy reception; to express that God's gift in the Sacrament is a gift special to the

[c] P. Lomb., l. iv. dist. iv.

Sacrament, "a work worked" by God, beyond and above human co-operation. "When Catholics say that Sacraments confer grace *ex opere operato*, they do not think that they confer it only from the merits of the receiver, either of condignity or impetratory, but by the virtue of the Sacrament itself, without which, even if such disposition preceded, it would not be given [d]." "It is said that Sacraments justify men, *ex opere operato*, because they do not justify by reason of the merits of the work of the minister, who confers the Sacrament, as far as it is his, as operating [*opus operantis*], viz. in what way he may be worthy of praise or blame: but the work of the minister is considered only in itself, be it done well or ill, so that it be done according to the Divine institution, because it hath this power, not by the virtue or merits of the minister, but by the virtue of the Author who instituted it" [the doctrine of our Article XXVI.]. The Council of Trent guarded the meaning of the *ex opere operato* by the words:—"If any one say that the Sacraments of the new law do not contain grace, or confer it *to those who place no bar to it;*" and in their rejection of those who confined the grace of the Sacraments to the elect:—"If any say that grace is not given through such Sacraments always to all, *as far as relates to God's part, although they duly receive them*, but sometimes and to some [e]." In which words they express the same limitation as our Article.

Of the number of the Sacraments little notice was

<hr>

[d] *Vazquez in* 3, P. d. 131, q. 1.   [e] Sess. vii. can. 6, 7.

taken in the Protestant confessions. Luther, regarding them as symbols for the purpose of confirming a man's faith in the forgiveness of sins, could necessarily see no sacramental character in many of those rites which had long been esteemed such. He admitted three,—Baptism, the Lord's Supper, Penitence [f]. Calvin also admitted only two Sacraments, in the sense in which he believed any Sacraments; viz. "outward symbols, whereby God seals to our consciences the promises of His good will towards us to support the weakness of our faith, and we, in turn, attest our piety towards Him, before Him, the angels, and men [g]." Baptism testifies that we *have been* cleansed and washed; the Eucharistic Supper, that we *have been* redeemed [h]." The "five falsely-named Sacraments" he rejected with much vehemence [i], whence there is no allusion to them in any of the original reformed confessions [j].

[f] The number is not defined in the Confession of Augsburg, but these are enumerated in Art. ix.—xii. The Apology, on Art. xiii., declares these three to be Sacraments, as "having the command of God and the promise of the grace of the New Testament. For in all three our hearts ought to settle, that God really forgives us for Christ's sake. Confirmation and Extreme Unction, it says, are rites received from the fathers, which the Church, too, does not require as necessary to salvation, because they have not the command of God." "If Orders be accounted the ministry of the word [i.e. preaching], we should undeniably call 'order' a Sacrament. Matrimony," it says, "if any one wills to call it a Sacrament, should be distinguished from the former, which are properly signs of the New Testament, and are testimonies of grace and of forgiveness of sins." (p. 155, ed. Tittm.)

[g] Inst. iv. n. i. [h] Ibid., n. 22. [i] Ibid., n. 19.

[j] The "declaratio Thoruniensis," the result of an attempt in Poland to unite Catholics, Lutherans, and Reformers, A.D. 1645, alone speak of them. It was received by the reformed in Brandenburg.—*Aug. Diss. Hist. Lit.*, in his *Corpus Libb. Symb.*, pp. 642, 643.

The septenary number of the Sacraments had long been held both by the Greek and Latin Churches, and there is no ground to deprive of a sacramental character the rites for which that character is claimed.

Peter Lombard is the first to formulize the number in the Latin Church. Before that nothing had been defined. Alexander Alensis[k] held that confirmation was not apostolic, but ordained by the Council of Meaux; Buonaventura[l] denies that it was established by Christ; Cajetan[m] denies that extreme unction is the ceremony mentioned in St. James. Rupertus Tuicensis says, "Sacred Baptism, the Holy Eucharist of His Body and Blood, the twin gift of the Holy Ghost. . . . These three Sacraments are the necessary instruments of our salvation[n]."

The language of the Article is awkward and embarrassed, whether it be that the use of the word "partly" did not at that time (as it certainly does not by the force of the word itself) imply a logical division into two classes, or that the framers of the Article used it illogically. But, certainly, the words could not have been intended to express any absolute division of the five Sacraments into the two classes spoken of, since, by no possibility, according to the principles of the framers, could Confirmation be classed in either. For the right interpretation of the Article, we need but these simple principles: 1. That the framers did not

---

[k] Alensis, p. 4, q. 9.   [l] Buonaventura, *Sent.*, l. 4, dist. 7, q. 2.
[m] Cajetan, *in Jac.* 5, p. 419, ed. Lugd., 1556.   [n] *De Victoria Verbi Dei*, l. xii. c. 11, cit. Owen.

mean to contradict the Homilies, which they praised;
2. That the writers, both of the Articles and the Homilies, did not use carefully guarded language without a meaning. The word "Sacrament" has notoriously been used in a wider and a stricter sense. The Homilies mention St. Augustine's description, "a visible sign of an invisible grace." In this respect they stand out from those other mysteries of the Christian life, which the fathers have here and there called Sacraments, such as prayer[o], or the Lord's prayer[p], or fasting[q], or Holy Scripture[r], or the Creed[p], or Martyrdom[s]; for although these are instruments of grace, through the blessing of God, they have not been marked out by any visible sign. Now, in this wider sense, " this Article does not deny the five rites in question to be Sacraments; it only denies them to be Sacraments in the same sense in which Baptism and the Lord's Supper are Sacraments,—'Sacraments *of the Gospel*,' 'Sacraments with an outward sign ordained by God.'" "If, then, a Sacrament be merely 'an outward sign of an invisible grace' given under it, the five rites may be Sacraments; but if it must be an outward sign ordained by God or Christ, then only Baptism and the Lord's Supper are in this sense

[o] St. Hilary, *in S. Matt.*, c. v. n. 1.

[p] "The Sacrament of the Creed, which they ought to believe; the Sacrament of the Lord's Prayer, how they ought to ask."—S. Aug., *Serm.* 228 *fin.*

[q] "Sacramentum esuritionis."—St. Hilary, *in S. Matt.*, c. xii. n. 2.

[r] St. Hil., ibid., c. xxiii. n. 4.

[s] St. Jerome, *Ep. ad Ocean.*, n. 6, p. 418, Vall.

'Sacraments.'" Now, in separating off these two Sacraments from the rest, the framers of the Article followed very high authority in the Latin, Greek, and Syriac-speaking Churches. To name no others now, St. Chrysostom, St. Augustine, and their contemporary St. Isaac the Great, gave special honour to those two Sacraments which flowed from the side of Christ[t].

These two, the Article calls "Sacraments of the Gospel," as being, as the Catechism says, "generally necessary to salvation;" or, according to the Homily, "having annexed to the visible signs the promise of free forgiveness of sins, and of our holiness and joining to Christ." "Orders," it has been said, "gives *power*, yet without making the soul acceptable to God; Confirmation gives light and strength, yet is the mere completion of Baptism; and Absolution may be looked upon as a negative ordinance, removing the barrier which sin has raised between us and that grace which

---

[t] St. Chrysos., *ad loc. in Hom.* 85; St. Aug., *in Joan.* 10. t. iii. tr. xlv. 9; *de Luct. Jacob, Serm.* 5, t. v. p. 30. "Faith came to me, and called to me, and said to me, that the Sacraments of the Church came forth from the opened side of Christ." (St. Isaac, *Serm. de fide ap. Assem. Bibl. Or.,* t. i. p. 243.) See also Tertullian, *de Bapt.,* c. 16, p. 263; St. Ambrose, *in S. Luc.,* l. x. § 135; St. Aug., *in S. Joh.,* Tract. cxx. n. 2, ix. n. 10, xv. n. 8; *de Civ. Dei,* xv. 26, xxii. 17; *c. Faust.,* xii. 39; St. Leo, *Ep.* xxviii. *Flavian.*; S. Paulin. Nol., *Ep.* xlii. *Florent.,* n. 4; Auct. *de Symb.,* l. ii. c. 6; *de cataclysm.,* c. iv.; in St. Aug. Opp. t. vi.; St. Cyril Al., and probably Apollinarius, *in S. Joh.* xix. 34; author of *Testim. de Adv. Dom.,* in St. Greg. Nyss.; St. John Damasc., *de Fid. Orthod.,* iv. 9. See in Dr. Pusey's Scriptural Doctrine of Bapt., pp. 294—297.

is by inheritance ours. But the two Sacraments 'of the Gospel,' as they may be emphatically styled, are the instruments of inward *life*, according to our Lord's declaration, that Baptism is a new *birth*, and that in the Eucharist we eat the *living* bread [u]."

But although these two great Sacraments are severed off from the other five, it has been observed, that so far from denying them to be Sacraments, the writers of all the formularies acknowledge or imply that they are in some sense "Sacraments." The Homilies directly call Marriage a "Sacrament [x];" and of Orders they say, "neither *it*, nor any *other* Sacrament else be *such* Sacraments as Baptism and Communion are [y]." So that we have two of the five expressly called "Sacraments," besides the allusion to "other Sacraments." The Article could not say that the five have not "*like* nature of Sacraments with Baptism and the Lord's Supper," unless the writers meant that they were in some sense "Sacraments." And the difference assigned (which is further remarkable) does not relate to the inward grace, but to the outward form. "For that," it continues, "they have not any visible sign or ceremony ordained of God." In the same way the Homilies expressly say, that "absolution" has the inward grace, "forgiveness of sins," only "not by express word of the New Testament, annexed and tied to the visible sign, which is imposition of hands."

[u] Newman on "Justification," Lect. 6, v. *fin.*　　[x] Sermon on Swearing, pt. i.　　[y] Homily on Common Prayer and Sacraments, p. 298.

It was said that the language of the Article, on the number of the Sacraments, is defensible :—

1. To state that there are only seven Sacraments, neither more nor less, is a mode of speech unknown to antiquity. The word was used, if not loosely, in a very extended sense. Christianity, being a religion of mystery, was full of Sacraments. It was the great sacrament of godliness itself, testifying as it did to God manifest in the flesh.

2. The Sacraments of Baptism and the Holy Eucharist are so pre-eminent over the other five, differ so in kind from them, and hang so closely together, that they may be bracketed off by themselves. What circumcision and the passover were to the Fathers, they are to the Israel of God. They alone are generally necessary to salvation.

3. Moreover, these two Sacraments alone have an outward sign, instituted by Christ Himself, being the means of conveying the inward grace. There is a marked parallelism between them in their previous announcement, actual institution, and subsequent administration.

4. As representing spiritual birth and spiritual food they are the very substance of the Church. All other blessings are subsidiary to these, both in the order of nature, and in the order of grace.

5. They stand also pre-eminent in that they and they alone, according to the Fathers, have flowed from the riven side of the Second Adam as He slept the sleep of death on the cross, and thus they constitute the mystic Eve, the bride, the Church.

The language of the Article is unfortunate, not in that it raised two Sacraments above the rest, but in tending to obscure the sacramental character of the other five rites by undue disparagement. Yet, happily, this Article is neither the exclusive, nor the main teacher of our people, according to the ancient principle, *lex supplicandi, lex credendi.* And, upon the simple principle, that documents should not be interpreted so as to contradict one another, where they can be harmonized the one with the other, since, in regard to Orders and Confirmation, in the service for each an outward sign is prescribed and an inward grace spoken of; and in Matrimony the benediction of the priest is appointed for those who would be married according to the law of the Church; and, in Penitence, there is a form appointed for conveying the grace of that Sacrament; it is clear that this Article must not be interpreted as denying that they are ordinances of God for the conveyance of spiritual grace. Of the fifth, the Anointing of the Sick, hereafter. It cannot be denied that seven ordinances have enclosed the whole Christian life in blessed bonds, not all necessary for all,—nay, in the highest form of Christian life there is no room for Matrimony; and in the first fervour of Christian love, *they* were the exception who needed to be restored by the Sacrament of Penitence,—but conveying, according to men's needs, the grace of which they are channels. They have ever been regarded to have a mystical significance of their own, and separately from the beginning have existed as practices in the

Church. To illustrate which truth, it may be well to dwell on each in order as follows :—

I. The Sacrament (in this inferior sense) by which the Holy Spirit is communicated to the faithful, to confirm and perfect in them faith and religion, is termed, on that account, the gift of the Holy Spirit; Confirmation; perfection; the seal; also, the Sacrament of the Spirit, the symbol of the Spirit, the Saqrament of Unction, the imposition of hands, unction, the mystic unction, the unction of salvation. An outward sign and an inward grace are both assigned in Holy Scripture, in that Peter and John were sent by the Apostles to those baptized in Samaria, "And they laid their hands on them, and they received the Holy Ghost [a];" and that the Holy Ghost came on the baptized [a], when Paul laid his hands on them. Baptism and Confirmation standing thus distinct in Holy Scripture, the intimate relation between them, and the custom of administering the one immediately upon the other, do not prove their identity. In matter, form, and character they are entirely different. Confirmation Tertullian names with Baptism and the Eucharist [b]; St. Cyprian gives it the dignity of a Sacrament [c]; St. Cyril, of Jerusalem, calls it "the seal of the fellowship of the Holy Ghost [d];" the author of the *de Sacramentis,* a special "spiritual seal," speaking of it under "Sacraments." The Council of Elvira speaks of the baptized as "perfected [e]" by it; that of Laodicea said the

---

[a] Acts viii. 17.   [a] Ibid. xix. 6.   [b] *Præs.* xxxvi.
[c] 70 *ad Januar.*   [d] Cat. xviii. n. 33.   [e] c. 38, 77.

baptized "ought after Baptism to be anointed with the heavenly chrism, and be partakers of the kingdom of Christ [f];" the Apostolical Constitutions call the unction "the confirmation of the confession [in Baptism], the seal of the covenants [g]." St. Cyril, of Alexandria, speaks of "the use of oil, contributing to perfection to those justified in Christ through holy Baptism," as a spiritual meaning of oil [h]; and says, "We are anointed with ointments, especially at the time of holy Baptism, making it a symbol of partaking the Holy Spirit [i]."

The Fathers, both Greek and Latin, speak of Confirmation being given with the imposition of hands, or with Unction with the Holy Chrism, or with both [k].

[f] c. 48.　　[g] iii. 16, 17.　　[h] In Joel ii. 23, t. iii. p. 224, Aub.
[i] On Is. xxv. 6, t. ii. p. 353, Aub.

[k] Some Marcosian heretics, denying (St. Irenæus says) "the Baptism of the regeneration to God," said, "it was superfluous to bring persons to the water; but, mingling oil and water with certain words, put it on the heads of those perfected. These, too, anoint with balsam." (St. Iren., i. 10, 1 and 4.) Tertullian mentions both as following upon Baptism, and speaks of them as the complement of Baptism :—"Then, going forth from the laver, we are anointed with the blessed unction according to the ancient discipline, whereby they used to be anointed to the priesthood with oil from a horn. So in us, too, the anointing runneth corporally, but profiteth spiritually; as the carnal act of Baptism itself, that we are immersed in water, is made spiritual that we are delivered from sins. Then the hand is imposed, calling and inviting by its benediction the Holy Spirit." (*De Bapt.*, c. 7.) Again, he places both between Baptism and the Holy Eucharist :—"The flesh is washed, that the soul may be unbespotted; the flesh is anointed, that the soul may be consecrated; the flesh is sealed, that the soul, too, may be guarded; the flesh is overshadowed by imposition of hands, that the soul, too, may be illumined by the Spirit; the flesh is fed with the Body and

"In the oldest Latin Sacramentaries and Pontificals only the laying on of hands and its form is prescribed."

Blood of Christ, that the soul, too, may be nourished from God." (*De Res. carn.*, c. 8.) St. Cyprian speaks of the sanctification of the oil wherewith the baptized are anointed. (*Ep.* lxx. *ad Jan.*) In the *Ep.* lxxiii., *ad Jubaian.*, having spoken of Peter and John " supplying what was wanted, viz. that, prayers being made for them and hands imposed, the Holy Spirit might be invoked and poured upon them ;" he adds, " the like whereto is done among us, that they who are baptized in the Church are offered to those set over the Church, that by our prayers and the imposition of hands they may obtain the Holy Spirit, and be perfected with the seal of the Lord." St. Firmilian speaks of the imposition of hands alone, (*Ep. ad S. Cypr., Ep.* lxxv.); as does the Council of Elvira (can. 38). The Luciferian in St. Jerome asks :—" Knowest thou not that this is the custom of the Churches, that on the baptized hands should afterwards be laid, and so the Holy Spirit invoked ? Askest thou where this is written ? In the Acts of the Apostles. Even if it were not supported by the authority of Scripture, the agreement of the whole Church herein would have the weight of a precept." St. Jerome answers thus far :—" I deny not that this is the custom of the Churches, that to those who have been baptized by Presbyters and Deacons, at a distance from larger cities, the Bishop goes forth, to lay on hands for the invocation of the Holy Spirit." (St. Jerome, *adv. Lucif.* n. 8, 9, Opp. ii. 180, 1, Vall.) St. Epiphanius mentions imposition of hands, yet speaking only of Acts viii. 17, 18, (*Hær.* xxi., *Simon.* n. 1) ; and St. Chrysostom, speaking of Acts xix. 6 only. (*In Actt. Hom.* xl., n. 1.) On the other hand, St. Cyril of Jerusalem mentions the anointing only. (Cat. xxi.) St. Basil instances the anointing of the baptized as an unwritten tradition. (*De Sp. S.*, c. 27.) Theodoret (as a mystical exposition of Cant. i. 2) :—" Remember the holy mysteries wherein those initiated [baptized], after denying the tyrant [Satan] and confessing the King, receive as the royal seal the Chrism of the spiritual ointment, receiving, as in the type, the ointment, the invisible grace of the Spirit." (Opp. ii. 30.) St. Augustine, in his *de Bapt.* (iii. xvi. n. 21), speaks only of the imposition of hands ; on Ps. xxvi. (in explanation of the *dum linitur* in the title, n. 2), *Cont. Litt. Petil.*, ii. n. 239 (in allusion to Ps. cxxxiii. 2), *de Trin.*, xv. 26 (on Acts x. 38), of the anointing only. The Apostolic Constitutions mention both in

In the formula sent by Clement IV. to Palæologus for the adoption of the Greeks, in view of union (in 1274), it is said of the Sacrament of Confirmation, "which the Bishops confer through imposition of hands, chrisming the regenerate [1]." The whole statement of faith was accepted in the letters sent to the second Council of Lyons, held in 1274 [m]:—but the Greeks asked to use the creed and the rites which they had before the schism; so that this is absolute evidence for the West only. The Synod of Mayence, in 1549, citing the Acts, states that "the Catholic Church received from the Apostles the rule of giving the Holy Spirit to the faithful by the hands of the Bishops, and that this Sacrament was from the beginning given by the imposition of hands alone; but that soon in the very time of the Apostles, by their tradition, it began to be conferred, with the use of unction." The ground it assigns is, that the Holy Spirit first descended visibly; when this was withdrawn, "the anointing began to be employed to represent the internal spiritual unction [n]."

A Confession of Faith published in 1662, by Nectarius

ii. 32, vii. 43, 44; unction only in iii. 16, vii. 22. St. Optatus (*Sch. Don.*, iv. 7.) alludes to both. Innocent I. (*Ep.* i. *ad Decent. Eugub.*, n. 3) says that a Priest can seal only with oil consecrated by a Bishop. St. Leo (*Serm.* 24, [*in Nat. Dom.*, iv.] c. 6) mentions Chrism only; in regard to returning heretics, baptized out of the Church, imposition of hands only (*Ep.* clix. *ad Nicet.*, c. 7), as being "what was wanting there;" (*Ep.* clxvi. *ad Neon.*, n. 2) " by imposition of hands, the power of the Holy Spirit invoked, which they could not receive from heretics. (*Ep.* clxvii. *Rust. Inq.*, 18.)

[1] Baron., A. 1267, n. 77.
Mich. Palæol. ad Greg. X.

[m] *Conc. Lugd.* ii., *Lit.*
[n] Can. 17, 18.

of Jerusalem, says that Confirmation was originally given by imposition of hands, but now by unction.

The blow bestowed on the cheek of the newly-confirmed person, was a usage imported from chivalry. It is not mentioned before the tenth century.

II. The second inferior Sacrament mentioned in the Article is that of Penance. According to the ancient faith, for those who had fallen into deadly sin after Baptism, there was established a Sacrament to restore the soul to grace, which is variously called Penance, Confession, Absolution, Reconciliation, the second Baptism, the Laborious Baptism, the second Repentance, the second raft after Shipwreck.

The inward grace, the forgiveness of sins, is promised in the most absolute terms by our Lord Himself, when He said to His Apostles, " Receive ye the Holy Ghost. Whosesoever sins ye remit, they are remitted unto them; and whosesoever sins ye retain, they are retained." This power was given in the Apostles to the Church, in the same way as the authority to baptize in the Name of the Holy Trinity, to preach the Gospel to all the world, to teach whatsoever Jesus had commanded, to celebrate the Holy Eucharist. All were primarily committed to the Apostles, to be transmitted by them to their successors. Since we continue to baptize, to teach, to celebrate the Holy Eucharist by virtue of a commission given to the Apostles primarily, it would be in the last degree inconsistent to deny the Church's power to absolve from sins in His Name.

There is absolutely no doubt that this mercy towards grievous sinners was exercised by the Church from the very first. The course of public penance, by which the soul was prepared for the grace of Christ in the Absolution, is mentioned by St. Irenæus, who speaks of an adulteress, who "having been converted, continued during the whole period [of her life] in a state of penitence" [ἐξομολογουμένη, *in exhomologesi*, old Lat.], "weeping and lamenting what she had undergone through the impostor[o]" Marcus the Gnostic, and of the women, who, having been led astray by him, had no courage to undertake the labours of penance[p]; by Tertullian, who shews how, by the disposition of divine goodness, penance purifies the soul from all sins whatsoever, — how it is a plank which should bear those sunk beneath the waves of sin to the haven of Divine mercy, — and how sin must not be concealed, but confessed sincerely[q]; by Lactantius, who observes as a distinctive note of the Church Catholic the advantage she has in having confession and penance as the cure of sin and of the wounds of the soul[r]; by Origen, who says the seventh means of obtaining the remission of sin, hard and laborious, is penance, when the sinner waters his couch with his tears, when his tears become his meat day and night, when he blushes not to discover his sin to the priest of the Lord, and seek a remedy for the ills of his

---

[o] i. 13, n. 5. [p] Ib., n. 7. [q] *De Pœn.*, ii., iv., ix., x. He asks :—"Is it better to be damned in secret, than absolved openly ?" [r] *Instit. Div.*, iv. 30.

soul[s]. The course of public penance was known by a technical Greek term, " exomologesis."

While the true dispenser of pardon is God in His Son Jesus Christ, our great High-Priest, the visible and earthly organ is the Christian Hierarchy; but no absolution of theirs is valid, without a true repentance arising from the love of God, and a steady determination by His grace never to fall into deadly sin again. Furthermore, perfect contrition, in virtue of the *ardor charitatis*[t] which is its form, without the sacrament, effaces all sin; yet no enlightened and instructed conscience would venture into the presence of its Judge with any of those sins unconfessed and unabsolved, of which He saith :—" They which do such things shall not inherit the Kingdom of God[u]."

[s] *In Lev. Hom.* ii. n. 4.

[t] Origen, in the same passage, in which he speaks of the remission of sins, according to the public penitential discipline of the Church, just quoted, sets, side by side with it, the remission, which is through abundance of charity :—" The sixth remission takes place through abundance of charity; as the Lord Himself, too, says, ' Verily, I say unto you, many sins are remitted to her, because she loved much;' and the Apostle says, ' For charity covereth a multitude of sins.' There is yet, too, a seventh, although hard and laborious, remission of sins through penance, when the sinner," &c., (as above.) Origen then contrasts these modes of obtaining forgiveness with different sacrifices of the Mosaic law :—" If that charity, which is greater than faith and hope, have abounded in thy heart, so that thou love thy neighbour, not only as thyself, but as He sheweth, Who said, ' Greater love hath no man than this, that a man lay down his life for his friends;' know that thou hast offered bread, too, of fine flour, kneaded in the oil of charity, in the unleavened of sincerity and truth. But if in the bitterness of thy weeping thou art subdued by sorrow, tears, and lamentation, if thou have macerated thy flesh and dried it with fasting and much abstinence," &c. (*l. c.*, t. ii. p. 191.)   [u] Gal. v. 21.

III. The rite whereby men were raised in the Church to the clerical state [x], was early called 'order,' the 'laying on of hands,' 'ordination,' the 'sacrament of the pontiff,' the 'priestly benediction,' the 'Levitical benediction.' Both the outward sign and the inward gift are named in Holy Scripture:—"Stir up the gift of God, which is in thee, by the laying on of my hands [y]."

From all antiquity the Church has firmly believed in a special and proper priesthood, having its undoubted title in the mission and authority it has received from Jesus Christ, and has expressed this belief in its outward life and organization. It has never denied the universal priesthood of those who are the members of Jesus Christ, our great High-Priest, who have received the unction of the Spirit, and who should offer themselves ever a living sacrifice to God; but this belief does not contradict the notion that our Lord has intrusted the ministry of the word and Sacraments, not to all the faithful, but to certain delegated individuals. While in one sense acknowledging our Lord to be the One Priest, she has ever firmly held the existence of a proper Priesthood, having an undoubted title in the mission and authority received from Christ. "Bishops and presbyters are properly termed priests [z]." That the right to administer the Sacraments is given to a corporation, and very strong language of a certain mediation between God and the people, is found through all the Fathers.

---

[x] "Ordo Sacerdotalis."—Tertullian, *Exhort. cast*, 7, p. 778, Rig.

[y] 2 Tim. i. 6.   [z] St. Aug., *Civ. Dei*, xx. 10.

The Marcionites were the first to misconceive the universal priesthood of Christians. In the Middle ages the Cathari and Flagellants denied the objective reality of the Christian Priesthood. Wickliffe maintained that a priest in mortal sin is thereby degraded from the priesthood, and loses the power of administering the Sacraments; whence it would follow that, the inward state of priests being known only to God, the validity of their clerical acts would become radically doubtful and uncertain.

Luther, insisting on the universal priesthood of Christians, absolutely denied any grace of orders, yet, to avoid anarchy, he admitted, though inconsistently, the necessity of ordination; yet by it he understood nothing else than an external delegation on the part of the Christian community, which can recall the power thus granted. Calvin allowed Ordination to be "a ceremony, taken from Scripture, not empty or superfluous, but a faithful symbol of spiritual grace." He only did not class it with the other two, he says, "because it is not ordinary nor common among all faithful, but a special rite to a certain function [a]." But to him Sacraments were as outward things, as seals to a parchment, pictures visibly representing the promises of God [b].

The Church has always recognised these orders in the dignity of the clerical state,—the Episcopate, the Priesthood, and the Diaconate.

St. Ignatius of Antioch is the earliest exponent of

[a] Inst., pp. 19, 28.　　　　[b] Ibid., pp. 14, 15.

a fact to which the universal consent of tradition bears witness.

IV. If marriage, even according to the Roman laws, was estimated as the mutual enjoyment of right, both divine and human (*jurium divinorum et humanorum consortium*), one may imagine how much more highly it was regarded in the purer atmosphere of Christianity. First in the actual life of the members of Christ, and then in the scientific development of the idea, we find a perfect revolution in the relations which obtained between the sexes. The prevalence of the Manichæan heresy and of Gnosticism, both of which depreciated Matrimony, was under God the means whereby the doctrine concerning it became submitted to Christian analysis, and therefore we find, in those authors who confuted these heresies, a scientific treatment of it. Especially is this the case in St. Augustine.

Matrimony, such as it exists under the Gospel, is the most mysterious expression of human love, shadowing out Divine. St. Chrysostom remarks the mystery in this, as laid down in Paradise, how, towards one, heretofore a stranger and unknown, it surmounts the highest love of relationship of parent and child, and parents rejoice to be forsaken for it, as being the earthly contentment of human love. But the Gospel made it more. Through grace, the full, self-forgetful, self-surrender of each to the other in all things lawful, in unfelt, unconscious, because love-ensouled self-denial, makes it a human shadow of that

Divine self-emptying love of Christ for His Church, wherewith "He gave Himself for it," and of the Church's fealty to its Lord and Head. The mysterious oneness of the married "signified the mystical union between Christ and His Church." St. Paul was speaking of Christian marriage when he said, "this mystery," or "Sacrament, is great, but I say with reference to Christ and the Church," i.e. the mystery of the conjugal union is great, in its bearing on the union between Christ and the Church. But marriage out of Christianity did not so picture that union, on account of the toleration (1.) of polygamy, (2.) of divorce. In any case, it is of Christian marriage that he is speaking, since he is giving a rule for living in it according to the greatness of its mystery. He is writing to Christians about themselves and their own duties.

Christian marriage being, then, so high a mystery, the Church from the first joined it in with sacred grace-conferring rites. "How can we find words," says Tertullian [c], "to describe the happiness of that marriage, which the Church joineth together, and the oblation confirmeth, and the blessing sealeth, the angels report, the Father ratifieth!" St. Siricius says [d], "that among the faithful it is a sort of sacrilege, if that blessing, which the priest places upon one about to marry, were violated by any transgression," [viz., if one betrothed to one were to marry another.]

[c] *Ad Uxor.*, ii. 8, *fin*. See the beautiful sequel, pp. 430, 431, Oxf. Tr.   [d] *Epist. ad Himer. Tarrac.*, n. 4.

St. Jerome[e] says that matrimony, so far from being disapproved by the Church, is on the contrary conferred by her. If Marius Victorinus, St. Zeno of Verona, St. Chrysostom, St. Epiphanius, content themselves by recognising in general terms the profound and mysterious signification of marriage; St. Augustine frequently calls it in the most express terms a Sacrament[f], even predicating of it an indelible character as in Baptism and Confirmation[g].

In 1179 it was forbidden to receive fees for it, "as for other Sacraments[h]." Yet several of the middle-age theologians do not express themselves very strongly on the subject. Abelard and Peter Lombard denied that Matrimony conveyed grace. Durandus, granting that the theologians of his age held it to be a Sacrament properly so called, maintained that it was not so in a proper and rigorous sense, but only taken largely.

V. The unction of the sick is the lost pleiad of the Anglican firmament. One must at once confess and deplore that a distinctly Scriptural practice has ceased to be commanded in the Church of England. Excuses may be made of " corrupt following of the Apostles," in that it was used, contrary to the mind of St. James, when all hope of the restoration of bodily health was

---

[e] *Adv. Jovin.*, l. i.

[f] *Gen. ad lit.*, c. ix. n. 12, 7 ; *Bon. Conjug.*, c. vii. n. 7, xxiv. n. 32 ; *Nupt. et Concup.*, i. xii. n. 13, xvii. n. 19 ; *Pecc. Orig.*, xxxiv. n. 39, xxxvii. n. 42.

[g] *Adult. Conj.*, ii. 4 ; *Nupt. et Concup.*, i. x. n. 4, xvii. n. 19 ; *de bono Conj.*, c. vii. ; *de Gen.*, l. c.

[h] *Lateran.*, 1179. Can. vii.

gone; but it cannot be denied that there has been practically lost an Apostolic practice, whereby, in case of grievous sickness, the faithful were anointed and prayed over, for the forgiveness of their sins, and to restore them, if God so willed, or to give them spiritual support in their maladies. "Is any sick among you ? Let him call for the elders of the Church. And let them pray over him, anointing him with oil in the Name of the Lord. And the prayer of faith shall save the sick, and the Lord shall raise him up, and if he have committed sins they shall be forgiven him [1]."

On whatever ground, the earliest notice which occurs of the unction of the sick [k], is in an Epistle of Innocent I., A.D. 416. For, although Origen quotes the text of St. James, he does so, exclusively in relation to the power of the keys, and the course of public penitence [1], as Bellarmine acknowledges [m], in regard both to him and St. Chrysostom [n]. Yet, since the object of Innocent was to inform Decentius as to the practice at Rome, as being the only Apostolic Church in the West [o], his answer conveys not his own judgment only but a knowledge of that practice. The question

----

[1] St. James v. 14, 15.

[k] Baronius (H. E. 63, xvi.) separates off as altogether distinct from "the Sacrament of unction," the mention of miraculous cures by the use of oil, such as Tertullian mentions to have been used by Proculus (*ad Scap.*, c. 4); or as Egyptian monks used to expel diseases (Sozom., vi. 20 and 29; Ruffin. H. E. ii. 4); and St. Martin, according to Severus (*Vita S. Martini*, n. 15); and St. Hilarion, as related by St. Jerome (*vit. S. Hilarion.*)

[1] *In Lev., Hom.* ii. n. 4.   [m] *De Sacr.*
[n] *De Sac.*, iii. 6.   [o] Inn. I., *ad Decent.*, Præf. and Resp. viii.

of Decentius was, whether a Bishop might anoint the sick; Innocent's answer was, certainly he might, since according to St. James, presbyters might. But the answer brings out the facts, that the Chrism for that object was prepared by the Bishop, and that the laity might use it in any needs of themselves or their friends. Only those under penance, being in fact excommunicate, could not have it, being a Sacrament, since they were debarred from all Sacraments.

"There is no doubt that this [the passage of St. James] ought to be understood of the faithful, when sick, who can [*possunt*] be anointed with the holy oil of Chrism, which, being made by the Bishop, not the Priest only, but all Christians may use, by anointing, in their own or their friends' necessities. But it was added needlessly, that it was doubted as to Bishops, in what, there is no doubt, is allowed to Presbyters. For it is therefore said [in St. James] of Presbyters, because the Bishops, being hindered by other occupations, cannot go to all sick persons. But if a Bishop either can or thinks it meet to visit any one, *he* can unhesitatingly bless and touch with the Chrism, to whom it appertaineth to make the Chrism itself. For on penitents it cannot be poured, because it is a kind of Sacrament. For to whom the remaining Sacraments are denied, how can it be thought that one kind is allowed P ?"

St. Cæsarius, of Arles, exhorts persons in sickness to

P Resp. viii.

have recourse to the remedies of the Church, not to charms:—"As soon as any illness supervenes, let the sick person receive the Body and Blood of Christ, and then anoint his poor body, that that which is written may be fulfilled in him; 'If any is sick among you,' &c.   See, brethren, that he who in sickness has recourse to the Church, will both receive health of body and obtain forgiveness of sins.   Since these two-fold benefits can be found in the Church, why do hapless men strain to bring on themselves manifold evils through enchanters, or soothsayers, or diviners[q]?"   The passage of Cæsarius agrees with that of Innocent I. in presupposing that the sick man *anointed himself*.

In the Eastern Church, the early reference to the text relates (as we have seen) to "the power of the keys;" in Origen and St. Chrysostom no mention of, or allusion being made to the sick, much less to any anointing of them.   The passage of Victor, of Antioch, was made to bear upon it, only through an inaccurate Latin translation.   Victor himself, while explaining the meaning of St. Mark[r], adduces the passage of St. James

---

[q] *In App. S. Aug.*, t. v. *Serm.* 265, *olim. S. Aug. de Temp.*, *Serm.* 215.

[r] On St. Mark vi. 13, Greek Catena, *in S. Marc.*, p. 125, ed. Possini, Rom. 1673, p. 324, ed. Cram., Oxon.   The whole passage is:—" Things like this, Luke, too, sets forth; but the 'anointed with oil' [Peltanus glosses 'de *mystica* unctione et olei usu,'] Mark alone said; to whom James, too, said the like in the Catholic [Epistle] : 'Is any sick among you, let him call to him the presbyters of the Church, and let them pray over him; and the prayer of faith shall save the sick, and the Lord shall raise him up.'   The oil then applied signified both the mercy from God, and the cure of the disease, and the enlightening of the heart.

as akin to it, but speaks of the anointing and the prayer accompanying it, as a thing of the past, so that the natural inference would rather be, that it was not used in Antioch in his time. He ascribes emphatically the whole effect to the prayer. St. Cyril, of Alexandria, also quotes the text barely, in the course of an abstract argument about heathen incantations[*]. If people thought that the titles of God would dispel their diseases, he bids them, praying for themselves, utter the words. " *Thou*," he says, "wilt do better than *they* [the evil spirits], offering glory to God and not to the foul spirits. I will mention the Divinely-inspired Scripture too, which saith, 'Is any sick among you let him call,'" &c.

The meagreness of tradition is, however, replaced in some measure by the agreement of the Greeks, the Armenians, the Nestorians, and all the Orientals, with the Latins on this subject; so that one cannot doubt that a sacramental use of anointing the sick has been from the beginning.

Our Abp. Theodore, A.D. 680, contrasts the customs of the Greeks and Latins, in that " according to the

For it is manifest to every one, that the prayer effected the whole, but the oil, *as I deem, was* the symbol of these things." [Pelt. paraphrased, " But *it may be said* that prayer effect*eth* all these things, but that the oil *is* only an outward symbol of all those things which *take place*."]

[*] *De Adorat.*, l. vi. t. i. p. 211, Aub. Palladius, the other speaker in St. Cyril's Dialogue, being satisfied on this subject of augury, St. Cyril goes on to speak of false-swearing. Anastasius Sinaita, qu. 23, on the power of evil spirits to produce miraculous effects, extracts this with other passages.

Greeks a Presbyter may make the Chrism for the sick, if need be ; according to the Romans, it is not allowed, save to the Bishop only[t]." Ecgbert, Abp. of York, A.D. 732, in his extract *de jure sacerdotali*, has the rule, " That according to the enactment of the holy fathers, if any is sick, he be diligently anointed with sanctified oil together with prayers[u]." Among the canons enacted under King Edgar, it is enjoined, that " every Priest give unction to the sick, *if they desire it*," and " have both baptismal oil and unction for the sick[x]," and an enactment occurs, as to his report of himself, " when he fetches Chrism," i.e. from the Episcopal city. The unction of the sick "*if* the sick layman desire it," is enjoined in the canons of Ælfric[y]; and a separate portion of the consecrated Chrism is directed to be kept for that use[z]. It appears from the ritual, alike of the Western[a] and

[t] Cap. Theod. in Thorpe, Ang. Sax. Laws, ii. 63.

[u] Excerpt. Ecgb., n. 21.   Ibid., ii. 100.

[x] Can. 65, 66, 67.   Ibid., ii. 259.   [y] Can. 47.   Ibid., 385.

[z] Ælfr., *Ep.*, Ibid., 391.

[a] " O Lord God, Who hast said by Thy Apostle James, ' Is any sick among you ? let him call the presbyters of the Church, and let them pray over him in the Name of the Lord ; and the prayer of faith shall save the sick, and the Lord shall alleviate him ; and if he be in sins, they shall be remitted to him ;' Cure, we beseech Thee, our Redeemer, by the grace of the Holy Spirit, the languors of this sick person, and heal his wounds, and forgive his sins, and expel from him all dolours of mind and body, and mercifully restore full health within and without, that, restored by the help of Thy mercy, he may be repaired for his former duties ; who," &c. " Holy Lord, Almighty Father, Everlasting God, Who, pouring the grace of Thy blessing into sick bodies, with manifold love guardest Thy creature, be present, of Thy goodness, at the

Eastern[b] Church, that restoration to bodily health was, and is still, according to the belief of the Church, a primary object of the anointing. Mabillon[c] traces the change to the popular superstition about the beginning of the thirteenth century.

"Of old," he says, "it was used before the viaticum," [and probably some time before, whence it would follow, that, since it was used once only in the same illness, it would not be used at the last]. Hence he explains the fact, that there is no mention of unction in the life of St. Gertrude (died A.D. 678), of St. Eustasius (died about A.D. 625), of St. Richarius (died about 645), although there is mention of their receiving the viaticum. The anointing with the holy oil *before* the viaticum is mentioned in Sugerius' life of Louis VI., as to his Queen St. Chrotildis, and in the contemporary but anonymous life of St. Hernigundis (died about A.D. 660).

Mabillon says, moreover, that it came to be called "*extreme* unction" [probably, originally, the last of

Invocation of Thy Name, and, freeing Thy servant from sickness and granting him health, raise him up with Thy right hand, strengthen him with might, protect him with power, and, with the longed-for prosperity, restore him to Thy Holy Church, through," &c.—*Rituale Rom. Paul V. jussu, edit.* Antw. 1669.

[b] "Holy Father, healer of souls and bodies, Who didst send Thine Only-Begotten Son, our Lord Jesus Christ, healing every disease and redeeming from death, heal this Thy servant also of the sickness of soul and body which encompasses him, and quicken him through the grace of Thy Christ;—for Thou art the Fountain of healings, O Christ our God, and to Thee we send up the glory, to the Father, and the Son, and the Holy Spirit."—Euchologion, p. 417. Paris, 1647.

[c] *Praef. ad* tom. i. *Actt. S. Ordinis Benedict.*

the unctions used in the rites of the Church during the Christian's life], "not before the close of the 12th century." For that "the name '*extreme* unction' does not occur in the Sacramentaries published by Menard; nor in Uldaric, in the *Consuetudines Cluniacenses;* nor in Lanfranc, Anselm, Peter Damiani, Peter de Honestis, in the *regula Clericorum;* nor in St. Bernard or P. Lombard." Yet that "it was called '*extreme* unction,' before it was placed after the viaticum, as appears from the contemporary life of William, Abp. of Bourges, died A.D. 1209, in Bollandus, Jan. 10." "This custom," he says, "continues intact till now only among the Cistercian monks, and perhaps certain Churches."

The first appearance of the superstition cited by Mabillon, occurs in Constitutions of Richard, Bishop of Salisbury, about A.D. 1227:—"Let the Priest, moreover, say and announce confidently, that after the use of this Sacrament, it is lawful to return to the use of Marriage."

It occurs, however, two centuries before in Ælfric's Pastoral Epistle, from which it appears, that some, as a religious act, vowed, in case of recovery, to abstain from the use of marriage; others, who had not vowed, held themselves to be so bound, looking upon it as a sort of ordination. Ælfric had to say that those who had not vowed were free in these things, and that unction might be repeated, if any should again fall sick[d]. From the Canons of Ælfric, it appears that

---

[d] If the sick layman desires to receive unction, let him then confess him and forgive every grudge before the unction; and if he recovers and after the unction become sick, he may, unless he have

some so dreaded the anointing, that they would not consent to receive it. Confession of sin to the Priest was required before the unction could be used[e]. The superstition was condemned by the sixth statute of the Synod of Exeter, A.D. 1287. There it was found necessary to enjoin, that it should be publicly declared through the parochial presbyters[f], that that Sacrament, as also some others, may be repeated as often as there is need. And thus, because some unskilled laity, thinking unwisely concerning this Sacrament, so abhor it, and refuse to receive it even *in extremis*, foolishly thinking that after its reception, the eating of flesh, walking barefoot, and even tokens of love from one's lawful wife, are entirely forbidden[g]; the Synod speaks of it as a heresy. This enactment is itself repeated almost *verbatim* in the Synodal Constitutions

vowed the contrary, enjoy the society of women, and flesh, if he himself will. In the unction there is healing and forgiveness of sins, and it is no ordination as some men imagine. And if the man be again sick, let him again receive unction, when it be needful." (Ælfric, Past. Ep., n. 47, 48. Thorpe, ii. 385.)

[e] "The priest shall have allowed oil apart for children, and apart for sick men, and always anoint the sick in bed. Some sick men are fearful, so that they will not consent to be anointed in their illness. Now we will tell you how James, the Apostle of God, taught hereon :— 'If any among you be sick, let him pray with one mind and praise his Lord !' 'If any one among you be sick, let him order to be fetched to him the mass-priests of the Church, and let them sing over him, and pray for him,' &c. Thus spake James the Apostle concerning the unction for sick men; but the sick must confess with inward groaning to the priest, whether he has any crimes unatoned for, before he anoints him, as the Apostle has before enjoined; and no man may anoint him before he pray for this, and do his confession."

[f] Wilkins, *Conc.*, ii. 295.

[g] Ibid., tom. ii. p. 135; see *Statuta Scotiæ*, tom. ii. 278.

of H. Wodlake, Bishop of Winchester, about A.D. 1308[h]. But the popular dread of the Sacrament prevailed ; and Mabillon thinks it probable, that " on account of such phrenzies, the anointing of the sick began to be reserved for the point of death, and that that custom was gradually extended to all Churches."

But *abusus non tollit usum.* The Church of England acted more in conformity to its declared adherence to antiquity, by appointing, in the first instance, a service for the anointing of the sick in her first English Prayerbook. This was among the losses in those unhappy times just before the accession of Mary, and although everything of that earlier liturgy was praised by those who removed it, it has never been restored. Since, however, the Visitation of the Sick is a private office, and uniformity is required only in the public offices, there is nothing to hinder the revival of the Apostolic and Scriptural custom of anointing the sick, whensoever any devout person may desire it. It is, indeed, difficult to say on what principle it could be refused. The rite was restored by the nonjuring Bishops. Meanwhile, until it can be generally restored, it may be observed, that it was never considered necessary to salvation, as is formally laid down by St. Thomas[i]. It was rather a privilege of the devout.

[h] And in the *Statuta Ecclesiæ Scoticanæ*, No. 62 (Robertson, *Statuta,* vol. ii. p. 34), and No. 119 (Rob., ii. 58), where we find the remarkable expression, " Proponat autem sacerdos nihil infirmo quod ante ægritudinem fuerat licitum post convalentiam per extremam unctionem reddi illicitum."   [i] iv. dist. 23, q. i. art. 1, *fin.*

ARTICLE XXVI.

DE VI INSTITUTIONUM DIVINARUM, QUOD EAM NON TOLLAT MALITIA MINISTRORUM.

QUAMVIS in Ecclesia visibili bonis mali semper sunt admixti, atque interdum ministerio verbi et Sacramentorum administrationi præsint, tamen cum non suo, sed Christi nomine agant, ejusque mandato et authoritate ministrent, illorum ministerio uti licet, cum in verbo Dei audiendo, tum in Sacramentis percipiendis. Neque per illorum malitiam, effectus institutorum Christi tollitur, aut gratia donorum Dei minuitur, quoad eos qui fide et rite sibi oblata percipiunt, quæ propter institutionem Christi et promissionem efficacia sunt, licet per malos administrentur. Ad Ecclesiæ tamen disciplinam pertinet, ut in malos ministros inquiratur, accusenturque ab his, qui eorum flagitia noverint, atque tandem justo convicti judicio, deponantur.

" Of the Unworthiness of the Ministers, which hinders not the effect of the Sacraments.

" ALTHOUGH in the visible Church the evil be ever mingled with the good, and sometimes the evil have chief authority in the ministration of the Word and Sacraments; yet, forasmuch as they do not the same in their own name, but in Christ's, and do minister by His commission and authority, we may use their ministry, both in hearing the Word of God, and in the receiving of the Sacraments. Neither is the effect of Christ's ordinance taken away by their wickedness, nor the grace of

God's gifts diminished from such as by faith and rightly do receive the Sacraments ministered unto them, which be effectual, because of Christ's institution and promise, although they be ministered by evil men.

"Nevertheless, it appertaineth to the discipline of the Church, that inquiry be made of evil ministers, and that they be accused by those that have knowledge of their offences; and finally, being found guilty by just judgment, be deposed."

Some special prerogatives and responsibilities of the Christian ministry have with more or less logical consistency been acknowledged by every sect and Church. Even those who have taught that the ministerial power is a mere delegation of power from the congregation, have yet recognised a certain authority, and demanded a certain morality as a consequence thereof. What is venial in the ordinary member is not so in the case of the minister. A higher standard is demanded of those whose position is that of the chosen and selected teachers of the congregation.

But if this be so in the case of those sects who claim no sacramental authority for their ministers, how much more is it so with those who recognise the divine hierarchy; who hold that the Christian priesthood is a delegation from the priesthood of Jesus Christ, according to the words, "As My Father sent Me, so send I you;" who recognise in 'the sacerdotal power a transmission from above, not a representation from beneath, according to the words, "Obey them that are set over you in the Lord," and who regard the sacred office as the medium of certain mysterious blessings, the holders of that office being " stewards of the mysteries of God."

Where this belief prevails, not only is a higher standard demanded of the officers of religion, but anything like sin or immorality is regarded with the greatest abhorrence. That any so invested with the gifts of ordination should partake in the vices or worldlinesses of those around them, is offensive in the highest degree to Christian instincts. A specially holy life is the correlative of specially holy gifts, and therefore, like " the hedge of the law" among the Jews, certain amusements and occupations, not in themselves wrong, are proscribed by the spiritual sense of the Church, and termed unclerical, meaning thereby that they are unworthy of the thoughts of the *clerus*, or Lord's heritage.

Moreover the measure of proportion indicated in the old law, where it is said, " as with the priest so with the people," is observable under the new law. The vices and virtues of the clergy will form a pretty accurate gauge of the religious condition of a Church, and while every reformation and revival has been attended or preceded by increasing strictness on the part of the clergy, (as in the great Cistercian movement in the twelfth century,) all periods of religious decay have been caused or accompanied by a corresponding degradation of the character of the clergy. The state of things indicated by the manners pourtrayed in Chaucer's " Canterbury Tales," is sufficient proof of this.

Or take the scornful picture given by Dante[a] :—

> " Venne Cephas : e venne el gran vasello
> De lo Spirito Santo magri e scalzi
> Prendendo 'l cibo di qualunque hostello
> Or voglion quinci e quindi chi rincalzi
> Le moderni Pastori, e che li meni
> Tanto son gravi : e chi dirietro gli alzi.
> Cuopron de' manti loro i palafreni,
> Sì che due bestie van sott' una pelle :
> O Patienza che tanto sostieni."

But while the sensitiveness of the conscience of the Church touching the virtues of the clergy must be recognised and admired, the student of history cannot fail to notice from the earliest period a tendency to forget the institution in the individual, and to ignore the organic commission in the qualities of the person commissioned. Nothing but a well-grounded faith in the hierarchical structure of the Church will prevent men falling into this extreme, and as a matter of fact, from very ancient times there have been sects who made the validity of the Sacraments depend on the worthiness of him who administered them, and it is against these that the Article is directed.

Now the very nature of a Sacrament implies that it not only signifies grace given, but actually bestows it, in virtue of the institution of Christ. The Thomists held that the Sacraments worked as *physical* causes, the Scotists as *moral* causes of grace, but both maintained that they operated not *per accidens* but *per se ;* that is,

[a] Paradiso, xxi. 119.

in conformity with their divine purpose and by the virtue attached to them by our Lord, they always obtain their end, and confer their peculiar grace in all cases universally, where man imposes no obstacle. But a further question arose: could that obstacle be found in the moral state of the administrator? It was granted that certain moral conditions in the case of the recipient could mar the effect of the Sacrament, but what about him who ministered it? The Church has always held that his unworthiness could put no obstacle to grace, nor foul the source whence flowed the streams of Christ's benediction. "He who receiveth is not injured, even if he who bestows should seem unworthy; nor are the unspotted mysteries defiled, should the priest exceed all men in wickedness, ($\pi\alpha\rho\epsilon\lambda\acute{\alpha}\sigma\epsilon\iota\epsilon\nu$ [b])." St. Augustine points out that if this were not so, man would lose all his motives for confidence in God, and God would cease to be his only hope [c]. St. Optatus shews that they who baptize are the labourers, not the householder; and that the Sacraments are holy *per se;* and that it is to shut God out of His gifts to maintain otherwise [d].

Yet from an early period this truth was resisted, 1. by the Novatians, who rejected the Baptism of the Church [e], ascribing, an ancient writer says [f], the

[b] S. Isid., l. iii. *Ep.* cccxl.: see also Greg. Naz., *Orat.* 40; Chrys., in *Matth. Hom.* l. n. 3.   [c] *Cont. Lit. Petil.,* i. 4. n. 5, and i. 3. n. 4; 6. n. 7.   [d] *De Schism. Don.,* v. 4.

[e] St. Cypr., *Ep.* lxxiii. n. 2. p. 243, Oxf. Tr.

[f] *Quæstt. V. et N. T.,* ap. q. 102, in St. Aug., Opp. t. iii. App., p. 98, Ben.

efficacy of the Sacraments to the character of him who administered them; 2. by the Donatists, who, regarding the piety of the administrator as the condition of the efficacy of the Sacraments, refused to recognise the ordination of Cæcilian by Felix of Aphthonga, whom the Donatists accused falsely of having been a traditor, that is, having in the persecution delivered up the sacred vessels and books, under threat of death [f].

At the great revival of mental thought in the middle ages, this notion, probably caused by the exceeding corruption in the lives of the ecclesiastics, was again and again produced. Arnold of Brescia, and his adherents, taught it. The Vaudois maintained that priests in mortal sin could not consecrate the Eucharist, and that the transubstantiation took place not in the hand of the unworthy celebrator, but in the mouth of the worthy communicant; that a bad priest could not absolve; that it was better to confess to a pious laic than to a wicked clergyman. Wicliffe, and Huss, though he is not always consistent, pretended that a priest in mortal sin is thereby degraded from his priesthood, and from his power to operate Sacraments. It will be seen that as the inward state of the clergy is known to God alone, the validity of

[f] It appeared subsequently, from the curious Acts of the Synod of Cirta (in St. Aug. *c. Crescon.*, iii. 27, 28), that those who originated the Donatist schism by consecrating Majorian in the place of Cæcilian, had themselves been "traditores," and had at that Synod accorded each other a mutual amnesty.

their acts on this theory becomes radically doubtful and uncertain [h].

This led on to another error at the time of the Reformation. The efficacy of the Sacraments was held no longer to depend on the interior disposition of the minister. Not the beneficial effect only, but the reality also of the Sacrament was held to depend on the interior disposition, the faith of him to whom the Sacrament was administered [i].

Our Article condemns both these notions. It lays down that the Sacraments have an objective value in virtue of their institution. Sacraments "be effectual because of Christ's institution and promise," therefore they do not depend on the state of the recipients. It also lays down that the clergy, who have chief authority in the ministration of Word and Sacraments, do not minister in their own name, but in Christ's; therefore neither do they depend on the state of the celebrant. The Article, however, thinks it right to bring prominently forward the necessity of men being in a fit state for the beneficial partaking of these ordinances, and therefore dwells on the fact that the grace of God's gifts in the case of wicked clergy is not diminished from such as "by faith and rightly" receive them.

[h] Vide Gerson, *Responsio ad Error. de orat. privat. fidelium*, tom. ii. p. 654; Du Pin, D'Argentie, *Collect. Judiciorum de nov. err.*, tom. i. p. 2; p. 168.

[i] Luther, *Capt. Bab.*, tom. ii. ed. Gen. p. 286; *Conf. Aug.* xiii. *Apol.* art. iii. n. 155.

"Nevertheless, it appertaineth to the discipline of the Church that inquiry be made of evil ministers." That the vices of the clergy helped to produce the Reformation is a fact allowed on all hands. In the Provincial Council held in 1549 at Edinburgh, it is declared "that the two main roots and causes of the evils which have occasioned the disturbances, and the heresies which the Synod met to check, are the corruption of manners and profane indecency of life of the clergy on the one hand, and the gross ignorance of good letters and all arts on the other [k]." The same convention exhorts the prelates and beneficed clergy in the bowels of Jesus Christ and for zeal of piety, in order to meet heresy, to amend their ways, "lest they should proceed to correct the morals of others, themselves entangled in notorious crimes, to the great scandal of the people, and increase of heresy [l]." The pictures of the habits of the clergy given by these canons is terrible. To forbid the unblest offspring of unhallowed alliances to remain in the parsonages, to condemn implication in secular business, to repress sumptuousness of apparel, to enforce some sustentation for poor people out of their benefices, to order decency in their families, which families were most ill-ordered, to enforce preaching at least four times a-year, to regulate the schools and the quality of those ordained and presented to benefices, to repress pluralities, were among some of the efforts made to turn the tide of the Reformation in Scotland; but it was too late. The very effort

[k] *Conc. Prov. Eccl. Scot.*, ii. p. 81, ed. Robertson.   [l] Ibid., p. 118.

to restore discipline drove over some of the younger abbots and beneficiaries to the cause of the Reformed to escape Reformation. Perhaps sin and fear had paralysed the energies of those who made the laws. Of the six bishops present at the Synod of 1549, three at least were stained with the worst crimes condemned; the salt had lost its savour, and the violence of the subsequent changes becomes the measure of the corruption which occasioned them.

In England it was not so bad, though even here there was much to amend. The succession of earnest prelates never wholly died out, even to the last. Witness the praise of Warham by Erasmus, and Fuller's less generous testimony to the eminent merits of Fisher.

That a false opinion, that had created the great schism of the Donatists in Africa, should be condemned, is not surprising. No body such as the English Church could continue to maintain an organic existence, if the efficacy of its sacramental rites depended upon the inward condition of its ministers. But the condemnation is remarkable when we remember that the opinion here censured was the centre-point of the reforming theories both of Wicliff and of Huss. According to these, the wicked or unworthy priest was no priest. An immoral Pope was no true successor of Peter, or Vicar of Jesus Christ. The great popularity of the name of Wicliff, as the great forerunner of the English Reformation, has blinded men to the real character of the communistic and anti-social theories in State craft which he advocated; and it is a remarkable thing that one of the Articles of the Reformed Church of England should in such trenchant terms deny his theory of the priesthood. The solution of the difficulty seems to be that although Wicliff had told profoundly on the conscience of England, (we find this in the conduct of Robert Hallam, Bishop of Salisbury, at the Council of Constance, who not only inveighed against the vices of Pope John XXIII., but objected to the burning of Huss,) nevertheless as a party the Lollards were never popular in England, (Shakspeare is said to have called Falstaff, Sir John Oldcastle, in his first draft of Henry IV.,) and therefore it is doubtful whether these earlier Reformers are the true fathers of the later ones. Probably, so far as the destructive side was concerned, the earlier denunciations of the scandals did much to break down the faith of the people in the old objects of reverence, either persons or things, but they did not go to construct anything of the late Reformation. On the contrary, the distinctive tenets were, as in the case of the present Article, condemned by the Church, and the notions found a more congenial home in some of the wild sectaries who gave so much trouble in the later days of Elizabeth's reign.

ARTICLE XXVII.

DE BAPTISMO.

BAPTISMUS non est tantum professionis signum, ac discriminis nota, qua Christiani a non Christianis discernantur, sed etiam est signum regenerationis, per quod tanquam per instrumentum, recte baptismum suscipientes Ecclesiæ inseruntur, promissiones de remissione peccatorum, atque adoptione nostra in filios Dei per Spiritum Sanctum visibiliter obsignantur, fides confirmatur, et vi divinæ invocationis gratia augetur.

Baptismus parvulorum omnino in Ecclesia retinendus est, ut qui cum Christi institutione optime congruat.

" Of Baptism.

"BAPTISM is not only a sign of profession, and mark of difference, whereby Christian men are discerned from others that be not christened; but it is also a sign of regeneration or new birth, whereby, as by an instrument, they that receive baptism rightly are grafted into the Church; the promises of forgiveness of sin, and of our adoption to be the sons of God by the Holy Ghost, are visibly signed and sealed; faith is confirmed, and grace increased by virtue of prayer unto God. The baptism of young children is in any wise to be retained in the Church, as most agreeable with the institution of Christ."

To be severed from the mass of mankind, to be distinguished as the little flock to whom it has pleased the Father to give the kingdom, is no small privilege, yet this is the first and lowest conception of the Sacrament of Baptism. It is a mark of difference "whereby Christian men are discerned from others that be not christened" (Lat. *a non Christianis*). But it is something infinitely higher than this, and the gifts therein bestowed are classed by the Article under the following four heads.

First, "it is a sign of regeneration or new birth, whereby, as by an instrument, they that receive Baptism rightly are grafted into the Church."

Here observe, first of all, that the word "sign" is the technical word for the outward part of any Sacrament, and therefore, it means that the aspersion of the neophyte with water, or his immersion therein, accompanied by a definite form of words, is the outward act which conveys regeneration or new birth; such Sacrament acting instrumentally (*per instrumentum*), that is, as the instrument ordained by Almighty God, the result of which is, by a strict law of cause and effect, that the person receiving Baptism rightly is grafted into the Church. Of this engrafting St. Chrysostom says[a]:—"Blessed be God, Who alone with wonders made all things, and changeth all. Behold they enjoy the calm of freedom who a little before were held captives; they are denizens of the Church who were

---

[a] *Orat. ad neophytos apud Augustinum contra Julianum*, lib. i. paragraph 21.

wandering in error ; and they have the lot of righteousness who were in the confusion of sin. For they are not only free, but holy ; not holy only, but righteous ; not righteous only, but sons ; not sons only, but heirs ; not heirs only, but brethren of Christ ; not brethren of Christ only, but co-heirs ; not co-heirs only, but members ; not members only, but a temple ; not a temple only, but instruments of the Spirit. See how many are the free gifts of Baptism : and whereas some think that the heavenly grace consists only in the remission of sin, lo ! we have accounted ten glories thereof. Wherefore we baptize infants, although they have no sins, that holiness, righteousness, adoption, inheritance, brotherhood with Christ, may be added to them ; that they may become His members."

Secondly, " The promises of forgiveness of sin, and of our adoption to be the sons of God by the Holy Ghost, are visibly signed and sealed," (*visibiliter obsignantur*). Again, says St. Chrysostom :—" The being sealed is a mark of great Providence ; that we are not set apart only, not taken by lot only, but sealed. For as one would make manifest those who fell to him, so also God set us apart that we should believe, He has sealed us that we should inherit the things to come. Again, through the things that are passed, He establishes those to come. For if it is He Who establisheth us to Christ, (that is, Who suffereth us not to be broken from the faith toward Christ) ; and He also Who anointed us, and gave the Spirit in our hearts, how shall He not give us the things to come ? For, if He gave the beginnings, and the foundations, and the root, and the fountain, that is, the true knowledge of Himself, the participation of the Spirit, how shall He not give the result thereof?"

The Liturgies of the East and West agree in calling Baptism a seal, an impress, a guardian mark to those baptized. The baptized themselves are, in the language of the Revelations, called "the sealed;" and while they use the word "seal" chiefly of the great sacramental act of Baptism itself, they regard that great mystery as casting a portion of its radiance before and behind, and giving efficacy to other acts connected with it. The Church regards our Lord as favourably allowing the charitable work of bringing new members to Him, and so believing that He anticipated a portion of His grace to preserve them during the interval until they are fully prepared for Baptism, they ventured to affix His seal on catechumens; or, after Baptism, they again visibly and formally affixed it, thereby representing to the mind what has first been worked invisibly by the Holy Spirit. As this was done in the form of the Saviour's cross, and the term "seal" applied to that act of impressing the cross, it is probable that the word "sealing" was connected with a corresponding outward act, such as the sealing of the forehead actually spoken of by St. John; so that, we may infer that the use of the cross in Baptism was coeval with Christian Baptism itself, which imparts to us the saving virtue of the Passion of Christ [b].

[b] cf. Dr. Pusey's Tract on Baptism, p. 140.

Thirdly, "Faith is confirmed." In the ancient rituals, at the beginning of the service, the god-parents were asked in the name of the child to be baptized, "What seekest thou of the Church?" and the answer is, "Faith." This teaches us that, whereas God's first or prevenient grace brings men to Faith and Baptism, and a certain pre-disposition of faith along with repentance is bestowed in that holy ordinance, yet, as a consequence of our incorporation in Christ, fuller measures of assisting grace are bestowed upon the recipient, and that faith, which in its inchoate state obtained the grace of Baptism, is by that same Baptism increased and confirmed according to the blessed promise of God, "Open thy mouth wide, and I will fill it."

Fourthly, "Grace is increased by virtue of the invocation of the divine name" (*vi divinæ invocationis*), for thus the Latin version of the Article teaches us to understand what in this connection would be unintelligible, viz. the expression in the English Article, that "grace is increased by virtue of prayer to God." This in its literal sense would be a truism, but, rightly interpreted, it asserts the great religious truth that Baptism not only confers but increases grace, bestows more abundantly the help and assistance of God according to the enlarged capacities of the new man in Christ, makes the soul more and more radiant and beautiful in the eyes of God.

The question of infant baptism, while not without its authority, according to the terms of the Article, in the inspired Word of God, rests mainly upon that of the Church. Perhaps nothing tends to exhibit in so striking a manner the objective nature of the Sacraments of the new law, than the practice of conferring them upon those who are incapable of reason, in the belief that from such a ceremony any possible good result shall follow. This difficulty has not only perplexed many good Christians, but forms the ground of defence of the advocates of adult baptism.

The doctrine can in no way be explained away, or its edge blunted. True, that beyond certain indications of the existence of baptismal grace and growth herein exhibited in the lives of some favoured servants of God, we have ordinarily no direct evidence of the new principle of spiritual life therein imparted. But faith needs not external tokens of what God has promised. We have nothing to do but to submit our reason to what the Church has taught us, firmly convinced that since our Blessed Lord suffered the little children to come unto Him, and since St. Paul pronounced the children of his converts to be holy, we may be sure that the bounty and goodness of God works invisibly in His elect, anticipates by grace the first risings of the lower motions of our nature, determines the soul to good from earliest days, tends it from youth up with fostering hand, arms it in the beginning for the battle of life, and prevents it in all its doings with His most gracious favour.

The Article expresses itself distinctly but cautiously on the subject of infant Baptism. It asserts that " it is in any wise to be retained," and grounds that retention on the dogmatic fact, that it is most congruous with the institution of Christ, (*cum institutione Christi optime congruat,*) i.e. just what we should expect from that law of benediction, supernatural power, and unmerited grace, which the Gospel emphatically exhibits.

And this very much represents what Holy Scripture indicates on the subject. While there is no direct command for the practice, all analogies and all inferences are in its favour. The practice of infant circumcision, and of the infant baptism of proselytes among the Jews; the universality of the injunction "to teach all the nations, baptizing them[c];" the absoluteness of what our Lord said to Nicodemus[d], coupled with the "Suffer the little children to come unto Me[e];" the assertion that the children of Christians are "holy[f]," which implies a cleansing from original sin; the practice of the Baptism of households[g], all are in favour of the practice, which actually from St. Justin[h], Tertullian[i], Origen[k], and others, we find to have obtained, although in later times the practice of deferring Baptism became common, out of fear of forfeiting the fulness of its gift by grave subsequent sin[l].

The reader will remember what has been said under Article XVI. as to the effect of the Sacrament of Bap-

[c] St. Matt. xxviii. 19. [d] St. John iii. 5. [e] St. Mark x. 14.
[f] 1 Cor. vii. 14. [g] Acts xvi. 15, 33 ; 1 Cor. i. 16.
[h] *Apol.*, i. 15, p. 11, Oxf. Tr. [i] *De Bapt.*, c. 18.
[k] *In Luc., Hom.* xiv. [l] See St. Aug. Conf., i. n. 17, 18,
pp. 10, 11, Oxf. Tr.

tism on sin [m]. It is in amplification of what was there stated that we assert the general effects of Baptism to be as follows:—

I. According to the words of Ezekiel [n]: "Then will I sprinkle clean water upon you, and ye shall be clean: from all your filthiness, and from all your idols will I cleanse you;" and those of the Apostle: "So many of us as have been baptized into Jesus Christ were baptized into His death? Therefore we are buried with Him by Baptism into death: that like as Christ was raised up from the dead by the glory of the Father, even so we also should walk in newness of life. For if we have been planted together in the likeness of His death, we shall be also in the likeness of His resurrection: knowing this, that our old man is crucified with Him, that the body of sin might be destroyed, that henceforth we should not serve sin. For he that is dead is freed from sin. Now if we be dead with Christ, we believe that we shall also live with Him: knowing that Christ being raised from the dead dieth no more; death hath no more dominion over Him. For in that He died, He died unto sin once: but in that He liveth, He liveth unto God. Likewise reckon ye also yourselves to be dead indeed unto sin, but alive unto God through Jesus Christ our Lord [o]"—since all sin pertains to the oldness of life to which a man by his Baptism dies, and he thereby begins to live in newness of life, it follows that all sin is taken away by Baptism.

[m] p. 235. [n] ch. xxxvi. 28. [o] Rom. vi. 3—11.

II. As by Baptism a man is incorporated into the Death and Passion of Christ, (for if "we be dead with Christ, we believe that we shall also live with Him[p],") so the Passion of Christ becomes the remedy of each man just as if he had suffered in deed; but the Passion of Christ is a sufficient satisfaction for all the sins of mankind, and therefore he who is baptized is freed from the *reatus*, the liability to all the punishment due to his sins, as if he had fully satisfied for them. This happens by his being made a member of that Body, of which He Who suffered and satisfied is the Head.

III. Baptism takes away the penalties *of* this present life, but not *in* this present life; only in the resurrection of the just, when this mortal shall have put on immortality, shall these be removed. And this is as it should be, for two reasons.

1. It is meet that the incorporate members of the one Body should, like the Head, die and suffer, bear the cross, and win the crown.

2. Men must not come to Baptism to avoid the sufferings of this present life, but to gain the glories of the next.

IV. By Baptism graces and virtues are conferred upon men; for, being thereby incorporated into and made members of that Body, of which Christ is the Head, from that Head graces and the plenitude of virtues are derived unto all. "Of His fulness have all we received[q]."

V. By Baptism each one is born again into the spi-

[p] Ibid. 8. [q] St. John i. 16.

ritual life, which is by the faith of Christ, according to the Apostle, "The life which I now live in the flesh, I live by the faith of the Son of God[r]." But life can only exist in members united to their head, from which they receive sense and motion; so from the spiritual Head, Christ, are derived the spiritual sense, which is the knowledge of truth; and the spiritual motion, which is the instinct of grace.

VI. This of course opens up the question of the theological reasons for infant Baptism, for how can the knowledge of the truth and the instinct of grace be in those who have no will or reason? To this it is answered, that as the promises attached to Baptism by Christianity belong to all the members of Christ, they attach to children with all their concomitants; but grace and the infused virtues are the concomitants of that newness of life which is the special grace of Baptism, therefore children obtain them, in habit but not in act; of which, of course, they are incapable. Just as one asleep may have the habit of virtue, but while sleeping he is precluded from exercising it. St. Augustine[s] beautifully illustrates the theory of sponsorship:—"Mother Church, in dealing with her babes, uses for them others' feet that they may come, others' hearts that they may believe, others' tongues that they may confess." So that they believe, not by their own act, but by the faith of the Church communicated to them.

---

[r] Gal. ii. 20.   [s] *Serm.* x., *de Verb. Ap.*, 176, t. v. 840, Ben.

VII. The next grace of Baptism is the opening of the Kingdom of Heaven, which was signified miraculously[t] at the Baptism of our Saviour. To open the door is to remove the impediment which prevents entrance; but that impediment is the *culpa* and *reatus pœnæ*, both of which are removed by Baptism, in that it incorporates men into the Passion of Christ.

VIII. The effects of Baptism are, as to its essence, the same in all, but not, of necessity, its accidental effects. Essentially, it was ordained to regenerate all men into the spiritual life; but accidentally, in the case of adults, coming with more or less devotion, they may receive more or less of the grace of newness: also the divine virtue, in the extinction of the law of sin in the members, may in some cases miraculously work to its entire destruction, according to a special ordination of divine Providence[u].

IX. A serious question arises, how far does a feigned Baptism hinder its effect. It is almost too horrible to suppose such a thing, but a fiction may arise, either from unbelief, or from contempt of the Sacrament, or from a celebration of the ordinance in such a way as would vitiate the Sacrament, or from an indevout access to it. The answer is, that in all cases *Character,* the invisible seal upon the soul, is conferred; but the other effects are for the time suspended, and emerge when the fiction is destroyed by penitence[x].

[t] St. Luke iii. 22.   [u] St. Aug., *de Peccat. Merit. et Remiss.*, c. 39.
[x] St. Thos. 3ª qu. 69, 1—10.
Baptism holds the first place among the Sacraments, because it is

K k

the gate of the spiritual life ; by it we are made members of Christ, and become of the Body of the Church.   It was instituted by our Lord before His Passion, as we learn from the third chapter of the Gospel of St. John.   Baptism is divided into Baptism *fluminis, flaminis,* and *sanguinis;* yet the first only is the Sacrament, the others, in defect thereof, are sufficient for the justification of the sinner.

Yet beyond these cases, Baptism is necessary to salvation, *necessitate medii.*

The matter of Baptism is twofold, proximate and remote.   The proximate matter is the ablution of the body, which should be such that it may be perceived that the water touches the body ; this may be, either by immersion of any part of the body into water, or by the affusion of water on the body, or by the aspersion of sufficient water to wet the body.   The remote matter is natural water, either cold or hot, or bitter or sweet, or rain or river, or well or spring, or bath or sea, or turbid or muddy, or sulphurous.   Also melted snow or condensed steam are valid.   But oil, any bodily excreta, wine, milk, juices, are invalid vehicles of the grace.   Distilled water and broths are doubtful.   Where from necessity baptism has been administered in doubtful material, it is best to rebaptize *conditionaliter.*

The form of Baptism in the Latin and English Church, is, "I baptize thee," &c.   In the Greek Church, " Be the servant of God baptized in the Name," &c.

For the essence of the form of Baptism four things are required. There must be expressed, 1. The person " Thee ;" 2. The action of the minister " I baptize ;" 3. The invocation of the adorable Trinity "in the name of the Father, and of the Son, and of the Holy Ghost ;" 4. The assertion of the Unity as well as Trinity conveyed by " In the name of."   The expression " In the power of," would not be valid.

Baptism in the name of Christ, or in the name of the Lord Jesus, in spite of a Canon of Pope Nicholas I. (*A quodam Judæo* 24 *de Consec. dist.* 4) is generally held to be invalid.   The passages in the Acts of the Apostles do not mean that this was the primitive form, for that were to contradict the direct command of our Lord ; but that the Apostles administered the baptism of Christ, not that of John, or of Paul, or of Cephas ; that it was instituted by Christ, and admitted men into His Communion and covenant. St. Cyprian (Ep. lxxiii.) says :—" Peter makes mention of the Lord Jesus, not in the way of omitting the Father, but that the Son may be joined with the Father." (See also St. Aug., lib. iii. *cont. Maximin.,* 17.)   The ordinary minister of Baptism is he who has ordinary jurisdiction. A deacon may baptize, by commission from the bishop, in defect of priests.

In case of necessity any one, having the use of reason, who baptizes with water in the name of the Holy Trinity, is accepted,—priest, deacon, layman, male, female, heretic, or excommunicate. Persons are not to be re-baptized who are baptized with the proper form and words by heretics, even by Calvinists who deny that Baptism remits sin, unless there be a doubt of the sufficiency of the administration. The Baptism of adults is properly in the hands of the Bishop, if he wills to do it solemnly, otherwise it belongs to the parish priest.

Priests of another parish baptizing against the will of the incumbent are to be severely punished, for usurping jurisdiction contrary to the mind of Christ.

One person ought to be baptized at a time, except in extreme necessity.

A parent ought not to baptize his child, except in case of necessity. No one can baptize himself.

Every man, and man only, while on earth is the subject of Baptism. Children, idiots, madmen, monsters are all subjects of Baptism. It is not the custom of the Church to baptize the children of unbelievers against the will of both their parents, but if one parent be Christian, or if there be the immediate approach of death, or if, arrived at the age of reason, they themselves require it, they may be baptized.

No moral disposition is required in children or idiots, but in adults to receive Baptism validly and fructuously are required three things, 1. The consent of the will; 2. Faith, at least actual; 3. Repentance.

The external confession of sin is not of necessity. (*Tract. de Sacr.*, *ap. S. Ambr.*, 3, 2; S. Thos. 3ª. qu. 68, art. 6.) A dying man who has lost his senses may be baptized, if one only witness has heard him express the desire of it. A person coming to Baptism without faith or contrition receives the character of Baptism, for it is valid, but in his case for the time infructuous. He may, however, repent and believe, and then the Sacrament is not to be reiterated.

ARTICLE XXVIII.

DE CŒNA DOMINI.

*Cœna Domini non est tantum signum mutuæ benevolentiæ
Christianorum inter sese, verum potius est Sacramentum
nostræ per mortem Christi redemptionis.*

*Atque adeo, rite, digne, et cum fide sumentibus, panis quem
frangimus est communicatio corporis Christi : similiter
poculum benedictionis est communicatio sanguinis Christi.*

*Panis et vini transubstantiatio in Eucharistia ex sacris
literis probari non potest ; sed apertis Scripturæ verbis
adversatur, Sacramenti naturam evertit, et multarum
superstitionum dedit occasionem.*

*Corpus Christi datur, accipitur, et manducatur in Cœna,
tantum cœlesti et spirituali ratione.   Medium autem
quo corpus Christi accipitur, et manducatur in Cœna,
fides est.*

*Sacramentum Eucharistiæ, ex institutione Christi non ser-
vabatur, circumferebatur, elevabatur, nec adorabatur.*

" *Of the Lord's Supper.*

" The Supper of the Lord is not only a sign of the
love that Christians ought to have among themselves
one to another; but rather it is a Sacrament of our
redemption by Christ's death: insomuch that to such
as rightly, worthily, and with faith receive the same,
the bread which we break is a partaking of the Body
of Christ, and likewise the cup of blessing is a partaking of the Blood of Christ.

" Transubstantiation (or the change of the substance

of bread and wine) in the Supper of the Lord, cannot be proved by Holy Writ, but is repugnant to the plain words of Scripture, overthroweth the nature of a Sacrament, and hath given occasion to many superstitions.

"The Body of Christ is given, taken, and eaten, in the Supper, only after an heavenly and spiritual manner. And the mean whereby the Body of Christ is received and eaten in the Supper, is faith.

"The Sacrament of the Lord's Supper was not by Christ's ordinance reserved, carried about, lifted up, or worshipped."

1. The awful and tremendous mystery of the Sacrament of our Lord's most sacred Body and precious Blood, the holy of holies of the new law, the Shechinah of the Christian dispensation, is the subject of the Twenty-eighth Article. It begins by denying the low and grovelling conception of Zwingli, who maintained that the Supper was no more than a *tessera*, or sign of communion between man and man. Zwingli eliminated all supernatural influence from the act. In the plainest sense he taught an entire absence of spiritual grace. The Article also denies the doctrine of Œcolampadius, who saw nothing more in the Eucharist than a symbol whereby one is bound to sacrifice for one's neighbour, after the example of Jesus Christ, one's body and blood, as baptism is a sign by which one binds oneself to give up one's life for the faith which one professes. The Anabaptists also, seeking in their false enthusiasm to establish an abstract mo-

tism on sin [m]. It is in amplification of what was there stated that we assert the general effects of Baptism to be as follows:—

I. According to the words of Ezekiel [n]: "Then will I sprinkle clean water upon you, and ye shall be clean: from all your filthiness, and from all your idols will I cleanse you;" and those of the Apostle: "So many of us as have been baptized into Jesus Christ were baptized into His death? Therefore we are buried with Him by Baptism into death: that like as Christ was raised up from the dead by the glory of the Father, even so we also should walk in newness of life. For if we have been planted together in the likeness of His death, we shall be also in the likeness of His resurrection: knowing this, that our old man is crucified with Him, that the body of sin might be destroyed, that henceforth we should not serve sin. For he that is dead is freed from sin. Now if we be dead with Christ, we believe that we shall also live with Him: knowing that Christ being raised from the dead dieth no more; death hath no more dominion over Him. For in that He died, He died unto sin once: but in that He liveth, He liveth unto God. Likewise reckon ye also yourselves to be dead indeed unto sin, but alive unto God through Jesus Christ our Lord [o]"—since all sin pertains to the oldness of life to which a man by his Baptism dies, and he thereby begins to live in newness of life, it follows that all sin is taken away by Baptism.

[m] p. 235.   [n] ch. xxxvi. 28.   [o] Rom. vi. 3—11.

II. As by Baptism a man is incorporated into the Death and Passion of Christ, (for if "we be dead with Christ, we believe that we shall also live with Him [p],") so the Passion of Christ becomes the remedy of each man just as if he had suffered in deed; but the Passion of Christ is a sufficient satisfaction for all the sins of mankind, and therefore he who is baptized is freed from the *reatus*, the liability to all the punishment due to his sins, as if he had fully satisfied for them. This happens by his being made a member of that Body, of which He Who suffered and satisfied is the Head.

III. Baptism takes away the penalties *of* this present life, but not *in* this present life; only in the resurrection of the just, when this mortal shall have put on immortality, shall these be removed. And this is as it should be, for two reasons.

1. It is meet that the incorporate members of the one Body should, like the Head, die and suffer, bear the cross, and win the crown.

2. Men must not come to Baptism to avoid the sufferings of this present life, but to gain the glories of the next.

IV. By Baptism graces and virtues are conferred upon men; for, being thereby incorporated into and made members of that Body, of which Christ is the Head, from that Head graces and the plenitude of virtues are derived unto all. "Of His fulness have all we received [q]."

V. By Baptism each one is born again into the spirality on the ruins of dogmatic faith, desired only to recognise in the Eucharist a symbol of the mutual devotion which Christians ought to have for each other.

2. The first positive statement of the Article is that it is "a Sacrament of our redemption by Christ's death." This is equivalent to the expression of Theodoret, μυστήριον σωτήριον[a], or to that used by St. Augustine on the occasion of his mother's death[b], *Sacramentum pretii nostri.*

"Insomuch as to such as rightly, worthily, and with faith receive the same, the bread which we break is a partaking of the Body of Christ, and likewise the cup of blessing is a partaking (in the edition of 1553 'a communion') of the Blood of Christ." This expression, being the embodiment of Holy Scripture, must mean, of course, what God the Holy Ghost meant in Holy Scripture, and of that meaning the consent of the ancient Church is a better interpreter than any of us. The word κοινωνία everywhere in Holy Scripture means an actual participation or communion of that which is spoken of.

The Scripture word κοινωνία, as applied to the Body and Blood of Christ, means not only that we receive that Body and Blood, but that we become one Body and one Blood with Him, as St. Paul explains in 1 Cor. x. 17: "For we, being many, are one Bread." On which Theophylact says: "He does not say, μετοχή, but κοινωνία, a more excellent word, as if he would imply the closest union. What he says is of the act:

---

[a] In 1 Cor. xi. 23.   [b] Conf., ix. 36.

' It is that which flowed from the side of Christ, and receiving of it we commemorate, that is, we are united to Christ. Are you not ashamed, O Corinthians, to return to the cup of idols, after that cup which hath delivered you from idols?'" St. Chrysostom also notes this difference: "Why said he not participation? Because he intended to express something more, and to point out how close are the unions; in that we commemorate not only by participating and partaking, but also by being united. For as that Body is united to Christ, so also are we united to Him by this Bread[c]." It will be seen, therefore, that the word "partaking" in the English translation is no adequate rendering of the Latin, which is the Scriptural *communicatio*.

This patristic explanation of the word κοινωνία disposes of the formula whereby Calvin endeavoured to steer a middle course between the Lutheran teaching on the one hand, and that of Zwingli and Œcolampadius on the other. He taught that the Body of Christ is truly present in the Lord's Supper, and that the believer partakes of it; but he only meant that simultaneously with the bodily participation of the material elements, which in every respect remained what they were, and merely signified the Body and the Blood, a power emanating from the Body of Christ, which is now in heaven only, is communicated to the Spirit. Framed originally under the pressure of the confusions among the Reformed, this middle opinion made its way among them, and included many of the Lutherans

[c] *Hom.* xxiv.; 1 Cor. x. 17.

themselves, as its advocates employed, without hesitation, the expression that Christ is really present in the Eucharist, and His Body and Blood given to believers for participation. In England, in consequence of the great authority of Richard Hooker, who, in the gradual process of working himself out of Puritanism, had on this mysterious doctrine attained to Catholic feeling, while he adhered to Calvinistic definition, this view has obtained to an extent remarkable in view of its intrinsic inanity. It does not satisfy the letter of Scripture, which distinctly predicates the affirmative proposition, "This *is* My Body." It contradicts the testimony of the primitive Church, as we shall presently proceed to shew from a long catena of authorities. It has exhibited its unsatisfactoriness in never having been able to maintain an abiding existence, either rising into the Catholic doctrine, or, more commonly, degenerating into a bare Zwinglianism, and has only found favour with those who, unwilling to accept the profound mystery of the Holy Eucharist with all its consequences, are unable to bring themselves to an absolute denial of any presence of Christ, and, therefore, in this formula find a sop to the cravings of an intellect which dreads to carry to conclusions the premises which in reason only lead to the acceptance of the Catholic doctrine.

The word κοινωνία disposes also of what has been termed the theory of virtualism or equivalence — a theory which proposes to attempt the impossible task of reconciling the high and mysterious expressions of our Lord Himself, His holy Apostles, and the primitive Fathers, with such a view of the doctrine of the blessed Sacrament as practically amounts to the real absence of our Lord therefrom. A virtual Presence, as it is sometimes incorrectly called, means, when we examine it, a bestowal of the grace, efficacy, virtue, or influence of the atoning Death of our Lord. It supposes the bread and wine to be equivalents for the absent Body and Blood, so that to partake with faith of the former is virtually and in effect as though we partook of the latter. The very Body and very Blood are supposed to be absent. They are not actually "given" or "taken." They are neither present by consecration nor present in devout reception. Somewhat of this nature was that theory of a school of the Nonjurors, which owed its existence to John Johnson, the learned author of "The Unbloody Sacrifice." It was, that the Body of our Lord, which had been conceived by the Holy Ghost, and born of the Virgin Mary, had ascended into heaven, there to remain till the restitution of all things; but that in the Divine mysteries, on consecration, the Holy Ghost descended upon the gifts of bread and wine, which had been offered in sacrifice to God, and joining Himself with them, made them the Body and Blood of Christ in power and efficacy.

Moreover, it is not said in the Article that we are partakers of Christ, or of a grace from Christ, but the Bread which we break, i.e. the Bread which has been blessed and consecrated by our Lord's words, "This is

My Body," through the operation of the Holy Ghost, is the communion or participation of the Body of Christ; and the Cup of Blessing, i.e. the Cup blessed by the words, "This is My Blood," is the partaking of or communication of the Blood of Christ.

In adducing the following passages from the Fathers, I would only premise that I have selected such passages as contain the doctrine of the Real Objective Presence, —I mean that the Body and Blood of Christ are so sacramentally present in, or under, the consecrated Bread and Wine, that the Fathers either called the whole, the outward and the inward part together, or even the outward part alone, by the name of the inward part, the Body and Blood of Christ. I have passed over all the passages (which are naturally far more numerous) in which the Fathers speak of our "receiving the Body and Blood of Christ," "that saving Body, Christ Himself;" that we "eat His Body," or "drink Blood from His side;" "receive Him and lay Him up in ourselves, and place the Saviour in our breasts." All passages which speak only of the "reception" I have omitted.

St. Ignatius[d], consecrated Bishop of Antioch by St. Peter, says of the Docetæ who did not believe in the reality of our Lord's Body :—"They confess not that the Eucharist is the Flesh of our Saviour Jesus Christ, which suffered for our sins, which the Father in His mercy raised again."

Justin Martyr, a disciple of Apostles, in giving an

<hr>

[d] *Ep. ad Smyrn.*, n. 7.

account of the Christian worship to the Emperor :—
" We do not receive it as *common* bread, or as *common* drink, but in what way Jesus Christ our Saviour, being through the Word of God Incarnate, had both flesh and blood for our salvation, so also have we been taught that *the Food, over which thanksgiving has been made* by the prayer of the word which is from Him (from which [food] our blood and flesh are, by transmutation, nourished), is the *Flesh and Blood of Him, the Incarnate Jesus.* For the Apostles, in their records which are called the Gospels, have delivered that Jesus so commanded them, that He, having taken bread and given thanks, said, ' Do this in remembrance of Me. This is My Body.' And, likewise, having taken the cup and given thanks, He said, 'This is My Blood[e].' "

St. Irenæus, who says that he remembers the times of his youth with Polycarp (the disciple of St. John) better than recent things, argues against the Gnostics : —" If the Lord belonged to another Father, how was it just that taking bread, of this our creation, He confessed that it was His own Body, and He affirmed that the mingled drink of the cup was His Own Blood[f] ?"

In the Harmony ascribed to Tatian or Ammonius, the words of the Gospel are paraphrased thus :—" And then, having taken bread, and afterwards the cup of wine, He bare witness that it was His Body and Blood, and bade them eat and drink, for that it was a memorial of His coming suffering and death[g]."

[e] *Apol.*, i. § 66.　　　[f] iv. 33, 2.　　　[g] *Harm.* iv. *Evang.*, Bibl. Patr., ii. P. ii. p. 210, A.

Tertullian, on whose antiquity the Homily lays such stress, speaks to this effect :—" The zeal of Faith might speak on this head all the day long, mourning that the Christian should come from the idols into the Church ... that *he should approach those hands to the Body of the Lord*, which bestowed bodies on demons. Nor is this enough. It were a small matter that they should receive from other hands that which they defile, but they themselves also deliver to others that which they have defiled. Makers of idols are chosen into the ministry of the Church. Horrid sin ! The Jews laid violent hands. but once upon Christ ; *these every day assault His Body*. O, hands worthy of being cut off ! Let them now consider whether it were said only in a figure, ' If thine hand offend thee, cut it off.' What hands ought more to be cut off than those by *which the Body of the Lord is offended* [h] ?"

And here, in order of time, comes in the Greek inscription found at Autun, which is assigned to the second century, because, in A.D. 202, the Greek Church in France was laid desolate. The antiquity of this part of the inscription, and its testimony to " the Divinity of our Lord, and the divine dignity of the Sacraments," are recognised with satisfaction by Dr. Christopher Wordsworth. As the inscription has only been known for these few years, but is of extreme value for the simplicity of the faith expressed by it, it is right to cite his words from his printed letter to Cardinal Pitra, the Benedictine editor [l]. The inscription relates to

[h] *De Idol.*, § 8, p. 228, O. T.   [l] *Spicil. Solesm.*, t. i. p. 563.

the two great Sacraments, and affirms only what all
Catholic Christians must hold in common, the Real
Objective Presence. "Quam valida vero ad catholicam
veritatem stabiliendam et ad hæreticam pravitatem de
Christo Deo, de divina Sacramentorum dignitate, pro-
fligandam, testimonia suppeditet non sine summa volup-
tate videmus. Et hanc priorem inscriptionis partem
antiquitus in marmore extitisse . . . pro comperto
habeo." Dr. Wordsworth does not say anything about
the definite date of the inscription, but he believes it
to be ancient, "antiquitus." The lines relating to the
Holy Eucharist are:—"Receive the honey-sweet [food]
of the holy things of the Saviour;" or, as others, "of
the Saviour of the holy." "Eat, drink, having Jesus
Christ, the Son of God, the Saviour, in thy hands."
The well-known anagram $IX\Theta Y\Sigma$ occurs at this same
time, both in the Greek and Latin Church; in the
Greek, in a hymn ascribed to St. Clement of Alexandria; in the Latin, in Tertullian. In St. Clement of
Alexandria, as well as in this inscription, it is used in
reference to the Eucharist[k]. It occurs in the recently
discovered works attributed to St. Melito. It occurs
also in Origen, St. Hilary, St. Ambrose, St. Optatus,
Severian, Bishop of Gabala, the rival and enemy of
St. Chrysostom, Sedulius, St. Paulinus, St. Augustine,
St. Peter Chrysologus, St. Prosper, the African author
of the *De Promiss. Dei*, and St. Cyril of Alexandria[l].
There can neither be a simpler nor a fuller statement

[k] See Dr. Pusey, Real Presence, p. 338, note.
[l] See the passages collected in *Spicil. Solesm.*, t. iii. p. 527.

of the Objective Presence of our Lord, God and Man, in the Holy Eucharist, received in the hands to be food to the faithful than in this inscription, which the Providence of God has brought to light.

Author of the *Carmina adv. Marcion* [m] :—" From what creation suppose ye the Bread and Wine are, and must be confessed to be, His Body and Blood? Proved not He Himself the Maker of the world by deeds? And, at the same time, that He bare a Body of Flesh and Blood?"

Origen:—" We, rendering thanks ($\epsilon\dot{v}\chi\alpha\rho\iota\sigma\tauο\hat{v}\nu\tau\epsilon\varsigma$) to the Creator of the universe, eat the Bread, offered with thanksgiving ($\epsilon\dot{v}\chi\alpha\rho\iota\sigma\tau\iota\alpha\varsigma$) and prayer over the things offered, which [bread] becometh, for the prayer's sake, *a certain Holy Body,* which halloweth those who use the same with a sound purpose [n]."

Note the reserve in this passage. The author is arguing with a heathen, to whom it was not right to expose the Mystery, and therefore uses reserve :—" Ye who are wont to be present at the Divine Mysteries, know how, when ye receive the Body of the Lord, ye keep It with all care and veneration, lest any particle of It should fall, lest any of the consecrated gift should escape you. For ye believe yourselves guilty (and ye believe rightly) if any thereof fall through negligence ; but if ye use so great caution, and rightly use it, in preserving His Body, how do ye think it a less guilt to have neglected the Word of God than His Body [o] ?"

---

[m] *L. 5, ap. Tertull.*   [n] *Cont. Cels.,* 8, c. 33.

[o] *In Exod., Hom.* xiii. § 3, p. 176.

St. Dionysius the Great, of Alexandria, who was consulted in most questions of moment by other Churches:—"For I could not venture to renew from the beginning (i. e., to re-baptize) one who had heard the Eucharist, and joined in answering the Amen, and stood by the table, and stretched forth his hands to receive the Holy Food, and had received it, and for a long while had partaken of the Body and Blood of our Lord Jesus Christ[p]." "For I do not think that women, who are faithful and devout, would venture, in such a state, to approach the Holy Table, or to touch the Body and Blood of Christ[q]."

St. Cyprian:—"For how do we teach or provoke them to shed their blood in confession of the name, if, when about to engage, we deny them the Blood of Christ[r]." "Let us also arm the right hand with the 'sword of the Spirit,' that it may boldly reject the deadly sacrifices, that, mindful of the Eucharist, the hand which has received the Lord's Body, may embrace the Lord Himself, from Him to receive hereafter the reward of heavenly crowns[s]." "Those mouths sanctified by heavenly food, after the Body and Blood of the Lord, loathed the profane contagion, and the relics of idol feasts[t]." "A violence is offered to His Body and Blood, and they sin more now against the Lord with hand and mouth, than when they were denying Him[u]."

[p] Euseb. H. E. vii. 9.   [q] *Ep. ad Basilid.*, can. 2. p. 114.
[r] *Ep.* lvii. *ad Cornel.*   [s] *Ep.* lviii. *ad Thibarit.*, § 10.   [t] *De Lapsis*, § 2, p. 154, Oxf. Tr.   [u] Ibid., 11, p. 163.

See how St. Dionysius the Great, Origen, St. Cyprian, agree with the Inscription of Autun in speaking of communicants as having in their hands "the Body of Christ."

Magnes:—"For it is not a type of the Body, nor a type of the Blood, *as some have blindly and idly said*, but is in truth the Body and Blood of Christ[x]." "Through that union whereby I am united, the Holy with the earthly, I give Bread and Wine, commanding them to be My Body and Blood[y]."

Hipparchus and Philotheus, martyrs in the persecution of Maximian, about A.D. 297:—"Three years have now passed since we received Baptism in the Name of the Father, and of the Son, and of the Holy Ghost, from the hand of a priest of the true faith, whose name was James, and he gave us continually the Body of Christ and His Blood[z]." When they had converted James, Pyragrus, Rumono, and another, this same priest "baptized them in the name of the Trinity, and imparted to them the Body and Blood of Christ."

Eusebius, the historian:—"On every day before the Sabbath [Friday] we make a remembrance of the Saviour's Passion, through the fast which the Apostles then first fasted, when the Bridegroom was taken from them; on every Lord's-day, quickened by the *consecrated Body* of the same Saviour's Passion, and sealed in our souls by His precious Blood[a]."

---

[x] *Frag. ap. Gall.*, iii. 541.   [y] Ibid., § 2.   [z] *Assem. Acta Mart.*, ii. 123.   [a] *De Pasch. in Maii Scriptt. Vett.*, i. 257.

St. James of Nisibis (one of the foremost of the Nicene Fathers, who had the gifts of miracles and prophecy) :—" Abstain thou from all uncleanness, and then receive the Body and Blood of Christ, and carefully guard thy mouth, through which the King hath entered ; nor mayest thou, O man, any more bring forth through thy mouth words of uncleanness[b]." "From that place where He kept the Passover, and gave His Body that they should eat, and His Blood that they should drink, He went away and departed thither with His disciples, where they took Him. When then His Body was eaten, and His Blood drunk, He was 'counted among the dead.' For our Lord with His own hands gave His Body for food, and when He was not yet crucified He gave His Blood for drink[c]." " When He had washed His disciples' feet, He sat down at the table, and then gave them His Body and Blood[d]."

St. Athanasius :—" Thou wilt see the Levites (deacons) bearing bread and a cup of wine, and placing them on the table ; and so long as the supplications and prayers have not yet taken place, *bare* ($\psi\iota\lambda\acute{o}s$) is the bread and the cup ; but when the great and wonderful prayers have been completed over it, then the Bread becometh the Body, the Cup the Blood of our Lord Jesus Christ[e]." " Let us come to the consecration of the mysteries. This bread and this cup, so

[b] *Serm.* iii. § 2, p. 46, ed. Rom. §4, p. 341. [d] Ibid., p. 346.

[e] *Serm.* xiv. *de Pasch.*, [e] *Serm. ad Baptizat. ap. Eutych. de Pasch. Maii Scriptt. Vett.*, ix. 625.

long as the prayers and supplications have not yet taken place, are *bare* elements, but when the great prayers and holy supplications have been sent up, the word cometh down into the bread and cup, and it becometh His Body [f]."

Juvencus, a Spanish poet about A.D. 330, thus paraphrases the history of the institution of the Lord's Supper:—"When He said these things, He brake the Bread with His hands, and being broken He gave it to them, and having holily prayed, He taught His disciples that He gave them His own Body." "Then the Lord taketh the cup, and it being filled with wine, He sanctifieth It with mighty words, and giveth It them to drink, and taught them that He had divided His own Blood. And He saith,—'This Blood will remit the sins of the people, This My Blood drink ye [g].'"

St. Julius, Bishop of Rome :—"An inquiry concerning Christ's Blood and Christ's Body [on occasion of the false accusation that St. Athanasius had broken a chalice] is carried on before an external judge, in the presence of catechumens, nay, worse than that, before heathens and Jews, who have so bad a name in regard to Christianity [h]."

Council of Alexandria, A.D. 339 :—"Our sanctuaries are now, as they have always been, pure, and honoured only with the Blood of Christ, and His pious

[f] Ibid.   [g] *Hist. Evang.*, L. iv. B. P. iv. 74.
[h] *Ep. ad Euseb. in S. Ath. Apol. ag. Arians*, § 31.

worship[i]." "For to you only it appertains to have the first taste of the Blood of Christ, and to none besides. But as he who breaks a sacred cup is an impious person, much more impious is he who insults the Blood of Christ[k]."

Julius Firmicus:—"We drink the immortal blood of Christ; to our blood is the Blood of Christ united; this is the healthful remedy for thy wickedness[l]."

St. Thecla, Maria, Martha, Maria, Ami, Persian martyrs under Sapor, A.D. 337, to the apostate priest, who, with a drawn sword, endeavoured to make them apostatize:—"Is this that holy propitiatory Thing which we received from thy hands? Is this the life-giving Blood which thou usedst to bring near to our mouths[m]?"

St. Hilary:—"If the Word was truly made Flesh, and we, through the food of the Lord, truly receive the Word made Flesh, how must He not be thought to abide in us by the way of nature, Who, being born Man, took to Himself the nature of our Flesh, now inseparable from Him, and, *under the sacrament* of the Flesh to be communicated to us, hath mingled the nature of His own Flesh with His Eternal Nature[n]." "Was He unwilling to suffer? but, before, He had consecrated the Blood of His own Body, which was to be shed for the remission of sins[o]." "What

---

[i] *S. Ath. Apol. c. Arian.*, init. p. 14, O. T.   [k] *In S. Ath. Apol. ag. Ar.*, § 6, p. 20, O. T.   [l] *De err. Prof. relig.*, p. 44. [m] *In S. Maruthas, Assem. Acta Mart.*, i. 125.   [n] *De Trin.*, viii. 13. [o] *In Matt.*, c. 31, § 7.

frenzy didst thou exercise against the Church of Thoulouse? The clergy were beaten with clubs; the Deacons were crushed with boxing-gloves armed with lead; and on Himself, as the holy will understand, on Christ Himself hands were laid [p]."

Arian Council at Philippopolis:—"Presbyters were dragged naked by him to the market-place, and (what must be said with tears and grief) he openly and publicly profaned the *consecrated Body of the Lord*, hung to the necks of the priests [q]." It is to be observed that they use the same phrase as Eusebius. It was then probably a received phrase. But to speak of the "consecrated Body of the Lord," must mean that that of which he speaks became such by consecration. "Sinning profanely and atrociously against the Body of the Lord and His mysteries [r]."

St. Damasus, "learned in the Scriptures [s]:"—

" Tarsicium sanctum Christi sacramenta gerentem,
   Cum male sana manus voluit vulgare profanis,
   Ipse animam potius voluit dimittere cæsus,
   Prodere quam canibus rabidis cælestia membra [t]."

St. Optatus :—" For what is the Altar, but the Throne of the Body and Blood of Christ [u]?" "Wherein had Christ offended you, Whose Body and Blood dwelt here at stated times?" . . . . . "In this way ye

---

[p] *c. Const. Imp.*, § 11. [q] *Ap. S. Hil. Fragm.*, iii. 9.
[r] Ibid., § 23. [s] St. Jerome, *Ep.* xlviii. *ad Pamm.*, n. 17.
[t] In Baronius, A. 381, n. 21, from *Antiq. Inscrip. App.*, p. 1174, n. 2.
[u] *De Schism. Donat.*, vi. 1. p. 90, ed. Dupin.

have imitated the Jews; they laid their hands on Christ on the Cross; by you He was smitten on the Altar [v]." "This great crime has been doubled by you, in that ye brake the chalices too, which bear the Blood of Christ [x]."

St. Ephrem:—"'Standing on their feet!' because one sitting may not receive the living Body; 'and no stranger shall eat thereof,' because no one unbaptized eateth of the Body [y]." "This was fulfilled in our Lord, when in the Mount of Jerusalem He brake His Body and divided His Blood, and said, 'This ye shall do for a remembrance of Me [z].'" "Thou wilt not burn the hand which received a portion of Thy holy Body, together with the hand which smote Thee on Thy cheek, Thee, the Creator. The mouth which ate Thee will not howl, together with the mouth which spat on Thee, on Thy face [a]." "Whom Thou hast made meet to administer in the Sanctuary, and to distribute Thy Body and Thy Blood to Thy flock, may his pasture be with Thy lambs [b]." "He brake His Body before thee, and mingled His Blood and gave it thee [c]."

St. Basil:—"Thou introducest higgling into spiritual things and the Church, where we are entrusted with the Body and Blood of Christ [d]." "Let him not bless either publicly or privately, nor distribute the

[v] Ibid., p. 91. [x] Ibid., c. 2, p. 92. [y] On Exod. xii. t. i. p. 213. [z] In Isa. xxv. 26, t. ii. p. 61. [a] Can. 12, t. iii. p. 246. [b] Can. 18, p. 247. [c] Paræn., 16, p. 439. [d] Ep. liii. Chorepisc., § 1, iii. 147.

Body of Christ to others, nor perform any liturgical office; but, satisfied with his rank, let him weep before the Lord, that his sin of ignorance may be forgiven him [e]."

St. Gregory of Nyssa:—"Wherefore also He who ever *is*, sets Himself before us as Food, that we receiving Him in ourselves, may become that which He is [f]." The Bread, again, is up to a certain time *common* bread, but when the mystery shall consecrate it, it is called and becomes the Body of Christ [g]. "Well do I believe that now, too, the bread, sanctified by the Word of God, is trans-made (μεταποιεῖσθαι) into the Body of God, the Word [h]." "For both there [in the Lord's Natural Body] the grace of the Word hallowed that Body, whose composition was from bread, and which itself, too, was in a manner bread; and here [in the Sacrament], in like way, the bread (as the Apostle says) is hallowed by the Word of God and prayer, not through meat and drink passing on into the Body of the Word, but trans-made (μεταποιούμενος) straight into the Body of the Word, as it was said by the Word, 'This is My Body [i]!'"

St. Gregory of Nazianzum:—"One of those who approach to the approaching God, and is accounted worthy of the holy station and order [k]." "Whoever besides ministers about the holy Table of God, and approaches to the approaching God [l]."

---

[e] *Ep.* cxcix. (Can. 2), Can. 27, p. 294.　　[f] *In Eccles.* iii. 8. *Hom.* viii. t. i. p. 456.　　[g] *De Bapt. Christi*, iii. 870.　　[h] *Orat. Catech.*, c. 37.　　[i] Ibid.　　[k] *Orat.* xxi. c. 7.　　[l] *Orat.* xlii. c. 26.

"And thou, wretched man, wilt thou boldly receive
In thy palms the Mystic Food, or God embrace
With hands, wherewith thou hast dug up my grave[m]."

Cæsarius (brother of St. Gregory of Nazianzum) :—
"He trampleth under foot God the Word, the Son of
God, who, in covetous hands lifted up against his neighbour, receiveth fearlessly the Sacramental elements, accounting them like *common* bread and wine, which, in
the eyes of the faithful mind, are contemplated, God[n]."
"And yet we believe the Divine Revelation, that not
as being equal or like, yet that still properly and
fitly, It is the Divine Body which is consecrated on
the holy Table, and is indivisibly distributed to the
whole sacred band, and partaken of without ceasing
to be[o]."

St. Amphilochius (friend of St. Basil and St. Gregory
of Nazianzum) :—"He, the Father, is both greater and
equal, greater than He who receives vinegar to drink,
equal to Him who poureth out as wine His own proper
blood, τοῦ τὸ οἰκεῖον οἰνοχοοῦντος αἷμα[p]."

Esaias Abbas :—"If thou willest to take the Body
of Christ, take heed that there be no anger or hatred
in thy heart against any one[q]."

St. Ambrose :—"So often as we receive the Sacraments, which by the mystery of the sacred prayer are
transfigured into Body and Blood, we shew forth the

<hr>

[m] *Carm.*, l. ii. § 2, Epigr. 69. [n] *Interrog.* 140, *Dial.* 3 ;
Gall. vi. 98. [o] Ibid., *Int.*, pp. 127, 169. [p] *Serm. adv.
Arian. in Maii Script. Vett.*, iv. p. 10. [q] *Reg. ad Monach.*, 50.

death of the Lord [r]." "What more noble than Christ, who in the Feast of the Church both ministers and is ministered [s]?" "Where His Body is, there is Christ [t]." "And in the ministering of the Apostles is set forth the future distribution of the Body and Blood of the Lord [u]." "Where Christ, the Head of all, is daily consecrated [v]." "At the same time, it is shewn what sort of person he ought to be who ministereth to Christ. For, first of all, he must be free from the allurements of various pleasures, shun inward drowsiness of mind and body, that he may administer the Body and Blood of Christ. . . . . See what thou doest, O priest, and touch not with feverish hand the Body of Christ [x]." "How in such hands wilt thou receive the all-holy Body of the Lord? how wilt thou bear to thy mouth the Precious Blood, having in thine anger unlawfully shed so much blood [y]?" "But if human blessing was of such avail as to change nature, what say we of the Divine Consecration itself, wherein the very words of our Lord and Saviour operate? For that Sacrament which thou receivest is consecrated by the Word of Christ. But if the word of Elijah was of so great power as to bring down fire from Heaven, shall not the Word of Christ avail to change the nature of the elements? Of the works of the whole world thou hast read,—'He spake, and they were made; He com-

---

[r] *De Fide*, iv. 10.   [s] *De Cain et Abel*, i. 5, § 19.   [t] *In Ps.* cxix. *Serm.* viii. § 48.   [u] *In S. Luc.*, l. vi. § 84.   [v] *De Virg.*, i. 11, § 65.   [x] *De Vid.*, c. x. § 65.   [y] *In Theodoret, Eccles. Hist.*, l. v. c. xvii. t. iii.

manded, and they were created.' The word of Christ, then, which could make of nothing what (as yet) was not, cannot it change the things which are into that which they were not? For it is not a less thing to give new natures to things, than to change natures. But why use we arguments? Let us use His own example, and build up the truth of the mystery by the example of the Incarnation. Did the wont of nature precede, when the Lord Jesus was born of a Virgin? If we inquire for the order of nature, woman united with man was wont to bear. And this Body which we consecrate is from the Virgin. Why inquirest thou here for the order of nature in the Body of Christ, when, against nature, the Lord Jesus Himself was born of a Virgin? True is the Flesh of Christ, which was crucified, which was buried; true therefore is the Sacrament of that Flesh. The Lord Jesus Himself declares, 'This is My Body.' Before the blessing of the heavenly words, another kind is named; after the consecration the Body is *signified*. He Himself saith, it is His Blood. Before consecration it is called other; after the consecration it is named Blood. And thou sayest, Amen, i.e. it is true; what the mouth speaketh, let the inward mind confess; what the speech uttereth, let the affection feel [x]." "In that Sacrament Christ is: because it is the Body of Christ; it is not therefore bodily food, but spiritual. Whence, too, the Apostle saith of its type:—' Our fathers did eat spiritual meat, and did drink spiritual

[x] *De Myster.*, §§ 52—54.

drink.' For the Body of God is a spiritual Body; the Body of Christ is the Body of the Divine Spirit [a]."

Author of the *De Sacramentis* (a Bishop, and probably a disciple of St. Ambrose): — "The Altar is a figure of the Body, and the Body of Christ is on the Altar [a]." "You say, perhaps, 'my bread is common bread.' But that bread is bread before the words of the Sacraments; when the consecration is added, from bread it becomes the Flesh of Christ. How can that which *is* bread, *be* the Body of Christ? By Consecration. And the Consecration, in whose words is it? The Lord Jesus'. For all the rest which had been said before is said by the priest; praises are offered to God; prayer is made for the people, for kings, for the rest. When the Venerable Sacrament is to be consecrated, the priest now no longer uses his own words, but he uses the words of Christ. So, then, the word of Christ consecrates the Sacrament. What is the word of Christ? That by which all things were made. The Lord commanded, the heaven was made; the Lord commanded, and the earth was made; the Lord commanded, and the seas were made; the Lord commanded, and all creatures were brought forth. Thou, seest, then, how powerful in working is the Word of Christ. If, then, there is such power in the Word of the Lord Jesus, that those things which were not should begin to be, how much more is it operative that the things which *were should still be, and be changed into something else!* So, then, that I may

<hr>

[a] *De Myster.,* § 58.

answer thee, it was not the Body of Christ before the Consecration, but after the Consecration I say to thee that now it is the Body of Christ—'He spake, and it was made; He commanded, and it was created.' Before it is consecrated, it is bread; when the words of Christ are added, it is the Body of Christ. Then hear Himself saying—'Take and eat ye all of this, for this is My Body.' And before the words of Christ, it is a cup, full of wine and water; when the words of Christ have operated, the Blood of Christ is caused to be there, which redeemed His people [b]." "So, then, not idly dost thou say, Amen, already thereby confessing in spirit that thou receivest the Body of Christ. The priest saith to thee—'The Body of Christ,' and thou sayest, Amen, i.e. true [c]."

St. Jerome:—"God forbid that I should speak anything unfavourable of these; for, succeeding to the Apostolic rank, with holy mouths they make Christ's Body, through whom also we are Christians [d]." "But let us hear that the bread which the Lord brake and gave to His disciples was the Body of the Lord our Saviour, since He Himself said to them, 'Take, eat; this is My Body;' and that the cup was that of which He said again, 'Drink ye all of this; for this is My Blood of the New Testament, which is shed for many.' That is the cup of which we read in the Prophet— 'I will receive the cup of salvation.' And in another place—'Thine inebriating cup, how good is it!' If,

---

[b] Ibid., c. iv. § 14, 15; c. v. § 23; § 25.   [c] iv. 2, § 7.
[d] *Ep.* xiv. *ad Heliod.*, § 8; comp. Hooker, v. 77, 2.

then, 'the bread which came down from Heaven' is the Lord's Body; and 'the wine which He gave to His disciples is the Blood of the New Testament, which was shed for many for the remission of sins [d],' " &c. " Nought richer than he who carries the Body of the Lord in a wicker basket, His Blood in a glass [e]." " What ails the minister of tables and of widows (the deacon), that he swells and lifts himself up above those (bishops and priests) at whose prayers the Body and Blood of Christ is made [f] ?"

Luciferian, quoted by St. Jerome :—*Lucif.* " It is not the same thing to shed tears for sins, and to handle the Body of the Lord. It is not the same thing to fall at the feet of the brethren, and from on high to administer the Eucharist to the people [g]."

Jerome of Jerusalem :—" Many of those in the world often experience workings of such grace and of the Holy Spirit; those, I mean, who assist at the altar, and who approach to partake of the mysteries of Christ. For on a sudden they are filled with tears and joy and gladness. Whence also the Christian is fully convinced that he doth not receive mere (ψιλὸν) bread and wine, but in truth the Body and Blood of the Son of God, sanctified by the Holy Ghost [h]."

Theophilus, of Alexandria :—" Nor do we call the bodily substance vanity, as he (Origen) thinketh (falling, in other words, into the doctrines of Manichæus),

---

[d] *Ep.* cxx. *ad Hedib.*, § 2.　　　　[e] *Ep.* cxxv. *ad Rust.*, § 20.

[f] *Ep.* cxlvi. *ad Evang.* § 1.　　　　[g] *Adv. Lucif.*, § 3.

[h] *Comm. Christian. xtil.*, Gall. vii. 529

lest the Body of Christ also should be subject to vanity, through the eating whereof we, being satiated, daily ruminate on His words, 'Unless a man eat My Flesh, and drink My Blood, he has no part in Me[1].'"

St. Gaudentius, of Brescia:—"Himself then the Creator and Lord of Nature, who 'bringeth forth bread from the earth,' of bread again (for He both can, and hath promised), makes His Own Body; and He who of water made wine, makes also wine of His Own Blood[k]." "That you may not think *that* to be earthly, which has been made heavenly through Him who passeth into it, and made it His Body and Blood." .... "When He reached forth the consecrated Bread and Wine to His disciples, He said, 'This is My Body; this is My Blood.' Let us believe Him Whom we have believed. Truth cannot lie."..."But that He appointed the Sacraments of His Body and Blood to be offered in the form of Bread and Wine, there is a twofold reason[l]."

St. Isaac the Great:—"I beheld that her cup was mingled, and instead of wine it was full of Blood, and instead of bread, a Body was placed for her in the midst of her table. I saw the Blood and trembled; and the Body, and fear seized me; and she [Faith] made a sign to me, 'Eat, and be silent; drink, child, and scrutinize not.' ... She shewed me a Body slain, and placed thereof between my lips, and cried to me sweetly, 'See what it is thou art eating.' She gave

---

[1] *Epist. Pasch.*, A. 401, § 11; *ap. S. Jerome, Ep.* xcvi. i. 564.
[k] *De Pasch.*, tr. ii. B. P. v. p. 946.   [l] Ibid., p. 947.

the pen of the Spirit, and bade me subscribe ; and I took, I wrote, and I confessed, 'This is the Body of God [m].'"

St. Paulinus, of Nola, friend of St. Ambrose and St. Augustine, wrote as part of an inscription for an altar, under which a piece of the Cross was to be placed :—

"Cuncta salutiferi coeunt martyria Christi,
    Crux, Corpus, Sanguis, martyris ipse Deus."

St. Maruthas (a very great man, a friend of St. Chrysostom) :—"Now as often as we approach to the Body and Blood, and take It in our hands, we believe that we embrace the Body, and that we are of His Flesh and His Bones, as it is written. For Christ did not call it a type and a likeness, but that in truth 'This is My Body, and this is My Blood [n].'" And so St. Maruthas, in his Liturgy, paraphrases our Lord's words of Consecration : — "Jesus took bread into His holy hands, and giving thanks to the Father, blessed, sanctified, brake, and divided to the disciples, and said, Take eat, believe and be certain, and so proclaim and teach, that this is My Body which is broken for the salvation of the world, and to those who eat It and believe in Me, giveth expiation of sins and life eternal [o]." And in like way he paraphrases the words of Consecration of the Cup.

We now come to the testimony of the great St.

[m] *Serm. de Fide ap. Assem. Bibl. Or.*, t. i. p. 220.   [n] *Comm. Evang. in Assem.*, i. 179.   [o] *In Renaudot. Liturg. Or.*, ii. 263.

Augustine:—"For on this account it seemed good to the Holy Spirit, namely, that for the honour of so great a Sacrament, the Lord's Body should enter the mouth of a Christian previously to other food [p]." "And when the Apostle said this, the discourse was upon the subject of those who, treating the Lord's Body like any other food, took it in an undiscriminating and negligent way. If, then, this man is rebuked who does not discriminate, that is, see the difference of, the Lord's Body from other meats, how must he be damned, who, feigning himself a friend, comes to His Table a foe [q]!" "Christ was carried in His Own Hands, when commending His Own Body, He said, 'This is My Body.' For that Body He carried in His Own Hands [r]." "That Bread which ye see on the Altar, sanctified by the Word of God, is the Body of Christ. That Cup, rather what the Cup holds, sanctified by the Word of God, is the Blood of Christ [s]." "For the Blood of Christ hath a loud voice on earth, when, on receiving It, all nations answer, Amen [t]."

St. Chrysostom:—"O marvel! O love of God for man! He who sitteth aloft with the Father, is at that hour held in the hands of all, and giveth Himself to those who will, to enfold and embrace [u]." "For when they were eating and drinking, He took bread, brake it, and said, 'This is My Body which is broken for

[p] *Ep.* liv. *ad Januar.*, § 8.   [q] *In S. Joh.*, *Hom.* lxii. § 1.
[r] *In Ps.* xxxiii. [xxxiv.] *Serm.* i. n. 10.   [s] *Serm.* 227, *in Die Pasch.*, iv.   [t] *Cont. Faust.*, xii. 10, t. viii. p. 231.   [u] *De Sacerdot.*, iii. 5, i. 382.

you for the remission of sins.' The initiated know
what I mean: and again, the Cup, saying, 'This is
My Blood, which is shed for many for the remission
of sins.' And Judas was present when Christ said this.
This is the Body which thou, O Judas, didst sell for
thirty pieces of silver; this is the Blood for which,
a little before, thou madest that shameless compact
with the reckless Pharisees[x]." "The same who adorned
that Table, adorneth this too now. For it is not man
who maketh what lieth there to become the Body and
Blood of Christ, but Christ Himself who was crucified
for us[y]." "For indeed His Body is set before us
now; not His garment only, but even His Body;
not for us to touch It only, but also to eat, and be
filled. . . . . Believe, therefore, that even now it is that
Supper, at which He Himself sat down. For *This* is
in no respect different from *That*. For neither doth
man make This and Himself the Other, but both This
and That is His own work. When, therefore, thou
seest the Priest delivering It unto thee, account not
that it is the Priest that doeth so, but that it is Christ's
Hand that is stretched out. . . . For He that hath given
the greater, i.e. hath set Himself before thee, much
more will He not think scorn to distribute unto thee
of His Body. Let us hear, therefore, both priests and
subjects, what we have had vouchsafed to us; let us
hear and tremble. Of His Own Flesh He hath granted
us our fill; He hath set before us Himself sacrificed[z]."

<hr>

[x] *De Prodit. Jud.*, § 5.　　　　　　　[y] Ibid., § 6.
[z] *In S. Matt., Hom.* L. § 3.

"That Table at that time was not of silver, nor that cup of gold, out of which Christ gave His disciples His Own Blood: but precious was everything there, and awful, for that they were full of the Spirit [a]." "Purer than what sunbeam should not that hand be, which is to sever this Flesh, the mouth that is filled with spiritual fire, the tongue that is reddened by that most awful Blood [b]?" "I would give up my life rather than impart of the Lord's Blood to the unworthy; and will shed my own blood rather than impart of such awful Blood contrary to what is meet [c]." "I say now, if even a man's garment be what one would not venture inconsiderately to touch, what shall we say of the Body of Him who is God over all, spotless, pure, associate with that Divine Nature, the Body whereby we are, and live; whereby the gates of hell were broken down, and the sanctuaries of Heaven opened? How shall we receive This with so great insolence? Let us not, I pray you, let us not slay ourselves by our irreverence, but with all awfulness and purity let us draw nigh to It; and when thou seest It set before thee, say thou to thyself, 'Because of this Body am I no longer earth and ashes, no longer a prisoner but free; because of This I hope for heaven, and to receive the good things therein, immortal life, the portion of angels, converse with Christ; this Body, nailed and scourged, was more than death could stand against; this Body the very sun saw crucified, and turned aside his beams; for This, both the veil was rent in that

[a] Ibid., § 3.　　　[b] *Hom.* lxxxii. § 5.　　　[c] Ibid., § 6.

M m

moment, and rocks were burst asunder, and all the earth was shaken. This is even that Body, the blood-stained, the smitten, out of which gushed the saving fountains, the one of blood, the other of water, for all the world[d].' " " And these things thou doest when thou hast enjoyed the Table of Christ, on that day on which thou hast been counted worthy to touch His Flesh with thy tongue. Whosoever thou art then, that those things be not so, do thou purify thy right hand, thy tongue, thy lips, which have become a threshold for Christ to tread upon[e]." " For it is in no common manner that our lips are honoured when they receive the Lord's Body[f]." " And then, thus scrupulous as thou art in this little matter, dost thou come with soiled soul, and thus dare to touch It? And yet the hands hold It but for a time, whereas into the soul It is received entirely[g]."

Council of Carthage (under Aurelius), A.D. 398 or 401 :—" That if need compel, the Deacon may, in the presence of the Presbyter, at his bidding, deliver to the people the Eucharist of the Body of Christ[h]."

Philo Carpasius, of Cyprus, A.D. 401 :—" These (the deacons) bear the Body of Christ and His Blood, the Head of the Church[i]."

Apostolical Constitutions, doubless a very ancient and authoritative work[j] :—" Those who bestow upon

---

[d] In 1 Cor. x. 16, *Hom.* xxiv. § 7. [e] *Hom.* xxvii. § 7.
[f] *Hom.* xxx., 2 Cor. xiii. 12. [g] On Ephes. i., *Hom.* iii.
[h] c. 38. [i] *In Cant.*, c. 37. [j] See Dr. Pusey on the Real Presence, pp. 605—8.

you the Saving Body and the Precious Blood[k]."
"Let the Deacons after the prayer, some attend exclusively to the offering of the Eucharist, ministering to the Lord's Body with fear[l]."

St. Cyril, of Alexandria:—"What is the cause and efficacy of the mystical Eucharist? Why do we receive It within us? Is it not that It may make Christ to dwell in us corporeally also by participation and communion of His Holy Flesh[m]." "We shut to the doors, and Christ appeareth to us all visibly and invisibly—invisibly as God, and visibly again in the Body, and He permitteth and giveth us to touch His Holy Flesh. For according to the grace of God, we approach to the participation of the mystical Eucharist, receiving Christ in our hands, that we too may firmly believe that He hath truly raised His own Temple[n]." "If any one should dare to say that the Word of God was transformed into the nature of the Body, one might very reasonably object to him, that He, on giving His Body, did not rather say, 'Take, eat, this is My Divinity which was broken for you,' and 'This is—not My Blood, but rather—My Divinity, which is shed for you.' But since the Word, being God, hath made the Body, born of a woman, His Own, without undergoing any alteration or change, how was it not right and true that He said to us, 'Take, eat, this is My Body?' For being Life, as God, He made it both Life and Life-giving[o]." "I hear that

---

[k] ii. 33.   [l] l. ii. c. 57.   [m] On St. John xv. 1, l. x. c. 2.
[n] Ibid., in xx. 16.   [o] *Adv. Nest.*, iv. 5. t. vi. pp. 118, 119.

they say that the mystic Eucharist is unavailing for blessing, if a portion of it remain to the next day. They are mad who say this. For Christ is not altered, nor shall His Holy Body be changed; but the power of the Eucharist and the life-giving grace is abiding in it [p]."

St. Isidore, of Pelusium:—"If our God and Saviour, being made Man, gave the Holy Ghost to be the completion of the Divine Trinity, both as being, in the invocation of Holy Baptism, numbered together with the Father and the Son as freeing from sins, and as, upon the Mystical Table, making the common bread the Very Body of His own Incarnation [q]," &c. "The fine linen that is spread out underneath the ministry of the Divine gifts, is the ministration of Joseph of Arimathea. For as he, having wrapped the Body of the Lord in fine linen, committed to the tomb that Body, through which our whole race has gained the fruit of the resurrection, so we, consecrating the shewbread upon fine linen, find undoubtedly the Body of Christ, gushing forth for us with that incorruptibility, which He whom Joseph attended to the tomb, the Saviour Jesus, rising from the dead bestowed [r]."

Theodotus, Bishop of Antioch, died A.D. 427:—"As the king himself and his image are not two kings, neither are the Very Personal Body of Christ, (αὐτὸ τὸ Χριστοῦ σῶμα τὸ ἐνυπόστατον), which is in heaven, and the Bread, the antitype thereof, dis-

[p] *Ep. ad Calosyr.*, t. vi. P. 2, p. 365.　　[q] l. i. *Ep.* 109, *ad Marathon.*, p. 34.　　[r] l. i. *Ep.* 123, p. 38.

tributed to the faithful by the priests in the churches, two bodies." Thus he asserts the identity of the Body of Christ in heaven and on the altar, and yet, in that he speaks of the antitypes, distinguishes the outward and inward parts.

Paulinus, the Deacon:—"Honoratus also, priest of the Church at Vercellæ, when he had laid himself down to rest in the upper part of the house, heard three times the voice of one calling him, and saying to him: 'Arise, make haste, for he is now about to depart.' He, going down stairs, offered to the Saint the Body of the Lord[s]."

Eusebius, of Alexandria:—"Be early then in the Church of God, approach the Lord, confess to Him thy sins, repent with prayer and a broken heart, abide during the Divine and Holy Eucharistic service, complete thy prayer, on no account leaving before the dismissal. Behold thy Lord, divided in pieces and distributed and not expended; and if thou hast thy conscience clean, approach and communicate of the Body and Blood[t]."

St. Maximus, of Turin:—"Fitly then, and as though for a sort of fellowship, was it appointed that the martyrs should be buried *there*, where the Lord's death is daily celebrated, as He Himself saith: 'As often as ye do this, ye do shew forth My death, till I come.' So should they who died for His Death rest under

---

[s] *Vita S. Ambrosii*, n. 47, *ap. S. Ambrosii* Opp. t. ii., App. p. xii.

[t] *Orat. de Die Dom. init.*, Gall. viii. 252, about A.D. 444.—See for an account of this Father, Dr. Pusey, Real Presence, pp. 449, 450.

the mystery of His Sacrament. Fitly, I say, and as though for a sort of fellowship, is the tomb of him who was slain placed *there*, where the Lord's slain Body is placed, that they whom the cause of one suffering had bound with Christ, the sanctity of one place might unite [u]."

Theodoret :—" Do not we, enjoying the holy Mysteries, communicate with the Lord Himself, whose Body and Blood we say they are? For we are all partakers of that one Bread. How can we communicate with the Lord through His precious Body and Blood, and again with devils through meat offered to idols [v] ?"

As the "meat offered to idols" is something orally received, "*through* which" idolaters communicated with devils, so, plainly by force of the contrast, " the Body and Blood" was orally received, "through which they communicated with Christ."

While Theodoret states, that "after the consecration the mystic symbols do not depart from their own nature, for they remain in their former *substance*, and figure, and form, and can be seen and touched as before [x];" he adds, "but in thought they are conceived, and believed, and adored as being those things which are believed [x]." Moreover, he distinctly says, " we call the mystic fruit of the vine, after the consecration, the Lord's Blood." . . . " Thou knowest that God hath called Bread His own Body [y]," assuredly not untruly nor unreally.

<hr>

[u] *Serm.* 73, *de Sanctis, præcip. S. Cyprian.*   [v] In 1 Cor. x. 16, 17,
iii. 228.   [x] *Dial.* ii. t. iv. p. 126, Sch.   [y] *Dial.* i., Ib. p. 25.

Theodotus, of Ancyra (he took a prominent part against Nestorius in the Council of Ephesus) :—" He who then drew the Magi with unspeakable might to holiness, hath now also to-day gathered together this joyous assembly : He, no longer laid in the manger, but lying on this saving Table. For that manger was the mother of this Table. For that cause did He lie in that [manger], that on this [table] He might be eaten, and might to the faithful become Saving Food [z]."

St. Peter Chrysologus :—" The woman touched His raiment, and was healed, and was freed from her long weakness. Wretched we, who daily handle and receive the Body of the Lord, and are not healed of our wounds [a]." " Let Christians, who daily touch the Body of Christ, hear how much medicine they can take from the Body Itself, when the woman seized all her health from the hem only of Christ [b]." " Himself is the Bread, which, sown in the Virgin, leavened in the Flesh, kneaded in His Passion, baked in the furnace of the Sepulchre, laid up in Churches, placed on the altars, provides heavenly Food daily for the faithful [c]." " He is Himself the Bread which cometh down from Heaven: . . . . which is daily brought to the Table of the Church for heavenly Food: which is broken for the forgiveness of sins, which feeds and nourishes them who eat It to life everlasting: this Bread we daily ask to be given to us, until we enjoy

---

[z] *Hom: in Nativ. Dom. in Conc. Eph.*, p. 3, c. 9.
[a] *Serm.* 33.　　[b] Ibid. 34.　　[c] Ibid. 67.

It wholly in that endless day [d]." " He transmitted
His Body to the Table of the Church, that It might
be heavenly Flesh for the nations to eat unto salvation [e]." " I grieve, truly do I grieve, when I see
that the Magi poured gold around the cradle of Christ,
and I see that Christians have left empty the Altar
of the Body of Christ [f]."

St. Proclus:—" By such prayers then they looked
for the descent of the Holy Ghost, that by His Divine
Presence, He might make and declare the Bread offered for sacrifice, and the wine mingled with water,
that very Body and Blood of our Saviour Jesus Christ;
which takes place no less even until now, and shall
take place unto the end of the world [g]."

St. Leo:—" Since the Lord says, 'Except ye eat the
Flesh of the Son of Man, and drink His Blood, ye
have no life in you,' ye ought so to communicate of
the holy Table as to doubt nothing of the truth of
the Body and Blood of Christ; for by the mouth is
that received which is by faith believed; and vainly
is Amen answered by them who dispute against what
they receive [h]." " They neither learn by hearing, nor
understand by reading, what in the Church of God
is so concordantly in the mouth of all, that not even
by tongues of babes is the truth of the Body and
Blood of Christ in the Sacrament of the Communion
passed over in silence [i]."

<hr>

[d] *Serm.* 71.   [e] *Ibid.* 95.   [f] *Ibid.* 103.   [g] *Tract. de
Tradit. Liturg. Div.*   [h] *Serm.* 91.   [i] *Ep.* lix. *ad Cler.
et. Pleb. Const.*, § 2.

St. Nilus:—"A leaf of paper made of papyrus and size, is called mere (ψιλὸς) paper, but when it receives the signature of the Emperor, it is (as is well known) called Sacra. So conceive with me also of the Divine Mysteries, that before the Intercession of the Priest, and the descent of the Holy Ghost, the oblations are *mere* (ψιλὸν) bread and *common* (κοινὸν) wine; but that, after those dread invocations, and the coming of the Adorable, Good, and Life-giving Spirit, the Oblations, laid on the Holy Table, are no more *mere* (ψιλὸν) bread and *common* (κοινὸν) wine, but the Precious and Immaculate Body and Blood of Christ, the God of all, 'purifying from all iniquity' those who communicate with fear and great longing[k]." "Then [the Angels] dispersed hither and thither over the whole holy House, co-operating, each of them, with the Bishops, Priests, and all the Deacons, there present, who were administering the Body and venerable Blood, they aided and strengthened them[l]." "Let us not approach to that Mystic Bread, as to *mere bread* (ψιλῷ ἄρτῳ). For It is the Flesh of God; Flesh Venerable, and Adorable, and Life-giving. For It quickens men dead in sins[m]."

St. James, of Sarug:—"From what time He took it [the bread] and called it His Body, it was not bread, but His Body, and they ate it, marvelling; eating His Body, and He lay with them at the table, and drinking His Blood, and hearing the

---

[k] l. i. *Ep.* 44.   [l] l. ii. *Ep.* 294.   [m] l. iii. *Ep.* 39.

voice of His teaching[n]." Again, on the Real Presence:—"Our Lord divided His Body with His own Hands at the table, and who dareth to say now that it was not His Body? He said, 'This is My Body,' and who averreth it not? If any aver it not, he is no disciple of the Apostolate. The Apostles averred it, and while He was alive, and lay at table with Him, they ate Him." He adds the reason:—"Faith stoops not to questionings. She knows how to accredit: to scrutinize she never learnt. The chosen disciples were anxious to hold true what the Son said; not, to scrutinize or ask as shameless ones. The bread which He brake, and called His Body, they knew to be His Body: and so they accounted it, as if in very deed its Blood were trickling[o]."

After stating the Supper of the Lord to be a Sacrament of our redemption by Christ's death, the Article proceeds, " Insomuch that to those who regularly, worthily, and with faith receive the same, the Bread which we break is a partaking of the Body of Christ."

Admitting the distinction of a Sacrament being generally necessary, *necessitate medii* and *necessitate præcepti*, and holding that the Holy Eucharist is thus necessary on the latter ground[p], it will be seen that to a beneficial reception, everything must be done which is necessary to secure on man's part the subjective appropriation of the work of Christ. If Christ

---

[n] *Serm.* 66, *de Pass. Dom.* in *Antirrhet.*, 2, cap. 9, p. 46, *S. Ephr. Opp. Syr.* t. ii.

[o] Ibid., c. 12, p. 50.   [p] *Lugo. De Euch., Dist.* iii. § 11.

on the cross be the Objective Atonement, Christ in the Holy Mysteries rightly, worthily, and with faith received is its subjective appropriation. The importance of these words cannot be exaggerated. First, the sacrament must be received *ritè*, all that the Church requires in the way of previous preparation of repentance, according to the present discipline of the Church, must be gone through. "Let a man examine himself, and so let him eat of that bread." He must interpose between his sins and the Holy Mysteries such means as the Church has laid down in different times, to secure a prosperous approach. This has varied in different times. The penitential Canons shew this in the early Church; in the modern Roman and Greek Church alike auricular confession is obligatory before Communion in case of every mortal sin; whereas the Anglican Church admits all on contrition, with the practice of confession in case of an unquiet conscience, and of consequent scruple or doubtfulness, viz. whether a person should or should not communicate.

And next it must be received *dignè*. This applies to the inward disposition of the heart. Not till a man is really contrite for his sins is he justified in approaching the Lord's Body. Confession and absolution without a hearty sorrow for sin, springing, at least, from detestation of its foulness, will not avail to destroy the past. We must repent for the love of Jesus, because we have offended the kindest and tenderest of friends, the Spouse and Lover of our immortal souls. Charity is the form of contrition. The supernatural love of

God is that which gives life to the sorrow for the past, which otherwise would work death, as the Apostle bears witness. Hence true sorrow for sin is lifelong, and hence, in spite of the fullest faith in the ordinances of grace and the fulfilment of the Lord's promises, the cry of the penitent Christian is still "Amplius lava me ab iniquitate meâ," and he dies crying to his Master, "Dimitte nobis debita nostra."

The question of "with faith" shall be treated more at length as we proceed in considering the Article.

The doctrine of the real objective Presence being certainly true, as being contained in our Blessed Lord's own words, "This is My Body;" and attested by the whole Christian Church from the times of the Apostles [q], it follows that some sort of change must have taken place as to the elements through consecration. "Before," as St. Athanasius says, "bare ($\psi\iota\lambda\grave{o}s$) is the Bread and the Cup; but, upon consecration, the Bread becometh the Body; the Cup, the Blood of our Lord Jesus Christ [r]."

This change was, in the oldest time, expressed by the simplest terms [s]; "It is," "It becomes;" or, in prayer to God, "consecrate," "perfect," "appoint," "make [s]." The Liturgy of St. Chrysostom, and others following him, use the words, "changing by Thy Spirit." There are also other more emphatic, yet

---

[q] See Dr. Pusey, "The Real Presence of the Body and Blood of our Lord Jesus Christ the Doctrine of the English Church;" and "The Defence of the Bishop of Brechin."

[r] See above, p. 509.   [s] See Dr. Pusey, pp. 252—254.

rare words, occurring once or twice only in each father who used them, "transmake," "transelement," "transfashion," "re-order," "transfigure," "transfer [t]."

Against any of these, the English Church has never made any exception; but only to a specified sense of the word "transubstantiate," which is popularly taken, not as implying a change in the οὐσία, or "essence," of a material thing, but the desition of the material substances of which that creature of God is composed. The word, "substance," "substantially," came to have stress laid upon it through the heresy of Berenger. That talented, bountiful, but vain-glorious and dishonest man, used the terms of the Church in an unreal sense. He made no difficulty in professing that "the Bread of the Altar, after consecration, is the very Body of Christ, which was born of the Virgin, which suffered on the Cross, which sitteth at the right hand of the Father; and the Wine of the Altar, after it is consecrated, is the true Blood, which flowed from the side of Christ [u]." But he meant, (as he explains him-

---

[t] μεταποιέω, once by St. Gregory of Nyssa, and once by Theodoret, trans'ating St. Ambrose; μεταστοιχειόω once in the same passage of St. Greg. Nyss.; μεταρρυθμίζω and μετασκευάζω, each once by St. Chrysostom; "transfiguro" twice by St. Ambrose; "transfero" in the Gallican Sacramentary.

[u] This was in the Council of Lateran, 1078. (See Martene and Durand, *Thes. Nov. Anecd.*, iv. 103.) Berenger states that the confession was accepted by Gregory VI., as clearing him from heresy at a convention of Bishops, on All Saints' Day [A.D. 1078]; that in a Council in the following Lent this amended form was substituted: "I believe in my heart and confess with my mouth, that the Bread and Wine, which are placed on the Altar, are, by the mystery of holy prayer and by the words of our Redeemer, substantially converted into

self,) only by representation [x]; he assailed impetuously
the belief, that the Body of Christ, which is at the

the true and proper and life-giving Body and Blood of Jesus Christ
our Lord; and are, after consecration, the true Body of Christ, which
was born of a Virgin, and which, offered for the salvation of the world,
hung upon the Cross, and which sitteth on the right hand of the
Father, and the true Blood of Christ, which was shed from His side, not
only by the sign and virtue of the Sacrament, but in its own proper nature, and the truth of its substance." (Ib. 104.) Berenger, after explaining these words away in his own fashion, says that he declined accepting them as an exposition of his meaning, understanding that the Pope
was satisfied with his own statement, but that finding he was required
to own, and "did own, prostrate on the ground, that" he "had up
to that time erred, in that when" he "said of the sacrifice of the
Church, that 'the Bread and Wine consecrated on the altar are the
Body and Blood of Christ,'" he "had not added, 'substantially.'"
This he recanted.　(Ib., pp. 108, 109.)

[x] The following statements, from his second answer to Lanfranc,
are pure Calvinism, but they agree with what Lanfranc says of him at
an earlier period :—" Not seen are the Body and Blood of Christ, which
are laid up in heaven, because if before the time of the restitution of all
things thou layest down that the Flesh of Christ can, (I say not, be seen
by the bodily eyes,) but be anywhere upon the earth, thou dost against
the prophecy of David, against the Apostle Peter, against his co-Apostle
Paul, against all authentic Scripture.　But thou dost lay down, that
the Flesh of Christ, being called down (*devocatam*), is, before the time
of the restitution of all things, present, when thou assertest that the
faithful receive nothing else from the altar except the Flesh and Blood
of Christ (*sensualiter*), which is so against the grounds of faith, that none
of the faithful ought to think that he receives to the refreshment of his
soul ought save the Flesh of his Lord God, whole and entire.　Yet not
called down from heaven, but *abiding in heaven*, which no reason
allows to take place by the mouth of the body; but that it should be
done by that most enlarged devotion of the heart, cleansed to see God,
is hindered by no indignity, by no difficulties; to which, i.e. to the
devotion of the heart, to the gaze of the soul, St. Ambrose necessarily
draws you, (will you, nill you,) in the book wherein he exhorts to
receive the Sacrament of the altar." (Bereng. *de S. Cœna adv. Lanfr.*,
pp. 157, 158, ed. Neander.)

right hand of God, is brought down thence so as to be present here ?. He rejects contemptuously the belief of

"Christ the Lord requires of thee, that thou shouldest believe that by His most pitying love towards the human race, it was wrought that He shed His Blood, and, *by so believing*, shouldest wash thee from all sin by His Blood (*sanguine* for *sanguinem*); He requires that, *having ever in memory that same Blood of Christ*, thou shouldest place the life of thy inner self in it, as a *viaticum* to accomplish the journey of this life, as thou settest the life of thy outer self in external food and drink." Then, after speaking of Baptism, "He requires that *through the bodily eating and drinking*, which takes place through the outward things, the bread and wine, *thou admonish thyself of the spiritual eating and drinking, which takes place in the mind* from the Body and Blood of Christ, while thou refreshest thyself in thy inner self with the Incarnation and Passion of the Lord, that according to the humility whereby the Word was made Flesh, and the patience whereby He shed His Blood, thou form the life of thy inner self with what humility thou oughtest, be eminent in what patience thou oughtest, that thou acquiesce in them, rejoice in them, as, in thy outer self, thou acquiescest in thy food and drink. For thou hast no reason to shrink from eating bread and drinking wine, because it is, as St. Ambrose says in this very treatise on the Sacraments, 'a wonted and known creature.' But making an inference from the washing, which takes place in regeneration through the Blood of Christ, in the refreshment of the altar, he says, as thou hast received the likeness of death, so thou drinkest the likeness of His precious Blood." (Ibid., pp. 222, 223.) Lanfranc had charged him with this, in his answer to the recantation of the confession, to which he swore at the Council of Rome :—"Thou holdest that the bread and wine of the Lord's table, at the consecration, remain, as to the substance, immoveable. That is, that they were bread and wine before consecration, and are bread and wine after consecration, and that they are therefore called the Flesh and Blood of Christ, because they are celebrated in the Church in memory of the crucified Flesh, and of the Blood shed from His side, that we, *being thereby admonished, may ever have in mind* the Passion of the Lord, and, so bearing it in mind, may unceasingly crucify our flesh with its vices and affections." Lanfranc well adds, "If these things be true, the Sacraments of the Jews were better and Diviner than the Sacraments of Christians." (B. P. xviii. 775, fin.)

? See in note x. He had said in his former book, "Who can either

Lanfranc in an actual substantial Presence, which he repeatedly calls by a scoffing term, (of which he knew that it did not express that belief,) " portiuncula carnis et sanguinis[z]." The term " substantialiter," which he complains of being required to add to his confession at the Synod at Rome, was necessary to prevent evasion, in that he confessed that the Bread

conceive by reason, or grant that by miracle it could come to pass, that bread is broken in the Body of Christ, which [Body], after the Resurrection, is perfect with entire incorruptibility, and, unto the time of the restitution of all things, remains in heaven *indevocable*." (B. P. xviii. 770, *in Lanfr. de Corp. Dom.*, c. 17.) Lanfranc answers, " As to this, that thou opposest the incorruption of the Lord's Body, and that, until the Day of Judgment, it cannot be called down (*devocari*) from heaven, as a ground of impossibility to our faith, whereby we believe that He is truly eaten by His faithful, thou either dost not understand our faith, or understanding it, strivest, by expounding it amiss, to deprave it to thy own destruction. For we in such wise believe that our Lord Jesus Christ is truly and healthfully eaten by those who receive worthily, as to hold most assuredly that He exists in the heavenly places, undefiled, uncorrupt, uninjured."

[z] The phrase occurs so often in his second book against Lanfranc, as evidently to have been a favourite term of reproach with him. He uses it also twice in his answer to Adelmann: " Mine, or rather the cause of the Scriptures, stood thus, that the Bread and Wine of the Lord's table, is not *sensualiter*, in a way cognisable by the senses, but intellectually, not by absumption, but by assumption, is changed, not into a *portiuncula carnis* against the Scriptures, but, according to the Scriptures, into the whole Body and Blood of Christ." And " it is not the opinion but the insanity of Paschasius and the vulgar, that in the altars a *portiuncula* of the Flesh of the Lord is now, too, broken with the hands, is now, too, crushed by the teeth of the outer man." (*Epist. Purgator. c. Almann in Martene and Durand. Thes. Nov.*, t. iv. p. 111.) His meaning under the term *portiuncula* must be, that whereas, according to his own opinion, he fed on Christ whole and entire, at the right hand of God, only a *portiuncula* of His Body and Blood could be present under the consecrated species. He calls it "*particula carnis Christi.*" (Ib.)

and Wine were the Body and Blood of Christ, but only as reminding us of them. It was the conviction of his contemporaries that this was his heresy [a], and the

[a] Adelmann states to Berenger what was said of him, both in Italy and Germany, that he seemed to think "of the Body and Blood of Christ, immolated daily on the holy Altars throughout the earth, otherwise than the Catholic faith holds; viz., (to use their words of thee) that there is neither true Body of Christ nor true Blood, but a certain figure and similitude." (*Ep. ad Bereng.*, B. P. xviii. 438.) Berenger, in his answer, evades this by saying that he "was never a Manichæan; i.e. that he believed that the Body of Christ was true and human." He adds, "When I grant that anything is given [*dari*, Mab.] to become the Body of Christ, then, since Christ had only a true Body, I must grant that it becomes the true Body of Christ. But I grant that the Bread and Wine of the Altar, after consecration, become, according to the Scriptures, the Body and Blood of Christ; and therewith I cannot but grant that the Bread and Wine are made *to faith and intellect* the true Body and Blood of Christ." Distinguishing the *res sacramentorum* from the *sacramenta*, he says :—"it is true nevertheless that the true Body of Christ is set forth on the very Table, *but spiritually true to the inner man;* that in it [the Table] the Body of Christ is spiritually eaten uncorrupted, uncontaminated, unattrite, by those only who are members of Christ." (*Epist. Purg. c. Almann.*, p. 110.) See also ab. note x. Hugo, Bishop of Langres, writes to him, "Thou sayest, speaking too largely, 'In this Sacrament the Body of Christ is in such wise, that the nature and essence of the Bread and Wine is not changed,' and thou makest the Body, which thou hadst said was crucified, intellectual, wherein it is most evident that thou confessest it incorporeal." (*Tract. de corp. et sang. Christi cont. Berengar.*, B.P. xviii. 417.) Abbot Durand treats the explanation of the Berengarians as mere colouring of their heresy. [Satan] "has persuaded some to think, and with cunning whispers to convey to others, that nothing in the Sacraments of the Lord is done according to truth, but rather that everything is enacted in figure and likeness. Who, cunningly to free themselves of the suspicion of heresy, and to shew their agreement with the Lord's teaching, cloak themselves with this cunning act, and so, tampering, colour their dogma of profane novelty, as to say that the Bread and Wine, which are brought to the altar, after consecration too, remain what they had been, and so are, in a manner, the Body and true Blood of Christ, *not*

Catechism of the Council of Trent says, that the cor-

naturally, but figuratively. But if this great perverseness be anywise
admitted, that in the mysteries of the Lord there be believed to *be no
truth, but a shadowy falsehood is alone* maintained, what remains but
that the whole teaching of the Christian profession perish ?" (*De corp.
et sang. Dom.*, P. i., Bibl. P. xviii. 420.) "God forbid that we should
be joined in like faithlessness with men so perverted, and from the
truth itself averted, and in the Holy Communion of the Lord's Body
and Blood, we should confess aught less than the Catholic Church
throughout the whole world preaches ; *in which there is, in truth, as
true Flesh of Christ and true Blood* as Christ Himself is truthful,
Who first sanctified them, and gave to His own thereafter the authority and form of sanctifying them by His own power." (Ib., P. ii. p. 421).
" It being understood that thou didst extol John Scot [Erigena], con-
demnest Paschasius, holdest things contrary to the common faith of the
Church, a sentence of condemnation was promulgated against thee,
depriving thee of the communion of the Holy Church, which thou
busiedst thyself to deprive of its Holy Communion." (Lanfranc (to
Berenger) *de corp. et sang. Dom.*, c. 3, B. P. xviii. 765.) "Berenger, of
Angers, formed a heresy after his own name, and contrary to Evangelic
truth, *presumed to deny the truth of the Body and Blood of the Lord ;*
asserting that, in the sacrifice of the Lord, the Bread and Wine are not
really or essentially, but *figuratively* only, converted into the Body and
Blood of the Lord. Pope St. Leo IX. then diligently examined the heresy
by the general judgment of a synod, and, after examination, condemned
it by a synodal judgment. Berenger himself he deprived of the communion of the Church, which he by his assertions wished to deprive of
the communion of the Lord's Body and Blood. Then he summoned
him to be heard at the then approaching synod, to be held on the next
September at Vercellæ. The Apostolicus by synodal judgment condemned
the opinion of Berenger, and the book of John Scotus on the Body of
the Lord, under anathema, and confirmed the faith, which all Catholics
have hitherto had and still have, of *the truth of the Body and Blood of
the Lord.*" "At the General Synod at Tours, Berenger anathematized
under oath his own heresy, and under the same oath promised that he
would thenceforth keep the common faith of the holy Church, as *to the
truth of the Body and Blood of the Lord.*" (*Auct. de Berengarii
damnatione multiplici* (written A.D. 1088, the year of Berenger's death)
in Conc. xi. 1425, ed. Col.) Of the Joannes Scotus, whom Berenger

rection of this error was the object of the definition of

professed himself ready to vindicate, Ascalinus says that he argued vehemently against the Real Presence. "I see that John Scotus strains with every nerve and his whole intent to this alone, viz., that this which is consecrated on the Altar is neither truly the Body nor truly the Blood of Christ. This he endeavours to establish from works of the Fathers, which he explains perversely : as the prayer of St. Gregory, 'Let Thy Sacraments, O Lord, perfect in us what they contain, that what we act in figure, we may receive in real truth.' In expounding this the aforesaid John, among other things contrary to the faith, says, ' these things are done in (specie) appearance, not in truth.'" Theodosius, in his letter to Henry I. of France, states the heresy to be that they [Bruno, Bishop of Angers, and Berenger, of Tours] maintain that the Body of the Lord is not so much a body as a figure and shadow of the Lord's Body. (*Conc.* xi. 1437, Col.) Guitmund alone says that some of his disciples ascribed to him "impanation." In answer to Roger, who mentions the common belief, "Berenger and those who follow him assert that the Eucharist of the Lord is not truly and substantially the Body and Blood of the Lord, but is only called so, because it is a sort of shadow and figure significant of the Body and Blood of the Lord," Guitmund says, that as far as he could extract from some Berengarians, "some say that there was nothing whatever of the Body and Blood of the Lord in that Sacrament, but that they are only shadows and figures. But some, ceding to the right reasons of the Church, yet not receding from their folly, that they may seem to be in some measure with us, say that the Body and Blood of the Lord are there really contained but in a hidden way, and that they may be received, are (so to speak) impanated. And this *they say* is the more subtle mind of Berengarius himself." (*De corp. et sang. Christi veritate in Euch.*, L. i. B. P. xviii. 441.) Undoubtedly Berenger often veiled his attack on the doctrine of the Real Presence, under the semblance of an attack on the belief that that which decayed was the Body of Christ. The then belief of some (e.g. of Guitmund himself) that the Holy Eucharist did not nourish, and that the consecrated elements never decay (Guitmund, ib., L. ii.), which the Roman Church has abandoned, gave him an advantage in this respect, in that some of his opponents shrunk back from an evident truth. But no one, I think, who knows Berenger's utter dishonesty, can doubt that this was but a veil of his real attack. The expression, too, of horror at his blas-

the Council of Lateran [b]. And, accordingly, the Canon uses the word, "is transubstantiated," but the whole stress is on the Real Presence. "[c] The Same is the Priest and the Sacrifice, Jesus Christ, Whose Body and Blood in the Sacrament of the Altar *are truly contained under the species of Bread and Wine;* the Bread being transubstantiated into the Body, and the Wine into His Blood, that for the perfecting of the mystery of unity, *we may receive of His, what He received of ours* [Flesh and Blood]." In the writings against Berenger, " truly" and " essentially" are used as equivalent to " substantially [d]."

Lanfranc, when appealing against Berenger to the

phemies (See *Conc. Brion. Conc.* xi. 1430, *Conc. Paris.*, ib., 1436) is not likely to have been elicited, had there been a reverent acknowledgment of the Real Presence.

[b] " Another means remains by which we may investigate the judgment of the Church on matters of faith, viz., the condemnation of the contrary doctrine and opinion : but it is a known fact that so universally diffused and disseminated throughout the Universal Church at all times, and so unanimously received by all the faithful, was the belief of the Real Presence of Christ's Body in the Holy Sacrament of the Eucharist, that when, five hundred years since, Berengarius dared to deny it, asserting that it was only a sign of Christ's Body, he having been promptly condemned by the unanimous voice of the Council of Vercellæ, convoked by the authority of Leo IX., anathematized his heresy ; subsequently returning to the same impious madness, was condemned by three other Councils, one held at Tours, the other two at Rome, of which latter two, one was convened by Nicholas II., the other by Gregory VII.; the same sentence was afterwards confirmed by Innocent III. in the great Council of Lateran ; and the faith of the same truth was subsequently more openly declared and established by the Councils of Florence and Trent." (*Cat. Rom.*, p. ii. c. 4, qu. 29.)

[c] *Conc. Lat.*, iv. can. 1.   [d] See above, note a.

faith of the Church throughout the world, uses no other language than we should use now. What he affirms of Latins, Greeks, Armenians, and all who are called Christians, he might have affirmed of us now. "If that is true which thou believest and supportest as to the Body of Christ, false is that which is believed and supported thereon by the Church throughout the world. For all who rejoice in being, and being called, Christians, glory that they receive in this Sacrament the true Flesh of Christ and His true Blood, both taken from the Virgin. Ask all who have received any knowledge of the Latin language and of our letters. Ask Greeks, Armenians, or any Christians whatsoever, of whatsoever nation,—they attest with one mouth, that this is their faith [e]."

It is self-evident that the English Article does not go directly against the Council of Lateran: (1.) because the term "transubstantiato" is a subordinate part of the Lateran Canon; (2.) because, (as we shall

---

[e] *Adv. Bereng.*, c. 22, B. P. xviii. 776. In like way we should all subscribe to Ascalin's protest to Berenger: "With Paschasius and other Catholics, I am not only minded, but with veneration I receive that the Very Body and Very Blood are taken by the faithful on the Altar under the species of Bread and Wine." (*Epist. ad Bereng. in Conc.* xi. 1434, Col.) Again, "We ought not to wonder or doubt that God can effect, that this which is consecrated on the Altar, is by the virtue of God the Holy Ghost, and the ministry of the Priest, united to that Body, which our Redeemer took of the Virgin Mary, (since each is a corporeal substance, each is visible,) if we remember that we ourselves are compacted of a corporeal and incorporeal, of a mortal and immortal substance; if, lastly, we firmly believe that the Divine and Human Nature met in One Person. Let dust and ashes unfold to me the explanation of the first and second, and then let it think that it suffices to make clear the first." (Ib., 1435.)

see hereafter) even of the statement in which it occurs, our Article does not even touch upon the most important part, the change "*into* the substance of the Body and Blood of Christ;" (3.) because there is ground to think that two entirely distinct meanings, and those not having the slightest bearing upon one another, have been given to the word "substance."

The solution of what difficulty remains will be found in the meaning attached to that word. Does the word mean natural substance? the component parts, the constitutive principles which chemistry makes known to us, or is it the subtle essence, subsistence, the *οὐσία*, which corresponds to personality in men and angels? This can only be determined by a comparison of the Article with other documents of the Church, and with the context of the Article itself.

I. The other document of the Church in which the doctrine of Transubstantiation is treated of is the Black Rubric at the end of the Communion Service, the history of which forms a significant commentary on our exposition.

It is well known that a declaration in form like this, but containing a mighty and vital difference, was, without the consent of the Church, and apparently without any authority but that of the Privy Council, appended to King Edward's Second Book. It had apparently been discussed among the bishops, and no determination come to, and at last, before publication, it was put out and bound up with that edition of the Prayer-book.

It disappeared from the Prayer-book of Queen Elizabeth, and was not taken in by King James.

At the last revisal in Charles the Second's time, to meet as far as possible the scruples of the Puritans, on their petition, it was agreed[1] that the Declaration should be for the first time assumed into the Prayer-book by competent authority as we should now hold, but a total and radical change was made before it was deemed orthodox and admissible. The courtiers of King Edward had denied that there was any "real or essential presence there being of Christ's natural flesh and blood." The divines of King Charles could not assent to this, so they altered the words, into "any corporal presence of Christ's natural flesh and blood." The emphatic word here is "corporal," which is a very different thing. Real or essential implies the *quidditas* or *substantia* of the Schoolmen; corporal, one of the qualities of the same.

Now in this document we find that it is not the metaphysical οὐσία that we are concerned with, but the natural substance. "The Sacramental Bread and Wine remain still in their very natural substances." Natural substance here is equivalent to the φύσις, or *natura*, of Pope Gelasius and Theodoret.

II. The context of the Article further confirms this interpretation.

Four results are said to spring from it. Four concomitants are in the tenor of the Article said to attend

[1] Cardwell's Confer., p. 322.

upon Transubstantiation.   1. That it cannot be proved by Holy Writ; 2. that it is repugnant to the plain words of Scripture; 3. that it overthroweth the nature of a Sacrament; 4. that it has given occasion to superstition.

1. and 2. Now it is perfectly clear, that so far from the μεταβολή in the Holy Sacrament being improbable on the grounds of the letter of Scripture, it is the sacramental theory which comes nearest to that letter; for our Lord did not say, ' This is joined with My Body,' or 'this signifies My Body,' or ' this represents My Body,' or ' this has the power and efficacy of My Body,' but "This is My Body."   It is evident that the letter of Holy Bible alludes to a deep inward mysterious change, whereby what was bread is called, and is, Christ's Body.

" The Bread and the Wine is not τύπος of the Body and Blood of Christ.   God forbid.   But it is the very (αὐτὸ) deified Body of that very (αὐτοῦ) Lord, who said, This is of Me, not the type of the Body, but the Body, and not the type of the Blood, but the Blood[f]."

Yet the plain words of Scripture, in that they freely use the word "bread" to describe the Blessed Sacrament after consecration, go against the desition of the *signum* therein.

3. The Article does not charge Transubstantiation with the common incorrect argument that it contra-

[f] St. John Dam., *Orth. fid.*, l. iv. c. 13.

dicts the senses, but that it overthrows the nature of a Sacrament. Now this greatly helps us in our view that it is not the abstract theory of a change, but the incorrect physics which are condemned. Such a change only is excepted against, as would involve a physical desition of what before existed in such wise, that the visible sign of That which is invisible should have no real existence.

There is no argument so strong against this abuse of the Scholastic theory of Transubstantiation as the natural one, connected with the thought of its destroying the nature of a Sacrament, derived from the controversies of the fifth century with regard to the Natures and Person of our Lord. The Monophysite heretics wished to teach that our Lord's Body was now changed into a Divine substance, and they illustrated it by the supernatural change of the sacramental symbols. This was met in the face by Orthodoxus:— " You are taken in the net which you have woven; the mystic symbols do not, after consecration, depart from their own nature; they continue in the former essence and shape, and are visible and palpable as before; but in thought they are conceived, and believed, and adored, as being those things which are the objects of faith [h]."

The same assertion is made by Pope Gelasius in his treatise *De Duabus Naturis*, a tractate which, though doubted by some Roman theologians, is quoted by St. Fulgentius only nine years after its publication,

[h] Theodoret, Eranistes.

and therefore must be genuine. An indirect argument
like this stands on the ground of circumstantial evidence, which, though hardly a safe guide where none
other exists, adds indefinitely to certainty when it
operates in confirming direct testimony. Granting
the existence of that whole class of authors who
admit that in the Holy Eucharist there is an earthly
and a heavenly nature, this incidental argument comes
in with tremendous power, nothing having been less
in the mind of the authors at the time, than to make
any declaration on the subject, so vexed in after times,
i.e. the desition of the *signum* in the Holy Eucharist.

And yet if this analogy is quoted for the continued
existence of the *signum*, it is only just that it should
be extended to that which is supplied by the similitude
of the entire doctrine of the Incarnation. Given that
our Lord exists in two natures, there is but one Divine
personality which determines the mode of existence of
those natures. Analogically, therefore, given that the
two natures remain in the Blessed Sacrament, the personal existence of it must be Divine, and therefore the
soul will not rest in the outward sign, but will rise to
the thought of the Thing signified, and dwell therein
by faith and loving contemplation. It is as a result of
this that the Fathers, when they speak of the Holy
Sacrament, speak of it only by the name of the inward part.

4. The last assertion is that the coarse view of Transubstantiation has given rise to many superstitions.
This goes very much to enforce what has been said

above. People would not have asserted that any honour was superstitious which was paid to the Presence of our Lord in the Sacrament, but they would say that it was superstitious to use the blessed Sacrament for purposes for which it never was intended, and which have never been sanctioned by the Church; for example, it would be superstitious to bury the Sacrament with the dead, or to mix It with ink for the purpose of signing the condemnation of a heretic, as was done in the case of the Synod of Rome in 648, in the matter of the Monothelites.

Again, it would not be superstitious to believe, that as in the case at Bolsena, (assuming the circumstance to be true,) our Lord attested the truth of His presence in the Sacrament by an appearance of blood; but it would be superstitious to believe that that appearance was physical, that it was our Lord's Blood, and as such be received. And so, it would be superstitious to believe that those appearances of Christ as a little child in the Sacrament, which have from time to time been vouchsafed to God's servants, was the actual body of our Lord in its natural condition.

All that the letter of the Article denies, is that by virtue of the words of consecration such a change takes place in the proportions and conditions of the elemental substances now mentioned, that the same component parts which before made up the forces of bread, now make those of flesh and blood. This is not the case even as to human food. Bread and Wine are commuted into flesh and blood; but the same physical component parts are not present in each[1]. Much less have we any occasion to think of anything so earthly, under the name "substance," i.e. "essence" of Bread and Wine, since it is confessed on all hands that "our Saviour Himself ever sitteth at the Right Hand of the Father in heaven, according to His natural mode of existence," while He is "sacramentally present with us by His own substance," not in any carnal way, but "by that mode of existing, which although we can hardly express in words, we may, through thought illumined by faith, understand to be possible to God[k]."

And here it is of moment to draw attention to another important change in our present Article. Bishop Gheast, who said of the Article, "that it was of mine owne pennynge," (that is, obviously so much of it as was new in the final revision), caused to be struck out all mention of the *terminus ad quem*, i.e. "into the

---

[1] The following analysis of the component parts of wheat, flesh, and blood, has been furnished to me by an eminent physiologist :—

	Wheat.	Flesh.	Blood.
Oxygen	43·40	21·39	21·43
Hydrogen	5·80	7·57	7·17
Carbon	46·10	51·83	51·95
Nitrogen	2·29	15·01	15·07
Sulphur	0·03	0·03	0·05
Phosp. Lime and Magnesia	1·06	0·64	0·29
Pot. and Soda, (Phosp., &c.)	0·75 (potass)	3·09	1·17
Chlor. Soda	(Salt in bread)	0·44	2·40
Iron (Ox. and Phosp.)	(?) occasional	(?)	0·47
Silicon	0.03 accidental from husks.		0·00
	100·00	100·00	100·00

[k] *Conc. Trid.*, Sess. xiii. c. 1.

substance of Christ's Body and Blood;" and restricted the rejection of the word Transubstantiation to the *terminus a quo,* "the change of the substance of the Bread and Wine." This alteration is much stronger than if the words which he omitted had never stood; for the omission was a deliberate act. It shews evidently that of the former complex explanation "the change of the substance of bread and wine into the substance of Christ's Body and Blood," the only point excepted against was a change in the substance of Bread and Wine.

It remains to consider what the Article means as to this, which alone remains as a difficulty.

Substanti*a* is manifestly, by the force of term, some one thing. It concerns us not so far, whether it be material or immaterial; only it may be observed that we do not know what matter itself is. Chemistry, whose employment is the analysis of the compound objects of which our senses are cognisant, has (at least as represented by one of its most eminent discoverers [1]) set aside the idea that matter is compounded of atoms. He says, "To my mind *a,* or the nucleus, vanishes, and the substance consists of the powers, or *m.* And, indeed, what notion can we form of the nucleus, independent of its powers? All our perception and knowledge of the atom, and even our fancy, is limited to the ideas of its powers. What thought remains, on which to hang the imagination of an *a,* independent

---

[1] Professor Faraday, in a paper on the Nature of Matter, in the "Philosophical Magazine," Feb., 1844, p. 141.

of the acknowledged forces. Now the powers we know and recognise in every phenomenon of the creation, the abstract matter in none; why, then, assume the existence of that, of which we are ignorant, which we cannot conceive, and for which there is no philosophical necessity ?"

All which we know of are certain "forces." What is the unity which holds them together we know not. But one thing cannot, at the same time and in the same sense, be many things. The substantia of bread and wine cannot be what we mean by the physical substances, i.e. all those component parts which are united in it. This is but to say that we use a singular and a plural in different senses. Every crumb of a piece of bread would, if detached, have its own substantia; but also every crumb of a piece of bread would have in it all those things which the whole has—oxygen, hydrogen, nitrogen, &c. And the component parts, or, as as we popularly call them, substances, cannot be the same as substance. "Substance" is something beyond them. St. Thomas says that "substance is discerned by the intellect alone, and not by sense." But these component parts of bread may, by analysis, be made discernible by sense. Now what those who, believing our blessed Lord's Presence in the Sacrament of the Altar, alone desiderate, is, not to be required to believe what, in things of which the senses are cognisant, would contradict them. The Catechism of the Council of Trent meets these difficulties by saying, that " the Eucharist is, after consecration, called bread, because it has the appearance, and still *retains* the quality, *natural* to bread, of supporting and nourishing the body[m]. It says that this natural quality is *retained*, not that it is restored by the creation of fresh materia, or by the bringing back of the old miraculously, or by any other miracle, which the explanations of the Schoolmen presupposed. All Christians must believe any miracle which comes to them by authority. But no authority is alleged for these. They are only opinions of the Schoolmen, and those, mutually contradictory. This "natural power of nourishing," of which our senses are cognisant, is the only remaining property of natural substances, which the Anglican formularies can include, when they speak of the "bread and wine remaining in their natural substances," i.e. that they have all the characteristic properties which our senses can discern. Those formularies do not refer to any abstract questions about "substance."

But now even natural philosophy comes in to our aid. It is pretty well agreed that material bodies consist of a number of unextended forces. "Some of these forces are permanent, others are visible; for while the substance remains the same, the phenomena are perpetually varying. Each body, therefore, may be considered to be a collection of changeable forces, resulting from the activity of a great substantial force. It is evident that the shifting forces may be looked upon as qualities, emanating and radiating from a central force, which is the permanent source of them

[m] P. ii. c. 4, q. 38.

all, and which is the substance. It is also clearly conceivable, that *these forces should remain* after the central force or substance is gone [n]."

Now this is just the distinction which was needed. We do not at all understand what the *οὐσία* or *substantia* of anything is. We can conceive *that* it is, not *what* it is. It seems, according to these last explanations, to be *that*, which constitutes a thing what it is, that which lies at the bottom of its being. It is deeper and more recondite than anything which affects our senses, even than those forces which "naturally support and nourish our bodies." If this be so, the question is at an end. There is but one belief as to the presence of Christ, that He, "our Saviour, Who now sitteth at the right hand of the Father in heaven according to His natural mode of existence, is yet present to us by His substance sacramentally [o]." The question has relation only to the Bread and Wine, what the Roman Church means by the "substanti*a*" which it affirms to cease to remain, and we by the "substanc*es*" which we affirm to remain. If "substance" means no more than its Greek equivalent, *οὐσία*, "essence;" and if the term, "is transubstantiated," means no more than those old words, "becomes," "is;" and if, by it, the Roman Church only means to guard with greater accuracy our blessed Lord's words, "This is My Body," not contradicting anything which we know by experience, not basing a theology upon a supposed illusion of our

[n] Dalgairns, "The Holy Communion," App., note F., p. 423.
[o] *Conc. Trid.*, l. c.

senses, but only asserting that that "quidditas" (whatever it be) whereby the bread was bread, is removed, leaving all those forces of which alone we are cognisant, then, God be thanked, Who has said to a great mountain which stood between us, "Be thou a plain." There is nothing in such a statement which our Article denies, or which could form a difficulty to any soul, which believed the blessed Presence of our Saviour, of His Body and His Blood.

"The Body of Christ is given, taken, and eaten, in the Supper, only after an heavenly and spiritual manner." One cannot exaggerate the importance of the words *given, taken,* and *eaten.* "The Body of Christ,"—observe how completely the Article adopts the old nomenclature; it does not say the Sacrament of the Body of Christ, but *Corpus Christi,* the Body of Christ, shewing that what was in a partial way described in the beginning of the Article, from its effects as a partaking of the Body, is objectively the Body itself. "The Body of Christ" is first *given,* that is, by the Priest, or rather by the Great High-Priest, through the ministry of His earthly representative. It is next *taken,* first into the hand of the communicant, therefore the Body is something external to him who takes it; it is objective and independent of anything in him. It is Christ's Body before he takes it. It is given to him in what the Priest gives him, and that, the Article says, is the Body of Christ. The heavenly and spiritual manner applies equally to all the three. It is given in a heavenly and spiritual manner, for the

whole action is supernatural. It is taken in a heavenly
and spiritual manner, for we have here to do with the
order of grace, not the order of nature. It is eaten
after a heavenly and spiritual manner, for " It is the
Spirit that quickeneth, the flesh profiteth nothing."
The explanation of the term "only," is best left to its
author, Bishop Geste.

Yet once more, the words, " The Body of Christ
is given, taken, and eaten, only after a spiritual and
heavenly manner," contain the doctrine of an Objective Presence. For it is said not only given and received, which might imply something which takes
place within the soul only, but given, *taken*, and eaten,
which implies an external act on the part of the person
receiving. The "taking" and "eating" are two distinct acts q.

q It is vain to say, as some have said, that this has no force. The
very arguments used to disprove its force add to it. It has been said
(and these are the strongest cases which they can produce) that even
Calvin says, " Nihil dubito quin et Ipse vere *porrigat* et ego *accipiam*."
Accipio, in Calvin's sense, is "receive," not "take."

The formula of the Conference at Poissy (1561),—" Confitemur Jesum
Christum in cœna nobis offerre, dare, et vere exhibere substantiam sui
corporis et sanguinis, operatione Spiritus sancti, et nos *recipere* et *edere*
spiritualiter et per fidem verum illud corpus quod pro nobis mortuum
est" (quoted from Hospinian, *Hist. Sacram.*, ii. p. 520),—was not
a genuine, "reformed" statement, but a form in which the reformed
statement had been re-moulded by the Roman Catholic theologian
Despense. It has also an important qualification at the close, which
Beza supplies in his account of the Conference.—(*Histoire Ecclesi-
astique des Eglises Réformées*, t. i. p. 382, ed. 1841.) Nothing could
be more hollow than this attempt to state the Calvinistic doctrine, so
that it might pass with the Queen Mother and the French politicians
and the Gallican divines.

The accurate language of this clause is further illustrated by what was deliberately rejected on revision. In the Articles of 1553, there had been a sentence in these terms :—" Forasmuch as the truth of man's nature requireth that the body of one and the self-same man cannot be at one time in diverse places, but must needs be in one certain place : therefore the Body of Christ cannot be present at one time in many and diverse places. And because (as Holy Scripture doth teach) Christ was taken up into heaven, and there shall continue unto the end of the world, a faithful man ought not either to believe or openly to confess the real and bodily presence (as they term it) of Christ's flesh and blood in the Sacrament of the Lord's Supper." In the Parker Latin MS. of 1563, the following clause was here added, but struck out in the Synod :—" Christus, in cœlum ascendens, corpori suo immortalitatem dedit, naturam non abstulit; humane enim nature veritatem (juxta Scripturas) perpetuo retinet, quam uno et definito loco esse, et non in multa, vel omnia simul

The real meaning of this ambiguous statement is further illustrated by Beza himself :—" Jesum Christum, verum Deum et verum hominem per visibilia signa nobis offerri, ut mentes nostræ fide in cœlum, ubi nunc est Christus, sublatæ Illum spiritualiter contemplentur, et omnibus Ipsius bonis et thesauris perfruantur : idque tam certo et vere quam nos videmus accipimus edimus et bibimus corporalia et visibilia signa." —(Ib., p. 514.) Beza's party explained the "Sancti Spiritus operatione" to be that " fide et Spiritus S. operatione, mentes nostræ, quarum hic est præcipuè cibus, in cœlum elatæ perfruantur corpore et sanguine præsente."—(Ib., p. 521.) Beza also maintains,—" Quærendum esse in cœna Christum eo modo quo esset antequam carnem induisset."— (Ib., p. 513.)

loca diffundi, oportet. Quum igitur Christus in cœlum sublatus ibi usque ad finem seculi permansurus, atque inde, non aliunde, (ut loquitur Augustinus,) venturus sit, ad judicandum vivos et mortuos, non debet quisquam fidelium, et carnis ejus et sanguinis, realem et Corporalem (ut loquuntur) præsentiam in Eucharistia vel credere vel profiteri [r]." The dogmatic importance of these deliberate rejections must not be undervalued.

The clause in the Article which we are considering, contains first the fact that the subject we have treated of is the Body of Christ in the Supper. And all the assertions made concerning it are that its mode of existence is absolutely supernatural. What is heavenly and spiritual cannot be liable to the laws of physics. It is something emphatically mysterious. The relation of the Body of Christ to the species of Bread and Wine is so wondrous that the mind fails to grasp it, and only dares to use language with regard to it which has been sanctioned by the Church. Thus we may properly say without figure that the Body of Christ is fed upon, but only in an improper sense may we say that it is broken, according to the words—

> " Nulla rei fit scissura
> Signi tantum fit fractura."

All these matters find their ultimate term in the difficult question whether it can be said that Christ is locally in the Sacrament [s], " of which we may in brief

---

[r] See Hardwick, pp. 312, 313.

[s] St. Thos., quæst. 75, art. 1, and 76, art. 5.

lay down, that the Body of Christ, if it be compared with the form of bread, is not in them as in a place, because as the substance of bread is not said to be in its accidents as in a place, so neither does the Body of Christ which succeeds to it under those accidents. But, if the Body of Christ be compared with the place of the species, it can be so compared in two ways; either as the Body of Christ according to itself, or as denominated by and invested with the species. In this second consideration, the Body of Christ may be said to be in that circumscribed place, not properly, but improperly, and *secundum quid*; for as, by reason of the species, we in an improper sense say it is seen and handled, because the species are seen and handled, so, for the same reason, we may improperly say that, because the species are circumscribed by space, It also is. Lastly, if the substance of the Body of Christ according to itself be compared to place, it is not said to be in place physically and in a circumscribed fashion or quantitatively; for although it be there properly, yet it is not by a circumscription *ubi*, because the *res ubicata* corresponds with the parts of space by its own parts, and in this sense St. Thomas denies that the Body of Christ is locally in this sacrament [t]."

We proceed to consider "the means whereby the Body of Christ is received and eaten."

The words of the Article must, both (1) on account of the literal meaning, and (2) in reference to the context, be confined to the subjective act of communi-

[t] Lugo, Disp. vi. § iii. ed. Migne, 228.

cating. The passage does not mean that Faith makes the difference between its being the Body of the Lord, or not the Body of the Lord which is received and eaten ; it does not mean that Faith is that which makes the distinction between a real presence and a real absence of the Body of Christ: but it means that the condition of reception on the part of the recipient, according to Christ's ordinance and the intention of the Church,—that is, for the spiritual good of the said recipient,—is Faith.

Observe the words " received and eaten." These, in their literal sense, are essentially subjective. They describe what is necessary on the part of the communicants to a *beneficial* partaking, and they mean no more, for we must now compare the words with the preceding clause of the Article. The preceding clause has stated the supernatural and mysterious nature of the whole transaction. "The Body of Christ is given, taken, and eaten in the Supper,"—there is the whole action,—after a Heavenly and Spiritual manner, in a way that transcends the senses, in the order of grace and not in the order of nature ; and Bishop Geste, the author of the Article, tells us that his own insertion of the word " only" does not militate against the objectivity of the Presence. But when we come to consider the office of Faith in the matter, there is a remarkable omission. It is asserted that the whole action is Heavenly and Spiritual, by avouching that the Body is *given, taken,* and *eaten ;* when we speak of Faith it is said merely that it is received and eaten.

The word "given" is the *differentia* between the two statements, and in the word "given" there is bound, up the whole question of the reality and objectivity of the Presence.

This view of the real meaning of the Article is supported by the response in the Scottish Communion Office at the awful moment of reception. The communicant is directed to answer to the words of the minister, "Amen." What does this mean? It means what it meant in the ancient Church, from which the custom is derived. In the early Church the earliest words were alone, "the Body of Christ, the Blood of Christ," to which the faithful assented "Amen." The disciple of St. Ambrose gives the interpretation, "So then not idly dost thou say Amen, already thereby confessing in spirit that thou receivest the Body of Christ. The Priest sayeth to thee, the Body of Christ, and thou sayest Amen, i.e. true. What thy tongue confesseth let thy affections retain [a]."

The statement in the Article is in perfect harmony with the language of the ancient Church. It would be unnatural if in the glowing language of Liturgies and Fathers the high office of Faith should not be fully recognised.

When, in 1661, the words "with faith" were added to the words "draw near" in the English office, the apparent source from which they were taken was the Liturgies of Armenia, Jerusalem, St. Chrysostom, and St. Basil. All say, "Approach with the fear of God,

[a] *De Sacr.*, L. iv. c. iv.

and *faith* and love." The love is omitted in the Armenian. What was this but to say to the people, It is by Faith that you will profitably partake of these holy mysteries.

And this again is most emphatically set forth in the Confession of the Eucharistic Faith, which, in various forms, is so prominent in the Liturgies of Egypt and Ethiopia[x]. As for example :—

" The holy, precious, living, and very Body of our Lord and Saviour Jesus Christ, which is given for remission of sins and life eternal to those who receive it *with faith*.   Amen.

" The holy, precious, life-giving, and very Blood of our Lord and Saviour Jesus Christ, which is given for remission of sins, and eternal life to those who receive it *with faith*.   Amen.

" This is the Body and Blood of Emmanuel, in very truth. Amen. I believe, I believe, I believe, henceforth and for evermore.   Amen.

" This is the Body and Blood of our Lord and Saviour Jesus Christ, which He took of the holy and pure Virgin Mary . . . .

" I believe, I believe, I believe that His Divinity was not divided from His humanity, no, not for an hour, nor the twinkling of an eye. He gave Himself for us to salvation, remission of sins, and life eternal, to those who receive them (the Body and Blood) *with faith*.   I believe, I believe, I believe, henceforth and for ever."

[x] Renaudot, vol. i. p. 520.

This is only the richest specimen of a class of these Confessions. For another, taken from the Coptic Liturgy of St. Basil, vide Neale's "Introduction to History of the Eastern Church." So also in the Western Church [y]. From the Leonine Sacramentary, take the following:—"Adesto quæsumus Domine plebi tuæ; ut quæ sumsit *fideliter*, et mente simul et corpore, te protegente, custodiat."

So also St. Gregory:—"Da nobis . . . ut sancta tua . . . semper *fideli* mente sumamus [z]."

This language of primitive antiquity bears witness to the fact that faith is the appointed instrument for reception of that which (in the sublime words which the ancient Liturgy of the West, embodying, as we may believe, the tradition of the Apostles, has not feared to put in juxtaposition with the very words of the divine Consecrator,) is emphatically *Mysterium Fidei*.

The necessity of the office of Faith in devout reception must be ever present in our view. It is indeed *Mysterium Fidei* in ways and senses far beyond what the course of controversies has elicited, or indeed what our mind can ever exhaust. If ever faith have an office in our approaches to God, it is when we kneel before His altar.

"The Sacrament of the Lord's Supper was not by Christ's ordinance reserved, carried about, lifted up, or worshipped."

The Latin version here is suggestive. Hitherto the

---

[y] *Muratori Lit. Rom.*, i. 369.   [z] Ibid., ii. 48.

rendering of the term "Lord's Supper" has been *Cœna Domini;* here, as in the preceding clause touching Transubstantiation, we have the ancient word *Eucharistia, Εὐχαριστία* [a]. And it is necessarily used not for the ceremony, but for the Divine Gift; that which was the result of consecration; the "Elements," as they are popularly termed by a phraseology in which the common language has preserved a sense of the unspeakable mysteriousness of that most august Sacrament [b].

The Article does not prohibit the practices mentioned, but merely states that the reservation, circumgestation, elevation, and adoration of the *Sanctissimum* is no part of Christ's institution. "Such ceremonies may be, and are, omitted without breaking our Lord's enactment touching the Eucharist. The Church might leave them out, and yet leave the whole of His institution untouched. So much is really the whole amount of the prohibition, as far as the sentence is concerned [c]."

That the Sacrament of "the Eucharist," as the later Articles term it, was not by Christ's ordinance reserved is admitted on all hands. The Council of Trent asserts that "it was instituted that it might be received [d]," but the Church has from the earliest times reserved the Holy Sacrament, regarding it as a most precious pledge from heaven and the miracle of divine love.

---

[a] See the word *Eucharistia* in Ducange's Glossary.

[b] Ignat., *Smyrn.*, n. 7; *Phil.*, n. 4; Justin, *Apol.*, i. 65, Iren. iv. 18, n. 5.　　　[c] J. Keble.　　　[d] Sess. xiii. cap. 5.

St. Justin Martyr says, that after celebration, the Eucharistic Elements were sent by the hands of the Deacons to those not present[e]. A touching instance of this is recorded in the act of the martyrdom of St. Lucian[f]. In the second century it was the custom for Bishops to send It as a token of peace and unity[g]. That the Eucharist was reserved in the Church under both kinds from the fourth century, is proved by St. Chrysostom in his letter to Pope Innocent[h], where the Saint describes the outrages of the soldiers in the church of Constantinople. At Nola It was kept . in a golden casket[i], which was laid up in the sanctuary. And this is probably the meaning of what Anastasius writes in his Life of Pope Nicholas, "Fecit autem ut in Basilicâ Salvatoris — cruces de argento purissimo quæ pendent ante figuram substantiæ carnis ejusdem Dni. N. J. C.[k]"

St. Basil not only mentions that in times of persecution the faithful were constrained to take the Communion into their own hands, and that the solitaries in the desert had to have recourse to the same practice, but mentions that it was the ordinary use of the Church of Alexandria, and asks, "Ought they not to believe that That which they carry home[l] in their

<hr>

[e] *Apol.*, i. 68, p. 52, Oxf. Tr.   [f] *Act. S. Luc. ap. Sur.*

[g] *Ep. Irenæi ad Victor. ap. Euseb.* H. E., v. c. 24.

[h] *Ep. ad Innocent., PP. apud D. Constant.*, t. i. p. 783.   [i] Amb., *Ep.* iv. n. 4.   [k] Vide Ducange.

[l] "*Eucharistiam domum delatam et in* arcâ servatam, *scribunt* Tertullianus sub finem libri *ad Mart.*, lib. ii. *ad uxor.* S. Cyp., *lib. de lapsis.* S. Aug., lib. iii. *Cont. Crescon.*, cap. 11; Bas., *in Epist.* cclxxxix.; *Joan.*

hands, is the Same Thing which they receive in church at the hands of the Priest [m]." This custom, which was universal, is believed to have lasted till the Papacy of Hormisdas, A.D. 514, and to have been retained even longer in the East. It was also reserved in long journeys by land and by sea [n]. The custom lasted till the Crusades [o].

Becket carried It round his neck on the occasion of his going in search of Henry II. When the ordeal by fire was proposed to be resorted to, to test whether the Pope was right in excommunicating Savonarola, his friend, Fr. Dominic, who was to make the fiery trial, held It in his hand.

Anciently the Sacrament was reserved at the consecration of bishops and at the ordination of priests, to be consumed by them during the forty days after the ceremony [p], and it was frequently buried with the dead [q].

So also for the communion of infants and of the sick, and for the *Missa Præsanctificatorum* both in the Roman, Greek, and Milanese Churches. In fact, till

Moschus, cap. 29. 79; Verum id Canon 3 Conc. Cæsaraugustani vetitum, quo anathematizatur is qui Eucharistiæ Gratiam acceptam in ecclesiâ non consumpserit. *Vide* Baron., An. 57, n. 149, 150; An. 293, n. 2. *Conc. Tolet.*, i. cap. 14; *Capitul.*, lib. vii. cap. 473." Ducange *in verb. Eucharistia.*

[m] *Ep.* cclxxxix. *ad Ces. Pat.*

[n] S. Amb., *de Mort. Sat.*; S. Greg., *Dial.*, iii. 37, &c.

[o] *Vit. S. Lauren. O'Toole, Archiep. Dub., Apud Surium.* 14 *Nov.*; cap. 8, t. vi. 813; *Vit. S. Ludovici, Reg. Fr.*, 25 *Aug.*; t. iv. 912.

[p] *Ord. Romanus, Epist. Fulbert ad Erhard.*

[q] S. Greg., *Dial.*, ii. 24.

the thirteenth century, we have distinct evidence that in different ways, sometimes in a ciborium, sometimes suspended over the altar enveloped in veils, sometimes in tabernacles in the form of a dove, sometimes in aumbries beside the altar, sometimes along with images and relics of the saints, sometimes under baldachins, and sometimes in towers a few feet from the high altar, the blessed Sacrament was reserved with great dignity and honour. The practice of reserving the blessed Sacrament for the sick has obtained in the Scottish Church, by an unwritten tradition, since the days of the Non-jurors.

The carrying about of the Blessed Sacrament in solemn procession is a ceremony of the Western Church. It does not exist in the orthodox Eastern Church, nor in the English Church; neither do any of the Eastern heretical Churches practise it. It is impossible to fix the exact date of the commencement of the practice. On the one hand, the opinion of those who would maintain that it took its rise in Pavia in 1404, on the authority of Donatus Bossius, a jurisconsult of Milan[r], is contradicted by history; on the other hand, that of those who make it synchronize with the authorization of the *Festum Corporis Christi* by Urban IV. in 1264, is confuted by the silence of Durandus writing in 1286. It is, however, alluded to in documents of the Church of Chartres, 1339; of Sens, 1320; of Tournay, 1323. Cassander maintained that it is certain that the Feast was not

[r] *Chron. a Mundi init. ad an.* 1492.

instituted by Urban IV. for the exposition of the
Blessed Eucharist, but that the faithful should assemble in great numbers in the churches, there to
sing the praises of God, and to prepare themselves
by acts of piety to participate worthily on that day,
and receive it with respect. The celebrated Cardinal
Groper, the ornament of the Church of Cologne, inveighed against many of the abuses connected with
this ceremony, so late as 1560. St. Carlo Borromeo,
in the acts of the Council of Milan, puts restrictions
on the public exposition of the Blessed Sacrament[s].
The feast was celebrated at Liege fourteen years before the Bull of Urban, and did not become universal
till after the Council of Vienne in 1311.

"The Sacrament was not by Christ's ordinance lifted
up." In spite of the text in St. Paul's Epistle to the
Galatians, where in allusion to the divine mysteries,
it is said that Jesus Christ is set forth verily crucified
before their eyes[t], we cannot trace back this custom
to Apostolic times. In a certain form we find something of the kind very anciently practised in the
Greek Church[u].

In the Western Church there is no allusion to it in
the early Sacramentaries of Gelasius, Leo, or Gregory,
nor in the works of St. Isidore of Seville, or Rabanus, or

---

[s] *Tit. De Sac. Euch. De Expos. in orat.*, 40 horarum.

[t] Gal. iii. 1.

[u] "Longe post orationem dominicam brevi tamen ante communionem
spatio, juxta Jacobi, Basilii et Chrysostomi Liturgias, Dominicum
Corpus, non ita ut a populo conspicatur elevat Græcus Sacerdos."
(*Goar*, not. 158, *in Miss. Chrys.*, p. 143. col. 2.)

Walafride, or any of the ancient writers who explain the ceremonies of the Church. It is when we come to mediæval times, that the practice is recognised, such as in the *Speculum Ecclesiæ* of Hugh of St. Victor; in Hildebertus of Le Mans[x] (A.D. 1136). It is constantly alluded to in the Provincial Synods of the thirteenth century, as also by Durandus[y]. The elevation of the chalice does not obtain among the Greeks, and is by no means universal among the Latins.

It is unnecessary to go into the question of the worship of our Lord in the Sacrament, after the exhaustive treatise of John Keble, τοῦ μακαρίτου, to which the reader is referred.

[x] *De Offic. Miss.*

[y] *Rationale Div. Off.*

ARTICLE XXIX.

De manducatione Corporis Christi, et Impios illud non manducare.

Impii, et fide viva destituti, licet carnaliter, et visibiliter (ut Augustinus loquitur) Corporis et Sanguinis Christi Sacramentum, dentibus premant, nullo tamen modo Christi participes efficiuntur. Sed potius tantæ rei Sacramentum, seu Symbolum, ad judicium sibi manducant, et bibunt.

" Of the Wicked which eat not the Body of Christ in the Use of the Lord's Supper.

"THE wicked, and such as be void of a lively faith, although they do carnally and visibly press with their teeth (as St. Augustine saith) the Sacrament of the Body and Blood of Christ, yet in no wise are they partakers of Christ, but rather to their condemnation do eat and drink the sign or Sacrament of so great a thing."

This Article was first published in 1571. It is wanting in all the printed copies till that date. It is found in the Parker Latin MS. of 1563, and in the Parker English MS., 1571; also in the Latin edition of 1571, printed by John Day, and published by the Queen's authority. It does not appear in the early

printed copies of the Articles as finally put forth [a].
The passage from the supposed treatise of St. Augustine, which, extruded by the Benedictine editors from that author, is found in Bede, Alcuin, and others, was distinctly verified by a reference to the treatise from whence it is taken [b]. The Twenty-ninth Article was re-adopted on the 11th of May, 1571, and finds its place in all the printed copies of that date, whether English or Latin. We must account for the hesitation with regard to its enunciation on the grounds either of Queen Elizabeth's own feelings, or on those of the scruples of her advisers. In fact we know that an interview took place on the subject between Parker and Cecil [c], where the latter called in question the fairness of the quotation from St. Augustine.

The doctrine concerning That which is received by the wicked in the Holy Sacrament, stands in a middle position between two truths, with either of which it must be reconciled. On the one hand, regarding the blessed Sacrament as the food of the soul and the subjective appropriation of the merits of Christ, remembering also that the Sermon on this doctrine, in the sixth chapter of St. John, is entirely silent on the subject, we must hold that there can be no beneficial reception to those in a state of sin; that it cannot act as a charm in the case of those who are unprepared; that so far are they from the blessedness

---

[a] Hardwick, p. 128, n. 2.   [b] Ibid., p. 140.
[c] Strype's Parker, p. 331.

of union with Christ, that it were far better that they had not approached those holy mysteries. On the other hand, it is equally true that the Holy Communion is such by virtue of consecration; that Christ's presence does not depend upon the mental emotion and spiritual condition of the recipient; that the Sacrament is what it is by the power of the institution of Christ. If this be so, wherein shall we reconcile these apparent contradictions? It is found in the fact that Christ is, in certain cases, present in the Sacrament, not to bless, but to judge—that reception of the Sacrament by the wicked conveys something more serious than a negation—that the wicked not only do not receive grace, but do receive judgment.

The language of the Article means that the *res Sacramenti* is received by the wicked; and the great voice of antiquity, with the exception of some passages in St. Augustine, supports this view.

It is in entire conformity with the teaching of the Epistle to the Corinthians:—"Wherefore whosoever shall eat this bread and (or) drink this cup of the Lord unworthily, shall be guilty of the Body and Blood of the Lord. But let a man examine himself, and so let him eat of that bread and drink of that cup. For he that eateth and drinketh unworthily, eateth and drinketh judgment to himself, not discerning the Lord's body [d]."

Unless the Bread and the Cup be what we believe

---

[d] 1 Cor. xi. 27.

Them to be, how can an unworthy communicant be guilty of the Body and Blood of Christ? On any other theory he may be ungodly, irreverent, profane, even sacrilegious; but on this theory alone can these terrible words be used in their truth, "Guilty of the Body and Blood of the Lord." What else *can* they mean than that to receive the inward part, the Body and Blood of Christ, unworthily, is to be guilty in that very respect?

Again, in the next verse, the Apostle supplies the way and means towards avoiding that profanation— "Let a man examine himself." The whole Church system of penitence is here placed between past sin and the Holy Communion. The lapsed Christian is to purge his unworthiness by examination, and its concomitant exercise of repentance.

And all this in view of the dreadful results of a neglect of these-means, for he that eateth and drinketh unworthily eateth and drinketh $\kappa\rho\hat{\imath}\mu\alpha$, 'judgment,' which our translators have rendered by the very strong word 'damnation;' and why? because they do not discern "the Lord's Body." Bengel says, "Domini Antonomasia, i.e. Jesu. Ecclesia non dicitur corpus Jesu aut corpus Domini, sed corpus Christi, hic igitur de proprio corpore Domini Jesu agitur."

How could the Lord's Body be discerned, if It was not there? Why should St. Paul give this reason for these fearful condemnations falling upon the irreverent sinner, if there were no presence of the Lord to be violated—no ineffable condescension to be disdained.

In the words of St. Chrysostom[c], commenting on the words, "Not discerning the Lord's Body,"—"not searching, not bearing in mind as he ought, the greatness of the things set before him—not estimating the weight of the gift,—For if thou shouldst come to know accurately, *Who* it is that lieth before thee, and *Who* He is who giveth Himself, and to whom, thou wilt need no other argument, but this is enough for thee to use all vigilance."

The argument from St. Paul rests partly on the whole tenor of what he says in this passage, partly on his very express words. That first argument from the whole context may be stated syllogistically in this fashion :—

Unworthy communicants either receive something besides bread and wine, or they do not.

If they receive nothing but bread and wine, their sin is not greater in kind than the misuse of any other ordinance, e.g. prayer.

But St. Paul plainly teaches that it is greater in kind, that it is something *sui generis*, a sin standing by itself. It is to be guilty of, or in relation to, the Body and Blood of Christ.

Therefore they who are so guilty cannot be receivers of nothing but bread and wine.

And there being no alternative between real absence and real presence, they must in some sense receive Christ, the inward part of the Sacrament.

But, distinct from, and over and above this, is

---

[c] Hom. 28, in 1 Cor., sect. 2.

St. Paul's remarkable phrase, the most characteristic and doctrinal expression in the passage, that which St. Paul assigns as the ground why to "eat and drink unworthily," is to eat and drink damnation to themselves, viz. μὴ διακρίνων τὸ σῶμα τοῦ Κυρίου, μὴ διακρίνων, that is, not discerning in the Latin sense—not discriminating between the Body of the Lord and all other foods. But there would be no blame in not so discriminating between the Body of the Lord and other food, unless that Body were present there.

If these words of the Apostle may be turned aside from their meaning, there is no safety for the retention of any plain and explicit statement of the Word of God.

The formularies of the Church rightly understood support the view that the *res Sacramenti* is received by the wicked.

1. In the exhortation before the actual reception we are told—"For as the benefit is great, if with a true penitent heart and lively faith we receive that Holy Sacrament (for then we spiritually eat the Flesh of Christ and drink His Blood; then we dwell in Christ, and Christ in us: we are one with Christ, and Christ with us); so is the danger great if we receive THE SAME unworthily." Whether "the same" here applies, according to the strictness of construction, to "the Flesh of Christ," or to the antecedent word "Holy Sacrament," we arrive at the same result, and that is, that that which is received by the good, *the Same* is received by the wicked and unworthy.

2. Moreover, in the warning before the Communion, we are exhorted "to consider the dignity of that Holy Mystery, and the great peril of the unworthy receiving *thereof;*" where we again see that what is provided for the good may be unworthily received by the evil.

3. Again, the same "Holy Sacrament" is described to be "so divine and comfortable a thing to them who receive it worthily, and so dangerous to them that will presume to receive *it* (that is, *the same*) unworthily."

4. Then, the Church commits herself to the belief that Judas received the Holy Sacrament, according to the almost unanimous consent of antiquity, and deduces a warning lest, after the taking of the Holy Sacrament, certain evil results follow.

5. So also the receiving the Holy Communion unworthily is said to "do nothing else than increase the sinner's damnation."

It must be observed that here, in an address to the people, the word Sacrament is taken in the popular sense, not to mean the *Sacramentum,* or outward part only, but the whole ordinance.

6. In the prayer of Humble Access the emphatic word "*so* to eat the Flesh of Christ, that our sinful bodies may be made clean by His Body," implies thereby that there is such a way of eating the Flesh of Christ as that men may not be cleansed thereby.

7. In the second Post-Communion Prayer, or public thanksgiving, beginning "Almighty and ever-living God," emphasis is laid on the word "duly."

But the Article under consideration affords another proof of the position.

At the end of Article XXV., in speaking of the Sacraments generally it is said:—"The Sacraments were not ordained of Christ to be gazed upon, or to be carried about, but that we should duly use them. And in such only as worthily receive the same they have a wholesome operation, but they that receive them unworthily purchase to themselves damnation, as St. Paul saith."

Here, though the passage is put under the head of the Sacraments in general, it is clear that the Holy Eucharist is specially alluded to, for no one then gazed on Baptism, nor could they carry it about; but the other Sacrament was both gazed upon and carried about. Assuming then that it is the Holy Eucharist which alone is alluded to, we find in the end of this Article the same doctrine which we have found in the Exhortations, and therefore, under pain of detecting a fearful inconsistency, we must believe that the true sense of Article XXIX. must be in accordance with this. It is also to be observed that by connecting this passage of Article XXV. with Article XXIX. we are led to identify the statement, that in worthy receivers only Sacraments have a wholesome effect or operation, with the statement that unworthy receivers are in no wise partakers of Christ. In other words, to be a "partaker of Christ," in the sense of Article XXIX., is to have in one's self that wholesome operation, which is identical with the "strengthening and refreshing" of the Catechism—which strengthening and refreshing is distinguished by the Catechism from the Body and Blood, as the *Virtus Sacramenti* from the *Res Sacramenti.*

Moreover, it must be mentioned that there is much that is curious about the reception of this Article. It is a well-known fact that Queen Elizabeth never, in the midst of her worldly policy, lost her faith in the Objective Presence of our Lord in the Holy Sacrament. Peter Heylin mentions[f], in close connexion, these two anecdotes:—"That when Dean Nowell of St. Paul's spoke less reverently in a sermon preached before her, of the Sign of the Cross, she called aloud to him from her closet window, commanding him to retire from that ungodly digression, and to return unto his text." And, "that, on the other side, when one of her divines had preached a sermon in defence of the Real Presence on the day commonly called Good Friday, in 1565, she openly gave him thanks for his pains and piety."

She was not likely then to accept this Article in any other sense than one consistent with this belief. Now the Article appears to have been composed in the end of 1562, and submitted to the Convocation of that date by Archbishop Parker[g]. It was accepted by the Upper House, but rejected by the Lower, unless, as has been thought, its omission in the authorized text, as settled after the Synod, was the result of Queen Elizabeth's will[h].

[f] Hist. Ref., p. 296, ed. 1674.

[g] Hardwick, Hist. Art., p. 128, ed. 1851.   [h] Ibid., 136, 139.

In the Convocation of 1571, the Article was restored. It is noteworthy that this was the very Convocation in which the bishops, by the famous canon *Conciona-tores*, imposed upon the clergy, as their guide in the doctrinal interpretation of Scripture, the authority of the Catholic Fathers and ancient Bishops.

Now, if there is any fact in theological history capable of demonstration, I think it is this, that the Catholic Fathers and ancient Bishops did teach, alike in liturgies and in treatises, that *in some sense* the unworthy communicants do receive the Body and Blood of Christ to their condemnation. This, to say the very least, must throw a strong light upon the interpretation of this Article.

The words of the Article cited as St. Augustine's, are not in the treatise as fully as there quoted. The interpolation is that of Venerable Bede, in the eighth century; such an interpolation being in consistence with the faith of Bede, who most emphatically taught that "the Holy Body and Precious Blood were offered up" in "sacrifice" on the altar.

It is right, however, to say that the interpolation is wholly in accordance with the mind of St. Augustine. It becomes our duty, therefore, from other passages in this great Father, to deduce what he really meant. We must premise that, amid the many and conscientious retractations by which in his latter days he corrected any mis-statements even in minute matters in his early teaching, no trace of retractation is to be found on this point. We may therefore arrive at a pretty strong probability as to what he really felt on the subject.

1. The following expressions appear to be in unison with the famous passage quoted in the Article :—"The sign which shews that one has eaten and drunk is this, if he dwelleth and is dwelt in, if he inhabiteth and is inhabited, if he cleaveth that he be not abandoned [1]." "There are persons who have not only in the Sacrament, but in reality, eaten Christ's Body, being placed in that very Body of His, of which the Apostle saith, 'We, being many, are one Bread and one Body.' He who is in the unity of that Body, in the coherent mass of the members of Christ, of which Body the faithful communicants are wont to receive the Sacrament from the Altar, he is truly to be said to eat the Body of Christ, and to drink the blood of Christ [k]." "The wicked are not to be said to eat the Body of Christ, because they are not to be accounted among His members," and adds that Christ's words, "Whoso eateth My Flesh and drinketh My Blood dwelleth in Me, and I in him," "shew what it is to eat the Body of Christ, and to drink His Blood, not as to the Sacrament only, but in truth ; that is, to abide in Christ, so that Christ also should abide in him [1]."

The key-note to many of the dicta of St. Augustine is his theory of perseverance. Alike as to Baptism and the Holy Eucharist, he often seems to speak as though a gift that was not retained was not really possessed,

[1] *Tract.* 27, *in S. Joh.*
[k] *Civ. D.,* xxi. 25.　　　　[1] Ibid., 25, *s. f.*

i.e. as if in the sight of God any existence of good which was not permanent was actually unreal. It is, in short, a Christian application of the heathen maxim, "Count no man happy before his end." This is one-sided language, and such as men do not usually employ.

2. This language, then, must be held in combination with such other Augustinian language as follows :—

On St. Paul's words, "Guilty of the Body," &c., St. Augustine says "that the Apostle was discoursing on those who, treating the Lord's Body like other food, took it in a negligent and indiscriminating way[m]."

"Do so many who, either in hypocrisy eat that Flesh and drink that Blood, or who, after they have eaten and drunk, become apostate,—do they 'dwell in Christ and Christ in them?' Yet assuredly there is a certain manner of eating that Flesh and of drinking that Blood in which whosoever eateth and drinketh It dwelleth in Christ. He, then, doth not dwell in Christ and Christ in him who eateth the Flesh and drinketh the Blood of Christ in any manner whatever, but only in some certain manner[n]."

"Any one who unworthily receives the Sacrament of the Lord does not, because he himself is evil, cause it to be evil, nor because he receives not unto salvation, has he received nothing, for that was no less the Body and Blood of the Lord to those also to whom the Apostle said, 'He that eateth and drinketh

---

[m] *Tract.* 62, *in S. Joh.*　　　　　　　[n] *Serm.* 71.

unworthily eateth and drinketh damnation to himself °.'"

3. These expressions arrive at their intensity when
they are brought to the crucial point whether the
wretched Judas did or did not receive the Lord's
Body.

St. Augustine says :—" The Lord allows Judas to
receive among the innocent disciples what the faithful
know to be our Ransom P."

" Of one Bread hath Peter and Judas received. Peter
received unto life, Judas unto death ᵠ."

How shall we reconcile this apparent discrepancy ?
It is reconciled by St. Augustine himself.

He says, " the good, together with the bad, eat and
drink the Body and Blood of Christ, but with a great
distinction, for these are clad in the wedding garment,
but those have it not. . . . And hereby, although at one
and the same feast, these eat Mercy, those Judgment ʳ."

In both cases there is a reception of the Body and
of the Blood of Christ, but there is only a profitable
reception to the good, for, as we have seen, St. Augustine uses Real as if it meant beneficial, in conformity
with his views on final perseverance. Those who, in
the language of the liturgies, keep what they have received, who persevere in the spiritual union of Christ's
mystic Body, are said by St. Augustine " so to partake
of Christ as to dwell in Him."

° De Bapt., c. Don., v. 8.   ᵖ Ep. xliii.

ᵠ Tract. 50, in S. Joh. See other passages of St. Aug. in Dr. Pusey's
"The Real Presence the Doctrine of the English Church," pp. 262—265.

ʳ Ad Donat. post Collat., n. 27.

To sum up the teaching of St. Augustine, it must ever be borne in mind, in seeking to ascertain his meaning, that he holds, as it were, two inward parts or *res* in the Sacrament: 1st. Christ's real but now spiritual Body, which He took of the Blessed Virgin; 2nd. His mystical Body, the Church of God's elect, and that all receivers partake of the first, and only worthy receivers of the other.

This will be yet more clearly seen, if we observe the context of that passage from which the Article quotes. Our author is there speaking of a *res*, of which only worthy communicants partake, and this *res* is, strictly speaking, a permanent inherence in the mystical Body of Christ. This mystical aspect of the Holy Communion—which, it will be remembered, is so beautifully illustrated in that prayer of our Church which speaks of due receivers of the holy mysteries as "very members incorporate in the mystical Body of" our Lord, and in its holy fellowship,—was by no means absent from the mind of Fathers like St. Chrysostom and St. Cyril, who would not have agreed with St. Augustine on the question of the decrees of God.

But the Article does not in any way stand committed to St. Augustine's view of predestination. It does not even use his precise language in the very place which it quotes from him. It gives its genuine meaning, but it substitutes words which express that meaning for his own. St. Augustine in that passage says, "Who dwelleth not in Christ, and in whom Christ dwelleth not, doth neither eat His Flesh nor drink His Blood, but rather, unto judgment to him-self, eat and drink the Sacrament of so great a thing." Bede rightly explained St. Augustine's words by add-ing the word "spiritually," i.e. to the health of his spirit, or, in other words, so as to be "partaker of Christ." As St. Jerome says, "His blood we drink, and without Him we cannot drink." Without Christ, we cannot be "partakers of Christ." This, which St. Augustine shews to have been his meaning, the framer of our Article directly expresses. Instead of saying that "the wicked cannot eat the Flesh of Christ, or drink His Blood," i.e. as St. Augustine himself shews that he meant these words, "cannot *so* eat the Flesh of Christ and drink His Blood as to be partakers of Christ," the Article at once uses the scriptural phrase. "The wicked are in no wise partakers of Christ." By the necessity of the case they cannot be. *They* can-not be "partakers of Christ" of whom Holy Scripture uses the awful language, that they are " none of His." They abide not in Christ, nor He in them. They, He says, are "cast forth as a branch and withered." To be a " partaker of Christ," is the language of St. Paul. Our Article uses St. Paul's language in St. Paul's meaning. No one ought to attempt to maintain that our Article uses the words of Holy Scripture in a non-scriptural sense. There can be no beneficial reception to those in a state of sin. It is impossible to point out any distinction between the statement of the Article, that " the wicked are in no wise partakers of Christ," and that " there can be no beneficial reception to those in a state of sin." Whatever our bias may be, we dare not affix to words of Holy Scripture used in our Articles any other than their scriptural meaning. The words "partakers of Christ," in the Article, must mean the same as "partakers of Christ" in Holy Scripture, from which our Article has taken them. But in Holy Scripture, to be "a partaker of Christ" is to have a share, so to speak, "in Christ and of Christ," to be united with Him, to have a share of the blessedness, the graces, the acceptance which is in Him and from Him. No paraphrase expresses the depth of those simple words of Holy Scripture, "partakers of Christ." For whatever blessedness flows from Him, what they primarily mean is, share in Christ Himself. This the Article denies of the wicked. To those who remain such unto the end, Christ tells us that He shall say, "I never knew you." However near they approach to Him, they are none of His; and since by His grace alone we can partake of Himself, they who have not His grace cannot "partake of Christ," can have no share of Him.

The framer of the Article altered St. Augustine's words. He brings out St. Augustine's meaning by changing the concise words which St. Augustine used, and by substituting the scriptural phrase, which, as appears from the other places of St. Augustine, expresses what that Father really meant. And this meaning we must have taken, whether it made for or against our views. For we are bound to take the words of our Articles in their strict, grammatical meaning, and we must take a scriptural phrase in its scriptural meaning. But we now happen to know, over and above, that this was the meaning of the framer of the Article.

It appears from Archbishop Parker's Letter to Lord Burleigh, that he alleged St. Augustine's authority in this Article only up to a certain point. Parker wrote: "Sir,—I have considered what your Honour wrote to me this morning concerning St. Augustine's authority in the Article, in the first original agreed upon, and I am still advisedly in mine opinion *concerning so much, wherefore they be alleged in the Article.*" Now, as has been observed, to say that the words of St. Augustine were alleged only "*concerning so much,*" implies that there was some further point for which it might be supposed that they could be alleged. Now, St. Augustine's own words might (though not in their true meaning) have been taken to deny that "those who dwell not in Christ, nor Christ in them," in any way receive within themselves the Body and Blood of Christ. People have so understood them. Archbishop Parker says that the Article stops short of some further point. But there is no further point of which the Article could stop short, but that the wicked in some way receive within themselves the Body and Blood of Christ. The words, "are in no ways partakers of Christ," exclude all benefit from the reception—any share of Christ Himself. There is only one further point for which Parker could say that the Article stopped short of alleging St. Austin, viz. that they received in themselves, though they have no share in them, no benefit from them, the Body and Blood of Christ.

Even supposing that we had no light thrown on the true interpretation of this Article from St. Augustine, from other Fathers, or from the Prayer-Book, it seems that its own words, "*but rather to their condemnation*," are the key to the whole. The Article is antithetical. One member of the antithesis, is, "In no wise are they partakers of Christ." The other is, "But rather to their condemnation they eat and drink," &c. These two members must be logically opposed. The idea denied in the first must be the opposite to that which is affirmed in the second. But the idea affirmed in the second is that of *condemnation*. Therefore the idea denied in the first must be that of *justification*. Justification, then, must be implied in the partaking of Christ; in other words, the partaking of Christ means a beneficial reception only.

The popular objection has no weight at all, except by importing into the words of the Article a meaning which they will not bear. The Article does not deny (God forbid!) that we receive orally the Body and Blood of Christ; it does not say, that by faith we feed on Christ at the Right Hand of God, contemplating Him there. It is speaking of beneficial reception only. It had said, that "to such as rightly, worthily, and with faith receive the same, the Bread which we break is a partaking of the Body of Christ."

Q q

It anew states this, " Faith is the mean whereby we beneficially receive it."

An argument has been drawn from the heading of the Article, " which eat not the Body of Christ," that the Church of England meant to deny that they receive it at all, not to assert that they receive no benefit from it. But since the body of the Article only says that " the wicked are in no wise partakers of Christ," (which, plainly, they cannot be,) then the heading cannot be held to contain more than this. For no heading of an Article or Canon (any more than of an Act of Parliament) may lawfully be employed to introduce into the substance of such Article or Canon, a meaning which the grammatical structure of the words of such Article or Canon does not admit. Nor can the heading of an Article form a proposition, binding upon us, distinct from the meaning of the body of the Article. For this would be to make such heading a 40th Article, which is, of course, inadmissible. Both statements must mean the same. But this they do, if we understand the words " eat not" in the sense which they have in St. John, &c., whence they are taken, " eat not so as to dwell in Christ and He in them*."

* See Dr. Pusey " The Real Presence the Doctrine of the English Church," pp. 252—259.

ARTICLE XXX.

DE UTRAQUE SPECIE.

CALIX Domini laicis non est denegandus; utraque enim pars Dominici Sacramenti ex Christi institutione et præcepto, omnibus Christianis ex æquo administrari debet.

Of both Kinds.

" THE Cup of the Lord is not to be denied to the lay people; for both the parts of the Lord's Sacrament, by Christ's ordinance and commandment, ought to be ministered to all Christian men alike.

The Utraquist controversy involves principles even more important than the actual point ruled. Right as it is that in an ordinance " so mysterious, so closely appertaining to the Sacrament of our Lord's Passion and of our redemption, there should be no infringement of our Lord's commands[a]," the change from that which was in the beginning divinely instituted, involves nothing less than that the living Church has the power to alter not only that which stood upon an unbroken tradition of nearly twelve hundred years, but that which was done " by Christ's

---

[a] Cyp., *ad Corc., Ep.* lxiii.

ordinance and commandment." It was not till the time of the Schoolmen that the mind of the Church seriously set itself to the matter in hand. The danger of irreverence had suggested before this means for securing the consecrated elements from profanation. In the Greek Church the Body of the Lord had been administered with a spoon, after it had been dipped in the Blood. The Blood had been received through a golden pipe to prevent any accident. It was reserved for the Scholastic era to solve the difficulty by the withdrawal of the Chalice from all but the celebrant. This was not effected without resistance. In Bohemia, as all know, it was the occasion of wars and persecutions. In England, the Cup could not be withdrawn without the introduction of an unconsecrated drink, which was given ostensibly to assist in the deglutition of the Blessed Sacrament under the form of Bread, but probably to pacify the people for the loss of the Divine Chalice [b].

The question was one of the chief subjects of decision at the Council of Basle. The subject, on the Roman Catholic side, is treated at great length in the speech by Johannes de Ragusio, which is given among the Acts of the Council [c].

He lays down—1. that Communion under both kinds is not necessary for all the people, *necessitate medii;* 2. neither is it so *necessitate præcepti;* 3. nay, in view of the custom and law of the Church, it is not only not

---

[b] See some interesting papers by F. C. H., in " Notes and Queries," 1st Series, xii. 477; and 2nd Series, i. 143.

[c] *Conc.,* Labbe and Cossart, t. xvii. p. 817.

useful but actually hurtful. He passes briefly by the first point, on the ground that God has not so tied His power to Sacraments, as not to be able to save souls but in that way, and devotes himself to the next head, which he maintains 1. by the divine law; 2. by the practice of our Lord; 3. by the authority of General Councils; 4. by the dicta of doctors.

1. Under the first of these heads he quotes three texts in the sixth chapter of St. John, where there are so many allusions to the true Bread and none to the true Wine.

2. Under the second, he draws an analogy from the multiplication of the loaves; also he cites the Lord's Prayer, " Give us this day our supersubstantial bread."

3. Under the head of Councils, after some special pleading for a Canon in the Sixth General Council, he tries to turn the Canon of the eleventh of Toledo, where a previous Canon with regard to reception had been modified, to a very opposite purpose from what was intended. He thinks that the second Canon of the Council of Rheims testifies to the practice. He also cites the Council of Worms.

4. He rests much on the custom of the Church, shewing, that though the custom varied, there were early testimonies to the practice. He quotes Pope Innocent allowing consecration in one kind only, in regions where wine cannot be got, and adduces many of the Schoolmen:—Alexander Ales, Albertus Magnus, St. Thomas, St. Bonaventura, Petrus de Tarantasia, and Ricardus de Media Villa. After going into ab-

stract reasons for the practice, he states that the motives which induced the Church to insist on it was the danger of spilling the species; the danger of corruption; the practical assertion of the truth that Christ is *totus sub utraque specie;* the special honour of the sacerdotal state, and the recognition of a state of languor which had come over the Church, the laity in the days of martyrdom having pressed for the communion of the Chalice, a condition which no longer existed.

Not a word is said of " They all drank of it[d];" nor of the authority of St. Paul in the Corinthians.   He does not meet the distinct testimony to the universal practice of the early Fathers, such as Justin Martyr[e], or of St. Cyprian[f], or the evidence supplied by all the Liturgies, or the witness of all the Fathers and Popes till the time of the Schoolmen.   But it must be remembered that even the Schoolmen themselves admit the blessing of the Chalice, " Because the use of the faithful and the unity of the mystic body is not perfectly signified without the double sign, and therefore in virtue of a Sacrament both ought to be had[g]."

The most remarkable testimony in favour of the practice is that of Pope Gelasius, which has come to us through Gratian[h].   " A Priest ought not to receive the Body of Christ without His Blood.   So Pope

---

[d] St. Mark xiv.   [e] *Apol.,* i. 65.   [f] *De Lapsis,* cxxxii.
[g] *Alb. Mag.,* 4 sent. dist. viii. 13.   [h] *Corpus Jur. Can. Decr.,*
iii. pars ; *De Consecr.,* dist. ii. c. 12.

Gelasius to Bishops Majoricus and John :—' But we have learnt,' says Gelasius, ' that certain persons, after having received only the portion of the sacred Body, abstain from the Chalice of the sacred Blood. Which persons, without doubt (because they are said to be bound by I know not what superstition), should either partake of the Sacraments in their entirety, or be excluded from the entire Sacraments, BECAUSE THE DIVISION OF ONE AND THE SAME MYSTERY CANNOT TAKE PLACE WITHOUT GREAT SACRILEGE.' " Before him, St. Leo[1] excommunicated certain African Manichæans, who from their wicked principles objected to the Sacramental Cup.

However, while we have the evidence that universally in the public and solemn Liturgy of the Church, the faithful received the Blessed Eucharist under both species till the twelfth century, it is due to historical truth to state that there were certain practices which shewed that in cases of necessity, communion under one kind was considered lawful. For example, the early Christians carried home the Blessed Sacrament in a linen cloth called a dominicum, but we have no record of the holy Blood being reserved in a phial. In St. Cyprian[j] we have an account of a child being communicated under the species of wine. It was carried on the breast, at sea, in an orarium, as in the case of St. Birinus, Apostle of Wessex. Again, the saints in the desert carried away the Blessed Sacrament in the species of bread, and in some cases the

---

[1] *Serm.* iv. *Quadr.*   [j] *De Lapsis,* vi. 16.

sick when communicated from the reserved Sacrament received in that kind only. Children, as we have just seen, received only under the species of wine[k]. These instances, and they go over a great range, not only serve to console one under the contemplation of the fact that the Occidental Church causes all but the celebrant to abstain from the Sacrament of the Cup, but also illustrate how the mind of the Church became trained to the thought that it might dispense with the Chalice without danger of invalidating the Sacrament. They shew that those thus deprived lose not any grace necessary to salvation. Still it is to be deplored that the matter has been thus ruled, for :—

I. It brings the practice of the Church into an unhappy antagonism with Holy Scripture, for, however we may insist on St. Paul's alternation "Whosoever shall eat of this bread, or drink ($\mathring{\eta}$ $\pi i \nu \eta$) of the cup of the Lord," or on the celebration being termed the breaking of the Bread, there is no gainsaying the "drink ye all of it," especially as interpreted by the practice of twelve centuries. It is due to truth to say that Roman Catholics meet the text by holding that our Lord spake to the Apostles as in the character of Priests, and that therefore the question of the laity does not come in; but then the real question is, that the Chalice is not held back from the laity as such, but from all priests and laity, save only the celebrant.

II. It has given rise to painful scruples of conscience,

---

[k] Cyp., *de Lapsis.*

and to persecution and treachery, as in the case of John Huss, and the Bohemians. However defended on the score of reverence, it ought never to have formed a cause of such severities as were practised. The whole story is a sad one, and discreditable to the persons concerned therein.

III. But the most serious thing is, that according to the best theologians something is lost by the deprivation. While the Sacrament under one kind conveys all the graces necessary to salvation, the Chalice has a special grace of its own—the grace of gladdening. If the Sacraments cause that which they signify, the species of bread and wine must signify in different ways; and that diversity will refer, both to the sign, and to the mode of the signifying, and to the thing signified. Therefore, the effect of the two will not be common but diverse. Both species together signify the plenitude of the heavenly feast and the perfect satisfaction of the soul, which each by itself does not signify.

While it is granted that either species refects us by causing habitual grace, there are certain secondary effects of the spiritual meat and drink: that of the meat is to strengthen the weak, as it is written, " and bread to strengthen man's heart;" that of drink is to give joy to the sad, "and wine that maketh glad the heart of man [l]," is that spiritual transport, the *inebriatio animæ*, of which the Scripture speaks [m].

[l] Ps. civ. 15.   [m] Vide Lugo, *de Sacramento Eucharistiæ*, dist. xvi. sect. iii. p. 488, ed. Migne, 1841.

Indeed, to say that the Cup has not a gift over and above the other species, would be to contradict the Church, which after reception of the Body, directs that the words be used, " the Blood of our Lord Jesus preserve thy body and soul unto everlasting life."

ARTICLE XXXI.

De Unica Christi Oblatione in Cruce perfecta.

Oblatio Christi semel facta perfecta est redemptio, propitiatio, et satisfactio pro omnibus peccatis totius mundi, tam originalibus, quam actualibus. Neque præter illam unicam, est ulla alia pro peccatis expiatio ; unde missarum sacrificia, quibus vulgo dicebatur Sacerdotem offerre Christum in remissionem pœnæ, aut culpæ, pro vivis et defunctis, blasphema figmenta sunt, et perniciosæ imposturæ.

" Of the One Oblation of Christ finished upon the Cross.

" The offering of Christ once made is the perfect redemption, propitiation, and satisfaction for all the sins of the whole world, both original and actual: and there is none other satisfaction for sin but that alone. Wherefore the sacrifices of masses, in the which it was commonly said that the Priest did offer Christ for the quick and the dead, to have remission of pain or guilt, were blasphemous fables, and dangerous deceits."

"The breaking of the Bread and the Prayers," which are the terms used for the worship of the primitive Church [*], have from the beginning been invested with

* Acts ii. 42.

a sacrificial character. The Greek original of the New Testament brings this out much more strongly than the English translation. Thus, in the Acts of the Holy Apostles, the expression, " as they were ministering," is rendered by the hieratic word λειτουργούντων; the Christian ministers in the person of Christ, τῶν ἁγίων λειτουργὸς [b], are διακόνοις τῆς καινῆς διαθήκης [c]; the worship of the Church of the Gentiles as elected on the ruin of the Jews is the πρόσφορα τῶν ἐθνῶν; not only εὐχαὶ and δεήσεις ('prayers and supplications') but εὐχαριστίαι are to be offered for all men; it is asserted that ἔχομεν θυσιαστήριον, the old Levitical words adscara, 'sacrificial commemoration,' rendered ἀνάμνησις, and asah rendered ποιεῖν, by the LXX, are adopted by Christianity; and St. Paul, animated entirely by the sacerdotal idea, calls himself λειτουργὸν Ἰησοῦ Χριστοῦ εἰς τὰ ἔθνη, ἱερουργοῦντα τὸ εὐαγγέλιον τοῦ Θεοῦ, ἵνα γένηται ἡ προσφορὰ τῶν ἐθνῶν εὐπρόσδεκτος, ἡγιασμένη ἐν Πνεύματι Ἁγίῳ [d]. Accordingly, in the very earliest ages, we find such expressions, προσφορὰ, θυσία, ἱερουργία, oblatio, Sacrificium Dominicum, Dominicum, freely used, and the sacrificial aspect of the Holy Eucharist is clearly stated by St. Clement, of Rome [e], and by St. Ignatius [f]; and St. Justin speaks of the Eucharistic Sacrifice being pre-signified by the pure offering mentioned by the Prophet Malachi [g]. St. Irenæus [h], after relating the institution, adds this

[b] Heb. viii. 2. [c] 2 Cor. iii. 6. [d] Rom. xv. 16.
[e] 1 Cor. n. 40, 45. [f] *Eph.* n. v.; *Magn.*, n. vii.; *Phil.* iv.
[g] *Tryph.*, 41, 117. [h] S. Iren. iv. 17, n. 5.

remark : " Thus Jesus Christ has established the Sacrifice of the New Testament, which the Church offers to God throughout the whole world, according to the teaching handed down by the Apostles." He states that it is the Word Who is offered in this Sacrifice [1].

Origen [k] asserts that in the Christian Churches there is a Sacrifice, at once commemorative and propitiatory, that is to say, the Eucharist.

St. Cyprian [l], who had occasion to enter upon the consideration of the doctrine of the Holy Eucharist with a view to satisfying the scruples of certain ignorant and simple persons who demurred at the use of wine in these holy mysteries, asks :—" Who is more a Priest of the Most High God than our Lord Jesus Christ, Who offered a sacrifice to God the Father, and offered the same which Melchisedek had offered, i.e. bread and wine, namely, His own Body and Blood?" In the same letter he says :—" If Jesus Christ our Lord and God is Himself the great High-Priest of God the Father, and first offered Himself a Sacrifice to the Father, and commanded this to be done in remembrance of Himself, surely that priest truly acts in Christ's stead, who imitates that which Christ did; and he then offers a true and full sacrifice in the Church to God the Father, when he begins to offer it according as he sees Christ Himself offered it."

St. Cyril of Jerusalem, in his " Catechism," which is very important as shewing the actual practical in-

---

[1] St. Iren., iv. 18, n. 4.   [k] *In Lev. Hom.* xiii. n. 3.
[l] *Ep.* lxiii.

struction of the Church of his time, says, without ora-torical periphrasis, " We offer Jesus Christ immolated for our sins [m]."

But a still clearer evidence of the faith of the early Church is to be found in the early Liturgies. The parts of these which are found in all, and are thus traced up to a common ancestry of unwritten tradition, are so venerable in their antiquity, that many great scholars have maintained that they are more ancient than the later epistles. In any case, they are docu-ments of the highest authority, and unimpeachable witnesses to primitive practice. Now, in all these without exception, we have the distinctest enunciation of the Sacrificial character of the Holy Eucharist. In spite of the insertion of the prayer of St. Chrysostom into our morning service, which was in 1544 appended to the Litany, it is probable that the English Re-formers were not conversant with the Eastern Litur-gies, otherwise we cannot conceive how they could have preferred the Second to the First Book of Ed-ward, or have rested content with the emendations at the beginning of the reign of Elizabeth.

Bearing in mind, then, the hieratic language of Holy Scripture, the unbroken tradition of Church doc-tors from the earliest times, the witness of the ancient Liturgies, (a witness corroborated by the fact that many of these have been used by bodies which have been alienated from the Catholic Church since the Council of Chalcedon, and so become an independent testi-

[m] *Myst. Cat.*, xxiii. n. 10.

mony,) we are safe in accepting the truth, that in view of the imperfection of the Levitical rites, and of His Eternal Priesthood after the order of Melchisedek, our Lord,—although He was about to offer Himself once for all upon the altar of the Cross to His Father, by means of His death to obtain eternal redemption for us, yet because His is an abiding Priesthood, in order that He might leave to the Church a visible rite whereby the bloody Sacrifice once for all to be accomplished on the Cross might be represented, remembered till the end of the world, and its virtue applied to the remission of sins as they are committed,—at the Last Supper, in the night that He was betrayed, offered to God the Father His own Body and Blood under the form of Bread and Wine, delivered Them to the Apostles, and, by the words "This do in remembrance of Me," commanded them and their successors thus to shew forth His death till He come again.

One cannot find any contradiction between this Article and the Catholic doctrine of the Eucharistic Sacrifice thus stated. In the words of Mr. Palmer[n]: "The Article condemning the sacrifices of masses, in which it was commonly said that Christ was offered for the quick and dead for the remission of pain or guilt,"—" rightly censures that erroneous view of the Sacrifice, but does not declare against the doctrine of the Eucharistic Sacrifice rightly understood." And elsewhere: "The Thirty-first Article is directed against the vulgar and heretical doctrine of the *reiteration* of Christ's Sacrifice

---

[n] Treatise on the Church, vol. i. p. 400, ed. 1842.

in the Eucharist. It was those ' missarum sacrificia, quibus vulgo dicebatur sacerdotem offerre Christum in remissionem pœnæ, aut culpæ, pro vivis et defunctis,' which are pronounced ' blasphema figmenta et perniciosæ imposturæ ;' but not ' missarum sacrificia,' as understood by the Fathers, and in an orthodox sense. The Article was directed against the errors maintained and countenanced by such men as Soto, Hardinge, &c., who, by rejecting the doctrine of a Sacrifice by way of commemoration and consecration, and not literally identical with that on the Cross, and by their crude and objectionable mode of expression, countenanced the vulgar error that the Sacrifice of the Eucharist or mass was in every respect equal to that of Christ upon the Cross, and that it was, in fact, either a reiteration or a continuation of that Sacrifice," i.e. actively a continuation. "The Article was not directed against the doctrine of the Eucharistic Sacrifice, as explained by Bossuet, Veron, and others, with which we have no material fault to find°."

Or if it be right to claim Episcopal sanction for this view, it is to be found in the words of the present Lord Bishop of Exeter : "Again I see the same high authority numbers among the errors of Rome which our own Church has renounced, that a propitiatory virtue is attributed to the Eucharist ᴾ." "I am not aware of our Church having anywhere condemned such a doctrine. That it has condemned (as we all from our

---

° Treatise on the Church, vol. ii. p. 347.
ᴾ Pastoral Letter of 1851, p. 53.

hearts condemn) 'as blasphemous fables and dangerous deceits,' 'the sacrifices of masses, in the which it was commonly said that the Priest did offer Christ for the quick and dead to have remission from pain or guilt,'— we know and heartily rejoice. But this is very far, indeed, from saying or meaning that the Eucharist hath not 'a propitiatory virtue,' and we must be very careful how we deny that virtue to it. The consecrated elements ought not to be separated in our minds from the propitiation for our sins, continually presented for us before the throne of God. Whether we regard them in correspondence with the meat-offerings and drink-offerings of the Old Testament, as memorials of the one great Sacrifice, and so, in union with that Sacrifice, by virtue of Christ's appointment, representing and pleading to the Father the atonement finished on the Cross—or as answering to those portions of the typical sacrifices which were eaten by the Priests and offerers — in either case, they are intimately united with the altar in heaven and with its propitiatory virtue. 'In these holy mysteries,' in an especial manner, heaven and earth are brought together. *Sursum Corda.* 'Therefore with angels and archangels, and all the company of heaven, *we* laud and magnify Thy holy Name.' The partakers of the Sacrifice, are partakers of the altar and of all its inestimable benefits, the first of which is the propitiation for our sins. For, in the Eucharist, as a *Sacrament,* 'we eat our *ransom,*' as St. Augustine says,—we receive spiritually 'the Body of our Lord Jesus Christ which was given for us,' 'the Blood which was shed for us;' in the same Eucharist as *a Sacrifice*, we, in representation, *plead* the one great Sacrifice which our Great High Priest continually presenteth for us in heaven. In heaven, He presenteth ever before the Father, in person, Himself,—mediating with the Father as our intercessor; on earth He invisibly sanctifies what is offered, and makes the earthly elements, which we offer, to be sacramentally and ineffably—but not in a carnal way—His Body and Blood. For although once for all offered, that Sacrifice, be it remembered, is ever LIVING AND CONTINUOUS, made to be continuous by the resurrection of our Lord. Accordingly, St. John tells us, in Rev. v. 6, 12, that he beheld, and lo in the midst of the throne stood a Lamb as it had been slain, and to Him is continually addressed the triumphant song of the *heavenly* host, 'Worthy is the Lamb that was slain to receive power, and riches, and wisdom, and strength, and honour, and glory, and blessing.' To Him His Church on earth, in the Eucharistic Service, in like manner, continually cries, 'O Lord God, Lamb of God, Son of the Father, that *takest* away the sins of the world.' Not that tookest away, but still takest—'Agnus Dei, qui tollis peccata mundi.' As, then, the Sacrifice is continuous, its propitiatory virtue is continuous, and the fulness of the propitiation is pleaded for the whole Church, wheresoever the commemoration of it is exhibited in the Holy Eucharist."

The key to the meaning of the Article is in the

words " wherefore" and " satisfaction." Any construction which condemns a doctrine of Eucharistic Sacrifice consistent with the first sentence of the Article, makes it self-contradictory, inasmuch as the Article expressly confines itself to excluding any notion which would militate against the perfection of the offering of Christ once made upon the Cross, as being the only " satisfaction for sin." For " there is but one real, true, and proper Sacrifice, viz. the offering which the Incarnate Son of God made of Himself upon the Cross to the Eternal Father."

The Sacrifice in the Eucharist is substantially the same as the Sacrifice of the Cross, because the Priest is the same in both, and the Victim is the same in both; just as the Sacrifice which Christ the eternal Priest is now presenting to His Father in heaven, is the same which He offered upon the Cross, because He Himself is the same Victim and Priest both in one. But there is a difference. There is a difference in the manner of offering. In heaven Christ is not offering Himself in the same manner as He did upon the Cross. We cannot rightfully censure or approve the first part of this proposition, without consideration of the second. If we deny the first as contradictory to the Article, we must deny the second, for it also affirms a Sacrifice of Christ distinct in the manner of offering from that on the Cross,—distinct both as not meriting any more, and as not accompanied by suffering—and so far both statements stand in the same relation to the statement in the Article; if the second is not contradictory, neither is the first. Are we prepared to say that the second statement in the proposition, "The Sacrifice which Christ the eternal Priest is now presenting to His Father in Heaven, is the same which He offered upon the Cross," is contradictory to the Article, and is equivalent to setting up another meritorious Sacrifice? If not, there is no confusion of thought. While the Sacrifice is continuous, the Satisfaction, properly so called, is not so. The "atonement," as meritorious, was finished upon the Cross.

If the doctrine be said to be antagonistic to the statement, "Christ in His Holy Gospel hath commanded us to continue a perpetual memorial of that His precious death until His coming again," it must be recollected that we are dwelling on the act of our blessed Lord in meritoriously dying upon the Cross, an act in time which being past can be commemorated. If we withdraw our thoughts for one moment from the Blessed Eucharist to the action of our Lord in heaven, we find that there, by the presentation of His Humanity, He does make a memorial of His act upon the Cross. In that celestial service we find the two elements of a real presence and a commemorative offering, and if we believe a real presence in the Holy Sacrament, with the change from a natural to a supernatural condition, we can apply this reasoning to establish an analogous offering in the Church below.

That a memorial of a Sacrifice may be the Sacrifice itself, is plain from the case of the Paschal Lamb;

which, offered as it was year by year continually, was in kind the same sacrifice with that originally offered in Egypt, yet truly a memorial of it. When, therefore, the Homily says, " we must be careful that we do not of a memory make it a Sacrifice," we may not understand it as though the two ideas were inconsistent, but rather as follows: ' It is not to be accounted a distinct and independent Sacrifice; we must never use it or think of it apart from its relation to the One Great and True Sacrifice which had gone before.' And this is no doubt St. Chrysostom's meaning, when having said, " we celebrate no other Sacrifice, but the same always," he as it were qualifies his words, adding, " or rather we make a remembrance of a Sacrifice ;" i. e. it was never to be forgotten that this rite, though most truly a Sacrifice, was so by being the memorial of the One Sacrifice on the Cross. Memory, then, is not inconsistent with Sacrifice. If it were, there could be no Sacrifice of the Altar at all.

The next point which requires to be considered is the assertion of the futility of the sacrifices of masses in reference to the quick and the dead. It is not inconsistent with this to assert that ' We pray that the whole Church may receive, through this Sacrifice, the benefit of the Lord's Passion, each, of course, according to his need and capacity of receiving. Whence the Eucharist is called by some of the Fathers a Sacrifice for the Living and the Dead.' Where a word is absolutely necessary to convey a meaning, the use of that word must be risked, but always with

careful explanations. We are not content with saying the Church simply, nor yet the whole Church, but
we say "all the whole Church ⁱ," that there may be
neither limitation nor reserve in our application of
the Sacrifice. And as the Church, in the amplitude
of its extent, embraces both worlds, the visible and
the invisible, we must be understood to pray and to
offer for all the living members of Christ's Body, whether
sojourning with us here on earth, or departed hence in
the Lord—for we cannot offer for all the whole Church
unless we do, when we comprehend all who are in it,
all who are united to Christ, all who are *one* with us
in that mystical Body which is the fulness of Him
Who filleth all in all. It is no new use of the term
to apply the very peculiar expression of "all Thy
whole Church," to those in the intermediate state;
many English divines have done so without blame.

However people may wish to disparage the testimony of the early Liturgies, it is a fact which
cannot be gainsaid, that *in every one of them*, without exception, there is a commemoration of the faithful departed. The entire universality of the practice must remove any ground for doubt on the subject. Much has been said about the difficulties of
arriving at what the ancients believed, but here
over the whole Christian world we have evidence for
this truth from the most solemn documents which
may be traced up to the highest antiquity, documents which with the strongest evidences of a com-

ⁱ Communion Office, Book of Common Prayer.

mon origin, yet vary sufficiently to become concurrent testimonies in favour of any doctrine which they agree in expressing.

And secondly, it may be further said that the application of the blessed Eucharist to the departed, must in our Church stand and fall with the practice of prayers for the dead. In its aspect of the great oblation, the Holy Communion may be considered as prayer in its most intense and highest form. If it is unlawful to pray for the faithful departed, it must be unlawful to remember them in the sacred mysteries; but if the first practice be permitted, the second must be so likewise. The Church of England has judicially ruled in her Supreme Tribunal, that prayer for the Dead is not unlawful[r].

It cannot be doubted that in the very earliest and purest ages of the Church, it was universally believed that the celebration of the Holy Eucharist had special reference to the faithful departed. Tertullian[s]:—
" Wherefore does she pray for his (her husband's) soul, and begs for him in the meantime refreshment, and a share in the first resurrection, and offers for him on the anniversary of his death." St. Cyprian[t], providing against the clergy becoming executors, says that the Bishops who preceded him resolved that there should be no oblation for such, nor should the sacrifice be celebrated for his repose (" nec sacrificium pro dormitione ejus celebraretur"). The passage in St. Cyril's

---

[r] Case of Woolfrey *v.* Breeks, Stephens's Clergy Law, i. 191.

[s] *De Monog.*, n. x.　　　　[t] *Ep.* i. *ad Cler. et Pleb. Furnis.*

Catechism is well-known :—" Also on behalf of the holy Fathers and Bishops who have fallen asleep before us, and of all in spirit who have already fallen asleep among us, believing that it will be of very great assistance to the souls, for which prayer is raised while the holy and most awful Sacrifice lies before us." St. Macarius[u], of Alexandria, discusses the subject of the advantage that accrues to the soul when " an oblation is offered up to God in the Church for the dead." St. Epiphanius, in controversy with Aerius[v], asserts and defends the practice of making a commemoration of the just, and on behalf of sinners : " on behalf of sinners supplicating for mercy from God, and for the just . . . in order that on account of the honour that we pay to Christ, we may separate Him from the race of men." St. Ambrose[x] :—" Give the heavenly Sacrament, let us follow the soul of the grandson with our oblations." St. Chrysostom[y] describes the actual ritual of his time as obtaining $\pi\alpha\rho\alpha\mu\nu\theta\ia$ for the dead. The reader will also remember the last injunction of St. Monica to St. Augustine.

One common argument against the Eucharistic Sacrifice is that, according to this belief, one must hold and teach the blasphemy, that the Sacrifice in the Eucharist must be substantially, virtually, and essentially, although not as He appeared on Calvary, Christ still laying down His life for the sheep, still shedding

<hr>

[u] *Serm. de Excess.*, n. 3—5, p. 238, t. vii. Galland.   [v] *Adv. Hær.*, 75.   [x] *De obit. Valent.*, t. ii. p. 1189, s. 56.
[y] *In Act. Apost. Hom.* ix. ; also xli. in 1 Cor. iii. *ad Philip.*

His Blood for our redemption, still discharging the
yet unpaid penalty for human guilt; that the sacrificial work, in all its essentials of suffering, dying, and
atoning, instead of being finished, must be still only
in progress of accomplishment; that, in fact, there
is a propitiation of the same merit, nature, power, and
efficacy, that Christ's offering on the Cross was not
the alone satisfaction for sin; that one must deny
that the oblation of Christ was finished upon the
Cross; that one must believe that that Sacrifice of
the Holy Eucharist re-enacts the Sacrifice of the Cross
in all its essential entirety; that one must hold our
Lord's eternal Priesthood to consist in His being an
eternal victim, that is, suffering and dying to atone;
that this belief, to be consistent, implies not only that
Christ undergoes in another mode the Sacrifice of the
Cross, but that His Sacrifice of Himself was insufficient,
inasmuch as a repetition is tantamount to insufficiency
of the first act of sacrifice.

Now all this is more than met by the thought that
that one Sacrifice and its all-sufficient merits live on,
as in our Lord's perpetual presentation of Himself in
heaven, so in our Eucharistical Oblation of His Body
and Blood sacramentally present on our altars. We
have nothing apart from that One Sacrifice; our
Eucharistic Oblation is not something in and for itself;
something independent of that One Sacrifice, even
while it pleaded it. Such is its union with that Sacrifice, that it is a perpetual application of its virtue;
yet not as something distinct, but as united with it

through the oneness of that which is offered, that same
Body of Christ offered on the Cross to make atonement
for the sins of the whole world and for each one of us,
offered and presented to the Father, in heaven and in
the Church below, on the " altar above," and on the
Holy Table, in pleading and for application of the
Atonement once for all wrought upon the holy Cross.
On the Cross that offering was made once for all with
shedding of Blood; on earth the offering is made in
an unbloody manner, as the ancient Church attests.
On the Cross, that offering merited the salvation of
the world; on the Altar, Christ being risen from the
dead, dieth no more, but the fruit of that death is
made over to the faithful. On the Cross, the full satisfaction was paid; on the Altar, the memorial of that
satisfaction is made to the Father, in correspondence
with the memorial made upon the celestial Altar.

To shew the harmony between the doctrine of the
Eucharistic Sacrifice as taught by the Fathers, and
the teaching of the Article, while on the one hand we
are bound to receive as true what has been taught
ubique, semper, et ab omnibus, the Church's concurrent
exposition of the Word of God " in the best and purest
ages;" on the other hand it must be consistent with
that other truth of God, which the Thirty-first Article
declares, out of St. Paul. And the solution is found in
the oneness of that which was sacrificed,—the Body of
Christ, offered in satisfaction for our sins, with blood-
shedding on the Cross, offered mystically, sacramentally, ἀθύτως and ἀναιμάκτως, as the Fathers speak,

without shedding of blood, or without sacrificial slaying, on the Altar. And this is further illustrated 1. by a comparison of our acts on earth with our Lord's everlasting Priesthood in heaven. Since His perpetual presentation of His pleading Body there, (by which continual intercession He obtains for us all grace,) does not interfere with the completeness of the Sacrifice on the Cross, so neither does the corresponding presentation on earth in the Eucharistic Sacrifice. 2. Other objections are to be met by stating the belief of the Fathers,—1. that there is a real sacrifice in the Holy Eucharist; 2. that what is offered is the Body and Blood of Christ, invisibly and sacramentally present with us, but still the same Body which our Saviour offered for us in His own meritorious Sacrifice on the Cross; (for although His Body is present with us in a different way, it is still the same Body, for our Blessed Lord hath not two Bodies, but one only;) 3. that by offering and pleading this, we, if there be no let or hindrance on man's part, obtain the more readily the grace of God which we entreat for.

The matter may be made clearer by the distinction between "the active and passive sacrifice," i.e. sacrifice as "the action of offering," and sacrifice as "the thing offered." It is simply an ambiguity in our language, in which we use the same word (as is noticed in Johnson's Dictionary,) for 1. "the act of offering;" 2. "the thing offered." Theologians use the word "sacrifice" in the one English sense, of "the thing offered ;" those who object to their teaching take it in the other, of " the act of offering." Article XXXI. uses the word sacrifice in the sense of "the *act* of offering." In this sense every one must affirm what the Article affirms, (it is a simple and fundamental matter of faith.) As an act of immolation, atonement, satisfaction, the offering of Christ was "finished once for all."

With all which men, educated in imperfect systems of theology, say on the perfectness and all-sufficiency of our Lord's act of oblation—His active Sacrifice—one must most entirely concur. It is a matter of rejoicing (amid the misbelief in many quarters at the present day) to observe the jealousy for the maintenance of these most vital truths; amid our many sorrows, it is gratifying to find, on the part of men even of extreme views in one direction, such harmony with the ancient faith on the blessed Atonement of our Lord. No Christian can say otherwise, than that the Sacrifice of the Cross was " the one oblation of Christ," *oblatio unica,* " the offering of Christ once made," *semel facta,* "for all the sins of the whole world, and there is none other satisfaction for sin but that alone," *præter illam unicam neque est ulla alia.* It stands alone in all respects. It is one and singular in *the victim, the act, and the result.* There is only one Christ, one offering for sin, one purchase of man's redemption. The Sacrifice of the Cross was Christ's offering of Himself, performing an act which was unique in itself, and securing a purchase which was entire in itself. Although extending in its effects throughout eternity, the Sacrifice of Christ—i.e. His act of sacrificing Himself, His shedding of His precious Blood for man's salvation, His dying for us, atoning for us, meriting for us, making intercession for us,—is, in time, place, and circumstances, a thing of the past. It was *laying down His life*, dying, voluntarily submitting to death; and death, when really fulfilled, is an accomplished fact, a thing past and complete in itself. Again, the Sacrifice of Christ *was offered upon the Cross;* it was the act of a certain specific time and place, as distinct from all other occasions and places. The Sacrifice of the Cross was, moreover, *a perfect act of atonement and satisfaction* for the sins of the whole world, which Christ alone was able to make, and did make by the single act of dying, and which, when made, was ended as complete and sufficient for its purpose.

Every Christian must believe this. And so, on the other hand, every Christian must repudiate the fearful errors which are ignorantly supposed to follow from the true doctrine, " there never can be any other sacrifice (i.e. any other act of sacrifice) identical with the Sacrifice of the Cross." Assuredly not. No one ever said so. All that is said is with St. Chrysostom, What *we* offer is the Same which our blessed Lord then offered for us. Obviously, to say or imply that Christ was still laying down His life for the sheep, still shedding His Blood for our redemption, still discharging the yet unpaid penalty for human guilt, is more than a contravention of the Thirty-first Article ; it is blasphemy.

But it has sometimes been said, the distinction between "the action of offering," which was completed, perfected, finished, once for all upon the altar of the Cross, "and the Thing offered," must be set aside on the ground that where the offerer is the same and the thing or person offered the same, the act of offering must be the same also. Will the reasoning hold? Apply it to the ritual of the Day of Atonement. It was the same pontiff who immolated the victim outside the tabernacle, and who presented its blood within the holy of holies ; the latter function being described by the Apostle as the *offering* of the blood[z] ; a phrase, most momentous in relation to the anti-typical part of the subject. It was also the same victim in both cases. But who will say that the act of offering, when the sacrifice was slain, and the act of presenting its blood within the holy of holies, was one and the same act? Again, apply this inference to the sacerdotal work of our Lord. He was the Offerer on the Cross, and is the Offerer before the Throne. On the Cross and before the Throne there is but one Thing or Person offered ; one Sacrifice, in that passive sense in which theologians have used the terms. But, on the above assumption, it would follow that the "action of offering," on the Cross and in Heaven, was one and the same ; in other words, that the satisfaction or Atonement which belongs to

[z] Heb. ix. 5.

our Lord's meritorious death on Calvary would not be "perfect," or "once made," but continuous.

The Fathers mean by their saying, that our Blessed Lord, now too, "is the Offerer and the Oblation," that "the Sacrifice here below is part of His Melchizedekean priesthood. He invisibly consecrates; He invisibly offers." Our Lord invisibly offers, in that He invisibly consecrates. St. Ambrose says :—"though Christ is not now seen to offer, yet Himself is offered on earth, when the Body of Christ is offered; yea, Himself is plainly seen to offer in us, Whose Word sanctifieth the Sacrifice which is offered*." Christ now, also, doth invisibly and efficaciously all which is done in His Name. Christ baptizeth, although not in the same mode as He baptized on earth. Christ absolveth, although not in the same mode as when He said to the penitent before Him, "Thy sins are forgiven thee." Christ consecrateth, Whose word of power consecrates, although not in the same mode as on the night before His Passion. Christ is the only Teacher, although not in the same mode as when He spake the Sermon on the Mount. He comforteth, though not in the same way as when He said on earth, "Be of good cheer," or "Peace be unto you." So neither does it follow, nor is it true, that because our Lord, by His word, still consecrates our offering, He is the Offerer in the same way as when, on the night before He suffered, He anticipated the assault of the Jews, "according to the mode of His priestly act, ineffable

* In Ps. xxxviii. § 25, p. 852.

and invisible to man, and offered Himself as an Offering and Sacrifice for us, Priest at once, and 'the Lamb of God, who taketh away the sins of the world[b].'" He offered Himself by anticipation at the last Supper; He offered Himself in deed by His meritorious death on the Cross; He offereth Himself by presenting Himself, our High-Priest for ever, in the presence of the Father in heaven; He mystically offereth Himself in the Holy Eucharist, not only in that He consecrateth by His word the gifts which He has taught us to offer for a memorial of Himself, but that, being Sacramentally present, He is "precious in the eyes of the Father." Yet because He Himself is the agent in all, it follows not that He acts in the same way in all. On the Cross, He *made* the offering; in heaven, He *presents* it, and as God-man, pleads it; on earth He giveth it to us to plead, in that He consecrates that Offering, whose very Presence pleads, in that it is, in a mystery, the Body which was broken, the Blood which was shed for us.

But it may be argued that the assertion " An eternal Priesthood implies, by the necessity of the case, a perpetual victim, and that perpetual victim is the offering of the Body of Jesus," is completely opposed to Scripture, because a victim is one enduring death for others, and a perpetual victim is a contradiction in terms.

Neither the Latin *victima* (as used either in classic writers, or in a theological sense by the Fathers,)

[b] S. Greg. Nyss., *in Christ. Resur.*, Or. i. t. iii. p. 389.

nor the English "victim" means "one enduring death." The Latin means, if we accept the authority of Facciolati, "a thing *destined to be* sacrificed," or "which has been sacrificed." For the English, Johnson gives the original and metaphoric meaning: 1. "A sacrifice, something *slain* for a sacrifice. 2. Something destroyed." The act of being offered was ordinarily so brief as not to be taken into account. The only idea which the word "victim" had *not*, was "enduring death." It continued a victim, after death, until it was consumed. Animal sacrifices perish; our Great Sacrifice abideth. The title belonged to Him before He was slain. For He is the Lamb slain from the foundation of the world. It applied to Him in the same sense, and in the same sense only, while He was dying. For His Death consummated the Sacrifice. It applies to Him equally now, as the Lamb which hath been slain, and is most especially applicable to Him who "appears," or "exhibits Himself," continually before God for us, with all His saving wounds, the tokens of His Passion. An eternal Priesthood implies, by the necessity of the case, *something to be perpetually offered*, and that which is perpetually offered for us by our Melchizedek is the Body of Jesus.

Many of these objections flow from an inadequate belief in the doctrine of the perpetual Priesthood of our Lord and His unceasing intercession for the whole Church. It is to be feared that some hold, rather, that having made His one Oblation upon the Cross, He has now ceased from any exclusively priestly function. Is their idea of His intercession more than that of an oral all-prevailing prayer? But God hath said, "Thou art a High-Priest for ever." And He is not in such wise a High-Priest, that He can be imagined separate from the Sacrifice which He once offered. For that Sacrifice was Himself. That Sacrifice is His Manhood, never to be divided from His Godhead. He has carried within the veil that Holy Body, once wounded for our transgressions, and those very wounds, which He shewed to St. Thomas, now resplendent in glory, still move the Father to look upon the face of His Anointed, and for His sake freely to give us all things. And as this is no derogation from the oneness and completeness of our Lord's atoning act on Calvary, so neither is it a derogation therefrom that we, in the Holy Eucharist, with all our prayers, present unto the Father the same Holy Body, present in an ineffable way by the words of consecration.

Note on ' adscara' and ' asah' p. 600.

עָשָׂה, "2. f. fecit, i.e. paravit victimam vel hostiam Deo offerendam (sacrificia enim diis convivii instar parata offerebantur), inde obtulit. Thus, Ps. lxvi. 15; Exod. xxix. 36, 38, 39, 41; Num. vi. 17; &c. (Cf. gr. ἱερὰ ἔρδειν, ἱερὰ ῥέζειν, et omisso acc. ῥέζειν θεῷ, Il. 2, 400; 8, 250; Od. 14, 251, lat. *sacra, res divinas, facere,* et ellipt. *facere,* i.e. sacrificare, Cic." Gesenius ad verb. Thes. p. 1075, 6. אַזְכָּרָה 2. " Verbale Hiphil ab ea radicis significatione, quæ supra no. 1, bb. exposita est, pr. ' sacrificium memoriale, in memoriam revocans.' LXX. Vulg. μνημόσυνον, memoriale. Sic appellabatur ea fertorum pars, quæ una cum thure in altari comburebatur, cujusque suavis odor in coelum ascendens ejus, qui sacrum obtulerat, memoriam numini commendare credebatur. Lev. ii. 2, 9, 16, v. 12, vi. 8. Num. v. 26." Ib. v. זָכַר, p. 417.

ARTICLE XXXII.

De Conjugio Sacerdotum.

*Episcopis, Presbyteris, et Diaconis nullo mandato divino
præceptum est, ut aut cœlibatum voveant, aut a matri-
monio abstineant. Licet igitur etiam illis, ut cæteris
omnibus Christianis, ubi hoc ad pietatem magis facere
judicaverint, pro suo arbitratu matrimonium contrahere.*

" Of the Marriage of Priests.

" BISHOPS, Priests, and Deacons, are not commanded
by God's law either to vow the estate of single life,
or to abstain from marriage: therefore it is lawful for
them, as for all other Christian men, to marry at their
own discretion, as they shall judge the same to serve
better to godliness."

The first point here to be observed is the title, and
though we have observed that there is a certain loose-
ness in the use of terms in the titles of the Articles,
yet here and there there are indications of a set purpose in the phraseology used. Now both the title and
the contents of the Article of 1571 differ from the
earlier digest. In the title of Article **XXXI.** of 1553,
it is laid down categorically, "The state of single life
is commanded of no man by the word of God;" or as
it is said in the Latin, *Cœlibatus ex verbo Dei præcipitur*

nemini. This *præceptum* of the title is changed in the body of the Article into *mandatum,* " neither is any one compelled, *jure divino,* to abstain from matrimony." The revised Article uses the expression *De conjugio sacerdotum.* The language in the second place is a little strengthened, and both the ideas of *mandatum* and *præceptum* are conjoined—*nullo mandato divino præceptum est;* and it then goes on to add that the clergy in this respect may act as other Christian men. Now not only is the marked contrast of the clergy with other Christian men an observable thing, but the use of the word *sacerdotum* shews how entirely the English Reformers repudiated the idea of a mere minister, and assumed that of a λειτουργος or *sacerdos.* Had the word stood alone we might have supposed it to be a slip, but bearing in mind the employment of it in Article XXXI., we may suppose that it was no *incuria,* but intentionally done. If so, we have the identity of the priesthood before and after the Reformation asserted, just as actually we find maintained in the amended Statutes of Corpus Christi College, where it is held that the Fellows, " though discharged from massing," were still of necessity to be Priests [a].

And the word, in being used to cover the three sacred orders, adds to the importance of the phraseology; for though in the primitive Church, in St. Cyprian, St. Augustine, St. Ambrose, the word is used for the Episcopate, just as the corresponding term ἱερευς is used by St. Chrysostom; and though after-

---

[a] Vide Statutes, Corpus Christi College.

wards it was sometimes with and sometimes without the specification *secundi ordinis*, used for the Presbyterate; the including the Diaconate in the term, shews how high in the Article is the estimate of all the orders according to the old definition: — " Sacerdos, quasi sacrum dans, a Dei mysteria administrando[b]." The early use of *sacerdos* and *levita* for Priest and Deacon, derived into the Christian phraseology through the Vulgate, shews how completely the new law was looked upon as the continuation and supplement of the old law.

The proposition that the celibacy of the priesthood is not *jure divino* is absolutely Catholic. It has ever been regarded as a matter of pure discipline, varying with the different ages, and the necessities of the Church. The law might be relaxed to-morrow over the whole world; but it is the distinguishing feature of Christianity to be at once both real and ideal. It throws itself into the world, accepts the complex phenomena of civilization, and deals with men as it finds them. And yet it never loses sight of the thought that its real home is not on earth but in heaven, and that it has to transmute the elements of this world into a higher order. Compounded of the divine and the human, it has to subdue and elevate its inferior nature, and the actions of this mixed creation are referred to celestial personality. The divine Person of our Lord shines down upon His work, and just as it was the Divinity and not the Humanity which supplied the

[b] Ducange, *ad verb.*

Personality to Him, so in His work on earth it is the
nobler element that must dominate. In our Divine
Lord the Godhead determined the operation of the
Humanity, which was assumed as the instrument of
the Divinity; His Personality was not human, but
Divine; His Human Will ever followed His Divine
Will; His Human acts were deified; of that Humanity
we are partakers, and through It, St. Peter says, we
are "partakers of the Divine Nature[c]." The tendency,
therefore, of religion will always be to the ideal; it
will at least recognise a high standard, however far
it may come short of it.

Now we find that this actually was the fashion, on
which our Lord promulgated the Gospel. While He
came not to destroy the law, but to fulfil it, to give
it a fresh sanction and larger grace, while He was
manifested that He might elevate the ordinary society
of men, and make them live so as that by His merits
they might attain everlasting life, He also instituted,
as we have seen in a previous Article (XIV.), what are
termed Counsels of Perfection. He gave the rule of
a higher life, formed upon His own most holy life, for
"such as could receive it." Voluntary poverty, in
imitation of Him who had not where to lay His head;
voluntary obedience, as following Him Who for our
sakes was subject to Joseph and Mary, the works
of His hand; virginal purity, at the foot of Him
Who was the Virgin Son of a Virgin Mother, become
those higher exceptional graces—the ideal, in short, of

[c] 2 Pet. i. 4.

Christianity, the highest manifestations of the results of the Gospel; a law, not for all but for the few: yet these few, lights of the world in their several generations.

A view like this could not but profoundly affect the sacerdotal requirement. Even in the lowest types of Christianity, as has been already stated under Article XXVI., it is always expected that the clergy shall be an example to the flock, shall lead a somewhat stricter life than others, shall abstain from certain harmless amusements, and deny themselves in what is permitted freely to their people. Still more was this the case in the early Church, when the new religion in all its strength was the regenerating power of the world; when, in the face of a corrupt and effete Paganism, it was giving new life to society. Then the demand for any high qualifications in the clergy naturally took the shape of an exaction of adherence to the Counsels of Perfection. Yet neither our Lord, nor His Apostles, nor again their successors the early Bishops, strained human nature beyond what it could bear. While our Lord laid down the rule of perfection for such as could bear it, He allowed the Apostles to choose as clergy men who were married once[d]. St. Paul makes provision for the conduct of

[d] "He [St. Paul] says that a Bishop must be blameless, husband of one wife. He so saith, not enacting this as a law, but hindering unrestrainedness." St. Chrys. *in* 1 *Tim.*, *Hom.* x. The Bishop of Thyatira, consecrated probably by St. John, was, according to the undoubted reading (Rev. ii. 20), married, though his marriage turned out ill. "*Thy* wife, Jezebel." "The word σου is in the best and oldest

such married men, and for the regulation of their families. While recognising the claims of "the present necessity" freely, he allows St. Timothy and St. Titus to ordain as Bishops once-married men who were blameless and well conducted in the ordinary rules of life[e]. The injunction to St. Titus at least, implies that such as were married, were married before ordination. The Greek Church was very strict in enforcing this limitation.

The Apostolic Canons, or Ante-Nicene Eastern Code, while they forbid any of the three sacred orders to put away their wives on plea of religion, exclude digamists and those who have married widows or divorcees; and absolutely forbid marriage after ordination[f]. At Neocæsarea, in 314, Priests married after ordination are to be degraded[g]. At Ancyra the same rule is laid down, but Deacons signifying their intention of marrying before ordination may do so[h]. The Synod of Gangra condemned those, who, misled by the heretical teaching of Eustathius, the Semi-Arian Bishop of Sebaste, on marriage, would not receive communion from a married priest, as though he ought not to minister[i].

The abuse of the συμπαρεισάκτοι or *subintroductæ*,

MSS., the Syrian and older Latin version (in Cyprian and Primasius 'uxorem tuam'), and is therefore rightly received into the text by Meyer, Lachmann, Tischendorf, and Buttmann. Only Düsterdick rejects it, manifestly on grounds other than critical, for the evidence is overwhelming in its favour."—(Döllinger, "First Ages of the Church," p. 293, not. 2. Eng. Tr.)

[e] 1 Tim. iii. 2 ; Tit. i. 5, sqq.   [f] Can. v., xvi., xvii., xxv.
[g] Can. i.   [h] Can. x.   [i] Can. i.

however, implies a co-existent life of celibacy both of
men and women. For to celibates only could there
either be temptation to, or plea for, this strange and
perilous custom. There are notices of its extending
to some few clergy, and this implies an existing custom
of clerical celibacy. For when corrupt ways or self-
deceits are noticed, it implies that such self-deceit
was an exception. The abuse was the resource of
those, who having, in whatever way or on whatever
ground, given up marriage, wished for the solace of
the intimate society of the other sex, meaning no sin,
though too often, after a time, involved in it. St. Cyprian, indeed, who first mentions the abuse, expressly
states that one Deacon only was involved in it; and
he was at once excommunicated[j]. But in Antioch,
which the heathenized Paul of Samosata did what in
him lay to demoralize (A.D. 260), a formal name (συν-
εισάκτοι) was invented by the inhabitants for those
virgins who were domiciled among men. Paul himself had several such with him, as had his Presbyters
and Deacons[k]. This, then, is a trace of celibacy of
clergy, even in the luxurious Antioch. They were
living as celibates, till Paul corrupted them. Leontius,
who, when a Priest, was deposed for this practice in
an aggravated form[l], was also an insulated case; yet

[j] See St. Cypr., *Ep. ad Pompon.*, p. 7, and note in Oxford Translation.
In *Ep.* xiv., St. Cyprian speaks of the Presbyters and Deacons as restraining these evils.

[k] *Ep. Synod. Conc. Ant. in Eus.*, H. E. vii. 30.

[l] St. Ath., *Apol. pro fuga*, § 26; *Ep. ad Mon.*, § 38. The Synod of
Ancyra forbade virgins to live as " sisters" with any, can. 19, but with-

each such bad case implies that celibacy had an eminence, which bad men wished to attain without its sacrifices.

At the Council of Nicæa it was proposed to forbid the use of marriage to Bishops, Priests, and Deacons, who had married as laymen. It was "vehemently resisted" by St. Paphnutius, an aged confessor, as "a heavy yoke which ought not to be imposed on consecrated men, lest from excessive preciseness the Church should be injured." His authority, the more strong because he himself had led a virgin-life, was sufficient to prevent any law being made upon the subject. Marriage, then, among the clergy remained unforbidden. St. Gregory Nazianzen was the son of the bishop of that see. Eusebius and Socrates have many instances of a married clergy [m].

Custom, however, had gone further than law. The Canon of Nicæa, which forbade that "any Bishop, Priest, or Deacon, or any other of the clergy, should have a *συνείσακτος* with him, unless it were mother, sister, or aunt, or person liable to no suspicion [n]," implies

out any allusion to clergy. St. Clement, of Rome, in his first Syriac Epistle, c. 10, warns against the custom of those "who dwell with virgins under pretence of piety." Later, St. Jerome mentions the "Agapetæ and the virgins who daily fall." (*Ep.* xxii. *ad Eustoch.*, n. 13, 14.) St. Chrysostom has two homilies on *subintroducti* and *subintroductæ*, but with no reference to the clergy. Gieseler's statement, that "this custom chiefly burst in among unmarried clergy," is unsupported by evidence. His statement also, that it is alluded to in Hermas, *Pastor*, l. iii. sim. 9, § 11, is altogether a mistake; nor does there seem to be any allusion to *this* abuse in Tert. *de jej.*, c. 17.

    [m] Socr., i. 11; Soz., i. 23.   [n] Can. iii.

an extensive clerical celibacy, which it protects from scandal. St. Epiphanius says, that "the priesthood sets out mostly from virgins, or, if not, from monks; but if they suffice not for the service, from such as are continent as to their own wives, or are widowers from a single marriage [o]." "This," he says, "prevailed as to Deacon, Priest, Bishop, and Subdeacon, especially where the Canons of the Church were accurately observed [p]." "In some places," he adds, "Presbyters, Deacons, and Subdeacons had children, because men's minds had grown relaxed, and, for the multitude, Clergy were not found." St. Jerome, who says that some Bishops required those whom they ordained to be previously married, and that the people sometimes preferred to elect married Priests to be Bishops, lays it down broadly as the rule of the East [i.e. the Patriarchate of Antioch] and Egypt, as well as Rome, that the Clerks should be either virgins or continent, whether out of or in marriage [q]. Yet his saying that there were "as many twice-married Bishops as at Ariminum [r]" [300], though vaguely said and spoken apparently of such twice-married, as had married once only since their Baptism, implies an extensive married clergy.

Origen had laid down, as the ground of clerical continency, St. Paul's words, that the married were not to defraud one another, except by consent for a season, that they might give themselves unto prayer. If so,

<hr>

[o] *Expos. fid.*, n. 21. [p] *Hær.* 59, n. 4.
[q] *Adv. Vigil.*, n. 2. [r] *Ep.* lxix., *ad Ocean.* § 2, 3.

"it is certain that the perpetual sacrifice is impeded to those subject to conjugal necessities. Whence it seems to me, that to offer the perpetual sacrifice belongs to him alone, who should have devoted himself to unceasing and perpetual chastity[s]." Eusebius follows him, when comparing the Gospel with the old law. He quotes St. Paul's words, "the husband of one wife," but adds, "but for the consecrated, who are engaged in the service of God, it is fitting that they refrain themselves from marital intercourse[t]." St. Cyril, of Jerusalem, uses the argument, "if he, who fulfils *well*[u] the office of Jesus' Priest, refrains himself from women[x]," against those who denied the Incarnation. St. Gregory, of Nyssa, urges Moses' command[y], as a ground of sacerdotal continency[z].

The Œcumenical Council of Chalcedon prefaces its prohibition to Readers and Cantores to wed with Pagans, Jews, or heretics, unless they promised to accede to the orthodox faith, with the words, "Since in some Eparchies they are allowed to marry." Yet in the East, after this, we find Bishops having children by their lawful wives during their Episcopate. The discipline in the East was stereotyped by the Council at Trullo. It forbade clergy who had risen to the Subdiaconate to marry after ordination; but it allowed those who should marry previously, to live with their wives, except at their turn to celebrate, that they

---

[s] *Hom. 23 in Num.*, n. 3; Opp., ii. 358.   [t] *Dem. Ev.*, i. 8; *fin.* p. 33.   [u] καλῶς.   [x] Lect. xii. n. 26, p. 136, O. T.   [y] Ex. xix. 15.   [z] *De Virgin. fin.*, Opp., iii. 178.

might gain what they ask of God [a]. Bishops were forbidden to do this, on pain of deposition [b]. If a married Priest was advanced to the Episcopate, his wife, having first been separated by mutual consent, was, after his consecration, to enter some distant monastery, being provided for by the Bishop [c].

In the West, Tertullian stated it to be an admitted rule, that a second marriage excluded from orders. "I remember some twice-married to have been deposed from their order." "No other *can be* a Priest, than he who, as a layman, had only once been a husband [d]." Elsewhere he insults the Catholics for having twice-married Bishops [e]. The inconsistency is nothing strange in Tertullian; perhaps the solution may lie in the different senses given to 'digamus,' which sometimes includes those only who married twice after their baptism, sometimes those also, who, as Christians, had married once only [f]. Hippolytus, however, in the *Philosophumena*, makes it one of the charges against Pope Calixtus, that they had begun to be lax on this subject. "In his time digamous and trigamous Bishops, Priests, and Deacons, began ($\mathring{\eta}\rho\xi\alpha\nu\tau o$) to be advanced to the clericate. If any also who was among the clergy ($\grave{\epsilon}\nu$ $\kappa\lambda\mathring{\eta}\rho\varphi$ $\mathring{\omega}\nu$) married, such an one remained

---

[a] Can. vi., xiii.

[b] Can. xii. The Canon speaks of the custom as prevailing in Africa, Libya, and other places, and of the offence which it occasioned to the people.

[c] Can. xlviii.   [d] *De Exhort. Cast.*, c. 7.

[e] *De Monogamia*, c. 12.

[f] See Dr. Pusey on Tertullian, note N, pp. 420—432.

in his office as if he had not sinned[g]." In Spain, the Council of Elvira, A.D. 309, forbade marital intercourse to the three orders, on pain of remotion from their office[h].

The law presupposes, however, the *previous* marriage of many clergy, which is recognised also in another Canon[i], prohibiting a Bishop or any other Clerk to have any other with him, except a sister or a daughter dedicated to God. This implies also that the clergy were of mature age. "Very many (*plurimi*) Priests and Deacons, however, continued to have children in, or even out of marriage," (as St. Siricius states in his answer to Exuperius of Tarragona, A.D. 398,) maintaining this custom on the ground of the Old Testament law[k]. Laymen also were ordained, who had been more than once married[l], and this the Spanish bishops did, as if it had been enjoined rather than forbidden[m]. St. Siricius lays down that, on the principles of the old law, "all we, Priests and Deacons, are bound by an indissoluble law, to give hearts and bodies to sobriety and chastity." Those who used marriage in the priesthood were to be deposed; but it was allowed to live in single marriage till thirty, which was fixed as the age of the Diaconate[n].

The second Council of Toledo, A.D. 405, required that those dedicated by their parents to Holy Orders,

---

[g] *Philosoph.*, ix. 12, p. 290.   [h] Can. xxxiii.

[i] Can. xxvii.   [k] *Ep. ad Exup.*, n. 7.

[l] "Quibus fuerint numerosa conjugia," ib., n. 8.   [m] Ibid.

[n] Ibid., n. 9. Five years more were required for the Presbyterate; ten more for the Episcopate.

and educated under the Bishop's eye, should, at eighteen, be interrogated publicly, as to their wish to marry. From those who so will, they say, " we cannot take away what is granted by the Apostles," but such were to be admitted to Holy Orders only in advanced age, when, by mutual consent, they had renounced the use of marriage[o].

In Africa, in the Council of Carthage, A.D. 428, the same enactment was made as at Elvira, that " what Apostles taught, and antiquity observed, we, too, may keep[p]."

St. Innocent I., in his answer to Victricius, Bishop of Rouen, A.D. 404, abridging the arguments of Siricius, lays down the continence of Priests and Deacons as an Apostolic tradition, observed in the Roman Church[q].

St. Leo's answer to the enquiry of Rusticus, Bishop of Narbonne, whether Deacons were allowed the use of marriage, lays down, as the recognised law of the Church, that the ministers of the altar, equally with the Bishops and Presbyters, were prohibited from this.

[o] Can. i. The eighth Council of Toledo, A.D. 636, forbids the marriage of Subdeacons, as a breach of previous law.

[p] *Conc. Carth.* ii., can. ii. In the fifth Council of Carthage, A.D. 438, (*Cod. Eccl. Afr.*, can. xxv.), this enactment was received as " having been established in diverse Councils." Those who infringed it were to " be removed from the ecclesiastical office."

[q] " For the sake of those who, through ignorance or sloth, do not maintain ecclesiastical discipline, and venture on many things not to be ventured on, thou hast rightly asked that in those parts the form be observed which the Roman Church holds, not so that any new precepts be commanded, but that we wish that those things, which have been neglected through the sloth of some, be observed by all, which yet were constituted by Apostolic tradition and of the fathers."

"In order that from a carnal, it should become a spiri
tual marriage, they must not send away their wives,
yet they must have them as though they had them not,
that the love of wedlock may be unimpaired, and the
act of marriage may cease[r]." In his letter to Anastasius, Bishop of Thessalonica, he expressly includes
the Subdeacon as bound by this law, and lays down
that none was to be advanced to the three higher
orders, who was found not to have so refrained[s].

In Gaul, the Council of Turin, A.D. 401, forbade
those who had children, while in the ministry, to be
admitted to higher orders[t]. The first Council of
Orange, A.D. 441, forbade any married men to be ordained, unless, with purpose of conversion, they should
first profess chastity; Deacons, who used marriage, were
to be deposed[u]. The second Council of Arles, A.D. 452,
forbade any one in the bond of wedlock to be raised
to the priesthood, unless he should first be converted;
a Deacon, or any upwards, who for his solace should
have any woman, except grandmother, mother, sister,
daughter, granddaughter, or wife, converted with him,
was excommunicate[x]. It also adopted the two Canons
of the Council of Orange[y]. The first Council of Tours,
A.D. 460, relaxed a consitution of their fathers, which
withheld from communion any Priest or Deacon who
continued to have children, but forbade such to offer
sacrifice to God, or minister to the people, or to rise

---

[r] *Ep.* clxvii. *Inq.* 3, p. 1422.   [s] *Ep.* xiv. c. 4. p. 687.
[t] Can. viii.   [u] Can. xxii. Can. xxiii. provided that
a Deacon, breaking this rule, should be put aside from his office.
[x] Can. ii., iii.   [y] Can. xliii., xliv.

to any higher order[e]. The Council of Agde, A.D. 506, enforced "the rule of ecclesiastical life and discipline which had gone from Bishop Siricius to the provinces," incorporating a portion of the letter of Innocent I.[a] The third Council of Orleans, A.D. 538, renewed the old Canon about clerical continency. The second Council of Tours, A.D. 567, had still to re-enact, "that a Bishop should have a wife as a sister;" and that "a Bishop, who had not an *episcopa*, was not to be followed by any crowd of women, but that the ministers of the Church, especially the Clerks who serve the Bishop and ought to guard him, should have liberty to eject strange women from frequent co-dwelling[b]." The Council also states that "not indeed all, but many [*plures*] Archpresbyters of villages, Deacons, and Subdeacons, were suspected by the people of remaining with their wives." It enjoined that they should be accompanied by other Clerks. A Presbyter, Deacon, or Subdeacon, found with his *presbytera*, or *diaconissa*, or *subdiaconissa*, was to be excommunicated for a year, and deposed from all clerical office[c]. The wives, however, of married Priests or Bishops were not withdrawn into convents, as appears from the history of Stephania, wife of Pope Adrian II. In A.D. 868, Eleutherius, who had deceived and married her daughter, being already espoused to another[d], murdered mother and daughter.

The greater strictness of law in the West led to

---

[e] Can. ii.   [a] Can. ix.   [b] *Præf.* and can. ii.   [c] Can. xii., xiii., xix.   [d] Hincmari Remensis *Annales*, A. 868, in Pertz, *Mon. Germ.*, i. 476.

greater laxness of practice. The Western Councils of
the ninth century[f], and still more in the tenth century[g], indicate that concubinage prevailed, and a sort
of half-recognised marriage was very common. There
were frequent Canons of Councils that no son should
succeed to the benefice of his father.

The Council of Mayence, A.D. 888, had absolutely
to prohibit the clergy from having any females whatever, even the allowed relations, in their dwellings,
much guilt, even incest, having been the result[h]. The
Council of Metz, in the same year, made the like
enactment, though alluding only to the evils[i]. The
constitution of Riculfus, Bishop of Soissons[k], A.D. 889,
and a Council of Nantes (exact date unknown) refer
to the same, and speak of other sins by reason of the
attendants[l]. Even a saint, St. Peter Damiani, had to
write against horrible sins of the clergy, which one
can neither name nor even remotely allude to[m]. The
work was stolen, and suppressed for a time, because he
could not but speak plainly[n]. But one remedy, the
marriage of the clergy, became extensive. Leo VII., in
a letter to the Kings, Dukes, Bishops, Abbots, Counts,
and specially to the Bishops of Salzburg, Ratisbon,
Frisingen, Seben, and the rest of the Bishops throughout Gaul, Germany, Bavaria, Swabia, A.D. 939, speaks
of the clergy taking wives, like the rest of Christians[o].

---

[f] Aux. 836, Mayence, 888.   [g] Poitiers, 1,000, can. vi.

[h] Can. x.   [i] Can. v.   [k] c. 14.   [l] Can. iii.

[m] *Liber Gomorrhianus*, Opusc., 7.   [n] See Baron., A. 1049, n. 10—15.

[o] *Epist.* 3.

Guido, early in the eleventh century, says that this was done throughout Italy [p]. Benedict VIII., in the preface to a Council of Ticino, inveighs against the publicity and extent of these marriages, which, by the provision made for the children, impoverished even wealthy Churches. He re-enacted the old laws, which were confirmed by the Emperor Henry II. (This was between 1014 and 1024). The name *presbyterissæ* was a recognised name, and appeared in public instruments [q]. The instance of the Church of Milan, in which "all the Priests and Deacons," and even the Archbishop was married [r], was the more remarkable on account of the proverbial excellence of its clergy [s]. They had even a tradition that St. Ambrose formally allowed single marriage [t].

The laxity infected even Monastic bodies. In the Celtic provinces of Europe the Church lands came to be hereditary in the Abbot's or Priest's family. Sacerdotalism became hereditary, and the names Mactaggart, the priest's son; MacNab, the abbot's son; Mactavish,

---

[p] *Disciplina Farfensis*, in *Vetus discipl. Monast.*, Paris, 1726, p. 37.

[q] *Aventinus*, l. v. p. 346. From stress of time the following facts are put together from the authorities given in Gieseler's *Kirchengeschichte*.

[r] Heribert, A. 1019—1046. *Chron. Mediol. in Murat. Scriptt. Rer. Ital.*, t. iv. p. 122, quoted by Gies.

[s] "Mediolanum in clericis, Papia in deliciis, Roma in ædificiis, Ravenna in Ecclesiis." (Landulf, *Hist. Mediol.*, iii. 1.) Gieseler quotes also Anselm of Lucca (Alexander II.), "Unless all the Priests and Deacons of this city had wives, in preaching and in other good manners they were very effective." (Ib. 4.) "The Papal legate, P. Damiani, attested, that 'verily he had never seen such a clergy.'" (Arnulf., *Hist. Med.*, iii. 12.) Ib.

[t] *Land.*, i. 11, quoted ib.

the nun's son, are abiding testimonies of the laxity of the discipline of the Scoto-Irish Church. It was the same throughout Europe, as an accurate historian, Sir James Mackintosh, one by no means likely to over-estimate the work of a great Church-reformer, has declared his opinion, that Gregory VII. intended to save religion in Europe from becoming a caste-religion, like Brahminism, with all the withering influences which such caste-religion implies.

One of that Pontiff's weapons in restoring discipline was the enforcement of clerical celibacy. This was adopted with certain modifications by Lanfranc in 1076, an exception being made for the country clergy who had already married wives; but St. Anselm, in 1102, at the Council of Westminster, forbade marriage, separated those married, suspended them *a divinis*, and forbade the faithful to be present at their services. The law of the English Church, thenceforward till the Reformation, exacted celibacy in the clergy.

But, "quid leges sine moribus vanæ proficiunt?" An old Saxon Chronicle says, "all those decrees had no effect; all retained their wives, by the king's permission, as they had done before ᵘ." For the Bishops "left it to the king to judge as to the *focariæ* of the priests; and the matter ended with the gravest scandal. For the king took infinite money from the Presbyters to redeem their *focariæ* ˣ." In 1208, in the reign of King John, all the house-keepers (*focariæ*) of the Presbyters and Clerks throughout all England were taken

<hr>

ᵘ *Ad* A.1129, in Wilkins' *Conc.*, i. 411.   ˣ Matt. Paris, A. 1129.

by the king's officers, and obliged to redeem themselves at a heavy sum. So it was in other Northern kingdoms. The rule of clerical celibacy was enforced with difficulty, and broken. The long list of decrees of Councils against "the concubines, house-keepers (*focariæ*), and servants (*pedissequæ*)" of the clergy [y], is an indication of the efforts to maintain clerical celibacy, and of their failure. Sometimes the Bishops connived at its breach; at times, it is said, "for money or some other temporal advantage [z]," more often, it is to be hoped, looking upon the forbidden quasi-marriage as the least of two evils [a]. The gloss on the decree, that those Clerks, who had offspring, "should be removed from the sacerdotal office [b]," said, "But it is commonly said that for simple fornication one ought not to be deposed, since few are found without that vice." A Chancellor of Paris said publicly, "in the hearing of his whole school, which was full of so many men, of so great account and learning," "that never did the old enemy, in any matter, so circumvent the Church of God as in the utterance of that vow [c]" [of

[y] Schröckh (K. G. Th. 27, pp. 205, 6) enumerates 24, between A. 1207—1302.

[z] Prelates, who should do so, are sentenced to the like penalty with the offenders, by *Conc. Lat.* iv. A. 1215, can. xiv. Both rules were enforced in the *Constitt. Edmund. Cantuar.*, A. 1236, c. 4.

[a] Such quasi-marriages were often, however, contracted with a bad conscience; some changing the person repeatedly [*totiens mutent*], all putting them away *in extremis*. *Antigraphum Petri*, (written between A. 1153—1173) in Gieseler, par. 3, Abschn. 3, § 65, n. d.

[b] *Dist.* 81, c. 6.

[c] Peter Comestor, reported by his pupil, Giraldus Cambr., an ear-witness, in Cave, *Hist. Lit.*

the continency of the clergy]. A celebrated summist
lays down, "that a Confessor, who advised an Acolyte,
who had not the gift of continency, to marry secretly,
evading the eyes of his Bishop, commits no great sin.
For we believe it to be a less sin to retain his benefice
[contrary to law] with a secret marriage, than to have
fornicaria against the divine prohibition. But if subsequently he be compelled by his prelates to come to
Holy Orders, we believe that it is a less sin, *uxore uti*,
than to fornicate with another, if he will not wholly
to contain [d]." William Durand, Bishop of Mende, suggested whether, since all the efforts of Councils and
Popes had been unavailing, "it would be expedient
that, in the Western Church, the custom of the Eastern
Church, as to the vow of continency, should be retained
in regard to those to be advanced [to Holy Orders],
especially since in the time of the Apostles the custom
of the Eastern Church was observed [e]." In Hungary,
Synods allowed the marriage of the clergy in the
eleventh century. Compulsory celibacy was first established there, in Denmark, Sweden, and Poland in
the thirteenth. In Silesia, a Bishop of Breslau wrote
against it in the twelfth; and in Bohemia, in the
thirteenth century, complaints were made to Innocent III. of an Archbishop of Prague, who notoriously had a wife, by whom he had children [f].

[d] *Summa quæ incipit Commiserationes Domini*, c. 165, in *Flacii
Cat. Test. Verit.*, ii. 662, Lugd. 1597.

[e] *De modo gen. conc. celebr.*, p. ii. rubr. 46. f. xxxv. v.

[f] See authorities in Gieseler, l. c.

In the fourteenth century, a fresh indication of existing evils appears, in that the laity compelled the clergy to take concubines, thinking it necessary for the safety of their own families [g]. In some parts of Ireland and Norway, it was the custom of the country that the Bishops and Priests should have concubines publicly; they accompanied the Prelates on visitations; the *amasiæ*, or wives of the Presbyters, took rank; Presbyters who had none paid double procurations, as infringers of their country's custom [h]. "Much the same ways as to luxury were altogether observed, as to the priests of Gascony, Spain, and Portugal, and the countries contiguous to Africa; whence in all those parts there were more natural than legitimate children, and more such were openly promoted and preferred in the grant of ecclesiastical titles [h]." In Spain, Asturia, Gallicia, and elsewhere, Presbyters and others in Holy Orders married publicly [i]. In Italy fines were imposed by successive Councils [j]; that of Bergamo, A. 1311,

---

[g] The Council of Palencia, A. 1322, c. 7, fin., excommunicated individuals, and laid an interdict on any community who should do so. Nic. de Clamengis says that "in most parishes they would not tolerate a Priest who had not a concubine, so persuaded were they of the universal incontinency, and that even this precaution sufficed not." (*De Præsul. Simoniacis*, Opp., p. 165.) In the next century the Frisons with difficulty allowed of any other, on the same ground. Æneas Sylvius, A. 1440. (*Cosmogr.*, ii. 35.)

[h] *Theod. a Niem. Nemus Unionis, Tract.* vi. 35.

[i] *Alv. Pelag. de planctu eccles.*, ii. 27. "With a marriage-feast, as if lawful wives. Sometimes with a public instrument, promising not to part with them, especially noble ladies, and endowing them with the goods of the Church."

[j] *Ravenn.*, A. 1317, rubr. 4; 10 libræ for having or permitting sus-

imposed twice as large a fine on a Prelate as on an ordinary Clerk[k]. The Council of Presburg, A. 1309, imposed on *concubinarii publici* the forfeiture of one-fourth of the income of the benefice, avowedly as being more effective than excommunication[l]. The Council of Mayence, A. 1300, imputes its revival to the avarice of some who counted gain to be godliness[m]. Bishops were said not to presume to rebuke as being themselves tainted[n]. The Emperor Charles IV. threatened to sequestrate the revenues of those who gave occasion to this scandal, but was checked by Innocent VI., as interfering with the freedom of the Church[o].

The complaints of previous centuries heightened in the fifteenth. In the beginning of the century, it was said for certain that clergy of the Roman Curia still had their concubines without shame, notoriously to all[p]. Card. Julian assigned as his ground for acquiescing in the Council of Basle, to which he had been indisposed; " the deformity and dissoluteness of the clergy of Germany, whereby the laity are beyond measure irritated

pected persons; *Benevent.*, A. 1331, c. 55, 56; *Constitt. Eccl. Ferr.*, A. 1332, c. 31.

[k] Ten libræ of Pavia for a Prelate or Rector, five for a common Clerk. Rubr. 6.   [l] *Conc. Posoniens.*, c. 5.

[m] Nic. de Clamengis complained that "in most dioceses Rectors of parishes commonly and publicly have concubines at a fixed price settled with their prelates." (*De ruina Eccl.*, c. 22.)

[n] Theobald, *publ. conq. in Conc. Const.*, in v.d. *Hardt. Conc. Const.*, t. i. P. xix., p. 909. He made stronger charges.

[o] iv. *Ep. ad Carolum.*

[p] P. de Pulka in C. of Constance, A. 1416. On the horrible state of the Court at Avignon, something is quoted from Petrarch, more alluded to in Milm. Lat. Chris., v. 500, n. g.

against the clerical order, induced me to come here.
It is much to be feared that, unless they mend, the
laity will, as they publicly declare, like the Hussites,
burst upon the whole clergy. A deformation of this
sort gives great boldness to the Bohemians, and greatly
colours their errors, because they inveigh chiefly against
the foulness of the clergy. Wherefore, even if a General Council had not been instituted here, it would have
been necessary to form a Provincial Council—for reforming the clergy; since it is, in truth, to be feared,
that unless that clergy correct itself, even if the heresy
of Bohemia should be extinguished, another should be
aroused [q]." The Council of Paris, A. 1429, states, that
" for the crime of concubinage, whereby many ecclesiastics and religious are infected, the Church of God
and the whole clergy are held in derision, abomination,
and reproach among all nations; and that most abomin-
able wickedness has so prevailed in the Church of God,
that simple Christians do not now believe that fornication is mortal sin [r]." The fine on concubines was
forbidden [s], but practised [t], probably in the hope that

[q] *Epist. Julian. ad Eug.* iv. *in Fasc. rer. fug. et expet.*, Lond.,
p. 56.   [r] c. 23.

[s] By *Conc. Paris.*, A. 1429, c. 23; *Conc. Dertus.*, A. 1429, c. 2. The
Council of Basle prohibited it, "under pain of eternal malediction, and
a fine of the double of such receipt; required prelates to remove the
persons, if need be, by aid of the secular arm, and not to permit
the sons so born to remain with their father." (*Sess.* 20, *Decr.* 1.)

[t] "A penalty of ten florins for not dismissing concubines or *focariæ*,
or other women suspected of incontinency," was imposed by a Synod
of Breslau between 1447 and 1458. (*Hartzheim Conc. Germ.*, v. 445.)
"Complaints were made of this by *Fel. Hammerlin, Dionys. Carth.*

the mulct might deter at least the poorer clergy. Those,
who so offended, boasted of it[u]; the laity were sometimes scandalised, sometimes copied it[v]. It is a grave
and pious Abbot, no mere declaimer against the vices
of his times, who says of the clergy, "By the exceeding badness of their lives, they slay miserably the
sheep of Christ—'Pro libris sibi liberos comparant, pro
studio concubinas amant.'—Let not then the Priests
wonder that the laity despise them, since themselves
despise the commands of Christ. I fear vehemently
that shortly graver things will arise against the
clergy[x]." Popes would ordinarily be selected from
the better clergy; but, besides that the century closed
with the thirty years of Sixtus IV., Innocent VIII.,
Alexander VI., Æneas Sylvius, afterwards Pius II.,
answers with levity his father's blame, that he had
had a son from sin, treating it as a matter of course.
"Wide-spread is this plague, if plague it is to be called,
to do what is natural[y]," &c. "Let a Presbyter be avaricious, an usurer, glutton, &c., if he be not incontinent,

(*de vita et regim. Archidiac.*, Art. 19, "against the dangerous, vicious,
and damnable custom of visiting and receiving money from *fornicarii*.")
Herm. Ryd. de Reen (*de vita et honest. cleric.*, c. 1). Theodoric, Archbishop of Cologne, ᴀ. 1423, commanded under severe penalty the dismissal of the concubines, but changed soon. "The Bishop took money
from the priests, and left them their concubines; perhaps he knew not
how to meet the wickedness of the times by any other remedy, or,
scared by the number, he despaired of effecting anything." *Jac. Sibert.*
(*de calamit. huj. temp.*)

[u] Steph. Episc. Brandenb. *comm. ad Orat. Domin.*, c. 17.

[v] Ludov. Episc. Spir. in summons to *Martini Synod.*, ᴀ. 1486.

[x] Trithemius Abb. Spanh. *instit. vitæ Sacerdot.*, c. 1, about ᴀ. 1485.

[y] L. i. *Ep.* xv. He relates his seduction of the mother.

he is accounted by all to be holy and honest [a]." "The priesthood was held so low, and daily lower, that many were ashamed to become Clerks, or allow their people to become so [a]." One only token there was, that God had not forsaken His Church, that while the world was full of satires on these excesses [b], earnest men in every portion of it complained of it [c]. "In no century," it is said, "were there so many decisions of Synods and Bishops against *concubinarii* as the fifteenth [d];" or so many complaints of their uselessness. Stringent measures in Italy produced, it is said, still worse evils and a more degraded clergy [e].

[a] *Lavacr. Consc.*, c. 6. "Why is it that the rest of mankind, of whatever condition, hate us? Certes, we cannot say, that the children of this world persecute us, as children of light—for we are not children of light, but of darkness. No other ground occurs to us, except that we are transgressors of the law." Ib.   [a] Ib., c. 7.

[b] Gieseler quotes several. The contemporary Epigram on Innocent VIII. was but too forcible; the more so, for its allusion to his title, as Pope, the "father."

[c] Gieseler refers to the following well-known names: St. Laurence Justinian, Patriarch of Venice (*de complanctu Xt. Perf.*, Opp., ii. 6); Tostatus, Bishop of Avila (*c. cleric. concub.*, Opp. xxv. 58); St. Antoninus, Archbishop of Florence (*Summa Conf. P.* iii. *de cler. præl. Ep.*, c. 10–16); Dionys. Carthus. (*de vita et regim. Præsul.*, art. 18, 27 sqq. 39, *de vita et regim. Archid.*, art. 19 sqq., *de vita Canon.*, art. 12, *de vita Curat.*); Rod. Sancius, Bishop of Zamora and Referendary of Paul II. (*Spec. vit. hum.*, ii. 19); the *Lavacrum Conscientiæ* (c. 4, 13, 15, 17); Baptista Mantuan., General of the Carmelites (*Alfonsus*, l. iii., *de calamit. temp.*, l. iii.); Joh. Trithemius (*Instit. vit. sacerdot.*, espec. c. 2); and others.

[d] Gieseler, referring to the documents in *Theiner, die Einführung d. erzwungenen Ehelosigkeit u. ihre folgen*, &c., b. 2, Abth. 2, p. 642, sqq. *Carové, völlst. Samml. d. Cölibatgesetze für d. Kath. Weltgeistl. mit Anm.*, p. 342, sqq.

[e] J. F. Picus, Lord of Mirandula, *Orat. ad Leonem P. M. et Cono. Lat. de reform. mor.*, A. 1517, in Brown's *Fasc.*, p. 419.

These scandals had become so intolerable at the time
of the Reformation, that it is not wonderful that there
should be a mighty reaction. The Church had, indeed,
struggled against the abuses. The Council of Basle
had, in its twentieth Session, ordained that "any
cleric, of whatsoever state, condition, religion, dignity,
even Papal and otherwise eminent, who shall after
due notice ... be a public concubinary, shall in the
space of three weeks be, *ipso facto*, suspended, and deprived of the fruits of his benefice; if he dismiss not
his concubine, or take her back when dismissed, he
shall be deprived of all his benefices." A public concubinary is defined to be, "he who retains a woman
suspected of concubinage and defamed, who, when admonished by his superior, does not in effect dismiss
her." These canons had been re-affirmed by various
provincial synods: in Scotland, so late as the Provincial Synods of Linlithgow and Edinburgh in 1549,
and again in 1558 and 1559; but they had failed. The
Church had to be reminded, as it is in the terms of the
Article, that clerical celibacy is not of divine institution, and that, being a matter of discipline, it was in
the power of the Church, in view of the intolerable
corruption of the times, to allow men to marry at their
own discretion, "as they shall judge the same to serve
better to godliness." This had seemed to some the only
remedy in the fifteenth century. Setting aside the
sort of proverb of Pius II., as Pope, "With great
reason marriage had been withdrawn from the Priests;
with greater, it seems, would it be restored[1]," (for

---

[1] *Platina de vitis Pontif.*, p. 762, ed. 1645.

his own previous history takes away its weight [s]), the well-known Canonist Panormitanus (himself an Abbot and afterwards Archbishop) discusses the ques-

[s] He had said, however, earnestly, as Æneas Sylvius, "Perhaps it would be no worse, that very many [*quam plures*] should be married, since many might be saved in a married priesthood, who are damned in a sterile Presbyterate." (*Hist. Conc. Bas.*, l. ii. p. 86.) As Cardinal, he anticipated that another Pope [perhaps himself] might give dispensations. (*Ep.* cccvii.) See also, in Gieseler, extracts from the so-called Reformation Sigismunds, "an important voice from that time," and the so-called " Reformation Friederichs III. ;" *Fel. Hammerlin* (*de lib. Eccl.*) ; *Alain Chartier*, Secretary of King Charles VI. and VII., who says, " The avaricious disorders of Priests have detached Bohemia from the Church of Rome. Why say I, Bohemia ? nay almost all Christendom. For the people of the Church have by their faults so debased themselves and their office, that they are despised by all in the Church, great or small, and hearts are estranged from the obedience of holy Church by the dissoluteness of her ministers. For, as was said, they have left espousals, but they have taken instead lawless, vague, and dissolute luxuries. What has the law against the marriage of Priests effected, but to turn lawful generation into adultery, and honest co-habitation with one wife into multiplication of scandalous luxury ? " Card. Joh. Ant. in S. Georgio said, that " this command gives occasion of ensnaring many souls, and therefore he believes that as the Church brought in this precept of continence, it will at some time revoke it. And such revocation will be conformable to the Apostle's saying, 'as to virgins, I have no commandment, but I give counsel.' " Editor of *Aur. et singul. lectura super* iv. *decretalium ad tit.* vi., "Qui clerici vel voventes matrimonium contrahere possunt." The desirableness of revoking the prohibition was advocated by Jo. le Maire, Historiographer of Louis XII., *de Schism. et Conc. Eccl. univ. diff.*, P. i. c. 2, P. iii. c. 15 ; Polyd. Verg., *de rer. invent.*, v. 4. Adolf, Bishop of Merseburg, Prince of Anhalt, " The immoral unmarried life of the clergy was before his eyes. Wherefore he and many thought it good, that marriage should be again allowed them in Council, since otherwise this evil was not to be hindered." (*In Georg. Fürst zu Anhalt, Vorr. zu d. Pred. v. d. falsch. proph.*) Bapt. Mant., the Carmelite, dwells on men's censures against the prohibition, *Fasti*, l. i., *de S. Hilario*, Opp., t. ii. f. 252.

tion, and decides in favour of the removal of the prohibition : "Can the Church at this day enact, that a Clerk may contract marriage, as do the Greeks? I believe that it can; and I not only believe that the Church has the power of enacting this, but I believe that it would be a healthful statute for the good and salvation of souls, that those who wish to use continence and to merit the more, should be left to their will; but those who will not to contain, may marry : for experience teacheth, that quite the contrary effect follows from that law of continence, since at this time they do not live continently nor are pure, but are stained by unlawful intercourse, with gravest sin to themselves, whereas with their own wife it would be purity, as it is said, *cap. Nicæna*[h]; whence the Church ought to act, like a good physician, and if experience shews that a medicine rather hurteth than profiteth, should take it away. And would that this were done in all positive constitutions, that at least they should bind, as to the penalty, not as to [involving] fault. For positive statutes have so multiplied, that scarce any can be found who have not corrupted their ways[l]."

Nothing is said in the Article to the disparagement of the single state. On the contrary, the tone of the Article and of the Marriage Service is at variance with modern notions on this subject. They by no

---

[h] *Decret. Gratian.*, p. i., *Dist.* xxxi. c. 12.

[l] *Lect. sup. c. cum olim, De clericis conjugatis, Decr. Greg.*, l. iii. tit. iii. c. 6.

means regard marriage as a matter of course, upon the part either of the clergy or people. The Article claims for the clergy the same freedom as the people; but it sets before both, as the one ground, which "shall serve better to godliness?" Not earthly happiness, nor "Isaac's pure blessings and a verdant home," not the union of souls in holy love, nor anything else on this earth, is proposed as its measure; but this only, "Is marriage likely or not to benefit the immortal soul?" The question implies, that what is, in itself, free, is not free to each. For no one can be free to do that which, to *him*, does not, in his judgment, serve best to godliness. The Marriage Service goes further, by speaking of marriage as, with other motives, a remedy for those who "have not the gift of continency." For those who have any gift of God clearly are responsible for it. Much more the clergy, by how much their office brings them nearer to God. When God bestows the gift, the argument for such celibacy is founded on the very words of our Saviour Himself, where He commends a single life, and concludes with the significant comment, "He that is able to receive this saying, let him receive it." Contrasting the Law of Moses, in which divorce was allowed on account of the hardness of men's hearts, with the law of grace and divine strength which He came to announce and to inspire, He rests the benediction of the single life on those additional graces whereby under the new covenant men are able, in a higher degree than under any previous dispensation, to fulfil the will of God.

The next argument is found in the counsels of St. Paul[k], with regard to virginity. Plainly, the "present necessity" is not, as has been sometimes supposed, the condition of persecution in which the early Corinthian converts were presumed to live. For in neither Epistle is there any evidence of such persecution. On the contrary, the Christians in that community were living on perfect terms of friendship with the heathen around them. The "present necessity," therefore, must apply to the world under Christianity, and so the spirit of St. Paul's counsels must apply to all time.

Again, in that primeval religion handed down by early tradition among the heathen, which, in its foreshadowings, omens, and prophecies, is such a strong proof of the adaptation of the eventually-revealed Christianity to the wants and aspirations of man, we find side by side with sacerdotal caste, which implies a hereditary married priesthood, a higher and holier ideal, in which the virgin life is made the condition of ministration in the most sacred functions. Among the Indo-European races, the Greeks, the Romans, and the Indians, as well as among those Oriental races, where the malignity of matter and the purity of mind were distinguishing principles, we find that the ideal of heathenism had handed on the tradition of those earlier truths which had ever subsisted in the old and simple religions of nature.

Moreover, as there lurked in the old heathenism

---

[k] 1 Cor. vii.

a certain appreciation of the highest ideal of life, so even in Gnosticism we see a caricature and distortion of the same. It is Gnosticism, which St. Paul describes and condemns where he speaks of the early heretics forbidding to marry; they erred in maintaining the body to be absolutely sinful, and the work of an inferior demiurge. The truth in this system was a certain aspiration after the higher life. The Church at once met the error, and the truth; the error, by asserting the sanctity and quasi-sacramental character of marriage, the truth lurking in Gnosticism, which was the sanctity of nature and the immaterialism and spirituality of the human mind, by elevating virginity[1].

As the Jewish Priests, during their ministration, were obliged to abstain from their wives, when they commemorated God's mercies to the Jewish people, propitiated Him for their sins, and lived in habitual communion with Him; so the Christian Priest, who is not bound to a mere monthly attendance at the temple, but to a constant service, would seem to have a more continual call to the continent life.

Upon whom or how many in any given period, God is or would be pleased to bestow the gift of continence; whom, among men, He has created for the virgin life, lies in the secrets of the Divine Predestination. It is for individuals to learn for themselves, whereto God has called them, and neither to hold back from His calling, nor thrust themselves, uncalled, into a vocation for which God has not fitted them. Individuals, doubt-

---

[1] See Möhler's Criticism on the Memorial of the Freiburgh Professors, in the *Vermischte Schriften*, p. 177.

less, may obtain, as well as lose, a vocation for themselves; but they must obtain it before they venture upon it. It is a problem for the Church, to provide, as far as in her lies, that none should miss that vocation, whom God, in His eternal counsels, has created for it, and, on the other hand, to secure that those, who have not that calling, should, as St. Paphnutius advised at the Council of Nice, not have a burden laid upon them which they are unable to bear, God not having designed them for it. The Church has tried different ways. The Greek Church has one stereotyped plan of gathering into monasteries those who have the calling to the celibate life, and, while requiring of her Priests that they should marry before the priesthood, selecting for the Episcopate those who have ever led the virgin life, or who, being widowed, have been withdrawn from secular to monastic life. Of old, in the Western Church, together with the enforcement of continence on the three higher orders, there was a provision, more or less extensive, that those destined for the Clericature, who did not feel, in themselves, the gift of continency, should marry very early, so that children might be born to them, for some twelve years, before they should enter upon the service of the altar[m]. The middle ages witnessed an attempt and failure to enforce an universal celibacy of the clergy from the first. Since the Reformation, a more careful training of the future clergy in the Clerical seminaries has guarded those who would be guarded from that knowledge of sin, which increases tenfold the difficul-

[m] See above, pp. 634, 635.

ties of continence when the trial-time comes. "They are pure as angels," said a French Bishop of his seminarists. The Church of England has, as yet, left this, as well as other matters relating to the soul, purely to the consciences of individuals. It leans to the celibate; it does not enjoin it. But as men's souls are stirred more and more by the Spirit of God, it must be, that celibacy, among men too, and especially among those whom God calls to the priesthood, will become a recognised religious vocation. Wise will be her course, if she follows the Apostle's advice, and, without limiting the freedom which he admitted, directs her sons, as the more excellent way, to that which he chose.

After what has been said, it is unnecessary in a treatise of this kind to enlarge upon the increased influence, the capacity for labour, the disentanglement from the world, the economy of living, the increased facilities for missionary and hospital work of a celibate priesthood. At the price of much individual suffering, a mighty engine for the conversion of the world is thus recognised in clerical celibacy, as the fruit of self-devotion upon the call of God. And the spirit of St. Paul, reflected in the Apostolic Constitutions and Canons of the fourth century, finds its highest interpretation in such self-dedication, where the matured will, after having tested its powers, yields itself a living sacrifice to duty and to God.

ARTICLE XXXIII.

De Excommunicatis vitandis.

Qui per publicam Ecclesiæ denunciationem rite ab unitate Ecclesiæ præcisus est, et excommunicatus, is ab universa fidelium multitudine (donec per pœnitentiam publice reconciliatus fuerit arbitrio Judicis competentis) habendus est tanquam ethnicus et publicanus.

" Of excommunicate Persons, how they are to be avoided.

"That person which by open denunciation of the Church is rightly cut off from the unity of the Church, and excommunicated, ought to be taken of the whole multitude of the faithful, as an heathen and publican, until he be openly reconciled by penance, and received into the Church by a judge that hath authority thereunto."

To cut the offending member from the body is a power which natural law grants as inherent in every society. The expulsion of unruly members, or of those who refuse to obey the conditions of the implied contract which membership presupposes, is necessary to its well-being. All this holds in an increasingly true sense where we have to deal with supernatural ideas; and with more or less consistency every form of religion has arrogated to itself the right of expulsion;

and in the measure that highest spiritual privileges are attached to incorporation and visible communion, therewith the importance of the power for such expulsion must be conceived of. The highest notion, of course, is where the consequences of the deprivation of visible communion tell upon the soul in the next world, even to the endangering of salvation. Under the Jewish law the cutting off from the people, though sometimes meaning death by the judgment of God, or by the hand of man [a], was latterly understood of excommunication, which was either *niddui*, excommunication for a month; or *cherem*, excommunication accompanied with imprecations, the intensest form of which was *shammatta*. In the earliest times we find that the Christian Church wielded this terrible power, and made it the basis of all its discipline. With a graduated scale of Church censures, she reserved excommunication as the ultimate term of her jurisdiction. St. Irenæus mentions the final excommunication of Cerdon. Origen bears witness to the practice of the expulsion from communion of offenders, especially the incontinent. Tertullian, in view of his Montanist ideas, gives us much insight into the discipline of the Church during his time. The Canons of the Church not only lay down rules for the exercise of this discipline, but actually enforce many of their own enactments under penalty of anathema [b].

[a] 1 Kings xiv. 10; Exod. xxxi. 14, 15; Levit. xvii. 4.

[b] Vide Appendix to Sermon upon Evangelical Repentance by the Bishop of St. Andrew's. Oxf., 1841.

When the kingdoms of the earth became Christian, and had in certain cases to be dealt with by the Church in a corporate capacity, the theory of excommunication and interdict received further development.

It is unnecessary here to dwell at length upon the public discipline of the ancient Church, how the penitents were divided into weepers, hearers, kneelers, and co-standers; how crimes were visited by long terms of penance in proportion to the magnitude of the offence; how some were only reconciled in the article of death, and how some crimes were thought too great for restitution to communion in this life, though the mercy of God was hoped for them in the next. The Article distinctly asserts the duty of the faithful to take part with the justice of the Church, and strengthen the bands of her discipline by holding the excommunicate person as a heathen man and publican in the very terms of the Gospel[e], and in these words the present Church of England in theory, and to a certain degree in practice, adopts all the ancient teaching on this awful subject. It must not be concealed that certain complications arising from State establishment, from the predominance of a legal school which has given undue prominence to the assertion of temporal rights and to the protection which civil law gives to character, have crippled the exercise of godly discipline. Nevertheless, the Church has never ceased to deplore its decay, and to pray for its restoration.

[e] St. Matt. xviii. 17.

The teaching and practice of the Church on the subject of excommunication have been thus formularized in the Latin Church, and as the theory of the Church of England is intimately connected with it, some of the details are here given, with a view to clearness. An excommunication is an ecclesiastical censure, by which a Christian man is separated from the communion of the Church. It depends on the power of binding and loosing granted to her prelates by Christ, "If he neglect to hear the Church [d]:" observe also the practice of the Apostle handing the offender over " to Satan," on which St. Austin says, " Because the devil is without the Church as Christ is in the Church, so he is given over to the devil who is removed from the communion of the Church." Excommunication is nearly the same as anathema, but the latter is the more solemn form of the process, nay, in general, is more awful.

Excommunication is divided into the greater and the lesser. The greater is that ecclesiastical censure, whereby the Christian is separated from the communion of the faithful absolutely and simply; i.e. is deprived of all common blessings, such as the Sacraments of the Church, both as to administration and reception, as well as common prayer and society. The minor is that whereby the Christian is deprived only of the passive reception of Sacraments. When excommunication is spoken of indefinitely it means the greater. Again, excommunication is divided into 1. *ex-*

[d] St. Matt. xviii. 17.

communicatio latæ sententiæ, and 2. *excommunicatio sententiæ ferendæ*. The first is that which is incurred *ipso facto*, either by the perpetration of the crime, or by the sentence of the judge; *excommunicatio sententiæ ferendæ*, is that, which though held as established in law, yet is not at once and *ipso facto* incurred before the sentence of the judge.

Thirdly, excommunication is divided into that which is carried out by the law, and that which is carried out by the individual. Excommunication *quæ a jure fertur*, is when anything is prohibited by law, canons, constitution, or decree, under penalty of such, or of anathema. That *quæ a judice fertur*, is that which for any crime is inflicted by the judge. Hence, censure in kind is one thing, in law another as regards the individual; inasmuch as the first is of perpetual obligation, till revoked by legitimate authority, the other depends on the life of the censurer.

In the Roman Church there is the further distinction of reserved and unreserved excommunication.

All Bishops and other Ordinaries can excommunicate in their territories and dioceses, so chapters *sede vacante*, heads of orders, General Councils.

Only Christians, in this life, gravely and continuously offending, capable of reason, and subject to the jurisdiction of the excommunicator, can be excommunicated. Jews, Pagans, Saracens, and other infidels, cannot, because they have never been baptized nor are within the Church; but heretics can, because they have been baptized, and have taken on them the faith of Christ. The dead cannot be, for the binding is, " whatsoever thou shalt bind on earth," not under the earth. Next, gravity and contumacity are necessary, and not even against the contumacious, unless they have been summarily warned.

The judgment of God rests on the truth, which neither deceiveth, nor is deceived; but the judgment of the Church sometimes rests on opinion, which can easily err and cause to err, whence it sometimes happens that he who is bound by God is loosed by the Church, and he who is free with God is bound by the sentence of the Church. *Clave errante* is a recognised ground of appeal.

The first effect of excommunication is to deprive the excommunicate person of the active and passive use of the Sacraments.

2. Of the common suffrages of the Church, and the spiritual blessings which flow from the public offices of the clergy and the sacrifices of the faithful.

3. Of the right to assist at the divine offices. He may, however, hear sermons, recite prayers in private.

4. Of Ecclesiastical sepulture.

5. Of Political communion with the faithful.

6. In some countries he cannot be judge, advocate, or witness.

7. All his ecclesiastical acts are invalid, except the election of the Pope, no excommunication of a cardinal invalidating that.

8. It renders him incapable of receiving ecclesiastical revenues.

9. The excommunicated person is incapable of holding benefices.

10. He cannot obtain any rescript of grace or justice from the Apostolic See, unless in the actual case of excommunication, on appeal, it may be obtained for the defence of the excommunicate person.

11. It renders him suspect of heresy if he do not purge himself within the year.

12. It renders excommunicate (at least so far as the minor is concerned) all those who communicate with the excommunicate person.

The effect of the minor excommunication is three-fold :—

1. He may not partake in any Sacrament.

2. If without necessity he administers a Sacrament, he sins at least venially.

3. He cannot be elected to an ecclesiastical benefice.

Absolution, in the case of excommunication *a jure*, may be granted not only by Bishops and Prelates holding jurisdiction, but, so far as the *forum internum* is concerned, by parish Priests and simple confessors.

From excommunication *ab homine*, carried out by special sentence, none can absolve but he who laid it on, or his deputy, or his successor, or the superior of the censurer having plenary jurisdiction, but not as Archbishop in respect of his suffragans, except in case of appeal.

A man may be absolved out of confession, in absence, against his will; after death, if he died penitent, he may be so far absolved as to be capable of Christian burial, and of the suffrages of the Church.

Absolution may be given absolutely, or on condition, or *ad cautelam,* or *cum reincidentiâ;* that is, he may fall again under it if he neglect to do what he has promised, or for a special purpose as a judicial examination. No one can be absolved from the greater unless he swear to obey the commands of the Church, and not to sin in the kind again; also, he must make restitution so far as he can. Yet if he neglect to fulfil this, he does not relapse into the excommunicate state, but should be again excommunicated. Yet he who absolves without an oath, absolves illicitly though validly. Absolution extorted from fear is invalid.

Nothing will place before the student the awful character of excommunication in so striking a light, as the form of service which has for many centuries, with various modifications, been used in the Western Church, since the ninth or tenth century. Before that, no special form was prescribed. Martene gives some very terrible forms, but what is here exhibited is sufficiently striking and awful.

When the anathema, i.e. solemn excommunication for grievous faults, is to be inflicted, the Bishop, dressed in amice, stole, and cope, of violet colour, with a simple mitre, assisted by twelve surpliced Priests, having all burning candles in their hands, shall sit on a faldstool before the altar, or in some other public place as shall please him; he shall there pronounce and emit the anathema in this manner:—" Inasmuch as *N.,* by the persuasion of the devil, laying aside

by apostacy that Christian promise which he made in
Baptism, has not feared to lay waste the Church of
God, to despoil the ecclesiastical property, and vio-
lently to oppress Christ's poor ; therefore, anxious
lest he perish, by the pastoral negligence for which in
the tremendous judgment we shall have to give an
account before the Chief Pastor, our Lord Jesus Christ,
according to that which the same Lord terribly
threatens, saying : ' If thou shalt not announce to the
wicked his sin, his blood will I require at thy hand,'
We have warned him canonically once, twice, thrice,
and even four times, in order to convince him of his
wickedness, inviting him to emendation, satisfaction,
and penance, and correcting him with paternal affection. But he, alas! despising salutary counsels, in-
flated with the spirit of pride, disdains to give satisfaction to the Church which he has injured. Verily,
information is supplied by the precepts of the Lord
and His Apostles how we ought to act with regard to
such transgressors. For the Lord says, ' If thy hand
or thy foot offend thee, cut it off and cast it from
thee ;' and the Apostle says, ' Put away the evil thing
from among you ;' and again, ' If any one who is
called a brother is a fornicator, or covetous, or an
idolater, or an evil speaker, or a drunkard, or a robber,
not to take food with him.' And St. John, the beloved disciple of our Lord, forbids us to salute such
a wicked one, saying, ' Receive him not into thy
house, neither bid him God speed, for whoso biddeth
him God speed, communicateth in his wicked works.'
Fulfilling, therefore, the precepts of our Lord and

His Apostles, let us cut off this putrid and incurable member, which will not take medicine, by the sword of excommunication from the body of the Church, lest the remaining members of the body become tainted as by poison, by such pestilent disease. Therefore, since he despises our admonitions and frequent exhortations, and when thrice summoned according to our Lord's precept, he has neglected to repent and amend, since he has neither bethought himself of his fault, nor confessed it, nor sent an embassage to make any excuse, nor hath asked pardon; but, the devil hardening his heart, has persevered in the wickedness on which he hath entered, according to tho words of the Apostle, 'according to his hardness of heart and impenitence, hath treasured up for himself wrath against the day of wrath.' Therefore, him, with all his accomplices and supporters, by the judgment of God Almighty, Father, Son, and Holy Ghost, and of blessed Peter, Prince of the Apostles, and of all saints, also by the authority of binding and loosing in heaven and in earth bestowed upon our mediocrity by God, we separate from the reception of the precious Body and Blood of our Lord, and from the society of all Christians, and we exclude him from the thresholds of holy mother Church in heaven and earth, and we decree him excommunicate, and anathematized, and damned with the devil and his angels, and all the lost in eternal fire, till he recover himself from the snares of the devil, and return to amendment and penance, and satisfy the Church of God which he hath injured; delivering him to Satan for the destruction of the flesh, that his soul may be saved in the day of judgment."

" Then all shall answer ' Fiat, fiat, fiat !' Which being done, the Bishops and Priests ought to cast to the earth the candles which they held in their hands. Then a letter must be sent through the parishes, and even to the neighbouring Bishops, containing the name of the excommunicated person, and the cause of his excommunication, that no one henceforth through ignorance may communicate with him, and thus cause of excommunication may be taken from all."

It will be seen how in the midst of all these terrors, the emendation of the sinner is held in view, and provision made for his restoration. The same spirit animates the Article. The excommunicate person is to be taken of the whole multitude of the faithful as a heathen and publican, only till he be openly reconciled by penance, and received into the Church by a judge that hath authority thereto. If there be a remarkable fact in the history of the discipline of the Church, it is her great tenderness with regard to sinners, imitating her Divine Head. She embraces the returning prodigal, and on the slightest indications of repentance restores him to her Sacraments. She has again and again resisted the rigorous spirit of individual members since the days of her condemnation of Novatianism.

ARTICLE XXXIV.

DE TRADITIONIBUS ECCLESIASTICIS.

TRADITIONES atque cæremonias easdem non omnino necessarium est esse ubique, aut prorsus consimiles. Nam ut variæ semper fuerunt, et mutari possunt, pro regionum, temporum, et morum diversitate, modo nihil contra verbum Dei instituatur.

Traditiones, et cæremonias ecclesiasticas, quæ cum verbo Dei non pugnant, et sunt authoritate publica institutæ, atque probatæ, quisquis privato consilio volens, et data opera, publice violaverit, is, ut qui peccat in publicum ordinem Ecclesiæ, quique lædit authoritatem Magistratus, et qui infirmorum fratrum conscientias vulnerat, publice, ut cæteri timeant, arguendus est.

Quælibet Ecclesia particularis, sive nationalis, authoritatem habet instituendi, mutandi, aut abrogandi cæremonias, aut ritus ecclesiasticos, humana tantum authoritate institutos, modo omnia ad ædificationem fiant.

" Of the Traditions of the Church.

" It is not necessary that traditions and ceremonies be in all places one, or utterly like; for at all times they have been divers, and may be changed according to the diversities of countries, times, and men's manners, so that nothing be ordained against God's Word. Whosoever, through his private judgment, willingly and purposely doth openly break the traditions and ceremonies of the Church, which be not repugnant to the Word of God, and be ordained and approved of common authority, ought to be rebuked openly, (that others may fear to do the like,) as he that offendeth against the common order of the Church, and hurteth the authority of the magistrate, and woundeth the consciences of weak brethren.

"Every particular and national Church hath authority to ordain, change, and abolish ceremonies or rites of the Church, ordained only by man's authority, so that all things be done to edifying."

The word 'tradition,' in the sense in which the Article means it to be taken, is synonymous with the term *consuetudo*, meaning such a custom as is produced by the simultaneous and frequent action of the greater part of a community. It is divided into *consuetudo facti* and *consuetudo juris*. The first, which leads to the second, is the repeated use of the community to do anything, without the obligation of so repeating it. The second is a right constituted by such repeated acts. And this *consuetudo juris*, inasmuch as it tends to the introduction of new law, is, as it were, a second sort of law.

Taken generally, custom admits of a threefold division :—

1. Custom *præter legem*, which is also called constitutive law, is that which is found in those cases which are not defined by common law. It has the force of law, but to its obligation it is necessary that it should be introduced by an entire people, or, at least, the wiser

and greater part of it, with the intention of really bind-ing itself thereby. Hence customs of devotion, (such as bowing at the *Gloria*,) are not of obligation. In this sort of custom prescription is a necessary element.

2. Custom *secundum legem* is, that we suppose a pre-existent law, and either reduce it to practice, or, if it be doubtful, interpret it. It is important as confirming and strengthening existent law, and securing its being enforced.

Custom *contra legem* is that, by which the written law has either never been in use, or if in use has been abrogated by a contrary use. It cannot prevail against divine or natural right or law. No custom can abrogate the necessity of fasting, or the laws against perjury. But every positive human law, whether civil or canoni-cal, may be abrogated by a contrary custom, so that that custom be 1. reasonable, and 2. possess sufficient legitimate prescription.

1. The first condition implies that it shall not op-pose divine or natural law, nor be reprobated by the Canon Law, that it gives no occasion or licence to sin, and that it has no injurious effect on the public wel-fare. No custom can be pleaded that infringes on these.

2. Legitimate prescription must be a long time. In the Canon Law ten years is prescription; in the English Common Law sixty years; in the Scots Law forty years; in America twenty years are necessary. In civil matters a tacit abrogation on the part of the civil authority is implied by the toleration of the

X X

custom, therefore an exact rigorous time is not insisted on in civil matters [*].

Tradition, then, or custom, being in this manner the subject of time and action, the Article says rightly that it has at all times been diverse, and may be changed according to the diversities of countries, times, and men's manners. It adds the solemn caution, that by these fluctuations nothing be ordained against God's Word. That paramount authority of Holy Scripture which is so remarkable a characteristic of the XXXIX Articles, and which the Church of England inherited from the great teachers of the Middle Ages, supplies the limit to the diversity of the traditions of the Church.

It is the same with regard to her ceremonies. While the action of the Holy Ghost within the Body of Christ will be ever suggesting to her new forms of devotion and edifying rites, and these will be profoundly modified by climate, by the history of thought, and by the degree of civilization, there will ever be a check upon the revolution of the expression of the devotion of the Church in an ultimate appeal to God's Word, not only as the earliest historic record of Christianity and the first link in the golden chain of Catholic tradition, but also as a document possessing such authority as no other claims or has had conceded to it.

The in-dwelling of God the Holy Ghost will illumine the minds of the different nations without destroying their national characteristics, and therefore we shall

[*] From *Ferraris Biblioth. Canon. Jurid. v. Consuetudo.*

not be surprised to find many marked peculiarities in the services and ceremonies of the different Churches throughout the world.   The tone of the services of the Greek Church is markedly different from that of those of the Westerns; and even among the Westerns, in the more limited field of variation, strong points of individuality have been conserved.   The prevalence of direct prayer to our Lord in the Mozarabic rite preserves the recollection of the struggle with Arianism in Spain.   The Ectenæ in the Milanese rite are no doubtful indications of the originally Oriental source of the Ambrosian Office.   The great predominance of vernacular hymns in the Church of Germany testifies to an endeavour to supply that national demand for affective hymnody, which Luther, at the time of the Reformation, used with such mighty effect; as in such instances as are recorded in history, where a whole congregation, celebrating the Services after the fashion of their fathers, would suddenly burst forth into one of the German hymns of the new learning.   As a matter of fact, we know from history that this was the case, and the following quotation from the Ecclesiastical History of Sozomen exhibits to us the fact, that the diversities of ceremonies mentioned in the Article have been from the beginning.

" Different customs prevail in many Churches where the same doctrines are received.   There are, for instance, many cities in Syria which possess but one Bishop between them; whereas, in other nations, a Bishop is appointed even over a village, as I have my-

self observed in Arabia and in Cyprus, and among the
Novatians and Montanists of Phrygia. Again, there
are but seven Deacons at Rome, answering precisely to
the number ordained by the Apostles, of whom Stephen
was the first martyr, whereas in other Churches the
number of Deacons is unlimited. At Rome, Alleluia is
sung once annually, namely, on the first day of the
Festival of the Passover; so that it is a common thing
among the Romans to swear by the fact of hearing or
singing this hymn. In this city the people are not
taught by the Bishop, nor by any one in the church.
At Alexandria the Bishop alone teaches the people;
and it is said that this custom has prevailed there ever
since the days of Arius, who, though but a Presbyter,
broached a new doctrine. Another custom also prevails at Alexandria, which I have never witnessed nor
heard of elsewhere, and this is, that when the Gospel is
read, the Bishop does not rise from his seat. The
Archdeacon alone reads the Gospel in this city, whereas
in some places it is read by the Deacons, and in others
only by the Presbyters; while in many Churches it is
read on stated days by the Bishops; as, for instance,
at Constantinople, on the first day of the Festival of
the Resurrection. In some Churches the interval called
Quadragesima, which occurs before this festival, and is
devoted by the people to fasting, is made to consist of
six weeks; and this is the case in Illyria and the
Western regions, in Lybia, throughout Egypt, and in
Palestine: whereas it is made to comprise seven weeks
at Constantinople, and in the neighbouring provinces,

as far as Phœnicia. In some Churches the people fast three alternate weeks, during the space of six or seven weeks, whereas in others they fast continuously during the three weeks immediately preceding the festival. Some people, as the Montanists, only fast two weeks. Assemblies are not held in all Churches on the same day, or upon the same occasions. The people of Constantinople and of several other cities assemble together on the Sabbath as well as on the next day, which custom is never observed at Rome or at Alexandria. There are several cities and villages in Egypt where, contrary to the usages established elsewhere, the people meet together on Sabbath evenings, and, although they have dined previously, partake of the mysteries. The same prayers and Psalms are not recited, nor the same passages read on the same occasions, in all Churches [b]."

The tendency of modern Church legislation is in the direction of uniformity of worship. In our own Church the necessities of the time make the maintenance of the Prayer-book in its integrity a sacred duty. In Scotland an influential school have done what they could to get rid of the national Office for the Celebration of the Holy Communion. In France the Ultramontane party have toiled sedulously to expel the local and Diocesan Breviaries, and to substitute the Roman Office. There is something to be said for this substitution: perhaps there is more to be said for the retention of the older forms. As union is strength, so, no

[b] Sozomen, "Ecclesiastical History," bk. vii. c. 19.

doubt, a vast wide-spread uniformity of rite will tend to stereotype and strengthen those ideas, of which that rite is the type and watchword. On the other hand, much beauty, the evidence of much thought, must be lost by the abandonment of any service which has gained a real hold upon a people. It is unwise in any sense to weaken the antiquarian and sentimental value of any rite, and, above all, there may be deep theological reasons which, having suggested and maintained the peculiar practice, it were wrong to controvert. Perhaps, to sum up, it may be said that by uniformity of rite, strength and concentrated energy are gained at the expense of that passive power which unbroken tradition ever gives, and of that sense of largeness and freedom which is so important an element and so conducive to the health and action of the Body of Christ.

The next clause in the Article is a caution against those persons, who, of their private judgment, openly break the traditions and ceremonies of the Church.

The order of the words is observable. The evils arising from such infringement are stated to be 1. "offending against the common order of the Church; 2. hurting the authority of the Magistrate; 3. wounding the consciences of the weak brethren." The authority of the Church in these matters, although not involving any matter of faith (for the Article is treating only of *Adiaphora*), is placed first; and then only injury done to the authority of the Magistrate. For since, according to ancient custom, the Magistrate gave a civil sanction to customs, or "the common order of the Church," then, to infringe that, to which he had lent this sanction, was to lower his authority also. The wont of giving such civil sanction to the laws of the Church dates back to the earliest times of the converted Empire. To "confirm" the decrees of a Council became a technical term. The fathers of the second General Council wrote to Theodosius; "We pray your Clemency, that you will confirm with the writing of your Piety the decree of the Council, so that, as you honoured the Church by the letters which convoked it, you may set your seal to the conclusion which we have decreed[c]." The fathers of the Council of Ephesus applied to the younger Theodosius, that "the things set forth by the Œcumenical and holy Council for the confirmation of godliness against Nestorius and his impious doctrine, may have their own strength, being corroborated by the assent and approbation of your Piety[d]." The Emperor Marcian speaks of "confirming the holy Synod" [of Chalcedon] "by the decree of our Clemency[e];" and the fathers, in their Synodical Epistle to St. Leo, speak of the Emperor's having "confirmed by a law the judgment of your Piety." Justinian directed the Patriarch Mennas to send to the Metropolitans of his diocese "what had been decreed by the Chief Priests and *confirmed* by the Empire." Constantine Pogonatus

---

[c] *Epist. Syn. Conc. Const. ad Theodos.*
[d] *Conc. Eph.,* Art. 5.   [e] *Conc. Chalc.,* Art. 6.

confirmed by his "sacred edicts;" the sixth Council against the Monothelites; and "the decree of the Synod and the Emperor's edict" were spoken of by Leo II. "as a two-edged sword of the Spirit, by which that error was stricken through." Of particular Councils, the first Council of Orleans, A.D. 511, applied to King Clovis, that "if what we have ordained is approved to be right by" his "judgment also, the consent of so great a king and lord may, with the greater authority, confirm the sentence of so many priests." The recitation of the Nicene Creed, as settled by the Council of Constantinople, before the Communion of the Body and Blood of Christ, was decreed in the third Council of Toledo, A.D. 589, at the suggestion of King Recared, and "corroborated" by him. Three days' litanies in Advent, by which "every Christian soul should make humble amends to the Lord of heaven," were decreed in the fifth Council of Toledo, A.D. 636, at the exhortation of King Suintilla, and, as well as the sixth Council, A.D. 638, were "confirmed" by him. Ecclesiastical regulations as to benefices, suspension of any negligent Bishop, the appointment of three rogation-days in every month, were enacted by the sixteenth and seventeenth Councils, A.D. 693, 694, at the suggestion of King Egiza, and confirmed by him. The Council of Arles, Mayence, Rheims, Tours, Chalons, were held by Bishops at the command of Charlemagne for the correction of the condition of the

---

' *Ep. Const. Pog. ad Leon.*

Church, A.D. 813. "The Bishops sought the remedies of the evil in Holy Scripture and the Canons." The Councils of Mayence and Arles expressly submitted them to Charlemagne for revision; the Councils of Chalons and Tours state, that "the Canons made in each Synod were collated before the Emperor in the General Council at Aix, when they were confirmed, so as to have the force of law. Justinian, in his *Novellæ Constitutiones*, and Charlemagne, in his *Capitulare*, embodied the ancient Canons, to which they gave the force of law. Lothaire carried on the work of his grandfather, and formed a *Capitulare*, "to be kept as a law by all the lieges of the Holy Church of God, or of ourselves in the kingdom of Italy." Pope Leo IV. bound himself to observe "those capitula and precepts of Lothaire and his predecessors in all things[g]." A minute collation of our Anglo-Saxon ecclesiastical and civil laws, shews that the kings gave a civil authority to what had been previously enacted by the Bishops. It is, then, in accordance with ancient precedent, that the Article gives a secondary but real place to the sanction of the Civil Magistrate. The civil power usurped, cajoled, bribed, corrupted, oppressed; but the principle, implied by the Article, that the Civil Magistrate could give a civil sanction to the law of the Church, which, if given, was to be respected, was consistent with ancient precedents.

"Every particular or national Church hath autho-

---

[g] *C. de Capitulis*, dist. 10, ap. Gratian. The above is epitomised from Dr. Pusey on the Royal Supremacy, §§ ii., xiv., xv., xvii.

rity to ordain, change, and abolish ceremonies or rites of the Church."

The question, what constitutes nationality, is one of those which at this moment is perplexing the politicians of Europe, and has been the great pretext under which the Revolutionists of this century have advocated their designs. The present state of the world is to be upset, because the political circumstances of past ages have bound together divers races under one form of government. It is said that government is essentially conterminous with nationality; and yet it is very difficult to say in what nationality consists. It cannot consist in unity of race; for the most perfect polity that ever existed, the ancient Roman Empire, was an aggregate of many; and the form of the American Republic, which the necessities of the nineteenth century in the Western hemisphere have evolved, includes the emigrated subjects of almost every European state and their descendants. It cannot be a question of language; for we see the same language prevailing in monarchies and republics, the conditions of which make fusion and identification impossible. We are therefore driven back upon history, and the only definition of a nation which will satisfy rigorous criticism, is a polity organized under one supreme head, constituted of such individuals as, from the circumstances of past history, by conquest, marriage, or treaty, have been united into one concrete whole. From this definition it will be seen that unity of religion can no longer enter into the essence of a nation. It was not so at the time of the framing of the Articles. The Eastern Empire broadly embraced the Eastern Church. The Armenian religion was, above all, the symbol of a passionate nationality; while in the West the great Latin Church ruled the wills and consciences of Roman and Teuton. Then came the Reformation. The old habits of order, the ignorance of the political possibility of toleration, suggested to the reforming Kings of Germany and their Theologians no other basis but nationalism as the foundation of the new Creeds. Having no Episcopate, and regarding all Christians as equally Priests, they had no unity except in the person of the Sovereign. The Sovereign was their Bishop. And, therefore, we are struck in the history of the continental Reformation with the amount of the personal influence of the individual potentates, the difficulties which the preachers had in dealing with the civil authority, and generally with a confusion of ideas as to the relative spheres of Church and State. We have seen Lutheranism and Calvinism, if not chemically combined, at least blended into a new Evangelical Church at the will of an energetic Sovereign.

In England this tendency prevailed, but under different conditions. It was held in check by the existence of a spiritual body, which Henry was obliged to own, and through which his successors hoped to rule. The fact that she was an island tended greatly to insularity of thought. In one sense the Reformation was only the final act in a long struggle between the *Regale* and *Pontificale*, which, with dif-

ferent successes at different times, had been fought
out since the days of William the Conqueror.

Many things contributed to an Anti-Italian feeling.
The English kings carefully nursed it. The bitter
recollections of the national humiliation in the reign
of King John, which, but for its consequences, would
have died away, as all past things do, was kept alive
and aggravated by the continued exactions of the
Roman Curia [h], and the conferring of English benefices
upon Italians, who knew not the language of the
people, nor the face of their flock [i]. These often died

[h] The complaints in Matthew Paris are well known. The expression
of a Pope that England was "an inexhaustible well," became unhappily
notorious. The reputed venality of the Roman Court was admitted by
Honorius III. (M. Paris, A. 1226). John Andreæ mentions, that at the
Council of Vienne a commutation was spoken of (of which he himself
approved), whereby the Pope and Cardinals should have one-twentieth
of the clerical revenues of all Europe, in lieu of tenths, first-fruits, &c.,
payments to legates and nuncios. (*Comm. in Decr. Greg.*, i. tit. 32,
c. 15.

[i] The *Epistola Universitatis regni Angliæ*, addressed to Pope Innocent
IV., at the Council of Lyons, says that "beside the aforesaid subsidies
[to the Pope], the Italians (of whom there is now an infinite number),
are now enriched by churches belonging to the patronage of the religious, who are called their Rectors," the Italians "taking no cure of
souls, neither knowing their sheep, nor known by them; using no hos-
pitality nor almsgiving (as the statutes of the Church prescribe), but
only exporting the income out of the kingdom, impoverishing the kingdom not slightly, and seizing its revenues." "The Italians, deriving in
England more than 60,000 marks annually (besides other sources of
income), derive from the kingdom a larger revenue in bare money than
the king himself." (In Matth. Paris, p. 666.) These complaints were
repeated after the Council in letters from the king, the Archbishop of
Canterbury and his suffragans, the Abbots, the *Universitas Angliæ*.
(See in Brown. *fasc. rer. exp. et fug.*, ii. 420, sqq.)

at Rome, and their places were filled up with other Italians, before the patrons knew of the vacancy[k]. Sagacious minds foresaw impending evil[l]. The English kings made political capital of these grievances in the way of strengthening the realm, by exciting indignation against all foreign interference, and especially all foreign taxation. Henry VIII. dexterously seized the weak points of the Roman Court, professing to relieve his people from the evils involved by appeals to Rome, and the money-demands of its Court. He would take off the yoke of Rome, in order to make way for, and make fast his own.

There could be no doubt that in his resistance to the Roman Court, Henry VIII. at first carried with him the great mass of the English people, and it was only when men began to see whither events were irre-

[k] Ibid.

[l] The above letters to the Pope end with heavy prognostications. The Abbots close theirs, " Let your Holiness provide that the kingdom and priesthood be no wise divided; for if the English Church should be brought to ruin, a division being made between the kingdom and priesthood, both people and priest may groan, and the ruin of many follow without delay." " The peers, clergy, and people" end theirs, " unless the things aforesaid be speedily corrected by you, let your Holiness hold for certain, that it may with reason be feared, that such peril will impend both on the Roman Church and on the king, as cannot easily be remedied." (See further in *Eirenicon*, pp. 80—82.)

Durandus, Bishop of Mende, quoted " the vulgar proverb," " who wishes all loses all." " The Roman Church claims to itself all things (*universa*), whence it is to be feared that it will lose all things; for as Solomon says, ' Whoso squeezeth vehemently, draweth blood.' An example of which is in the Church of the Greeks, which is said, on this ground, to have departed from the obedience of the Roman Church." (*de modo cel. gen. Conc.*, p. ii. tit. 7.)

sistibly dragging them, that the Pilgrimage of Grace, and the Lincolnshire and Exeter Rebellions, exhibited the continued existence of the opposite spirit. When the breach with Rome was effected, on no other ground could the Reformation be justified and defended but on that of nationalism; and putting out of the question the Celtic populations of Ireland and Wales, the unity of race that generally prevailed through the island, and the separation by the sea from all other kingdoms save that of Scotland, enabled the experiment to be tried under the most favourable circumstances.

It now remains to be seen how far the principle of nationalism may be extended into things of religion. Obviously, nationalism must in no ways affect the faith. The faith is one everywhere, and in all times. But what is claimed in the Article is only that every particular or national Church hath authority to ordain, change, and abolish ceremonies, or rites of the Church, ordained only by man's authority: and to this proposition every one must give his assent. It had for its example the national Churches under the Empire; Africa, Spain, (perhaps Portugal,) and Gaul, each used their own code; as the Greeks had before the Council of Nice.

The passage just quoted from Sozomen, which in so few words brings strikingly before us the variations of practice in things non-essential in the Early Church, is confirmed by the Great Council of Nicæa itself[m], where it says, " Let the ancient customs prevail;" and

[m] Can. vi.

antiquity shews us that from the beginning, even in regard to the administration of the very Sacraments themselves, there were variations of form: and if such was the case with regard to these, how much more is this permissible in such inferior matters as discipline, ceremonies, and whatever else tends to edification! Variations have taken place both with times and places, and the same Churches have not always observed the same rites.

To any one who studies the structure of the present service-books of the Church of England, it will be evident that, while this principle was admitted in some cases to a degree with which we do not sympathize, there was a wise adherence to what had gone before. The old forms in spirit remained the same, except where they were actually and advisedly altered, and thus the identification of the Church before and after the Reformation, where it was possible, was vigorously maintained.

This principle is fully admitted by the great founder, under Christ, of the present English Church. St. Gregory the Great, writing to St. Augustine of Canterbury, who had requested information how he was to act, that wise and sagacious Pontiff writes :—" But it pleases me, that whatsoever you have found either in the Church of Rome, or of those of Gaul, or in any Church whatever, which would please Almighty God better, you would carefully select ; and into the Church of England, which at present is new in the faith, introduce by your instruction and care the most exalted things you have been able to collect from many Churches; for we must love not things for places, but places for things. Out of each Church, therefore, choose those things which are religious, pious, and right; and these, collected, as it were, in a bundle, deposit in the minds of the English for their practice." In this he followed the well-known example of St. Ambrose, as quoted by St. Augustine in the 54th Letter to Januarius. Indeed, the diverse forms for the administration of the ordinances of religion, such as Absolution and Extreme Unction, as illustrated in the Greek and Latin Churches, and, again, in the rites of the Eastern heretics, as well as those forms which were in use in the Middle Ages in Western Europe, are sufficient confirmation of the truth of the position laid down in the Article, that grace is not absolutely tied to one form of sacramental words, and that, *à fortiori*, with regard to the ordinary forms of prayer, a large latitude may be conceded. In fact, at the Council of Florence, a Canon was made in the exact sense of this very Article, that every one should observe the rites and customs of his own Church, which it is not lawful for any one to change by his private authority.

ARTICLE XXXV.

De Homiliis.

Tomus secundus Homiliarum, quarum singulos titulos huic articulo subjunximus, continet piam et salutarem doctrinam, et his temporibus necessariam, non minus quam prior tomus Homiliarum, quæ editæ sunt tempore Edwardi Sexti : Itaque eas in Ecclesiis per ministros diligenter, et clare, ut a populo intelligi possint, recitandas esse judicavimus.

De Nominibus Homiliarum.
[These are given in English, as under.]

" *Of Homilies.*

" THE second book of Homilies, the several titles whereof we have joined under this Article, doth contain a godly and wholesome doctrine, and necessary for these times, as doth the former book of Homilies, which were set forth in the time of Edward the Sixth ; and therefore we judge them to be read in churches by the ministers, diligently and distinctly, that they may be understanded of the people.

" *Of the Names of the Homilies.*

" 1. Of the right use of the Church.
" 2. Against peril of Idolatry.

" 3. Of repairing and keeping clean of Churches.

"4. Of Good Works: first of Fasting.

"5. Against Gluttony and Drunkenness.

"6. Against Excess of Apparel.

"7. Of Prayer.

"8. Of the Place and Time of Prayer.

"9. That Common Prayers and Sacraments ought to be ministered in a Known Tongue.

"10. Of the Reverent Estimation of God's Word.

"11. Of Alms-doing.

"12. Of the Nativity of Christ.

"13. Of the Passion of Christ.

"14. Of the Resurrection of Christ.

"15. Of the Worthy Receiving of the Sacrament of the Body and Blood of Christ.

"16. Of the Gifts of the Holy Ghost.

"17. For the Rogation-days.

"18. Of the State of Matrimony.

"19. Of Repentance.

"20. Against Idleness.

"21. Against Rebellion."

From the very beginning of Christianity, the preaching of Sermons and Homilies has formed a very important department of the teaching office of the Church. It mainly took the form of commenting upon the inspired records, hence the usual term was " tractare." In the time of St. Cyprian, at least in the Church of Africa where the sees were very small and numerous, preaching was the special office of Bishops. Even elsewhere, it was contrary to usage that a Presbyter should discourse in the presence of a Bishop. In the Alexandrian School, however, we have the catechetical lectures of Origen. After the age of the Apologies, when the faith had to be vindicated from the attacks of open enemies, we find that the edification of the faithful by exhortations from the Holy Scriptures forms a great part of the literature of the Church. St. Cyril, of Jerusalem, has given us his Sermons on the Mys-

teries of the Faith, delivered in preparation for the
Easter Baptism and Communion of the neophytes of
Jerusalem; and St. Chrysostom, he of the golden mouth,
is emphatically the great sermon-writer of the East.
Eusebius preserves his great Sermon at the consecration of the Basilica at Tyre. Other Fathers also in
the East, as SS. Gregory of Nyssa and Nazianzen,
and Basil, have come down to us in the exhortations
they gave to their people; while in the West, St.
Ambrose, St. Augustine, and St. Leo, are the most
prominent of the many sermon-writers, who, like
St. Zeno of Verona, St. Maximus of Turin, St. Gaudentius of Brescia, fulfilled one solemn function of
the episcopal office in preaching the Word of God.
St. Cyril of Alexandria is said by Gennadius, of
Marseilles, who flourished about sixty years after St.
Cyril's death, to have composed very many Homilies,
which "are committed to memory by the Bishops of
Greece." There seems to be an allusion to something
of this in St. Cyril himself, in a very curious exegesis
of the words, "When thou comest into thy neighbour's vineyard*," &c., although of his popular sermons but few have reached us, except the glowing one
on the Mystic Supper, and those on St. Luke, preserved in a translation by the Syriac Christians, and
lately brought to England and translated. He says
on the passage above mentioned: "I think it not unfit
for us to apply this to some others, who, plucking as
it were some spiritual food the words of the teachers

* Deut. xxiii. 24.

in the Churches, which are, may be, somewhat suddenly uttered, are not content with this, but going on to speak beyond bounds, and, as it were, putting them into a vessel, commit them to their tablets, with love of learning indeed, but wronging, in respect of understanding, the brethren, in that what is treated off-hand they commit to writing, as if it had been finished with much care.   And yet the Law, my good friends, would I say to them, clearly commanded to put nothing into a vessel[b]."

Many of these teachings lived on beyond the fall of the Empire into the Dark Ages, and we cannot doubt that the exposition of Scripture in Homilies must have been one of the methods whereby the fresh nations of the North were won under the dominion of Christ. But as love waxed cold, the duty of preaching became less insisted on, and the habit of preaching varied with the langour of the Church.   Among the very popular writers of the ninth century was Haymo, Bishop of Halberstadt.   His Homilies for the Sundays and principal Saints' Days, were printed in Paris in 1545.   In the East, preaching gradually died out, so that at present it hardly forms any part of the public worship of the Church; but in the West it never entirely ceased in the worst times.   There was perhaps little original in the teaching till the time of St. Bernard, when the Crusades, stimulated by the trumpet-voice of Peter the Hermit, called all Western Christendom to fight for the Sepulchre of the Lord.

[b] *De Adoratione*, lib. viii. p. 267.

These public appeals, however, were not the only sermons of the period. In the Cistercian Order, following St. Bernard, there rose up a school of mystical interpretation of the Word of God, which spoke to the consciences of men, and drew them to faith and obedience by the tenderest persuasion. That School passed away, and, in opposition to the Manichæan and Socialistic errors of the twelfth century, the powers of preaching were again called forth by the formation of the Dominican Order; and the eternal wisdom of God, sanctifying the intellect of man, was invoked to the crushing of error and inculcation of religious truth. From this Order emerged the celebrated Thauler, who had so profound an effect on Luther, and many others of distinction. This School, debased by the scandals of the century before the Reformation, recovered itself. For in 1612 Bernard Gualtier published an anonymous volume by some members of the Dominican Order, called *Sermones Discipuli*. Perhaps the *Discipulus* was John Herolt, whose *Sermones Quadragesimales* were printed at Maintz in the same year. Neither were there wanting in the Seraphic order, which inculcated a more mystical and effective theology, preachers of renown. St. Anthony, of Padua, is renowned for the wonderful effect of his simple exhortations in making many conversions to God; shewing that it is unction and not learning only, the blessing of God and not the ability of the preacher only, that touches the soul of man. In the fifteenth century a well-known collection was made with the quaint title of *Dormi Securè*, and was published. The full

title was "Sermons for Sundays, with Explanations of
the Gospels throughout the Year, sufficiently notable
and useful for all Priests, Pastors, and Chaplains:
which under another name is now called, Sleep se-
curely, or sleep without care, because they can without much study be incorporated and preached to the
people."

There exist many copies in MS. of the Sermons of
John Felton, Vicar of St. Mary Magdalene, in Oxford.
A selection from the names of the authors of the sermons that were printed soon after the discovery of
the art of printing, will show what was deemed best
worth preserving of the mediæval sermons:—There
are those of Robert Caraccioli di Licio, printed in
1473; F. Bartholomæus de Ursinis, 1473; Joannes
Gritsh, 1477; Ambrosius Spiera, the Servite, 1497;
Antonio de Vercellis, Minorite, 1491; Bartholomæus
de Pisis, Minorite, 1498; Leonardus de Utino, 1471;
Matthias Bosso, of Verona, 1495; Blessed Michael
Carchano, of Milan, 1476; Thomas de Haselbach,
1478; Herman de Pitrâ, 1481; Jacobus de Clusa,
1474; Frater Peregrinus, 1480; Paul Wann, 1497;
Hugo de Prato Florido, 1484; Meffret, 1487; Jacobus
a Voragine, 1485; Gabriel Biel, 1496; Joannes Nider,
1489.

But by the time that the Reformation had arrived,
much of this had lost its savour. The quality of the
preaching, according to the testimony of Berthold, had
greatly deteriorated. It is matter of history how it
was used by the venders of indulgences. Nay, even

as to the quantity of the Sermons, the neglect of
preaching by the clergy of all ranks was a never-
failing subject of complaint and invective in Scotland
for many years before the Reformation. "The Prelates certainly are dumb dogs," says the reforming
monk of Cambuskenneth, in 1536, "unable to bark
in the cloister. They associate with kings and princes
in cities and palaces, and therefore their voice is
not heard in the cloister. Wherefore, in the day of
anger and vengeance, the blood of their brethren will
be demanded at their hands[c]." Dunbar and Lindsay,
as satirists and Protestants; Quentin Kennedy, and
Ninian Wingate, as Catholics and apologists, alike
bear witness to this fact. We know from the satirists
of the day, into what a state the public preaching
had been degraded. Probably the parochial clergy
in England had very much abandoned the practice, and
left it to the ignorant and superstitious friars. In any
reform that must take place, fresh life must be infused into this department of Christian theology. As
a matter of fact, the Reformers, before the breach
with Rome, began to use it for their own purposes.
It was not to be supposed that the Church of England should neglect this weapon in doing the work
of those times.

The First Book of the Homilies was the first book
pertaining either to the public worship or teaching of
the Church, which was put forth in the reign of

[c] Fr. B. Richardin, *Exeg. le Can. D. Augustini*, fol. 188, 189.
See *Statuta Ecclesiæ Scoticanæ*, tom. ii. p. 288.

Edward VI. Henry died in January, 1547, and the Homilies bear the date of July 31 of the same year. Taverner had had Cranmer's sanction for the publishing of his "Postils," and the Bishops in the Convocation of 1542 had agreed "to make certain Homilies for stay of such errors as were then by ignorant preachers sparkled among the people." The project took none effect then, but five years afterwards the present First Book was printed by Grafton, with a preface running in the King's name, in which all the clergy, having cure of souls, were commanded to read it through to their parishioners again and again, until the King's pleasure should be further known. Nine editions were printed before the end of 1547, but they were very ill received. If the Priest misliked them, he read them unintelligibly; if the people, there was such talking and babbling in the church that nothing could be heard. In 1549, when the Prayer-book was put out, to make them less distasteful, they were divided into parts. In March, 1552, they obtained the express sanction of Convocation in the Thirty-fourth of the Forty-two Articles. On the accession of Elizabeth, a bill of Uniformity passed both Houses, with the Book of Common Prayer annexed to it. This, by the rubric in the Communion Service, carried with it the Homilies. In the editions a few verbal alterations were made, the only doctrinal one being the substitution of the word "governor" for "supreme head over all," in the Homily of Obedience. It was printed separately, but uniformly with the Second Book. The two books were not incorporated till near the end of the reign of James I.

It was intended in King Edward's time to put forth fresh Homilies, as may be seen from the rubric in the second Prayer-book, but death prevented him. Bonner published some Homilies in Queen Mary's reign, and on the accession of Elizabeth the Second Book of the Homilies, in which the number of subjects treated was twenty, while the number of treatises were thirty-eight, was published. In 1573, on the occasion of the two rebellions, the Homily against Rebellion gave six parts more. Much time passed before the book was ready, but at length, with the Thirty-nine Articles, it was submitted to the famous convocation of 1562, and received its approbation; yet Convocation had not much to do with them, as it only began to sit on the 12th of January, and the Articles involving the Homilies were passed on the 5th of February. The Queen took much longer time for her consideration of them. They did not come out of her hands untouched. The exact date of publication is not ascertained. They were, however, in the hands of the public Aug. 1, 1563. Six editions were speedily published. At first, it was necessary to enjoin the clergy to read the Homilies distinctly, on account of their dislike of the innovations contained in them. In process of time the aspect of things changed, Puritanism became the enemy to be dreaded, and the Homilies were enjoined to be read by way of stifling the prophesyings; James, for the same reason, sought assistance from the Homilies, as is noticed in his directions concerning preachers, dated Aug. 4, 1622. Then came forth the first folio edition of 1623, in which the two books are for the first time united into one volume. Some changes were made in the style, but the only modification of·teaching is contained in two brief marginal notes, referring to the conduct of St. Ambrose and the Emperor Theodosius.

The authorship of the Homilies in every case has not yet been ascertained. Some, however, have been distinctly traced to their writers. In the First Book :—

1. "The Exhortation to the Reading of Holy Scripture," is probably by Archbishop Cranmer.

2. "Of the Misery of Man," is certainly by Archdeacon Hartsfield.

3, 4, 5. "Of Salvation," "Of Faith," and "Of Good Works," are all by Cranmer.

6. "Of Charity," by Bishop Bonner.

7. "Of Swearing," by an anonymous writer who made use of Becon's invective against swearing.

8, 9, 10. "Of Falling from God," unknown; "Of Fear of Death," unknown ; "Of Obedience," unknown.

11. "Against Adultery," by Thomas Becon.

12. "Against Contention," unknown.

The authorship of the Homilies in the Second Book is much more uncertain, though Burnet speaks of the great share which Bishop Jewel had in compiling them :—

1, 2, 3. "Of the Right use of the Church," "Against

peril of Idolatry," "Of repairing and keeping clean of Churches," are probably from the same hand. The second is based upon a document under the title of "A Treatise of Master Nicholas Ridley," purporting to be an address to King Edward, but really presented to the Queen by Archbishop Parker. It again is derived from a work of Bullinger.

4. "Of Fasting," probably by Bishop Grindal.

5. "Against Gluttony and Drunkenness," partly from a Homily by Bishop Pilkington, and partly an adaptation of a discourse of Peter Martyr.

6. "Against Excess of Apparel," perhaps by Bishop Pilkington.

7, 8, 9. "Concerning Prayer," "Of the Place and Time of Prayer," "Of Common Prayer and Sacraments," probably Jewel.

10. "Of certain Passages in Scripture," a few sentences taken from a tract of Erasmus.

11. "Of Alms-deeds," the author is greatly indebted to St. Cyprian.

12. "Of the Nativity," unknown.

13. "Of the Passion for Good Friday," from Taverner's Postils.

14. "The Second Sermon of the Passion," unknown.

15. "Of the Resurrection," from Taverner.

16. "Of the Sacrament for Whit-Sunday," ascribed to Jewel.

17. "For Rogation-week," unknown.

18. "Of Matrimony," half from Veit Dietrick, of Nuremberg, and half from St. Chrysostom.

19. "Of Repentance," two thirds of the first part are translated from Rodolph Gualther.

20. "Against Idleness," perhaps by Jewel.

21. "Against Rebellion," added on the occasion of the rising in the North in 1569.

The measure of authority claimed for the Homilies is one that has been affected by the views of those that have quoted them. One party, in order to gain authority for their tone of doctrine, have sought to elevate them almost into the position of a standard of doctrine, not seeing how any such attempt would recoil upon themselves. Others have used them with more skill as bearing witness to many truths obscured by a current teaching, yet distinctly enunciated or presupposed by them. It is enough to say that, in the words of the Article, " they contain a godly and wholesome doctrine;" that the great truths of Christianity are borne witness to; that at the time of the Reformation some of these truths, having become obscured by superstition, needed to be re-asserted; that therefore the Homilies were " necessary for these times." To extend the expression " these times" to the present epoch seems to do violence to the natural meaning of the words. It would become an insulated passage in the Articles, in which the words were no longer to be taken in their original grammatical meaning, and which the Convocation which imposed them could not have imagined without the gift of prophecy. If any meaning in relation to the *present* times were to be forced into the words, it must be that they should be retained as witnesses of a past phase in the history of the Church, and as warnings against the return of such a state of things as brought on the Reformation.

The last clause in the Article, " we judge them to be read in the Church diligently and distinctly," was to meet the case of the lower clergy who disliked the changed tone of thought in the Homilies, or many of their statements, some of whom neglected to read the Homilies at all, while others read them in such a way that they were utterly unintelligible to the people, as has been mentioned in discussing the body of this Article.

ARTICLE XXXVI.

De Episcoporum et Ministrorum Consecratione.

Libellus de consecratione Archiepiscoporum et Episcoporum, et de ordinatione Presbyterorum et Diaconorum, editus nuper temporibus Edwardi VI. et authoritate Parliamenti illis ipsis temporibus confirmatus, omnia ad ejusmodi consecrationem et ordinationem necessaria continet, et nihil habet quod ex se sit aut superstitiosum, aut impium: itaque quicunque juxta ritus illius libri consecrati, aut ordinati sunt, ab anno secundo prædicti regis Edwardi, usque ad hoc tempus, aut in posterum juxta eosdem ritus consecrabuntur, aut ordinabuntur, rite, atque ordine, atque legitime statuimus esse, et fore consecratos et ordinatos.

" Of Consecration of Bishops and Ministers.

" The book of consecration of Archbishops and Bishops, and ordering of Priests and Deacons, lately set forth in the time of Edward the Sixth, and confirmed at the same time by authority of Parliament, doth contain all things necessary to such consecration and ordering, neither hath it any thing that of itself is superstitious and ungodly. And therefore whosoever are consecrated or ordered according to the rites of that book, since the second year of the forenamed King Edward, unto this time, or hereafter shall be consecrated or ordered according to the same rites, we decree all such to be rightly, orderly, and lawfully consecrated and ordered."

Our Lord is the immediate founder of the hierarchy, because it was He who ordained the Apostles Bishops, when He said to them: "As My Father sent Me, so send I you; receive the Holy Ghost; go ye into all the world and make disciples of every creature; whatsoever ye shall bind or loose on earth shall be bound or loosed in heaven." These words denote a power without limit, its measure is the wants of humanity, its field of action the world. At the beginning of the Church there was one general Episcopate.

Of this oneness His promise to St. Peter had been the type and earnest. In St. Cyprian's well-known words, "The Lord saith unto Peter, 'I say unto thee, that thou art Peter, and upon this rock I will build My Church, and the gates of Hell shall not prevail against it. And I will give unto thee the keys of the kingdom of heaven, and whatsoever thou shalt bind on earth shall be bound also in heaven; and whatsoever thou shalt loose on earth shall be loosed in heaven.' To him again, after His resurrection, He says, 'Feed My sheep.' Upon him, being one, He builds His Church; and though He gives to all the Apostles an equal power, and says, 'As My Father sent Me, even so send I you; receive ye the Holy Ghost, whose soever sins ye remit, they shall be remitted to him, and whose soever sins ye retain, they shall be retained,' yet, in order to manifest unity,

He has by His own authority so placed the source of the same unity, as to begin from one. Certainly the other Apostles also were what Peter was, endued with an equal fellowship both of honour and power, but a commencement is made from unity, that the Church may be set before us as one."

St. Peter, then, and the rest of the Apostles left Bishops in their stead, deriving their authority immediately from themselves, and through them from Christ. St. Clement says, in the well-known passage of his Epistle, written to allay the dissensions in the Church of Corinth, " Our Apostles knew, through our Lord Jesus Christ, that there will be contention about the name of the Episcopate. For this cause, then, having received perfect foreknowledge, they settled the aforesaid [Bishops and Deacons], and meanwhile gave a rule of succession, that when they should fall asleep, others, approved men, should succeed to their ministry ^a." And St. Irenæus speaks of the Apostolic succession of the Bishops, as a proof of their Apostolic doctrine; as in the celebrated passage, " The tradition of the Apostles, manifested in the whole world, all who wish to see the truth may behold in every Church, and we can enumerate those who were instituted Bishops in the Churches, and their successors down to us, who neither thought nor knew aught of the phrenzies of these men. For had the Apostles known hidden mysteries, which they taught the perfect, apart and unknown to the rest,

---

^a *Ep.* i. n. 44.

they would even specially deliver them to those, to whom they committed the Churches themselves also. For very perfect and blameless in all things, they wished them to be, whom they left also as their successors, delivering to them their own office of instruction, since, if these acted well, great good would result; if they fell, extremest calamity [b]."

It is probable that the Apostles chose cities and towns for their chief ministry, since these were the heart of each country, whence the Gospel would reach most easily to the smaller places. It is in cities, where we hear of Apostles abiding; they are cities which, in the main, they address. The metropolis of the country or province became naturally the ecclesiastical metropolis, the see of the first Bishop of that province. Such grouping of sees occurs even in the Apostolic Canons. "The Bishops of each nation must own him who is first among them, and regard him as head, and do nothing extraordinary without his mind [c]." The Council of Antioch, making the terms of this more definite, speaks of it as "the Canon of our fathers," and assign the reason. "The Bishops in each Eparchy must own the Bishop presiding in the metropolis, and submit to his thought for the whole Eparchy, because in the metropolis all from all sides who have matters meet together; whence it seemed good that he should be first in honour, and that the other Bishops [d]," &c. The Council of Laodicea requires that "the Bishops should be set in their ecclesiastical rule by the judg-

---

[b] iii. 3, 1.   [c] Can. xxxiii.   Can. ix.

ment of the metropolitans, and the Bishops around [e]."
The Council of Eliberis speaks of "the place in which
the first see of the Episcopate is established [f]." The
Council of Nice lays down that "a Bishop should be
appointed by all the Bishops in the Eparchy; but if
this should be difficult on account of a pressing necessity or length of way, that three should meet together,
the absent Bishops concurring, and agreeing by letter;
but that the validity of what took place should in each
Eparchy be assigned to the metropolitan [g]." It has
alike no other title for the highest sees than "the
Bishop in Rome," "the Bishop in Alexandria [h]." The
substance existed without the name.

This subdivision, which was made, in no way in-
terfered with the oneness of the Episcopate, which is
expressed in St. Cyprian's characteristic words, *Episco-
patus unus est, cujus a singulis in solidum pars tenetur* [i].
And so Pope Symmachus: "After the pattern of the
Trinity, whose power is one and undivided, there is
one Priesthood among the many Bishops."

"It is a fact recognised universally in the Church,
and as certain as its existence, that Jesus Christ has
established in the person of His Apostles, a power invested with a holy and legitimate authority, and that
this authority, conferred on the Apostles to govern the
Church, has passed to Bishops instituted by them, and
is preserved in all the successions of those who have
followed them. The most ancient monuments attest
that nothing can be done without the Bishop; that

---

[e] Can. xii.　　　[f] Can. xxxviii.　　　[g] Can. iv.　　　[h] Can. vi.
[i] It. Cypr., *de Unitate Eccl.*

without them is neither Baptism, Eucharist, or absolution; that they are in God's stead, and on this ground claim authority in things divine; that it is by tradition, of which they are the living links, that the Canon of Scripture is ascertained; that it is by them that controversies of faith are to be determined; that it is by them that we are in the Church, that the Church itself subsists and can with certainty be recognised [k]."

This Article has not to do with the present Ordinal as given in the Prayer-book, but with one in temporary use from the second year of Edward VI. till the time of Charles II.; it is, however, of primary importance, that its sufficiency and canonicity should be asserted and proved, inasmuch as the strength of every chain being exactly the strength of the weakest link and no more, if orders conferred under this rite had been invalid, no supplementing in after times would have availed. Unless the ordainers and consecrators were true Bishops themselves, they could not by a more perfect rite confer grace which they had not, or in any way improve the ecclesiastical position of the community to which they belonged. On the other hand, if the rite was sufficient, they were free to make that rite more edifying, orderly, and impressive; and this is just what the later revision has done.

The act of King Edward ordained that such form and manner of making and consecrating of Archbishops, Bishops, Priests, Deacons, and other ministers of the Church shall be used, (observe the recog-

[k] Klee, *Hist. Dog.*, i. 116.

nition of the minor orders,) as by six prelates and six other men of this realm, learned in God's law, by the King's Majesty appointed, shall be devised for that purpose. The act passed the Lords :—Tonstal, Bishop of Durham; Oglethorp, of Carlisle; Heath, of Worcester, Thirlby, of Westminster; and Day, of Chichester, protesting.

From the earliest periods of the Church, ordination has been invested with the greatest solemnity. It has been entrusted to the Bishops only, ordination by Presbyters being a thing unknown, or if known, only known to be declared absolutely null, till Luther and Calvin.

In the Apostolic Constitutions[1], when a Priest is to be ordained, the Bishop lays his hand on his head, the Priests and Deacons standing by, while the Bishop says a prayer, invocating grace on him who has been elected by the suffrage and consent of all the Clergy. By the Canons of the Tenth Council of Carthage, when a Bishop is to be consecrated, two Bishops are to hold the New Testament over his head, and while one Bishop pronounces the prayer of consecration, the rest of that order present lay their hands upon his head. At the ordination of a Priest the Bishop makes the prayer, and all the Priests in church with him lay their hands on the head of him thus ordained. In the case of a Deacon, the Bishop only does so.

In the Pseudo-Dionysius it is said: " The Bishop

---

[1] Lib. viii. c. 16.

elect who comes for consecration is to kneel before the Altar, the Gospels are held over his head, he receives imposition of hands from the consecrating Bishop." There is likewise a solemn form of prayer used on this occasion. A Priest at his ordination, kneels likewise before the Altar, the Bishop laying his right hand on his head, and completing the ordination with solemn prayers. When a Deacon is made, he kneels before the Altar on only one knee, and then the Bishop, laying his hand upon his head, pronounces a prayer proper for those of that order. All these respective orders are signed with the sign of the cross, the names and degrees of the persons published, and lastly, they are saluted by the Bishop and the rest of the Clergy [m].

In the Greek Church, the Archbishop, standing before the Holy Table, prays for the descent of the Holy Ghost upon the elect, and holding his hands upon his head, reads the instrument of his election; then after some prayers, opening the Gospels, he lays them on the head of the person consecrated, the other Bishops also touching him. He likewise makes three crosses on his head, and pronounces the prayers of consecration. Then one of the Bishops assisting reads part of the Litany, the Archbishop with his hand on the head of the elect makes another prayer, takes the Gospels from off his head, invests him with the omophorion. Then he is saluted by all and conducted to the Bishop's seat [n].

[m] Pseudo-Dion., i. 363, 364, ed. 1634; vide Morinus, *De Sac. Ord.*, ii. p. 51.   [n] Vide Euchologion, p. 160, ed. Venice, 1854.

At the Ordination of Priests, the beginning of the Office is like the former; the three crosses are made, hands are imposed, and prayer made specifying the order to which the elect is advanced. The Litany is said by a Priest, the proper habit put on, and the kiss of peace given. Then the elements being unveiled, the Bishop puts a piece of bread into the hand of the person ordained, and laying his hand on his head bows his body over the Holy Table. Then the ordained person returns the bread to the Bishop, and receives the Sacrament before the rest of the Priests.

The *Missale Francorum*, given by Mabillon, follows exactly the form of the Council of Carthage[o].

In the ninth century supplementary rites come in; the ring and pastoral-staff were given to Bishops, and the sacred vessels to Priests. In the Sacramentary joined to the end of the *Ordo Romanus*, the last is done with the words, "Receive thou authority to offer sacrifice to God, and to celebrate mass both for the quick and the dead." The Sacramentary of Gelasius speaks of offering sacrifices, but there is nothing of the delivering the vessels.

Neither is this enjoined in the Pontifical of Corbey of the ninth century, though there the hands of the Priest are to be anointed, and his offering sacrifices for the sins and offences of the people is made mention of.

So in the English Saxon Ordinal, called Egbert's Pontifical, the Priest's hands are anointed with oil and chrism, his head anointed, and an officiating habit

* Collyer's "Church History," vol. v. p. 368.

placed upon him. The ordination prayers mention his offering sacrifice for the sins of the people, but not "for the quick and the dead." No rule is given for the delivery of the vessels.

The Schoolmen lay great stress on this delivery, and even go so far as to doubt the validity of ordination conferred without it; on the other hand, they have always granted the canonical character of the Eastern orders.

The modern teaching of the Church of Rome on the essentials of ordination is to be found in the *Homo Apostolicus* of St. Alfonso[p]. In his 17th Tractate on the Sacrament of Order, No. 15, we find the following words :—" The second question is whether the matter and forms of the Sacraments, especially of order, are all specifically determined by Jesus Christ. The first opinion denies this, along with St. Bonaventura, Bellarmine, Valentini, Morinus, Lugo, Salmeron, &c. Their only reason is, that otherwise there could not be different matter and forms in the Greek and Latin Churches, especially in the case of the Sacrament of Order, seeing that in the Greek Church both the priesthood and the diaconate are conferred by the imposition of hands only; while in the Latin the handing over the instruments is required, according to the decree of Eugenius IV., as has been already mentioned. Whereupon they assert that as regards Baptism and the Eucharist our Lord ordained specifically both the matter and the form; but regarding the other Sacraments,

[p] Vol. vii. p. 466 sqq., ed. Turin, 1848.

He instituted them in kind only, leaving to the Church the power of determining them specifically, by giving them the words and things that should express the effect of the Sacrament. This opinion is probable, but there is a more 'probable opposed to it, which holds that the matter and form of all the Sacraments were specifically determined by our Lord; so Merbes, Habert, Juvenin, Tournely, Petrocor., Concina, and many others with St. Thomas, who cannot be denied to be of this opinion, when he says: 'For that the sanctification of man is in the hands of God Who sanctifieth him, it belongs not to man by his own judgment to assume the things whereby he is sanctified, for this must needs be determined by the institution of God. And therefore in the Sacraments of the new law, by which men are sanctified, it is needful to use things determined by the Divine institution[q].' To this opinion Benedict XIV. adheres, who says there is no foundation to prove that this power was conceded to the Church by Jesus Christ, nay, that it is opposed to the Council of Trent[r], where it is said that the Church can do nothing touching the substance, but only touching the administration of the Sacraments. But as regards the diversity of the Greek and Latin Churches, it is answered that the giving of the instruments is not held as essential matter, only accidental though integral. And to the decree of Eugenius, we answer with Merbes, Tournely, and Concina, that the Pope then did not determine the matters essential to order, but only

[q] 3rd p. qu. 60, a. 5.   [r] Sess. 21, cap. 2.

wished to instruct the Armenians in the rites of the Roman Church to which they wished to be united."

"The third question is, what is the matter of the Priesthood, whether only the imposition of hands, or the giving the instruments, and what is the form?

"There are three opinions: 1. that of Fagnani, Soto and a few others, who hold that the only matter is the tradition of the instruments which the Bishop gives the candidate, and the form 'Take thou authority of offering sacrifice,' &c., and by this matter and form is bestowed the power not only of sacrifice but absolution. The sole motive of this opinion is taken from the decree of Eugenius IV., where it is said, 'The order of Priesthood is given by presenting with a cup with wine, and a paten with bread.' But this opinion is commonly not received by the doctors. 2. The second is that of Bellarmine, Estius, Scotti, Layman, Salmeron, Coninc, Holzm., Vasquez, who maintain that in the ordering of Priests there is a double essential matter, so that by the tradition of the instruments power is given over the real Body of Christ, viz. that of sacrificing, with the words, 'Take authority,' &c., and by the imposition of hands power is given over the mystical body of Christ, viz. that of absolving, with the words, 'Take the Holy Ghost, whose sins thou remittest they are remitted.' 3. The third opinion, that of Martene, Becanus, Tournely, Juvenin, Petrocor., Concina, and others with St. Bonaventura, to which Benedict XIV. also agrees, holds that both powers are given to the Priest by the sacred imposition of hands, namely, when the Bishop extends his hands over the candidate with the Presbyters attending, as the Council of Trent says, 'that the ministers of extreme unction are Bishops, or Priests rightly ordained by them by the laying on of the hands of the Presbytery.' This opinion is confirmed by the Council of Trent[*], 'that we are taught sufficiently in the Holy Scriptures what things are chiefly to be attended to in the ordination of Priests and Deacons, but that we have nothing else assigned as the matter of the Sacrament of Order than the imposition of hands: it must be said, that beside the imposition, nothing else in ordination is of essential necessity.' It is also proved by the Greek rite, whereby, as has been said, men are ordained solely by the laying on of hands, seeing that the validity of Sacraments depends essentially on the forms and matter instituted by Jesus Christ. To this must be added what Benedict XIV. with Martene mentions, 'that the giving of the instruments was not introduced into the Church before the eighth or ninth centuries'. . . . As to what the form according to this third opinion is, some say, 'Take thou authority,' but more probably Morinus and Tournely say it is the prayer which the Bishop says in the imposition aforesaid, and the words which he says at the end in the third laying on of hands, ' Receive the Holy Ghost,' are only declarative of the Spirit being already given. The third opinion is the more probable, but because the second is probable, at least extrinsically, that in practice is to be followed."

[*] Sess. 23, c. 2.

The question of the validity of Anglican Orders used to turn on three hinges, 1. Was Barlow, through whom alone the succession was supposed to come, himself consecrated ? 2. Is there sufficient documentary evidence for the Consecration of Matthew Parker ? 3. Were the form, matter, and intention sufficient to confer valid ordination ?

As to the first, using the words of Dr. Lingard [t], "For ten years Barlow performed all the sacred duties and exercised all the civil rights of a consecrated Bishop. He took his seat in Parliament as Lord Bishop of St. David's. He was styled by Gardiner 'his brother of St. David's.' He ordained Priests : he was one of the officiating Bishops at the Consecration of Bulkley, [and likewise of Skip,] yet we are now called upon to believe that he was no Bishop, and consequently that nobody objected to his orders, though they were known to be illegal : or to his ordinations, though they were known to be irregular ; nor to his performance of Episcopal Functions, though it was well known that each such function was a sacrilege !"

As to the second, 1. The Public Records shew that Parker was *elected* by the Dean of Canterbury and four canons on Sept. 6, 1559 : on the 9th the Queen issued her Commission to the Bishops to consecrate, and punished them on their refusal. On Cecil consulting Parker, he replies that, in conformity with the statute 25 Henry VIII., the King must direct letters patent to an Archbishop or to four Bishops to confirm and

<hr>

[t] Catholic Magazine, 1834.

consecrate the Archbishop elect: that the consecration must take place on a Sunday, in a certain place, and the Book of Edward VI. used. The difficulty remaining, six doctors of Canon Law were consulted, who, by an instrument still extant, gave opinion that the Queen could dispense with the rigour of the law, and empower the deposed Bishops to execute the functions required by the statute; wherefore, on Dec. 6, just three months after the election, (shewing how carefully everything was gone about,) a second commission was issued to six Bishops, any four of whom were to consecrate the Bishop Elect. This took place on the 17th. The event was boldly patent to the world. It was mentioned in letters of the extreme party to their friends at Zurich. Matthew Parker's own diary, with the touching address, "Heu Heu Domine Deus, in quæ tempora servasti me," is extant[u]. The narrative of the Consecration, with a duplicate at Cambridge, still exists, and gives the minutest account of what actually took place[x], describing the very dresses and ceremonies employed, noting specially as the fact that all four consecrating Bishops said, "Take the Holy Ghost," &c.

Therefore, the study of the document shews that the question does not turn on the validity of Barlow's consecration; for in order to make the consecration absolutely secure, every one of the four officiating

[u] The consecration is mentioned by Machyn in his Diary, under the same date; and in the reign of James I., when the Fable of the "Nag's Head" was first propounded, an aged nobleman bore solemn witness that he had been present on the occasion.

[x] See Appendix to Courayer, p. 332.

Bishops was ordered to use the sacramental words. Of these four Bishops, two were consecrated by the old Pontifical, and two by the reformed ritual of Edward VI., and the three had their descent quite independent of Barlow.

As to the third point,—the form, matter, and intention—it is said that the form of Anglican Orders is imperfect, inasmuch as the office of a Bishop was not specified when hands were laid on Matthew Parker. The four consecrating Bishops used the following words:—"Accipe, inquiunt, Spiritum Sanctum, et gratiam Dei, quæ jam per impositionem manuum in te est, excitare memento: non enim timoris sed virtutis, dilectionis et sobrietatis Spiritum dedit nobis Deus[y]."

It has been said that these do not determine the office, and would suit the case of a parish-clerk as well as a Bishop. To this it must be answered; 1. That the use of the words of St. Paul, in which he gives the charge to St. Timothy as Bishop of Ephesus, shews that it was in the minds of these consecrators to confer on the candidate the authority of a primitive Bishop. Next, that there were other prayers in the service which distinctly determined the meaning of the action; and 3rdly, that the reformed Bishops were in no worse case than their predecessors; for in none of the English Pontificals, except that of Exeter, (which never was used, there being no record of any Bishop of Exeter having taken the principal part in conse-

[y] Cardwell, "Doc. Annals," i. 278.

crating a Bishop,) is there any determining word at the
time of the imposition of hands. In the Sarum Pontifical it runs thus :—"Finitâ letaniâ surgant omnes
præter electum. Et duo Episcopi ponant et teneant
evangeliorum codicem super cervicem ejus et inter
scapulas clausum, et, ordinatore super eum fundente
benedictionem, reliqui episcopi qui adsunt manibus suis
caput ejus tangant et dicat ordinator Veni Creator, ut
supra in ordinibus. Sequatur: Oremus. Oratio. Pro-
pitiare Domine supplicationibus nostris et inclinato
super hunc famulum tuum cornu gratiæ sacerdotalis,
benedictionis tuæ in eum infunde virtutem; per Dominum Nostrum Jesum Christum Filium Tuum, qui Te-
cum vivit et regnat in unitate Spiritus Sancti Deus."

The formula, "Receive the Holy Ghost," belongs
to the time of the schoolmen. Martene acknowledges
that they were unknown to antiquity, so that they
are scarcely found in any Pontifical older than his date
by four hundred years. Of all that he had seen, those
of Arles, Angers, and that of William Durandus, were
the only Pontificals that had them. It was only then,
that not content with praying for the descent of the
Holy Ghost, they thought it right to add His bestowal
in the imperative mood. Bearing this in mind, all
that the Council of Trent has said is that it is not to
no purpose that the Bishop says, "Receive the Holy
Ghost."

The next collateral proof of the validity of Anglican
ordinations is to be found in the Brief of Julius III.,
under date March 8, 1554; the Pope, without any

distinction of the ordinations conferred in the reigns
of Henry VIII. and Edward VI., or allusions to the
difference of their respective ordinals, left it to the
judgment of Cardinal Pole to rehabilitate those whom
he should judge worthy, to allow them to use the consecration they had received, and to consecrate those
who were not yet consecrated. The passage in the original runs as follows :—" Necnon de personis quorum-
cunque Episcoporum vel Archiepiscoporum, qui Me-
tropolitanam aut alias Cathedrales Ecclesias de manu
laicorum etiam schismaticorum, et præsertim qui de
Henrici Regis et Edouardi nati ejus receperunt, et earum regimini et administrationi se injecerunt, et earum
fructus, reditus et proventus etiam longissimo tempore
tanquam veri Archiepiscopi aut Episcopi, temere et de
facto usurpando, etiam in hæresin ut præfertur inci-
derint, seu antea hæretici fuerint; postquam per te uni-
tati sanctæ matris Ecclesiæ restituti exstiterint, tuque
eos *re-habilitandos* esse censueris, si tibi alias digni et
idonei videbuntur, iisdem metropolitanis et aliis Cathedralibus Ecclesiis denuo, necnon quibusvis aliis Cathedralibus etiam metropolitanis Ecclesiis per obitum vel
privationem illorum præsulum, seu alias quovis modo
pro tempore vacantibus, de personis idoneis pro quibus
ipsa Maria regina juxta consuetudines ipsius regni tibi
supplicaverit authoritate nostra providere, ipsasque
personas iisdem Ecclesiis in Episcopos aut Archiepiscopos præficere : ac cum iis qui Ecclesias Cathedrales
et Metropolitanas de manu laicorum etiam schismaticorum ut præfertur receperunt, quod iisdem seu aliis,

ad quas eas alias rite transferri contigerit, Cathedralibus etiam Metropolitanis Ecclesiis in Episcopos vel Archiepiscopos præesse, ipsasque Ecclesias in spiritualibus et temporalibus regere et gubernare, ac *munere consecrationis eis hactenus impenso uti*, vel si illud eis nondum impensum extiterit, ab Episcopis vel Archiepiscopis Catholicis per te nominandis suscipere libere et licite possint."

But this is not all. The Bull goes on to provide for the possible consecration of priests ordained irregularly, i.e. by the ritual of Edward VI., if such be advanced to the Episcopate:—"Necnon cum quibusvis per te ut præmittitur pro tempore absolutis et rehabilitatis, ut eorum erroribus et excessibus præteritis non obstantibus, quibusvis Cathedralibus etiam Metropolitanis Ecclesiis in Episcopos et Archiepiscopos præfici et præesse, illasque in eisdem spiritualibus et temporalibus regere et gubernare; ac ad quoscunque etiam sacros et presbyteratûs ordines promovere, et in illis aut per eos jam licet minus rite susceptis ordinibus etiam in altaris ministerio ministrare necnon munus consecrationis suscipere, et illo uti libere et licite valeant, dispensare etiam libere et licite possis, plenam et liberam apostolicam auctoritatem per præsentes concedimus facultatem et potestatem."

At the Council of Trent, a discussion took place, which tended to shew that Anglican orders were admitted on every ground except that of their non-confirmation by the Pope[a]. The question arose incidentally

---

[a] Vid. *Le Plat, Collect. Trid.*, vol. v. p. 578, ed. Lovan.

out of the controversy as to the origin of jurisdiction, whether directly from God or from the Pope. After some discussion, O'Hairt, Bishop of Achonry in Ireland, shewed that for these reasons it could not be maintained that jurisdiction was immediately from God. 1. That in the hierarchy there would be many heads, so that it would rather bring anarchy, and all would be upset. 2. That thereby the opinion of the heretics would be strengthened; for that in England the King calls himself Head of the Church, and creates Bishops who are consecrated by three Bishops, and say that they are true Bishops, who are from God; but we deny that, because they are not *adsciti* by the Roman Pontiff, and we say so rightly; *and by this reason alone, and by no other, do we convince them*, for they themselves shew that they have been called, elected, consecrated, granted mission. This sentiment pleased the Synod.

It is plain from this that the Anglican Bishops, ordained by the Pontifical of the reign of King Edward VI., were acknowledged to have every element of the Episcopal character, except recognition by the Pope.

Given, therefore, the historical truths of the facts of Parker's consecration as attested by a regular notary—admitting the doctrine laid down by St. Alfonso—taking into consideration, in the way of corroboration, what passed upon the subject at the Council of Trent, it is *absolutely certain* that Anglican Orders are valid and regular, unless the Pope's recognition be essential. And that that recognition is not essential, is proved by the fact that the validity and regularity of the orders of the Eastern Church have always and by all persons been admitted.

But we may retort irregularity on the impugners of Anglican orders. While four Bishops were carefully warned each to use the consecrating words in the case of Parker, it had been in the occasional practice both of East and West to admit as valid Consecration by *one* Bishop. There is a case of a single consecration in the history of St. Athanasius, another in that of St. Heliodorus; and in the ancient Scoto-Irish Church, in spite of the great multitudes of Bishops that were in Ireland, the practice was constant.

Nay, even in the case of the Papal See, there were tremendous irregularities. If we may believe Luit-prandus[a], John XII. ordained a deacon in a stable, and another of the Popes, Pelagius I., was himself con-secrated by two Bishops and a Presbyter, as Anastasius bears witness[b].

To charges, moreover, of laxity, as to the enforce-ment of Episcopal ordination after the Reformation, as in the well-known case of Whittington, Dean of Durham, and the others who in Elizabeth's time were instituted into benefices; all one can say is, that it was wrong, exceptional, and speedily remedied. But more

---

[a] Lib. vi. chap. 7.

[b] " Dum non essent Episcopi qui eum ordinarent, inventi sunt duo Episcopi, Joannes de Perusio et Pisonus de Ferentino, et Andreas presbyter de Ostia, et ordinaverunt eum pontificem."—Vide Baronius ad Ann. 555.

than that, it was distinctly an inheritance of pre-Reformation times. Benefices and Bishoprics had been held by non-ordained persons, even by children [c].

Since the reign of Queen Elizabeth the Episcopal succession of the English Church has received two infusions of what may be termed foreign blood. The first of these is the introduction of that of the Irish succession by the part which Primate Hampton took in the consecration of Bishop Morton, and by the translation of Bishop Murray, of Kilfenora, to Llandaff.

The usually received fact that the present Irish succession is purely Irish, based on the supposition that all the Bishops save two conformed at the Reformation, is now denied. It is quite true that several Irish Bishops were present at the Council of Trent; Thomas O'Herlihy, Bishop of Ross; Donatus Mac Congail,

[c] Among the documents preserved in the archives of Magdalen College, Oxford, we find a Bull of Pope Nicholas mediating in a dispute between the Founder and the Bishop of Salisbury, touching the benefice of Bryghtwell, in which a layman, a medical man, by nation reputed to be a Greek, held the living for ten years, alleging a papal exemption from holy orders. He had had a curate (*procurator*), but that curate was now dead, and the Rector could not be found. Upon this the Bishop of Winchester, the patron, presented William Darsset. The Bishop of Salisbury refused to institute him, and he appealed to the Archbishop of Canterbury. He then received institution, whereon the Bishop proceeds to sequestrate the living, intending, as was supposed, to interfere with the Bishop of Winton's patronage, but alleging that it still belonged to Thomas French. The Bull enjoins the Commissioners to put an end to all debate between the parties, and if the recited premises are true, to put William Darsset in full and peaceable possession of the benefice, invoking, if necessary, the interference of the secular arm.—(Communicated by the Rev. H. R. Bramley, Fellow of St. Mary Magdalen College.)

Bishop of Raphoe; and Eugene O'Hairt, Bishop of Achonry, took part in the discussions. And Wauchope, Archbishop of Armagh, "the blind Bishop," who was forced by the Pope into the place of Dowdall during his lifetime, was present at some of the latter sittings; but these three Bishops are in the Council described as Pius IV.'s Bishops, and they, therefore, must have been appointed between 1560 and 1568. The two Bishops, who, in 1560, refused to sanction the removal of the Pope's jurisdiction, were Walsh, of Meath, and Leverous, of Kildare. With the exception of these, all the Irish Bishops remained in their respective Sees, and from them, in conjunction with Abp. Curwen, the present Bishops have derived their orders. Dr. Studdert has shewn how carefully the Irish consecrations were attended to. The Irish Act, 2 Eliz., c. 4, abolishes *congé d'élire* and substitutes collation by letters patent; enacts that the collation be signified to one Archbishop and two Bishops, or else to four Bishops; that every Archbishop and Bishop shall with all speed invest and consecrate; that if they refuse they shall incur the penalties of præmunire and provisors. Though the records of the actual consecrations are lost, there are directions about temporalities of Alexander Craike, Bishop of Kildare, and evidence of a *ritus papalis* (Cotton's *Fasti*) used in the case of Roger Skiddie, Bishop of Cork and Cloyne in 1562. Then came Loftus, Archbishop of Armagh, and Robert Day, of Kildare; and in the case of Christopher Gafney, Bishop of Ossory, the Queen orders all things requisite

and meet for electing, consecrating, and installing, to
be done, as in like cases is used. The same orders
are given in Latin in the case of James McCaghwell,
Bishop of Cashel[d].

But even if it be said that all these facts are only
probabilities, it is certain that the Irish Orders are
valid through Hugh Curwen. He was consecrated by
Bonner and other recognised Bishops, according to the
Roman Ritual in Queen Mary's reign; and even if his
consecrations were performed without assistant Bishops
(of which, however, all the proof lies the other way),
all that can be said is that they were irregular, not
invalid.

The other intervention of a foreign Bishop in the
line of English Bishops was by Marc Antonio de Do-
minis. This prelate, who was Archbishop of Spalato, in
Dalmatia, for a time conformed to the Anglican Church
in the reign of James I., and was by him made Dean
of Windsor. During his residence in England he
assisted at the consecrations of Bishops Felton and
Monteigne.

The only remaining point to be noticed is the argument against the validity of the Anglican Orders from
the want of intention. Bishop Barlow's opinions on
Holy Orders were very loose, but still we must believe
that he intended *bonâ fide* to do and to say, what he
actually did and said in the matter of the consecration.
He was required to perpetuate the succession of English Bishops. Oglethorp refused to have anything to do

[d] See Lee's Letter to Abp. of Dublin, 4to., 1866, p. 36.

with it. Kitchen, though mentioned in the commission,
failed the Queen at the last.   Meanwhile, the Bishops
of the Old Succession were dispossessed, and a new commission issued. Thus, there only remained beside the
suffragan of Hull, the Bishops to whom the commission
was sent, with Bale, who took no part in the consecration. Whatever view Barlow had of Orders, he evidently
intended to obey Elizabeth, and the questions put to
the Canonists by the Queen, and the strict rule laid down
ad majorem cautelam of all pronouncing the sacramental
words, shew that the whole matter had been seriously
considered. The Prayers also of the Service indicate
sufficiently what was meant by it, and this must satisfy
the real doctrine of intention; for if the doctrine of
intention be supposed to be influenced by the private
opinions of the minister, no one can be certain of any
single baptism or ordination. Intention is satisfied, if
a person really intend to do what he has to do seriously, not in jest. Barlow intended to make a Bishop
and did so. What opinion he had on the grace and
indelibility of Holy Orders has nothing to do with the
question.

The reason for the concluding clause of the Article
is the same as that which prompted the Act of Parliament, 8 Eliz., c. 1. "An Act *declaring* the making
and consecrating of the Archbishops and Bishops of
this realm to be good, lawful, and perfect." The
doubts which it recites in the preamble are on the
point whether the same were duly and orderly done
according to the law or not; the remedy is partly

to shew that it has been duly and orderly done according to the laws of the realm, and partly to provide for the more surety thereof. Bonner had alleged that the Ordinal, repealed along with the Prayer-book in the time of Queen Mary, had not been separately named in the revising Statute, 1 Eliz. c. 2. Both the Act and the Article are passed *ex majori cautela*, a valid consecration being the corner-stone of the whole ecclesiastical edifice.

ARTICLE XXXVII.

De Civilibus Magistratibus.

*Regia Majestas in hoc Angliæ regno, ac cæteris ejus
dominiis summam habet potestatem, ad quam omnium
statuum hujus regni, sive illi ecclesiastici sint, sive civiles,
in omnibus causis, suprema gubernatio pertinet, et nulli
externæ jurisdictioni est subjecta, nec esse debet.*

*Cum Regiæ Majestati summam gubernationem tribuimus,
quibus titulis intelligimus animos quorundam calumnia-
torum offendi, non damus Regibus nostris, aut verbi Dei,
aut Sacramentorum administrationem, quod etiam In-
junctiones ab Elizabetha Regina nostra, nuper editæ,
apertissime testantur; sed eam tantum prærogativam,
quam in sacris Scripturis a Deo ipso, omnibus piis Prin-
cipibus, videmus semper fuisse attributam : hoc est, ut
omnes status atque ordines fidei suæ a Deo commissos,
sive illi ecclesiastici sint, sive civiles, in officio contineant,
et contumaces ac delinquentes gladio civili coerceant.*

*Romanus pontifex nullam habet jurisdictionem in hoc regno
Angliæ.*

*Leges regni possunt Christianos propter capitalia et gravia
crimina, morte punire.*

*Christianis licet, ex mandato Magistratus, arma portare,
et justa bella administrare.*

" Of the Civil Magistrates.

" THE King's Majesty hath the chief power in this
realm of England, and other his dominions, unto whom

the chief government of all the estates of this realm, whether they be ecclesiastical or civil, in all causes doth appertain, and is not, nor ought to be, subject to any foreign jurisdiction.

"Where we attribute to the King's Majesty the chief government, by which titles we understand the minds of some slanderous folks to be offended, we give not to our Princes the ministering either of God's Word, or of the Sacraments, the which thing the injunctions also lately set forth by Elizabeth our Queen do most plainly testify; but that only prerogative which we see to have been given always to all godly Princes in Holy Scripture by God Himself; that is, that they should rule all estates and degrees committed to their charge by God, whether they be ecclesiastical or temporal, and restrain with the civil sword the stubborn or evil-doers.

"The Bishop of Rome hath no jurisdiction in this realm of England.

"The laws of the realm may punish Christian men with death for heinous and grievous offences.

"It is lawful for Christian men, at the commandment of the Magistrate, to wear weapons, and serve in the wars."

The subject of Article XXXVII. is the *Civil* Magistrates. First the supremacy of the Queen's Majesty in the realm over all estates, in all causes, is asserted. Next the Fact and the Propriety of its subjection to any foreign jurisdiction is denied.

After this comes an explanation that the term 'chief

government' does not extend to the ministering either the Word or Sacraments, but does extend over all persons, "all estates and degrees," and to restraining evil doers with the *civil,* not the spiritual sword.

The jurisdiction of the Pope in the *realm* is denied; the right of capital punishment is asserted; and the lawfulness of the use of arms and of war at the commandment of the Magistrate is asserted. The Latin article imports the consideration that the war must be *just.*

The question of Royal Supremacy is one as old as the State establishment in the time of Constantine. So long as the Christian Church was a persecuted community, it administered its own laws; its Bishops were its judges in secular things; and, according to the rule of St. Paul, men did not go to law before the heathens but before the saints. Externally the Christian aimed at being a good subject, prayed for the stability of the Empire, even for the heathen Emperor. He had no difficulty directly in serving in the imperial legions, though there existed an accidental difficulty from the homage that was required from him to the Roman Eagles, or tutelary deities of the army, and to the person of the Emperor. How property was held, (for even at that early period the Church, especially that of Rome, did possess property,) we do not know. The Archdeacon of Rome had the care of the sacred vessels, which at a very early period were remarkable for their costly material. The churches were apparently held in trust by the Bishop and clergy.

Even under the Pagan Emperors the Church possessed land, though without legal sanction. In the third century we have evidence of the possession of a see-house at Antioch, which Paul of Samosata wished to retain after he had been deposed[a]. After the confiscations of Diocletian, Constantine ordered the land to be restored, and by an edict of 321 he permitted the Church to receive bequests (*bona*) in real property. There is no contemporary record for any great grant of land by Constantine, the forged donation being first known to be in existence A.D. 860. By the time of St. Gregory the Church was very rich, and it is reasonable to believe that, the Emperor having opened the door to such bequests, wealth flowed in from the devotions of the faithful. Indeed, Valentinian had to make a law checking the scandalous practices connected with such gifts. If Anastasius is to be trusted, Constantine bestowed upon the Basilicas which he founded in Rome alone, property to the value of 235,527 gold crowns, of which 60,000 went to the income of the Pope. The aggregate weight of the ornaments given to the Sanctuary was 1,880 lbs. of gold, 19,513 of silver, and 7,420 of bronze.

It is needless to add, that the discipline as well as the doctrine of the Church was a purely internal matter, in which the State had no interest nor control. Beyond a growing suspicion of the existence of Christianity as a dangerous organization, and occasional fanatical outbursts, chiefly in the provinces, ending

[a] Theodoret, H. E., ii. 8; Euseb., H. E., l. vii. c. 30.

in a temporary persecution; the attitude of the Empire to the Church was a contemptuous suspicious toleration.

It was a wonderful thing that the community should govern itself by the help of one sanction. Excommunication, or the power of ejecting an erring brother, was the *ultima ratio* of the Church, but then that bore fruit in the world to come. The power of binding and loosing was the charter of all Church discipline, for it relegated the sanction of the visible Church into the unseen world. If salvation depended, *clave non errante*, upon Church membership, and Church membership under certain laws was in the hands of the Hierarchy, it placed the control of the Church absolutely in their hands. And the power of discipline came with it, as we have seen when we have treated of the Church having authority in controversies of faith; power with regard to doctrine also was included, for false doctrine being an excommunicable sin, the same absolute control which the Church had over morals extended to matters of belief.

The State establishment at once modified these conditions. On the one hand the Episcopal jurisdiction which, in the way of arbitration, had been used to settle the disputes among the faithful, was turned into a coercive judicial power, the remains of which are found among most of the Romanesque races of Europe, and the shadow of which has remained in England till our own time. On the other hand, the Civil jurisprudence of the State had to modify itself to meet the requirements of the new faith; Church and State here worked in harmonious alliance, and the world profited by the alliance. However, beside this mutual influence, the two systems, developing homogeneous codes of law, lived on in indifferent harmony with each other, ages after ages. The conflict between the Canon and the Civil laws in various countries was only the outcome of this state of things. In most countries the Civil law has generally superseded the other, as material interests have become greater and greater.

It was the same in Politics. The *ecclesia docens,* 'the clergy,' the Hierarchy, to a certain degree maintained their authoritative position, after that the State became Christian. However great was the predominance of the Civil power, it generally recognised certain functions proper to the Spirituality. It found that within its influence there was another power which it could not touch—the domain of conscience. In proportion as dogmatic questions assumed a concrete form, that domain of conscience extended itself to many mixed questions, and collisions between the temporal and spiritual powers became the inevitable result.

The history of the world from the fourth century is a record of this collision. Sometimes fought out on the plain principle, as in the fight of the Investitures, sometimes disguised under the appearance of factions, as the Guelphs and Ghibellines, the Bianchi and the Neri[b]; the question profoundly agitated the

[b] Dante's *Inferno,* xxxii. 6.

Church, and was asserted with different success till the Reformation. The Church, now represented by the see of Rome, ever pushed its pretensions to the utmost limit. The State did all it could to protect itself against encroachments, by pragmatic sanctions. When supernatural ideas were strong, the Church predominated; when they were weak, either from material progress, or the effect of the vices of the clergy, the Church became proportionately enfeebled. There was an element of Erastianism [c] in the Councils of Basle and Constance, the aristocratic and episcopal and national element in the Church itself was worked in the interests of the State, against the Papacy or purely spiritual authority; and one aspect of the Reformation was a resignation on the part of religion of the spiritual independence, and the laying at the feet of the Civil power many rights that had been contended for for many an age.

[c] Hallam's "Middle Ages," vol. ii. p. 363.

"Before the appearance of the early Reformers, a republican or aristocratic spirit in ecclesiastical polity, strengthened by the decrees of the Councils of Constance and Basle, by the co-operation, in some instances, of the Church with the State in redressing or demanding the redress of abuses, and certainly also by the vices of the Court of Rome and its diversion to local politics, had fully counterbalanced, or even in a great measure silenced, the bold pretensions of the school of Hildebrand. In such a lax notion of Papal authority, prevalent in Cisalpine Europe, the Protestant Reformation had found one source of its success. But for this cause the theory itself lost ground in the Catholic Church. At the Council of Trent, the aristocratic or episcopal party, though it seemed to display itself in great strength, comprising the representatives of the Spanish and Gallican Churches, was for the most part foiled in the question which touched the limitations of the Papal Supremacy. From this time the latter power became lord of the ascendant."

The loss of England at the Reformation led, if not to the institution of Concordats, at least to their frequent employment. The relation between the Civil and Ecclesiastical power now became a matter of treaty in each State. Sovereigns made the best terms they could, and wrung from the occasional weakness of the Papacy what it could not help granting. Still the *Curia Romana* has never bated its theoretical rights, and while the State has managed in most cases to insist on the right of the *placitum regium* or *Exequatur*, the power of preventing bulls being published within its limits, and the institution of an appeal from the abuse of spiritual power in the Civil Courts, both that *Exequatur* and that *appellatio ab abusu* have been condemned in the *Encyclica* of Dec. 8, 1864.

The principles of Nationalism had developed themselves two hundred years before the Reformation. England, not being a part of the Empire, had always maintained its insular character; and, in spite of the moral effect of the death of St. Thomas of Canterbury, had always struggled to carry on the traditions of the Constitutions of Clarendon. In France the influence of the lawyers who, in opposition to the Councils, had developed the royal power by the inculcation of the Code of Justinian, had tended, in union with the gradual absorption of the great fiefs, to give increased power to the Crown, while the traditions of the Holy Roman Empire, especially in their Ghibelline embodiment, had ever been in the direction of thwarting and opposing the theologico-political theories of the

Church, as expressed by the Papacy. Dante's language, where a submission to, and enlightened knowledge of, the profoundest doctrines of the mediæval Church, are coupled with the keenest and most openly-expressed scorn for the vices of the individual Popes, serves as an illustration of the position taken up by many of the thinkers of Europe long before the Reformation. His beautiful dream of an Universal Monarchy, if hostile to the notion of an aggregate of nationalities, at least developed a theory of the self-sufficiency of the State, which in the presence of actual facts, i.e. of the impossibility of such universality, tended much to consolidate the notion of the autonomic existence of nations.

The Great Schism and the Convocation of the Councils of Constance and Basle helped in this direction. The lawyers became a new power in the world, and did what they could to consolidate the Civil State. When, in 1418, Martin V. began to restore the Papacy after the Schism, we find him combating them in France, protesting against the Statute of Provisors in England, and dealing in no measured terms with the spirit of rebellion, which the previous degradation of the Spirituality had engendered [d].

Thus also in Scotland, ecclesiastical questions were discussed and determined in Parliament during the fourteenth century. A case of disputed election to

---

[d] Vide Bull, printed in Burnet's "Reformation." Edit. Pocock, vol. iv. p. 148. Also Archbishop Chichele's Appeal from the Pope to a General Council, ib., vol. v. p. 485.

a Benedictine house was appealed from the judgment of the Diocesan to the Conservator (the Bishop who presided in the Church before the establishment of the two Archbishoprics), but finally decided by the King in Parliament by the advice of the clergy then present in 1391. In 1401, any one, thinking himself unjustly excommunicated, might appeal from the Bishop to the Conservator, from the Conservator to the Provincial Council, where such questions should be determined so long as the schism should last. To this ordinance the clergy consented during the schism, like the rest of the King's lieges. In 1417, the question whether Martin V. was to be acknowledged was debated, not in a Provincial Council of the clergy, but in a General Council of the three estates of the realm. In 1425, the bishops are authorized to search for heretics and Lollards by Parliament. In 1427, Parliament framed a measure for expediting the procedure in the secular cases in the Ecclesiastical Courts, and next year made rules about the treatment of leprosy by the clergy. This boldness in dealing with ecclesiastical matters startled the Papal Court, and contentions arose which were only silenced by the confusions that sprung from the murder of James I.

But there was another aspect of the question beside the relations between the Regale and the Pontificale. That between sovereign and people was long undetermined. Against the traditions of the Empire in the Middle Ages, a host of communities, and sects, such as the Fraticelli, Beguards, &c., had sprung up, ad-

vancing the most extravagant views of Government:
even the Franciscan Order itself had strong democratic tendencies.   The Schoolmen had laid down
a sound doctrine, that while the Hierarchy is immediately from God through Christ, "As My Father
sent Me, so send I you," the civil power came from
God mediately through the people.   Without assuming the absurdities of an original compact, such
as formed the base of the social theories at the beginning of the century, they held that power was
for the sake of the governed, not of the governors.   But
still the tendency of the weakening of the Papal power
in the previous centuries, and of the breaking up
of the feudal system, especially in France, by the absorption of the great fiefs into the Crown, had been to
give very great power to the State.   Although the
Stuart theory of the divine right of kings was not yet
formulized, one phase of the earlier Reformation was,
as has been said, to give very great power to the
Sovereign. But soon reaction followed. Calvinism was
essentially democratic.   It sprung up in a republic; it
became the dominant religion of the most successful
republic of modern times; and it has given a republican tinge to every country that it has touched.
Geneva, Holland, and Scotland, are witnesses of this.
The conversation between Mary of Scotland and Knox,
on that monarch's first arrival in Scotland, turned
on the assumption, that if princes became enemies of
God (that is, do not support the Reformation), God's
servants owe them no allegiance.   The formula was, if

a father went mad and offered to kill his children, they might tie his hands, and take his weapon from him; in like manner, if princes would murder the children of God, it was no disobedience to restrain them from their evil purpose.

The first proposition of the Article, therefore, is an assertion of the chief power of the Queen's Majesty. That power claims such privileges as, inherited from pre-Christian times, had been derived into the Holy Roman Empire, which was emphatically the State, the successor of that Great Polity which ruled the earth at the time of the coming of our Lord. England had never been in a strict sense part of the Great Empire. The Romans had abandoned it; the northern Barbarians had invaded it: the Saxons, after growing from a heptarchy into one kingdom, had maintained independent relation with the Empire; the kingdom of England imitated the style and title of the emperors of New Rome; the Bretwalda became the Basileus; there was a great affectation of Grecian etiquettes; but the whole theory of England was that it was a free and independent kingdom. This is the first proposition of the Article. But next to that, after certain explanations of the autonomic claim, there is a certain jurisdiction to be renounced.

The jurisdiction here renounced was that jurisdiction which, supported and strengthened by the false Decretals, and formulized by individual theologians after the Council of Trent, had for nine hundred years been exercised over the Church of England. From the time of the mission of St. Augustine by Pope Gregory, reference had been made to Rome, although only very slightly from the time of Theodore to the Conquest 669—1066. The interference eventually extended to the most minute things. The documents lately published from the stores of the Vatican, touching the interference of the Church of Rome with those of Ireland and Scotland, shew that nothing was too great or too small for its exercise. From a question of the regency of a kingdom down to the proper shape of a monk's hat[*], all came under its consideration. The confirmation of Bishops and Abbots, the dispensations in matrimonial cases, appeals from episcopal sentences, the concession of privileges to orders, made the Supremacy be felt in every county of the kingdom, while the higher politics of the realm were profoundly affected by it. Not the least remarkable point was the drain upon the resources of the country by the exaction of annates, first-fruits, Peter's-pence, and the intrusion of Italian and other foreign personages into the benefices of the Church of England. It is a question how far, even in the zenith of the Papal power, the Italian interference was on the side of righteousness and truth. In spite of the presumption that injured innocence would find redress at the threshold of the apostles, and that a cause, removed from local passions and prejudices, had the best chance of being settled equitably at Rome, it is to be feared that the result was the paralysis of the ordinary jurisdiction of the Bishop.

[*] Theiner, *Vetera Monumenta Scotorum et Hibernorum*, p. 76.

Even Hildebrand could not, as Innocent III., have enforced justice, in opposition to the vast machinery of the Roman Curia, and its *vis inertiæ*. Appeals were made by the English Clergy on every occasion against their Bishop. They were seldom prosecuted; the result was the mere prostration of the Episcopal and Metropolitan authority. The loudest complaints of the venality of Rome are of the thirteenth century, and some even in the twelfth. In the fourteenth and fifteenth centuries, the power of gold was still said to tell in the decision of appeals, and, rightly or wrongly, an abiding sense of the venality of the Roman Curia possessed the mind of Europe. Long before the Reformation there was a strong anti-Italian party in the English Church, and it must never be forgotten that the actual breach was consummated by the Catholic Convocation of the Church, by Gardiner, and Bonner, and Warham.

Yet that the mediæval Papacy, with all its faults, had an office in God's kingdom and in the history of the world, cannot be denied. As the strongest concrete form of the Episcopate, it was the preserver and dispenser of moral and religious tradition. It knit together in visible unity the various races which, as powers of this world, succeeded to the Roman Empire, and enlarged it. The Apostle of England had been sent and guided by that great Pontiff, who was so marvellously raised up at a time very critical for the history of Christianity, St. Gregory the Great. St. Augustine of Canterbury impressed on England an enthusiastic devotion to the see of Rome; the Apostles of Germany, issuing from England, implanted it together with the Gospel itself among the people whom they converted. Christians, in whatever different lands, using whatever different languages, were one body. One was their faith; one, their discipline; one, their worship. And this unity was personified in him, who, throughout Western Christendom, was looked to as the common Father. The Pope, as the Head and Father of Christians, was, in theory at least, the earthly refuge of the oppressed. He wielded an authority, before which kings, or a barbarian aristocracy, trembled; which could rebuke vice, or tyranny, or brute force upon the throne, with an authority greater than its own. Even the forged decretals (unhappy, in its consequences, as any fraud must be) were framed, not by Rome, nor with its cognizance, but as a protection against lawless civil power. In the miserable tenth century the Papal authority was still exercised in the name of Popes, who themselves have left their names only as a proverb of reproach. Strange, that the decline of the Papal power began with one, who himself sustained its loftiest claims. Boniface VIII. found his authority at the zenith. His hermit predecessor had been reluctantly allowed to enact that he might himself abdicate. He himself acted nobly as the Pacificator of Europe. He commanded peace to such monarchs as the English Edward I. and Philip the Fair, with their allies; he was (as Benedetto Gaetani) accepted as the arbiter; an interdict was to lie on the infringement of some chief terms; he received Scotland as a fief of the see of Rome; he had given a king to Hungary; and had conferred the Empire on Albert. Millions (it was said "almost all Christendom") flowed to Rome to visit the shrines of St. Peter and St. Paul, at the Jubilee which he instituted; his Bull, *Clericis laicos*, exempted all Clergy everywhere from any tax, under excommunication; and in the *Unam sanctam* affirmed the absolute subjection of the civil to the Papal power. Yet he died, accused of every imaginable or unimaginable sin, (many charges *primâ facie* are utterly incredible,) required by the French king to defend himself before a General Council. His successor, Clement V., had to account it a gain that the French king abandoned the prosecution[f]. The Council of Vienne declared Boniface "a Catholic and undoubted Pope[g]." But the fact that a Pope should, at the instigation not of the French king only, but of the States General, with all the ecclesiastics present, and above seven hundred acts of adhesion[h], be tried, after death, before a General Council, for atheism, simony, incontinence, witchcraft, heresy, and unnamable crimes[i], must have had a very profound effect upon the mind of Europe. The Bull, May 1311,

---

[f] He speaks of it as an inspiration of God, *Diploma in Rayn. Ann.* A. 1311, n. 30. Villani says that Clement V. promised to Philip on the Blessed Sacrament, as one condition of his elevation to the Papacy, to "destroy and annul the memory of Pope Boniface." *Hist. Fior.* viii. 80. He is followed by St. Antoninus.

[g] *Anton.* 3. p. tit. 21, c. 3.　　　　[h] Bulæus, *Hist. Univ. Par.,* iv. p. 46 sqq.　　　　[i] Ib., p. 41 sqq.

pronounced that Philip, in all the proceedings against Boniface, was "moved by a just zeal and fervour for the Catholic faith." Everything which could reflect upon him was to be effaced from the Roman records. The Bull, *Clericis laicos*, was cancelled as a source of scandal[k]; the other Bull, *Unam sanctam*, was declared to make no change in the relations of France to the see of Rome[l]. The precedent of an appeal to a General Council against a Pope for supposed heresy or immorality, was virtually admitted by the praise of Philip, and the fact of the Council. On this followed, what has been called the Babylonish captivity, the seventy years' residence of the Popes at Avignon, subjects of the king of France.

The fiscal necessities of the impoverished Courts of Lyons and Avignon made the demand for money more and more peremptory. As the Papacy ceased to represent a Christian want and idea, it became more and more rapacious. John XXII. imposed the tax of annates, or first-fruits, on all benefices, to be paid into the Papal chancery; he *reserved* to himself all the bishoprics in Christendom. Benedict XII. assumed the right of disposing of all benefices vacant by cession, translation, or deprivation. After the return from Avignon, the Great Schism occurred. The shake to men's convictions by this event cannot be exaggerated. That the organ devised for the unity of the Church, as the Papacy with more or less distinctness had been recognised to be for centuries, in development of the

---

[k] Clement., l. iii. tit. 17.　　　[l] Extrav. Comm., l. v. tit. 7, c. 2.

teaching of St. Cyprian, should give way under the pressure and increasing strength of the adolescent nationalities of Europe, was a mighty blow to the Western Church. Humanly speaking, but for that, the Reformation would never have taken the shape it did. Men's minds for nearly a generation had got into the way of doubting who was Pope, and therefore the element of certainty, which had been so attractive a notion in dependence upon it, was lost; lost not only to that generation, but with more perilous results to those who succeeded.

The fifteenth century accustomed men's minds to a lowering of the Papal authority. It opened with the deprivation of the two rival Popes by the Council of Pisa[m], and the broken oath of the new Pope, Alexander V., to continue the Council, until it should have effected a reform[n]. On his decease, the Cardinals un-

[m] Sess. xv. Jur. 5. The "Sententia definitiva et privativa," runs: "The holy and universal Synod, representing the universal Church, and to whom the cognizance and decision of this cause is known to appertain, pronounces, decrees, defines, and declares, that Angelus Corario and Peter di Luna, both and each were notorious schismatics, and notorious heretics, departing from the faith, entangled with the notorious and enormous crimes of perjury and violation of vow, &c., that they are, *ipso facto*, rejected and deprived by God and the sacred canons; but that, nevertheless, the Council deprives both and each, inhibiting them and each of them from presuming to act as Supreme Pontiff."

[n] The oath was, that "if any of us shall be elected supreme Roman Pontiff, he will continue the present Council, and not dissolve it, nor allow it to be dissolved, as far as in him lies, until by him, with consent of this same Council, there be made a due, reasonable, and sufficient reformation of the universal Church and its condition, both in its head and members." Sess. xvi. Jur. 10.

happily chose one of notoriously disgraceful life, Bal-
thassar Cossa (John XXIII.), to succeed him; and no
one could dispute the righteousness of the act of the
Council of Constance, which, partly on the ground of
those notorious sins, deposed him°. The necessities
of the times supported the claim of the Council to have
authority over "any person, of whatever, even Papal,
dignity." Two Councils, Constance and Basle, claiming to be General Councils, and to have "their authority immediately from Christ," declared "the necessity
of a general reformation of the Church of God in its
head and members; claimed obedience herein and in
things which appertain to faith, and asserted the subjection of the Pope to a Council[p]. Specifically, the
Council of Basle removed many powers claimed by
the Popes, as Papal reservation of benefices[q]; it resisted appeals and interdicts[r], annulled annates[s], assigned to Cardinals the duty of admonishing the Pope;
if he would not correct himself, they were to delate
him to a General Council[t]. The Council of Basle,
indeed, undid its own work by its extreme measures
against Eugenius IV., when he removed the Council
to Ferrara; but the confidence, by which it was misled,
is an evidence of its popularity, and the fact that such

° Sess. Gen. xii. May 29, 1415. Seventy Articles were established
by evidence (v. d. Hardt., iv. p. 253), of which some were so offensive
that they were not read publicly. Ibid., pp. 237, 247.

[p] *Conc. Const.*, Sess. Gen. v.; *Conc. Bas.*, Sess. ii.

[q] *Decr. de elect. et confirm. Episc. et Prœl.*, Sess. xii.

[r] Sess. xx. Decr. 3, 4.   [s] Sess. xxi. Decr. i.

[t] Sess. xxiii. Decr. 4, *de num. et qual. Cardinal.*

decisions were made by a Council of undisputed Catholicity at the time, must have left a lasting impression. France continued to receive even the decrees of its later sessions during its conflict with Eugenius IV. (as that of the Immaculate Conception of the Blessed Virgin), as decrees of a General Council. Martin V., indeed, declared in a Constitution (A.D. 1418) any appeal from the Apostolic see invalid; Pius II. prohibited them [u]. Yet they continued, when occasion arose [v]. Exactions disgraced even the energetic reign of Martin V. Even when the Turks threatened Hungary, the attempts to promote a Crusade were regarded as mere occasions for succouring the Papal revenues. The purpose of Julius II. to lead a Crusade in person, which once would have roused all the religious enthusiasm of Europe, attracted a mere mob [x]. Had those who elected the three last Popes of the century, Sixtus IV., Innocent VIII., Alexander VI., had for their object to degrade the Papacy as a spiritual power, they would have chosen well. Yet the claims made for Papal authority never ran higher. Flatterers, on public occasions too, called the Pope "another God upon earth [y]." Alexander VI. dispensed with what was, or was accounted hitherto to be, Divine

[u] In a Bull, Jan. 23, 1460, "Execrabilis."

[v] On the part of the Elector, at Nürnberg, A.D. 1460; of the Emperor Sigismund, also 1460; by Charles VII. of France, also in 1460.

[x] *Vita Pii II.*, (in *Murat. Scriptt. Rer. Ital.*, iii. ii., p. 990); Card. Papiens., *Comm.*, l. i.

[y] Mentioned by Gerson, *Opp.* ii. 424, "Tu denique alter Deus in terris," said to Julius II. *in Lat. Conc.*, Sess. iv. Dec. 10, 1512.

law. To his married daughter Lucretia he gave licence
to marry, her husband still living[s], (of which she twice
availed herself, and her example was followed by Louis,
Duke of Orleans); he dispensed with orders to his
son Cæsar Borgia, a Deacon and a Cardinal[a], and he
first allowed of marriage with a deceased wife's sister,
which had, to a recent predecessor, been pronounced
beyond the power of the Pope[b].   His act was the precedent of that which furnished occasion for the breach
of Henry VIII. of England.   Indulgences given by
Julius II. for the rebuilding of St. Peter's, involved
the loss of half of Germany; it was the spark which
kindled the inflammable material.   The two last Popes
of that unhappy century became proverbs throughout
Europe, Innocent VIII. for his incontinence, and Alexander VI. for what in Popes was not allowed to be
simony[c].

To understand the position of England in reference
to the Papal power, and the degree of its repudiation,
it is necessary to go somewhat into detail concerning
the historic relations of Church and State.

Till the Norman Conquest in England there was no

[a] *Raph. Volat. comm. urb. Anthropol.*, l. xxii.
[a] Burchard in Eccard ii. 2096.
[b] Card. Joh. de Turrecremata to Eugenius IV. See Dr. Pusey's
Evidence on the Law of Marriage, Qu. 464, p. 27, ed. 8.
[c] That on Alexander VI. was,—

> Vendit Alexander claves, Altaria, Christum,
> Emerat illa prius, vendere jure potest."

It is said that it was sung in his time throughout the Christian world.
Lud. Tub., l. vi. § 7.

distinction of jurisdictions. All matters, spiritual as well as temporal, were determined in the Sheriff's tourn, the county court where the Bishop and Earl sat together[d]. As the legislative synods were mixed assemblies, so the executive was mixed also. The bishoprics being conterminous with the kingdoms, the archdeaconries with the counties, there was the closest connection between the civil and ecclesiastical laws: "The shyregemot shall be kept twice a year, and oftener if need require, whenever the Bishop and the Alderman of the shire shall be present; the one to teach the laws of God, the other the law of the land[e]."

The separation of the Ecclesiastical from the Temporal Courts was the act of William the Conqueror. No Bishop or Archdeacon was any longer to hold pleas of the laws episcopal in the Hundred, or draw a cause which belongs to the government of souls to the judgment of secular men. Whoever contumaciously refused the episcopal jurisdiction was to be excommunicated; and that, if need be, was to be supported by the King or Sheriff[f].

This was the reward of the support of the Pope, who sent two legates to England, with whom William held a synod when the Saxon Stigand was deposed, because he had no pall from Rome, and Normans were substituted for natives in many of the sees and abbeys. Yet, while the right to send legates was thus conceded, although not without royal licence in each case, no

[d] Burn's Eccl. Law, vol. ii. 81.   [e] Laws of Canute.
[f] *Carta Willelmi* in Thorpe's Ancient Laws, i. 495.

ecclesiastical decrees were passed without the royal assent, and William distinctly refused the oath of fealty to Gregory VII.

His successor, William Rufus, resisted the right of appeal.

In the reign of Henry I., the Pope obtained the patronage and donation of bishoprics and other benefices, Urban having decreed that no lay person should give any ecclesiastical benefice; and at the Synod of London, in 1107, the King yielded *investiture per annulum et baculum*, gaining the privilege that no foreign legates should be sent, but that the Archbishop of Canterbury was to be *legatus natus*. Both parties broke faith after St. Anselm's death, but the law remained. The settlement of 1107 was a compromise, the king resigning the form of investiture, but enforcing the homage of each prelate before he received the temporalities of his preferment.

A third point was gained in the reign of King Stephen. Appeals to the Pope were multiplied.

The power of the see of Rome still increased. In the reign of Henry II., clerks were exempted from the civil power. The Constitutions of Clarendon (1164), though for the time rendered inoperative by the moral effect of Becket's death, were the first great normal resistance to the Roman Court[f].

At last, in the reign of King John, the ecclesiastical power was in its zenith.

[f] See Johnson's English Canons, vol. ii. § 2. Anglo-Cath. Lib., Oxf. ed.

Henry III. owed his establishment in the kingdom to Pope Honorius; and the reigns of Edward I. and Edward II.,—with the exception of one Act in the thirty-fifth year of the first of these monarchs, prohibiting foreigners from holding benefices,—shewed no open resistance to the foreign power.

The accomplished Grossteste, Bishop of Lincoln, from 1235 to 1253, whose fame has hitherto mainly rested on a letter in which he resisted Innocent the Fourth's nomination of his nephew, Frederico di Lavagna, to a canonry at Lincoln, according to that evil practice of beneficing foreign, and especially Italian clerks, which was pursued till their incomes amounted in value to 70,000 marks[h], yet did what he could to support the Pope in obtaining the tax for the Crusades, the payment of which Henry III. had resisted[i]. Though his sense of episcopal responsibility induced him, at the risk of the anger of the Italians, to resist any improper nominations to benefices, " no one can exceed Grossteste in his reverence for the Papal power, and for Innocent IV. in particular[j]." He did much to promote the interest of the Friars, especially the Minorites. He was present at a Council at Lyons in 1245.

The foreign power of the Popes meanwhile had been making itself felt in many obnoxious ways, and the result was a passionate opposition, which found a legal expression in the Statutes of Præmunire.

The first of these, in 27 Edw. III., proceeds upon

---

[h] Luard's Preface to Grossteste's Works, p. lxxix.
[i] Ibid., p. xvii.   [j] Ibid., p. xx.

"the grievous and clamorous complaints of the great men and commons of the realm, how that divers of the people are drawn out of the realm to answer of things pertaining to the King's Court; and also that the judgments given in the said court are impeached in another court. Offenders shall have a day to appear to answer in their proper persons of the contempt done on this behalf. If they come not, they are put out of the King's protection, their lands are forfeit, and their persons subject to imprisonment."

No names are mentioned in this Statute, though it is plain what is pointed at; but in 16 Richard II., the language is more plain spoken. "Any one purchasing or procuring in the Court of Rome or elsewhere any translations of prelates, processes, sentences of excommunication, bulls, instruments, or any other things whatsoever, which touch the King; and they which bring within the realm or them receive, or make thereof notification, or any other execution whatsoever within the said realm or without, shall incur penalties of præmunire."

Meanwhile the secession to Avignon had weakened the Pope's authority. The pecuniary necessities of his Court, exiled from Italy, and domiciled first at Lyons and then at Avignon, made the exactions of money more peremptory; nay, it is to be feared that the needy ecclesiastics got into the habit of selling justice; at any rate, such was the abiding conviction of all Europe. All through the fourteenth century the influence of the French lawyers told in a very hostile way upon

the working of the Papal Court, and at last the Great
Schism brought matters to a crisis. In the reign of
Henry IV. Acts were passed prohibiting licences being
given by the King for the infringement of the Statutes
of Provisors, or for compositions with him[k]. The Council
of Constance, in 1418, tended to heal the schism, and
there is nothing in the history of Institutions more
striking than the way in which Martin V. did what
he could to restore the influence of the Papacy. His
relations with the English Church are well worthy of
study. The schism in the Papacy did more for the
Reformation, from an ecclesiastical point of view, than
later writers have recognised[l].

[k] "Pecock, *cir.* 1445, whose ideas on the subject of Papal Supremacy
were not at all in advance of his age, conceived that the Pope, as lord
paramount of the Universal Church and of all things thereunto pertaining, had a right, strictly speaking, to the entire proceeds of all
benefices, and that those whom he placed therein to enjoy them did no
sin in giving him (annates) of that which was his own, any more than
a bailiff does when he pays anything to the landlord of the soil."—
(Churchill Babington's Introd. to Pecock's Repressor, p. xvi.; cf. Repressor, p. 436—444.)

[l] I am indebted to a learned friend for the accompanying exhaustive analysis of the Papal interferences in the mediæval Church of
England :—

PAPAL PROCEDURE IN CASE OF PROMOTIONS.

1. *Metropolitans.* 2. *Suffragans.* 3. *Inferior Benefices.*

1. Metropolitans. (Most of the cases will be found in the first volume
of the *Anglia Sacra.*)

(a.) The gift of the pall, (1) originally recognising, (2) later confirming, (3) and finally conferring Metropolitan powers; coeval with
the establishment of Christianity in England, and as early as the
time of Egbert, Archbishop of York, 735, understood as necessary
for the completeness of the Metropolitan character.

From the period of the conclusion of the Wars of the Roses, the Papal power declined in England.   It

(β.) The right of refusing the pall to a new Archbishop, in case his character or mode of election is not entirely satisfactory; exercised by Nicholas II. in 1061, in the case of Ealdred, Archbishop of York; to whom, however, it was given by the same Pope almost immediately after. (*Flor. Wig.*, 1061.)

(γ.) The right of consecrating an elect Archbishop contrary to the will of the King and of the Archbishop of Canterbury; exercised by Calixtus II. in the case of Thurstan, Archbishop of York, in 1119. (*Orderic. V.*, 1119, and *Sim. Dun.*, 1119.)

(δ.) Right of determining an appeal carried before the Pope in a disputed election of two Archbishops, although previously decided by the legate; exercised by Eugenius III. in case of Archbishop Murdac, of York, the election of S. William, already consecrated, being quashed. (John of Hexham, and William of Newburgh.)

(ε.) A disputed election referred by appeal for confirmation to the Pope, who rejects both candidates, and prevails on the proxies of the electors to elect his own nominee; Stephen Langton. (M. Paris.)

(ζ.) A disputed election coming before him, he rejects both candidates, and in collusion with the English prelates, appoints a third person, *mero motu suo :* in 1229. (M. Paris.)

(η.) A disputed election coming before him, he persuades the candidates to resign, and in opposition to all parties provides his own nominee; as in the case of Robert Kilwardby, Archbishop of Canterbury in 1272. (*Anglia Sacra.*)

(θ.) An election coming before him for confirmation, he quashes it, and appoints his own nominee; case of John Peckham, Archbishop of Canterbury in 1278.

(ι.) An election coming before him for confirmation, he rejects the candidate, and in collusion with the King appoints the royal nominee; as in the case of Archbishop Reynolds in 1314.

Later cases are affected by the Statute of Provisors. (See below.)

2. Case of Suffragans.

(α.) Right of suffering and confirming *translations;* acknowledged from the time of the Conquest in the very few cases which occurred down to the end of the thirteenth century.

(β.) Right of nominating to a see vacant by translation, made by John XXII. (Parker's Antiq., p. 328.)

was a period of great agricultural and industrial advancement. The old Wiltshire manor-houses of the

- (γ.) The gradual aggression on the rights of the chapters proceeded much as in the case of the Archbishops; (1) by hearing appeals; (2) by deciding against both candidates, and persuading the proxies to elect the papal nominee; (3) by persuading the candidate or candidates to resign, and appointing a new man *mero motu*; (4) by persuading the proxies of all parties to leave the nomination to the Pope; (5) by providing absolutely, without regard to the wishes of King or Chapter.
- (δ.) Claim to fill up all benefices, vacated by the death of the Incumbent, at the Court of Rome.
- (ε.) Claim to provide for all bishoprics, either vacant or to be vacated: made early in the fourteenth century, and actually exercised in collusion with the King down to the time of the Reformation; during which time the right of the Chapters to elect, and of the Metropolitan to confirm was altogether in abeyance; the Statute of Provisors being systematically transgressed.
- (Concordat of 1373. See Rymer, ad ann. Adam Murimuth, p. 214, &c. Statute of Provisors, 25 Edw. III.)

3. Inferior benefices.

Provisions to these, whether in private or public presentation, are simply an usurpation without pretext, and as such resisted from the beginning. They begin by the demand of a prebend in each cathedral and collegiate church, and a portion in each monastery in the reign of Henry III., and may be traced in Matthew Paris almost to the end of the reign. These were made first for the purpose of maintaining the Papal Court, but very early became purchaseable. Forbidden by Statute of Carlisle and Statute of Provisors, 25 Edw. III.; and, owing to the opposition of private patrons, actually defeated in such cases from the time of the passing of the Statute.

LEGATIONS.

1. Simply missionary expeditions.
2. Embassies to obtain national recognition for the enactments of particular councils; e.g. mission of John the Chanter, Bede iv. 17, 18, and the Legatine Council of 787. (See Wilkins, *ad ann.*)

period testify to its civilization.   There was great
languor in religion; even Lollardism did not make

3. Embassies to consult the nation or the King, e.g. that of Armen-
   fred in 1062.   (See *Flor. Wig.*, *ad ann.*)

4. After the Norman Conquest; on the Hildebrandine theory, the
   Legate claims jurisdiction as the Papal Lieutenant. This is resisted
   (amongst others) by St. Anselm, who objects to the legation of the
   Archbishop of Vienne (*Ep.* iv. 2); by Henry I., who concludes an
   agreement with the Pope that no legate is to be sent to England
   without royal consent.   In 1125, John of Crema is suffered to hold
   a legatine visitation, but

5. The Archbishop of Canterbury himself accepts the office of legate
   in 1126, and thus helps to confound the metropolitan with the
   legatine authority.

6. Appointment of a Suffragan Bishop as legate, virtually super-
   seding the Archbishop, e.g. Henry of Blois, Bishop of Winchester in 1139.   A plan worked by Alexander III. during the Becket
   controversy.

7. From the time of Hubert Walter, 1193, the Archbishop is regularly *legatus natus*; and almost as regularly has a legatine commission.

8. Legate *a latere*—with powers to supersede the regular Legate, as
   the Legate had formerly superseded the Metropolitan; cases of
   Gualo and Pandulf, Otto and Ottobon, (see M. Paris); of a piece
   with the usurped provisions and taxes for false Crusades of the
   same period.

9. Archbishops of York occasionally made legates in the fourteeenth
   and fifteenth centuries, to the disparagement of Canterbury.

10. Martin V. threatens to take away Chichele's legatine commission,
    if he will not procure the abolition of the Statutes of Provisors and
    Præmunire. (Wilkins' *Conc.* ii., *sub* Chichele.)

11. Legation *a latere* of Wolsey, with unprecedented powers; con-
    nived at by the King, and afterwards made by him a plea for the
    oppression of the Church. (See Bulls in Rymer.)

APPEALS.

Case *before the Conquest* in marriage question. (See Hook's Life of
Dunstan.)

After the Conquest, appeals in disputed elections. (See above.)

itself sensibly felt. "Henry VII. possessed the undisputed right of nominating candidates to the Episcopal Sees. He was not satisfied with bestowing all the clerical promotions, he also appropriated to himself the half of the annates[m]." The see of Rome, occupied by Alexander VI. and Julius II., was ripe for attack, though the actual onslaught was postponed for a few years.

The question now comes, How far did the Statutes of the English Reformation affect the Church of England, as guardian of the faith, and as member of the great Christian polity? To estimate rightly the position, we must see what actually took place in Parliament and Convocation.

After the establishment of legates (1139), suits carried more frequently to Rome. Forbidden by Constitutions of Clarendon, 1164; but suffered after Henry the Second's abjuration in 1173; and constantly carried there down to the Statute of Præmunire, *temp.* Edw. III.

Throughout the whole of this time the administration in private suits at Rome was flagrantly mercenary; but the processes were analogous to those of ordinary courts of law.

PECUNIARY EXACTIONS.

1. Ancient Romescot or Peter's pence.
2. Money levied on appeals, privileges, &c., purchased at Rome.
3. First fruits, &c. (See Gibson's *Codex.*)
4. Sums raised by taxation for Crusades (false or pretended ones, as that against Frederick II.)
5. Sums raised as procurations for the legates, in the thirteenth century, which were very heavy, and were the great cause of popular discontent.
6. Sale of benefices or provisions (indirect).

[m] Ranke, i. 20.

In 1536, both Houses of Convocation acknowledged Henry VIII., " Ecclesiæ et cleri Anglicani singularem protectorem, unicum et supremum dominum, et quantum per Christi legem licet, etiam supremum caput ipsius majestatem recognoscimus [n]." They promised never to attempt to allege claim or put in ure any new canons without the King's licence; or to enact them without his assent; and lastly, they petitioned for a commission of thirty-two persons to revise the Church laws, to annul what was faulty, and to present the remainder to the Crown for fresh confirmation.

These enactments never took final effect, nor entered into the constitution of the Church. They are evidences of the temper of the Catholic clergy at the time. While they do not acknowledge that the power of Church legislation resides in the Crown, they place the exercise of it under Crown restraints. All corrective jurisdiction is definitely annexed to the Crown, though nothing is said of directive jurisdiction.

This Act was repealed by 1 and 2 Ph. and M., c. 8, and when the repealing Act was itself repealed, the repealing parts of it were saved in 1 Eliz., c. 1, except as to certain of the rescinded acts.

The 1 Eliz., c. i. sect. 17, provides " that such juris-

---

[n] In the preamble to 25 Hen. VIII., c. 19, it is stated " the Clergy of this realm of England, have not only knowledged according to the truth, that the Convocations of the same Clergy are, always have been, and ought to be assembled by the king's writ," &c., which is a distinct falsehood. See the history in Atterbury on Convocation, pp. 82 sqq.

dictions, privileges, superiorities, and pre-eminences, spiritual and ecclesiastical, as by any spiritual or ecclesiastical power or authority hath heretofore been, and may lawfully be, exercised or used for the visitation of the ecclesiastical state and persons, and for reformation, order, and correction of the same, and of all manner of errors, heresies, schisms, abuses, offences, contempt, and enormities, shall for ever by authority of this present Parliament, be united and annexed to the imperial Crown of the realm."

In the nineteenth section it provides that all Bishops and ecclesiastical persons shall take the oath of the Queen's Supremacy, as the only Supreme Governor of this realm, and of all other Her Highness's dominions and countries, as well in all spiritual and ecclesiastical things or causes as temporal. The clergy at ordination subscribe a clause similar to this oath, which in terms was repealed by 1 G. and M., c. 8.

It will be observed that neither the words of the Article, nor those of any of the documents still in force, make the Sovereign the source or fountain-head of ecclesiastical jurisdiction. The powers given are corrective not directive powers; for reformation of abuse, not for the ordinary administration of the offices of the Church.

One could not have said this in the days of Henry VIII. and Edward VI. in view of Cromwell's Vicar-Generalship, of the episcopal commissions taken out by the Bishops, of the title Head assumed by the monarch. But these statutes and practices were repealed. One

cannot exaggerate the importance of Elizabeth's change
of style from Head to Governor. So much resides
in a name, that although the actual power claimed by
Henry VIII. under the title Head, was no greater
than that of Elizabeth, the name Head might have
been developed into the claim of any amount of power.
The position then assumed was that certain ancient
jurisdictions which had belonged to the Crown had
been usurped by the Curia of Rome, and that this
must be remedied. The title, therefore, of the law
of 1 Eliz. is, "An Act to restore to the Crown the
ancient jurisdiction over the Estate Ecclesiastical and
Spiritual, and abolishing all foreign powers repugnant
to the same." This was afterwards explained in the
Queen's Injunction of 1559, that the Queen should
have sovereignty and rule over all manner of persons;
so that no other foreign power should have any authority over them, thus limiting the refusal of jurisdiction
to what was repugnant to ancient law. The 5 Eliz.,
c. i. sect. 14, refers to this as fixing the legal construction of the oath above alluded to. The ideal was
to restore such a state of things as existed in the times
of Constantine, Justinian, or Charlemagne.

What Elizabeth meant, or rather what she desired
people to believe that she meant, has been made very
clear in a remarkable document recently disinterred by
the industry of Mr. Froude from the recesses of the State
Paper Office, and it is the more germane to the present
matter that it bears the date of 1570, and in fact preceded
only by a few months the enforcement of the Thirty-

nine Articles [o]. The northern rebellion had just been subdued, and the unhappy agents in it had been hanged in hundreds. The Roman Catholics were subdued for the moment, but embittered and exasperated beyond imagination. The Regent Murray had been murdered by Hamilton of Bothwellhaugh, and the terror of assassination, a too commonly employed political weapon in the sixteenth century, menaced Queen Elizabeth. It will be seen in the document: 1. that she only claimed the authority that had from immemorial time attached to the English Crown; 2. that she challenged no superiority to define faith or change ceremony; 3. that the Royal Supremacy extended only to persons; 4. that she has to provide that the Church be orderly governed and established; 5. that she was so far tolerant that she did not mean her subjects to be molested in matters of faith, so long as they did not gainsay Scripture or the Creeds, and that they might retain their own opinions so long as they were outwardly quiet and resorted to Church; 6. she appealed to a free General Council, promising to abide by its award, so as the truth were not obtruded on her by threats of war and rebellion, by fulminations, or other worldly tyrannous violences or cruel practices [p].

[o] Froude, vol. x. p. 5, Domestic MSS., 1569—1579.

[p] Henry VIII. was excommunicated, and in the Bull his subjects were commanded to renounce their allegiance, and the nobles were ordered "sub ejusdem excommunicationis ac perditionis bonorum suorum pœnis," to unite with all Christian princes in expelling Henry from England. Elizabeth was excommunicated in pretty similar terms, but not until twelve years after her accession. In answer to a request from

" February, 1570. So much as to the general
management of the country. There remained to be
considered religion, on which her rule, ' specially from
abroad, had been most frequently and maliciously im-
pugned.' It was true, Elizabeth admitted, that ' the
external ecclesiastical policy of England differed in
some respects from that which was established in other
countries, and occasions had been sought to trouble
weak consciences on this ground. Simply, however,
she declared that she had neither claimed nor exerted
any other authority in the Church than had attached
from immemorial time to the English Crown, although
that authority had been recognised with greater or less
distinctness at different times. The Crown challenged
no superiority to define, decide, or determine any article
or point of the Christian faith or religion ; or to change
any rite or ceremony before received and observed in
the Catholic Church. The Royal Supremacy in matters
Spiritual means no more than this, that she being by
lawful succession Queen of England, all persons born
in the realm were subjects to her and to no other
earthly ruler. She was bound in duty to provide that

the Emperor and other Roman Catholic princes, that she would allow
the Roman Catholic places of worship, she replied that she would not
allow them to keep up a distinct communion, alleging her reasons in
these remarkable words, " For there was no new faith propagated in
England ; no religion set up but that which was commanded by our
Saviour, practised by the Primitive Church, and unanimously approved
by the Fathers of the best antiquity." The Roman Catholics, both in
England and Ireland, outwardly conformed to the services of the Church
for about ten years. (Phillimore's International Law, vol. ii. p. 417,
1855.

her people should live in the faith, obedience, and observance of the Christian religion; that consequently there should be a Church orderly governed and established; and that the ecclesiastical ministers should be supported by the civil powers, that her subjects might live in the fear of God to the salvation of their souls. In this, Christian princes differed from Pagan princes, who, when they did best, took but a worldly care of their subjects' bodies and earthly lives. And yet,' she said, 'to answer further to some malicious untruths, she never had any meaning or intent that any of her subjects should be troubled or molested by examinations or inquisitions in any matter of their faith, as long as they should not gainsay the authority of the Holy Scriptures, or deny the articles of faith contained in any of the Creeds received and used in the Church; they might retain their own opinions in any rites or ceremonies appertaining to religion, as long as they should in their outward conversations shew themselves quiet and conformable, and not manifestly repugnant to the laws for resorting to their ordinary churches.

"'So far and no farther the Crown of England claimed authority over the Church; and if any potentate in Christendom, challenging universal and sole superiority, should condemn the English princes for refusing to recognise that superiority, Elizabeth said she would be ready, in any free and general assembly, where such potentate should not be only judge in his own cause, to make such an answer in her defence as should in reason satisfy the university of good and faithful Christians; or, if she failed to satisfy them, as the humble servant and handmaid of Christ, she would be willing to conform herself and her policy to that which truth should guide her into for the advancement of the Christian faith and concord of Christendom; she would admit as truth, however, only that which Almighty God should please to reveal by ordinary means in peaceable manner, and not that which should be obtruded upon her by threatenings of bloodshed and motions of war and rebellion, or by curses, fulminations, or other worldly tyrannous violences or cruel practices.

"'With this general statement her subjects ought to be contented. She had done nothing which could justly offend them, and she intended to do nothing. Inasmuch, however, as some kinds of her people had been encouraged in disobedience by an opinion evil conceived of her lenity, she must and would, for the future, make use of the sword of justice against the obstinately disaffected. There should be no inquisition, no examination, no violence done to conscience in matters of faith; and that who would outwardly conform should enjoy the fruits of her former accustomed mildness: but sedition and rebellion should be speedily and promptly repressed ⁹.'"

⁹ Froude's History of England, from Fall of Wolsey to Death of Elizabeth, vol. x. pp. 6—8. Lond., 1866. The above address of the Queen was sent to every parish, and "hung up in some public place where every one could see it, and read aloud in service time from the

Such was the view of the Supremacy, which Eliza-beth, in terror of foreign invasion and intestine com-motion, probably also in entire conformity with her own real opinions, propounded to her subjects. She does not claim so much as Henry VIII. had acquired. Nothing is said as to any right absolutely to designate the person to be elected to any vacant see, or of the prohibition to enact any canons without the leave of the sovereign, which Henry VIII. had forced upon the Clergy. These had been made part of the law of the land; but Elizabeth does not claim them as part of her prerogative. They might, accordingly, be aban-doned at any time, without touching on the preroga-tive claimed for the Crown. She claims only a personal authority over all her subjects. Henry VIII., in his wily "Letter to the Clergy of the province of York, A.D. 1533, touching his title of supreme head of the Church of England [r]," pointed out that the meaning of the words, *caput Ecclesiæ*, were limited by those united with them, *et cleri Anglicani.* "It were too absurd," he says, "for us to be called Head of the Church, re-presenting the mystical body of Christ. And there-fore, although *Ecclesia* is spoken of in these words touched in the proeme, yet there is added, *et cleri Anglicani*, which words conjoined restrain, by way of interpretation, the word *Ecclesiam*, and is as much as to say, *the Church* i.e. *the clergy of England.* Which

pulpit." The original MS. is in the Rolls' House. (Domestic MSS., 1569—1579.

[r] In Wilkins' *Conc.*, iii. 763.

manner of speaking in the law ye have professed ye many times find, and likewise in many other places." And of the Clergy also, he claims only that their "persons, acts, and deeds should be under the power of the prince by God assigned, whom they should acknowledge as their head." And for this he thought it to suffice, that they were governed by ordinances, made in convocations assembled by authority of kings. "If you take *spiritualibus* for spiritual men, that is to say, priests, clerks, their good acts and deeds worldly, in all this both we and *all other princes* be at this day chiefs and heads, after whose ordinance, whether in general or particular, they be ordered and governed. For leaving old stories and considering the state of the world in our time, is there any Convocation, where laws be made for the order of our Clergy, but such as by our authority is assembled? And why should we not say, as Justinian saith, 'Omnia nostra facimus, quibus a nobis impartitur auctoritas?'" where Justinian means, that "the Sovereign makes, or adopts, as his own, all things to which he gives civil authority." In regard to judicial authority, he says, "some notable offences we reserve to our correction, some we remit by our sufferance to the judges of the Clergy; as, murder, felony, and treason, and such like enormities we reserve to our examination; other crimes we leave to be ordered by the Clergy, not because we may not intermeddle with them, for there is no doubt but as well might we punish adultery and insolence in priests, as Emperors have done, *and other princes at this* *time do,* which ye know well enough; so as in all these articles, concerning the persons of priests, their laws, their acts, and order of living, forasmuch as they be indeed temporal and concerning this present life only, in those we (as we are called) be indeed in this realm *caput,* and because there is no man above us here, we be indeed *supremum caput.*" Henry VIII. then proceeded to disclaim authority in things spiritual. "As to spiritual things, meaning by them the Sacraments, being by God ordained as instruments of efficacy and strength, whereby grace is of His infinite goodness conferred upon His people, forasmuch as they be no worldly nor temporal things, they have no worldly nor temporal head, but only Christ that did institute them, by whose ordinance they be ministered here by mortal men elect, chosen, and ordered as God hath willed for that purpose, who be the Clergy; who for the time they do that, and in that respect, 'tanquam ministri versantur in his, quæ hominum potestati non subjiciuntur; in quibus si male versantur sine scandalo, Deum ultorem habent; si cum scandalo, hominum cognitio et vindicta est.'" Here he asserts, again, the distinction of cases in which "the prince is the chief doer," and those "when by sufferance *or priviledge* the prelates intromit themselves therein*." On judgment as to heretical teaching, he does not speak; but he adds, "We be not in deed nor in name, to him that would sincerely understand it, head of such things, being not

---

* Something seems to have dropped out. It stands, "either the prince," &c., without any corresponding "or."

spiritual, as they be not temporal, and yet to these words spoken of us, *ad evitandam illam calumniam*, there is added, *quantum per legem Christi licet.*" Henry VIII. did not claim to interfere in things spiritual. In the Act " for restraint of appeals[1]," which lay as the foundation of the rest, and which is still part of the law of the land, while claiming for himself to be " furnished, by the goodness and sufferance of Almighty God, with plenary, whole and entire power, pre-eminence, authority, prerogative, and *jurisdiction, to render and yield justice* and final determination *to all manner of folks*, resiants, or subjects within this his realm, in all *causes*, matters, debates, and contentions, happening to occur, insurge, or begin within the limits thereof, without restraint, or provocation to any foreign princes or potentates of the world," yet claims no direct jurisdiction herein.   He only claims to be head of the whole body politic, spiritualty and temporalty, " the body spiritual whereof having power, when any cause of the law divine happened to come in question, or of spiritual learning, then it was declared, interpreted, and shewed by that part of the said body politic, called the spirituality, now being usually called the English Church, which always hath been reputed and also found of that sort that both for knowledge, integrity, and sufficiency of number, it hath always been thought, and is also at this hour, sufficient and meet of itself, without the intermeddling of any exterior person or persons, to declare and determine all such doubts, and to

[1] 24 Henry VIII., c. 12.

administer all such offices and duties as to their rooms spiritual doth appertain."

The Act of Parliament, which is still in force, stated that it belonged to the spiritualty to "declare, and interpret, and shew any cause of the law divine which might come in question." Elizabeth, following Henry VIII. both in what he claimed and in what he disclaimed, (except the title of "Head,") disclaimed "all superiority to define, decide, or determine any Article or point of the Christian faith."

And yet it is on this very point that imminent peril to the faith lies. It is now a principle of English justice that one charged with any offence is to be protected against criminating himself; it is also a principle that any doubt is to be given in his favour. On a doctrinal subject doubt might, in a given case, be raised as to the force either of the theological terms used by the Church, or of those in which a Clerk incriminated is alleged to have contravened them. In the former case, according to the 24th Henry, c. 12, it was clearly presupposed that the spiritualty would define, "declare, interpret, and shew" such point of doctrine. Elizabeth expressly denied that the Crown had any such power. And yet this power is practically exercised by lawyers, by authority of the Crown, and this with the avowed principle that doctrinal statements, by which the case is to be determined, are to be ruled to mean as little as they can anyhow be made to mean, and this by lawyers unfamiliar with the terms. The result has been, that vital doctrines have been successively made open questions. Discipline is utterly prostrate. Formerly, one with cure of souls, if suspected of teaching error for truth, of poisoning instead of feeding his sheep, had to clear himself of the charge. Now, the object of lawyers (according to the principle of acquitting one criminated if possible) is to evacuate the meaning of terms, whereby the Church has defined and guarded the faith. This power, inspired by lawyers, exercised in the direction of the casting down of all dogmatic truth, threatens the existence of Christianity in England, and it remains to be seen what power can cope with it. If not resisted, there seems no guarantee for the preservation of any one distinctive doctrine of the Christian religion. The first great blow to the theory. of the personal headship over the Church of England was given by the latitudinarian William. The establishment of Presbyterianism in Scotland introduced many difficult elements into the polity of England, which, in view of the strong political feelings of the time, were not appreciated. Among other things, it necessarily gave the *coup de grace* to the personal headship. The Crown is now no more head of the Church in England than of the kirk in Scotland. It retains in each the power of giving redress to any subjects in things temporal, as it has also in other religious bodies. It has whatever power Acts of Parliament have given her, but the Queen is "in all causes supreme," within the Church of England, in the same sense as she is in bodies external to it, and in no other.

Having premised these facts, it becomes us to see

exactly what the literal and grammatical sense of the Article implies.

1. "The Queen's Majesty hath the chief power in the realm of England and other her dominions." This implies an assertion of civil supremacy, such as was wielded by the Emperors in Germany, and a repudiation of vassalage to the Pope. King John had consented to receive back his crown as a gift, and his kingdom as a fief of the Holy See. The Pope was no longer to be the Suzerain of England.

In the early draft of the Article, "Ireland," which was specially claimed by the Popes, so that the King was only called Lord of Ireland, is mentioned. In the Elizabethan draft the word is made general, "other her dominions." As Queen Mary had lost Calais, the last English possession on French ground, the wider expression may have reference, either by a mere recognition of the popular style which attributed the kingdom of France to the Sovereign of England; or to Scotland, over which the English sovereigns had always aimed to rule, and into which she was at the time exceedingly anxious to introduce the Anglican Polity.

The next assertion is that to the Queen "the chief government of all estates of this realm, whether they be ecclesiastical or civil, in all causes doth appertain." This first strikes at the mediæval laws whereby clerks were exempted from the civil courts. It was a restoration of one of the Constitutions of Clarendon. The bad effect of these exemptions had been found. It was for the good of the clergy themselves that they were brought within the power of the civil law. The difficulty lies "in all causes." As the subject under consideration is "the civil magistrate," it must refer to property. In all causes where a question of property comes in (as we have seen in the earliest times in the instance of Aurelian and Paul of Samosata), the civil magistrate must interfere. No subject may divest himself of his right as a subject of claiming the protection of the law of the land. Any civil court may interfere in the disputes of a religious body, in the way of interpreting the condition of Church membership, the meaning of trust deeds, &c. It will be seen, as we proceed in the Article, that the expression "in all causes," is interpreted and limited by a subsequent clause. It is also interpreted by the words that the Queen's Majesty, "is not nor ought to be subject to any foreign jurisdiction." Now the word 'jurisdiction' is a technical one; it implies the enforcement of a system of law by means of courts.

Jurisdiction is defined as the faculty of any one having public authority and pre-eminence over others for their guidance and government. It is derived *a jure dicendo*, according to justice and the rules of law, which is one of the principal offices of public power.

1. It is divided into civil and ecclesiastical. The first is that which is concerned with secular causes and the temporal rule of the State. The second is concerned with causes pertaining to the worship of God and the

spiritual care of souls, and this jurisdiction is exercised, 1. in the *forum externum* of the courts; and 2. in the *forum internum* of conscience and the sacraments.

2. It is divided further into 1. voluntary, that exercised over willing subjects, such as manumission and adoption in things civil; or ordination, consecration, absolution, dispensation, institution in things sacred; 2. contentious, that exercised against unwilling subjects, such as summoning and punishing. The first, in some cases, may be exercised outside its proper territory, validly and licitly; the second not so.

3. It is divided also into 1. ordinary, that which belongs to any one by reason of his office or dignity, by law, canon, or custom; and 2. delegated, that which a man has, not by his own right, but solely by commission from another, for whom he acts.

4. Again, it is divided into *imperium* and simple jurisdiction. *Imperium* is that which is exercised by the *officium nobile* of the judge, which acts *motu proprio*, from its own power in punishing crimes, &c. Simple jurisdiction is that which is exercised by the *officium mercenarium* of the judge, when he proceeds to try at the instance of the agent.

Imperium is divided into *jurisdictio alta*, or *imperium merum*; and 2. *jurisdictio inferior*, or *imperium mixtum*. The first respects public utility only, as the punishment of malefactors; the second respects private utility, as appointing tutors.

Under *imperium* comes the right of inflicting every kind of punishment.

Ordinary jurisdiction may be acquired in three ways:
1. either by the privilege of the sovereign conceded to
the dignity or person; 2. or by law or canon; 3. or
by custom legitimately prescribed.

Ordinary jurisdiction does not expire with the death
of him who grants it, but delegated jurisdiction does so.

Jurisdiction is necessarily required in hearing confession, and absolution given by a priest without jurisdiction is null; yet, even according to the strictest Roman
rules, simple priests in the article of death may absolve not only from venial sins, and mortal sins elsewhere confessed, but even in reserved cases, for in such
cases the Church gives jurisdiction to all priests, even
degraded and excommunicated; and this is extended
to cases where there is a probable danger of death[u]. "It
will be seen from this that whatever irregularities as
to form have resulted as a consequence of the acts of
the sixteenth century, given the validity of Anglican
orders, even allowing (which we do not concede,) a
formal defect of jurisdiction, in article of necessity, any
person soever may be absolved from any sins whatsoever by any priest whomsoever." Before the Council
of Trent, jurisdiction was given in very various ways[x];
the direct licence or approval of the Bishop was not
required for receiving confessions previously to that
Council. One of the most remarkable extensions of
jurisdiction was that of " tacit consent" of the Superior,
which dispensed even with positive prohibitions.

[u] Ferraris, *Bibliotheca ad verb. Jurisdictio.*
[x] See in Dr. Pusey's Letter to Mr. Richards, pp. 30—81.

In Waterworth's Council of Trent it is stated that at the Council a discussion took place as to the source of jurisdiction. The Pope wished it to declare that jurisdiction came from the Chair of St. Peter. The answer was, it was a question whether it was not given in Holy Orders, and on that ground they refused to affirm it.

By the code of the Universal Church, all jurisdiction in the provinces is given by the Metropolitan, but the Metropolitan himself receives his jurisdiction from the Provincial Bishops. The Pope, if Universal Bishop, must receive his jurisdiction from all the bishops of Christendom; for, stripped of his patriarchal and universal powers, he is only an ordinary bishop. This militates against the Ultramontane theory, which maintains that the Pope is as much above a bishop, as a bishop is above a presbyter. Such a position would imply a direct ordination from Jesus Christ, which, though a logical consequence of the premiss, has never yet been claimed.

As the Queen of England was Suzerain and not vassal, so was she not subject to the Papal courts; not only is the law of the land declared paramount, but the Queen's Canon law comes to be substituted for the Pope's Canon law. The whole expensive foreign procedure, which had been so long the complaint of the English, was by the Church abolished. The Article gives ecclesiastical sanctions to the different Acts of Parliament in which this Reformation was carried out.

But now came an important modification, imported

into the Article at the last revision, in view of the political situation of the Queen, and of the intellectual progress of the controversies of the Reformation. These two reservations are that the Church, " we" the spiritualty, in whom the power of definition lies, " give not to our princes the ministering either of God's word or of the Sacraments ;" that is, neither the right to define doctrine, nor the discipline of the *forum interius* of the Sacraments. Not only is the right to preach and teach reserved, but the highest form of that teaching, dogmatic definition, as in councils, must be included in the expression of ministering God's word. None ever ministered God's word so efficaciously as the fathers of the Church in Council assembled. And so the inner jurisdiction of the Sacraments, the power of the keys, excommunication and its consequences, are by the letter of the Article withheld from princes.

Having stated negatively the abatement to the jurisdiction in all causes, the Article proceeds positively to state what prerogative the Church gives to them, viz. that given to all godly princes in Holy Scripture by God Himself. The ideal is the relation of the good kings of Judah to the Israelitish hierarchy, for the term 'godly' precludes the idea being extended to the relations between the early Christians and the heathen emperors.

But we are not left in doubt what is meant. The princes are, 1. to rule all states and degrees committed to their charge by God, whether they be ecclesiastical or temporal; and 2. to restrain with the civil sword (observe the distinction implied between the two swords and the indorsement of the mediæval interpretation of the text, *Ecce duo gladii*) the stubborn and evil doers; that is, to exercise over all a certain corrective jurisdiction.

The next proposition is that the Bishop of Rome—*Pontifex Romanus*—hath no jurisdiction in this realm of England,—not in this Church of England, but in this realm. The jurisdiction which has just been claimed for the Queen's Majesty cannot of course, by the force of the term, belong to the Apostolic See. The jurisdiction that is given to the one has been taken away from the other. They are correlative. It is a civil question, the subject of the whole article is the civil magistrate, therefore it must be a civil jurisdiction. It must be so; for plainly both the word and the Sacraments have been excepted, and therefore it touches the question between Pope and Queen, not between Pope and Bishop, except so far as the bishop is an English subject. It has to deal with the temporal side of spiritual things, not with the spiritual things themselves. So far as the article is concerned, it does not affect the question of the Scriptural $\pi\rho\omega\tau\epsilon\iota\alpha$ of St. Peter, or even that $\pi\rho\epsilon\sigma\beta\epsilon\iota\alpha$ granted by the early Councils to his successors in the see of Rome [y].

---

[y] Hallam speaking of the action of King Henry VIII. takes exactly the line adopted in the text, and says, " As for the Pope's merely spiritual primacy and authority in matters of faith, which are, or at least were, defended by Catholics of the Gallican or Cisalpine school on quite different grounds from his jurisdiction or his legislatorial power in points

We saw just now that the right of punishment was included in *imperium*. There are four theories on which the right of punishment is grounded, and these theories have distinguished the progress of human society. All have an element of truth in them: no one by itself is adequate to meet all the circumstances of the case. The first theory on which the right of punishment is grounded is that of expiation. The crime against society is here looked upon in its primary light, as an offence against God. This is the view of theocracies, and more or less of early society generally. God is a God of order. Civil society is His work. Every wrong, therefore, done to civil society is a wrong against Him. Again, human life is one of the most wonderful creations of God, and His special care; an attempt on human life, therefore, comes very closely into contact with Him. He has surrounded human life with special hedges and sanctions. Blood crieth from the ground. A Nemesis in this life dogs the heels of the murderer, in a way and degree that it dogs no other sin. Lastly, in early society crime, vice, and sin are not clearly distinguished, and the two first are referred to the last, of which they are indeed the species. Even *mala prohibita*, things not wrong in themselves, but only wrong because against lawful enactments, are sins, so that the

of discipline, they seem to have attracted little peculiar attention at the time, and to have dropped off as a dead branch, when the axe had lopped the fibres that gave it nourishment." (Hallam's *Const. Hist.*, vol. i. p. 67, ed. 1846.)

element of expiation comes in in the case of every punishment.

The next aspect of punishment is that of retaliation. An eye for an eye, and a tooth for a tooth. This is the principle of what is termed vindictive justice. The divine relation to man is here not so directly marked as in the former case, though in the abstract, God being Justice Himself, He really is considered under this theory. However, mainly, the question turns on the relations between man and man. So much injury inflicted must be compensated by so much suffering undergone; for so much property taken or destroyed, so much restitution made. An extreme form of this is the right of vendetta, namely, that when the retaliation has not taken place in the person of the offender, his heirs are still liable. In proportion as law is established, and provisions are made therein for the redress of individual wrongs, in that proportion an individual abdicates in favour of society his right to private vengeance.

The third theory of punishment, is that which finds most acceptance with modern thought. It is that which bases its right to inflict such pain as punishment necessarily implies, on the ground of prevention of crime. Here the idea of God is to a degree further eliminated, and the matter is based upon a theory of utility. This theory in its degree is perfectly legitimate, resting as it does on that self-love which God has implanted in man, but it may be exercised in a way that self-love may degenerate into selfishness, and so defeat its own end. Applied to the question at issue, utility holds that the whole principle of punishment rests on the right which society has, by all means to prevent or repress whatsoever injures or weakens it. Now every crime by so much injures society, and therefore society, in the instinct of self-preservation, may prevent it. So strongly is this theory held now, that the measure of suffering is now everywhere reduced to a fancied maximum of prevention, as where the severe penalties against forgery have been remitted, to secure, in all cases, the offender being brought to justice. Abnormal sins, which were formerly treated as crimes, are in the process of ceasing to be so, the effect of publicity having been found to have the effect not of prevention, but of turning public attention to such faults in the way of imitation.

A fourth theory, is the emendation of the offender. The education of children supplies an analogy to the treatment of men as members of the republic. Judicial punishment is one of the ways in which families are governed, and the same is a necessary evil on the larger scale. Public attention being now turned to the great mass of criminal population, which in the midst of our boasted civilization has grown up at our doors, moved, partly by humanity, and partly by fear, is doing all it can to abate the fearful nuisance. Among the remedies, education, refuges, criminal colonies, and the like, punishment is now inflicted in such way as will tend to benefit the criminal, especially in the case of the young offenders; this forms an important element in the nature and degree of the award inflicted.

All these four theories are distinctly recognised in Holy Scripture. The theory of expiation in those striking rites which were to be practised in the case of the barbarous slaughter; that of retaliation in many of the awards of the Mosaic dispensation, only that the retaliation was taken out of the hands of the individual injured, and was inflicted by the judge, as the representative of God. It was an embodying in written law, the rule of the Divine justice, " As I have done, so God hath requited me *." That of prevention and that of amendment in the theories of government put forth by St. Paul in his Epistle to the Romans.

Having laid down these principles, it remains for us to test the question of capital punishment by each of them. It is a tremendous thing that any class of men may judicially and in cold blood take the life of a fellow-creature, deprive him of that which they cannot restore, and abridge the term of probation and instruction which the life of each man is. A thoughtful school in the present day has greatly doubted, and in some cases absolutely denied, the lawfulness of this. Life, they say, is something so sacred that it is inviolable. Any punishment short of that is permissible, but on any account to violate the sanctuary of life is wrong. Moreover, it is maintained that society fares best by minimizing the measure of punishment in all cases, and that, if society can go on equally well without

* Jud. i. 7.

capital punishment, it is plainly the duty of society to do without it.

It will be seen that on every one of the four theories just mentioned, death-punishment is defensible. On the theory of expiation, we have the distinct recognition of Holy Scripture, "lest the land be defiled with blood;" on that of retaliation, blood must wash out blood. On that of prevention, it is clear that there are temptations to some crimes so strong, and the reward of others so great, that nothing but the fear of hanging for them will deter men. The greatest advocates for the abolition of capital sentences are significantly silent in the presence of a great State necessity, or in the chronic predominance of some brutal form of murder. Even the theory of the emendation of the criminal is in favour of death-sentences. A man who has committed a great crime has a better chance of a true repentance, if when condemned to pay the penalty of his crimes with his life, he knows that he has a fixed term only to live. He betakes himself to religion; he is attended by its ministers, and he has the four last things brought before him so forcibly, that there is every chance of his becoming really penitent. On the other hand, in the case of those tremendous imprisonments, sometimes for life, which society exacts where capital punishment is forbidden, to shut up a bad man with his own bad thoughts for a lifetime, is to do one's best to turn him into an incarnation of everything that is foul, lustful, and malignant.

The Article on the Civil Magistrate concludes by asserting the lawfulness of wearing arms and of war. Both these are permitted, on the ground that under certain circumstances man may take the life of his fellow. Individually he may protect life or property, even to the destruction of the life of his assailant. Hence the permissibility of arms, not only of defence but of offence. Our Lord sanctions the use of the sword. It is a terrible necessity, still it is a necessity. Of course as the civil government becomes stronger, and interferes more promptly and efficaciously in the redress of wrongs, that necessity diminishes, and there is perhaps no such test of the real civilization of a country as the non-necessity of the use of weapons for personal protection. From the time that the court-sword went out as a fashion, there was a marked advance in civilization. It is a degeneracy when men have to adopt the revolver and the bowie knife.

The last point treated of is War.

Cicero[*] describes war as a striving by force (*certationem per vim*), but custom has established that it is not an action but a condition, which is indicated by the word, so that it comes to mean the state of those who are striving by force. This applies both to public wars, wherein nations are concerned, and also to private wars, as where a traveller contends with a robber, and which are the first form of wars, for the word itself, *bellum*, is derived from *duellum*, ' a combat between two.'

[*] Grotius, lib. i. cap. 11, vol. i. p. 2. ed. Lausanne, 1751.

There is nothing against natural law in war, for the end of war is the preservation of life and members, and the retention or acquisition of the things which are useful for life. Society only forbids that violence which injures it. The force that does not injure the right of another is not unjust.

So there is nothing against the *jus gentium* in war. Nay, necessity and use have trained nations so that certain forms of war have been introduced, and hence we have the distinction of the *bellum solemne*, in which is a certain order and method along with justice; and the *bellum non solemne*, which retaining still the same element of justice, may be tumultuary, sudden, and informal (*incondita*).

Neither is there anything against the divine law, in spite of the Noachic precept against bloodshed, and the sixth commandment of the Decalogue. For, not to speak of the example of Abram and the kings of Canaan, the principle of death-punishment so clearly taught in the Bible, implies that it may be inflicted on a large scale, in defence of life, honour, matrimonial honour, or the stability of the state. Even under the Gospel the same principle may be admitted; for

I. The right of the sword is recognised [b] in the Prayers for the Civil Government, and its recognition as bearing not the sword in vain [c].

II. St. John the Baptist does not forbid the στρα-τευόμενοι, the militia against Aretas, to fight, but urges them not to maraud, and to be content with their pay.

[b] 1 Tim. ii. 1.   [c] Rom. xiii. 4.

III. War hangs on the same principle as capital punishment. Our Lord has forbidden neither the one nor the other.

IV. The early Christians followed the Jewish customs where they were not forbidden by our Lord, therefore war is lawful to Christian men.

V. The examples of Cornelius and of the various pious centurions in the Gospels, are evidences that there is no sin in bearing arms. Add the number of saints who have been soldiers.

VI. St. Paul had no hesitation in using the services of the soldiers, the four quaternions of men who conducted him from Jerusalem to Philippi. Also he refused not to die if guilty of breach of the law.

VII. Wars are predicted in the 18th chapter of the Apocalypse, with the manifest approbation of the saints.

VIII. Our Lord abrogated only the ceremonial law of Moses, by which the Gentiles were separated from the chosen people, but He left the natural law and what was deemed right and lawful by well-conditioned and well-moralled states.

In short, while we must deplore the necessity of war, its existence is a necessity of the present state of the world. A large army is the best guarantee for peace. The possibility of war, coupled with the knowledge of its misery, waste, and expense, acts as a pacificatory element on earth. Nay, actual war, though in one sense deplorable, is not wholly bad. It braces up the nerves of a nation, it developes heroism, and prevents men from resting too exclusively on a materialistic money-getting civilization.

It need hardly be said that, while on the one hand the providence of God employs war to scourge and amend men's corrupt ways, yet the necessity of war is a token of decayed Christian love. The Christian must mourn even over "just wars." At the Incarnation the herald-song was, " On earth peace, good will towards man." Ambitious wars, " What are they but a vast brigandage [d] ?" "Christians who originate an unjust war from lust of power or wealth, or from envy lest a neighbouring prince become too great or powerful, are not so much Christians as Pagans." But, says St. Augustine, " if war is waged out of the cupidity of man, this hurts not the saints. For there is no power but of God, either commanding or permitting. A just man, then, if perchance he be in military service under a king who is even a sacrilegious man, may rightly war at his command, keeping the due order of internal peace, (to which what is commanded is either certain that it is not against the command of God, or not certain whether it be,) so that perchance the injustice of the command may make the king guilty, but the due order of obeying may prove the soldier innocent [e]."

[d] *Grande latrocinium, S. Aug. de Civ. D.,* iv. 6.

[e] *S. Aug. c. Faust.,* xxii. 74, 75. On the opinions of the early Fathers, see Dr. Pusey's Note E on Tertullian against Gibbon's taunt : c. 15, n. 4.

ARTICLE XXXVIII.

DE ILLICITA BONORUM COMMUNICATIONE.

FACULTATES et bona Christianorum, non sunt communia, quoad jus et possessionem (ut quidam Anabaptistæ falso jactant); debet tamen quisque de his quæ possidet, pro facultatum ratione, pauperibus eleemosynas benigne distribuere.

" Of Christian Men's Goods, which are not common.

" THE riches and goods of Christians are not common, as touching the right, title, and possession of the same, as certain Anabaptists do falsely boast. Notwithstanding, every man ought, of such things as he possesseth, liberally to give alms to the poor, according to his ability."

An investigation into the origin of the notion of property is one of great interest, not only on philosophical and literary, but on practical grounds also. Such questions as the measure of relief to which the able-bodied poor are entitled, or the proportion of remuneration to be allotted to labour as against capital, bring the matter before our thoughts in a way that appeals to all. Yet it is difficult to lay down a comprehensive statement of the question; for jurists generally assume the idea of property as a postulate, use it as the foundation of law, deal with it as an ultimate fact, and confine themselves to the modifications and restrictions enforced by society on its unlimited use. The old civil law brocard, " Quod nullius est, fit occupantis," is tacitly assumed as indisputable.

" God bestowed on mankind in general a right over the inferior things of nature immediately after the Creation, and again at the Flood. All things, says Justin, were undivided and common to all, as if all had one patrimony. Hence it was that every one might take to his uses what he pleased, and consume what was to be consumed; which use of the universal right was then instead of property, for what any one had so taken, another could not without injury take away from him. Thus, Cicero* says, 'a theatre belongs to all, yet the place possessed by any one may be called his own.'

" It was not impossible that this condition of things could continue, if men continued to live either in great simplicity, or in a certain mutual charity. Communion, by reason of an exceeding simplicity, may be observed in some tribes of America; the other, the communion of charity, the Essenes practised, and then the Christians at Jerusalem, and now not a few who lead the ascetic life.

" The simplicity in which man existed at first, was

* *De Fin.*, iii.

shewn by his nakedness; there was in him rather the ignorance of vice than the knowledge of virtue. . . . But in this simple and innocent life men persisted not, but applied their minds to diverse arts. 'God made man upright, but they have found out many inventions[b].' The most ancient arts appeared in the first brothers. From the diversity of their courses arose emulation and then slaughter, and at length when the good were infected by the conversation of the bad, the giant life of violence prevailed. The world being washed by the Flood, there succeeded the desire of pleasure, to which wine ministered, and hence arose unlawful loves. But concord was more broken by ambition, at Babel; after which men parted asunder and severally possessed the various parts of the earth, yet so that afterwards there remained a community not of cattle, but of pastures. This lasted, till the number of men and cattle so increased that lands every where began to be divided, not among nations as before, but many families also; but wells in a thirsty land, every one made his own by seizure.

" Hence we learn wherefore men departed from the primitive community; 1st, of moveables, and, 2ndly, of immoveables also; viz., because when, no longer content to feed upon what grew of itself, to dwell in caves, to go naked, or clad in bark or skins, they had chosen a more artificial life, there was need of industry, which every one must use.

" The reason why the fruits of the earth were not

<hr>

[b] Eccles. vii. 29.

brought together for common use, was, 1st, the distance of places whereby men are separate, and, 2nd, the failure of justice and love, whereby it came to pass, that neither in labour nor in the consumption of those fruits due equality was preserved. Thus we learn how property arose, not only by an act of the mind (for they could not know the thoughts of one another, what every one would have to be his own, that they might abstain from it, and many might desire the same thing,) but by a certain covenant, either *express*, as by division, or *tacit*, as by occupation. Community of goods being given up, and no division being made, an universal agreement must be supposed, whereby each one should have belonging to himself what he occupied. ' It is allowed,' says Cicero, ' that every man may prefer himself before another in getting things useful for his life, nature not being repugnant hereunto.' To which is added the saying of Quinctilian; ' Granting that what is come into a man's possession is his own, certainly whatsoever is possessed by right is taken away by wrong.' And the ancients when they called Ceres, *Legifera*, and her rites *Thezmophoria*, signified this, that by the division of fields came up the original of a certain new right ͨ."

Yet a knowledge of the manners and customs of certain nations, and the history of religious and philosophical speculation on these subjects, shew that the postulate of the existence of property has been disputed.

ͨ Hugo Grotius *De Jure Belli et Pacis*, cap. ii. vol. ii. p. 53, ed. Laus., 1751.

For example, the notion was very much modified among the Celtic races. Their possessions accrued not to one, but to the tribe. Sismondi shews this with regard to the Highlands of Scotland; and the recent publication of the Brehon laws in Ireland, exhibits to us the picture of a simple state of society, not without its civilization, in which tribal possession forms a most important constituent. Analogous to this is the village-system in India, in which from time immemorial there has been a joint occupation and possession by the ryots. Dynasty after dynasty of conquerors, often foreign conquerors, utterly ignorant or regardless of this peculiar institution, have ruled in India; laws, such as those made by Lord Cornwallis in misunderstanding of what was dearest to the feelings of the poor villagers, have been enacted, but still the old system has survived to this day. Neither can this be said to be the characteristic of the Indo-European race, for the recent war in New Zealand, so deeply to be regretted on every ground, has arisen from an ignorance on the part of the British authorities of these peculiar tenures.

But, furthermore, the idea of property has been challenged both on theological and philosophical grounds; on the first by the Anabaptists, as indicated in the Article; on the latter by such communists as St. Simon, Fourier, and Proudhon, who boldly state the matter on the apparent paradox that it is property that is the theft.

With regard to the first, one cannot do better than quote the weighty words of Lord Stair, the eminent

Scottish Jurist: "It is a false and groundless opinion which some hold, that man by his fall has lost his right to the creatures, until by grace he be restored, and that the sole dominion of them belongs to the saints, who may take them by force from all others. For by the whole strain of the law of God, He still alloweth dominion and property of the creatures in man, without distinction, and prohibiteth all force or fraud in the contrary, which sufficiently cleareth that subtilty of man's forfeiture; for though sin maketh men obnoxious by way of obligation to punishments by God's exterminating him from the use and comfort of the creatures; yet that obligation doth not infer the actual ceasing of man's right, much less the stating of the rights of mankind in a small part of them [d]."

Nothing is so irritating for religionists, as to be outstripped in the course upon which they have entered, or to have their principles, by them often held in solution, precipitated and carried out into inconvenient results. Something of this kind was experienced by the Lutherans in the case of the earlier Anabaptists. At first they agreed entirely with them, except on the subject of infant-baptism, the rejection of which was only a legitimate consequence of Luther's dogma which, connecting the efficacy of the Sacraments with faith, rendered the baptism of infants wholly irrational. But soon this alliance became a deadly hatred. A fearful fanaticism drove these men into every species of violence; they were implicated in the war of the

[d] Bk. II. chap. i. p. 166.

peasants, and at last the outrages at Münster shewed to what terrible results sincere ill-guided zeal may lead men.

They had strong millenarian expectations. After foretelling the utter extirpation of all the ungodly, they announced the kingdom of Christ as immediately thereafter established upon earth. A new and perfect life, in common among Christians, would then be established, without magistrate or external law. Even the Bible was to be abolished; for the perfect children of God needed it not. Perfect equality and community of goods would prevail, and even marriage be no longer contracted. Of course war was unlawful, and oaths unnecessary, in this glorious kingdom of Christ. These high and ideal notions cannot but extort our admiration, but the Anabaptists wished to force these on men unprepared, and by violence. Many other errors were held by them, and it is to be feared that Antinomianism especially prevailed amongst some of them. "In the first Anabaptists we discern, beside the simplicity of the child, the fury of the wildest demagogue, who, to create a happy and holy world, destroyed in the most unholy and calamitous manner the actual one; and, as a blind instrument, ministered to the ambition, the avarice, and all the basest passions of the reprobate men, whom we so frequently meet with in the early history of the sect[*]."

The speculations of the Anabaptists are things of the past; but the questions which they raised are still

[*] Möhler, ii. 161.

unsolved. After the dark ages, with the very first dawn of intelligence, hungry mouths began to ask "why are we hungry?" Many of the heretical sects had social as well as religious errors in the catalogue of their opinions. In the ages of faith every question took a religious form, and therefore political economy expressed itself in the language of the soul. Begardi, the good men of Lyons, the Albigenses, and many others, thought that they were reforming the Church when they were only stating their political grievances. In the opinions of Huss and Jerome of Prague many of the propositions condemned are simply economics; for they endorsed the propositions of Wicliffe.

That the tyranny of the feudal system should generate such sentiments, or that God should seek to alleviate the sorrows of men by raising up the Franciscan Order to console the poor, are circumstances not to be wondered at. At a time when the oppression was at its worst, and when industrial wealth was beginning among the Lombards and Genoese to occupy a new place as a power in the world, Francis of Assisi by proclaiming the holiness of poverty on which he founded his order, and Jacopone da Todi by becoming the poet of the unfortunate, were made the instruments of God's goodness. The Seraphic Order in all its branches ever maintained a traditional recollection of the causes of its rise. It has ever been the poor man's friend, and has escaped much of the odium which has fallen upon other religious associations.

But after the institution of the Franciscans, with their various reforms, nothing was done for the poor. To burn Huss and Jerome of Prague was no real solution of the question. A terrorism might silence complaint; but the complaint was there still, and so the evil went on till the Reformation. It would be curious to trace the political causes of that event. In all countries it was influenced thereby. Calvinism made Holland and Geneva republican; it became the element of political disturbances in Scotland, the weakest of all royalties; and the Stuarts with their pet dictum, "no bishop no king," put strongly and truly the democratic element of the new system. It was the same in England, modified by the strong will of the Tudors, and the greater strength of the monarchical principle. In Germany, where the nobility were stronger than in any other country in Europe, the rise of the Anabaptists saved them by precipitating the element of communism that was held in solution, and giving the nobles an easy victory over them. In Italy and Spain, (with the exception of Venice,) the elements of Protestantism got trodden out simultaneously with those of political freedom; while in France, the struggle of the two principles was fought out in internecine feud, more than one half of France, nobility and all, being Protestant. The massacre of St. Bartholomew was a piece of cruel State-craft, as well as of religious persecution,—the revocation of the Edict of Nantes expelled with Protestantism the last efforts of political free-thought of France. Meanwhile, the absenteeism caused by the crushing of the political power of the nobility, and the consequent enforcement of their attendance at Court, added to the extravagance of the kings after the time of Mazarin and Richelieu, established a spirit of alienation between the ranks in society, and an impoverishment of the lower classes, which resulted in the first Revolution. The good side of that movement was a vindication of the rights of man as man; the misery was a denial of his rights as the creature of God. A political economy which eliminates God as the main factor in life is Sciolism.

The economic side of the democratic question was differently treated in England. The destructive Wars of the Roses prevented a surplusage of population, and the Commons were comparatively well fed. The nobility and squirearchy lived very much on their estates, the parochial system was strongly developed, and a kindly feeling existed between the different ranks of society. The immense mass of land, too, held in mortmain by the abbeys, while it prevented the full development of the resources of the country, had this effect, that a great many of the commons held their farms on easy terms, while the ready dole at the convent-gate afforded a subsistence for the poorer sort. As a matter of fact, no poor-law was required till the reign of Edward VI. Representative Government kept tyranny in check, if it did nothing directly to ameliorate the condition of the poor. The introduction of foreign trades, though at the time viewed with jealousy by the people, in reality was a boon to them. The national resources were not taxed by the existence of great standing armies, and therefore the outbursts of popular misery were few, and the demand for the solution of the questions affecting the rights of labour and capital respectively, never came to a bloody arbitrement.

It has been reserved to the nineteenth century, when industry has been developed to a degree that our fathers never dreamt of, when the discovery of gold has upset for a time the whole measure of prices, when increased locomotion has indefinitely thrown open markets, to call up all these questions again. For in spite of all material advancement, a hideous pauperism menaces society, and the enlightenment of the age is thereby terribly reminded of that Biblical truth it would fain deny or invalidate, that "the poor shall never cease out of the land." And the awful thing is, that the pauperism of an industrial civilization is more hopeless, more incurable, more degraded, than that of any prior state of things. When an oriental sovereign could compel a whole nation to build a pyramid, when the daughters and goods of the vassal were not safe from the lust and rapacity of the overlord, it was simply the misfortune of the unhappy ones, and their cry entered into the ear of the Lord God of Sabaoth; but now the pauperism of the age is the result of moral degradation, and drink, and every kind of sin, and the squalor of the external circumstance is the symbol of the foulness of that which exists within.

Poverty is one thing, pauperism is another. Poverty is the momentary or even permanent deprivation of the enjoyments of means; it is the state in which man is condemned to work for the necessaries of life: but pauperism is a chronic, normal, almost fatal state of misery, which hands over a notable portion of living humanity to moral degradation and physical suffering, while a small and privileged class live in the most unexampled luxury. For here is the awful fact, that pauperism is measured by the advance of industry, and progress in wealth goes on side by side with progress in misery.

A great man has said, " There is not a sadder sight than that which Great Britain offers, between a wealth and a luxury without bounds, and the exhaustion to which ten thousand of the poor, shut up in cellars, without light or air, are exposed. Misery, famine, and degradation, in the presence of our sumptuous abodes and our exhaustless profusion, strikes us more than any other misery in the world."

The chief causes of this disastrous state of things are, 1. the exaggerated preponderance of industrial over agricultural production, and the abnormal displacement of the powers of labour, so that on the occurrence of a crisis great distress is produced. 2. The separation of interest between master and workman, and the existence of combinations on either side for mutual aggression and protection. 3. The cessation of work at home, and the aggregation of labour in great workshops, and hence the creation of great industrial towns to the prejudice of the moral and physical health of the people. 4. The extreme division of labour, which makes man more and more of a machine, and impoverishes him mentally and morally. Lastly, the hideous mixture of the sexes in the workshops, and the abuse of the young, which produces in some cases a corruption unheard of in Christian times.

No wonder that all this produces pauperism, that pauperism is misery, and misery cries aloud, Why should these things be? No wonder that, unable to detect that much of its misery is of its own making, poverty should claim a hearing in the presence of inordinate wealth, and demand in the accents of despair, For what end has property been instituted?

It has been said that every heresy is the intellectual vengeance of some suppressed truth; in any case, there is often an underlying truth at the bottom of each aberration. What we have said of the image of God not being entirely obliterated by the Fall will induce us to acknowledge the fact that man still hankers in a feeble way after the Good and the True, does not naturally take up with the evil and the hideous, so that his errors are disguised in some specious form of virtue; otherwise error would not be so nearly synonymous with sin.

Now what was the underlying truth which lay at the bottom of the Anabaptist theories, which gave point to the paradox of Fourier and Proudhon? It was that in the eyes of God all property is held in trust for our neighbour. While in the order of nature and of civil polity, that state is most firmly established where the individuality of ownership is most strictly recognised and respected; in the order of grace it is otherwise. God permits the existence of property, but only as a necessary evil. To avoid a dead level of unprogressive barbarism, He allows one man to have, another to want; but in allowing this apparent injustice, He corrects the disparity by the sense of responsible stewardship. The children of the kingdom must have nothing selfish about them; their citizenship being in heaven, they must use what God has given them, for His glory, and for the benefit of His creatures. Civil society being His ordinance, has its claims on man; there is something due to the position of each rank and class of life. But there is beside and beyond this the kingdom of God and His righteousness, the interests of Christ and His members, and the sense of stewardship connected with these interests.

It will be seen how all this affects the luxury, the industrial power of modern civilization. That a certain refinement and grace of life, is not only not sinful, but actually a help heavenward, cannot be denied; that an industrial progress is compatible with the development of the resources of a Christian nation must also be admitted. But beyond such admission, it is very difficult to see one's way to lay down canons of right on such a question. While a well-appointed establishment, rich dresses, costly wines, circulate money and foster trade, one asks oneself, in spite of oneself, how many poor children would the same cost feed, clothe, and educate. While the development of industry gives work and wages to many a poor creature, and brings the necessaries of life by cheapness of production within the reach of the poor, it is awful to think of the terrible race which competition causes, the neglect of immortal souls in the training of those who by a horrid sarcastic truth are termed "hands," and the countless evils which spring from the system, not to mention the mutilations by machinery, the premature exhaustion of the physical powers, the creedless unlovely life, and the solitary workhouse-death.

It is needless to deplore evils which we cannot mend. At least, each one in his station should try and do his duty, and so mitigate the evils consequent on the necessary permission of property. Matters will not be mended by revolution, though we know from an awful experience, that evils of this kind neglected, are apt to end in revolution, and a country where its nobles and capitalists betray their trust is apt from time to time to be regenerated in their blood. The true course is, that each one in his station should live according to the rule of the "Sermon on the Mount:" live a Christ-like life on earth, the life of the brethren of Him who laid down His life for His friends; love his brother as himself, render to all their due, love as brethren, be pitiful, be courteous; so shall one step be gained towards the reign of righteousness and charity. The rest must be relegated to the great compensation day. "Son, remember that thou in thy lifetime receivedst thy good things."

ARTICLE XXXIX.

De Jurejurando.

Quemadmodum juramentum vanum et temerarium a Domino nostro Jesu Christo, et Apostolo ejus Jacobo, Christianis hominibus interdictum esse fatemur : ita Christianorum Religionem minime prohibere censemus, quin jubente magistratu in causa fidei et charitatis jurare liceat, modo id fiat juxta Prophetæ doctrinam, in justitia, in judicio, et veritate.

" Of a Christian Man's Oath.

" As we confess that vain and rash swearing is forbidden Christian men by our Lord Jesus Christ, and James His Apostle ; so we judge that Christian religion doth not prohibit, but that a man may swear when the magistrate requireth, in a cause of faith and charity, so it be done, according to the Prophet's teaching, in justice, judgment, and truth."

An oath is a tacit or expressed invocation of the Deity, as of the first and infallible Truth, in testimony of anything. It is a religious asseveration, made with the intention of swearing to the truth of anything, God being called in as witness and avenger. It is divided into the oath assertory, and the oath promis-

sory. Again, into the oath simple, and the oath solemn, such as homages and professions of faith.

Again, it is divided into the oath of attestation, the
oath of execration, the oath of threatening.

Three conditions, as the Article quotes from Jeremiah (chap. iv.), are requisite to a legitimate oath—
justice, judgment, and truth; justice, that the thing
be lawful and honest, and so the Name of the holy
God be not adduced in confirmation of injustice or
sin; judgment, in that the oath be not taken without
necessity or grave cause, or manifest advantage, with
prudent consideration of the mind, and pure and reverent affection of the will; and truth, that the thing
be true, or at least on reasonable grounds and *bonâ
fide* believed to be true; so that the holy Name be
not brought forward to testify to a lie, which were
perjury and a great sin.

An oath so taken, is not only no sin, but a religious
act. "Thou shalt fear the Lord, and swear by His
Name[a]."

But the habit of swearing without a cause, indis-
creetly and inadvertently, whether the thing be true
or false, is a mortal sin; so that such a consuetudinary
sinner, neglecting to amend his ways, sins grievously
by the force of the retention of such custom, as often
as he so swears. Being in proximate peril of mortal
sin from the habit, he sins also in not attempting to
cure himself.

The habit of swearing has very much gone out

[a] Deut. x. 20.

among the upper classes, partly from the censure of
society, partly, it is to be feared, from the materialistic
and unbelieving frame of mind into which uninter-
rupted prosperity, fulness of bread, and an unsupernatural mind, throw the soul. Men will not swear by
God, unless they realize His hand in all things. It is
not simple good, that has caused the abandonment of
this disgusting vice.

Among all people [b], and from the most ancient times,
very great has been the power of an oath. Our ancestors, saith Cicero, esteemed no bond of faith stronger
than this. Hence it has always been believed that
some heavy punishment hangs over the head of a per-
jured person, and even posterity paid for the sins of
their forefathers in this kind. Even the will, without
the actual deed, drew punishment along with it, as in
the story of Glaucus, as told by Herodotus.

To a valid oath, sanity of mind and deliberation of
purpose are required. Next, what is so sworn as the
mind of the swearer conceives it must be done, must
be kept. They perjure themselves, who, while saving
the words, disappoint the expectation of those to whom
they have sworn.

As to oaths deceitfully procured, if it be certain
that he who sweareth supposeth something done, which
indeed is not so, and that, unless he had believed it,
he would not have sworn, the oath will not bind.
But if it be doubtful whether he would not, even

---

[b] *Grotius de Jure*, lib. ii. c. 13, vol. iii. p. 1, ed. Laus., 1751.

without that, have sworn the same, he must stand to his word, because the greatest simplicity there can be agrees to an oath.

Yet the signification of an oath is not to be extended beyond the received custom of speech, as it is one thing to give, it is another thing not to require that which is taken away.

Above all things, an oath binds nothing made of unlawful matter. A sworn promise to do what is either naturally, or by the interdict of God, unlawful, does not hold good. It is sometimes against duty to perform a promise, or to keep an oath. If one's faith be pledged to commit a sin, it is strange to call it faith.

Also, an oath that hinders a greater moral good does not hold. We owe to God progress in good, and so may not take away from ourselves the liberty of so doing. A man who swears never to do another a good turn would not be bound.

No man, also, is held to fulfil what is impossible.

Next, as to the form of oaths. These may vary, but all agree in fact. The calling in God to be witness and avenger underlies the idea of every oath. Every oath terminates in imprecation upon the perjurer. Other names and things, as one's country, one's head, one's children, sometimes were associated with God, but pleonastically.

The effect of an oath is the settlement of controversies, as the greatest assurance among men. Some authorities maintain that even a forced oath is to be kept, out of reverence to God. The Hebrew kings were reproved by the prophets, because they kept not faith with the Babylonian conquerors. And the person alone to whom we swear is not to be respected, but He by whom we swear, God. This suffices to create an obligation; and therefore oaths to tyrants, and pirates, and other common enemies, are valid. In such bad cases, however, the heir of a man would not be bound.

An oath to another, being a solemn promise, the person who makes it is released from that oath, if he to whom it is made refuses to accept the advantage so promised. Neither is a man bound, if the quality under which he hath sworn to any, ceaseth; as, if a magistrate cease to be a magistrate. When a man resigns a place, the oath is voided by the loss of the place.

As to whether that which is done against an oath is unlawful only, or also void, in law, one must say that if one's faith only be engaged, an act done against an oath is valid, in law, e.g. a will, or a sale: it is not valid, if the oath be so conceived, that withal it contains a full abdication of the power to act.

The acts of superiors cannot so far prevail, that an oath, so far as it is truly obligatory, is not to be performed; for that it is of natural and divine right. But a superior may forbid the taking of oaths, or prevent their fulfilment.

Or a mixed case may be, where the superior ordains that the oath shall be of force, if approved by him.

On this ground is defended the power of dispensation in the Church.

Our Lord and St. James do not forbid the "assertory" oath, of which there are some instances in St. Paul, but the oath promissory of a future uncertain thing. "It is best and most profitable, and to the rational creature most convenient, to abstain from swearing, and so to accustom oneself to truthfulness, that one's word may be taken for an oath [c].

The most advanced schools of modern jurisprudence are more than doubtful as to the policy of using oaths in judicial processes. When a man determines to tell the truth, he will do so without an oath; when he has determined to lie, an oath will not hinder him. This is true; but, on the other hand, so illogical is the action of the human conscience, that there are many who will be deterred by an oath from stating what they would state without that sanction. In the popular mind there is a great gulph between a lie and a perjury, and besides the fact that perjury is punishable at law, an oath gives a further guarantee for the enunciation of the truth.

[c] Grotius.

THE RATIFICATION.

CONFIRMATIO ARTICULORUM.

HIC liber antedictorum Articulorum jam denuo approbatus est, per assensum et consensum Serenissimæ Reginæ Elizabethæ Dominæ nostræ, Dei gratia Angliæ, Franciæ, et Hiberniæ, Reginæ, Defensoris fidei, &c., retinendus, et per totum regnum Angliæ exequendus. Qui Articuli, et lecti sunt, et denuo confirmati, subscriptione D. Archiepiscopi et Episcoporum superioris domus, et totius Cleri inferioris domus, in Convocatione Anno Domini, 1571.

"*The Ratification.*

"THIS Book of Articles before rehearsed, is again approved, and allowed to be holden and executed within the realm, by the assent and consent of our Sovereign Lady Elizabeth, by the Grace of God, of England, France, and Ireland, Queen, Defender of the Faith, &c. Which Articles were deliberately read and confirmed again by the subscription of the hands of the Archbishops and Bishops of the Upper House, and by the subscription of the whole Clergy of the Nether House in their Convocation, in the year of our Lord 1571."

The Articles are primarily a State document, made ecclesiastical by the acceptance of the two Convocations in 1562 and 1571. This fact weighs much in a moral point of view in respect to our subjective treatment of them. One treats them very differently from the decrees of a Provincial Synod of the Church of England. Convocation, though by some said to be legally the Church of England by representation, is only so in the sense of certain civil results. It is not a Council in the strictly ecclesiastical sense. Its decrees do not bind the conscience from any intrinsic authority in themselves, or in the documents put out by it. It only binds the conscience as a result of subscription. It is immoral and wicked in itself, to deny the decree of a Council accepted by the Church. It is not immoral or wicked in itself to deny an Article, e.g. that the Homilies have certain qualities. It only becomes immoral and wicked, when a man has signed what he does not believe, or when a man denies what he has subscribed to.

A result of this will be that a very different degree of reverence will attach to the body of the document, and specially to the inferences to be drawn from it. In dealing with the language of a Council, emanating from the Holy Ghost, we speak with bated breath in discussing it, and we respect inferences that may be certainly gathered from it, though not expressed; but in dealing with a document of the nature of the Articles, we are under no such moral obligation. The plain literal and grammatical sense, interpreted by the hardest legal head, is all that we have to do with in accepting the text; and as regards the inferences, we have nothing whatever to do with them.

Lastly, they are not of eternal obligation. The offspring of a controversial age, they bear on their surface the evidence of their paternity. That age has passed away, and the questions then unsolved have received the fullest consideration, and much that then looked like actual opposition has been found to be mere logomachy. New enemies to the faith have sprung up since those days, of which they take no cognizance, and, in resistance to these, all parties in the sixteenth century would have united as against a common foe. Two camps are arraying themselves in battle against each other. Communities and men are taking their sides. All conscious misbelief is gravitating towards unbelief; all imperfect but sincere conviction tending to the Catholic Faith. As then believers, in opposition to infidels and miscreants, come to make common cause, that common cause will lead to common faith, and under such common faith there will be no need for such declarations as the Thirty-nine Articles; they will have done their work, so, having done their work, they will take their place among the things of the past.

And to this consummation, to this common cause and common faith, we have to ask ourselves, what course of events will tend. How is the present state of confusion in the Church of Christ to be remedied? What can be done to heal the divisions in the Body of the Lord? There has been but one answer in all ages of confusion. At the beginning of the troubles in Henry the Eighth's time, just after Wolsey's death, when the matter of the division had thrown everything into confusion, Sir Thomas More said that he desired three things, and one of these things was the Convocation of a Free General Council. It was the recognised means of healing the wounds of the Church desired by those enlightened men, who, while ‚they recognised and deplored the existence of scandals and corruptions, clung earnestly to the old faith[a]. Nor was this confined to them alone[b]. The reformers, such as Melanchthon and Archbishop Herman of Cologne, maintained their reforms to be provisional until a General Council[c].

Luther himself at one time used it as a weapon of offence against the Pope[d]. In this very volume we have seen that Queen Elizabeth appealed to a free synod to arbitrate on the Anglican position. If Bishop Jewel in so many words does not go so far[e], it is at least the legitimate outcome of his Apology. He

[a] In 1536 Convocation, in protesting against the Pope holding a Council "without the express consent, assent, and agreement of the residue of Christian Princes," says, "We, taught by long experience, do perfectly know, that there never was, or is, anything devised, invented or instituted, by our forefathers, more expedient, or more necessary, for the establishment of our faith, for the extirpation of heresies, and the abolishing of sects and schisms; and, finally, for reducing Christ's people into one perfect unity and concord of religion, than the having of General Councils." (Burnet, Ref., vol. i. App. b. iii. No. 5.)

[b] e.g. Erasmus, *Epist.*, lib. xxviii. 8. [c] Hardwick's Manual of Ref., p. 9, ed. 1856. [d] Ibid., p. 62, note.

[e] "Nos quidem concilia et episcoporum doctorumque hominum conventus et colloquia non contemnimus. Neque ea quæ fecimus, prorsus sine episcopis aut sine concilio fecimus." (Jewel's *Apol.*, p. 34; Wordsworth's Christian Institutes; see also *Apol.*, part vi. (vol. iv. 71, ed. Jelf.) Serm. ii. vol. vii. 384; *Ep. de Conc. Trid.*, viii. 102.

gives many reasons for not attending at Trent, but all the reasons presuppose the supreme authority of a Council really Œcumenical. The theology of King James I., which was really able, and which, from the moral deficiencies of its author, has not received the respect it intellectually deserves, was in harmony with the same notion. Isaac Casaubon in his dedication to James I. (chap. v.) says, " Et tamen adhuc illis temporibus stabat suum jus, et in ecclesiâ summa auctoritas conciliis universalibus : quæ etsi cogi semper non poterant, semper tamen fas fuit piis hominibus spe saltem consolari sese ejus remedii, quod solum ad componendas controversias et hæreses auctoritate ecclesiæ debellandas cum Scripturæ docuerunt tum prisci patres agnoverunt atque usurparunt."

Hooker[f] says, " The urgent necessity of mutual communion for preservation of our unity . . . maketh it requisite that the Church of God here on earth, have her laws of spiritual commerce between Christian nations ; laws, by virtue whereof all Churches may enjoy freely the use of those reverend, religious, and sacred consultations, which are termed Councils General. A thing, whereof God's own blessed Spirit was the author, a thing practised by the Apostles themselves, a thing always afterward kept and observed throughout the world, a thing never otherwise than most highly esteemed of, till pride, ambition, and tyranny, began by factious and vile endeavours

---

[f] E. P., lib. i. ch. x. 14, ed. Keble, p. 252.

to abuse that divine invention unto the furtherance of wicked purposes."

If the appeal to a Council, under certain possible circumstances, was in the minds of the divines of the time of King Henry and Queen Elizabeth, it assumed a still more prominent place in what may be termed the Constructive Epoch of Anglicanism. The great High Church school, in seeking to find a Catholic basis for their teaching, had of necessity to appeal to this.

Thus Archbishop Bramhall[g], in his replication to the Bishop of Chalcedon, after stating, "I submit myself and my poor endeavours to the judgment of the Catholic Œcumenical essential Church," continues, "Likewise I submit myself to the Representative Church, that is, a free General Council, or so general as may be procured; and until then, to the Church of England, wherein I was baptized, or to a national English Synod."

In his just vindication of the Church of England from the unjust aspersion of criminal schism, in his propositions for re-union, in speaking of the "necessary explications" to be made in view of that blessed object, he says they must "be made by the authority of a General Council, or one so general as can be convocated[h]." He moreover says, "To rebel against the Catholic Church, and its representative a General Council, which is the last visible judge of contro-

---

[g] Vo'. ii. p. 22, Anglo-Cath.   [h] Part i. d. 2, vol. i. p. 279.

versies, and the Supreme Ecclesiastical Court, either is gross schism, or there is no such thing as schismatical pravity in the world[i]."

So Archbishop Laud[j] says, "Therefore according to A. C.'s own argument, there will be some business also found (is not the settling of the divisions of Christendom one of them?) which can never be well settled but in a General Council; and particularly the making of Canons, which must bind all particular Christians and Churches, cannot be concluded and established but there."

So Bishop Overal[k], "And if in those troublesome times the peace of the Church were thus preserved, how much more now under Christian magistrates may it be strengthened, upheld, and maintained without the Pope, not only within their separate kingdoms, but likewise throughout (in effect) all these western parts of the world, if Christian Kings and Sovereign Princes would agree together for a General Council, to the end that all these heresies, errors, impostures, and presumptions, wherewith the Church of Christ has been long and is now miserably shaken and disturbed, might be at the last utterly suppressed and extinguished[i]."

A profound distrust of the motives of the Roman Catholic Church runs through the appeals to a Council on the part of the Elizabethan divines; it was felt

[i] Part i. d. 2, vol. i. p. 249.   [j] Conf. with Fisher, Works, vol. ii. p. 234, Anglo-Cath. ed.   [k] Conv. Book.   [l] Wordsworth's Christian Institutes, vol. iv. p. 146.

that under such auspices it could not be free. Recourse, therefore, was had to a theory of interference on the part of Christian kings, such as had actually been brought to act in the case of the early Œcumenical Synods; and later at Constance and Basle.

That appeal can no longer be made. Christian Europe (as representing the thought, civilization, and religion of the world) is no longer at one on the most important of all points. The Latin Communion is now represented (to speak broadly) by France, Spain, Austria, Bavaria, Portugal, Belgium. Italy as a nation is in semi-schism. Russia has been admitted as a potent factor into the politics of the West. Greece is a non-Latin kingdom, and the Provinces already possessed of a passionate nationality, are aspiring to their place in the royal houses of Europe. Prussia, for the moment the most powerful state in Europe, and uniting the force of all the vast north of Europe, is Protestant; so are the three Scandinavian kingdoms and Switzerland. It is obvious that not one of these possesses the adequate authority to move in the direction of the Convocation of an Œcumenical Synod. From the political side, such a conference is impossible.

Again, all modern theories of government are tending to treat religion only as a matter of police. The preservation of morals now concerns the civil magistrate, only so far as offences against them tend to breaches of the peace. The whole class of wrongs, which were in fact sins, are ceasing to be recognised as crimes. Above all, religious belief is being freed.

A man may believe what he pleases in the eyes of the State, so long as his belief does not assault public order, does not injure property or person. It is no longer recognised as a duty of the Supreme Civil power "to maintain truth." There is a re-action against the tyranny of the Reformation theory, which made over the consciences of the subject to the Crown.

Consequently, even if Civil Governments were at one as to the basis on which re-union was to be promoted, they could never consistently combine to call together a Council. The results of such a Council, if not a matter of indifference to them, would only become a subject of jealous dread, by the increase of power which it would give to the Catholic Church. The Elizabethan idea of such a convocation by the Christian princes, if it ever was more than an excuse for maintaining a separate position, is, in view of the actual condition of the world, and of the modern theories of dominion, an utter impossibility.

What, then, remains to be done? There is but one power on earth which is able to attempt this great work. Let the successor of St. Peter, Bramhall's *Principium Unitatis*, the holder of that see, whose *potior principalitas* was acknowledged by St. Irenæus, only rise above the miserable triumph of an immediate Ultramontane success; let him accept the high destiny which God has placed in his hand, of being, not as in past times the cause of disunion, but the principle of re-union in Christendom. Let him send forth his invitation, not merely to all the Bishops of his own subjection, assembled to register foregone conclusions, to give pomp and dignity to his own individual utterances; but let him invite first his own to testify to tradition and to judge freely in matters submitted to him. Then let him invite the ancient Eastern hierarchies, not as "prudent persons exercising ecclesiastical functions," but as the successors, as in fact they are, of the Ancient Thrones of New Rome, Alexandria, Antioch, and Jerusalem. Let him summon the Anglican prelates, not prejudging the doubts of their jurisdiction, but accepting them as they are historically, the occupants of the chairs of St. Austin and St. Paulinus. Let him call to himself all that is still sound in the Lutheran and Calvinistic bodies, whether they will hear or whether they will forbear,—and then in free Council assembled, under the inspiration of the Holy Ghost, let every question be discussed, every difficulty sifted. Let the fullest explanations be given of what has given-offence and promoted disunion; let the remaining superstitions left untouched by the Council of Trent be honestly dealt with; let the balancing and complementary truths that interpret the more startling assertions of the Church be enunciated; let the most candid and generous construction be placed upon the utterances of all the separated limbs of the Body of Christ; let a sound Catholic philosophy be sanctioned; let the deep underlying distinctions of race be allowed for; let the demarcation between faith and opinion be drawn with a firm and tender hand, so shall the great cause of re-union be promoted, the rent vesture of Christ repaired, the walls of partition broken down, and the reign of Christ the Lord over the world be inaugurated. "When in the day of His power, the people will offer Him free-will offerings with a holy worship [m]." "And I will make thy windows of agates, and thy gates of carbuncles, and all thy borders of pleasant stones; and all thy children shall be taught of the Lord, and great shall be the peace of thy children [n]."

Οἱ τῶν ἀποστόλων πρωτόθρονοι,
καὶ τῆς οἰκουμένης διδάσκαλοι,
τῷ Δεσπότῃ τῶν ὅλων πρεσβεύσατε,
εἰρήνην τῇ οἰκουμένῃ δωρήσασθαι,
καὶ ταῖς ψυχαῖς ἡμῶν τὸ μέγα ἔλεος [o].

SOLI DEO GLORIA.

[m] Ps. cx. 3.   [n] Isa. liv. 12.
[o] Hymn by Ephraim of Caria *apud Pitra Hymnographie de l'Eglise Grecque*, p. lxvii.

L'ENVOY.

I HAVE now come to the end of my task, and I submit my work to the judgment of the Church with a deep sense of the responsibility of my action. It is with the greatest diffidence that I have ventured to touch upon points, concerning which good men during more than three hundred years have come to such different conclusions. I can only say that I have tried to approach them in a candid, truth-loving, and conciliatory spirit. I have endeavoured to cultivate the loving spirit of the author of the *Considerationes Modestæ*, who, by his profound learning, pacific temper, and sincere piety, has illustrated the name I bear. I am well aware that my work is likely to provoke much hostile criticism. The office of mediator is proverbially a thankless one. I shall be accused of insincerity by some, of timidity by others. I shall be blamed for casuistical fine-drawing. I shall be taunted with not pushing my premises to their legitimate conclusion. My consolation is that it has been my constant effort to state the truth in love, without regard to consequences. On the one hand, I have never failed to exhibit the errors in speculation and practice which have from time to time prevailed, and to unfold the growth of those superstitions which have deformed the Christian religion; on the other hand, I have endeavoured to give due prominence to the statement and evolution of the true doctrine which underlies these errors, and the depravation of which has engendered those superstitions. Believing that there can be no sound Theological Science which has not its support in history, I have endeavoured to give its proper place to the argument from Antiquity, Universality, and Consent; at the same time, I have recognised that the Church of God is a living Entity, and that God the Holy Ghost speaks within her. I have also not passed over the mysterious fact that the action of the depraved and infirm free-will of man has been permitted to cripple the teaching office of the Church, as it has marred so much of the beautiful Creation and Re-creation of God.

In addition to the more general aid and revision of that dearest and most valued Friend to whom this attempt of mine is dedicated, which I have already acknowledged in the Preface, it is due that I should mention very large assistance in this present portion, in the extensive Patristic authorities with which Articles XXII. and XXV. are enriched, where his rare familiarity with the Fathers of the Church has furnished me with what else, the duties of my own calling leading me in other directions, I could only have but slightly gone into; and yet more in the labour so generously and ungrudgingly bestowed upon Articles XXXII. and XXXVII., in both of which large and important additions are due to him. Those who with me can see, even at a distance, that Life of unwearied, unceasing toil, a Life whose whole existence is for others; his own long-cherished works put off from year to year, in humility and gentle trustfulness, as other duties come before him one by one, will with me gratefully receive the fruits of his toil.

CHRIST CHURCH,
Sexagesima Sunday, 1868.

Printed by James Parker and Co., Cornmarket, Oxford.

www.ingramcontent.com/pod-product-compliance
Lightning Source LLC
Chambersburg PA
CBHW061413160726
47995CB00003B/588